RUBENS

AND HIS LEGACY

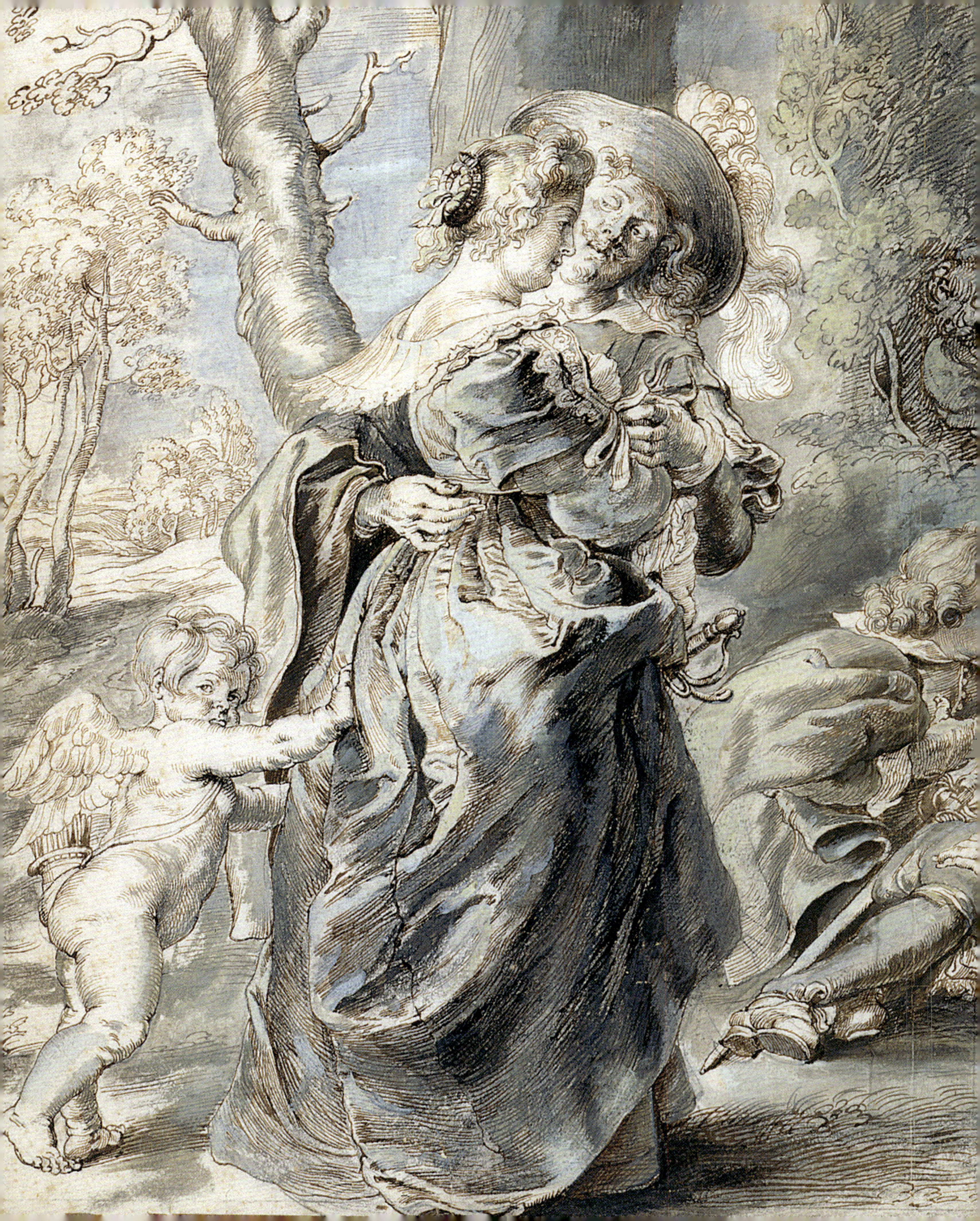

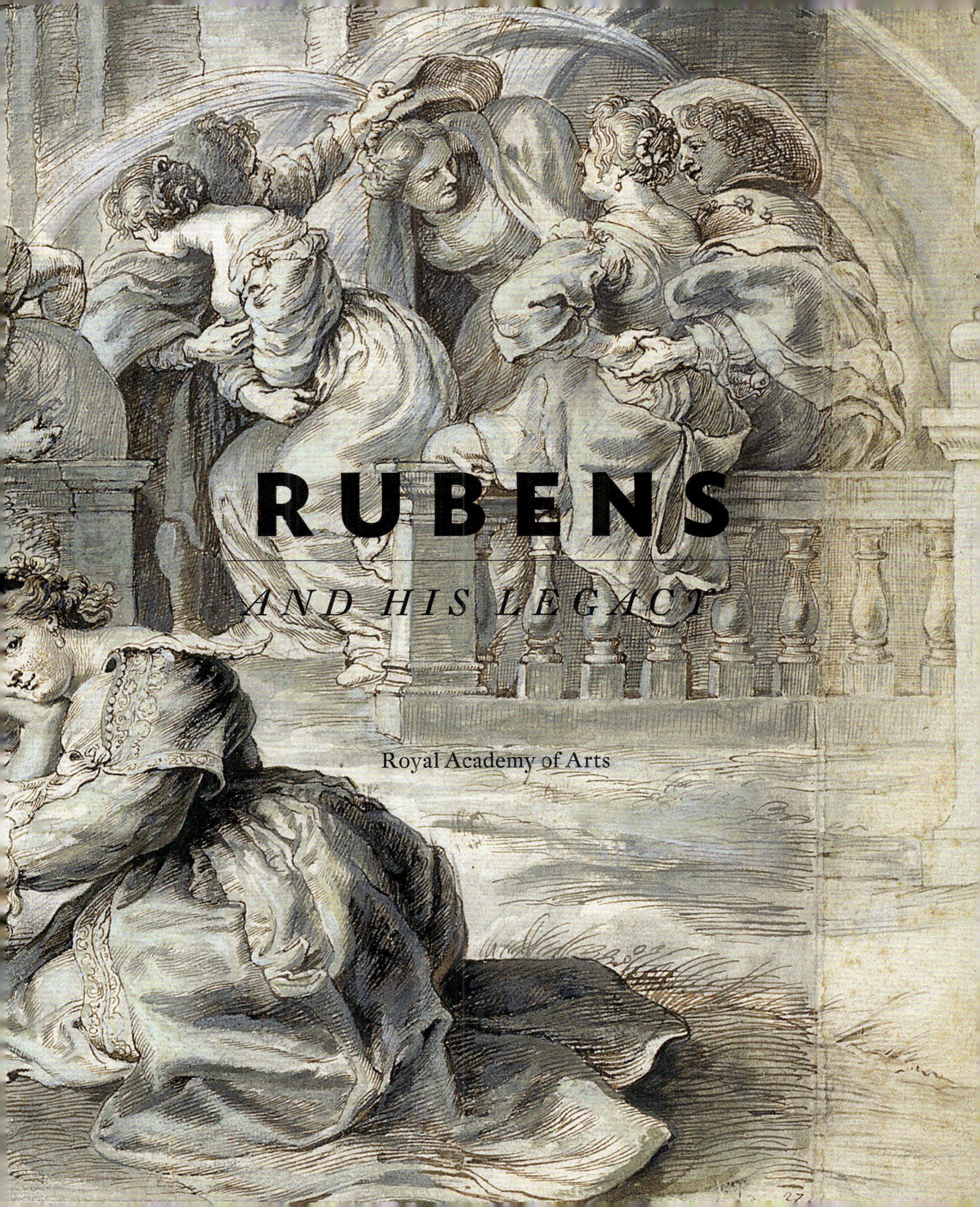
RUBENS
AND HIS LEGACY
Royal Academy of Arts

First published on the occasion of the exhibition
'Rubens and His Legacy: From Van Dyck to Cézanne'

BOZAR, Centre for Fine Arts, Brussels
25 September – 4 January 2015
Under the Patronage of Their Majesties The King and Queen of Belgium and of Mr Kris Peeters, former Minister-President of the Flemish Government; with the support of the Flemish Government

Royal Academy of Arts, London
24 January – 10 April 2015

Sponsored by

BNY MELLON
Partner of the Royal Academy of Arts

This exhibition has been made possible by the provision of insurance through the Government Indemnity Scheme. The Royal Academy of Arts would like to thank HM Government for providing Government Indemnity and the Department for Culture, Media and Sport and Arts Council England for arranging the indemnity.

Department for Culture Media & Sport

EXHIBITION CURATORS

ROYAL MUSEUM OF FINE ARTS ANTWERP
Nico Van Hout, Curator

ROYAL ACADEMY OF ARTS, LONDON
Arturo Galansino, Exhibitions Curator
with Katia Pisvin, Curatorial Assistant

EXHIBITION MANAGEMENT

ROYAL ACADEMY OF ARTS, LONDON
Idoya Beitia, Exhibitions Manager
Kitty Corbet-Milward, Rights and Reproductions Coordinator
Flora Fricker, Exhibitions Manager
Natalie Gibbons, Exhibitions Assistant
Jane Knowles, Exhibitions Manager
Tim Marlow, Director of Artistic Programmes
Francesca Sidhu, Temporary Exhibitions Manager
Anna Smith, Photographic and Copyright Coordinator
Andrea Tarsia, Head of Exhibitions Management

BOZAR, CENTRE FOR FINE ARTS, BRUSSELS
Nicolas Bernus, Technical Coordinator
Rocío del Casar Ximénez, Exhibitions Coordinator
Gunther De Wit, Publications Coordinator
Paul Dujardin, Artistic Director
Sophie Lauwers, Deputy Director of Exhibitions
Filip Stuer, Director of Marketing, Communication and Sales
Adinda Van Geystelen, Deputy Artistic Director

ROYAL MUSEUM OF FINE ARTS ANTWERP
Marjolijn Barbier, Financial Director
Veerle De Meester, Exhibitions Coordinator
Paul Huvenne, Administrator General
Elsje Janssen, Director of Collections
Vik Leyten, Director of Marketing, Communication and Education
Nathalie Monteyne, Registrar
Karen Wulgaert, Exhibitions Registrar

EXHIBITION CATALOGUE

ROYAL ACADEMY PUBLICATIONS
Beatrice Gullström, Production Coordinator
Alison Hissey, Project Editor
Elizabeth Horne, Managing Director, RA Enterprises Ltd
Carola Krueger, Production Manager
Simon Murphy, Project Editor
Peter Sawbridge, Senior Commissioning Editor
Nick Tite, Head of Publishing Operations

Translation from the Dutch (Nico Van Hout): Diane Webb
Translation from the French (Alexis Merle du Bourg): Caroline Beamish
Translation from the German (Gerlinde Gruber): Fiona Elliott
Translation from the Italian (Arturo Galansino): Caroline Beamish

Picture research: Sara Ayad
Design: Kathrin Jacobsen
Colour origination: DawkinsColour, London
Printed in Italy by Graphicom

British Library Cataloguing-in-Publication Data
A catalogue record for this book is available from the British Library

ISBN 978-1-907533-78-5 (paperback)
ISBN 978-1-907533-77-8 (hardback)

Distributed outside the United States and Canada by Thames & Hudson Ltd, London

Distributed in the United States and Canada by Harry N. Abrams, Inc., New York

EDITORIAL NOTE
Dimensions of all works of art are given in centimetres, height before width.

ILLUSTRATIONS
Pages 2–3: detail of cat. 138.1
Page 6: detail of cat. 58
Page 9: detail of cat. 96
Page 10: detail of cat. 36
Page 13: detail of cat. 23
Pages 14–15: detail of cat. 130
Pages 22–23: detail of cat. 2
Pages 76–77: detail of cat. 33
Pages 120–21: detail of cat. 55
Pages 176–77: detail of cat. 91
Pages 222–23: detail of cat. 104
Pages 258–59: detail of cat. 127

CONTENTS

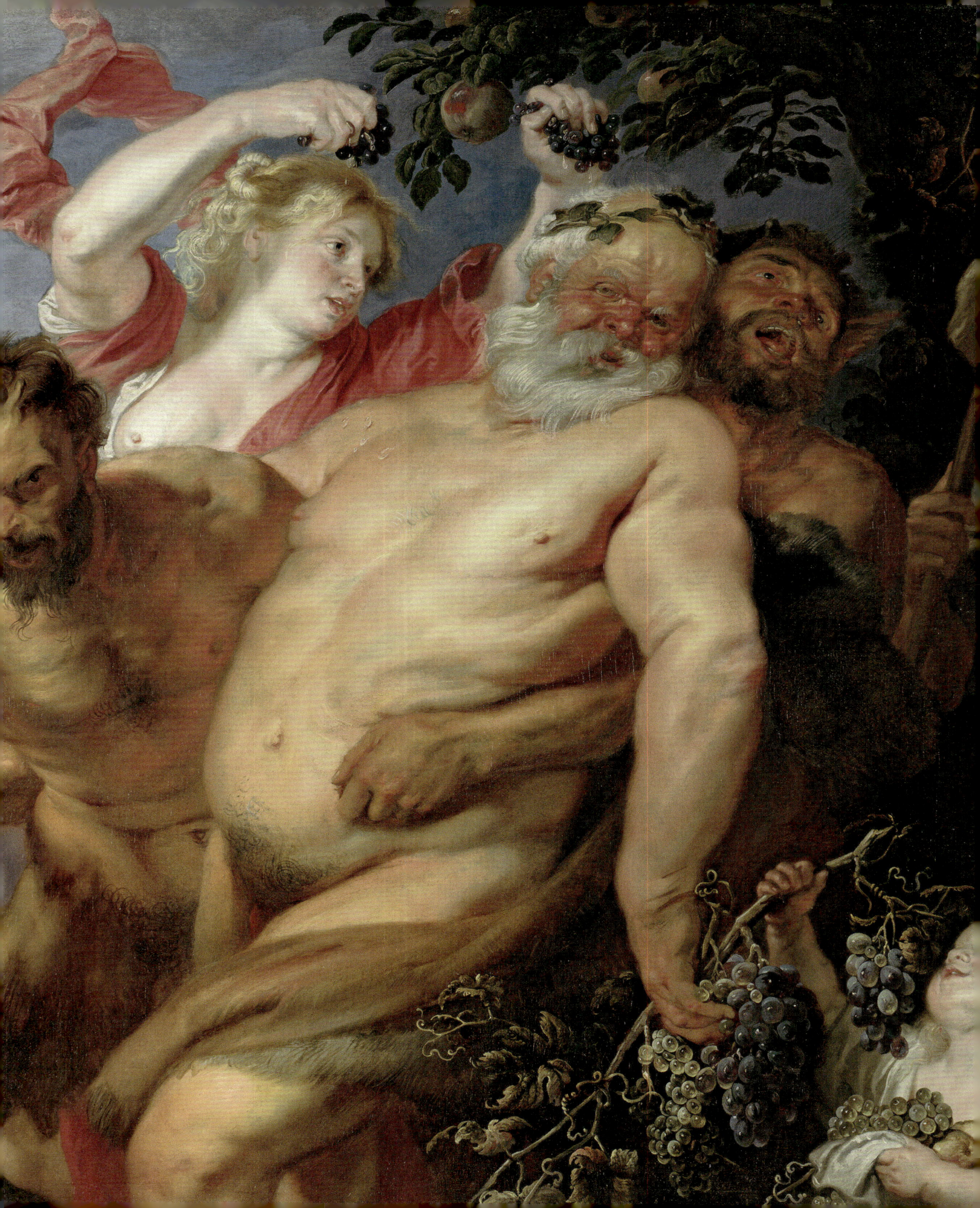

PREFACE

He travelled throughout Europe. The continent Rubens knew is not the Europe of today, and certainly there then existed nothing like the partnership that is now a defining feature of the European Union. The Europe of Rubens was shaped by royal absolutism, the Counter-Reformation, the Renaissance and humanism. But its internal boundaries posed no obstacle to this artist-diplomat, who served various kings, princes and clerics.

When one describes Rubens as the European artist par excellence, one speaks primarily of the European cultural heritage – from antiquity to the Italian Renaissance – that he eagerly assimilated and passed on. This prominence is pithily expressed in Pieter Steinz's cultural guide *Made in Europe. De kunst die ons continent bindt* (Made in Europe. The art that binds our continent) of 2014: 'Of all the Baroque painters, Rubens was the most European.'

The masterly way in which Rubens, through his art, wielded power was presented in 2013 with appropriate splendour in the exhibition 'L'Europe de Rubens', held at the newly opened Musée du Louvre-Lens. 'Rubens and His Legacy: From Van Dyck to Cézanne' is concerned less with the moment of power itself, rather it examines the influence that outlasts it – how Rubens's effect on the visual arts has continued, undiminished, for four centuries. Politicians can only dream of such enduring impact.

A man of his times, Rubens stole with his eyes. During his many journeys and commissions – from Mantua to Madrid, from Antwerp and Brussels to Vienna, from Rome to Paris and London – he kept his eyes wide open. While copying his predecessors, Rubens prised their secrets from them and forged these influences into an emotive pictorial idiom of his own. It is interesting to see how, after Rubens's death, the artists who appropriated his colossal *œuvre* did something similar, and how different aspects of 'Rubenism' came to the fore in different parts of Europe. British artists, for example, looked mainly at his portraiture and landscapes, while the Spanish were partial to Rubens as the ambassador of the Counter-Reformation, and French art history is indebted to the master's more 'frivolous' work. Rubens paved the way for both rococo and Romanticism. Do those varied views of this versatile artist tell us something about the much-lauded European 'unity in diversity'? Undoubtedly.

Few artists have succeeded in becoming an *-ism*, and few continue to appeal to the imagination to the extent that Rubens does. I hope you derive a great amount of enjoyment from this book, and from the lavish exhibition it accompanies.

Herman Van Rompuy
President of the European Council

FOREWORD

The artistic mastery of the painter, draughtsman, etcher and diplomat Peter Paul Rubens has made him not only a cornerstone of art history but also an immensely influential role model, both in his own time and for succeeding generations. Perhaps surprisingly, neither an exhibition nor a publication of this scale has been devoted to a comprehensive examination of his wider legacy.

The ambition of this exhibition and its catalogue is to do just that. The selection explores the Flemish master's universality, variety and inventiveness, and considers the ways in which his vital, fluid and expressive brushwork, the brilliance and luminosity of his colour, and his exuberantly sensual feeling for the tactile have been embraced down the centuries by painters as diverse as Van Dyck, Watteau, Daumier, Cézanne and Kokoschka.

'Rubens and His Legacy' has had a decade-long genesis. When refurbishment of the Royal Museum of Fine Arts Antwerp was proposed in 2004, the first idea to celebrate the museum's eventual reopening was a restaging of 'Le Siècle de Rubens', a survey show of the artist's seventeenth-century followers that had been mounted in Brussels in 1965. At the same time, however, it was recognised that Rubens's influence extends far beyond seventeenth-century Antwerp. The opportunity to create an international loan exhibition to consider his significance in a European context for the first time was rightly seized by Nico Van Hout, and, following our institutions' successful collaboration on the Van Dyck exhibition in 1999, the Royal Academy of Arts was delighted to join the project. In the meantime, a second phase of restoration in Antwerp had caused the reopening of the Royal Museum of Fine Arts to be pushed back to 2018. To enable the exhibition to open as planned in 2014, BOZAR, the Centre for Fine Arts in Brussels, which has staged many important and successful exhibitions with the Royal Museum of Fine Arts Antwerp in recent years, agreed to become the third partner in the project.

Numerous individuals across all three institutions have been involved in the exhibition's conception, development and delivery. Chief among them is Nico Van Hout, Curator at the Royal Museum of Fine Arts Antwerp. He has worked alongside Arturo Galansino, Exhibitions Curator, to deliver the exhibition at the Royal Academy, assisted by Katia Pisvin, Curatorial Assistant. An international team of specialist authors has worked with the Royal Academy's publications department to produce this handsome exhibition catalogue.

Without our many lenders, both public and private, no exhibition would have been possible. We are exceptionally grateful to them all for their generosity and for allowing us to share their works with our visitors.

We are also much indebted to the exhibition's London sponsors, BNY Mellon, Partner of the Royal Academy of Arts. No exhibition of this scope would be possible without the support of our long-term partners, whose belief in the project from the outset has been a great support. We thank them wholeheartedly.

It is our hope that the Antwerp–Brussels–London triangle that has brought this magnificent exhibition into being will give Rubens the pan-European dimension he deserves.

Paul Huvenne
Administrator General, Royal Museum of Fine Arts Antwerp

Paul Dujardin
CEO and Artistic Director, BOZAR, Centre for Fine Arts, Brussels

Christopher Le Brun PRA
President, Royal Academy of Arts, London

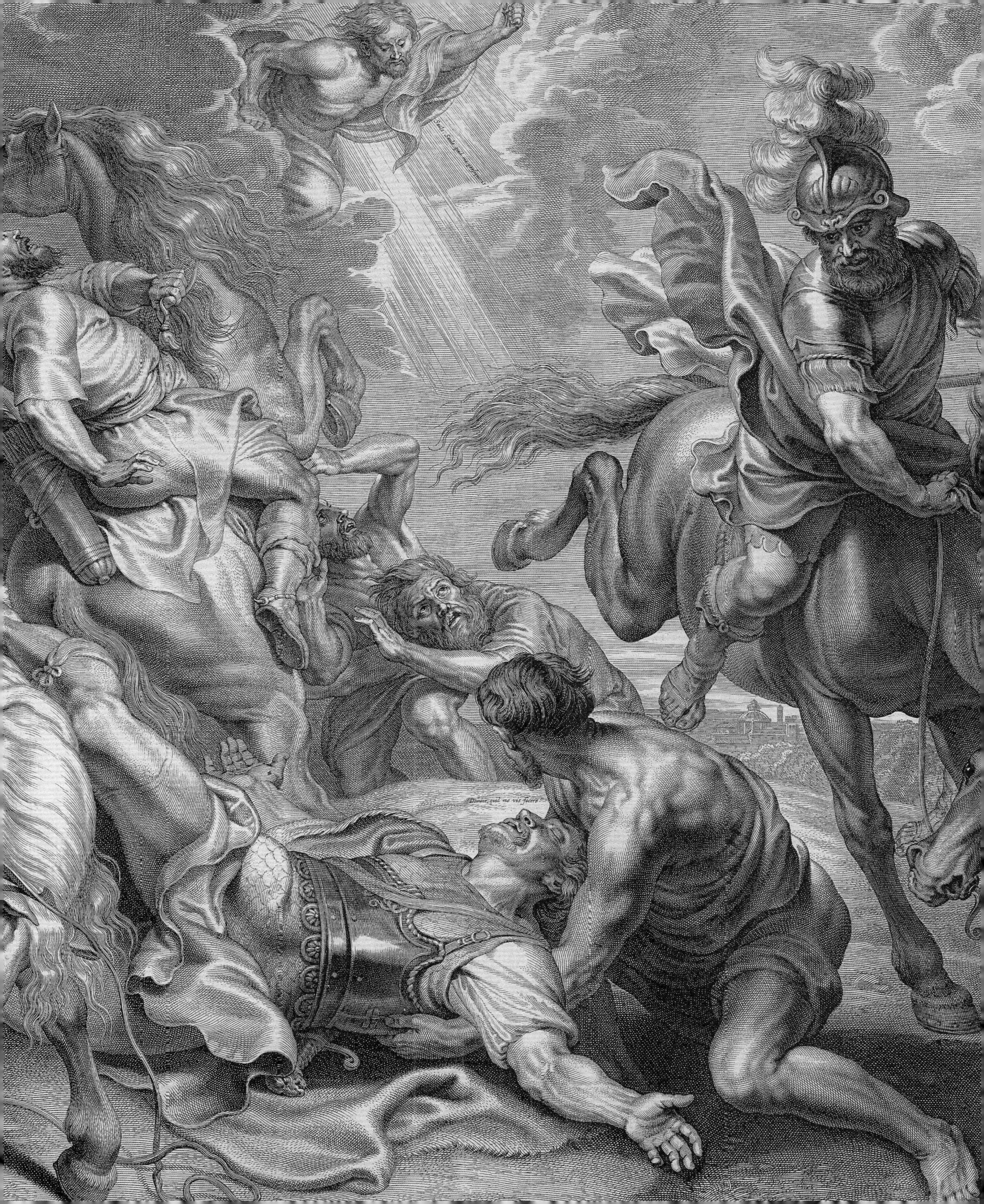
Saule, Saule, quid me persequeris
Domine, quid me vis facere?

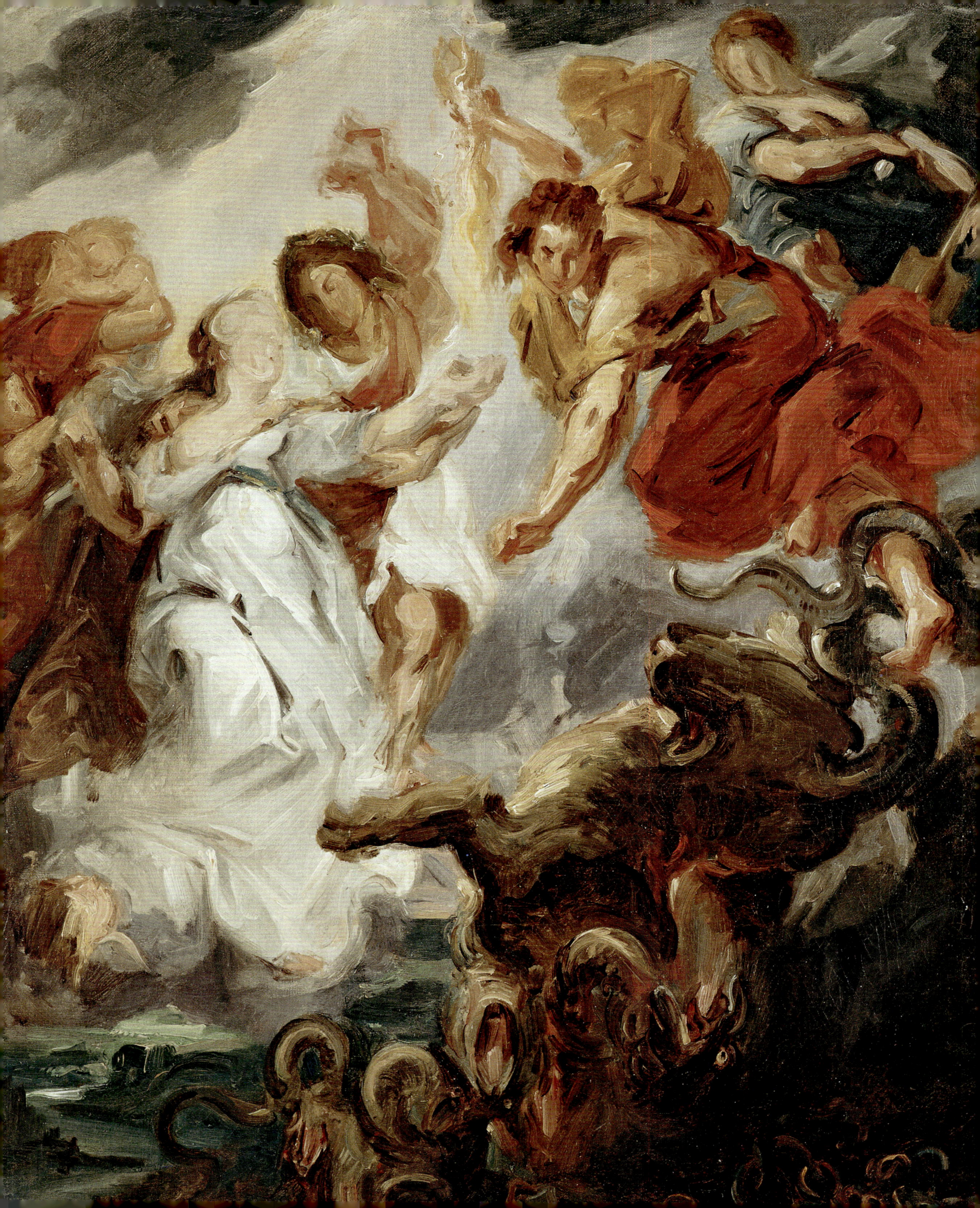

SPONSOR'S STATEMENT

It would be impossible to separate Peter Paul Rubens's successes as an artist from his activities as an art collector. At the time of his death, Rubens owned approximately a thousand works of art. Some of these were Old Master drawings, which he is known to have copied and corrected. Engagement with the legacies of other artists clearly inspired the Flemish artist, furnishing him with a storehouse of images that he could select from when creating his own works of art.

One of the works featured in the exhibition that speaks of Rubens's awareness of his own legacy is a drawing of the painting *The Defeat of Sennacherib*. Rubens's collaborative assistant and engraver Pieter Claesz. Soutman would probably have made this drawing while preparing a plate for a print, which would have been reproduced numerous times and distributed far and wide to help ensure the artist's legacy.

It is fitting that in 1978 this drawing was purchased for the National Gallery of Art, Washington DC, by the Andrew W. Mellon fund, which was instigated by the businessman and art collector's son, Paul Mellon. That the drawing features a number of horses, so beloved by Paul, is even more apt.

BNY Mellon is committed to supporting the arts as part of our global philanthropic endeavours and we have enjoyed a special partnership with the Royal Academy since 2007. Public access and education remain central to our international programme of arts sponsorship, and the Royal Academy strives to engage with the broadest possible audience through its exhibitions, events, publications and educational activities.

BNY Mellon is proud to support 'Rubens and His Legacy: From Van Dyck to Cézanne'. We hope you enjoy this fascinating exhibition about this legendary artist and his influence.

Michael Cole-Fontayn
Chairman of Europe, Middle East and Africa,
BNY Mellon, Partner of the Royal Academy of Arts

ACKNOWLEDGEMENTS

The curators of this exhibition would like to thank the following individuals for their invaluable assistance: Stijn Alsteens, Alessandro Bagnoli, Colin Bailey, Jean-Luc Baroni, Barbora Bartunkova, Xavier Bray, Duncan Bull, Bruno Claesen, Lai Couto, Anne Dary, Emmanuelle Delapierre, Rocío del Casar Ximénez, Willem de Ridder, Willy De Smedt, Simona Di Nepi, Ann Dumas, Mark Evans, Deborah Gage, David Jaffe, Guillaume Kazerouni, Friso Lammertse, Huigen Leeflang, Elizabeth McGrath, Aleksandra Medic, Norbert Middelkoop, Dr. Mirjam Neumeister, Geraldine Norman, Eric Pearson, Andrew Robinson, Pierre Rosenberg, Xavier Salomon, Béatrice Sarrazin, Nick Savage, Kathleen Soriano, David Taylor, Herwig Todts, Michael Tollemache, Cecilia Treves, Letizia Treves, Juliette Trey, Laura Turner, Christopher White, Humphrey Wine, Alexis Valticos, An Van Camp, Adri Verburg, Alejandro Vergara, Judy Watson

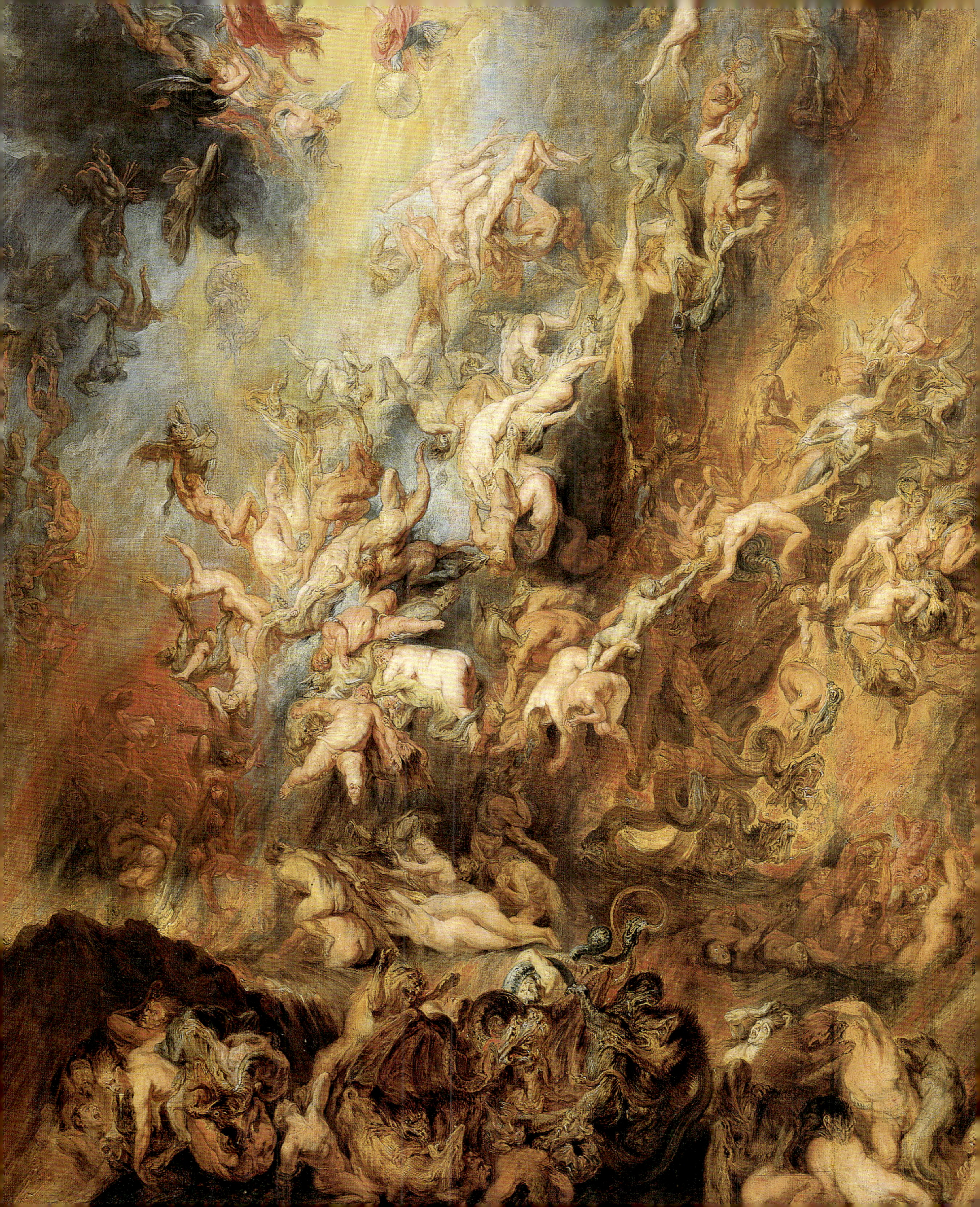

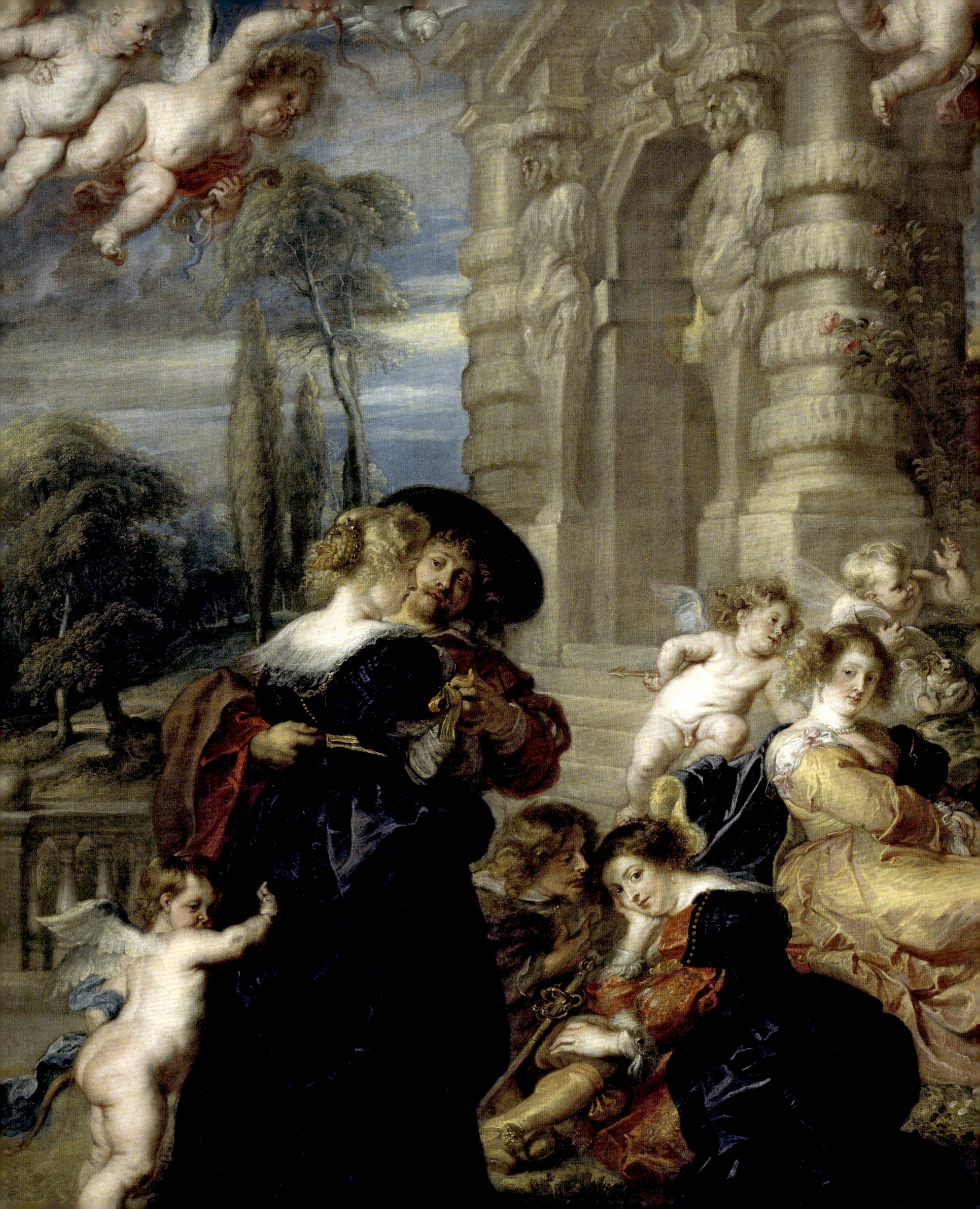

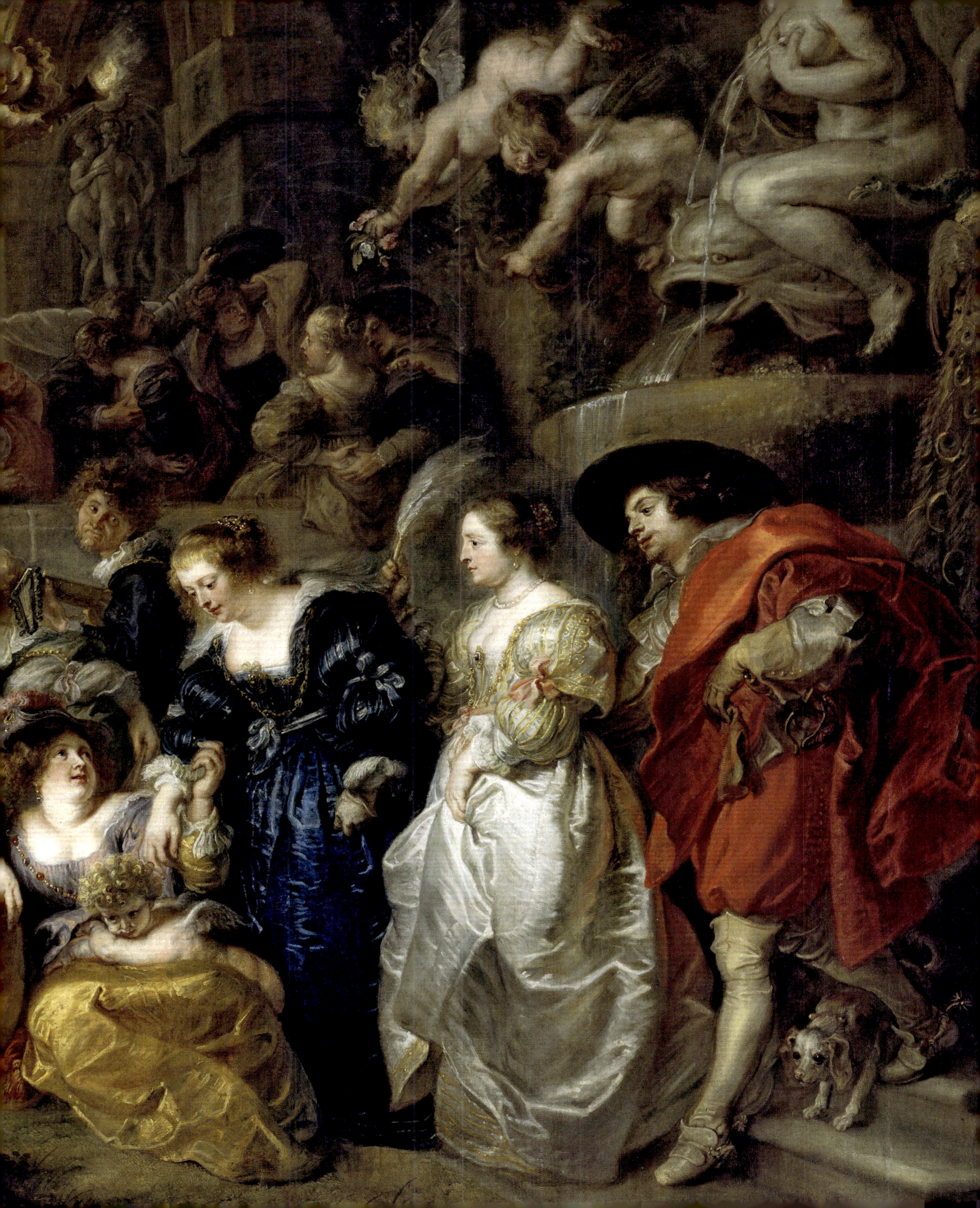

RUBENS AND HIS LEGACY: AN INTRODUCTION

NICO VAN HOUT

Seated regally beneath a portico in front of his easel, Peter Paul Rubens (1577–1640) is shown painting an allegory of peace 'from life' (fig. 1). He portrays Venus, the goddess of love, enthroned at the right, who turns and raises her hand to prevent her lover, Mars, from waging war. She endeavours to safeguard political power, whose attributes – the sceptre and the globe – lie in the left foreground. There we also see symbols of commerce and science (an astrolabe) and of the arts (a rolled-up manuscript, a mask, a score and a musical instrument), which can flourish only in times of peace. A putto releases the dove of peace, as Minerva and Abundantia, carrying a cornucopia filled with fruit and grain, descend on the scene.

The Italian painter Luca Giordano pays tribute in this canvas to the talent of his artistic hero – who had died twenty years earlier – and does so on a suitably monumental scale that would have met with his approval. Giordano refers in the painting to the famous allegories of peace that Rubens had painted for the King of England and the Grand Duke of Tuscany. That is no coincidence either; Roger de Piles, Rubens's biographer, also believed that no one else had ever treated allegorical subjects in such a clear and well-considered way: 'Because allegory is a kind of language and must therefore be justified by usage and understood by many, he [Rubens] introduced only those symbols that medals and other monuments of antiquity have made familiar to us, at least to the learned.'[1] The aristocratic image and success of Rubens – who had aspired to the mythic status of Titian – meant that he in turn became a role model for Van Dyck and the young Rembrandt.

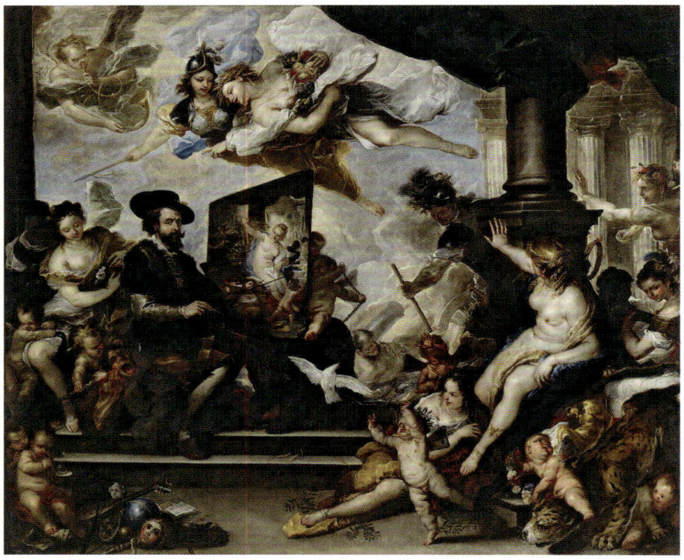

FIG. 1 Luca Giordano, *Peter Paul Rubens Painting an Allegory of Peace*, *c.* 1660. Oil on canvas, 337 x 414 cm. Museo Nacional del Prado, Madrid. Casón del Buen Retiro

Rubens also made an impression on Velázquez, who met him in Madrid in 1628 and visited Italy on his advice. And later on, both Sir Thomas Lawrence and Hans Makart attempted to equal the success of the court painter-cum-entrepreneur. In 1879 Makart even dressed as Rubens to march in a triumphal procession through Vienna.[2] Rubens's fame drove some artists mad. The Belgian painter Antoine Wiertz considered himself a reincarnation of the master, but his creations, as gigantic as they are hilarious, are among the most caricatural expressions of Rubenism.[3]

Rubens became known not only as 'the prince of painters' but also as 'the Homer of painting' – a true film director *avant la lettre*; notions that are firmly rooted in the art-historical literature. Johann Joachim Winckelmann stated that Rubens, like Homer, 'composed in accordance with the inexhaustible fertility of his mind ... he is rich to the point of prodigality. He sought the miraculous, just as Homer did, in fact just as any poetic and all-embracing painter does, particularly with regard to composition and chiaroscuro.' This German classicist was mainly attracted by Rubens's pictorial idiom of allegory, which he equated with the poetic and the sublime.[4] One of the most important characteristics of the painter is his universality, according to Charles Baudelaire in his *Salon de 1845*: 'Just as the epic poet, Homer or Dante, knows how to produce equally well an idyll, a narration, a speech, a descriptive passage, an ode, etc., so it is with Rubens, who, when painting fruit, paints fruit better than any specialist.'[5] The master's almost limitless range of subject-matter and boundless creativity also struck Hippolyte Taine, who wrote the following in 1869: 'the whole of human nature is in his grasp, save the loftiest heights. Hence it is that his creativeness is the vastest we have seen, comprehending as it does all types, Italian cardinals, Roman emperors, contemporary seigneurs, burghers, peasants and cowherding lasses, along with the innumerable diversities stamped on humanity by the play of natural forces and which more than fifteen hundred pictures did not suffice to exhaust.'[6]

The image of the painter-diplomat has persisted in exhibitions up to the present day. The show in Lille in 2004 told the story of Rubens's royal, ecclesiastical and bourgeois patrons, and those in Wuppertal in 2012 and in Lens in 2013 analysed the complex European politics of Rubens's day. These exhibitions affirmed the image of the artist as a servant of the Catholic establishment, a defender of absolutism and an architect of peace. Rubens was certainly all of those things, but that is only part of the story. If he were merely an outstanding painter of propaganda, he would have been quickly forgotten, but alongside the eloquent history painter there exists another Rubens: the creator of family portraits, landscapes and pastoral scenes, of peasant dances and gardens of love, a poetic Rubens who was present at the inception of rococo and Romanticism, a painter of sensuality as well as sensation, a Rubens who, in the imagination of Ferdinand de Braekeleer the Elder (fig. 2), immortalised the attractive Susanna Lunden in his garden pavilion in the famous *Chapeau de Paille* (fig. 35). Here the Belgian Romantic painter clearly pays tribute to that other Rubens, even though his loving 'reconstruction' tells us more about nineteenth-century taste than about seventeenth-century reality – as evidenced by the Biedermeier sofa, the footstool, and the table with a jug and dish of fruit.

Most exhibitions, however, feature the Homer of painting and his astonishing craftsmanship. The exhibition in Brunswick in 2004 presented Rubens as a painter of human emotions; in London in 2005 visitors were introduced to his sources of inspiration; and in Brussels in 2007 the genesis of a group of his works was reconstructed.[7] *Rubens and His Legacy* fits into this last category. The selection of works examines the relevance of Rubens's artistic legacy to other artists and invites visitors to look at the paintings before reading the labels, because, just like Michelangelo, Raphael, Titian, Rembrandt and Picasso, Rubens reshaped art history. That the face of the Baroque also belongs in this illustrious roll-call of masters is not in doubt, for the after-effect of the Flemish master extends across four centuries. Quite a few artists collected his prints, drawings, oil sketches and even paintings,[8] and yet the phenomenon of Rubenism has been investigated only narrowly and sporadically. In fact, the subject was long relegated to the bottom drawer of art-historical research. It was not until 1975 that the theme was examined in a small exhibition in Providence, Rhode Island,[9] and in 2004 academics delved into Rubenism again at a conference held in Lille.[10]

Of course, neither the exhibition nor its catalogue can present an entirely exhaustive overview of the broad art-historical subject of Rubenism. A number of interesting artists who were not essential to the conceptual framework of the exhibition fell by the wayside; these include the Frenchmen Jacques Blanchard and Joseph Parrocel, the Austrians Martin Johann Schmidt and Johann Michael Rottmayr, the Dutchman Jacob de Wit, the Mexican Cristóbal de Villalpando and the Belgian Gustaaf Wappers. Moreover, quite a few of the larger works, such as the painting by Luca Giordano discussed at the opening of this introduction, cannot travel. This is even the case with some of the smaller works, such as the iconic *Chapeau de Paille*, and the late landscapes that Rubens painted on fragile panels with complicated butt joints. In the interests of clarity and focus, sculpture has been excluded from the exhibition, despite Rubens's undeniable impact on Artus Quellinus, Georg Petel, Jean-Baptiste Carpeaux (fig. 3) and Auguste Rodin. The influence of his painting on works of sculpture is so complex that it merits a separate study and exhibition.

Rubens and His Legacy aims to continue in the vein of the London exhibition of 2005, which presented Rubens as the heir to antiquity and the Italian Renaissance. Six chapters explore specific facets of Rubens's *œuvre*: violence, power, lust, compassion, elegance and poetry. This division is only natural, for it was mainly in the portrayal of these themes that artists had recourse to Rubens. Court painters took an interest in his virtuoso engagement with allegory. For Spanish artists, it was his religious paintings that were important, for the British it was his landscapes and portraits, whereas French painters drew inspiration from his bucolic scenes. In fact, their interest was largely fuelled by the specific taste of Spanish, British and French art lovers, who appreciated not only the Flemish master's subject-matter, but certainly also his sumptuous palette, which Charles Baudelaire compared with many-coloured fireworks launched from the same place.[11] Or, in the words of Hippolyte Taine: 'Like an Indian deity at leisure, Rubens assuages his fecundity by creating worlds, and from the incomparable creased

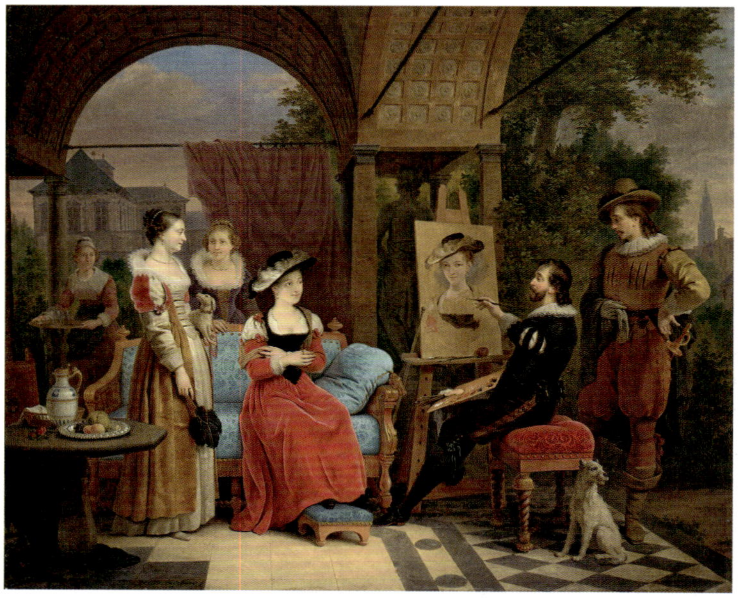

FIG. 2 Ferdinand de Braekeleer the Elder, *Peter Paul Rubens Painting the 'Chapeau de Paille' in His Garden Pavilion*, 1826. Oil on canvas, 100 x 123 cm. Musée du Louvre, Paris

and refolded crimsons of his robes to the snowy whites of his flesh or the pale silkiness of his blonde tresses, there is no tone in any of his canvases that does not appear there purposely to afford him delight.'[12]

Before the rise of the great European museums, the visibility of Rubens's *œuvre* was limited, and practically nothing was known about the stylistic evolution his work had undergone. Rubens's most accessible paintings were in the churches of the Southern Netherlands, in which many of his altarpieces were (and still are) to be found. Thus Sir Joshua Reynolds travelled around Flanders in 1781 with orders to buy paintings from private collections and at auctions selling the property of disbanded convents and monasteries.[13] It is no coincidence that Elisabeth-Louise Vigée-Lebrun accompanied her husband – an art dealer – that same year on a treasure hunt through the Low Countries. In those days Rubens's works could be admired in places other than their present homes, such as in the Palais du Luxembourg and the Palais Royal in Paris, and in the Elector's Picture Gallery in Düsseldorf. The rich Rubens collection in Madrid, however, went largely unnoticed for many years because it stood well outside the field of vision of those taking the Grand Tour to Italy. Not infrequently, artists and critics discovered the master's work in their patrons' collections. Roger de Piles, for example, described the works by Rubens in the possession of the 2nd Duke of Richelieu, while Watteau and Charles de La Fosse became acquainted with the master's paintings and drawings owned by their Maecenas, the banker Pierre Crozat, and Sir Thomas Lawrence admired the *Chapeau de Paille* that had been purchased by the statesman Sir Robert Peel in 1823.

There was, however, another way to form an idea of Rubens's work: the master himself had supervised the engraving of a large number of his compositions.[14] After his death, that selection quickly grew into a flood of prints that reproduced – not always faithfully – nearly his entire *œuvre*, long before the invention of photography. Prints after Rubens's religious paintings were frequently used for missionary work in Asia and the New World. Local painters copied his compositions, as a result of which his footprint can be found not only in Europe, but also in numerous churches in Mexico (fig. 4), Peru, the Philippines and Quebec.[15]

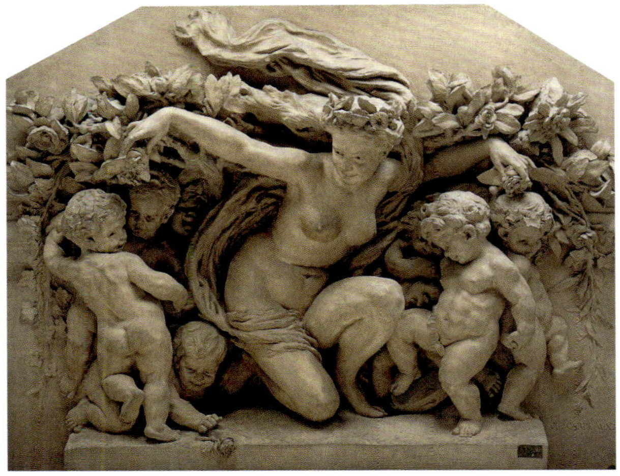

FIG. 3 Jean-Baptiste Carpeaux, *The Triumph of Flora*, 1863. Terracotta, 136.7 x 177 cm. Musée des Beaux-Arts de Valenciennes

Artistic influence occurs on various levels. At its most basic, the copy is an exercise in painterly technique. The next step up is the recycling of borrowed motifs in a new work. Resourceful artists, of course, would rather rework other artists' original ideas than make copies, so they subtly forge influences into a style of their own, and in the end their sources of inspiration are detectable merely as echoes, in the same way that a reaction between chemicals gives rise to a new substance. Manet used a composition by Rubens as the point of departure for several artistic experiments, the results of which cannot unreservedly be called Rubenesque (see cats 67 and 128).

Rubens was not universally admired; on the contrary, he became a target of criticism as early as the seventeenth century. The Italian biographer Giovanni Pietro Bellori reproached him for his unnatural and distorted forms, banal and insufficiently individualised faces, and a historically incorrect use of costume.[16] Both his palette and his reputed sloppiness in drawing were the subjects of an art-historical debate among French Académiciens in the late seventeenth century.

In the nineteenth century Rubens's reputation suffered at the hands of a Protestant and bourgeois public, in whom modesty and prudishness had been instilled. They showed little understanding of Catholic, erotic and exuberant subjects, which were considered offensive or immoral.[17] Criticism also came from an unexpected quarter: Delacroix, who thought that Rubens could not distinguish the main subject from matters of secondary importance, compared his paintings to an assembly at which everyone talks at the same time.[18] Compared to Titian, Rubens was 'exterior ... all surface', in the view of Renoir, who is nevertheless the painter who learned the most from the Flemish master.[19]

Bridget Riley rightly describes Rubens as a pragmatist, 'an artist whose aim it was to master the best of the past'[20] – in other words, an artist who sought to tell the stories of the past in a better way, as Horace tried to do.[21] This conclusion makes one wonder if it wouldn't be more correct to view Rubens as the last great master of the Renaissance, rather than the first painter of the Baroque. Admittedly, Rubens was no innovator, as Caravaggio and Rembrandt were, but he possessed an enviable talent for combining the most complex subjects and seemingly contradictory movements into a coherent and convincing

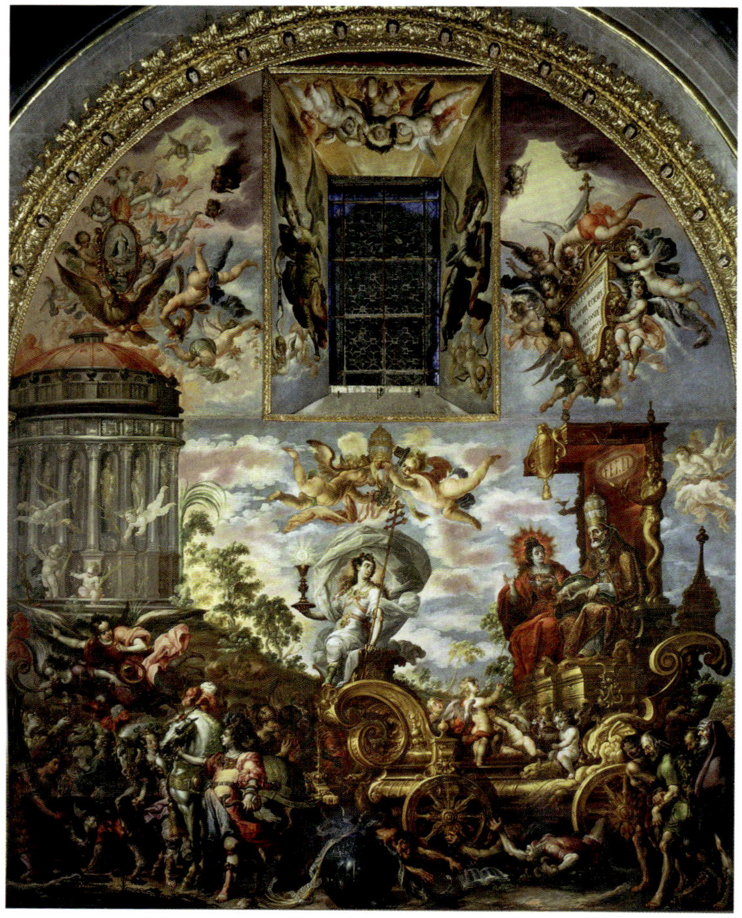

FIG. 4 Cristóbal de Villalpando, *The Triumph of Religion*, 1686. Oil on canvas, 899 x 766 cm. Sacristy of Mexico City Cathedral, Mexico

composition. Today, viewers who are unfamiliar with antiquity or Christian iconography look at Rubens's creations as Westerners look at Kabuki theatre: they are fascinated by the form, but the meaning escapes them. Rubens succeeded in orchestrating a rich palette with astounding ease, and his virtuoso brush strokes betray a level of self-confidence undreamt of by most artists. This was also observed by Velázquez, whose encounter with Rubens prompted him to work more efficiently and on a lighter ground.[22] It was for this reason, perhaps, that after the French Revolution painters and art lovers came to think of Rubens as an Old Master who was, admittedly, difficult to understand, though much could be learned from his brilliant *œuvre*. This is how he became a 'painter's painter'. Even though Van Gogh thought Rubens 'superficial, hollow, bombastic', he was at the same time stunned by his unparalleled manner of painting, 'precisely because he is, or rather seems, so supremely simple in his technique. Does it with so little, and paints – and above all draws, too – with such a swift hand and without any hesitation. [...] And how fresh his paintings have remained precisely because of the simplicity of the technique.'[23] Yet artists do not always admit that they, too, stand on the shoulders of giants. 'Well, regarding the influences in painting, I shall tell you about a personal experience,' Renoir confided in the art dealer Vollard: 'In the beginning I applied thick layers of green and yellow, thinking to achieve in this way more tonal values. One day in the Louvre I noticed that Rubens had achieved more sense of values with a simple scumble than I had been able to with all my thick layers of paint, on another occasion I discovered that Rubens used black to make silver. It goes without saying that both times I profited from the lesson, but does this mean that I am under the influence of Rubens?'[24]

At any rate, readers of this book will form their own opinions about Rubens and his impact on art history. It is important that they let themselves be led by their eyes and not by prejudices, preconceptions or reputations. The selection of works has been kept to a manageable size so that the viewer's gaze can roam undisturbed over the surface of the paintings. The image of Rubens's talent is invariably distorted by the many inferior studio pieces that bear his name. For the sake of more honest viewing, therefore, we have tried to select autograph works: in this case, less is more.

At the conclusion of this introduction, it is worthwhile to reflect for a moment on a comment made by John Ruskin, who had no natural affinity with the Baroque style: 'I have never spoken, and I will never speak of Rubens but with the most reverential feeling; and whatever imperfections in his art may have resulted from his unfortunate want of seriousness and incapability of true passion, his calibre of mind was originally such that I believe the world may see another Titian and another Raffaelle, before it sees another Rubens.'[25]

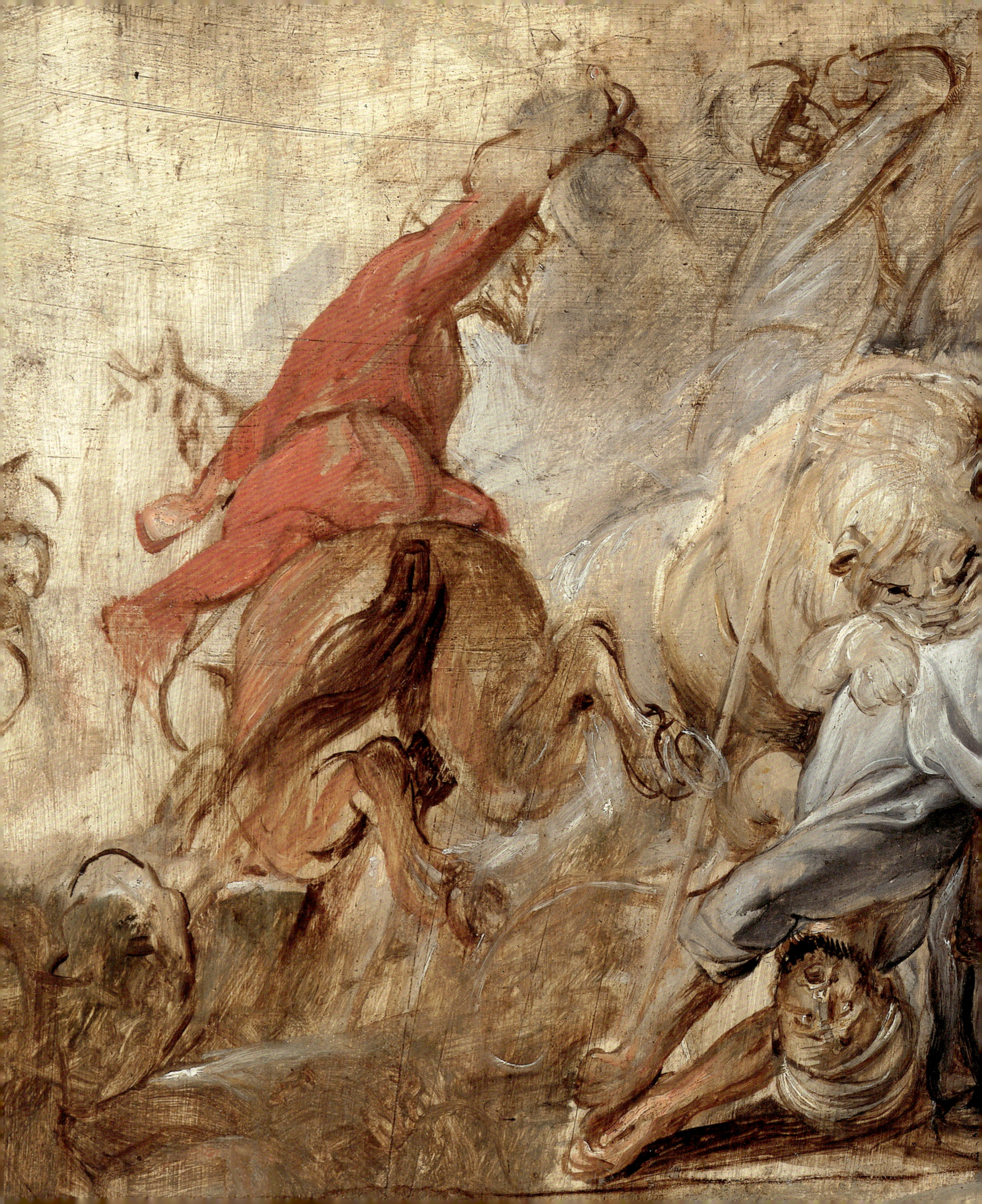

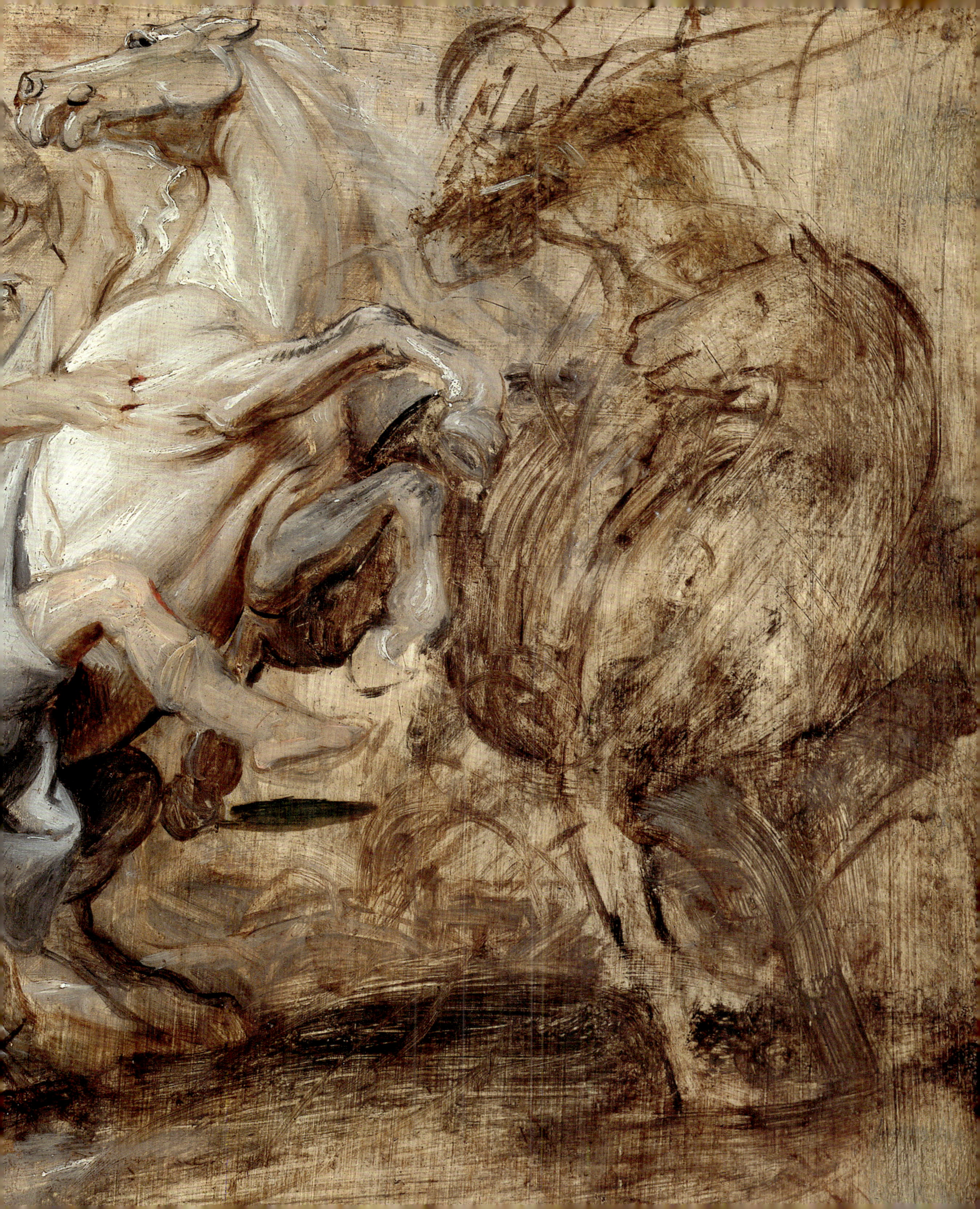

VIOLENCE

NICO VAN HOUT

At the end of her days the writer Johanna Schopenhauer – mother of the philosopher and friend of Goethe – looked back on her life, particularly at the journeys she had made around Europe in her youth. On one of those trips she had stopped at Düsseldorf to visit the Elector's Picture Gallery, which had helped to shape the artistic tastes of Diderot, Goethe, the Humboldt brothers and Thomas Jefferson.[1] Filled with admiration, she made her way through the rooms until she came to a halt in front of Rubens's *Great Last Judgement* (fig. 5). The ring of interwoven human beings, angels and devils made a violent and horrific impression: 'Out of inner fright I could scarcely bear the sight of it, nor turn away from it,' she observed.[2] Fifty years earlier, in 1790, Johann Georg Forster had indeed turned away from the altarpiece in disgust: 'No, it was none of the Muses that inspired the artist to paint such monstrosities,' wrote this natural scientist, who, with abhorrence, recognised 'in the dithyrambic fury that rages through the whole, in this grape-like cluster of people ... a cannibalistic meat market.'[3] Forster also stopped in Cologne, where he made an obligatory visit to *The Martyrdom of St Peter*, the master's 'last work'. 'Heaven help us,' he declared, deeply shocked, 'what kind of aesthetic feeling did many an acclaimed artist have! Are those subjects that deserve to be painted? Subjects that I would not wish to see in nature.'[4] Here the bourgeois taste and ethics of German Romanticism clash with the pictorial idiom of the Counter-Reformation, which glorifies suffering for a higher cause.

At the same time, however, an artist in Spain did venture to explore the caverns of the human psyche. For one of his famous 'black paintings' Francisco de Goya drew inspiration from a blood-curdling scene that Rubens had painted one hundred and eighty years earlier for the royal hunting lodge of Torre de la Parada. That is no coincidence, for Rubens's terrifying picture of old Saturn (fig. 6), his teeth pulling at the soft skin of one of his infant sons as he prepares to devour him, is a picture of madness that remains etched in the memory of every visitor to the Prado.

To present-day viewers, jaded by horror films and the reports of war correspondents, these reactions might sound rather melodramatic, yet they indicate the strong and enduring impact of Rubens's scenes of violence. Visitors to the Alte Pinakothek in Munich are still stunned into silence by Rubens's staggering representations of divine wrath and heavenly terror. In the *Great* and the *Small Last Judgement*, *The Fall of the Damned* and *The Fall of the Angels*, the artist emulates Michelangelo's *terribilità*, conjuring up forces that are beyond our comprehension. These are subjects that enabled Rubens to paint bodies in free fall, to demonstrate his skill in depicting the human anatomy from every possible angle. Rubens's horror scenes – nurtured by his own powers of imagination, by the realism of the Flemish tradition of painting, and by his knowledge of Caravaggio – are possibly even more shocking than those of his contemporaries. Just compare the unbridled aggression, thrown straight in the viewer's face, of Rubens's *Massacre of the Innocents* (1611–12; Art Gallery of Ontario,

FIG. 5 Peter Paul Rubens, *Great Last Judgement*, *c.* 1616. Oil on canvas, 606 x 460 cm. Alte Pinakothek, Munich

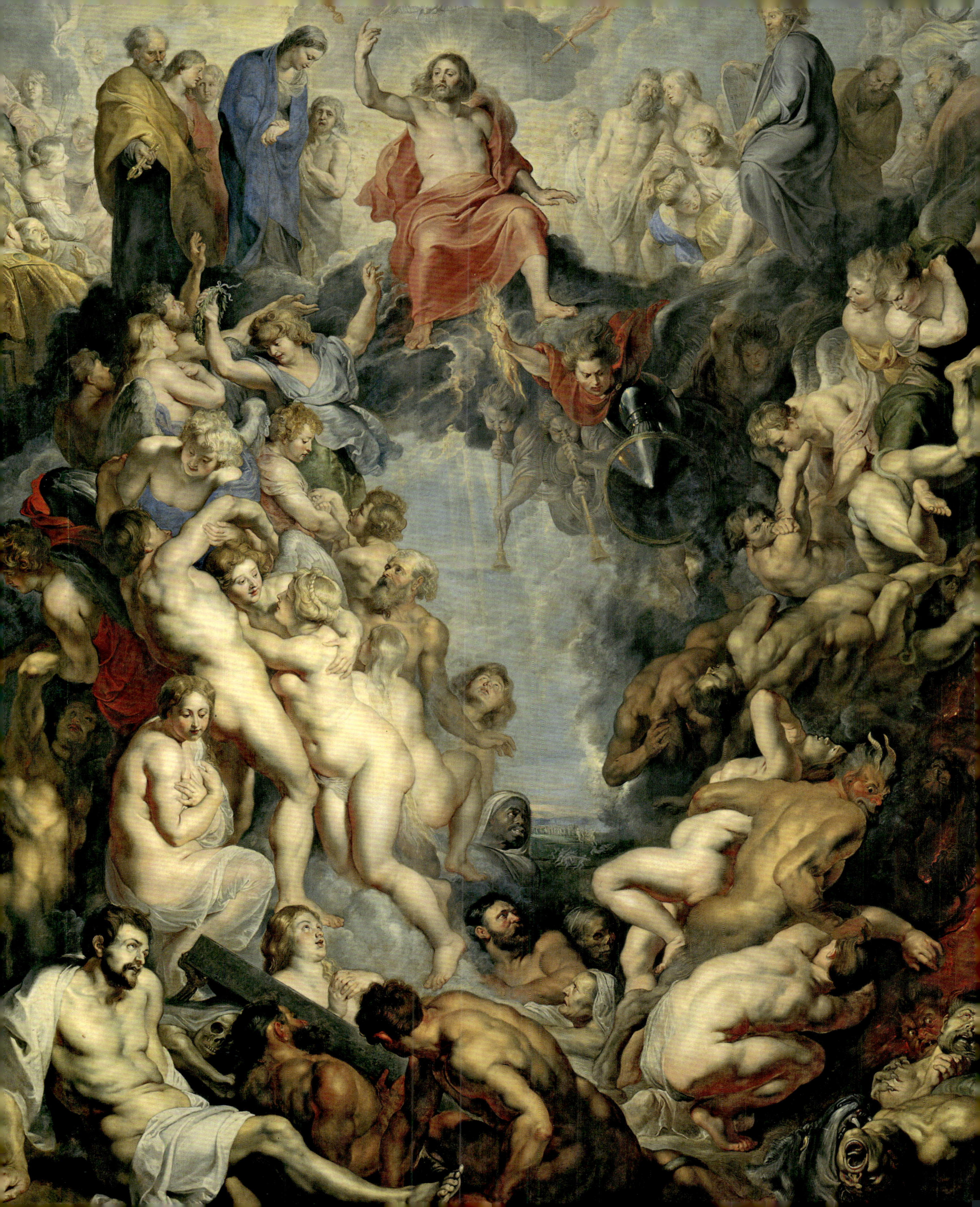

Toronto) with the stylised aesthetics of Poussin's paintings of the same subject (1625–29; Musée Condé, Chantilly and 1626–27; Petit Palais, Paris) or with Reni's anaemic interpretation of the theme (1611; Pinacoteca Nazionale, Bologna). Moreover, from 1630 onwards Rubens – under Titian's influence – made use of blurred contours to suggest movement and action, lending painted acts of violence an almost cinematic dimension. In fact, he was later criticised for using this stylistic device by the French Académiciens, who reproached his sloppy drawing. Charles Baudelaire showed more understanding, however, when he remarked – in his discussion of Delacroix's *Last Words of the Emperor Marcus Aurelius* (1844; Musée des Beaux-Arts de Lyons), shown in the Salon of 1845 – that 'this kind of drawing – which is analogous to that of all the great colourists, among them Rubens, for example – perfectly renders the movement, the physiognomy, the elusive and tremulous character of nature, which the drawing of Raphael never does'.[5]

The battle of the sexes likewise fascinated Rubens. The famous painting of the rape of the daughters of Leucippus by the unruly brothers Castor and Pollux (*c.* 1618; Alte Pinakothek, Munich) can still be seen as a passionate, surprise attack – a charm-offensive that got out of hand. By contrast, the sketch of the same subject in Oslo (cat. 21) and the sketch depicting the abduction of Proserpine (cat. 22) are rougher renderings of outrage. In terms of energy and dynamism, however, they are outstripped by Rubens's famous *The Battle of the Amazons* (fig. 7), a painting derived from a lost composition by Titian and – like the *Great Last Judgement* – ring-shaped in its conception.[6] Although Rubens had portrayed the subject previously, that painting (*c.* 1598; Schloss Sanssouci, Potsdam) cannot match the power of the work in Munich. *The Battle of the Amazons* is 'a piece full of heroic strength from the age of Theseus', according to Johann Jakob Wilhelm Heinse, an admirer of Rubens and one of the fathers of German Romanticism. 'The violence in men's shoulders and arms and fists holding murderous weapons, and in chest and knee: and in the rearing-up, the ever-changing leaping and violent jostling and head-tossing of warhorses.'[7] The revenge on all this male aggression is embodied by Rubens's depictions of strong *femmes fatales*, as in *Samson and Delilah* (*c.* 1609–10; National Gallery, London) – a work that clearly capitalises on male fears of castration. 'I love paintings ... from which one must turn away, provided it's out of terror and not out of disgust,' wrote Denis Diderot in his *Salon de 1761*. 'What is more horrific than the deed and the cold-bloodedness of the

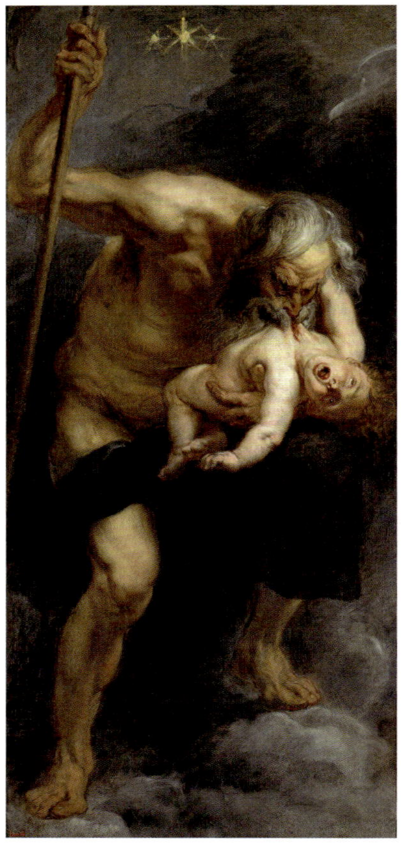

FIG. 6 Peter Paul Rubens, *Saturn Devouring One of His Sons*, *c.* 1636–37. Oil on canvas, 182.5 x 87 cm. Museo Nacional del Prado, Madrid

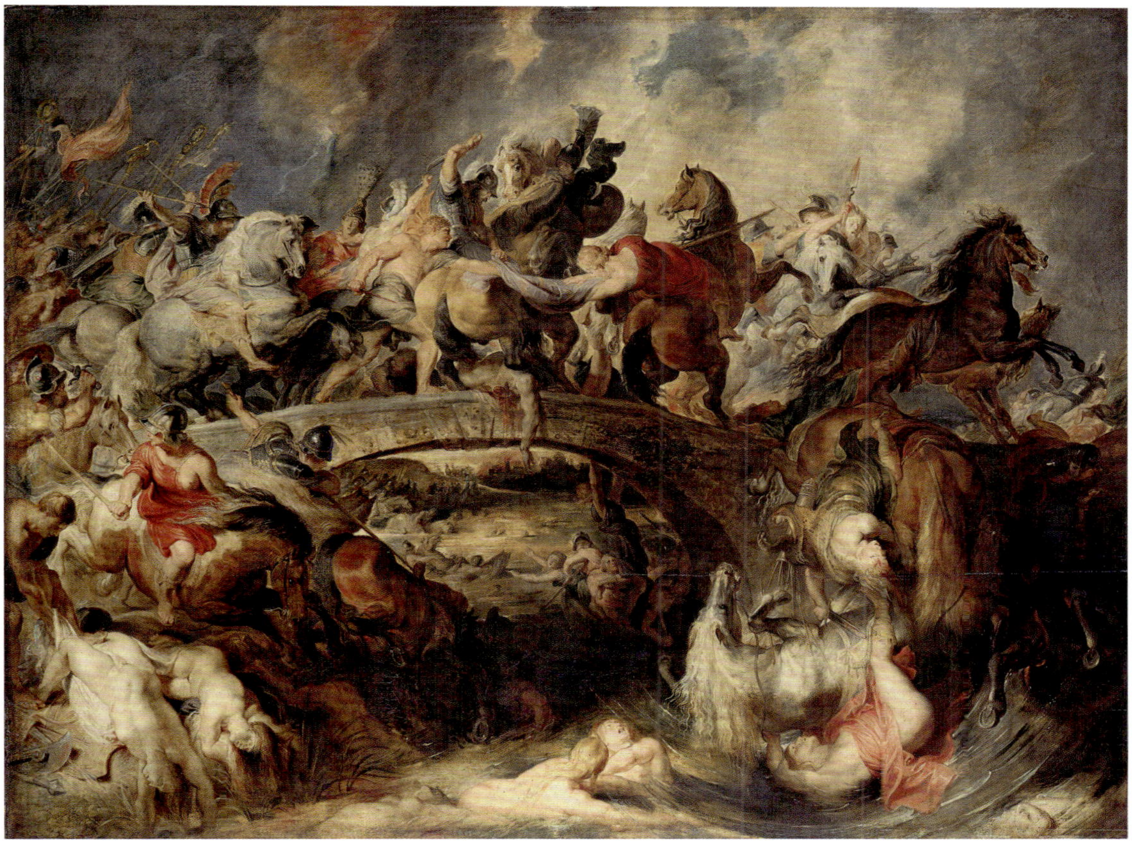

FIG. 7 Peter Paul Rubens, *The Battle of the Amazons*, *c.* 1615. Oil on panel, 121 x 165.5 cm. Alte Pinakothek, Munich

Judith by Rubens? She holds the sword, and calmly sinks it into Holofernes' throat.'[8]

Da Vinci's *Fight for the Standard* is considered the departure point of most of Rubens's battle scenes. Rubens owned a drawn copy, which he reworked (1602–06; Musée du Louvre, Paris), of that lost composition for the Palazzo Vecchio, Florence. Like the painters of the Renaissance, Rubens distributed the fighting over the entire surface area and lowered the horizon, so that the contours of the horses and their riders stand out clearly against the sky. Unlike his predecessors, however, Rubens approached the heroic tumult of battle as an autonomous artistic theme and was less interested in portraying a specific hostile encounter.[9] Rubens could flesh out the bygone battles of Decius Mus, Maxentius, and Licinius and Constantine the Great as he saw fit, with the exception of the Henri IV series, which was intended to document recent heroic deeds.[10] The same motifs recur in other contexts. For example, Rubens recycled the motif of the rearing horse and the rider tumbling backwards in the oil sketch of *A Lion Hunt* (*c.* 1614–15; National Gallery,

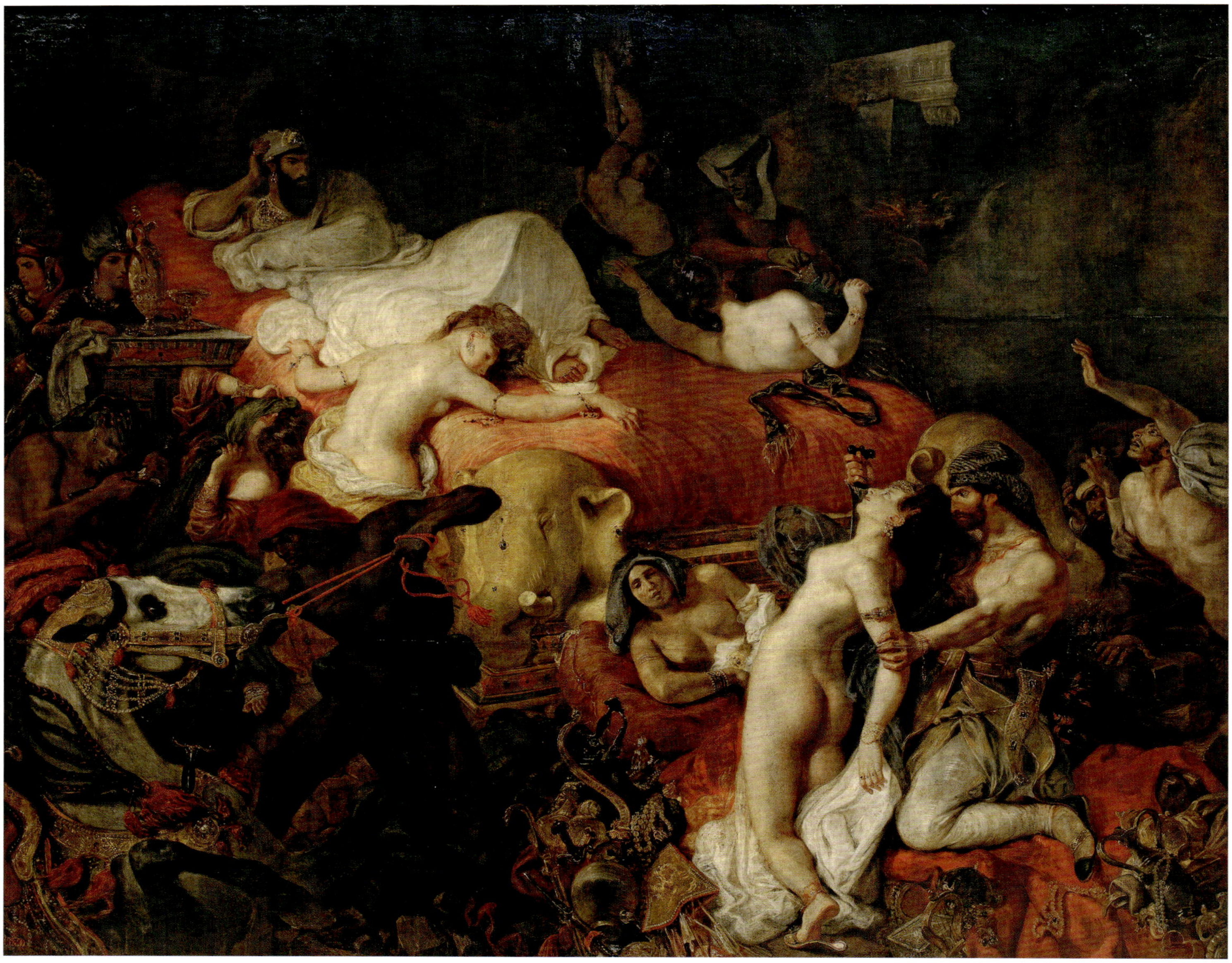

FIG. 8 Eugène Delacroix, *The Death of Sardanapalus*, 1827. Oil on canvas, 392 x 496 cm. Musée du Louvre, Paris

London), in *The Defeat of Sennacherib* (*c.* 1616; Alte Pinakothek, Munich), in the *The Death of Decius Mus* (*c.* 1618; Liechtenstein Collection, Vienna) and in the large battle scene from the Henri IV series (*c.* 1630; Galleria degli Uffizi, Florence).

In the nineteenth century, artists rediscovered Rubens as a creator of impressive scenes of violence. To begin with, his *œuvre* forms a complete catalogue of human and animal anatomy in all its movements. It is not surprising, therefore, that Théodore Géricault studied nudes by Michelangelo and Rubens for his portrayal of the desperate stranded people in *The Raft of the Medusa* (1819; Musée du Louvre, Paris),[11] and also copied falling figures from a print after Rubens. For the souls of the damned in his *Barque of Dante* (1822; Musée du Louvre, Paris) and the civilian victims in *The Massacre at Chios* (1824; Musée du Louvre, Paris), Delacroix drew inspiration from the outcasts, the sick and the resurrected dead in Rubens's representations of miracles (Kunsthistorisches Museum, Vienna, and St Martinus, Aalst). The use of allegorical imagery declined in the nineteenth century in all but official art, which continued to highlight heroism and martyrdom. This is illustrated, for example, by the figure of Victory in Sir David Wilkie's *Defence of Saragossa in 1808* (1828; Royal Collection). This Rubenesque camp follower subsequently inspired Wilkie's friend Delacroix to paint the figure of Marianne in *Liberty Leading the People* (1830; Musée du Louvre, Paris). Romantic artists frequently consulted Rubens's *œuvre* when painting their revolutionary canvases. Wilkie's *General Sir David Baird Discovering the Body of Sultan Tippoo Sahib* (1839; Scottish National Gallery, Edinburgh) extols the supremacy of the colonial ruler. This sinister painting also displays the monumental dimensions, the palette and the pathos of an *Entombment* by Rubens. Gustaaf Wappers constructed his overpopulated *Episode of the September Days of 1830 on the Grand Place in Brussels* (1835; Musées royaux des Beaux-Arts de Belgique, Brussels) around a dead martyr of the Belgian revolution. This composition plainly refers to a masterpiece that is a valuable part of the national patrimony: Rubens's *Deposition* in Antwerp Cathedral. Delacroix's choreography of *The Death of Sardanapalus* (fig. 8) – an Assyrian tyrant who has his wives and slaves slaughtered before he commits suicide – is based on a Rubensian model; its composition features an outer ring of bodies in action and a blood-red bed at its vortex. Here the sensual and the gruesome are bound by the century's fascination with Orientalism. Furthermore, the centrifugal *The Battle of the Amazons* provided the frame of reference for *The Battle of Taillebourg*, which Delacroix painted in 1837 for the Galerie des Batailles in Versailles. Abduction (and often, by implication, rape) as an artistic subject also made a comeback in the age of Romanticism.[12] In their search for usable material, artists inevitably came across Rubens's portrayals of this theme (such as cats 21 and 22).

But perhaps the theme most characteristic of Rubens is the trial of strength between humans and animals. Writing in the late nineteenth-century, Jacob Burckhardt attributed the artist's success to his 'strong desire to study and paint formidable beasts and supreme delight in all movement. There may be beauty and dignity in an animal at rest, but it is only the animal in free, powerful movement that can fully reveal its own peculiar life.'[13] Burckhardt referred to the series of dramatic and violent hunting scenes (such as fig. 9) that Rubens painted between 1616 and 1621 for art-loving clients among the royalty and the nobility.[14] Reviving this old genre was a calculated commercial move. Rubens did not confine himself to portraying European game, such as wolves and wild boar, but also depicted such exotic species as lions, tigers, leopards, crocodiles and a hippopotamus. Such animals are not to be found in the Netherlands, but the artist's thorough knowledge of anatomy and his skill with the brush enabled him to bring to life the fur and markings of tigers and leopards in the most miraculous way. Working from two stuffed baby animals, which a Neapolitan surgeon exhibited in Rome in 1601, Rubens became the first artist since antiquity to portray a hippopotamus (see cat. 10).[15] The artistic challenge of a hunting scene is to depict a number of dangerous situations simultaneously and to introduce order to the chaos. Rubens not only did this with consummate skill, but also proved to be a keen observer of the animal instinct. His creative quest for the best compositional solution ultimately led to the famous *Lion Hunt* in Munich (see cat. 2). The engraving by Schelte Adamsz. Bolswert (cat. 5) and the etchings by Pieter Claesz. Soutman made Rubens's hunting scenes known throughout Europe.

The hunting scenes of Rubens and his contemporary Frans Snyders aroused the enthusiasm of the Romantic British painter Sir Edwin Landseer. Although Landseer could rely on a solid native tradition of animal painting, he emulated, above all, the realism with which Rubens sought to depict wild animals. He travelled to Blair Atholl in the Scottish Highlands to observe wild deer in their natural habitat, and, like Rubens, hoped that his canvases would appeal to aristocratic hunters. The French appreciated Rubens's hunting scenes for their Orientalism and exoticism rather than for their realism. Rembrandt had been one of the first to recognise this quality in Soutman's prints (cats 6, 7, 8 and 10). These etchings were possibly lying on the drawing table of Carle Van Loo, Charles Parrocel and François Boucher when they were commissioned by the young Louis XV to design a series of exotic hunting scenes for the Petite Galerie in the Palace of Versailles (*c.* 1736–39; Musée de Picardie, Amiens).

Rubens's hunting scenes also exerted a considerable influence on the work of Eugène Delacroix (cats 12, 13 and 14).[16] The young Delacroix was fascinated by the behaviour of the lions and tigers in Paris's Jardin des Plantes, a botanical garden and zoo, and during his journey through Morocco in 1832 he was impressed by the wild horses he saw there.[17] It is asserted that Delacroix knew Rubens's hunting scenes only through Soutman's prints, but this seems unlikely.[18] In 1820 Rubens's spectacular *Wolf and Fox Hunt* (fig. 9) was sold in Paris to the art dealer John Smith, and four years later it was taken to London and resold to Alexander Baring, 1st Baron Ashburton, a patron of painters including Landseer and Sir Thomas Lawrence. It is not impossible that Delacroix saw the piece either on that occasion in Paris or in England, where he stayed from May to August 1825 in order to visit Wilkie and Lawrence. In September 1839 Delacroix undertook an art-historical pilgrimage to the Low Countries, to investigate the roots of his artistic heroes Rubens and Rembrandt. In the famous collection of King William II in The Hague, Delacroix made a copy after Rubens's *Landscape with a Boar Hunt* (fig. 10). In order to attend his brother's funeral, he travelled to Bordeaux, where he stayed the whole month of January 1846. As a great admirer of Rubens, Delacroix undoubtedly visited the Musée des Beaux-Arts in that city, where the master's impressive *Lion Hunt* of 1615–16 was on display (see cat. 6).[19] Perhaps this museum visit was what prompted him, in January 1847, to take Soutman's etchings in hand, and then later, in March 1854, when the French authorities asked him for a masterpiece to show at the Paris Exposition Universelle of 1855, to propose painting a huge lion-hunt scene. Delacroix hoped that this savage and exotic creation would enable him to emulate Rubens's great example with success, but his tour de force was not popular with either the public at large or the many connoisseurs who viewed it. However, the canvas opened the eyes of Charles Baudelaire, who compared it to an explosion of colour: 'Never before [have there been] colours more beautiful, more intense, or so penetrating to the soul through the channel of the eyes.'[20] This poet and art critic understood that the next generation of painters would not be afraid of colour.

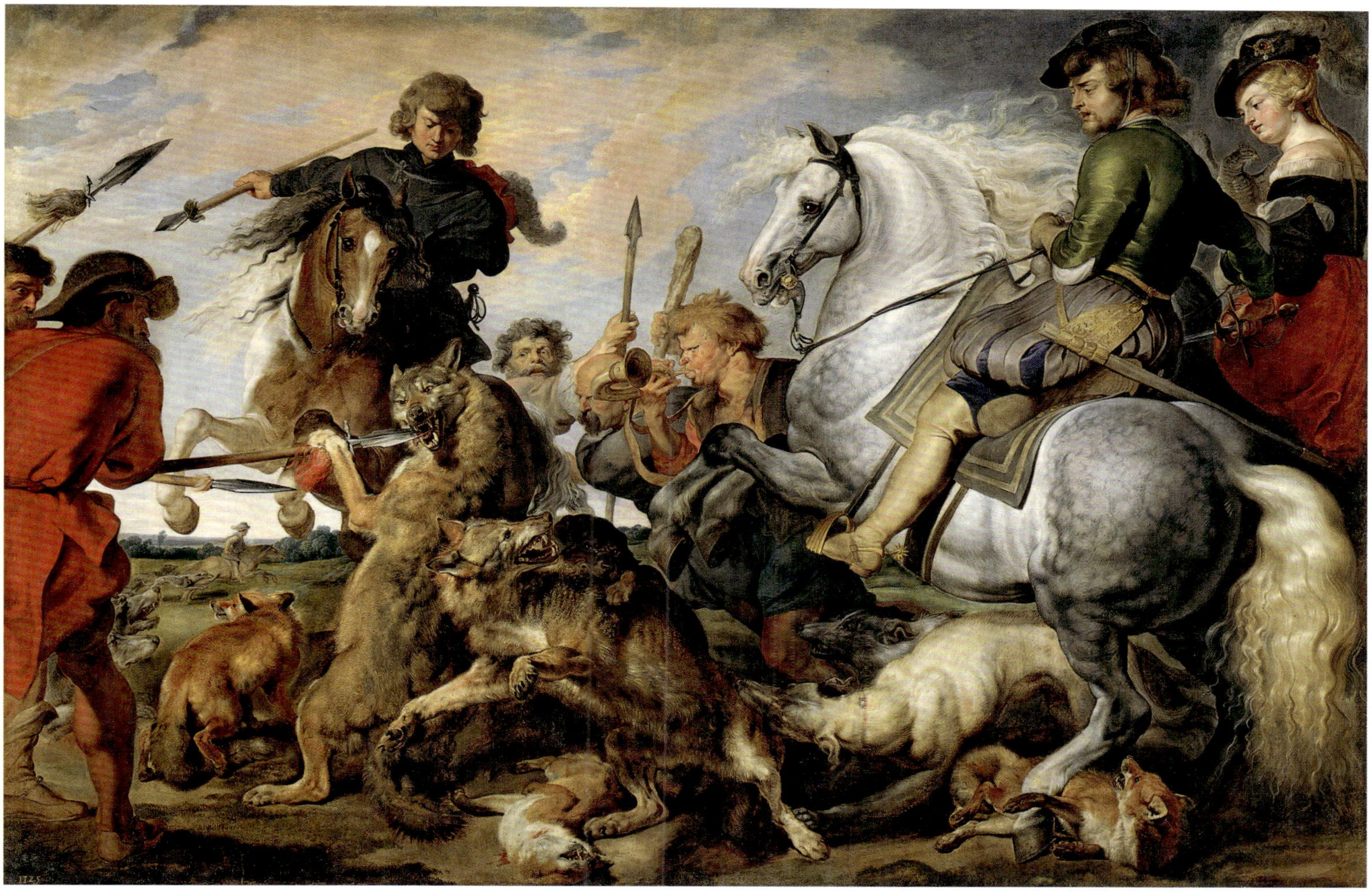

FIG. 9 Peter Paul Rubens, *Wolf and Fox Hunt*, *c.* 1616. Oil on canvas, 245.4 x 376.2 cm. The Metropolitan Museum of Art, New York

Rubens possibly painted the impressive Rennes *Tiger, Lion and Leopard Hunt* (cat. 1) in 1617, when he was working on the set of tapestries depicting the story of Decius Mus, a commission for which he signed a contract on 9 November 1616. The scene that depicts the death of the Roman consul (the first of three successive generations to sacrifice himself in battle) shows a horseman reaching backwards to spear his victim. Rubens recycled this figure, using it in reverse in the hunting scene. The *Tiger, Lion and Leopard Hunt* also contains a number of other elements that were originally used elsewhere. The horseman being attacked from behind by a wild animal can be found in a famous oil sketch (*c.* 1614–15; National Gallery, London). Rubens based the dead leopard at the right on a preparatory drawing (Morgan Library and Museum, New York) that he had previously made for *Daniel in the Lions' Den* (*c.* 1614–16; National Gallery of Art, Washington DC), and the Moorish rider with the turban has the same facial features as the *Portrait of Mūlāy Ahmad* (*c.* 1609; Museum of Fine Arts, Boston). The motif of the tigress taking her cubs to safety was inspired by a small bronze from Padua. Rubens succeeded in blending all these borrowings into a powerful and convincing image. The existence of the composition in numerous studio copies suggests that the artist considered it extremely successful.

The oil sketch in Munich (cat. 2) shows an oriental rider falling from his rearing horse and being bitten in the belly by a lioness. A horseman in the background flies at the wild animal with his sword as two of his companions race to his aid, one from each side. Rubens made this sketch (and another in the Hermitage) in preparation for his large *Lion Hunt*

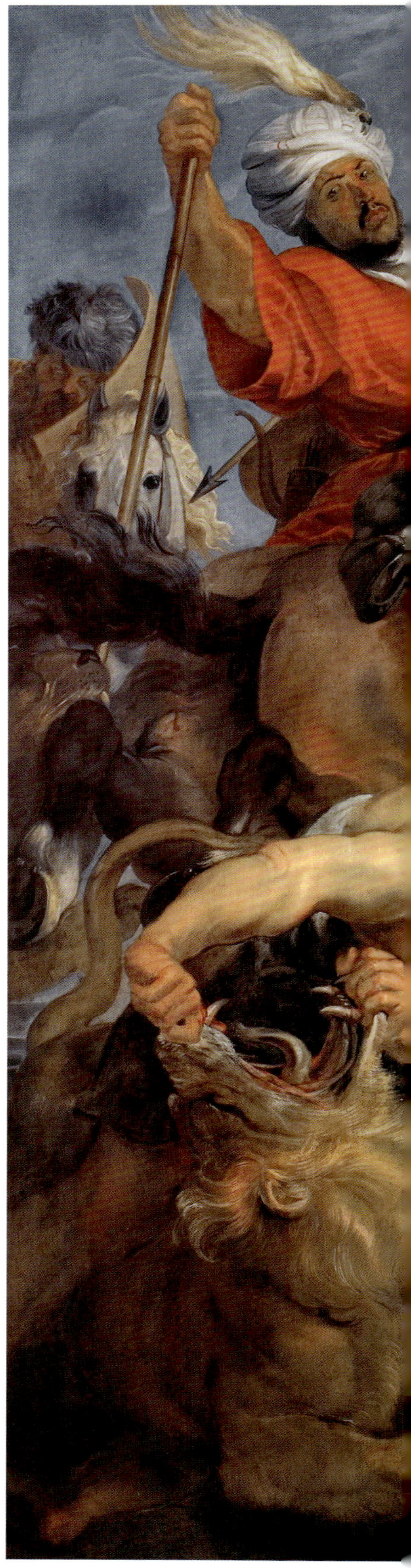

1

PETER PAUL RUBENS (1577–1640)
Tiger, Lion and Leopard Hunt, *c.* 1617
Oil on canvas, 256 x 324 cm
Musée des Beaux-Arts de Rennes, inv. 1811.1.10

PROVENANCE: purchased from Rubens by Duke (later also Elector) Maximilian I of Bavaria; Altes Schloss, Schleissheim; Neues Schloss, Schleissheim, 1761; confiscated by the French commissioner Neveu on 30 August 1800 and taken to Paris; assigned to the Musée des Beaux-Arts de Rennes in 1811 as part of a *deuxième envoi* ('second consignment')
SELECTED REFERENCES: De Piles 1681, p. 25; Rooses 1886–92, vol. 4, pp. 333–37, no. 1152; Held 1980, vol. 1, pp. 407–08, under no. 298, p. 632, under no. A16, p. 633, under no. A17; Balis 1986, no. 7, pp. 133–46

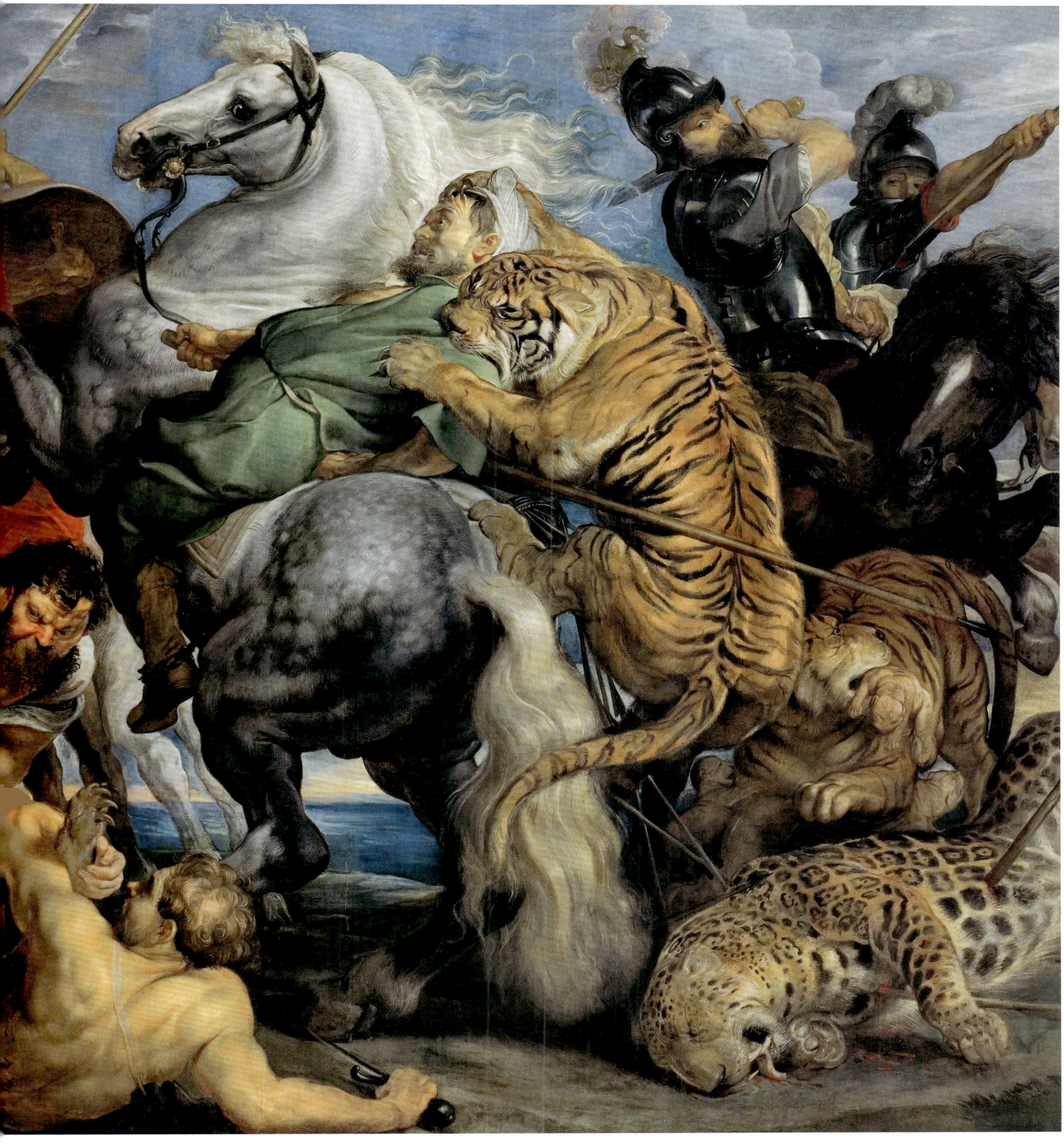

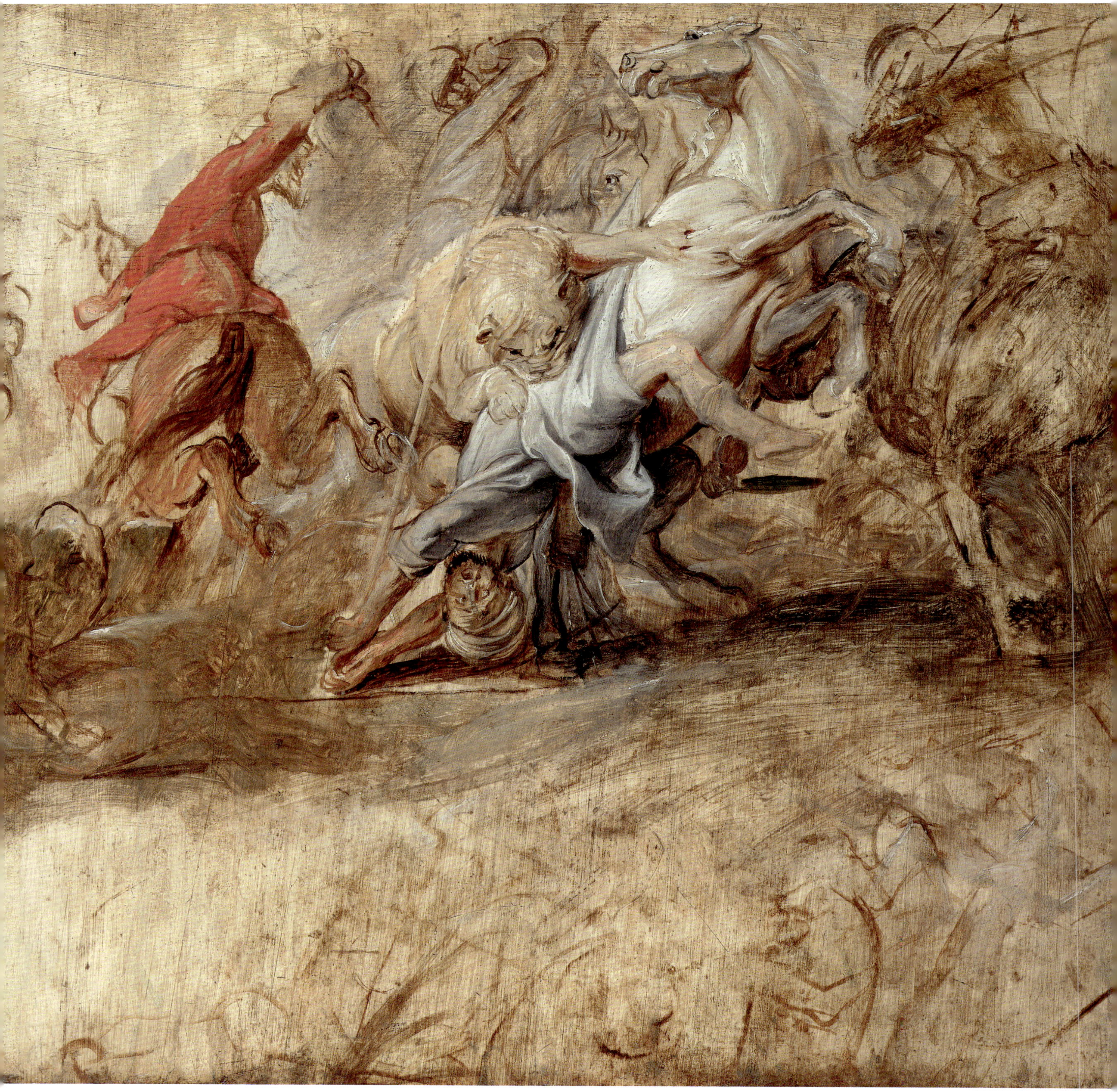

(Alte Pinakothek, Munich), a work that he completed in September 1621. The artist enhanced the subject's legibility by changing the shade of the oriental rider's tunic from blue to a lighter shade of bluish grey, so that horse and victim would form a whole. The sketch illustrates, above all, the master's dazzling precision and creativity. It is likely that the panel was originally larger, as evidenced by the lower and left edges, which cut through sketches begun in brown paint. In 1622 the artist re-used the small panel, making a design for one of the paintings in the Médicis cycle – Marie's marriage by proxy – on the verso and, at the same time, altering the format.

Another theme that enables an artist to portray the battle between man and beast is the story of Hercules and the Nemean lion. Rubens sketched this subject three times in red chalk on a sheet that is now in the British Museum (cat. 3).[1] The other scribbles on this sheet, one of which he corrected in ink, are related to another exploit of the mythical hero, namely his wrestling with Antaeus. The latter chalk studies are possibly related to the painting ordered by the King of Spain from the artist in 1639 (a work that Jordaens completed after Rubens's death).[2] The figures of Hercules or Atlas with the globe are also sometimes recognised among the scribbles. It is beyond dispute that Rubens's own creative wrestling presents a fascinating spectacle, for surely his quest for the perfect solution is the essence of his artistry.

That Rubens had a soft spot for this mythical superhero is also apparent from the woodcut of *Hercules Crushing Discord* (cat. 4) made by Christoffel Jegher under the master's supervision. An oil sketch (in the possession of the Museum of Fine Arts, Boston) for one of the oval allegories on the ceiling of Whitehall Palace, now the Banqueting House, in London, served as the model for this sheet. The impressive woodcut is proportionately narrower and higher, however, so adaptations were necessary. To increase its clarity, the left leg of crushed Discord was positioned lower and the club and raised arm of Hercules form a more vertical axis. A proof retouched by Rubens is preserved in the Bibliothèque nationale in Paris. Rubens certainly had this woodcut produced for commercial reasons, since portrayals of legendary musclemen such as St Christopher and Hercules traditionally enjoyed great popularity.

2

PETER PAUL RUBENS (1577–1640)
Recto: sketch for *Lion Hunt*, *c.* 1621;
verso: sketch for *The Wedding by Proxy of Marie de Médicis*, *c.* 1622
Oil on panel, 44 x 50 cm
Alte Pinakothek, Munich, inv. 15475.
Bayerische Staatsgemäldesammlungen
RA ONLY

PROVENANCE: sale (? Thomas) Major, London, 1751, lot 46, purchased by the 3rd Earl of Cholmondeley (1703–1770); Cholmondeley sale, Christie's, London, 10 July 1886, lot 220 (unsold); Lord Cholmondeley, Houghton Hall, Norfolk; purchased in 1994 by the Bayerische Staatsgemäldesammlungen with the support of the Kulturstiftung der Länder, the Bayerische Hypotheken- und Wechsel Bank and the Ernst von Siemens Kunstfonds
SELECTED REFERENCES: Held 1980, cats, 61 and 300; Balis 1986, no. 11b, pp. 174–75

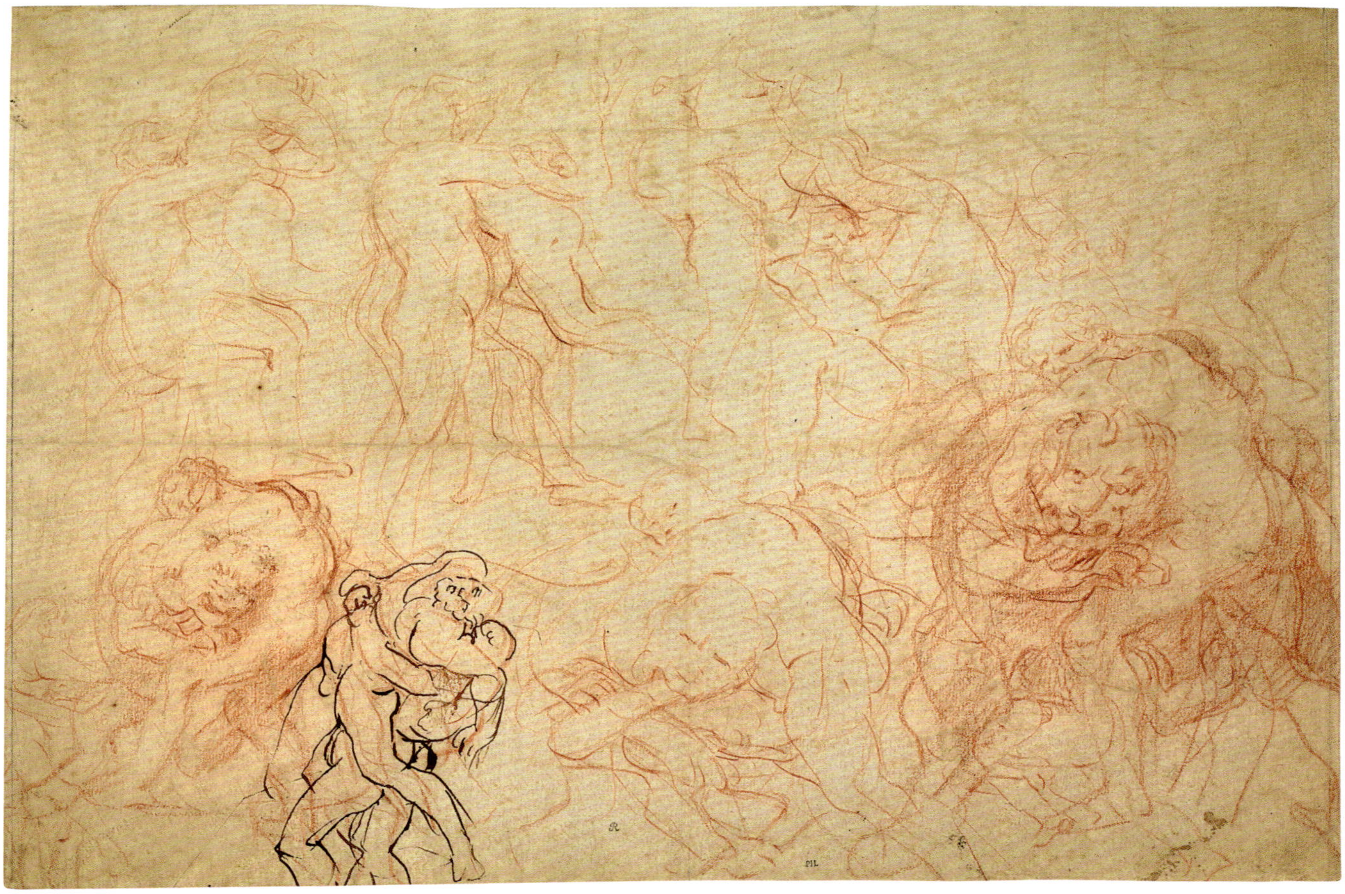

3

PETER PAUL RUBENS (1577–1640)
Recto: sketches for *The Labours of Hercules: Hercules Wrestles with Antaeus and three sketches of Hercules*, *c.* 1630–35; verso: two studies for a visitation: *The Virgin Embraced by St Elizabeth* and *Zacharias Greets Joseph* with a similar group at right, a spaniel at their feet
Red and black chalk with pen and brown ink, 31.1 x 47 cm
On loan from the British Museum, London, inv. 1897,0615.12. Presented by Henry Vaughan, 1897

PROVENANCE: Prosper Henry Lankrink; Jonathan Richard Senior; donated by Henry Vaughan in 1893
SELECTED REFERENCES: Burchard and d'Hulst 1963, pp. 295–301, no. 190; Rowlands 1977, no. 184; Held 1986, no. 217

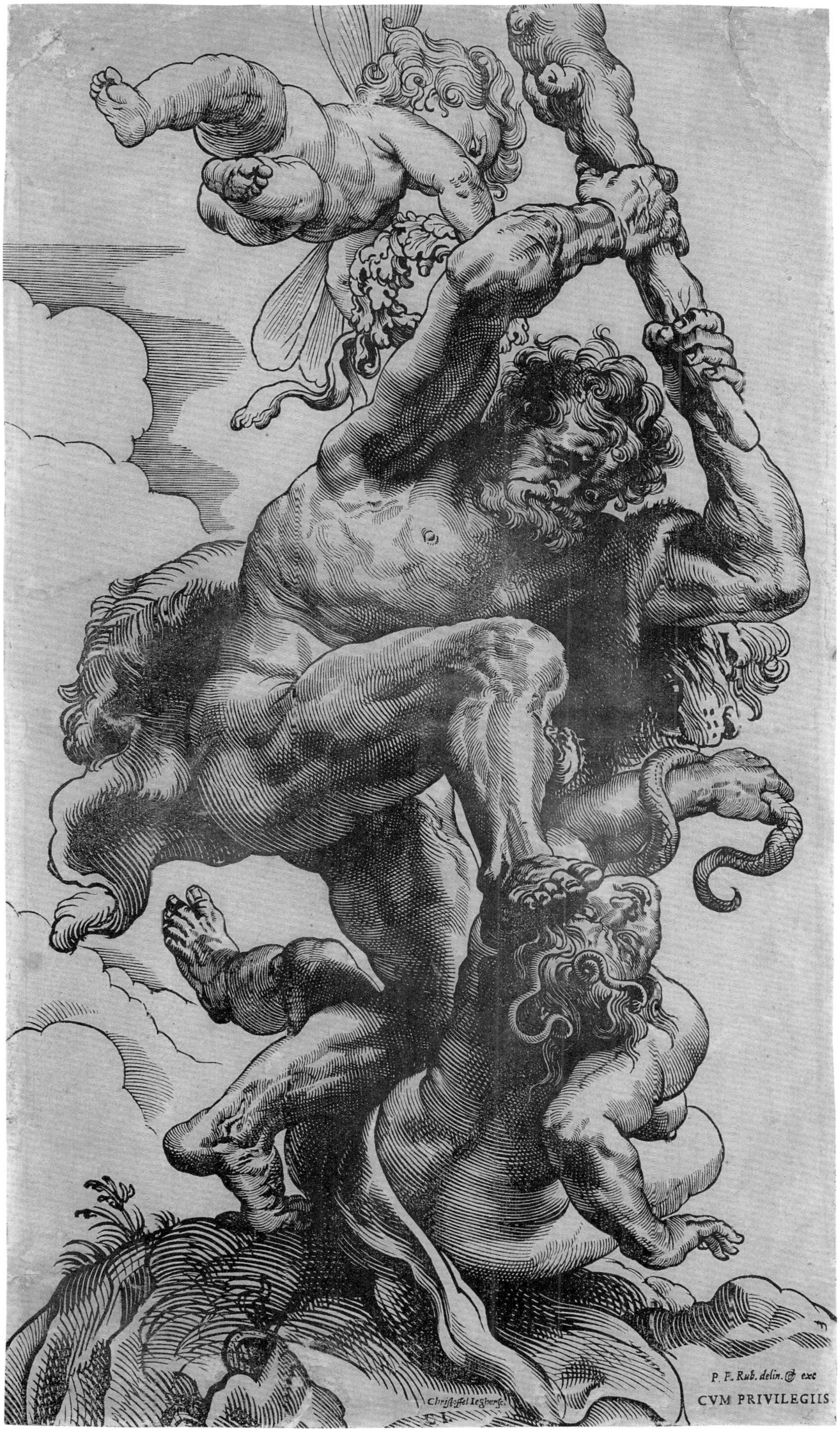

4

CHRISTOFFEL JEGHER
(1596–1652/53)
Hercules Crushing Discord, *c.* 1633–34
Woodcut, 60 x 35.7 cm
Royal Museum of Fine Arts Antwerp,
inv. 11139

PROVENANCE: Max Rooses collection, donated to the museum in 1900
SELECTED REFERENCES:
Van den Wijngaert 1940, no. 316;
Rome 1977, no. 155; Hollstein, 1949–2010, vol. 9, no. 15

Bolswert's *Lion Hunt* (cat. 5) is the only print after a hunting scene by Rubens that is certain to have originated under the master's supervision. Perhaps this is no coincidence, for in few other compositions did Rubens capture a life-and-death struggle so convincingly. Bolswert engraved the image sometime between 1625 (or 1626), when he enrolled as a master in the guild, and 19 August 1629, the date of death of the Prince of Chimay, to whom the print is dedicated.[1] It was previously assumed that Rubens had also commissioned the hunting prints by Pieter Claesz. Soutman (cats 6, 7, 8 and 10), who worked from 1616 to 1624 in the master's studio. However, the technique in which they were etched differs from that of the copperplate and wood engravings that Rubens preferred, and in the meantime scholars have come to the conclusion that Soutman must have etched the hunting scenes after 1636, when he was granted a privilege to publish prints in his native city of Haarlem.[2] The same is probably true for the *Lion and Leopard Hunt* (cat. 9) that was made by Jonas Suyderhoef under his supervision. *Boar Hunt* is the only sheet that bears a date – 1642 – but there is nothing to indicate that this was Soutman's first print. Clearly, this Dutch *peintre-graveur* was largely responsible for making Rubens's hunting scenes known to later generations of artists.

It seems likely that Rembrandt etched his *Large Lion Hunt* of 1641 (cat. 11) in response to Soutman's monumental prints. This is one of the few times that Rembrandt treated this subject in his graphic work,[3] and quite possibly he was aiming to surpass Soutman's etchings in terms of liveliness and truthfulness to nature when he produced this hunting scene. The chiaroscuro of Soutman's print may well do justice to the drama of the original painting, but the detailed and polished etching technique tempers its dynamism. The suggestion that Rembrandt was inspired by Rubens's oil sketches of hunting scenes seems less likely,[4] given their small number.[5] Moreover, according to a stipulation in Rubens's will, such studies – a mouth-watering pictorial archive – could not be sold until it became apparent that his youngest descendant would not pursue an artistic career, and this was not evident until 1657.[6]

It is possible that Eugène Delacroix had the impressive Bordeaux *Lion Hunt*, another canvas by Rubens, at the back of his mind when he began to scrutinise Soutman's prints on 25 January 1847 (see p. 30). The French painter thought that the composition of Soutman's *Lion Hunt*, which reproduces the Bordeaux work, made a confused impression and that the eye had no idea where to look first. In his view, Rubens did not distinguish enough between the main protagonists and figures of secondary importance.[7] However, he greatly admired the exuberant *Hippopotamus and Crocodile Hunt* (cat. 10). He was fond of the work's wild aesthetics, which differed so greatly from the sugary-sweet taste of the mid-nineteenth century.[8] 'In the reproductive print the painting seems to be inferior in every respect to the previous one; however, the deployment of the groups – or rather the single, unique group that comprises the entire picture – gives the imagination a shock that is renewed at every glance, just as the imagination is thrown into the same uncertainty of line in Soutman's *Lion Hunt*. In the *Hippopotamus and Crocodile Hunt* the monstrous amphibian occupies centre stage; riders, horses, dogs, all hurl themselves furiously at it. The composition presents something like a St Andrew's cross with the

5

SCHELTE ADAMSZ. BOLSWERT (c. 1586–1659)
Lion Hunt, *c.* 1625–29
Engraving, 42.2 x 58.6 cm
Royal Museum of Fine Arts Antwerp, inv. 10982

PROVENANCE: Max Rooses collection, donated to the museum in 1900
SELECTED REFERENCES: Voorhelm Schneevoogt 1873, 227.31.1; Balis 1986, no. 11e (copy 8); Hollstein 1949–2010, vol. 3, no. 298 (under Bolswert)

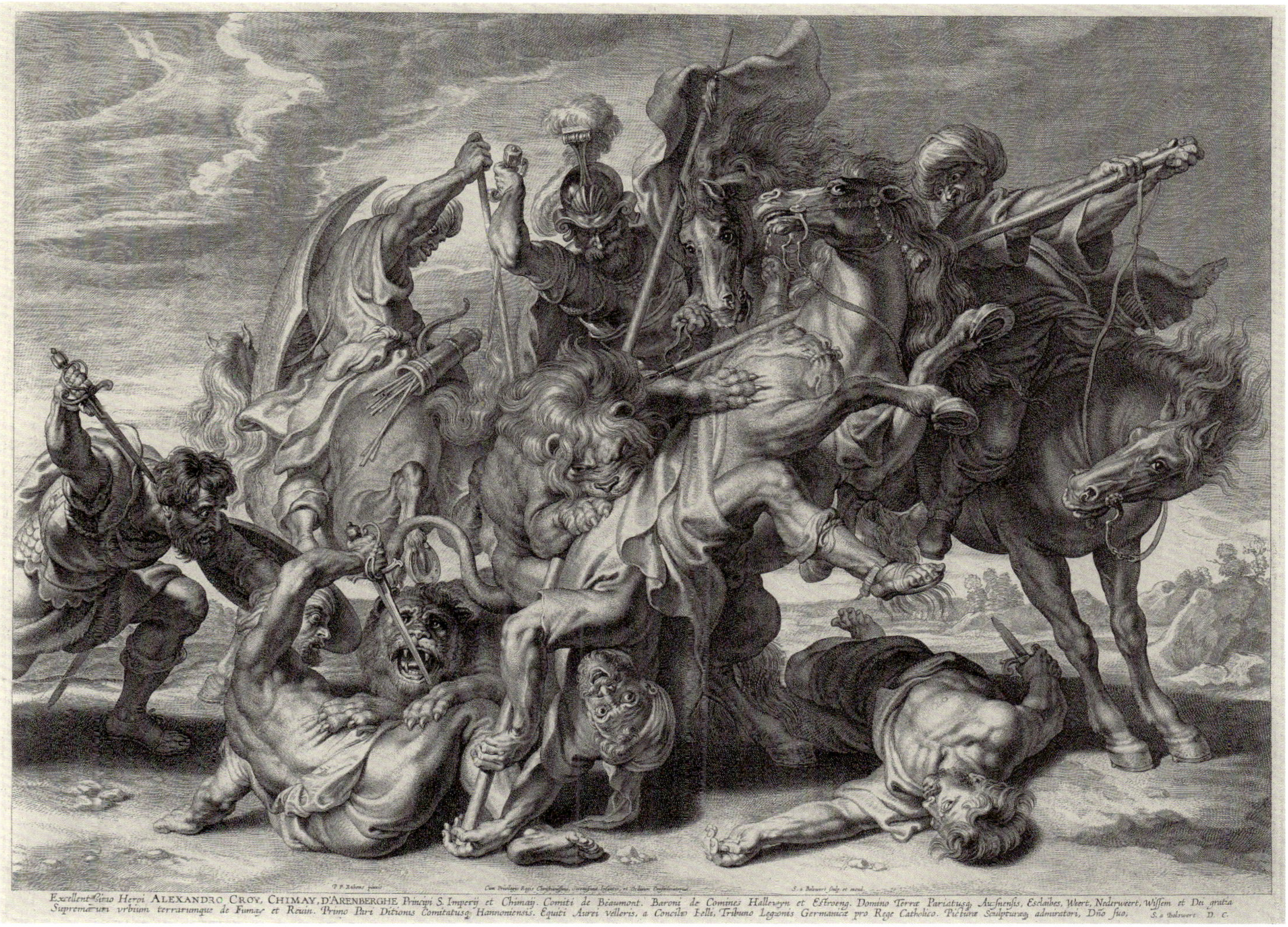

hippopotamus in the middle. ... And of incomparable effect is the large passage of sky framing the whole on both sides – particularly the left-hand passage, which is completely blank – which, by virtue of the simplicity of this contrast, lends the ensemble movement and variety and, at the same time, incomparable unity.'[9] These pertinent observations of Delacroix, which analyse the structure of Rubens's hunting scenes, remained valuable lessons, even for an experienced history painter.

6

PIETER CLAESZ. SOUTMAN (c. 1580–1657)
Lion Hunt, after 1636
Etching, 47.7 x 65.5 cm
Royal Museum of Fine Arts Antwerp, inv. 10985

PROVENANCE: Max Rooses collection, donated to the museum in 1900
SELECTED REFERENCES: Voorhelm Schneevoogt 1873, 227.31.3; Balis 1986, no. 6 (copy 6); Hollstein 1949–2010, vol. 17, no. 1 (under Soutman)

7

PIETER CLAESZ. SOUTMAN (c. 1580–1657)
Wolf Hunt, after 1636
Etching, 46 x 63 cm
Royal Museum of Fine Arts Antwerp, inv. 10988

PROVENANCE: Max Rooses collection, donated to the museum in 1900
SELECTED REFERENCES: Voorhelm Schneevoogt 1873, 227.31.5; Balis 1986, no. 2 (copy 11); Hollstein 1949–2010, vol. 18, no. 1

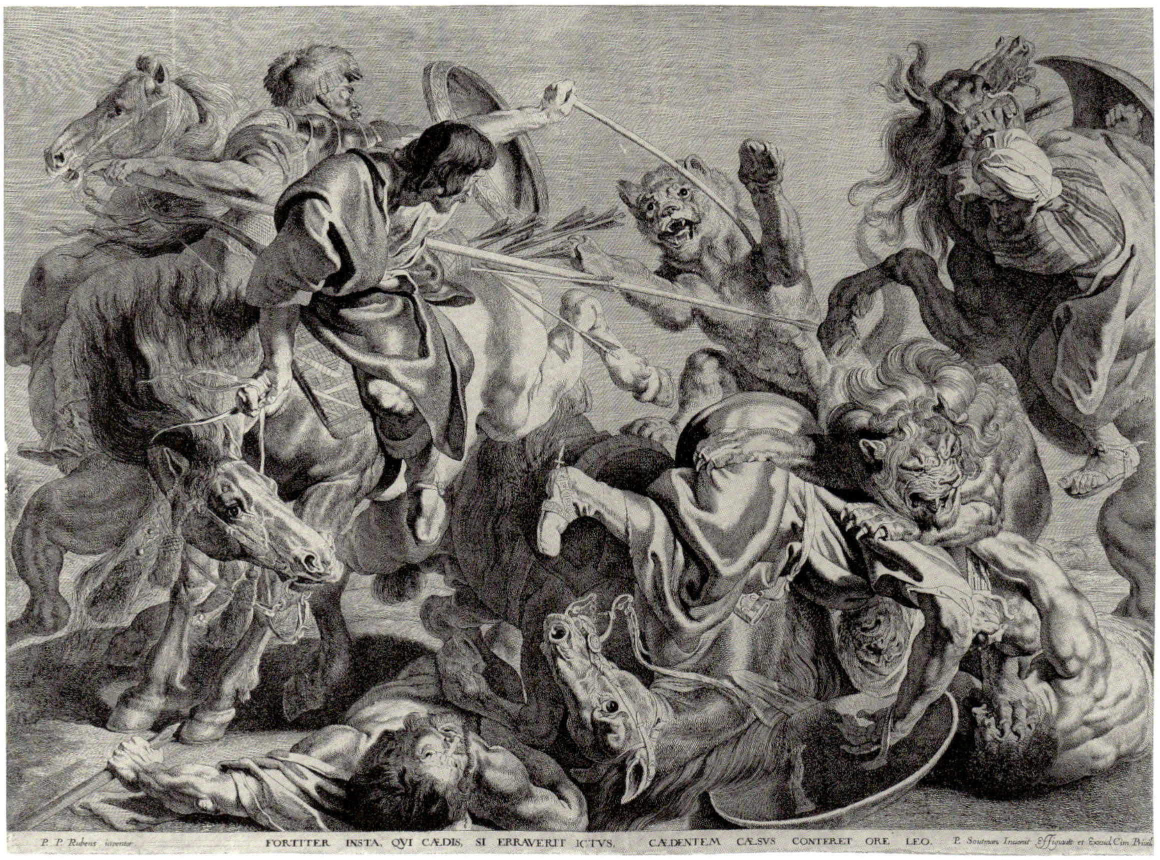

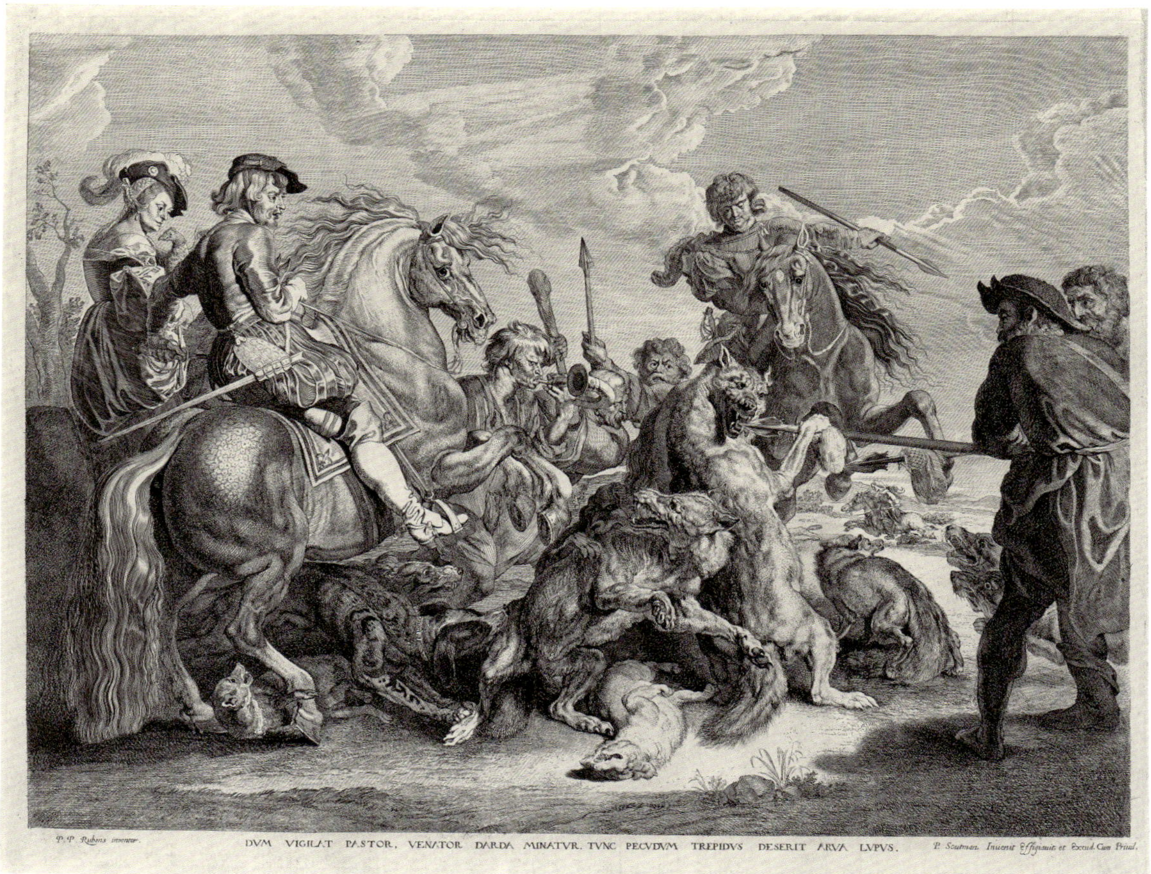

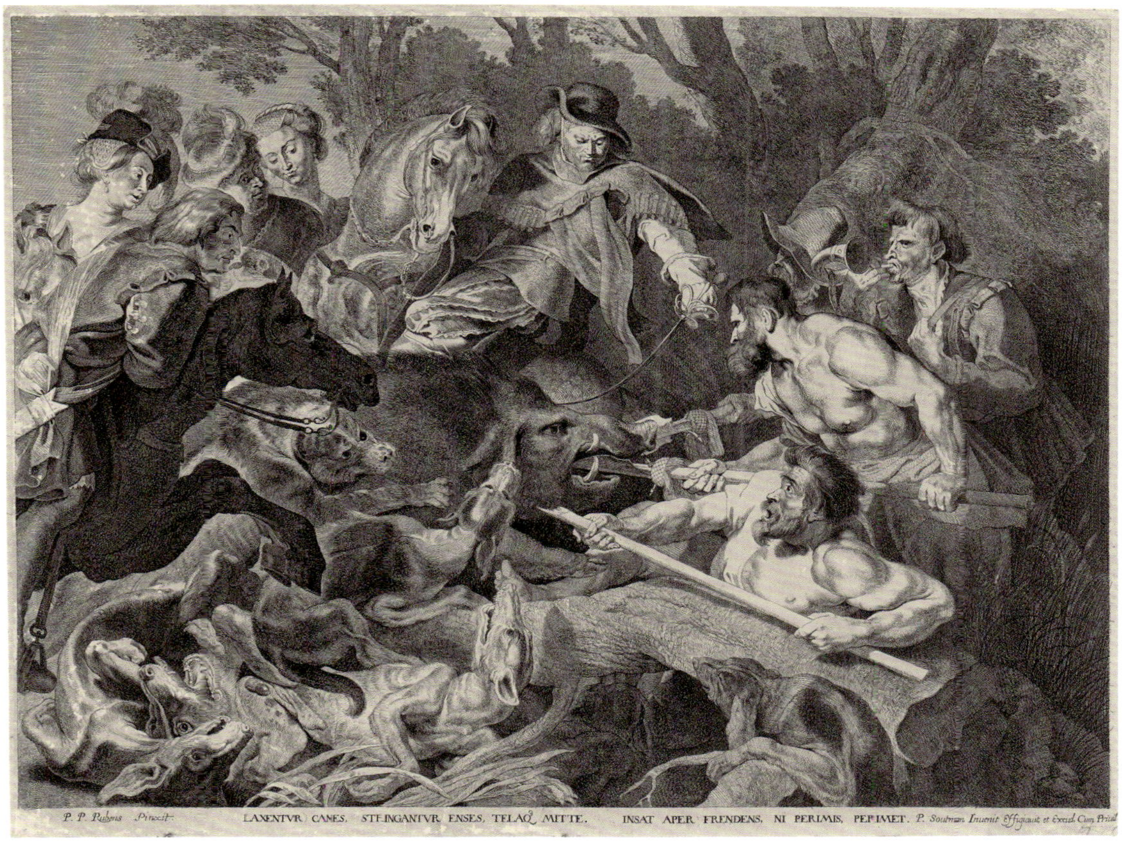

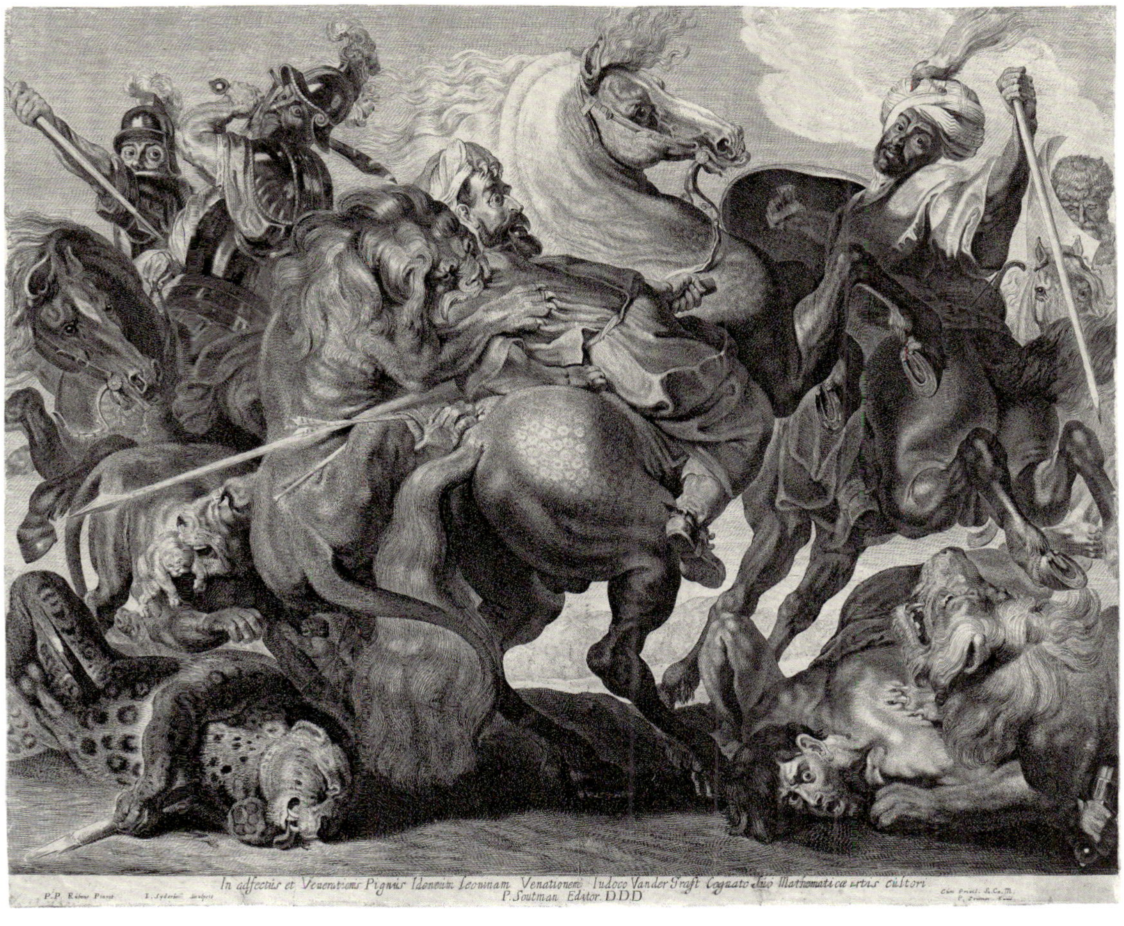

8

PIETER CLAESZ. SOUTMAN (c 1580–1657),
Bear Hunt, 1642
Etching, 47.5 x 63.9 cm
Royal Museum of Fine Arts Antwerp, inv. 10985

PROVENANCE: Max Rooses collection, donated to the museum in 1900
SELECTED REFERENCES: Voorhelm Schneevoogt 1873, 228.31.9; Hollstein 1949–2010, vol. 20 (under Soutman); Balis 1986, no. 18 (copy 10)

9

JONAS SUYDERHOEF (c. 1613–1686)
Lion and Leopard Hunt, after 1636
Engraving, 46.4 x 58 cm
Royal Museum of Fine Arts Antwerp, inv. 10986

PROVENANCE: Max Rooses collection
SELECTED REFERENCES: Voorhelm Schneevoogt 1873, 227.31.2; Balis 1986, no. 8 (copy 4); Hollstein 1949–2010, vol 28

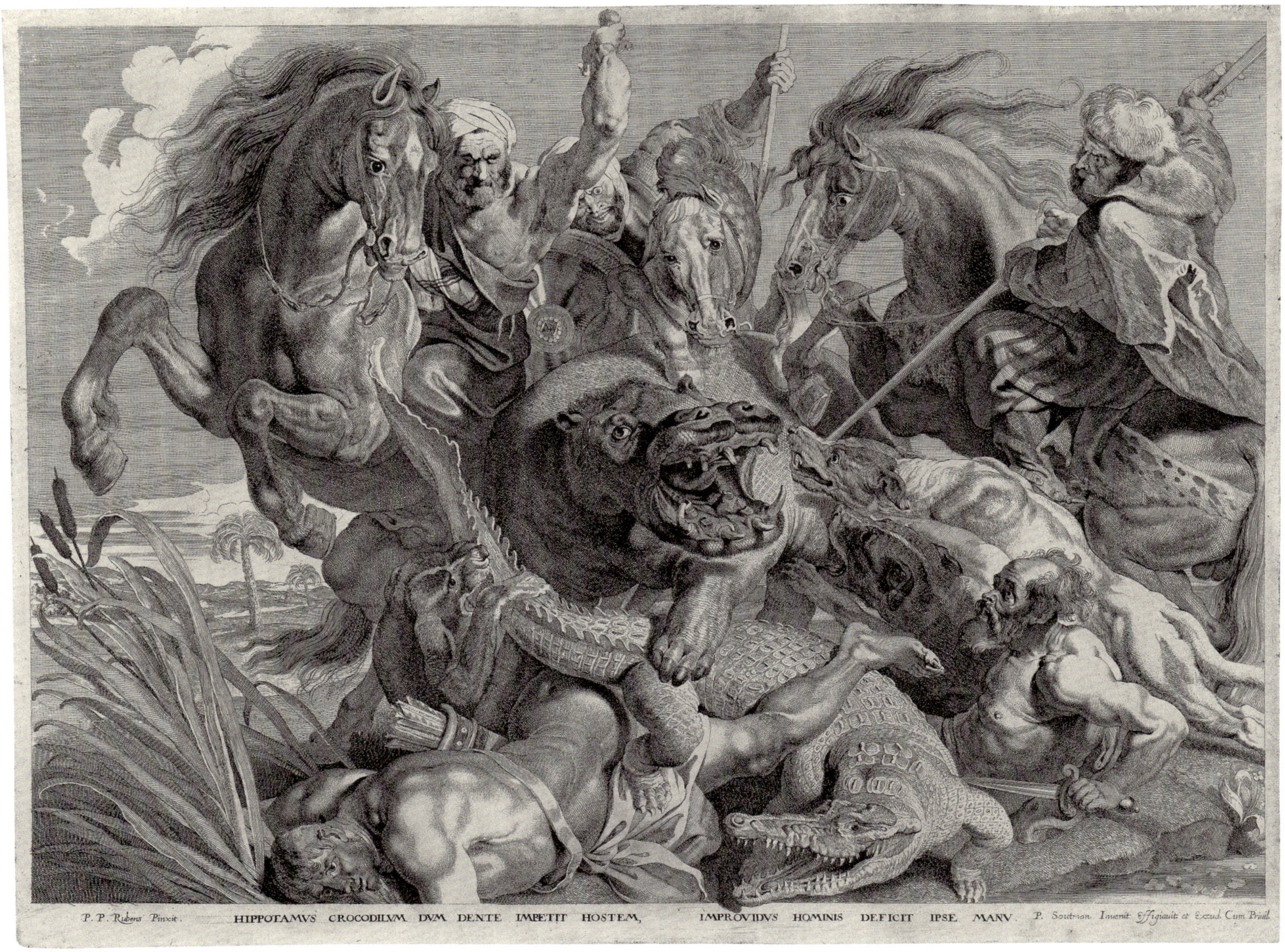

10

PIETER CLAESZ. SOUTMAN
(c. 1580–1657)
Hippopotamus and Crocodile Hunt,
after 1636
Etching, 44 x 62.8 cm
Royal Museum of Fine Arts Antwerp,
inv. 10994

PROVENANCE: Max Rooses collection, donated to the museum in 1900
SELECTED REFERENCES: Voorhelm Schneevoogt 1873, 228.31.11; Balis 1986, no. 5 (copy 14); Hollstein 1949–2010, vol. 21, no. 1

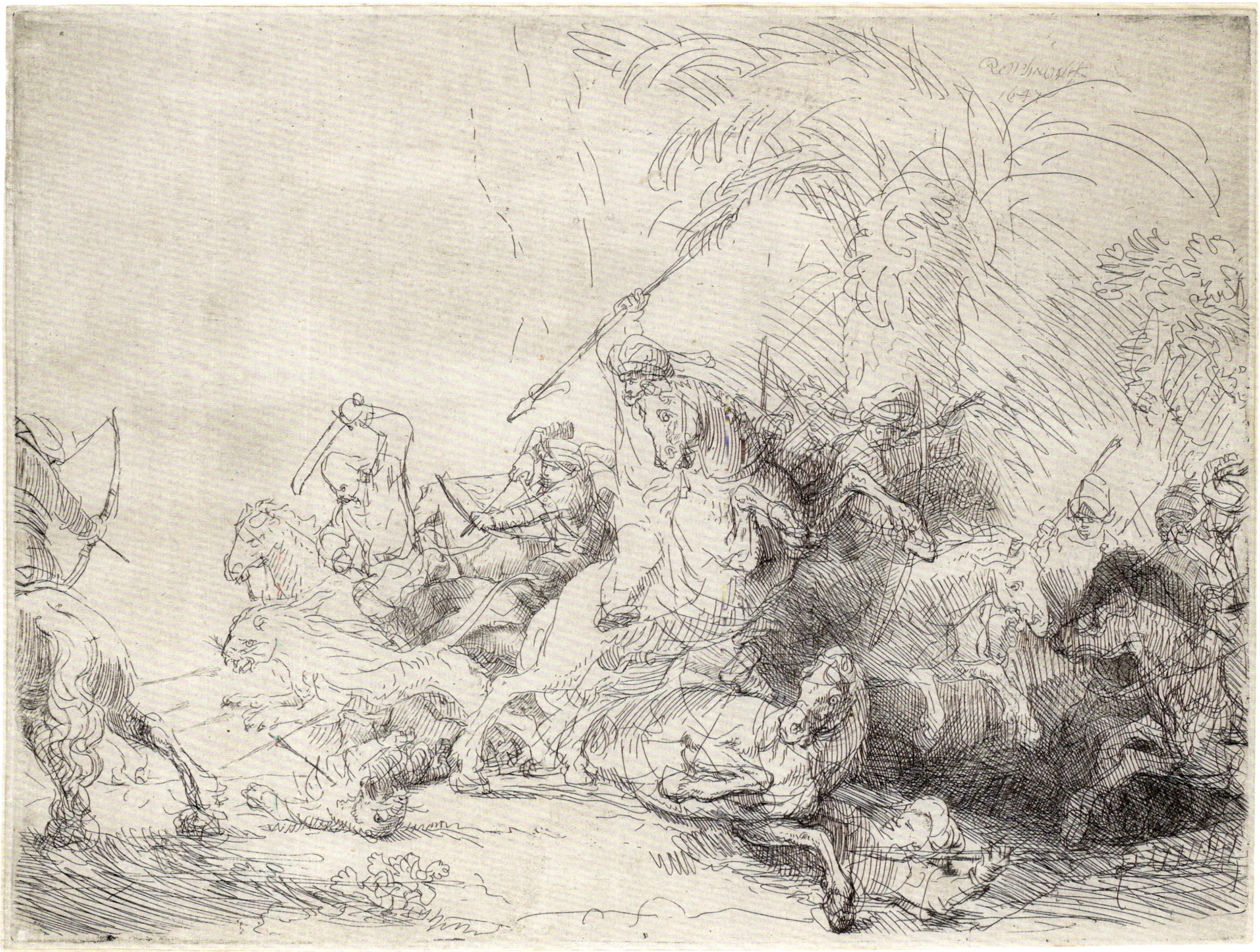

11

REMBRANDT VAN RIJN
(1606-1669)
Large Lion Hunt, 1641
Etching and drypoint, 22.2 × 29.8 cm
Rijksmuseum, Amsterdam.
inv. RP-P-OB-200

PROVENANCE: bequest of Mr and Mrs De Bruijn-van der Leeuw, Muri, 1961
SELECTED REFERENCES: White and Boon 1969, vol. 1, no. 114, second state; Hind 1915, vol. 1, no. 181, second state; London and Amsterdam 2000, no. 42

One of the first landscapes by Rubens that could be admired in England was the *Landscape with the Boar Hunt*, a work now preserved in Dresden. That painting was bought by the 1st Duke of Buckingham (1592–1628), the favourite of James I, and sold by the 2nd Duke in Antwerp in 1648. The young Van Dyck was possibly involved in its composition, since his hand can be recognised in a design in the Albertina in Vienna.[1] The famous *Study of a Fallen Tree* in the Louvre, which was the model for the gnarled tree at the left in the painting, is closer to Van Dyck than to Rubens.[2] The master himself was, however, responsible for the final execution of the painting. Even though such a working method, in which a resourceful assistant helped to develop an artistic concept, would seem to be the exception rather than the rule, it was nevertheless employed in this case. There are more and more indications that quite a few of Rubens's paintings were the result of creative teamwork.[3]

As was customary, Rubens's assistants made a number of copies of the *Landscape with a Boar Hunt*, the best of which is in Glasgow (fig. 10). The landscape passage in this piece is by Jan Wildens, to whom Rubens repeatedly entrusted background settings and other details. At the beginning of the nineteenth century, this painting belonged to the renowned collection of King William II of the Netherlands in The Hague, and it was there that Eugène Delacroix saw it in September 1839, when he and his mistress – the painter Marie-Elizabeth Boulanger – undertook an artistic pilgrimage to Belgium and the Netherlands.[4] Delacroix resolved to paint a scaled-down copy of it (cat. 12), as he had done shortly before with Rubens's *Education of the Virgin*, now in the Royal Museum of Fine Arts Antwerp.[5]

In the course of his life, Delacroix made nearly a hundred drawings after works by Rubens and painted some thirty copies in oil, most of them reduced in size – impressions that he executed in a rather loose style. Several of these *ricordi* reproduce the original composition in reverse, which shows that Delacroix also worked from prints. Approximately half of the copies were made at the Louvre, chiefly from the Médicis cycle (see cat. 34).[6] There are exceptions, however, for in the summer of 1825 he painted a copy (whereabouts unknown) of Rubens's *Apotheosis of the Duke of Buckingham*, which was then in the collection of his friend Sir David Wilkie. A few years later William Etty, it is supposed, also made a study of this oil sketch (cat. 43). Delacroix felt strongly about the importance of copying to the learning process: in his journal (published posthumously) he noted that Rubens, 'at the age of more than fifty, during the mission on which he was sent to the king of Spain, spent the time he didn't devote to business in copying in Madrid the superb Italian originals that are still to be seen there. He had done a great deal of copying in his youth. This exercise of making copies, completely ignored by the modern schools, was the source of immense knowledge.'[7]

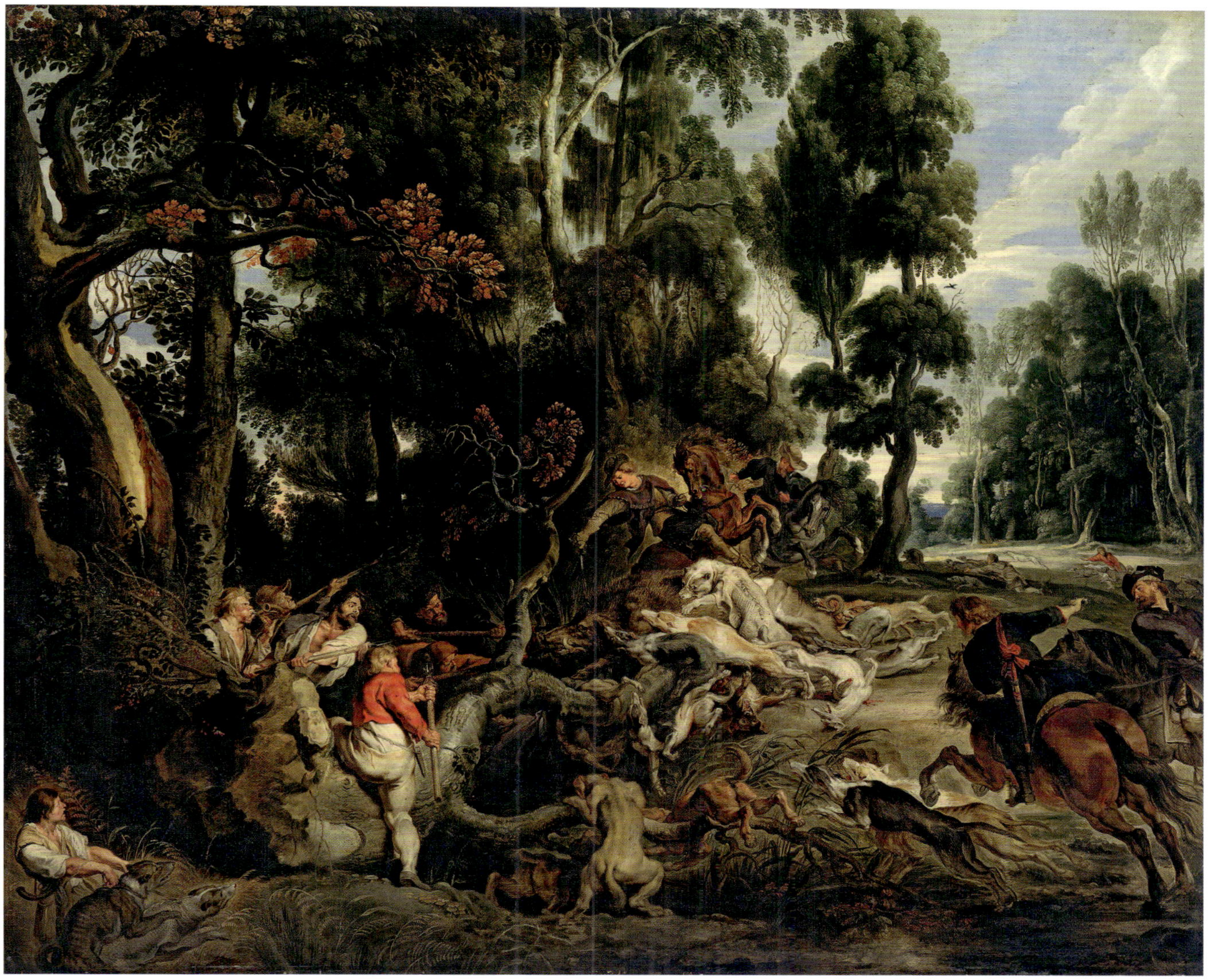

FIG. 10 Peter Paul Rubens, workshop and Jan Wildens, *Landscape with a Boar Hunt*, *c.* 1616. Oil on panel, 135.2 x 167.2 cm. Glasgow Art Gallery and Museum

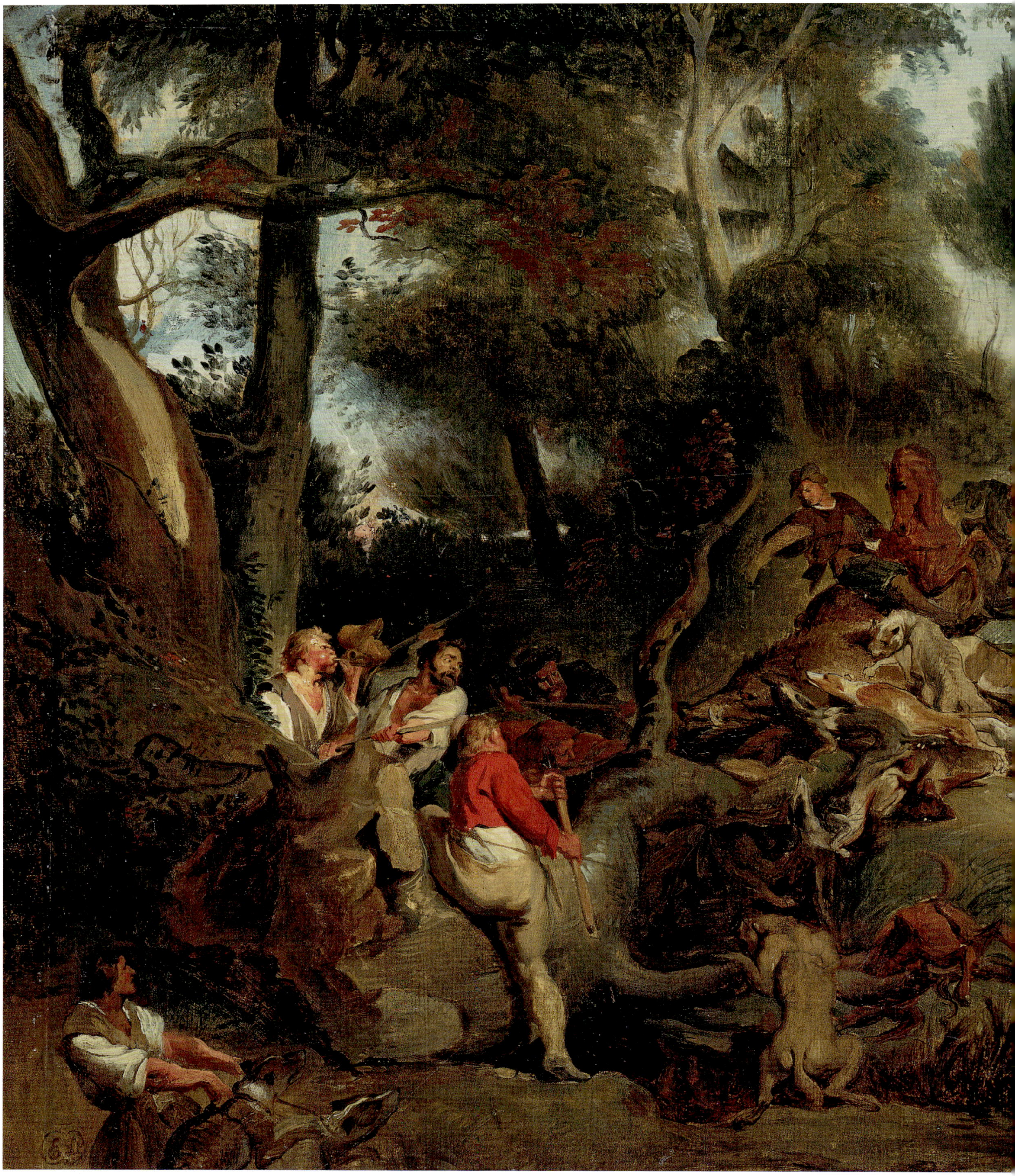

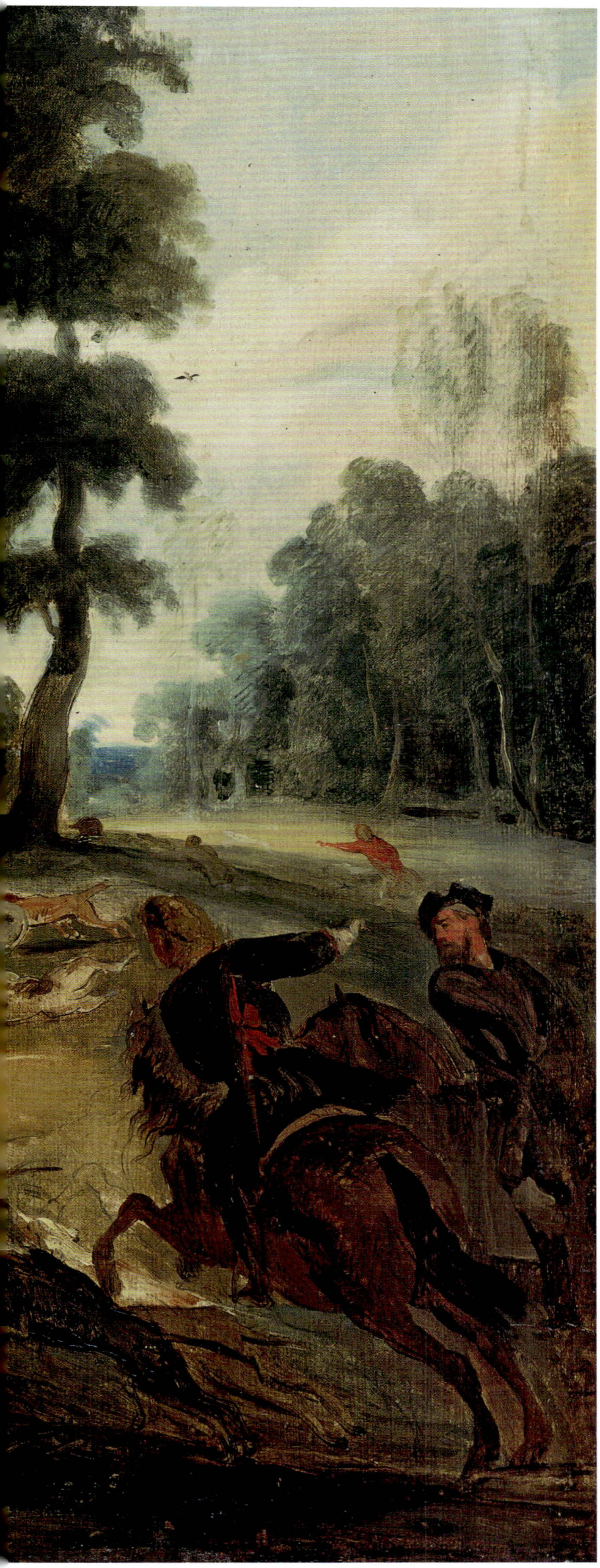

12

EUGÈNE DELACROIX (1798–1863)
Landscape with a Boar Hunt, 1839
Oil on paper, glued on canvas,
54.4 x 71.7 cm
Signed at lower left: *E D*
Neue Pinakothek, Munich, inv. 8717.
Bayerische Staatsgemäldesammlungen

PROVENANCE: Bessonneau Collection, Angers; Paul Cassirer; acquired in 1913 for the Neue Pinakothek
SELECTED REFERENCES: Ehrlich White 1967, no. 32

The Exposition Universelle in Paris in 1855 saw the confrontation of two diametrically opposed artistic movements: the academicism of Ingres – heir to Raphael, Poussin and David – and the Romanticism of Delacroix – heir to Titian, Rubens and Rembrandt. The French authorities commissioned Delacroix to paint a canvas that gave full expression to his artistic aspirations. The artist was to be paid 12,000 francs and was allowed to choose the subject himself, but he had to submit the design for approval. The work in question is possibly the beautifully detailed oil sketch in Stockholm (cat. 13). This study gives a good impression of what the complete composition must have looked like before the upper part of the canvas was destroyed by fire in 1870. As Rubens had done, Delacroix choreographed his composition by introducing groups of bright colours, with the intention of defining more clearly the violence of his subject. He began to paint on 30 July 1854 and from that day on his journal keeps us abreast of his progress, right up to the day of the opening, when he applied the finishing touches.

The painting was not a triumph, however. Members of the public soon began to express their objections to the aggressive subject, the vigorous, pastose manner and the loud colours. One critic described Delacroix's palette as extravagant madness, a complete denial of harmony.[1] Perhaps it is no coincidence that, after the exhibition, the painting was conveyed to a provincial museum (Bordeaux), where it joined Rubens's *Lion Hunt* (which was also destroyed by the 1870 fire). There Delacroix's work was copied by his former pupil Pierre Andrieu, by Odilon Redon and by Charles-François Daubigny.[2]

13

EUGÈNE DELACROIX (1798–1863)
Lion Hunt, 1855
Oil on canvas, 54 x 74 cm
Signed and dated at lower right:
Eug. Delacroix. 185[?5]
Nationalmuseum, Stockholm,
inv. NM 6350
BOZAR ONLY

PROVENANCE: possibly executed in 1854 as a design for the painting in Bordeaux, then further elaborated and signed and dated to be sold to the art dealer Détrimont; sold by Détrimont to Mr Goldschmidt or Goldsmith; Adolf Liebermann von Wahlendorf collection; his sale, Hôtel Drouot, Paris, 8 May 1876, lot 24 (unsold); Fop Smit, Rotterdam; Durand-Ruel, *c.* 1895; Henri Heugel collection; his sale, Galerie Georges Petit, Paris, 26 May 1905, lot 5; bought by M. Bauml; A. F. Klaveness collection, Oslo, *c.* 1929; Philip and Grace Sandblom Collection, Lund; by whom donated to the Nationalmuseum in 1970
SELECTED REFERENCES: Delacroix 1996, pp. 416, 420; Robaut 1885, no. 1278; Bjurstrom 1981; Johnson 1981–89, vol. 3, no. 199; Daguerre de Hureaux 1993, pp. 201, 204, 206, 326; Jobert 1997, p. 265; Paris 1998, no. 13

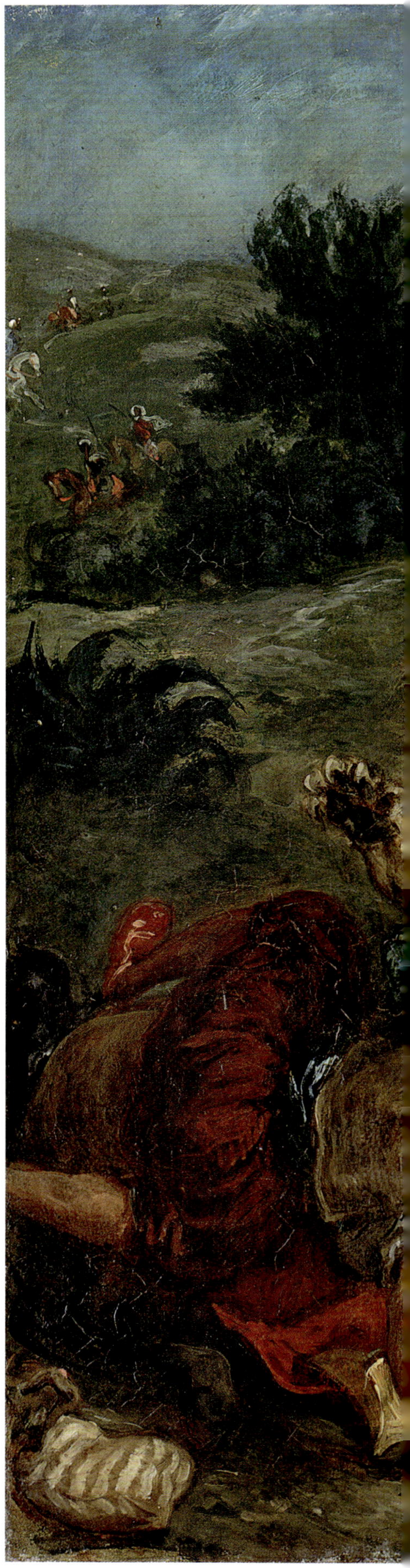

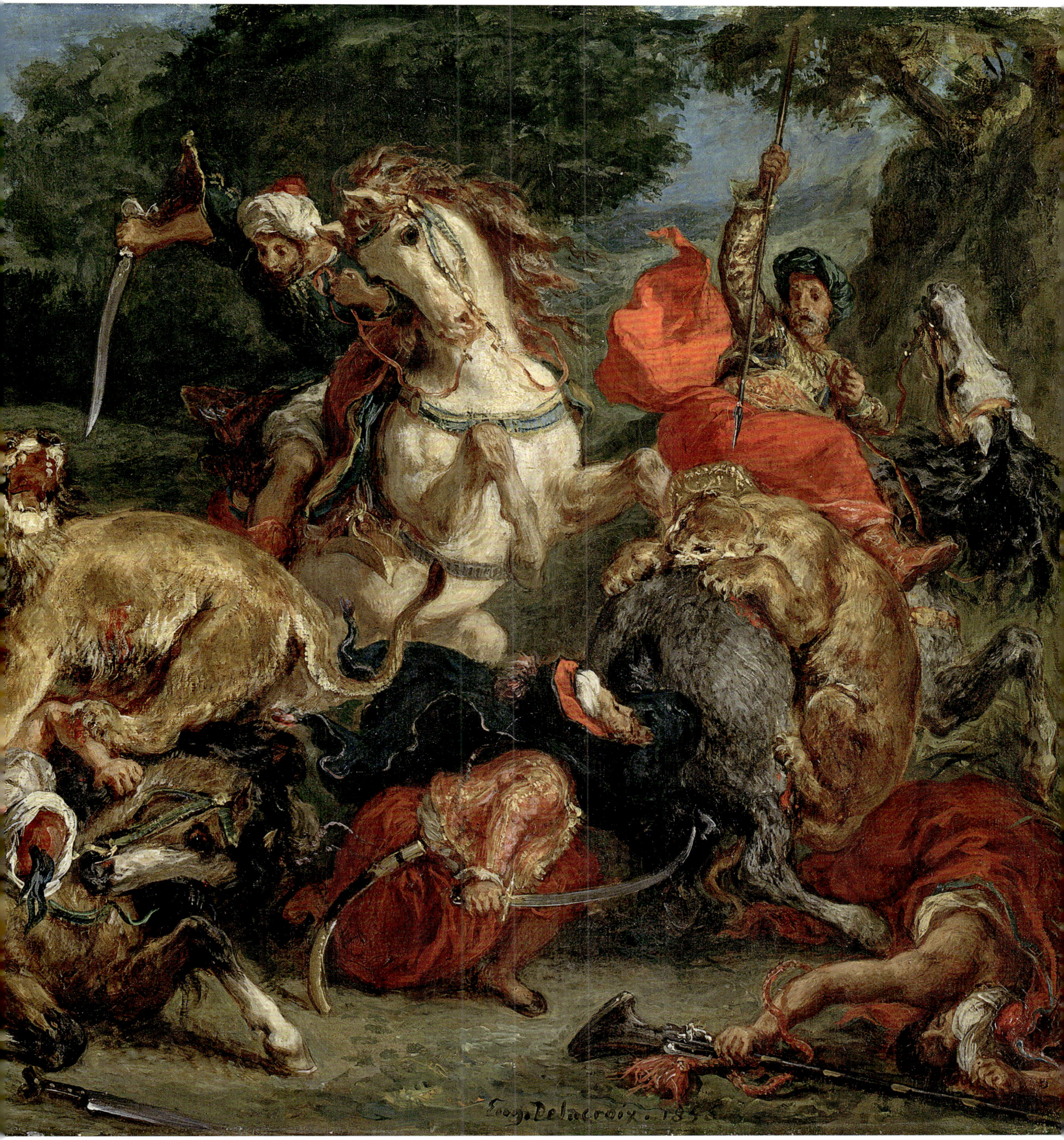
Eug. Delacroix. 185

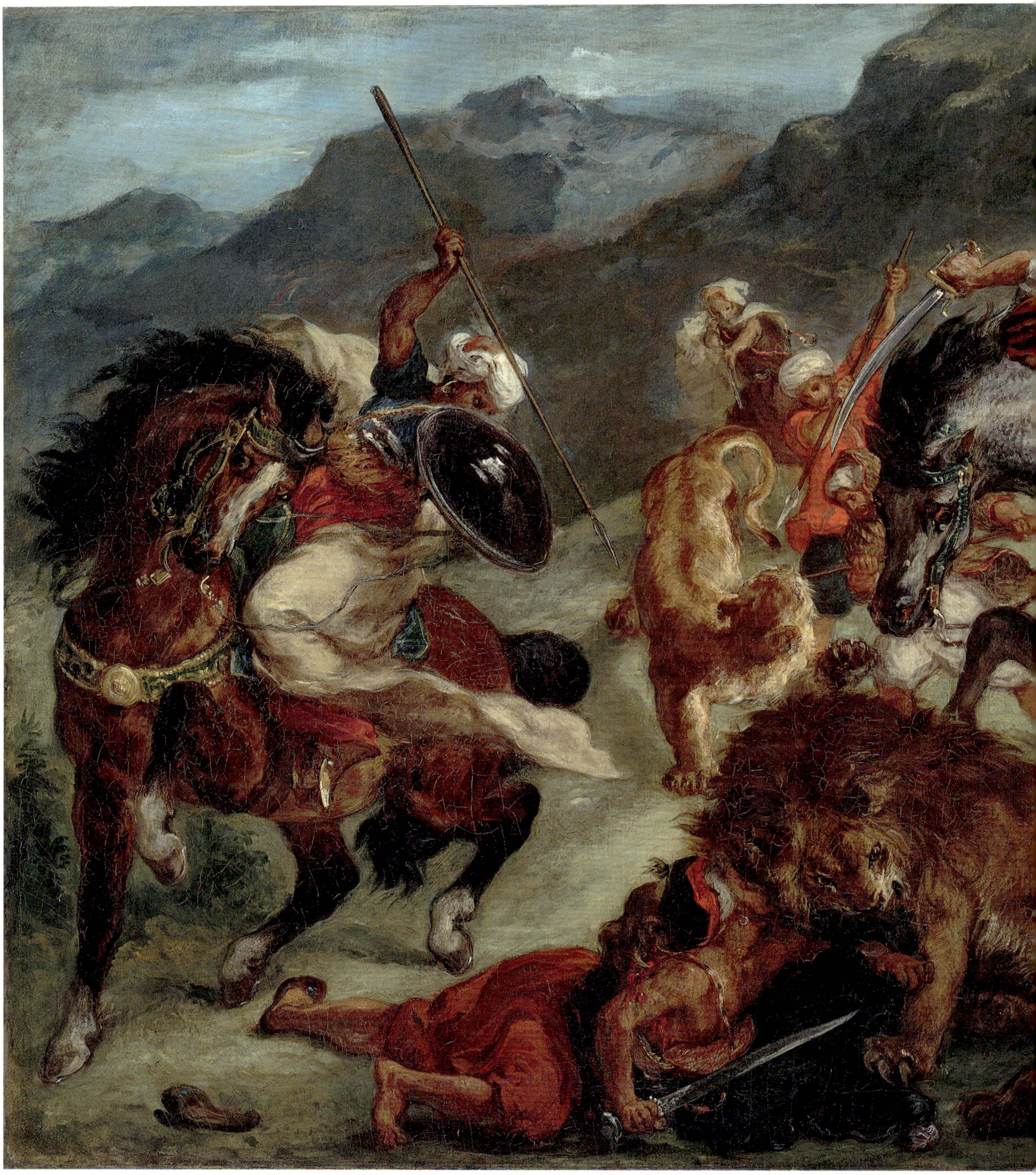

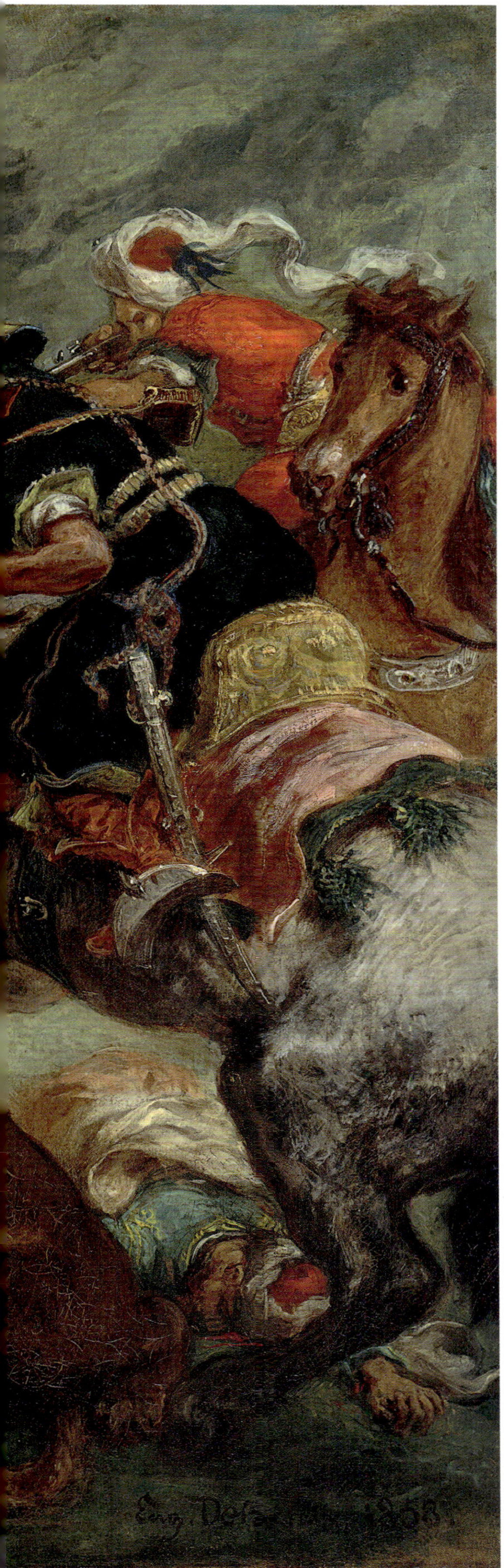

Three years later Delacroix painted the theme again, when he was commissioned – possibly by an art dealer – to paint a new *Lion Hunt* on a smaller scale (cat. 14). On 26 April 1858 he noted in his journal that he was making satisfactory progress and that the painting was nearly finished.[3] While at work the artist undoubtedly recalled what the critics had said about the *Lion Hunt* he had painted for the Exposition Universelle. He now simplified his composition, reducing the number of groups to four, with a lion and its victim appearing, partially shadowed, in the foreground. A rider at the left is about to throw his spear at the beast of prey, and at the right two horsemen rush to help the fallen man. In the background a lioness turns to face two attackers. Delacroix painted the exciting struggle in a subdued and rather dark palette. The intentionally bare background, which recalls North African mountain landscapes, increases the legibility of the whole.

14

EUGÈNE DELACROIX (1798–1863)
Lion Hunt, 1858
Oil on canvas, 92 x 117.5 cm
Signed and dated at lower right:
Eug. Delacroix. 1858
Museum of Fine Arts, Boston,
inv. 95.179. S. A. Denio Collection
– Sylvanus Adams Denio Fund and
General Income

PROVENANCE: anonymous sale, Hôtel Drouot, Paris, 30 March 1863, lot 9, sold to Durand-Ruel, Paris; 1867, sold by Durand-Ruel to Mr Adolph Edward Borie, Philadelphia; 1880, Mrs Adolph Edward Borie, Philadelphia; possibly sold to Erwin Davis, New York; 19 March 1889, Erwin Davis sale, Fifth Avenue Art Galleries, New York, lot 143; 1895, Durand-Ruel, New York; bought by the Museum of Fine Arts with the financial assistance of S. A. Denio
SELECTED REFERENCES: Delacroix 1996, p. 717; Robaut 1885, no. 1349; Sérullaz 1963, no. 492; Johnson 1981–89, vol. 3, no. 204; Daguerre de Hureaux 1993, p. 327; Paris 1998, no. 21

In 1803 the Maecenas and art collector Sir George Beaumont received a splendid present from his wife: *A View of Het Steen in the Early Morning* (fig. 40), a masterpiece by Rubens that is now in the National Gallery in London. The panel was exhibited in the studio of Benjamin West, President of the Royal Academy, where it made a deep impression on the animal painter James Ward. To demonstrate his talent to potential clients, Ward resolved to make a painting that would rival the old masterpiece: after all, he was dependent, as were most of the painters of his day, on commissions from aristocrats who wished to have their favourite horses, hunting hounds or children portrayed. He chose a panel of similar dimensions with a smooth surface, on which he could demonstrate his complete mastery of Rubens's transparency and brushwork. Instead of depicting Rubens's country estate, however, Ward painted St Donat's Castle in Wales, which in those days was a picturesque ruin (in 1925 the restored castle was sold to the newspaper magnate William Randolph Hearst and is now a reputable school). Ward borrowed the motif of the fighting bulls from George Stubbs. The completed *Bulls Fighting* (cat. 16) was admired by Beaumont and West, but in the eyes of John Constable it was little more than an imitation of an Old Master. The evocative cloudy skies and autumnal colours that Ward adopted from Rubens were certainly very popular with the bourgeois public in the first half of the nineteenth century. The Rubens revival of those years prompted this painter to take a number of other works by the Flemish master as points of departure for his own creations.[1]

Yet it was a Rubens hunting scene that would profoundly influence British animal painting. In 1824 Sir Edwin Landseer paid a visit to Sir Walter Scott at his home, Abottsford, near Melrose. The animal painter was fascinated by Scott's romantic novels and poems, and by the sagas and legends that were told in the Borders region of Scotland and England. Landseer also read the two ballads of Chevy Chase that Thomas Percy had published in *Reliques of Ancient English Poetry* (London, 1765). Both versions of the ballad tell the story of Lord Percy, the English Earl of Northumberland, who led a hunting party onto land belonging to the Scottish Earl of Douglas; the two enemies and both their clans perished in the ensuing battle. That same year Landseer saw the *Wolf and Fox Hunt*, a monumental canvas painted by Rubens in about 1616, which had been acquired by the politician and financier Alexander Baring (later 1st Baron Ashburton) – a painting now in the Metropolitan Museum of Art in New York (fig. 9). Landseer made a scaled-down copy of the canvas.[2] His fascination for the Middle Ages and the confrontation with Rubens's impressive hunting scene inspired Landseer to paint a masterpiece that successfully combines the Baroque idiom and medieval narrative. Two years later the painting (cat. 15) was exhibited at the Royal Academy, and the catalogue adapted some of the opening lines from the more modern version of the sixteenth-century ballad that Percy had published:

> *To drive the deere with hound and horne*
> *Erle Percy took his way;*
> *The chiefest harts in Chevy Chace*
> *To kill and beare away.*

15

SIR EDWIN LANDSEER (1802–1873)
The Hunting of Chevy Chase, c. 1825–26
Oil on canvas, 143 x 170.8 cm
Birmingham Museums and Art Gallery, inv. 1952P2

PROVENANCE: commissioned by the 6th Duke of Bedford; Bedford sale, Christie's, London, 19 January 1951, lot 186, purchased by the National Art Collections Fund; presented to Birmingham in 1952
SELECTED REFERENCES: Taylor 1955, p. 60; Boase 1959, pp. 167–68; Lennie 1981, pp. 64–68; Philadelphia and London 1981–82, no. 23

16 *(overleaf)*

JAMES WARD (1769–1859)
Bulls Fighting, with a View of St Donatt's Castle, Glamorganshire, 1803
Oil on panel, 132 x 228 cm
Signed: *J. Ward*
Victoria and Albert Museum, London, inv. 220-1871

PROVENANCE: donated by Charles Theobald Maud in 1871
SELECTED REFERENCES: Dayot 1908, p. 138; Grundy 1909, pp. 32–33; Nygren 1980, pp. 264–65

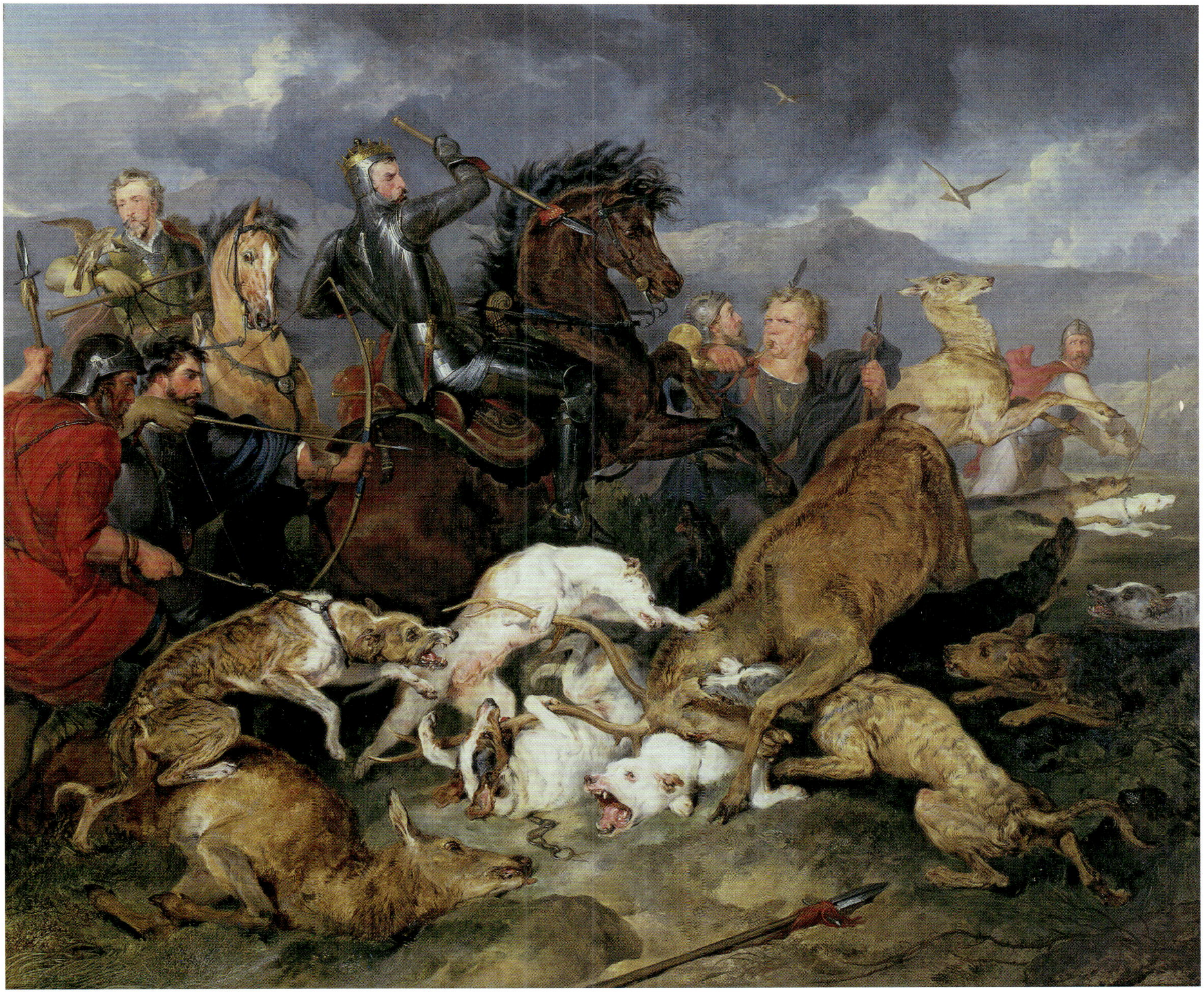

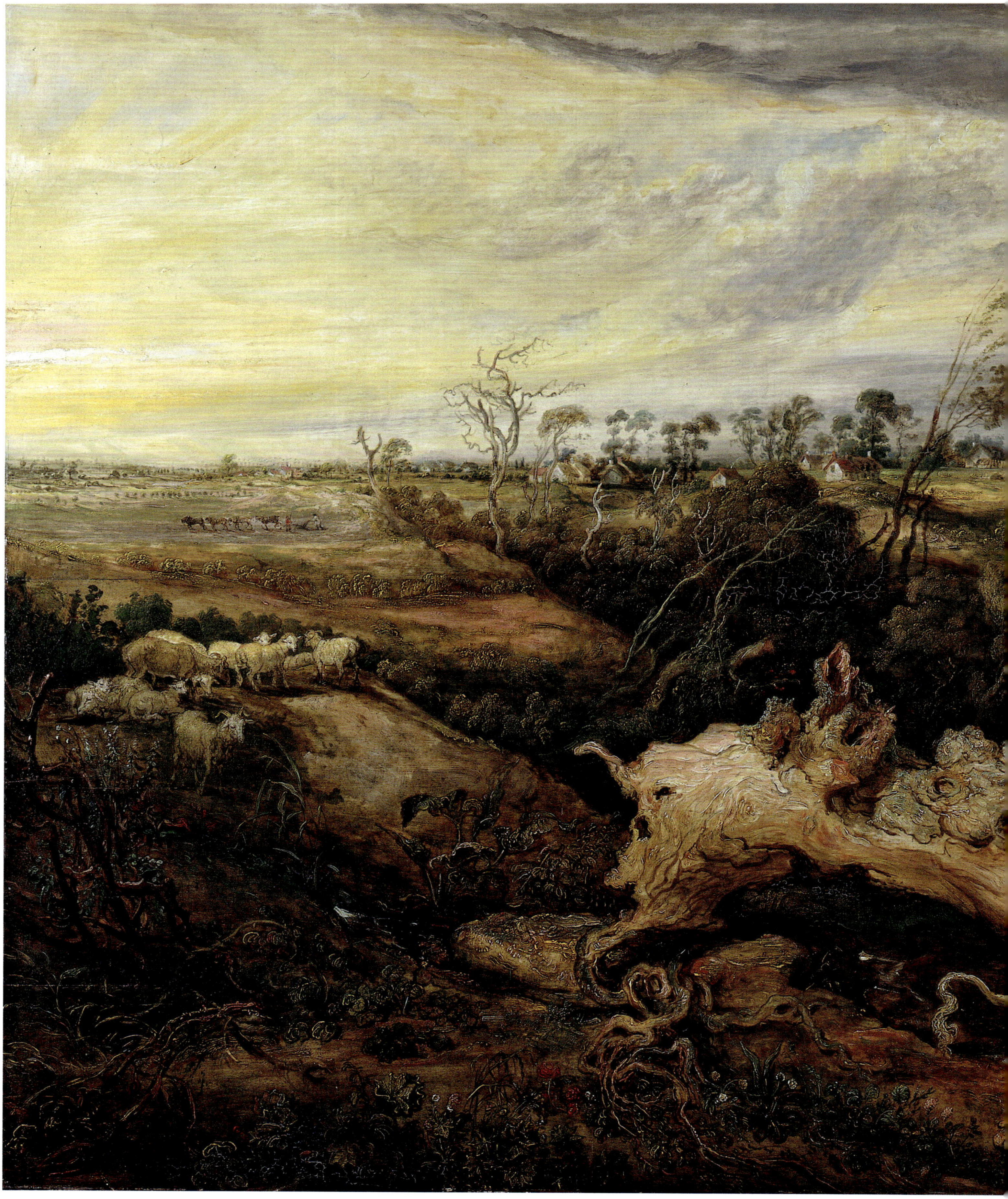

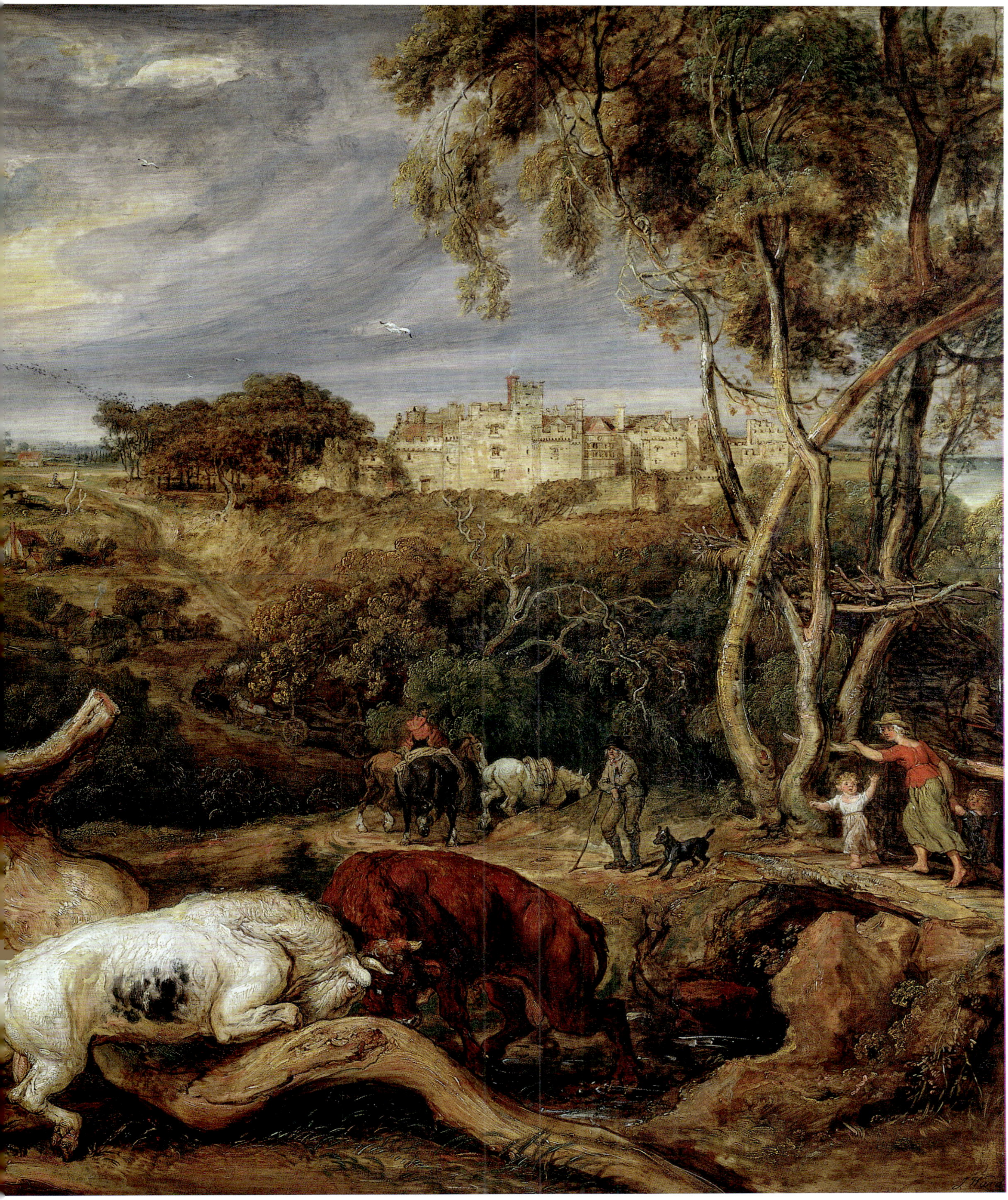

Théodore Géricault studied the work of Rubens mainly in the early years of his short career, even before he started to move towards realism. From 1810 he painted copies after works in what would come to be known as the Louvre Museum,[1] including Rubens's *Descent from the Cross* (whereabouts of the copy unknown), the *Wolf and Fox Hunt* (Ordrupgaard, Copenhagen), *Marie de Médicis at Pont-de-Cé* (Bühler Collection, Winterthur) and from *The Meeting of Marie de Médicis and Henri IV at Lyon* the detail of *Two Lions* (National Museum of Wildlife Art, Jackson, Wyoming). There is abundant evidence of Géricault's interest in Rubens as a colourist in his equestrian scenes with rearing horses and splendidly attired cavalrymen. But with an eye to his future creations, Géricault borrowed mainly the master's clever, tumultuous compositions, several of which were available as prints. The preparatory drawing (cat. 17) for one such print, after *The Defeat of Sennacherib* (*c.* 1616; Alte Pinakothek, Munich), can be seen here.

Géricault is known to have drawn a group of tumbling bodies from Jonas Suyderhoef's print after Rubens's *Small Last Judgement*.[2] This study played an important role in the development of his masterpiece, *The Raft of the Medusa*.[3] Rubens's *The Battle of the Amazons* (fig. 7) underpinned Géricault's preparatory drawing for *Horace at the Bridg*e (Musée des Beaux-Arts de Rouen). Around 1813–14, Géricault formulated in a sketchbook (now in Chicago) various compositional solutions for military scenes, including the page on display in this exhibition (cat. 18). While engaged in these exercises, he was inspired by Rubens's hunting scenes: after all, the famous paintings made for Maximilian I, Elector of Bavaria, were part of Napoleon's war booty.

Antoine Joseph Wiertz began his training in 1820 at the Koninklijke Academie in Antwerp, where he discovered the masterpieces by Rubens. From that moment on, he was seized by artistic overconfidence and a need for recognition. After winning the Prix de Rome in 1832, he lived from 1834 to 1837 in the Eternal City, where he made a monumental history painting full of heroism and bravura: *The Greeks and the Trojans Fighting over the Body of Patroclus* (Musée d'Art Wallon, Liège), of which a preparatory oil study is exhibited here (cat. 19). In using the complex diagonal composition, Wiertz attempted to rival Rubens's *Henri IV at the Battle of Ivry*[4] (Galleria degli Uffizi, Florence) and *The Consequences of War* (Palazzo Pitti, Florence). Even though the Raphael cult reached its apex around this time, Wiertz looked mainly to a home-grown hero: Rubens. Wiertz's painting was praised in Belgium, although one critic remarked caustically that 'the step from the sublime to the ridiculous has definitely been taken'.[5] In abandoned churches and factories, the painter created gigantic, nearly panoramic scenes. An apt example is *The Revolt of Hell against Heaven* (11.53 x 7.93 m!), completed in 1842, in which the satanic element taken from Rubens's *The Fall of the Damned* derails completely. Wiertz tried several times – in vain – to exhibit his own work next to that of his great role model. Official commissions were not forthcoming; but nevertheless, the Belgian government built a large studio in Brussels – the present-day Wiertzmuseum – to house the monstrous creations of this self-proclaimed genius.

Arnold Böcklin's *The Battle on the Bridge* (cat. 20) relocates the hostile encounter of Rubens's *The Battle of the Amazons* on a log bridge. A horde of naked blonde men on horseback tear

17

PIETER CLAESZ. SOUTMAN (c. 1580–1657) and
PETER PAUL RUBENS (1577–1640)
The Defeat of Sennacherib, *c.* 1618–20
Black chalk and pen and black ink with grey wash on laid paper, 35.2 x 45.4 cm
National Gallery of Art, Washington DC, inv. 1978.53.1. Andrew W. Mellon Fund, 1978

PROVENANCE: Jonathan Richardson, Sr (Lugt 2184)
SELECTED REFERENCES: Logan 1977, p. 405, no. 4

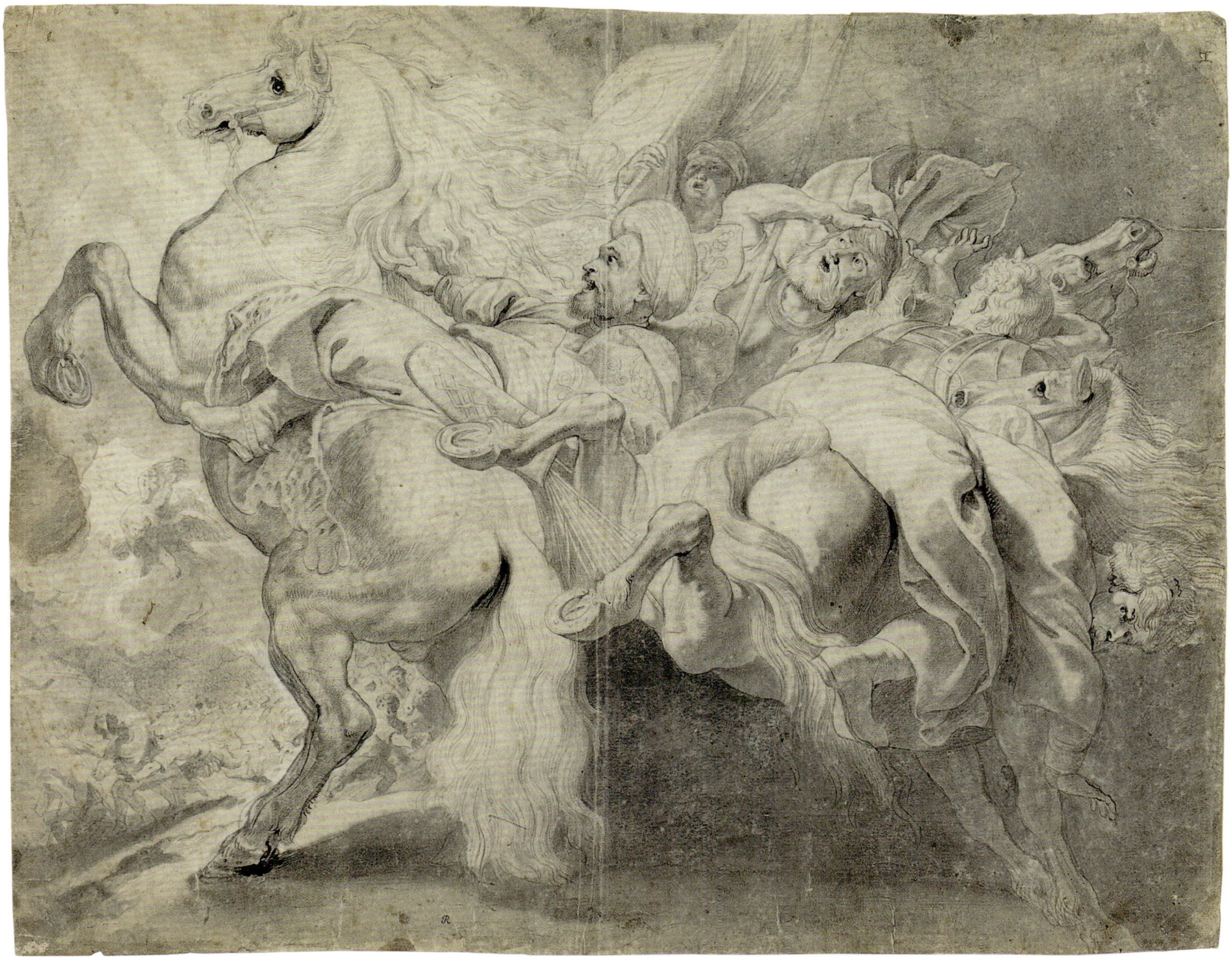

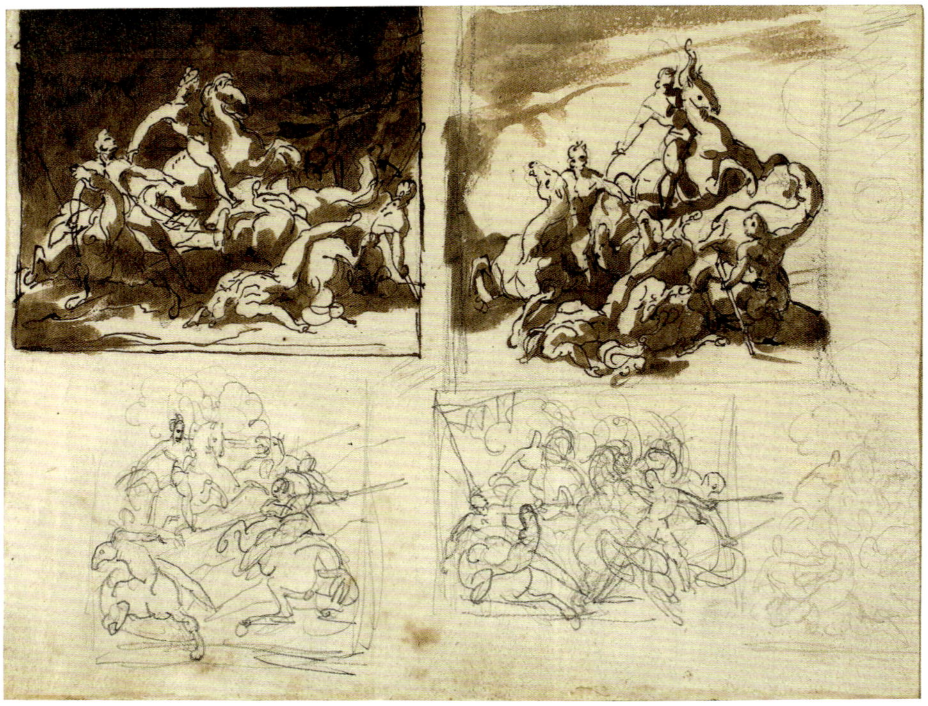

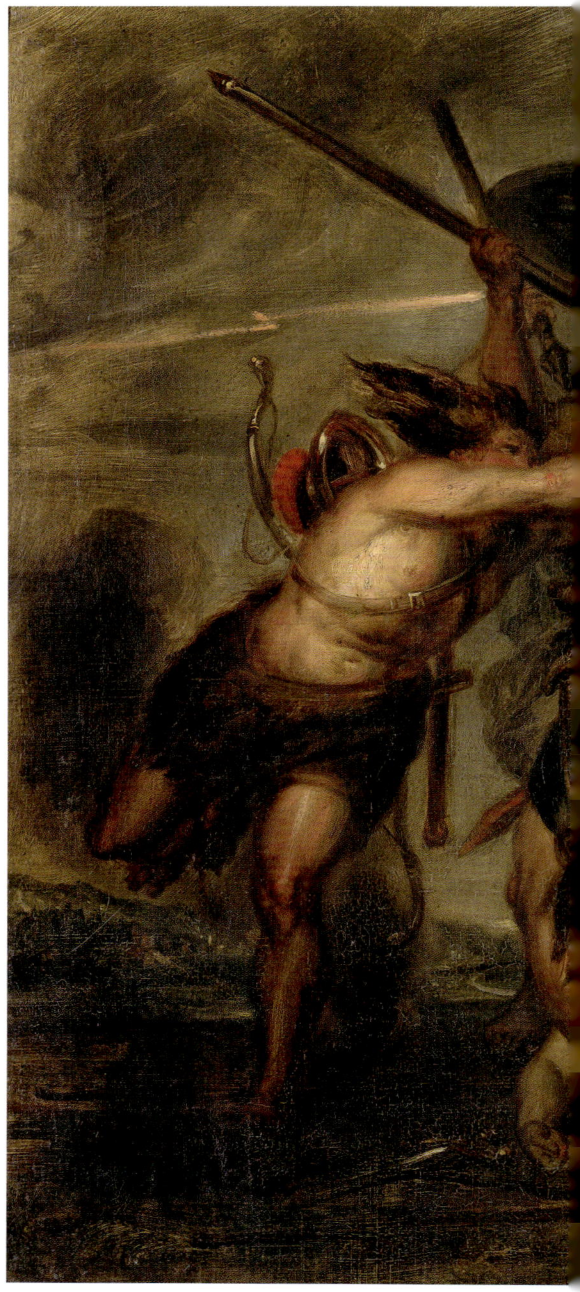

18

THÉODORE GÉRICAULT (1791–1824)
Five Sketches for a Cavalry Battle, *c*. 1813–14
Pen and brown ink with brush over graphite on paper, 17.2 x 22.8 cm
The Art Institute of Chicago, inv. 1947.35.50R

PROVENANCE: (?) Ary Scheffer, Paris; sale, Hôtel Drouot, Paris, 15–16 March 1859, lot 16, sold to Anatole-Auguste Hulot; sale, Hôtel Drouot, Paris, 11–13 January 1894; Baron Joseph Vitta (d. 1942), Paris; sold by César de Hauke to the Art Institute in 1947; Margaret Day Blake Collection
SELECTED REFERENCES: Eitner 1960, p. 39; Joachim and Haller Olsen 1978, pp. 65 and 80, no. 4B5; Bazin 1989, pp. 205–06, no. 875

into a group of warriors in battle gear, and in the foreground several warriors wade through the water to surprise their opponents' flank. The association with Teutons and Romans is obvious. As early as 1885, Böcklin made a first version of the subject,[6] and four years later another (Museum Georg Schäfer, Schweinfurt),[7] but the composition did not satisfy him, and he embarked on the present painting. Unlike contemporaries such as Turner and Menzel, who embraced technological progress, Böcklin's classical subject-matter deliberately runs counter to the industrialised society of the Gründerzeit.[8] In his 'anachronistic' works, Böcklin primarily sought to portray the primal instincts and Dionysian side of human beings: he not only rendered the joyful play of naiads and the effect of panic-stricken fear, but also portrayed centaurs hurling boulders and abducting nymphs. His pictures generally resound with black humour and his intention to surprise.

Böcklin found a kindred spirit in Rubens, the master who breathed new life into old myths and sagas. Thus the artist from Basel followed in the footsteps of his artistic mentor Jacob Burckhardt (1818–1897), the famous Rubens specialist.

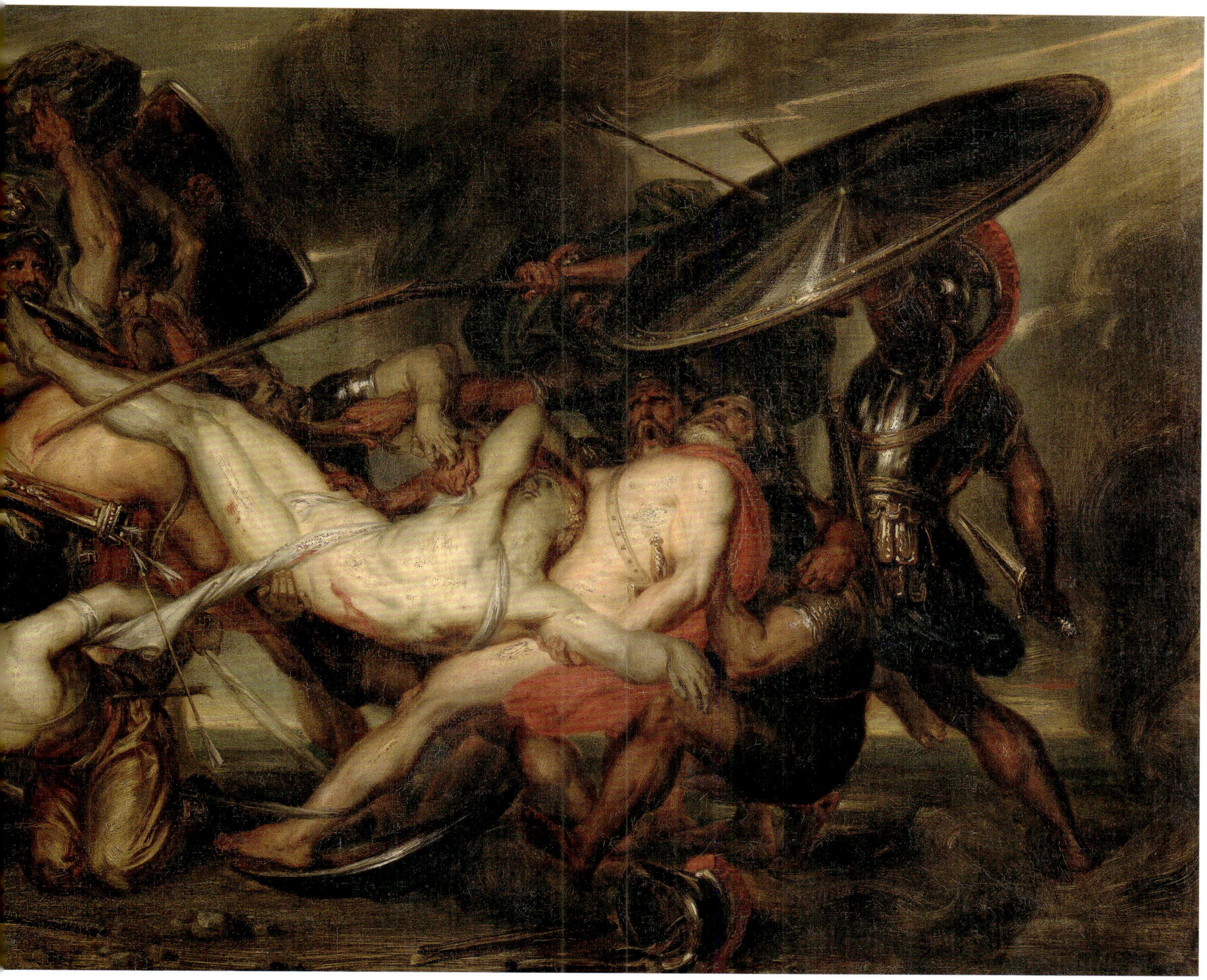

19

ANTOINE JOSEPH WIERTZ (1806–1865)
Study for *The Greeks and the Trojans Fighting Over the Body of Patroclus*, 1837
Oil on panel, 73.5 x 128.2 cm
Royal Museum of Fine Arts Antwerp, inv. 1183

PROVENANCE: bequeathed to the museum by Joseph De Bom in 1877
SELECTED REFERENCES: Brussels 1830, no. 948; Antwerp 1969, no. 312; Namur 2007; Antwerp 2013/14

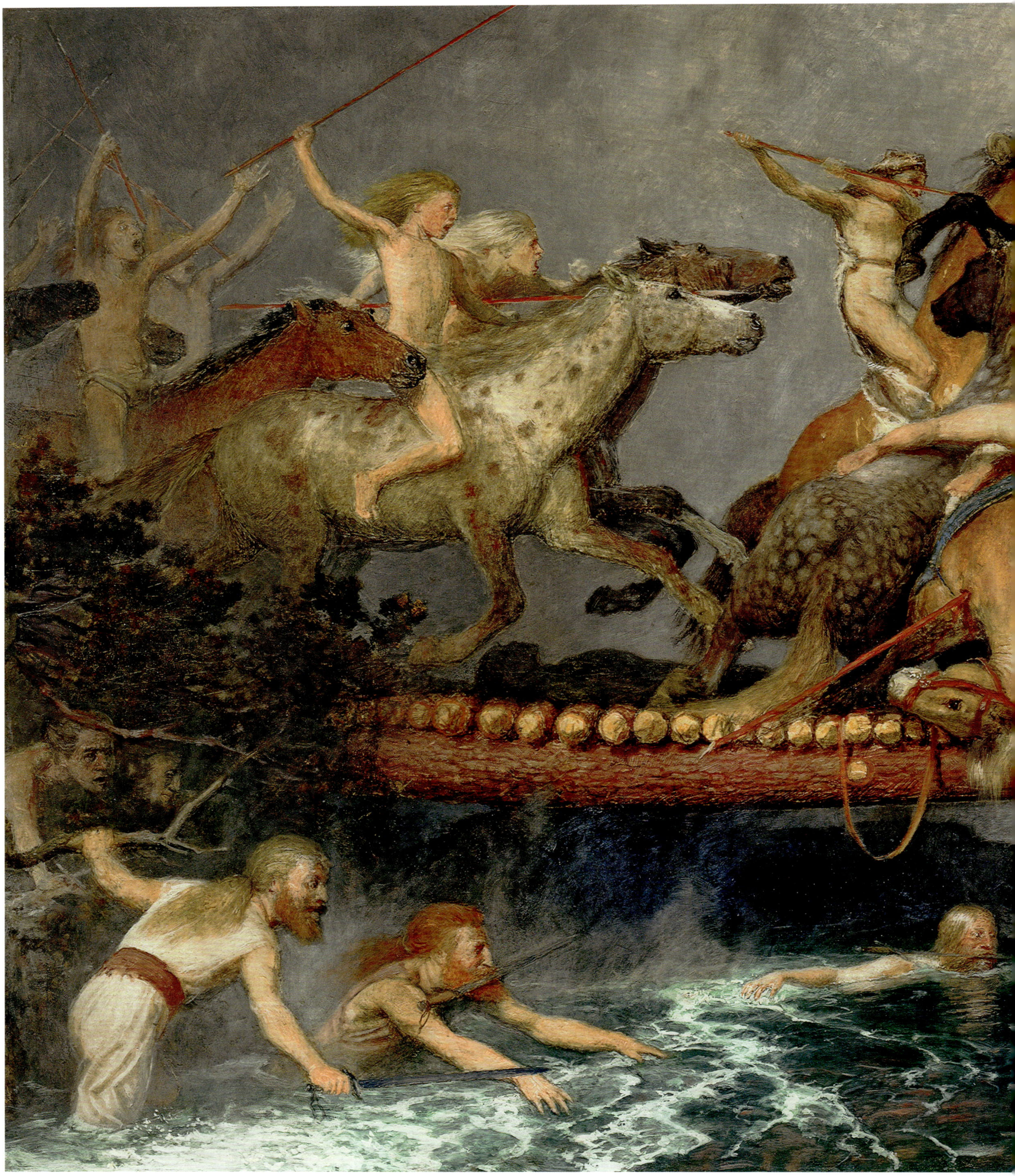

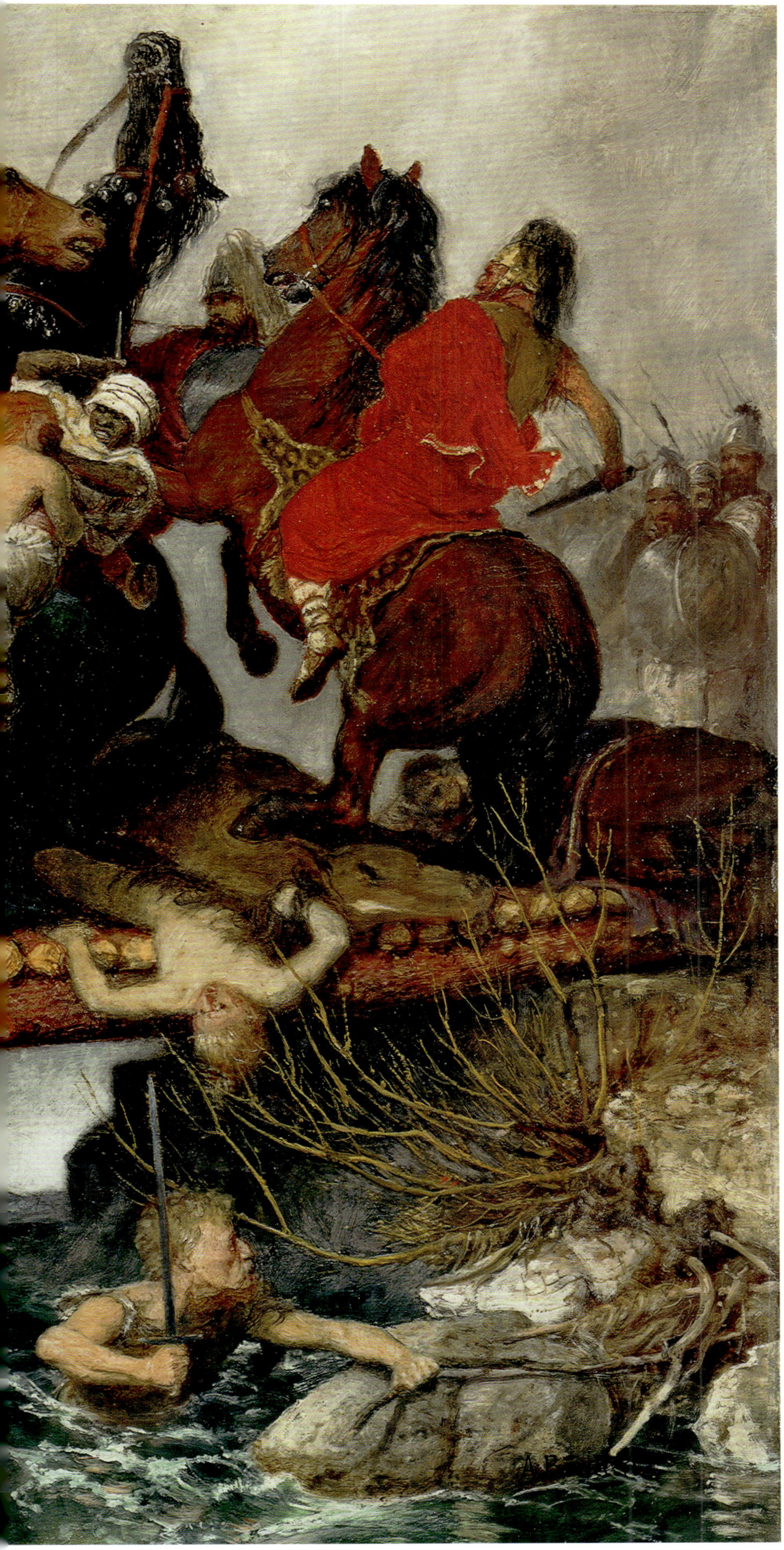

20

ARNOLD BÖCKLIN (1827–1901)
The Battle on the Bridge, 1892
Canvas affixed to panel, 100 x 142 cm
Signed *A. Böcklin* and monogrammed
at lower right
On loan to Kunsthaus Zürich.
Lent by a private collection

PROVENANCE: Theodor Klopfer, Munich, 1902; Hugo Helbing sale, Munich, 24 November 1908; Philipp Rosenthal, Berlin and Berg am Starnberger See, 1908; N. N. Böhmen; princely collection (?); Mr Leberecht, Berlin, 1943; Mrs Marie Leberecht, Berlin, 1973; Stenko Barnefsky, Berlin, 1973; sale Christie's, Düsseldorf, 13 November 1973; Stenko Barnefsky, Berlin, 1973; private collection since 1974
SELECTED REFERENCES: Schmid 1918, p. 240; Andree 1977, pp. 486–88, no. 418; Wichmann 1977, pp. 12–43; Winterfeld 1999, p. 169; Basel 2001, pp. 304–07, nos 80–81

Greek and Roman literature constitutes an inexhaustible repertoire from which painters of the Renaissance and the Baroque could pick subjects they considered visually attractive. Rubens was no exception in this respect. The themes he chose were often those that combined violence and lust, since the portrayal of these human passions resulted in dynamic and exciting compositions that capitalised on the taste of patrons and collectors: mythological stories usually provided an excuse for painting voluptuous female nudes thrashing about. Examples are the rape of the chaste Lucretia by the king's son Tarquinus (painted in about 1609–10 and held at the State Hermitage Museum, St Petersburg); the abduction of the Athenian princess Oreithya by Boreas, the north wind (*c.* 1615; Akademie der bildenden Künste, Vienna); the rape of the daughters of Leucippus by the twin brothers Castor and Pollux (*c.* 1618; Alte Pinakothek, Munich); the abduction of Hercules' wife, Deianeira, by the centaur Nessus (fig. 19, as well as studio pieces at Schloss Sanssouci, Potsdam, *c.* 1630); and the rape of Proserpine by Pluto, god of the underworld (*c.* 1636; Museo Nacional del Prado, Madrid).

Soon after returning from Italy, Rubens formulated the theme of the rape of the daughters of Leucippus in an oil sketch that is now in the National Museum of Art, Architecture and Design in Oslo (cat. 21). We recognise the Dioscuri – Castor and Pollux – by the stars on their heads. Until the publication of Julius Held's authoritative catalogue of Rubens's oil sketches, this panel was assigned to the master, but since this eminent scholar's negative verdict the work has sunk into oblivion.[1] The splendid Oslo sketch deserves to be rehabilitated, however: the vehemence and swiftness of Rubens's brush strokes, the manner in which he painted such details as the eyes and hands, and the dark palette are also seen in his studies (*c.* 1610; held by the Art Institute of Chicago and Thyssen-Bornemisza Museum, Madrid) for the famous painting of Samson and Delilah in the National Gallery, London. An X-radiograph reveals that the composition was painted over another, rather illegible, sketch. It is not known if the composition resulted in a large-scale painting of the daughters of Leucippus. Rubens recycled the motif of the floundering woman falling backwards in *Boreas and Oreithya* (Akademie der bildenden Künste, Vienna) and in his famous work *The Rape of the Daughters of Leucippus* (Alte Pinakothek, Munich). However, the aggression in the Oslo study gives way in the larger, famous version to a milder form of coercion.

Rubens's portrayal of the mythological rape of Proserpine was inspired by a long poem composed by Claudian (Claudius Claudianus, sometimes called the last poet of classical Rome). Venus, the goddess of love, asks Proserpine to pick flowers in a meadow. Pallas Athena and Diana propose to help the girl, but are infuriated when they realise that this is a trap set by Pluto to have the girl abducted. Athena raises her shield, decorated with the dreaded head of Gorgon; Diana restrains her, but only with difficulty, and prevents her from throwing a lance at Pluto. At the bottom left, the nymph Cyane, who tried to prevent the abduction, is transformed by Pluto into a fountain. It is difficult to believe that this lively composition is in fact derived from representations on two sarcophagi: one that Cardinal Scipione Borghese had mounted on the façade of

21

PETER PAUL RUBENS (1577–1640)
Sketch for *The Rape of the Daughters of Leucippus*, *c.* 1610–11
Oil on panel, 27 x 29 cm
The National Museum of Art, Architecture and Design, Oslo, inv. NG.M.01394

PROVENANCE: Patschinsky collection (according to a note on the back); the actor Koser, Berlin; Mrs Koser, Berlin; F. W. Lippmann, Berlin; purchased from Lippmann by Christian Langaard in 1915; by whom bequeathed to the Nasjonalgalleriet in 1923
SELECTED REFERENCES: Oslo 1973, pp. 178–79, no. 421; Held 1980, vol. 1, p. 633, no. 1; McGrath 1997, vol. 1, pp. 125–26 and note 74; Van Hout 2011A

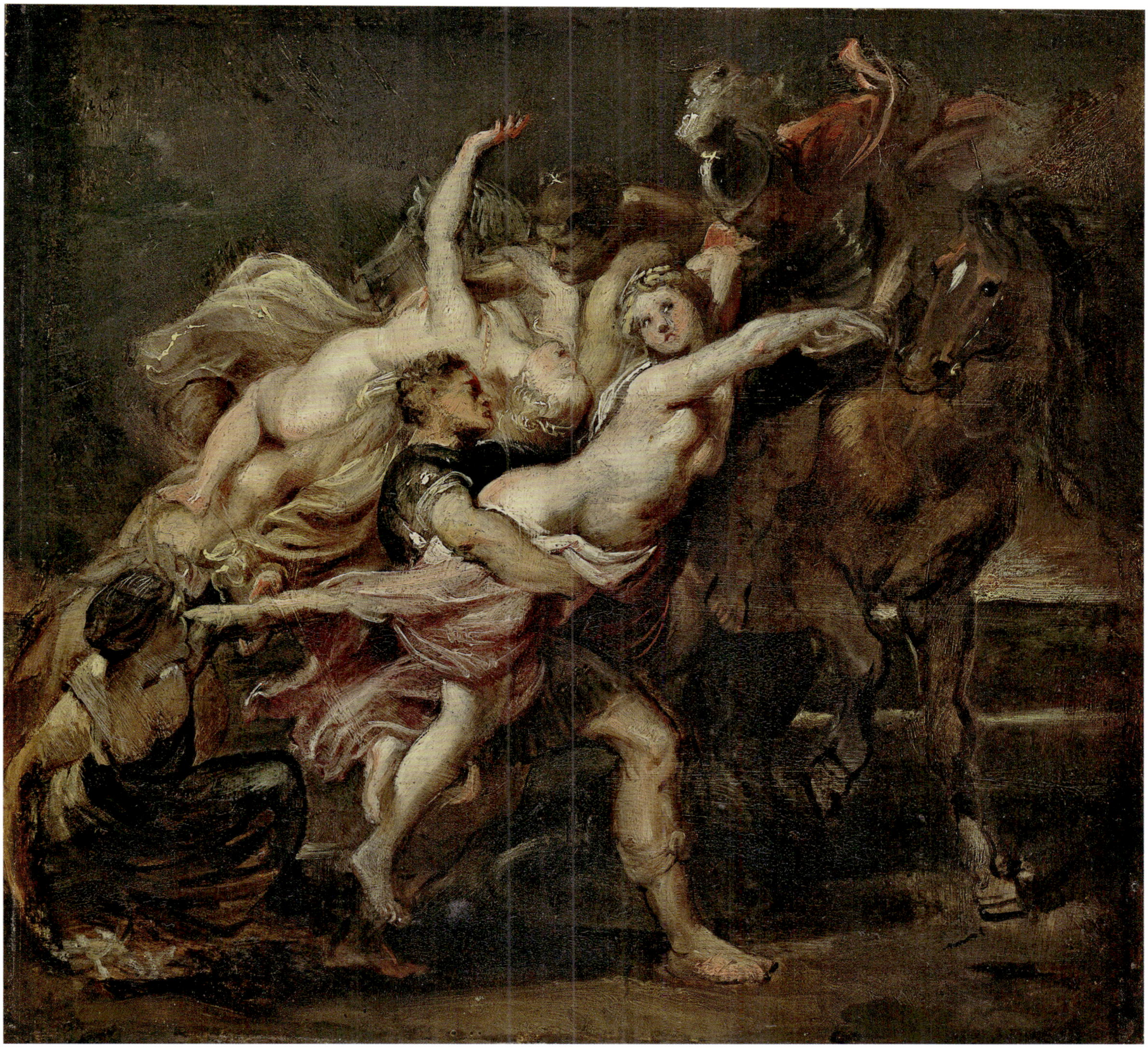

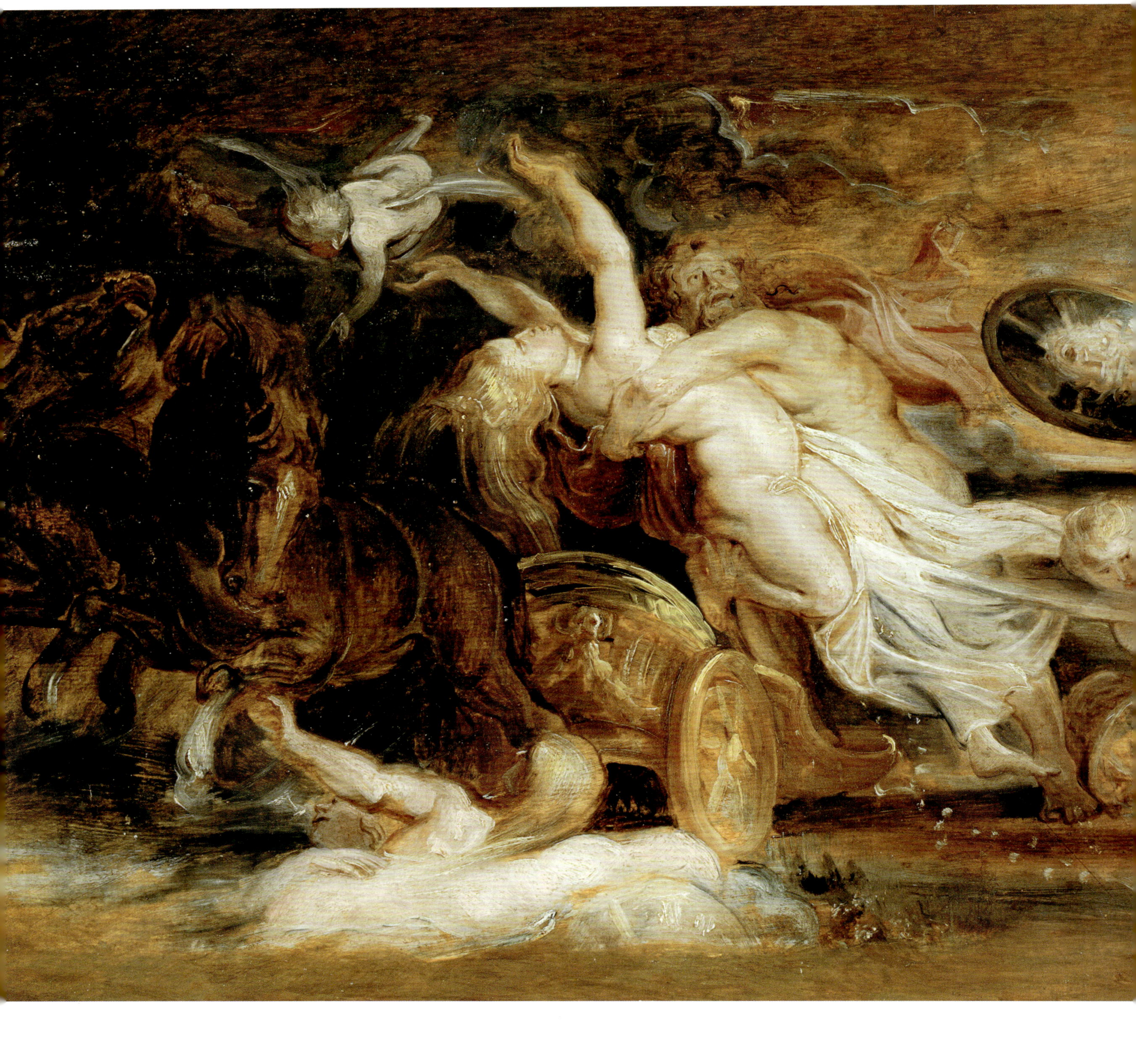

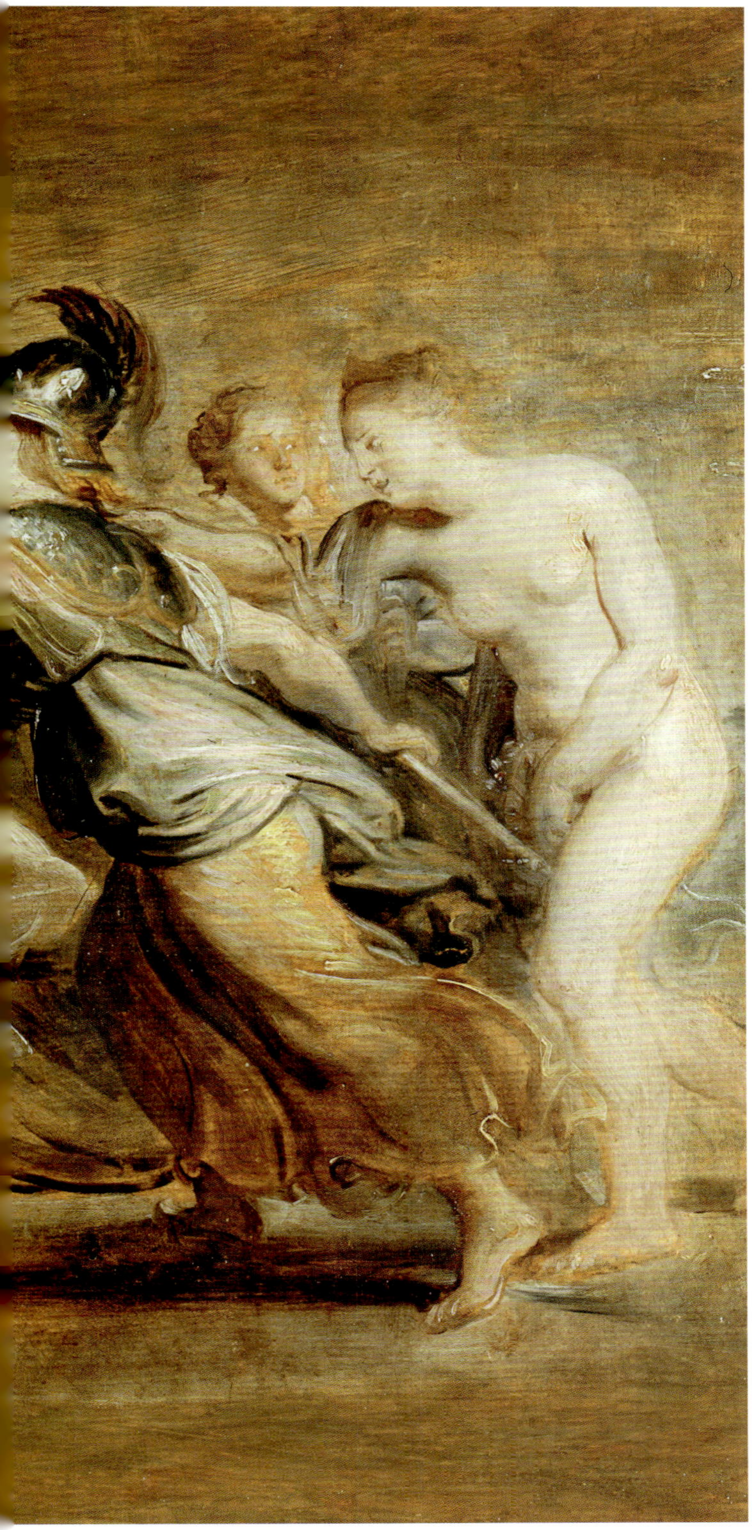

his residence in Rome in about 1607 (the present-day Palazzo Rospigliosi) and another that was then to be found in the Palazzo Accoramboni. The oil sketch (cat. 22) is perhaps a design for a large canvas that hung at Blenheim Palace, a work that was unfortunately destroyed by fire on 5 February 1861. A detailed model drawing for Soutman's etching of the same subject is preserved in the Ecole nationale supérieure des Beaux-Arts in Paris.

22

PETER PAUL RUBENS (1577–1640)
Sketch for *The Abduction of Proserpine*, *c.* 1614–15
Oil on panel, 38 x 67 cm
Musée du Petit Palais, Paris, inv. PDUT00954

PROVENANCE: Trouard sale, Paris, 22 February 1769, lot 94; Le Brun sale, Paris, 11 April 1791, lot 72; De Castelmore sale, Paris, 20 December 1791, lot 45; Cardinal Fesch sale, Rome, 17–18 March 1845, lot 200; Prof. Schrakner, Strasbourg; Auguste Dutuit; bequeathed to the Petit Palais in 1902
SELECTED REFERENCES: Rooses 1886–92, vol. 3, p. 153, no. 672 bis; Alpers 1971, pp. 157 and 258; Held 1980, vol. 1, no. 262, pp. 352–53

23

JAN BOECKHORST (1604–1668)
The Fall of the Damned, 1639–53
Oil on panel, 118 x 92 cm
On long-term loan to Suermondt-Ludwig Museum, Aachen, inv. GK 438. Lent by a private collection

PROVENANCE: Jan and Jeremias Wildens; (?) Jacques Stoop, Ghent, 1668; seen by Nicodemus Tessin (1654–1728) at Gelaude Habert's in Brussels in 1684; sold in Paris in 1756 (Colin); Dutartre collection, Paris, *c.* 1787; Dutartre sale, 19 March 1804, lot 17, sold to Paillet; Pitschaft sale, 11 April 1811, lot 140; Malvé collection, Paris, until 1864; bought by Barthold Suermondt and donated by him to the Aachener Museumsverein in 1882
SELECTED REFERENCES: Aachen 1883, p. 61, no. 115; Freedberg 1984, no. 52, (copy 1), pp. 228–30; Aachen 1994, p. 76; Gormans 1998; Braunschweig 2004, no. 43

Rubens's *The Fall of the Damned* is without doubt one of the Alte Pinakothek's most impressive paintings, a work whose huge size quickly draws the viewer into the infernal spectacle. The naked bodies in chaotic free fall are the souls of the damned, tormented by demons. Hovering above the violent maelstrom is the Archangel Michael with drawn sword. On the Day of Judgement he expels the serious sinners, and 'whosoever was not found written in the book of life was cast into the lake of fire' (Revelation XX, 15). Rubens was commissioned to paint this work by the Bishop of Antwerp, Marius Ambrosius Capello (1590–1676), who bequeathed it to the Dominicans of Ghent. Just as Van der Weyden, Bosch and Dieric Bouts had done before him, Rubens uncoupled the subject of the fall of the damned from the traditional iconography of the Last Judgement. In 1677 the 2nd Duke of Richelieu (1657–1715) bought the enormous panel 'that amazes all of Paris'.[1] De Piles wrote: 'there is no one who looks closely at the painting who is not gripped with fear and who doesn't feel himself descending, still alive, as it were, into hell. The ignorant unthinkingly praise it as well, as do the most knowledgeable connoisseurs; the former avert their gaze after looking at it for a while, because they cannot stand its terrible impact and because it seems to them that they are, in effect, seeing the truly damned, whereas with the connoisseurs, terror turns into admiration at this point'.[2]

In the painting, the French expert discovered allusions to the seven deadly sins: the proud snake, the covetous dragon, the lustful sow, the envious dog, the gluttonous monkey, the angry lion and the slothful donkey.[3] Later in the seventeenth century, Rubens's painting ended up in the collection of the Elector Palatine Johann Wilhelm in Düsseldorf, where it inspired the court sculptor, Gabriel Grupello, to design a human pyramid in bronze, which was unveiled in 1716.[4]

Jan Boeckhorst, a former assistant of Rubens, made a copy – greatly reduced in size – of *The Fall of the Damned* that is now preserved in Aachen (cat. 23). It is not an exact copy: Boeckhorst's figures are more slender (as one might expect from him), the fall of light has been altered as well, and the palette is more vivid than that of the original. The copy was presumably intended as a pendant to *The Resurrection of the Saved Souls*, a painting – now in the Staatsgalerie at Neuburg an der Donau – that was begun by Rubens and completed by another hand. The landscape painter Jan Wildens (1585/86–1653) bought this work at Rubens's estate sale.

The British Museum has a number of large, detailed chalk drawings (*c.* 75 x 50 cm) that depict falling demons and damned souls; these are partial copies of Rubens's composition. The sheet selected here shows the central group of corpulent gluttons (cat. 24). The modelling of the figures was worked up with virtuoso skill in watercolour and body colour, and it is no wonder that some are inclined to attribute this brushwork to Rubens himself.[5] Four other drawings – of lesser quality – from this series are to be found in the same collection and once belonged, successively, to the artists Prosper Henry Lankrink, Sir James Thornhill, Benjamin West and Sir Thomas Lawrence, as well as to the statesman Sir Robert Peel.[6]

Pieter Claesz. Soutman is thought to have used these drawings in conceiving his own version of *The Fall of the Damned* (cat. 25), a print executed with etching

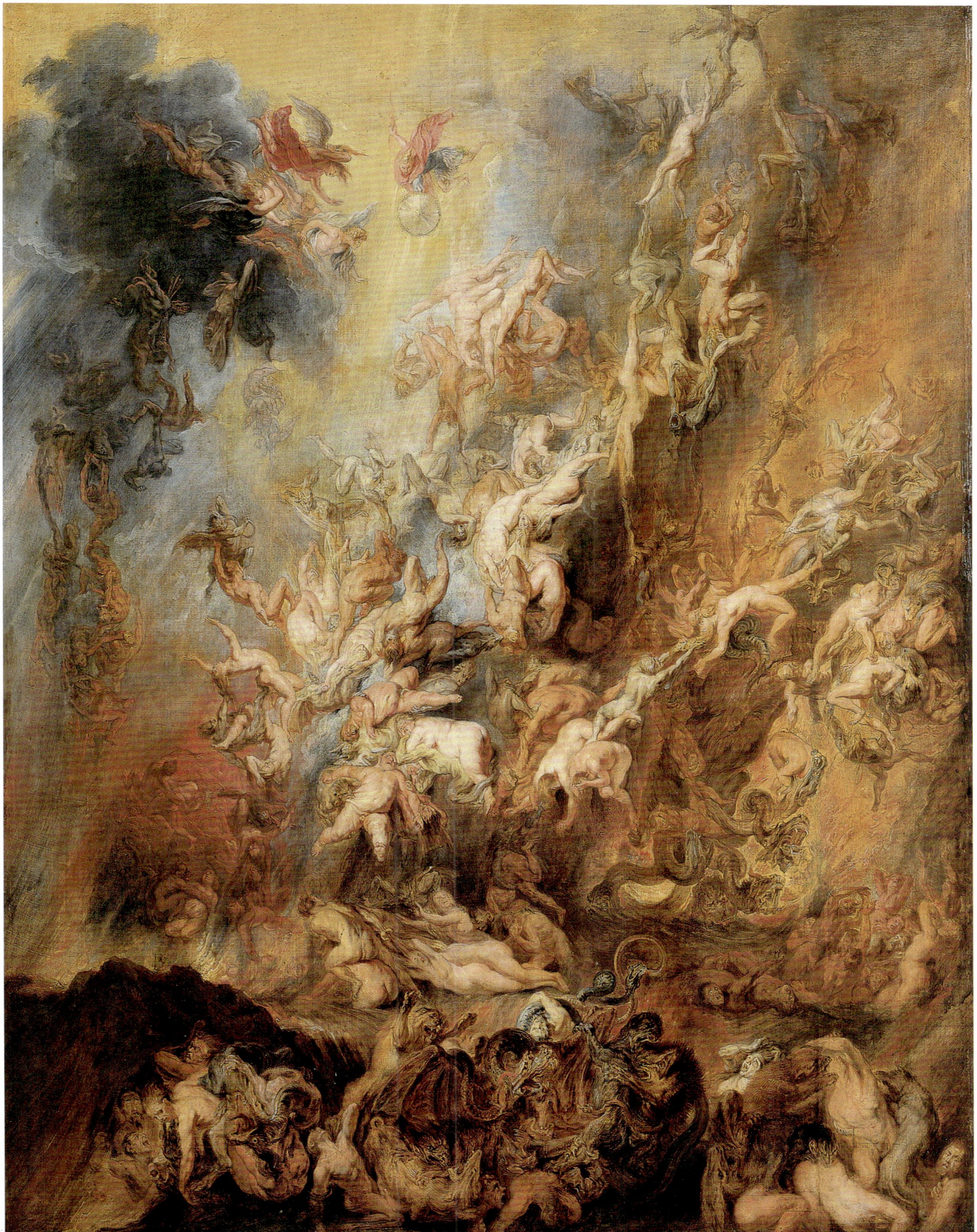

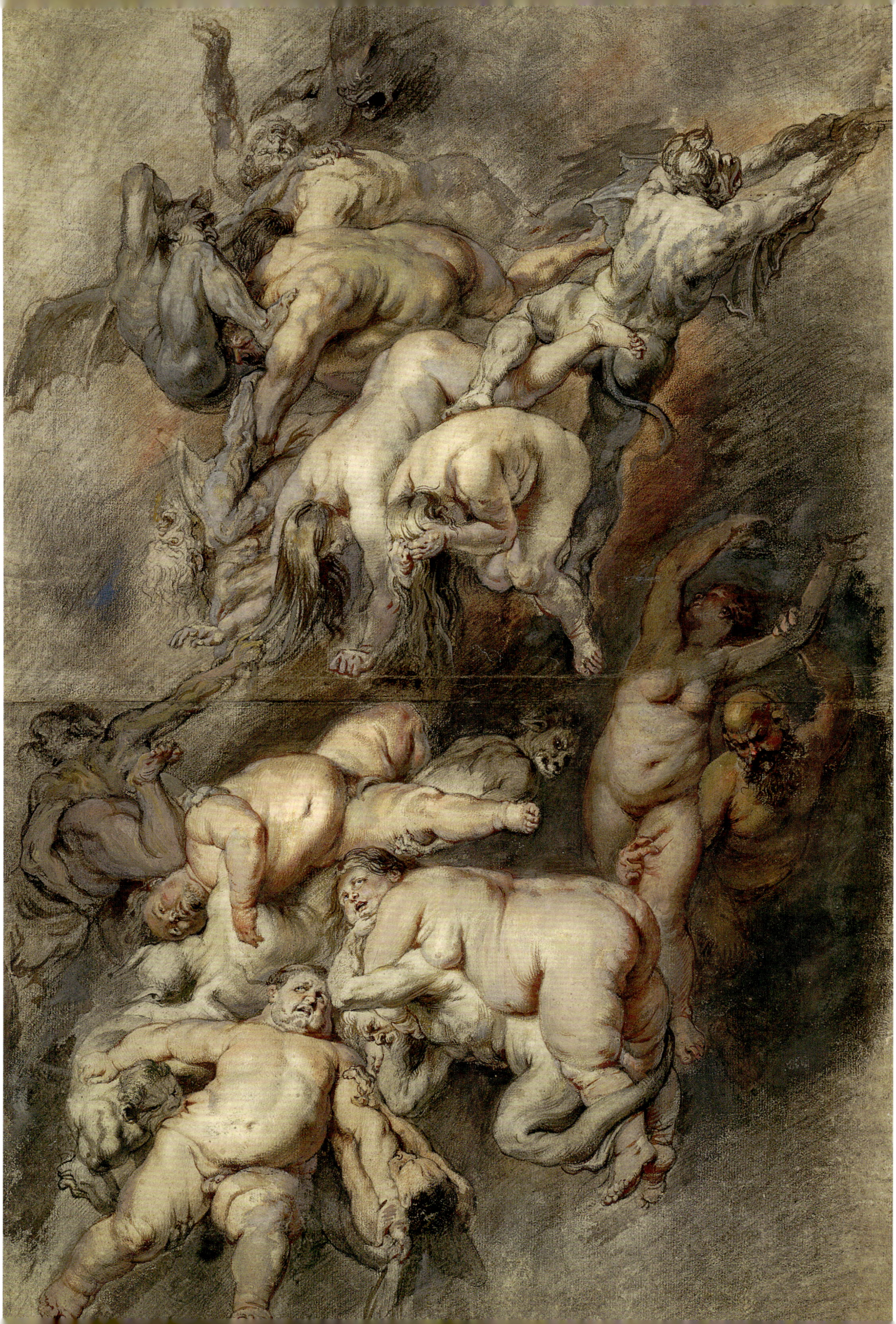

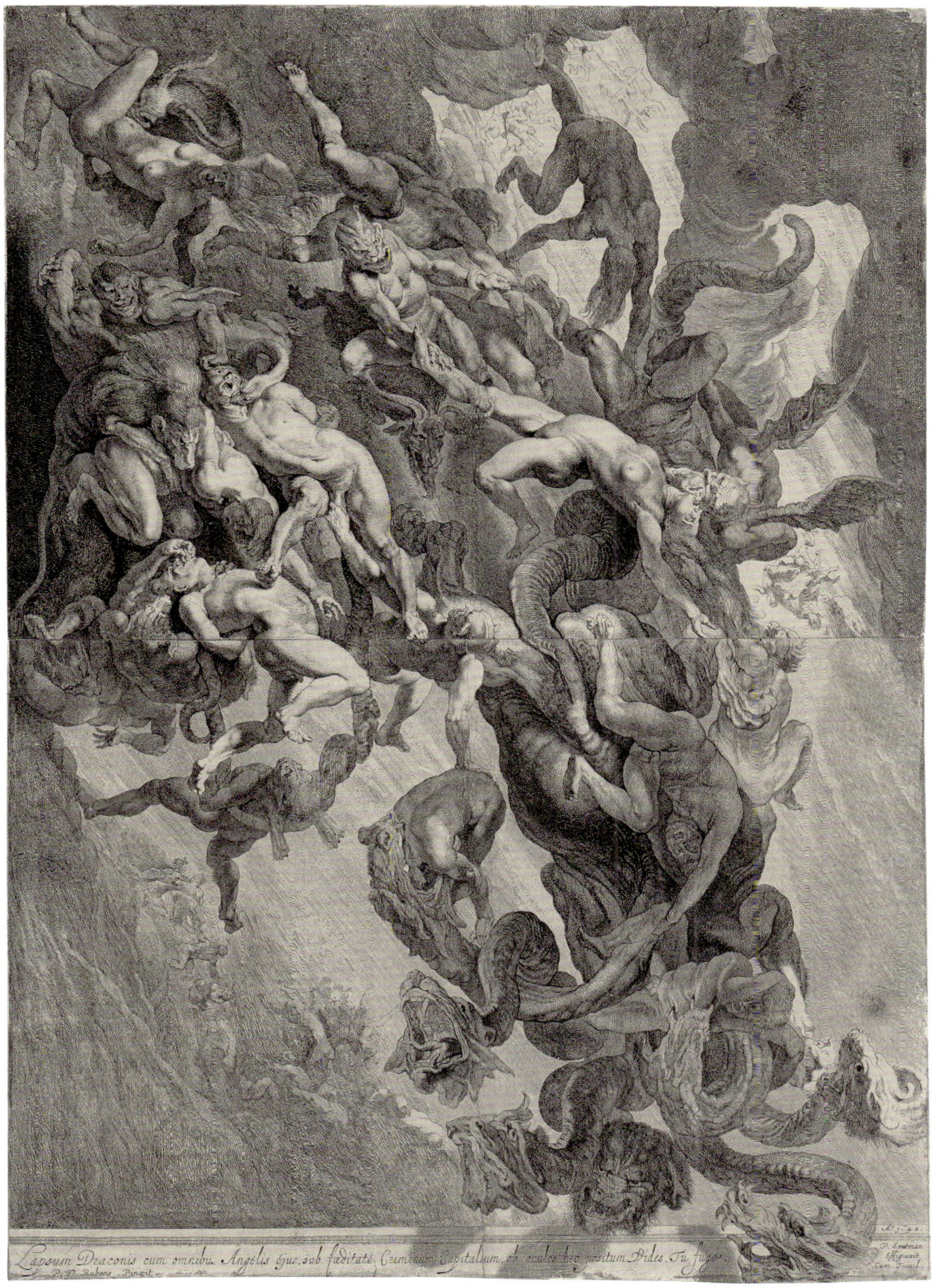

24

Attributed to
PETER PAUL RUBENS (1577–1640)
Sheet of studies for two groups in the upper half of *The Fall of the Damned*, *c.* 1614–18
Black and red chalk, watercolour and body colour, on two sheets conjoined, 70.9 x 47.4 cm
On loan from the British Museum, London, inv. Oo,3-9. From the bequest of Richard Payne Knight, 1824

PROVENANCE: Everhard Jabach (1610–1695); Pierre Crozat (1665–1740); Crozat sale, Paris, 10 April – 13 May 1741, lot 829; P. J. Mariette (1694–1774); Mariette sale, Paris, 15 November 1775 – 30 January 1776, lot 993; Le Brun sale, Paris, 11–13 March 1791, lot 266; Richard Payne Knight (1750–1824); by whom bequeathed to the British Museum in 1824
SELECTED REFERENCES: Hind 1915, vol. 1, no. 2; Rowlands 1977, no. 94; Freedberg 1984, no. 52, (copy 6)

25

PIETER CLAESZ. SOUTMAN (c. 1580–1657)
The Fall of the Damned, 1641
Etching and drypoint in two plates, 53 x 41.9 cm
Royal Museum of Fine Arts Antwerp, inv. 10116

PROVENANCE: Max Rooses collection, donated to the museum in 1900
SELECTED REFERENCES: Basan 1767, p. 40, no. 126; Voorhelm Schneevoogt 1873, p. 62, no. 458; Dutuit 1881, vol. 6, no. 126; Van den Wijngaert 1940, no. 634; Rome 1977, no. 27

26

JONAS SUYDERHOEF (c. 1613–1686)
The Fall of the Damned, 1642
Engraving, 64.0 x 53.5 cm
Royal Museum of Fine Arts Antwerp, inv. 10112

PROVENANCE: Max Rooses collection, donated to the museum in 1900
SELECTED REFERENCES: Voorhelm Schneevoogt 1873, no. 62.459; Hollstein 1949–2010, vol. 28, no. 2.1

needle (and drypoint modifications) that paraphrases Rubens's painting. As he did in the *Hippopotamus and Crocodile Hunt* (cat. 10), Soutman introduced in this print, a *trompe-l'œil* device: the dragon's head at the bottom seems to cast a shadow in the margin. Suyderhoef's version (cat. 26) differs markedly from the source.

Another artist who was impressed by Rubens's composition was Charles Le Brun, court painter to Louis XIV. During the construction of the chapel in the palace at Versailles, Le Brun was chosen to paint the ceiling. In 1679, however, it was decided by a narrow margin to demolish the chapel and replace it with a new building, which forced Le Brun to revise his plans completely. The definitive design shows the ceiling encircled by an illusionistic balustrade, which makes it look as though a chaos of damned souls are plunging into the room, while on the other side of the composition – above the high altar – a column of saved souls rises to heaven.[7] In this way Le Brun combines Rubens's composition with the perspectival ceilings in the churches of Sant'Ignazio (Pozzo) and Il Gesù (Gaulli) in Rome. In 1683, however, Le Brun's patron, Jean-Baptiste Colbert (Louis XIV's finance minister), died, and the scheming of the painter's rivals caused him to fall from grace under Colbert's successor, the Marquis de Louvois. In 1685 Le Brun made the painting that is now in Dijon (cat. 27). He intended to give this work to Louvois in an effort to turn the tide, but when the minister refused to accept it, the project foundered.

When painting stately interiors along Vienna's nineteenth-century Ringstrasse in neo-Renaissance and neo-Baroque styles, Hans Makart and Hans Canon were inclined to fall back on formulas that Rubens had come up with more than two centuries earlier. The celebrated Makart, who saw himself as the new Rubens, was commissioned to design the ceiling painting above the staircase in the Kunsthistorisches Museum (see cat. 28). The apotheosis of art (the victory of light over darkness) is a suitable theme. In the middle we see Apollo riding his sun-chariot; close to him hover Luna and Amor. Below them, Vices flee into the darkness, while several Virtues frolic in the clouds at the right. Just as he did in his other works, Makart drew inspiration from the compositions and the palette of the Venetian masters, as well as from Rubens and Delacroix. He had begun to paint the lunettes that border the ceiling, but his untimely death put an end to his work on this project. In the same period Canon designed his painting *The Cycle of Life* (see cat. 29) for the domed ceiling above the staircase in the Naturhistorisches Museum, the twin building opposite the Kunsthistorisches Museum. This is a secularised version of Rubens's *Great Last Judgement*. Rubens's supreme figure of Christ has been replaced by a contemplative Father Time, lower down in the painting, who is apparently indifferent to the medley of Rubensian motifs woven into a decorative ring behind him.

Early on, during his years at the Munich academy and after a short visit to Antwerp in 1884, Lovis Corinth entered into a dialogue with the masters of the Flemish Baroque and with Rubens in particular.[8] The young artist admittedly maintained that 'the time of Rubens and Brouwer and the history painters Gallait, Verlat and Leys was over'[9] and identified himself, rather, with the individualistic Rembrandt and with Frans Hals, whose works he later sought out in the Netherlands.[10] But his

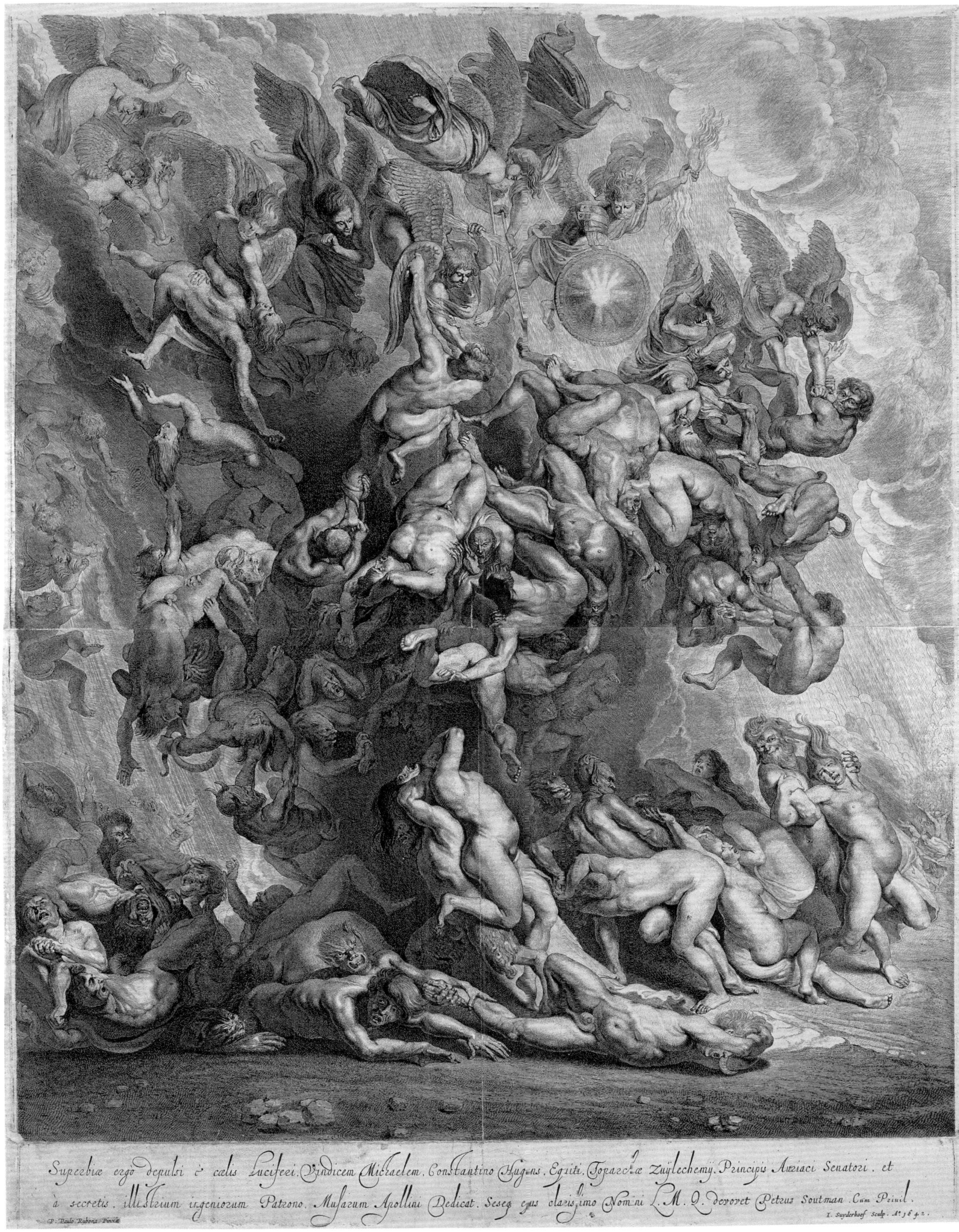
Superbiæ ergò depulsi è cælis Luciferi. Vindicem Michaelem. Constantino Hugens. Egiti. Toparchæ Zuÿlechemÿ. Principis Auriaci Senatori. et
à secretis. illustrium ingeniorum Patrono. Musarum Apollini Dedicat. Seseq eius clarissimo Nomini L. M. Q. devovet Petrus Soutman. Cum Privil.
P. Paulo Rubens Pinxit
I. Suyderhoef Sculp. A°. 1642.

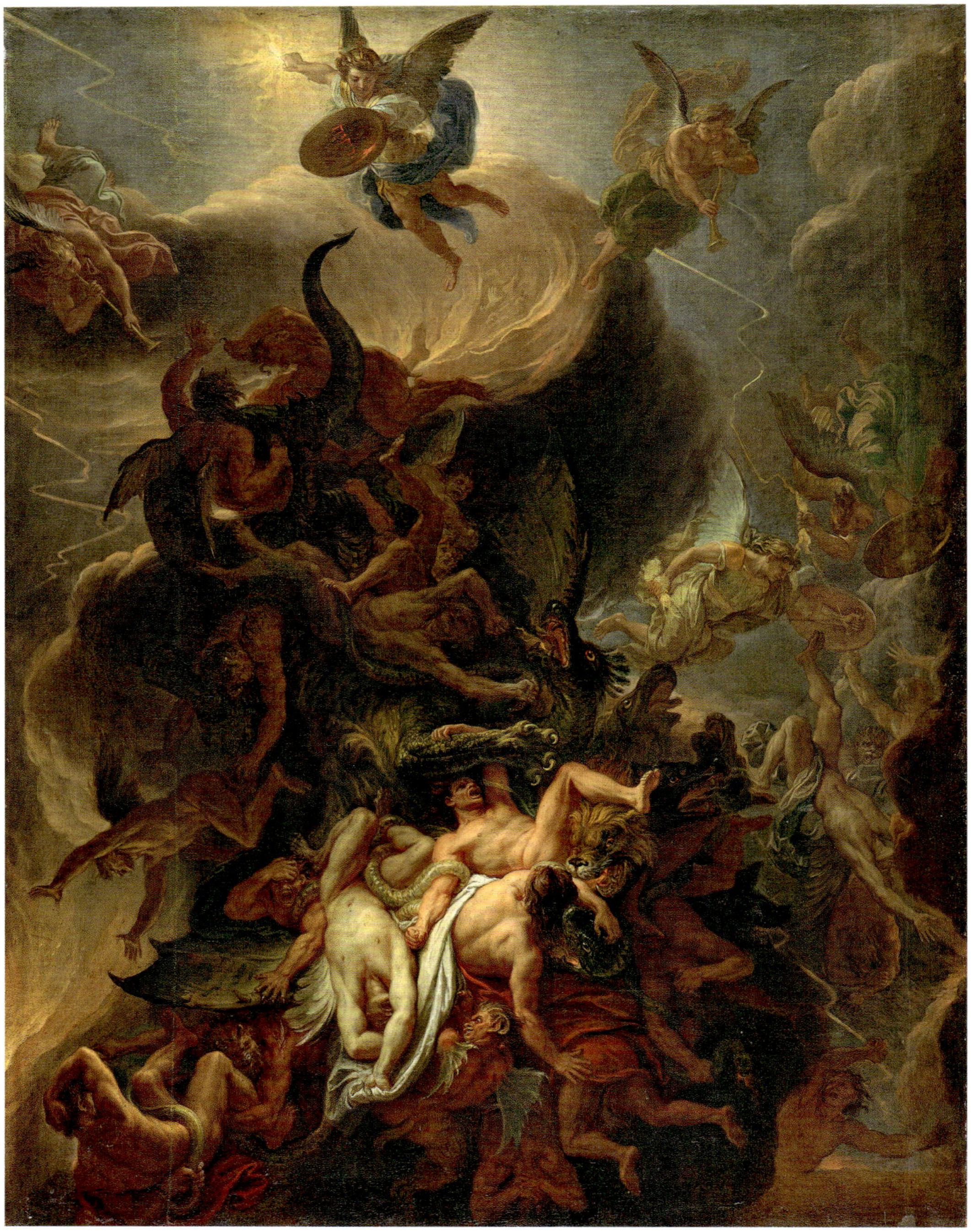

27

CHARLES LE BRUN (1619–1690)
The Fall of the Rebel Angels, 1685
Oil on canvas, 162 x 129 cm
Musée des Beaux-Arts de Dijon,
inv. D 1935-1-P

PROVENANCE: inventory of the royal collection at Versailles, 1695; Louvre, 1785; Musée des Beaux-Arts de Quimper, 1897; Musée de Versailles, 1921; Musée des Beaux-Arts de Dijon
SELECTED REFERENCES: Nivelon 1700, p. 300; Versailles 1963, no. 35; Thuillier 1967, pp. 263–64

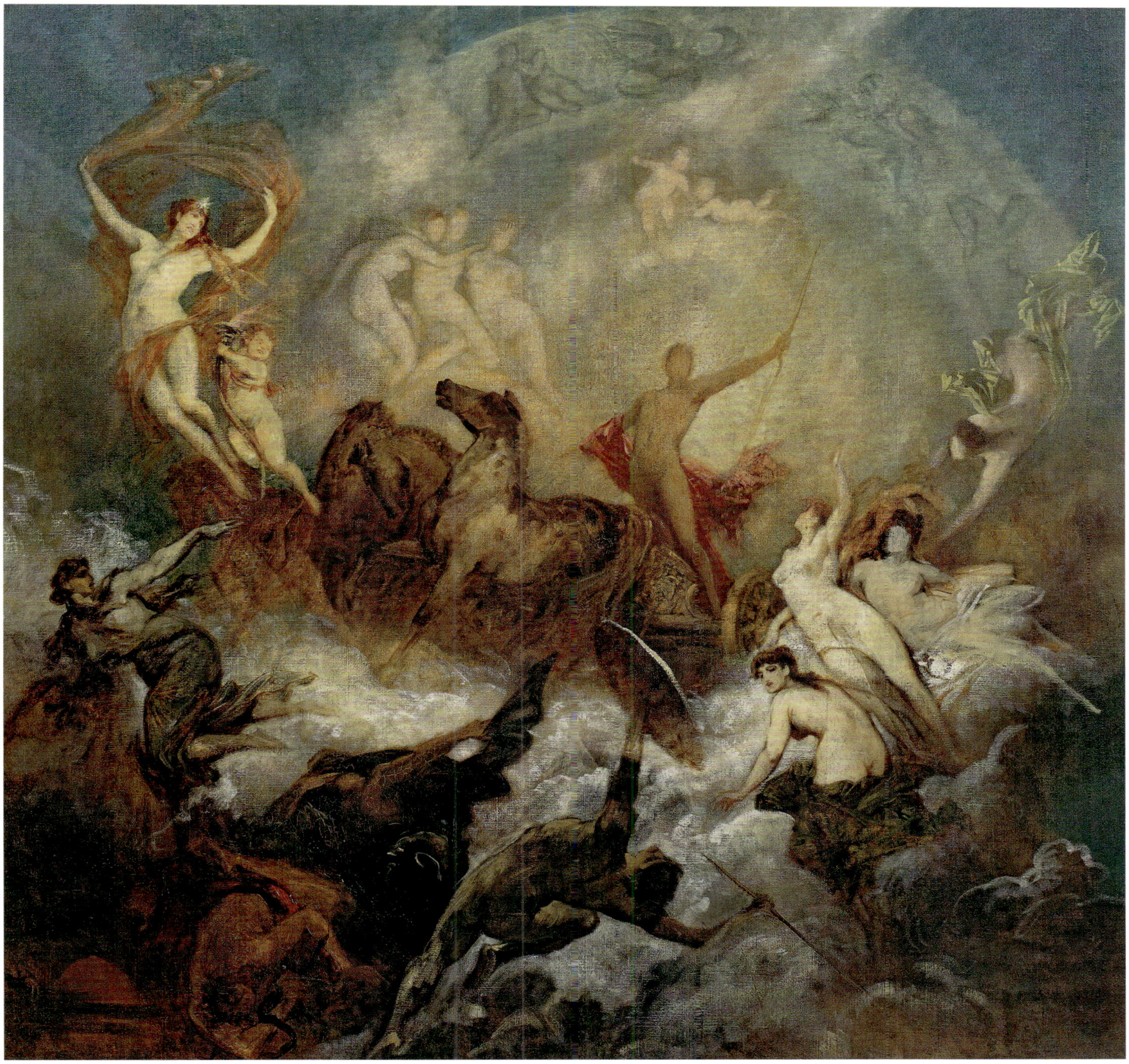

28

HANS MAKART (1840–1884)
Study for *The Victory of Light Over Darkness*, 1883
Oil on canvas, 184 × 170 cm
Österreichische Galerie Belvedere, Vienna, inv. 3756

PROVENANCE: donated by the Hofbaukomitee of the Kaiserliche Gemäldegalerie (Imperial Picture Gallery) in 1891
SELECTED REFERENCES: Schloss Halbturn 1986, no. 31

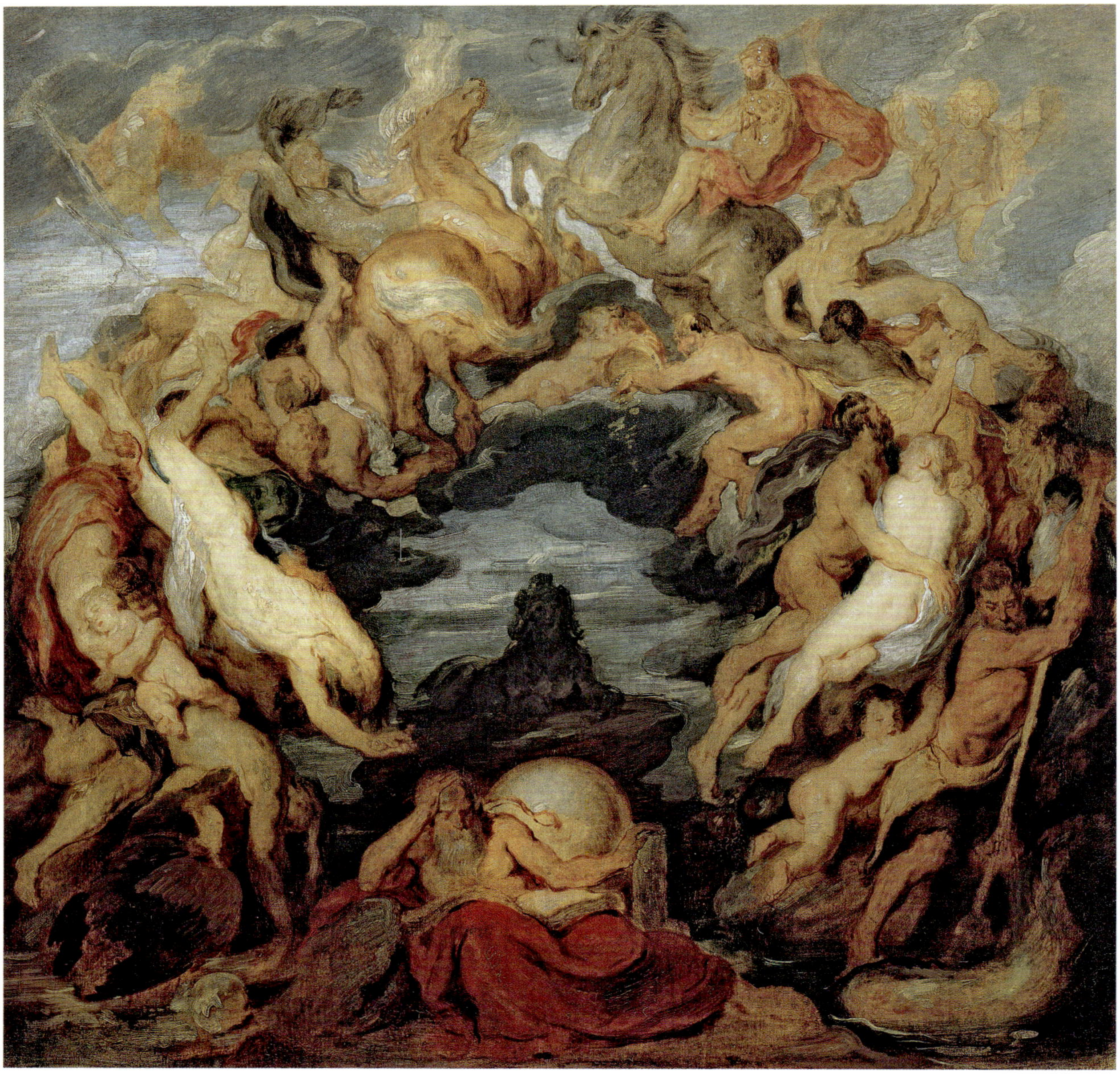

29

HANS CANON (1829–1885)
Design for *The Cycle of Life*, *c.* 1885
Oil on canvas, 110 x 117.5 cm
Österreichische Galerie Belvedere, Vienna, inv. 2084

PROVENANCE: donated by the Hofbaukomitee of the Kaiserliche Gemäldegalerie (Imperial Picture Gallery) in 1891
SELECTED REFERENCES: Lehmann 2007, p. 139

30

LOVIS CORINTH (1858–1925)
Hell (fragment), *c.* 1901
Oil on canvas, 102 x 41 cm
Scottish National Gallery of Modern Art, Edinburgh, inv. GML 793. Long Loan in 1997

PROVENANCE: none published
SELECTED REFERENCES: none published

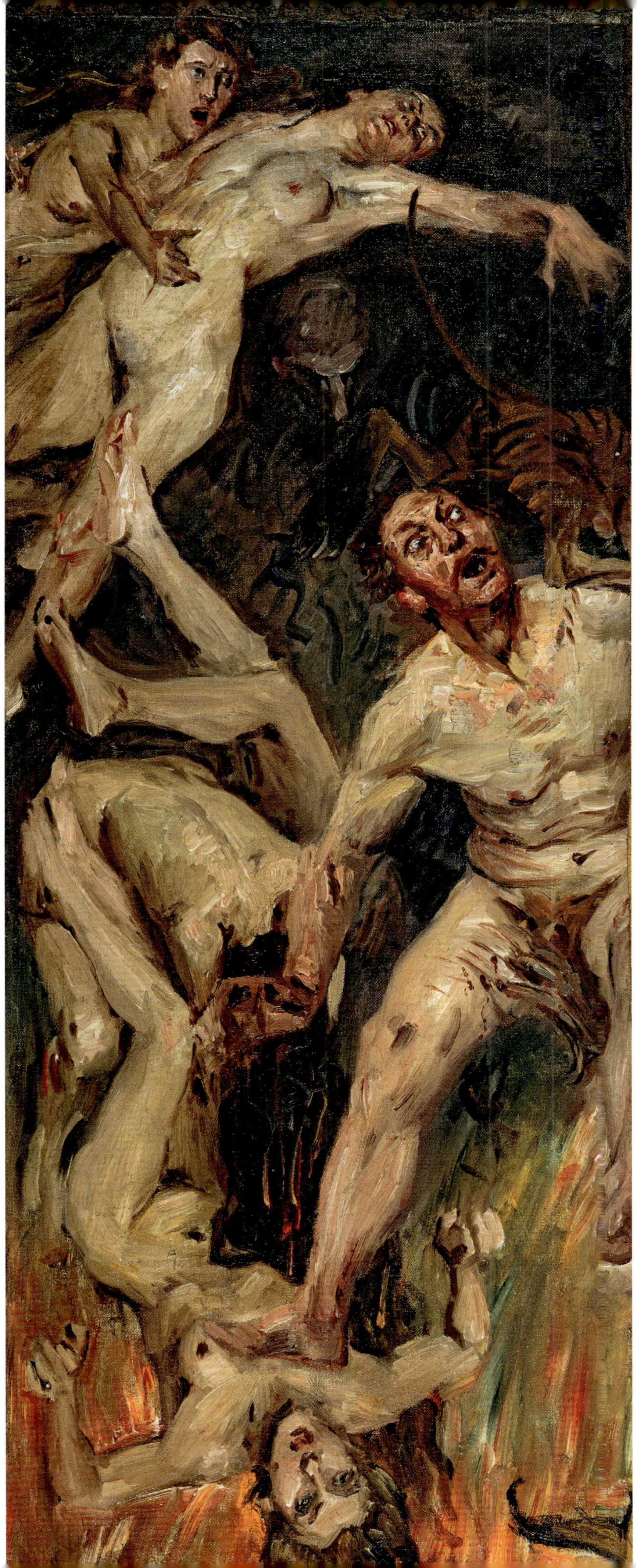

memories of Rubens's masterpieces in the Alte Pinakothek and the Royal Museum of Fine Arts Antwerp stayed with him: his palette became more colourful and his brushwork freer. Later canvases, such as *Diogenes*, *Ariadne on Naxos*, *The Childhood of Zeus* and *Susanna and the Elders* exude the energy of Rubens. In 1901 Corinth painted *Hell*, which refers to Rubens's *The Fall of the Damned*. He was dissatisfied with the painting, however, and kept only this fragment (cat. 30). Corinth painted the terrifying scene with the wild brush strokes that are his trademark.

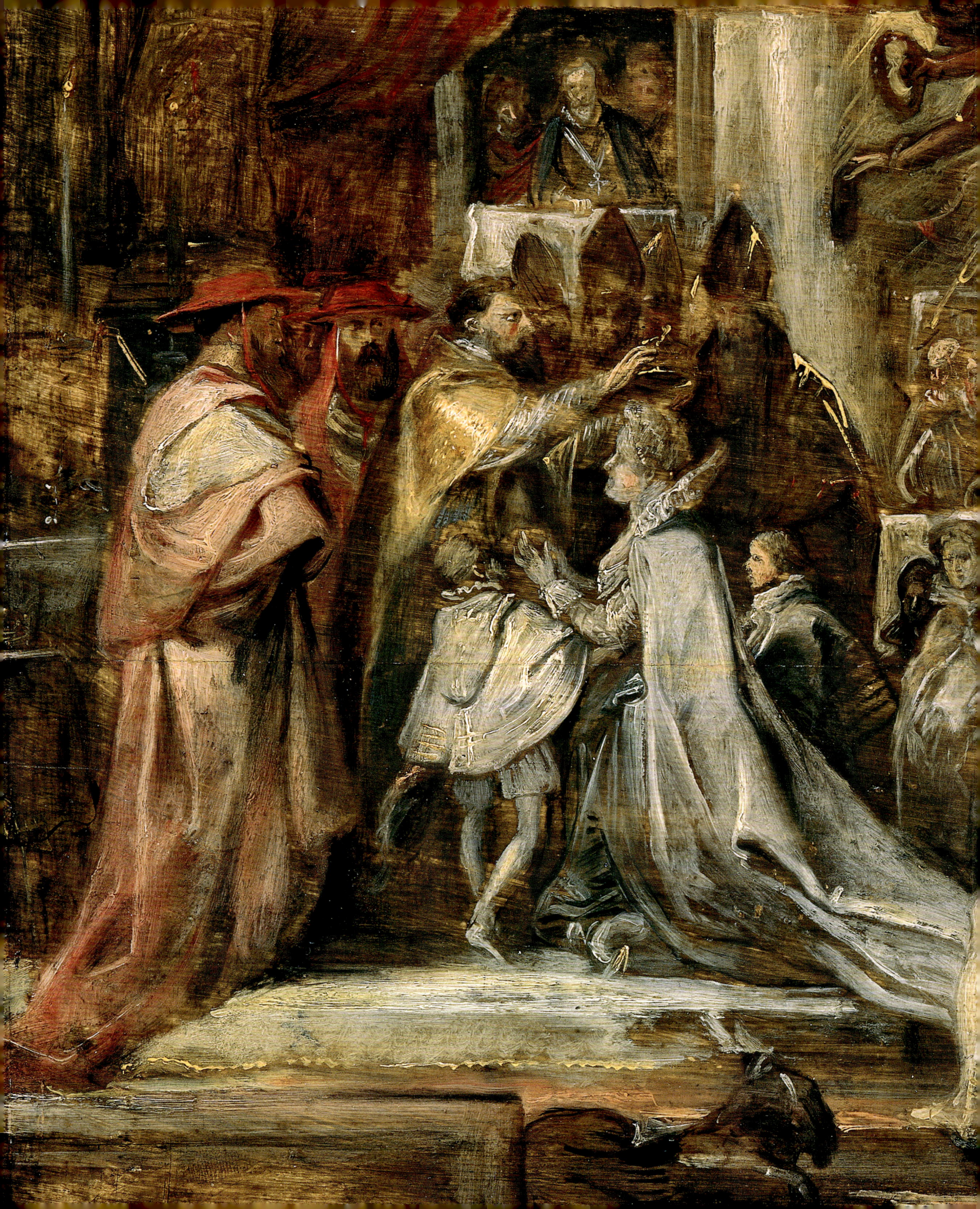

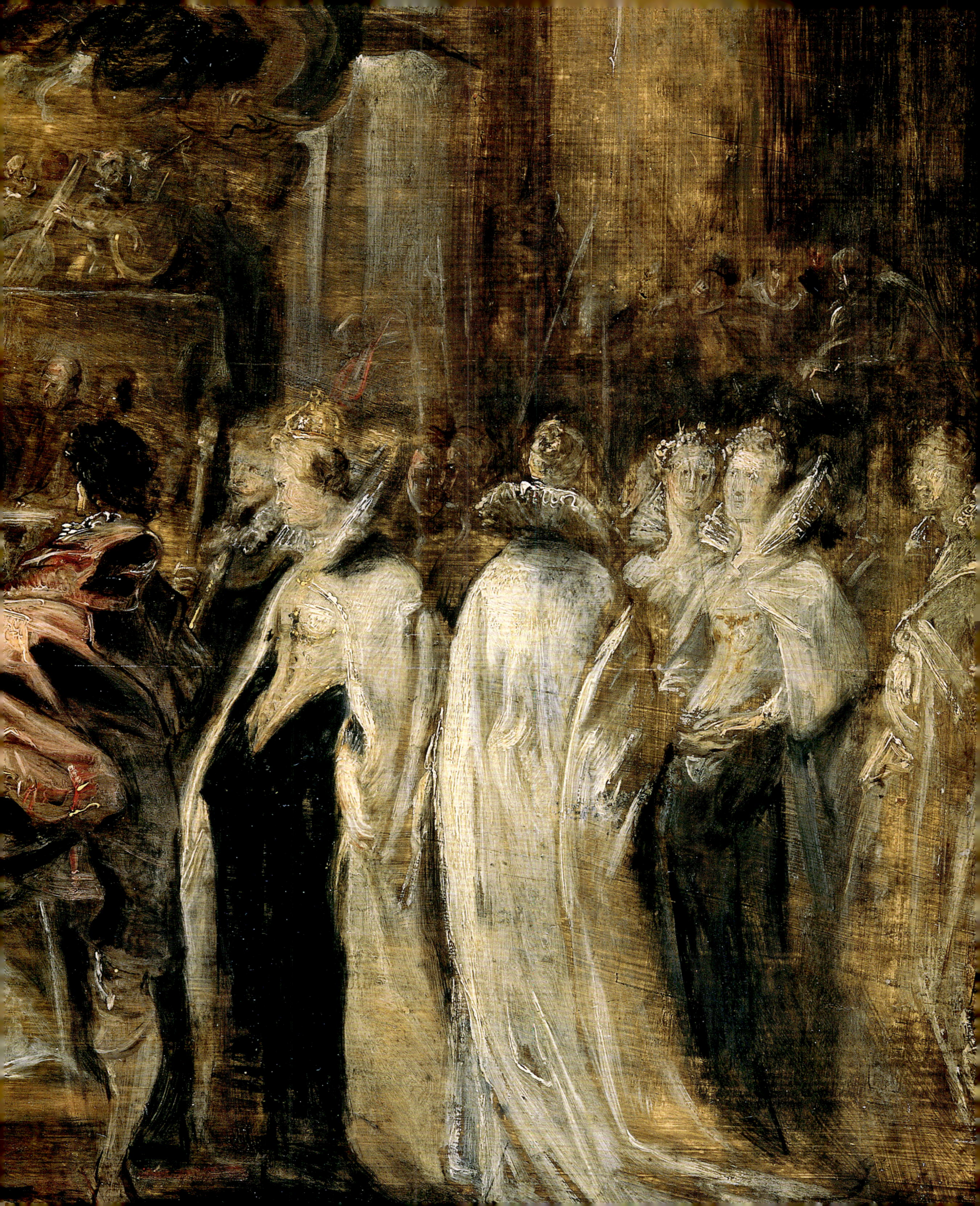

POWER

ALEXIS MERLE DU BOURG

POMP AND CIRCUMSTANCE: RUBENS AS APOLOGIST FOR POWER

Within the most prestigious collection of seventeenth-century engraved portraits – the *Iconographie* – Rubens appears at once as 'the Apelles of his age in Antwerp' (fig. 12), a paragon of the gentleman-painter, knighted by a succession of rulers, and as *homme d'Etat*, statesman, secretary to the privy council of the 'Catholic King'.[1] The printed letters on Van Dyck's engraved work sum up the unusual degree of overlap between art and politics in Rubens's life. Comparison with the most paradigmatic figure of Apelles can certainly be regarded as one of the most overused *topoi* of the modern age, but in this case for once the parallel seems justified: Rubens is enough of a heavyweight to hold his own against the main claim to fame of his distant predecessor, according to Pliny the Elder, painter by appointment to Alexander the Great. Rubens strove to glorify Vincent, Albert, Isabella, Marie, Henri, Philip, James and Ferdinand, plus a whole host of potentates, favourites and aristocrats, thereby providing us with a motley background to European history. In this very nearly exhaustive effort to celebrate the rich and powerful of his day he had only one rival in the history of European art: Titian, with whom he was locked in a fascinating creative competition during the whole of his career.

Of course, it was not Rubens's intention at the outset to paint mainly the great and the good.[2] The task required the combination of a formidable capacity for work, social mobility, tact and discretion cultivated from boyhood, and finally an international reputation consolidated through the 'promotional' use of the print.[3] At the height of his fame, Rubens could pride himself that the princes of Europe were competing with one another for his services, keen to honour the most illustrious living artist. This is why, after Charles I had ennobled Rubens in 1630, Philip IV felt obliged to follow his lead in 1631.

POWER MAGNIFIED, POWER AND THEATRE

Rubens's status as *primus inter pares* led first to the adaptation of the plastic language he created to the type of theatrical 'apologetics'[4] demanded by 'court society' and by the emerging modern state. One of the fundamental features of such apologetics has been described as the theatricalisation of existence.[5] Undoubtedly the feature of this language most specific to Rubens (and also the most challenging) was the representation of power – which had been shown as stiffly hieratic in form since time immemorial – in motion. Rather than conferring the signs of immutability on the holder of power, Rubens tended immediately to give him a 'kinetic' character (or to emphasise the intrinsic dynamism of the formulae he had inherited or created), while taking care not to alter his transcendental nature. Thus in 1603, in the equestrian portrait of the Duke of Lerma (fig. 11), predatory favourite of Philip III of Spain, Rubens found himself competing with Titian's *Charles V at the Battle of Mühlberg* (1548; Museo Nacional del Prado, Madrid). In his portrait, Rubens uncharacteristically chose a frontal pose that required strong acceleration of the

FIG. 11 Peter Paul Rubens, *Equestrian Portrait of the Duke of Lerma*, 1603. Oil on canvas, 290.5 x 207.5 cm. Museo Nacional del Prado, Madrid

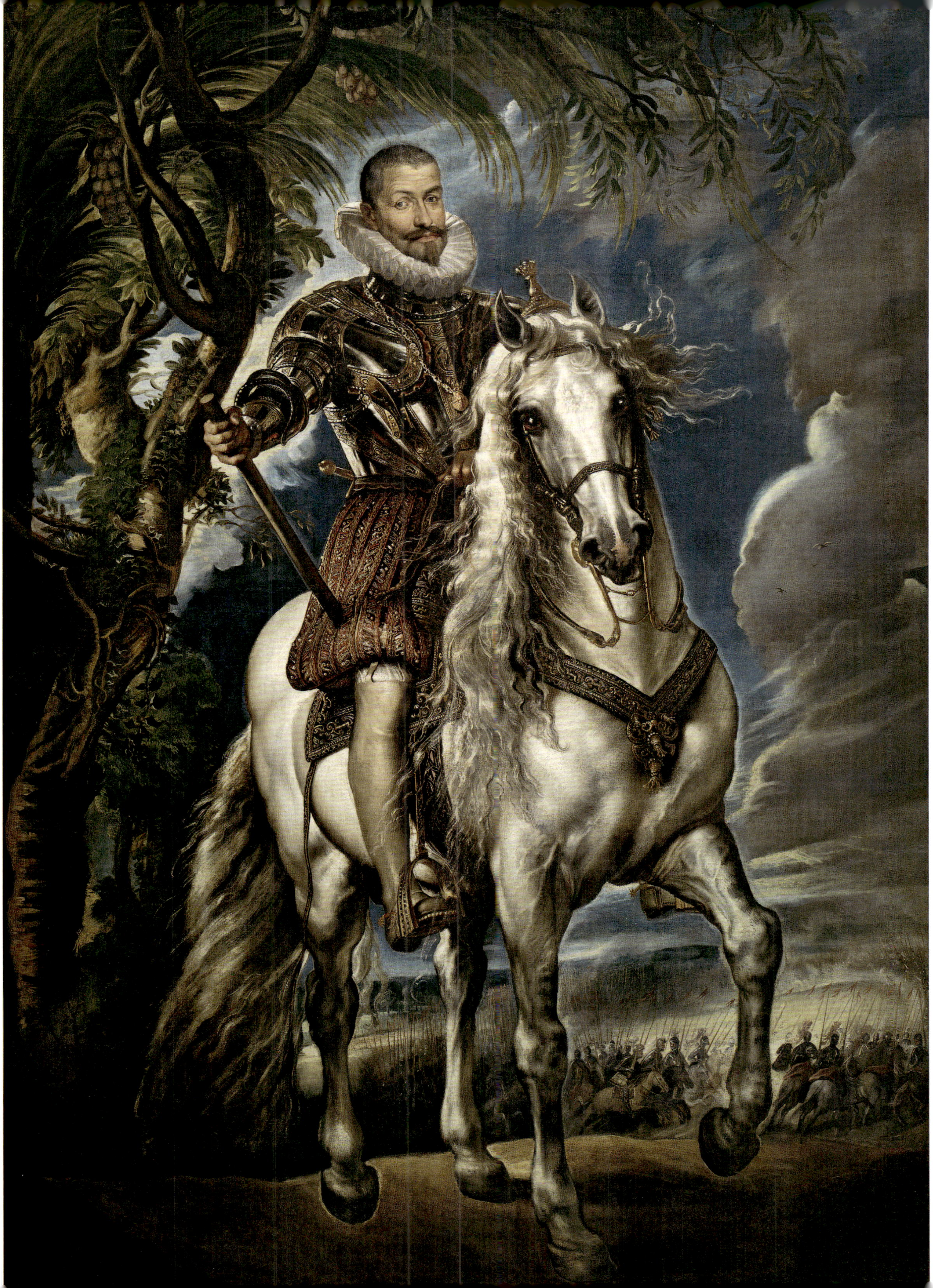

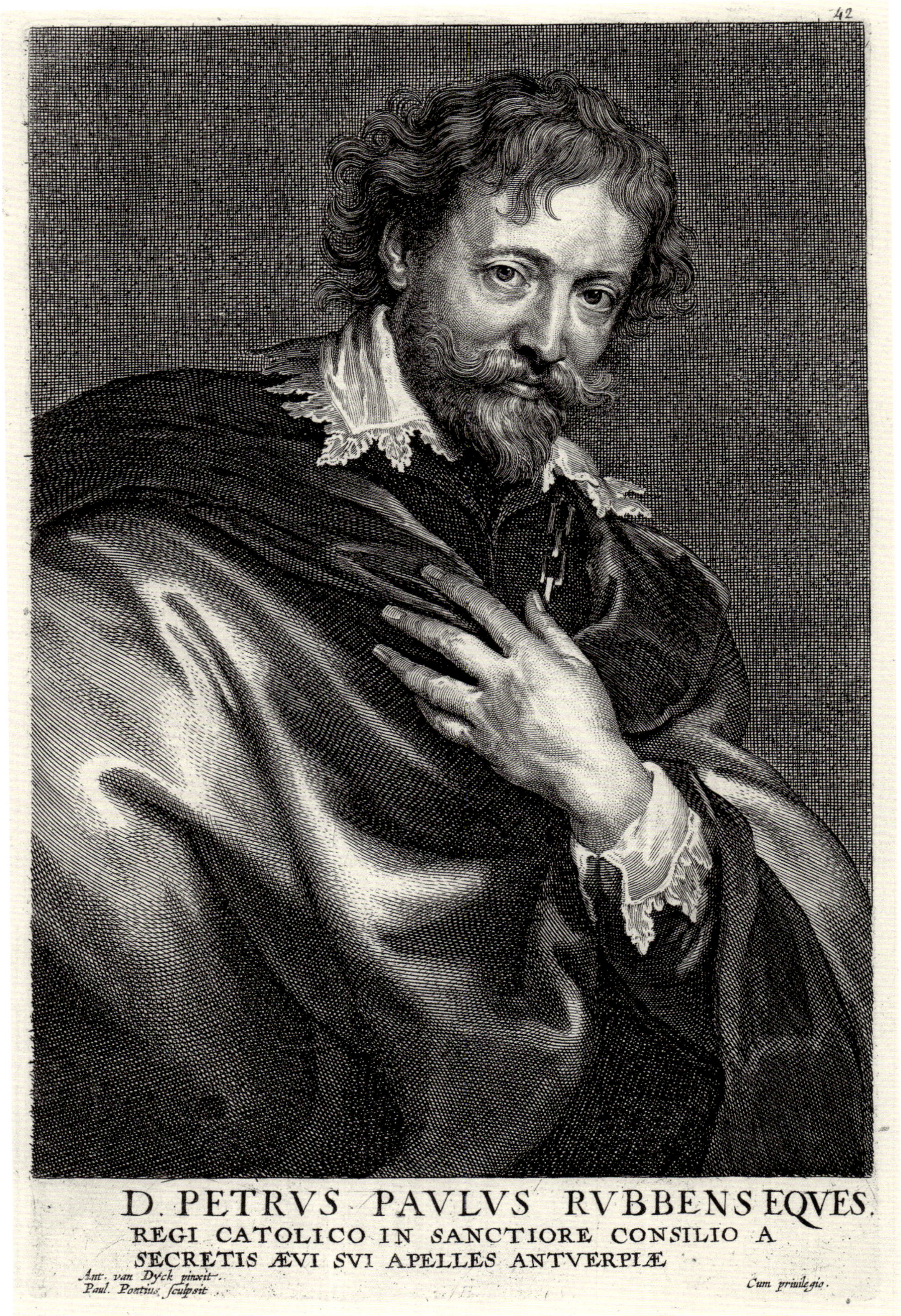
42
D. PETRVS PAVLVS RVBBENS EQVES.
REGI CATOLICO IN SANCTIORE CONSILIO A
SECRETIS ÆVI SVI APELLES ANTVERPIÆ
Ant. van Dyck pinxit.
Paul. Pontius sculpsit
Cum priuilegio.

perspective. Whereas Charles V had seemed suspended in majesty, Lerma – behaving like a king without a crown – is first and foremost a power on the move.[6]

The kinetic aspect of Rubens's exaltation of those in power has two characteristic manifestations: triumph and apotheosis. The time-honoured representation of triumph and the progression of the hero within an essentially martial situation provided a near-perfect match for the genius of an artist steeped in classical culture and supremely skilled at the presentation of pomp. The diffusion of humanist culture in Europe at the end of the Middle Ages and the beginning of the modern period had re-activated the triumphal iconography of ancient Rome; Rubens was in many respects following in the footsteps of Italian predecessors with whom he was closely familiar, most particularly Andrea Mantegna, Titian and Giulio Romano. The case of the 'apotheosis' was somewhat different, in that it constituted a kind of profane Ascension/Assumption of a prince or overweening noble. The Flemish artist played a key role in the renewal of this vertical representation of power (see pages 108–17) by merging the entire ascensional Christian repertoire with the Roman apotheoses that had been especially revealed by the rediscovery in Paris of the *Gemma Tiberiana*, a monumental cameo (said to date from the first century) that intrigued Rubens, the scholar Nicolas-Claude Fabri de Peiresc and their correspondents during the 1620s.[7]

The importance of the renewal of this allegorical language by Rubens was nevertheless no more remarkable than his introduction of *action* into the heart of his painted 'eulogies'. In the different means he adopted to celebrate those in power, Rubens in fact showed himself to be a virtuoso manipulator of allegory, peerlessly using its major modes, symbols and personification. It is in his dynamic use of personification – evolved from the twin heritage of antiquity and Christianity by embodying an abstract idea in an anthropomorphic figure – that the great artist proved himself most original. The monumental, though atypical, culmination of Rubens's work in this vein, the 24 paintings he executed for the Palais du Luxembourg that form the Galerie Médicis (1622–25; see cat. 34) and the abandoned decorative scheme begun for the Galerie Henri IV (1628–31; cat. 37), required him to represent contemporaries in close correlation with mythological figures from earth, air and water. Rubens and his French interlocutors developed an iconographic programme on an unprecedented scale – unrivalled in the complexity of the interaction between the figures and in the huge size of the scheme. One of the most unusual aspects of this combination, the outcome of the Mannerist notion of *pittura mista*,[8] lay in the fact that the mythological protagonists were no less convincing for it, offering the viewer the same corporeal substance, the same or even greater tangibility as the historical figures alongside them.[9] This seamless hybridisation of all the registers of representation – mimetic, narrative, eulogic and metaphorical – was achieved by an artist of enormous talent who offered extremely stiff competition to his rivals.

FIG. 12 Paulus Pontius, after Sir Anthony van Dyck, *Portrait of Rubens*, early 1630s. Engraving, 34.7 x 44.8 cm.

PROBLEMATIC POSTERITY

The rhetoric of apologetics produced with such consummate skill by Rubens found its earliest imitators in the circle of artists who worked from his models in Antwerp. Among them were Theodoor van Thulden and in particular, in the late 1640s and early 1650s, Jacob Jordaens, who in his decorative scheme for the Oranjezaal in the Huis ten Bosch showed himself to be Rubens's most able heir in the glorification of princes (see pages 102–05). In the seventeenth century this aspect of Rubens's legacy spread far beyond the Spanish Low Countries, even to France, a country that had for a time, it is alleged, rejected the painter who was the embodiment of the Baroque aesthetic. Such prejudice served to conceal how much French apologetic art of the century of Louis XIV owed to the art of the great Flemish painter.[10]

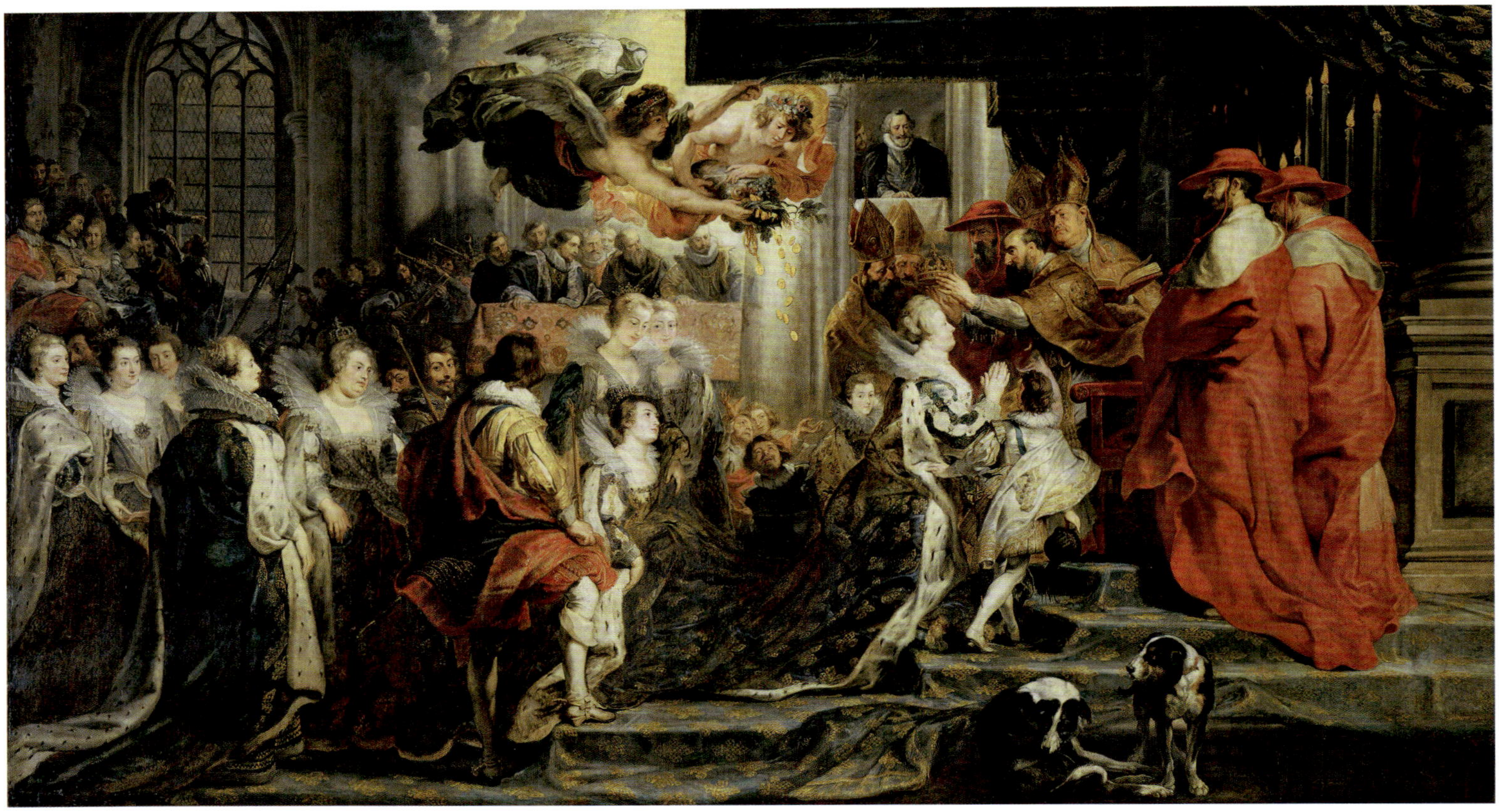

FIG. 13 Peter Paul Rubens, *The Coronation of Marie de Médicis*, 1622–25. Oil on canvas, 394 x 727 cm. Musée du Louvre, Paris

Rubens cut an ambivalent figure: wreathed in honour and fame, yet between the seventeenth and the nineteenth centuries the butt of constant criticism; he never managed to avoid disapprobation. Two aspects of his political work in particular incurred reproach. Writing in 1685 about the Galerie Médicis in his *Entretiens*, André Félibien revived the arguments that the combination of sacred and profane in Michelangelo's Sistine Chapel paintings had provoked in the sixteenth and seventeenth centuries. Although not free from insincerity (the reproach was made in the context of the altercation between the 'Poussinistes' and the 'Rubénistes'), the judgement should be related to the debate over the legitimacy of the 'pagan marvellous' circulating in contemporary literature throughout the century.[11] This rejection of mythological elements in episodes set after the beginning of Christianity bears witness, as Jean Seznec noted, to the gradual decline of the poetic emotion expressed in the fable.[12]

Heir to the syncretism of the Renaissance, Rubens was able to give his mythological figures startling presence and vitality. He had managed to mingle the two elements without

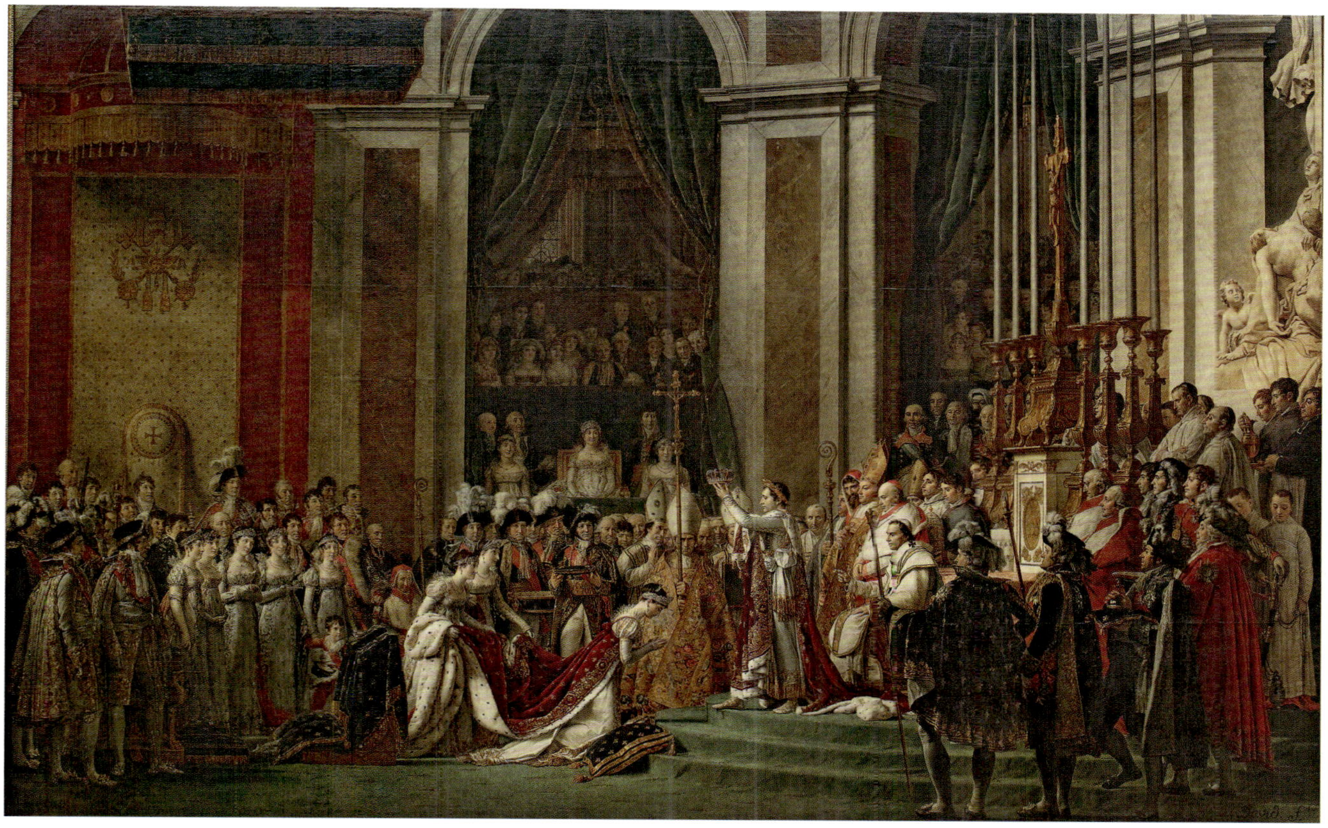

controversy for the contemporaries of Louis XIII, whose civilisation proceeded in the main from that of the previous century. This was no longer acceptable to the contemporaries of Louis XIV, whose taste was more refined. The scope of Rubens's apologetic language (and also that of Charles Le Brun at Versailles), represented by allegorical personification, was to become the object of growing public censure beyond the pious susceptibility of someone such as Félibien. The Abbé Dubos (*Réflexions critiques*, 1719),[13] Diderot (*Essais sur la peinture*, 1766),[14] Winckelmann (*Essai sur une Allégorie*, 1766)[15] and Sulzer (*Discours sur l'allégorie*, 1771–12)[16] are unanimous in denouncing the lack of verisimilitude to be found in Rubens's magical version of reality based upon the interaction of historical and mythological characters. A further, no less fundamental reproach relates to the obscurity and the multiple meanings of these figures, who defy interpretation. The deliberately equivocal nature of Rubens's political allegories can be ascribed mainly to court society's current craze for encryption, hermetics and *figure mistiche* (allegorical figures).

FIG. 14 Jacques-Louis David, *Coronation of the Emperor Napoleon I and Crowning of the Empress Josephine*, 1805–07. Oil on canvas, 621 x 979 cm. Musée du Louvre, Paris

It also signalled the artist's assimilation of the characteristics that were so indispensable in the busy, ruthless environment of a princely court: prudence and duplicity. Theorists of the Enlightenment no longer accepted this, arguing that *sign* and *meaning* should coincide without ambiguity.[17]

Even if this profound change in European sensibility did not quite sound the death knell of allegory in painting, it certainly led inexorably to its gradual decline. Paradoxically, the influence of Rubens's apologetic art was most compromised when the artist himself was exerting extraordinarily authoritative power over the course of European art. Jean-Antoine Watteau, who looked quizzically at Rubens's great princely celebrations – the Galerie Médicis or the decorations for the *Pompa introitus Ferdinandi* – before drawing inspiration from them in his quite light-hearted scenes from daily life,[18] was in no way eccentric; he embodied the spirit of his age. One might surmise that the gradual evolution of the great monarchies into administrative states, 'abstract' in some respects although embodied (and how!) in the person of a prince, must also have contributed to this decline. The shift of this paradigm helped to render the presentation of a ruler based on epic literature, or on theatre or ballet, less and less appropriate – indeed woefully miscast. Rubens's employers in Paris were not afraid to ask him to depict the Queen Mother in embarrassing, almost scandalous, circumstances – in the act of escaping or in flight. Times had changed. The representation of the King in the Galerie des Glaces at Versailles left no room for mishaps or misadventures; Louis XIV appears almost as much as a principle as a person (cat. 40).

In France, it was not until the 'hyper-personalisation' of the regime around the unique figure of Bonaparte at the end of the Directory, under the Consulate[19] and the Empire, that, paradoxically, the allegorical and triumphal language of Rubens regained some of its relevance. Again, it is worth noting that, during the Empire, the most celebrated of the works inspired by the Galerie Médicis, Jacques-Louis David's huge *Coronation of the Emperor Napoleon I and Crowning of the Empress Josephine* (fig. 14), bears certain affinities (which escaped nobody's notice at the time, probably not even the notice of Napoleon himself)[20] with one of the most prosaic, most descriptive and least allegorical compositions in Rubens's entire cycle: *The Coronation of Marie de Médicis* (fig. 13). Although David was not afraid of sacrificing historical truth to the demands of politics, as his predecessor had done, he was to exclude any allegorical reference from this composition, presenting it in a severely Neoclassical style; this is perceptible even in the palette, based on local colour, as far away as possible from the glinting play of light and shade employed by the Flemish master.

It is fascinating to see how James Ward (1769–1859) was inspired by Rubens, borrowing elements from his cycle known as *The Triumph of the Eucharist*[21] in his vast *Allegory of Waterloo* (1815–22; now lost); fascinating also that this London painter faced such severe censure for his work.[22] Of Ward's gigantic commission, only the *modello* remains (cat. 15),[23] but in it can be seen the influence of a scene from the *Eucharist* cycle known as *The Triumph of the Church*, which was disseminated in engravings (including those by Schelte Adamsz. Bolswert between 1648 and 1652).[24] Ward saw in Rubens's cycle a means of achieving the sublime atmosphere appropriate to his project to celebrate Wellington, but failed to realise that this heterogeneous language (which had also been used to glorify the Roman Catholic Church and its dogma) had simply become unpalatable to his contemporaries. The increasing advent – spasmodic but ultimately irresistible – of democratic culture in nineteenth-century Europe and the coming of the industrial age with its unprecedented social and aesthetic upheavals were to render Rubens's apologetics obsolete, the relic of a civilisation in decline.

Although the language (and in some respects the whole notion) of *eulogy*, used by Rubens in his great painted cycles in praise of princes, or in *The Triumph of the Eucharist*, had fallen into disuse, the same could certainly not be said of the wealth of formal and chromatic invention Rubens had produced. Generations of artists were to drink from this mighty spring,

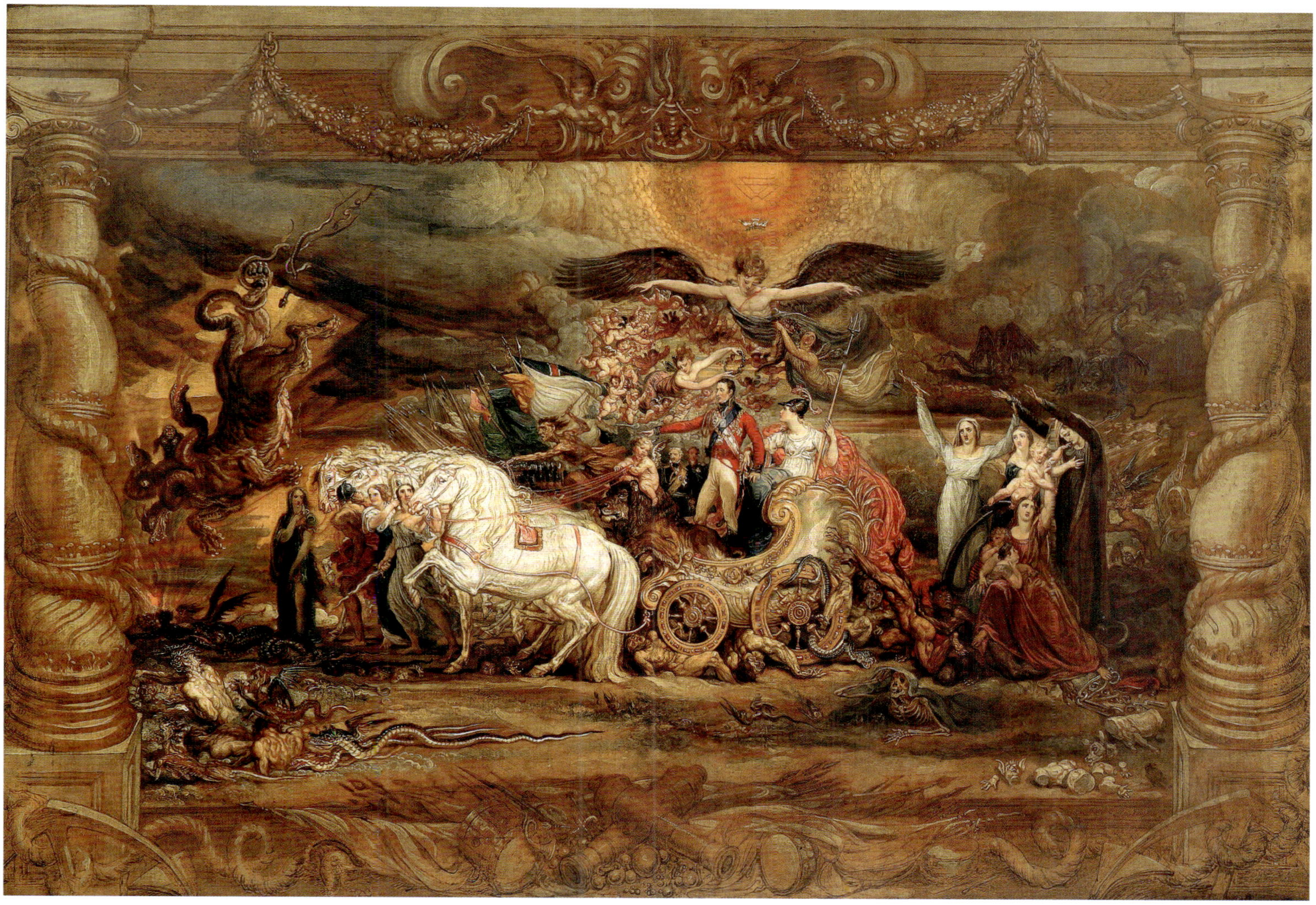

FIG. 15 James Ward, Sketch for the *Allegory of the Battle of Waterloo, 'The Triumph of the Duke of Wellington'*, 1815–16. Oil on canvas, 90 x 132 cm. The Royal Chelsea Hospital, London

each finding what he was looking for, sometimes even more than he was looking for.[25] Eugène Delacroix's attitude is a good example. His admiration for Rubens's sinuous sea nymphs frolicking in the water in the *Disembarkation of Marie de Médicis at Marseilles* (fig. 16) was shared by many other nineteenth-

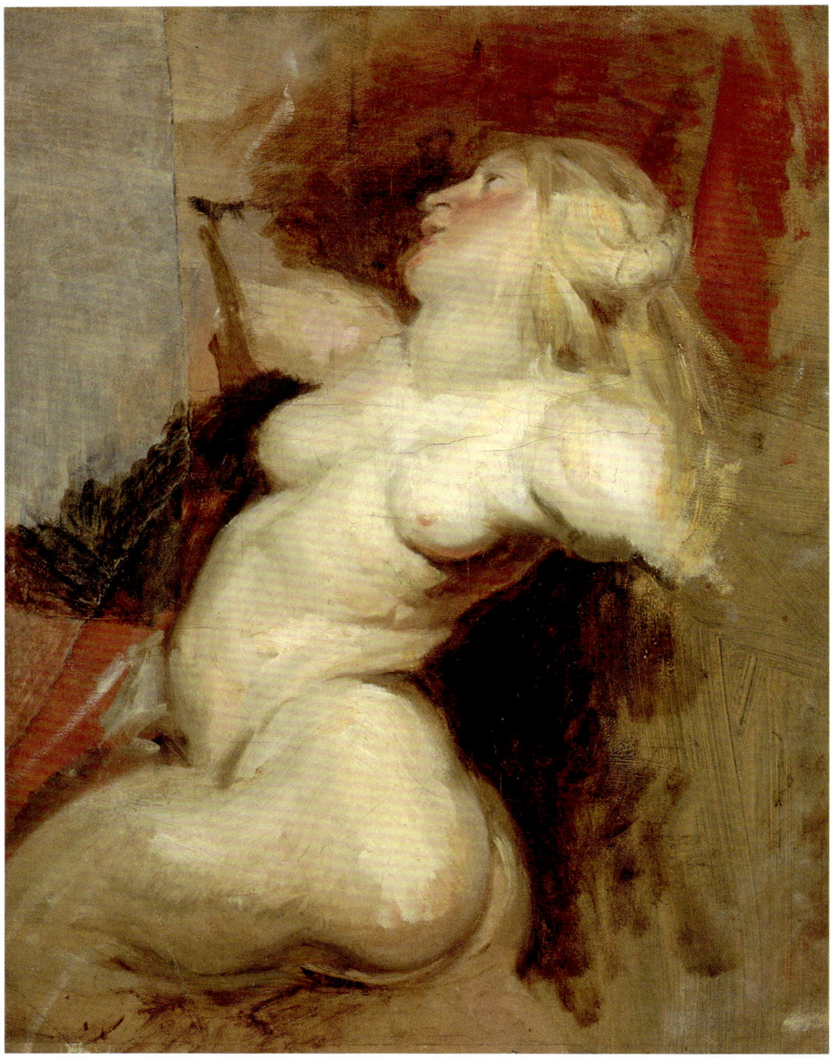

FIG. 16 Eugène Delacroix, *Nereid*, *c.* 1822; study after Rubens's *The Disembarkation of Marie de Médicis at Marseilles*, . Oil on panel, 46.5 x 38 cm. Kunstmuseum Basel, inv. 1602 (gift of friends of Professor F. Rintelen in his memory)

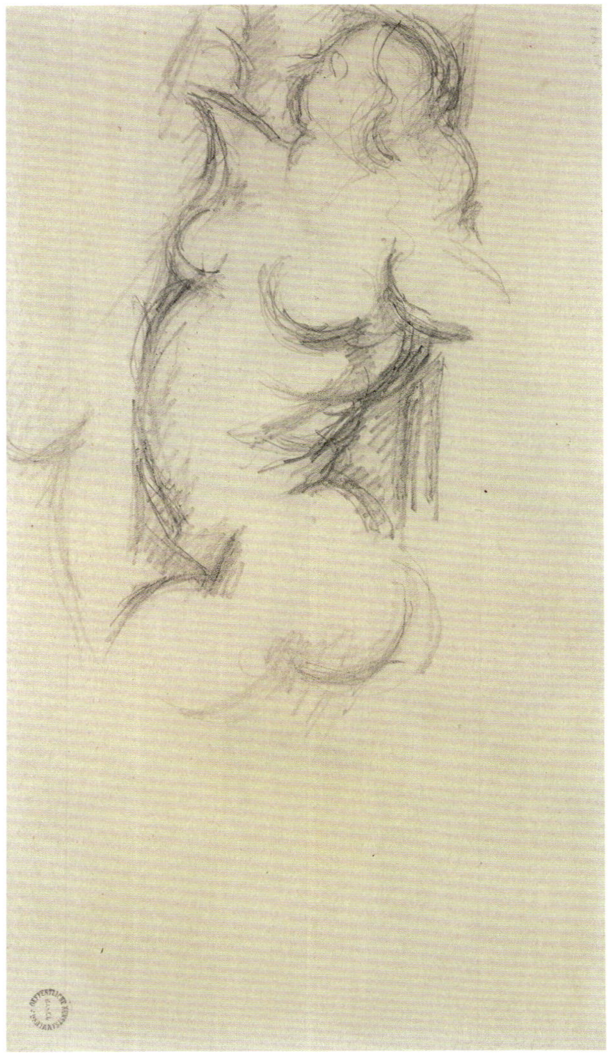

FIG. 17 Paul Cézanne, after Peter Paul Rubens, *Naiad*, 1895–98. Pencil, 20.8 x 12.2 cm. Kunstmuseum Basel

century artists, among them Etty, Fantin-Latour, Cézanne and Berthe Morisot.[26] In his case, however, the nymphs played quite a vital role, encouraging him, at the beginning of the 1820s, to experiment with the use of colour in two important areas: flesh tones and reflected light (the famous droplets of running water). It was through these aquatic figures that Delacroix began to seek a 'rational division of form into its component colours, independently of any *chiaroscuro*'[27] – this was one of the underlying principles of that key concept in modern painting, the complementarity of colours. The attitude of Cézanne who, between the beginning of the 1870s and the end of the 1890s,[28] endlessly presented the same sea nymphs (among a mass of other motifs from the Galerie Médicis) with a quite different aim, focusing on the articulation of volume (fig. 17), confirms that the great cycle in the Louvre inspired the crucial experiments in European painting in the latter half of the century.

The present selection of works demonstrates in stunning fashion, via Kokoschka's caustic *Loreley* (cat. 52), that the business of glorifying princes remained a lively affair in European artistic creation in the twentieth century; even though the Austrian Expressionist both revived and inverted the quintessential political allegory in order to denounce the apathy and suspicion of the British Empire towards those 'enemy aliens' living in Britain when the Second World War was declared. A few years earlier, in his defence of humanist values against fascism, Picasso – who did not like Rubens at all – may have remembered, this time without irony, the Flemish artist's use of pomp and circumstance.[29] As he worked on *Guernica* (1937; Museo Reina Sofía, Madrid),[30] Picasso might thus have considered, among many other sources, the profoundly political allegory, a genuine plea for peace, to be found in Rubens's *Horrors of War* (1637–38; Palazzo Pitti, Florence).[31] With regard to totalitarian regimes themselves – and although, like Rembrandt, Rubens has been the victim of attempts at ideological 'misappropriation'[32] – the propagandists seem never to have remembered the apotheoses of dynasties and princely triumphs of the Flemish master; this would have added insult to injury.

We might wonder about the capacity of our postmodern, hyper- (post-?) democratic society to cast a favourable and sympathetic eye over these vestiges of an institutionally non-egalitarian age, with its vanished values couched in abstruse language. The agility with which Rubens moved around princely courts, the nobility and wealth he acquired in the capitals of Europe, his diplomatic activities at the highest level – all kept him in the public mind for many years. None of this is compatible, however, with the generally accepted view of the *artist*, nor does it win public support today; Rubens's 'collusion' with those in power and his canny self-promotion arouse suspicion, if not downright disapproval (in 2001 a website described him as a 'fawning knave', sanctimoniously comparing him to the film-maker Leni Riefenstahl, propagandist of Hitler's regime).[33] Nevertheless, the fact that visitors from all over the world, despite knowing nothing about Marie de Médicis or the early Bourbons, continue to be bowled over at the Louvre by the huge paintings in the Galerie Médicis inspires a little optimism. Immeasurably mightier than its subject, the art of Rubens continues to win him followers, despite everything.

Preceded by two admirable preparatory oil sketches on panel (St Petersburg and Brussels),[1] the portraits of Longueval and Olivares bear witness to the depth of Rubens's involvement, during the 1620s, in the production of engraved effigies couched in highly sophisticated allegorical contexts. Charles de Longueval, Count of Bucquoy, an aristocratic inhabitant of the Spanish Low Countries and a prudent and methodical strategist in the service of the Habsburg monarchy, perished at the Siege of Ersekújvár (Neuhäusel) in Hungary at the beginning of the Thirty Years War. Rubens (most probably during summer of 1621)[2] provided his engraver Lucas Vorsterman with a design for a print – a 'patriotic' gesture as well as an expression of loyalty towards the Habsburgs – as promptly as he could, knowing that the demand generated in Flanders due to the death of the Count on 10 July 1621 would inevitably decrease over time.

Despite the disagreements that arose between Rubens and his brilliant engraver-interpreter,[3] the posthumous celebration of Longueval (cat. 31) remains a true masterpiece, unrivalled by the portrait of Gasparo de Guzmán (cat. 32), Count-Duke of Olivares and Philip IV of Spain's minister and favourite. On 8 August 1626 Olivares thanked the artist for the effigy engraved by Pontius, who had replaced Vorsterman as Rubens's printmaker 'by appointment'. The artist – who had not yet met the minister – and his engraver had taken their inspiration from two separate portraits of Olivares executed by the young Velázquez, the print being distinguishable from the Brussels *modello* by its more martial aspect. Whether the effigy was the outcome of a commission by the minister or of a self-seeking initiative on the part of the artist, the engraving marks an important stage in the rapprochement with the Court of Madrid; henceforward Rubens enjoyed frequent contact with Spain, on diplomatic as well as artistic matters. A virtuoso at the handling of allegory, and well prepared for this type of vertical composition by his activity, beforehand and simultaneously, as a designer of title pages for publishers (in particular for Balthasar Moretus [1574–1641] and the house of Plantin), Rubens here produced two works of reference in the field of commemorative, 'apologetic' engraved portraits.

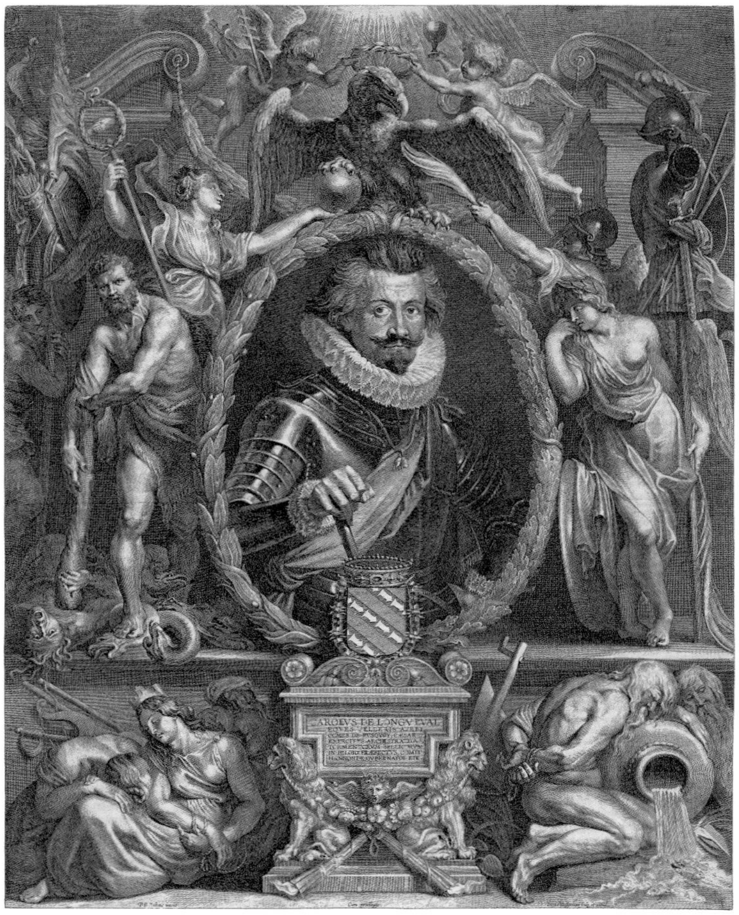

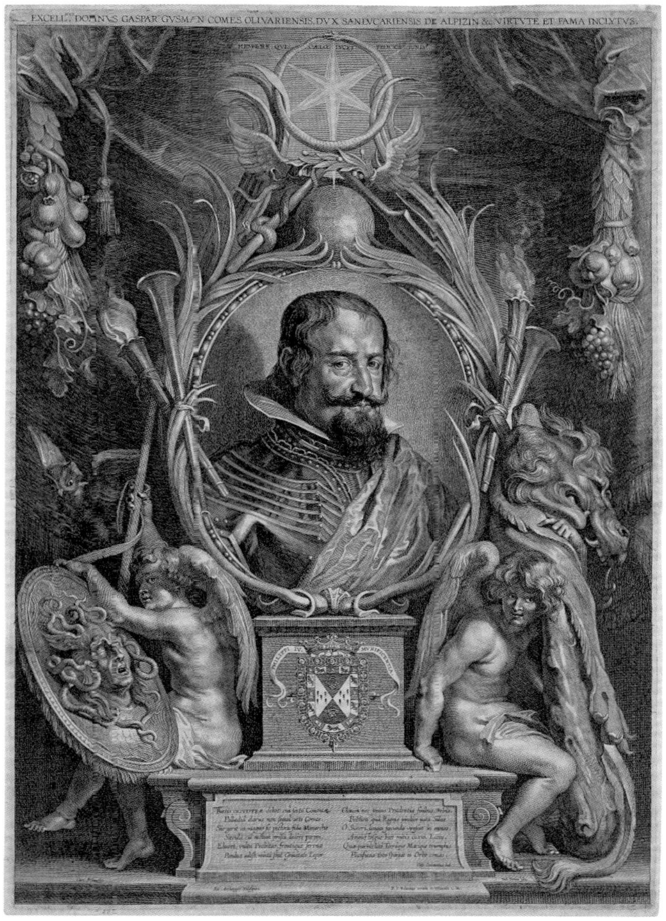

31

LUCAS VORSTERMAN THE ELDER (1595-1675)
Portrait of Charles de Longueval, Count of Bucquoy (1571–1621), probably printed after July 1622
Engraving (second state), 59.4 x 48.3 cm
Royal Museum of Fine Arts Antwerp, inv. 10876

PROVENANCE: the collection of Max Rooses, donated to the museum in 1900
SELECTED REFERENCES: Rome 1977, no. 140; Held 1980, vol. 1, no. 294; Vlieghe 1987, no. 82; Hollstein 1949–2010, vol. 43, no. 177; Van Hout 2004, pp. 48–51; Gritsay and Babina 2008, no. 309

32

PAULUS PONTIUS (1603-1658)
Portrait of the Count-Duke of Olivares (1587–1645), probably printed before August 1626
Engraving (first state), 61.2 x 44.1 cm
Royal Museum of Fine Arts Antwerp, inv. 10894

PROVENANCE: the collection of Max Rooses, donated to the museum in 1900
SELECTED REFERENCES: Rome 1977, no. 225; Held 1980, vol. 1, no. 295; Vergara 1999, pp. 34–36; Van Hout 2004, pp. 58–60; Brussels 2007, nos 13 and 15

33

PETER PAUL RUBENS (1577–1640)
Sketch for *The Coronation of the Queen in Saint-Denis*, probably between April/May and October 1622
Oil on oak panel, 49 x 63 cm
State Hermitage Museum, St Petersburg, inv. GE 516

PROVENANCE: possibly in the collection of Claude Maugis, Abbot of Saint-Ambroise (d. 1648), Paris; in the sale of François Ignace de Dufresne, Amsterdam, 22 August 1770, lot 138 (acquired by the 'antique dealer' Van der Schley for 890 florins); in the Hermitage collection since before 1774
SELECTED REFERENCES: Thuillier and Foucart 1967 (1969), p. 84; Held 1980, vol. 1, no. 67; Varshavskaya and Yegorova 1995, no. 23; Merle du Bourg 2004A, p. 59; Gritsay and Babina 2008, no. 314

During the summer of 1621 the future Cardinal Richelieu, 'comptroller to the household' of Marie de Médicis, invited Rubens to participate in the decoration of the Palais du Luxembourg, then being built in Paris[1] for the Queen Mother. Rubens was thus to consolidate his position as the leading decorative painter in Europe while securing the patronage of the most prestigious princess of the day: wife of the former king Henri IV, mother of the present king Louis XIII and mother-in-law of various sovereign princes. In a Paris contract dated 26 February 1622, Rubens had agreed to create 24 paintings illustrating 'the story of the most illustrious life and heroic deeds' of the Queen Mother, paintings that were mainly executed in the artist's studio in Antwerp. The 'inauguration' of the Galerie Médicis in the west wing of the palace rivalled the marriage by proxy of Charles I of England to Henrietta Maria, daughter of Henri IV and Marie de Médicis, in May 1625.

The project proved no easy task for Rubens. He had, for example, to manage the bad feeling that prevailed between the young Louis XIII and his mother: their strife had already brought the kingdom to the brink of civil war (1619–20). The correspondence between the artist and the scholar Peiresc[2] suggests that the Galerie Médicis was the fruit of a tricky compromise between the necessity to avoid offending the King (by recourse to what Peiresc terms in Italian *figure mistiche* – allegorical figures) and a plan designed solely to glorify Marie, all mingled with political special pleading *pro domo*, which could on occasion be remarkably aggressive. This need for dissimulation has made general interpretation of the Medici cycle very difficult; indeed, it has been laughingly compared to the Rorschach test.[3] The meticulously prepared compositions in the Galerie Médicis combine the hybridisation of a baroque apotheosis of a reigning monarch (to illustrate his ontologically superhuman nature), with an epic tale extolling the figure of a heroine who belongs way above the normal run of mankind thanks to her constant search for Glory.[4] The series of oil sketches, some monochrome, some lightly or sometimes more boldly coloured (now mainly divided between the State Hermitage Museum, St Petersburg, and the Alte Pinakothek, Munich),[5] allows the spectator to study the cycle at different stages of its production; the flexibility of Rubens's skill fills one with admiration – he was able to adapt to the inconsistencies of his employers regarding subjects, dimensions and the eventual placement of the large paintings. If we compare the St Petersburg sketch for *The Coronation of the Queen in Saint-Denis* (cat. 33), still quite compact and providing space for the gallery's door, with the Munich version or the large painting in the Louvre, which has a different layout – it is rectangular and inverted – we can gain some idea of the adaptability required of the great decorative painters.

Although not as overlooked as has sometimes been suggested, the Galerie Médicis did not at first attract the admiration it deserved. The public had to wait until 1710 for engravings of the scheme, produced on the initiative of Marc Nattier, who obtained royal permission to make engravings of Rubens's paintings in 1702 (plus a royal privilege to protect his enterprise). Nattier entrusted to his sons Jean-Baptiste and Jean-Marc the execution of the drawings, and these were used as models by eleven engravers between 1703 and 1710. The collection was published by one of the engravers, Duchange, and

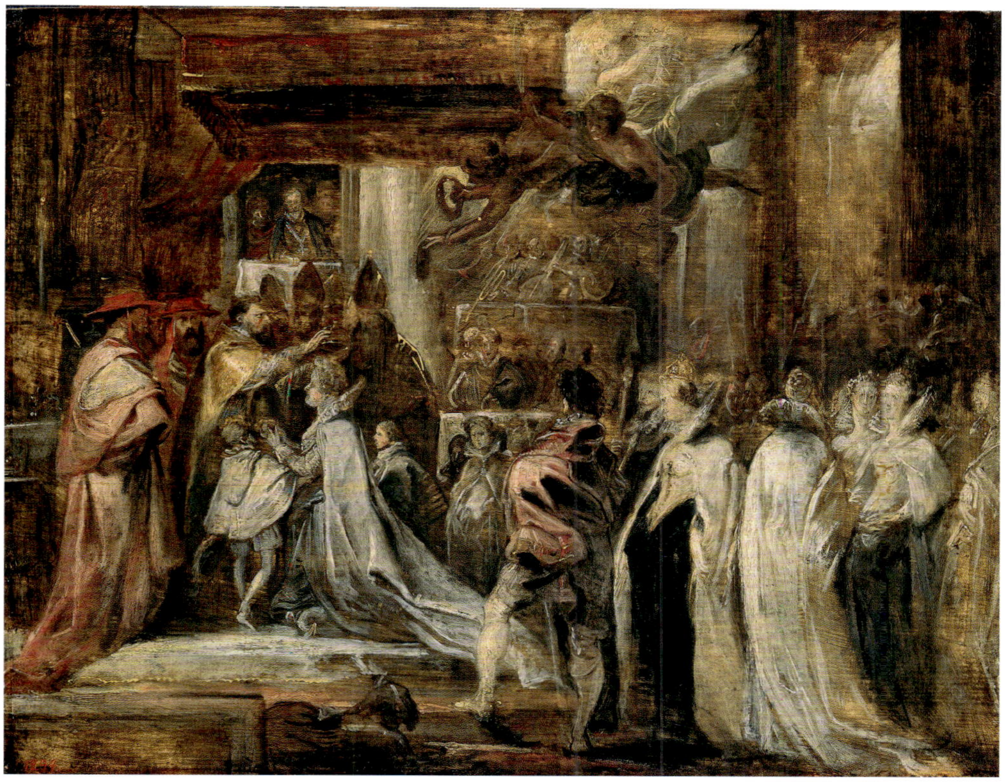

dedicated to the King in 1710; it was given the title *La Galerie du Palais du Luxembourg peinte par Rubens* (cat. 34). Notwithstanding the chilly, over-diligent reproduction of Rubens's compositions, the cycle had at last been reproduced in its entirety and faithfully, in large format and with captions that played an important part in the understanding (or lack of understanding!)[6] of the subjects until well into the twentieth century.[7]

After 1696, when Louis XIV obtained the reassignment to the reigning monarch of the palace built for his grandmother, the Galerie Médicis was regarded as one of the jewels of French cultural heritage and attracted artists from France and other countries; this attraction was to grow even stronger after the cycle of paintings had been removed to the Louvre (1815–16). In 1865 Fantin-Latour made a charcoal sketch entitled *Eugène Delacroix Being Welcomed into the Elysian Fields*, in which, interestingly, the deceased artist is welcomed by Rubens;[8] although usually reticent about using allegory, Fantin-Latour took his inspiration from the god Hymen fluttering in the seventh painting in the Galerie Médicis cycle. Both artists had copied parts of the cycle many times (cats 35 and 36) and both admired it unreservedly.

34.1–24

LOUIS DE CHATILLON (1639–1734)
GASPAR DUCHANGE (1662–1757)
ALEXIS LOIR (1640–1713)
JEAN AUDRAN (1667–1756)
ANTOINE TROUVAIN (1652/53–1708)
BENOÎT AUDRAN (1661–1721)
CORNELIS MARTINUS VERMEULEN (c. 1644–c. 1708)
BERNARD PICART (1673–1733)
CHARLES SIMONNEAU (1645–1728)
GÉRARD EDELINCK (1640–1707)
JEAN-BAPTISTE MASSÉ (1687–1767)
(Hand colouring with watercolour and gouache an anonymous eighteenth-century addition.)

A series of engravings, made between 1703 and 1710, (and published in Paris in 1710 as *La Galerie du Palais du Luxembourg peinte par Rubens, Dessinée par les Sr. Nattier et gravée Par les plus Illustres Graveurs du Temps*), made after the interpretive drawings of Jean-Baptiste and Jean-Marc Nattier. Plates of *c.* 51 x 25 cm, 51 x 38 cm and 51 x 83 cm
Royal Academy of Arts, London

All drawings after a cycle of paintings commissioned to decorate the Galerie Médicis in the Palais du Luxembourg, Paris, by Peter Paul Rubens. (Some of the titles given to these engravings differ from those of the original cycle.)

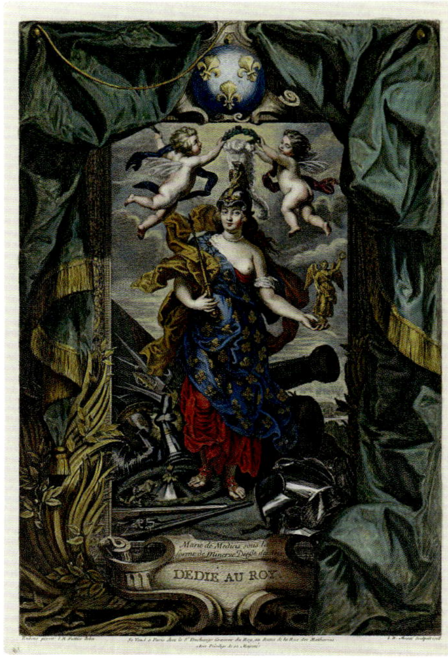

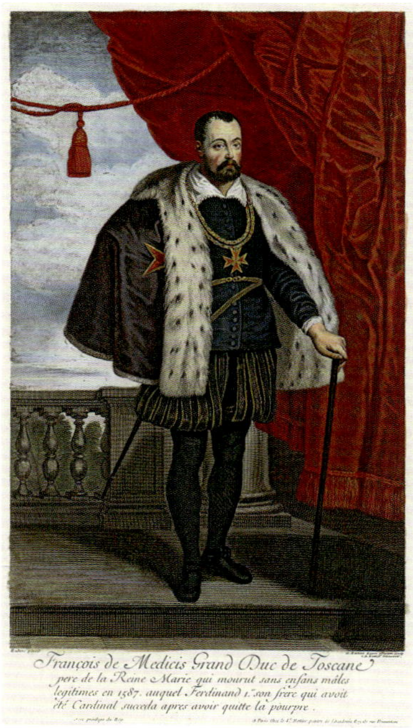

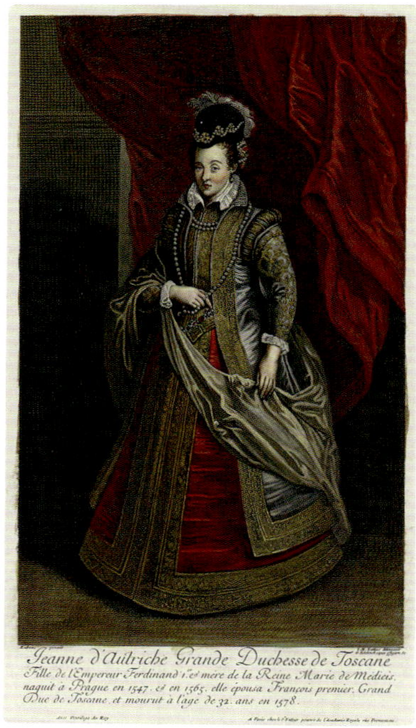

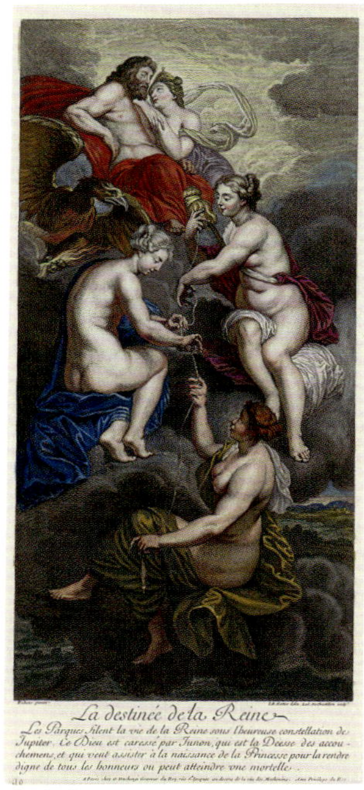

This page, from left to right:

34.1
Marie de Médicis in the Guise of Minerva, Goddess of Arts
(J.-B. M.)

34.2
François de Médicis, Grand Duke of Tuscany
(G. E.)

34.3
Jeanne of Austria, Grand Duchess of Tuscany
(G. E.)

34.4
The Destiny of the Queen
(L. D. C.)

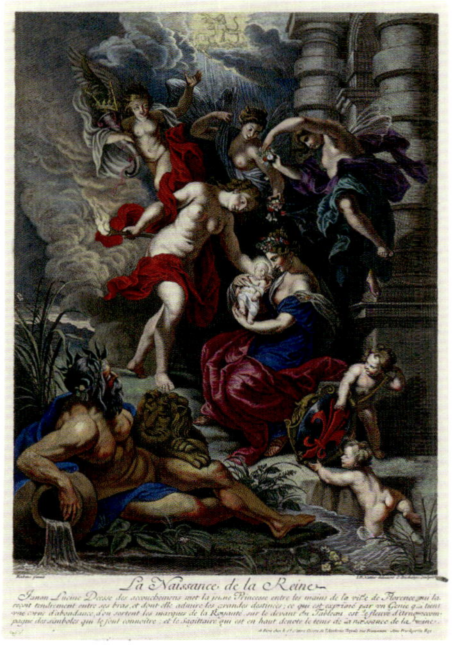

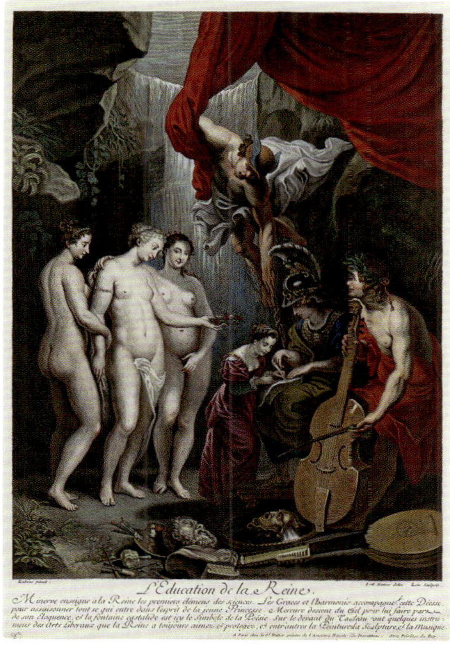

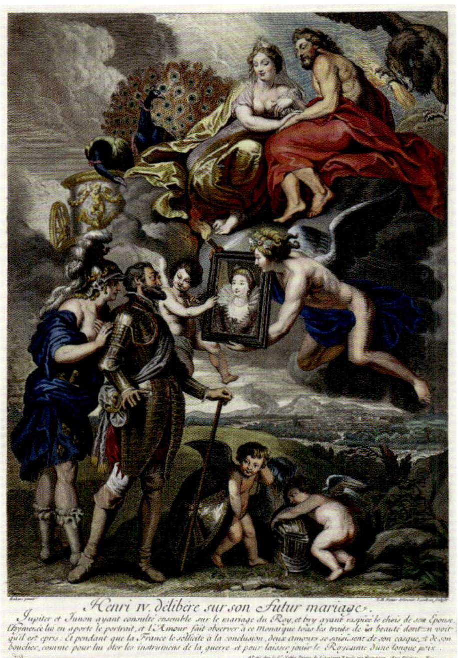

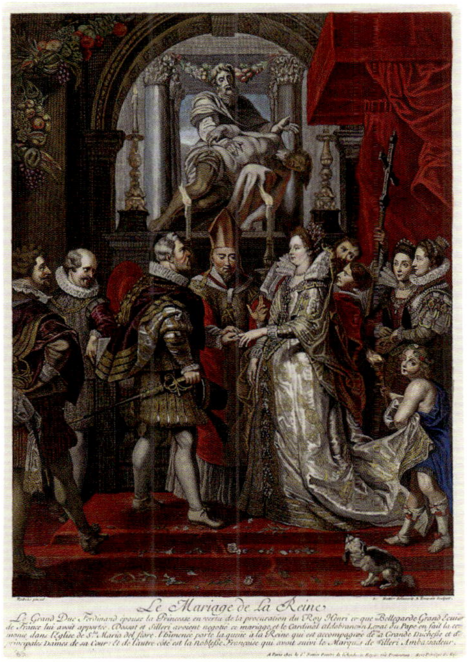

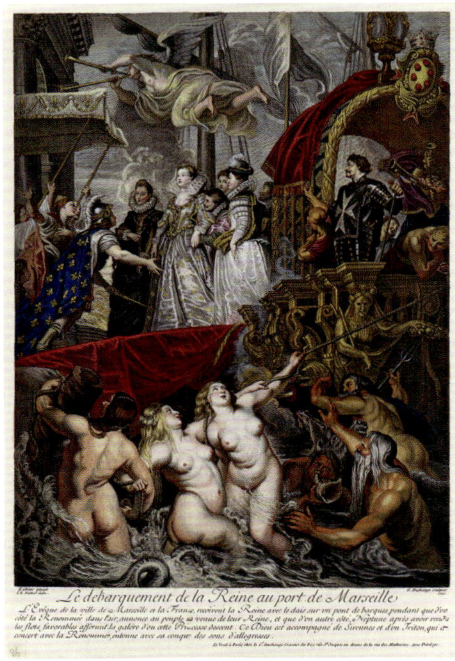

This page, from left to right:

34.5
The Birth of the Queen
(G. D.)

34.6
The Education of the Queen
(A. L.)

34.7
Henri IV Considers his Future Marriage
(J. A.)

34.8
The Wedding of the Queen
(A. T.)

34.9
The Disembarkation of the Queen at the Port of Marseilles
(G. D.)

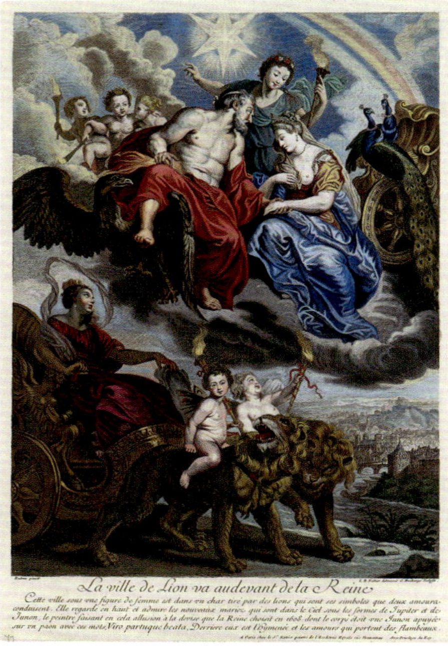
La ville de Lion va audevant de la Reine

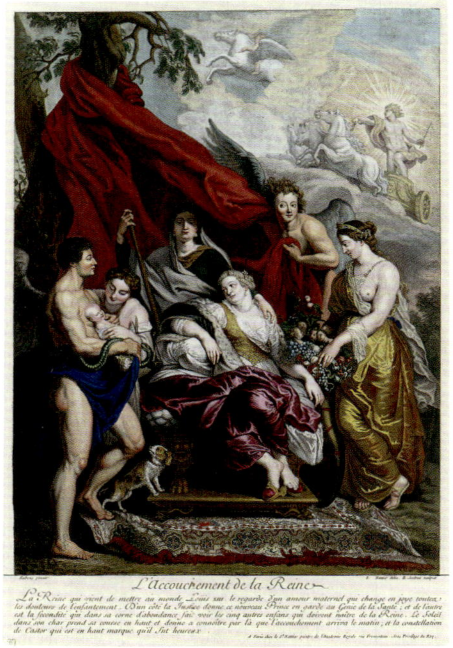
L'Accouchement de la Reine

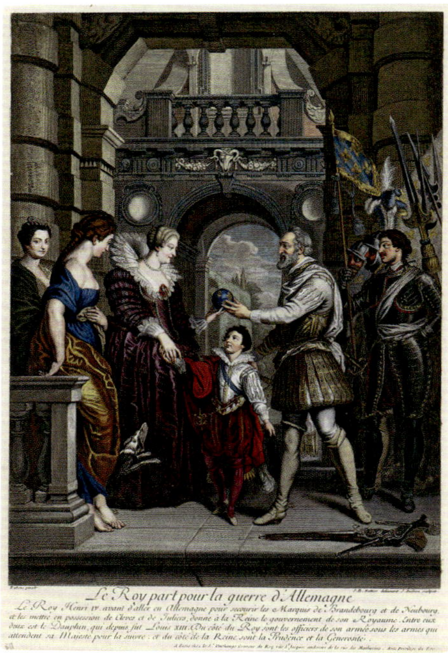
Le Roy part pour la guerre d'Allemagne

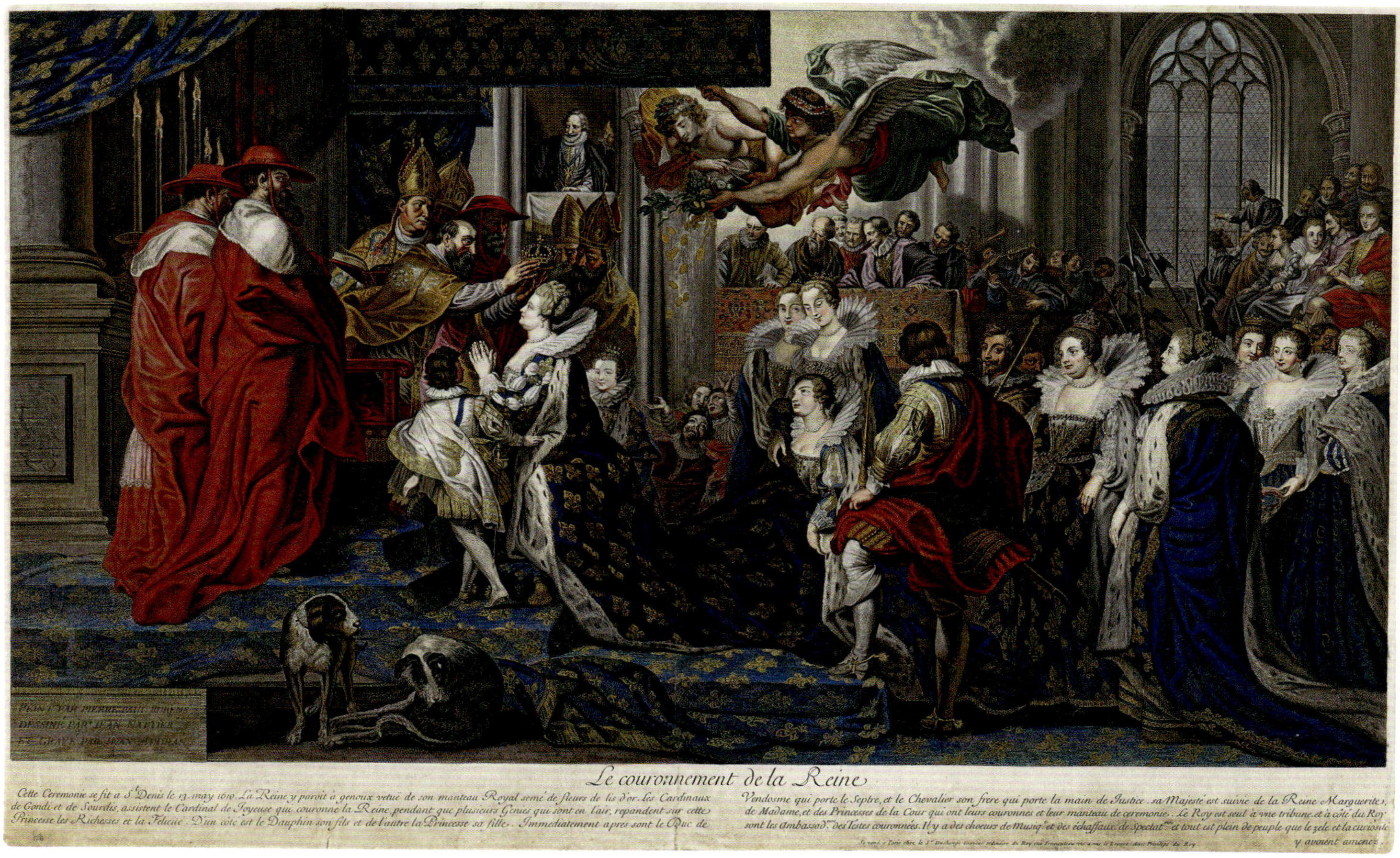
Le couronnement de la Reine
Cette Ceremonie se fit a S.t Denis le 13. may 1610. La Reine y paroit à genoux vetuë de son manteau Royal semé de fleurs de lis d'or. les Cardinaux de Gondi et de Sourdis, assistent le Cardinal de Joyeuse qui couronne la Reine, pendant que plusieurs Genies qui sont en l'air, repandent sur cette Princesse les Richesses et la Felicité. D'un côté est le Dauphin son fils et de l'autre la Princesse sa fille. Immediatement apres sont le Duc de Vendosme qui porte le Septre, et le Chevalier son frere qui porte la main de Justice. sa Majesté est suivie de la Reine Marguerite, de Madame, et des Princesses de la Cour qui ont leurs couronnes et leur manteau de ceremonie. Le Roy est seul à vne tribune et à côté du Roy sont les Ambassad.rs des Testes couronnées. Il y a des choeurs de Musiq.e et des échaffaux de Spectat.rs et tout est plein de peuple que le zele et la curiosité y avoient amenez.

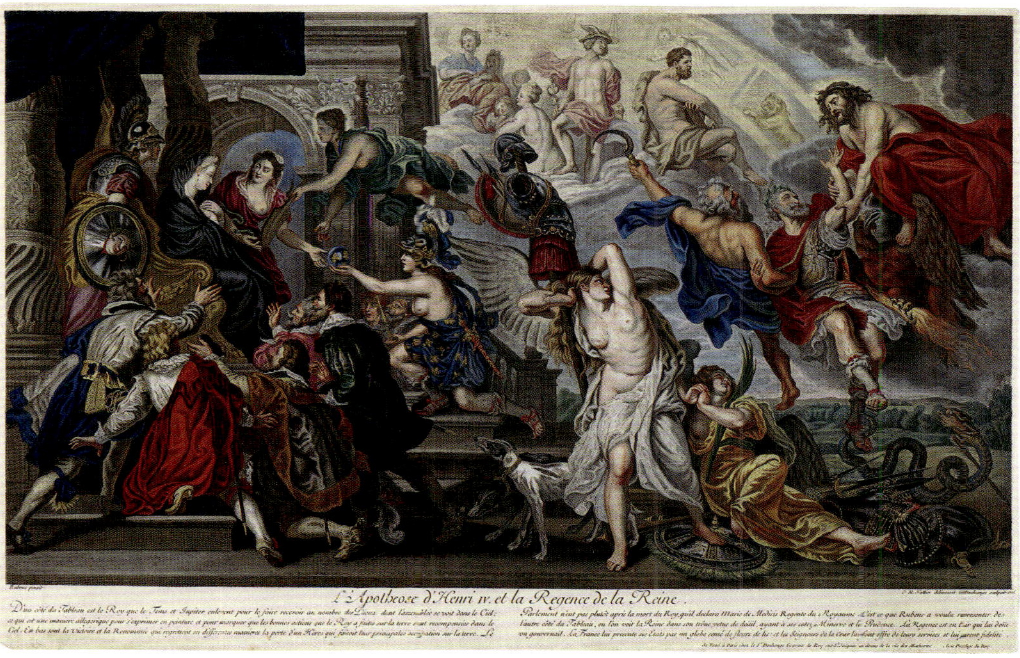

Page 94, from left to right:

34.10
The Town of Lyon Goes to Meet the Queen
(G. D.)

34.11
The Queen Gives Birth
(B. A.)

34.12
The King Leaves for the German War
(J. A.)

34.13
The Coronation of the Queen
(J. A.)

This page:

34.14
The Apotheosis of Henri IV and the Regency of the Queen
(G. D.)

34.15
The Government of the Queen
(B. P.)

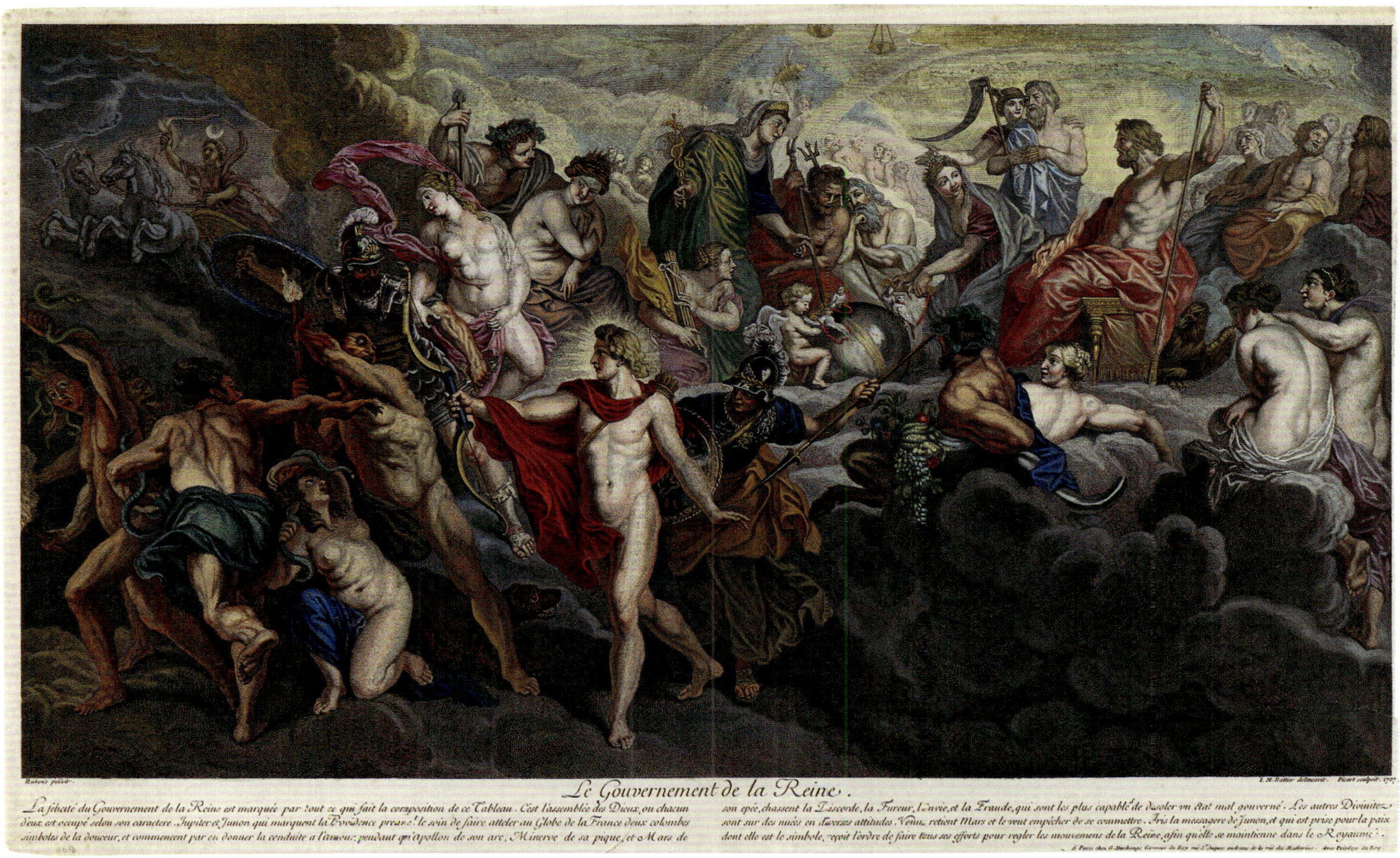

This page, from left to right:

34.16
The Voyage of the Queen to Pont-de-Cé
(C. S.)

34.17
The Exchange of the two Queens
(B. A.)

34.18
The Felicity of the Regency
(B. P.)

34.19
Louis XIII Comes of Age
(A. T.)

34.20
The Queen Flees the city of Blois
(C. M. V.)

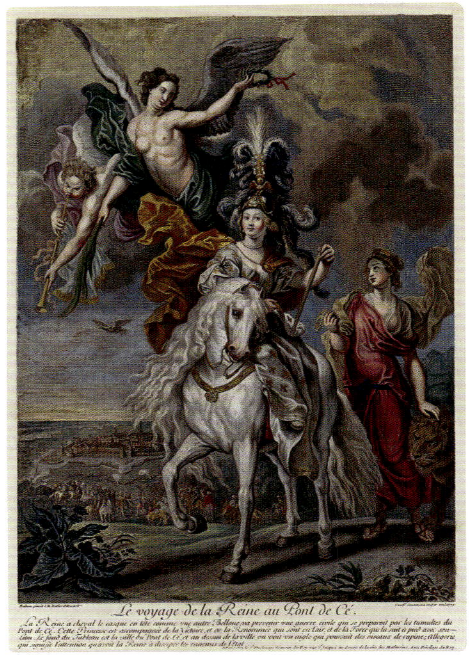

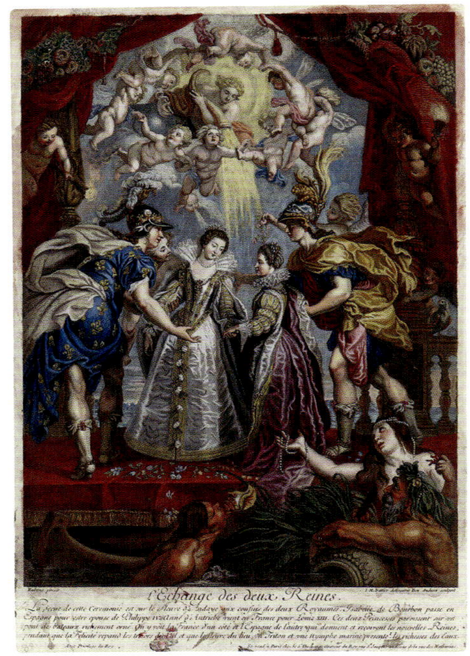

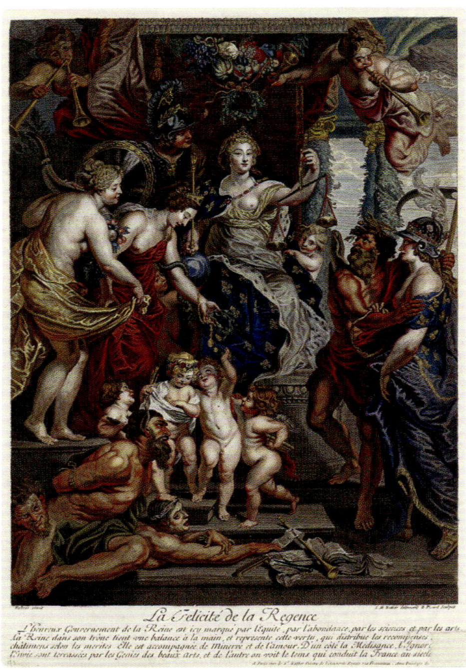

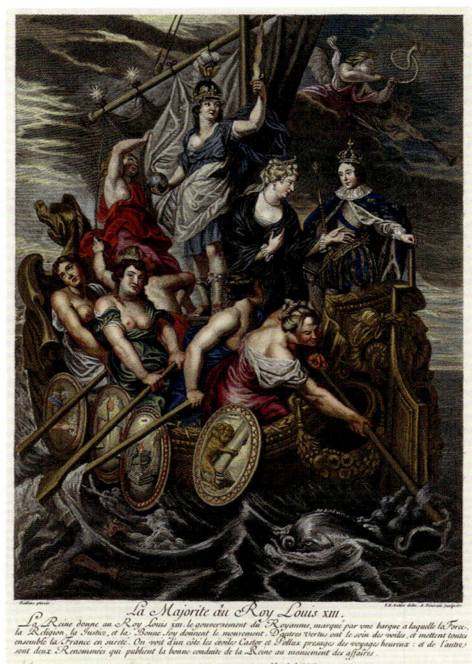

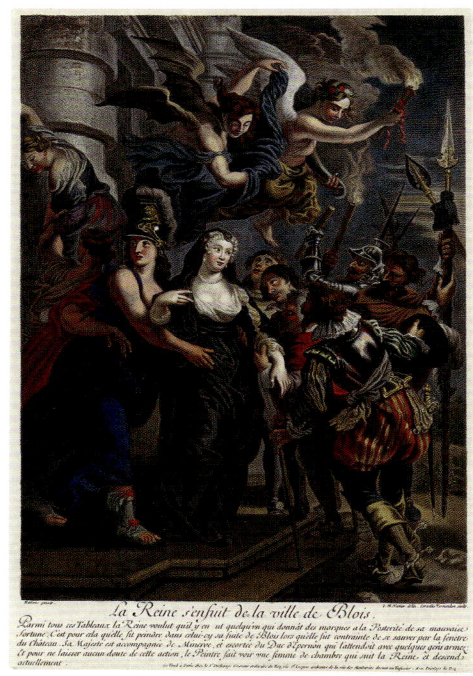

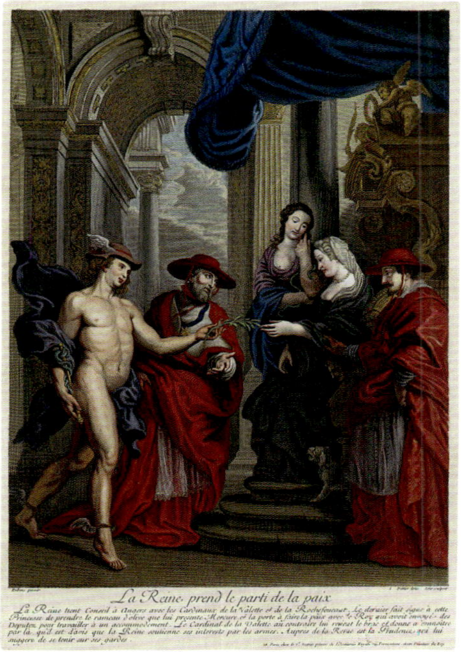

This page, from left to right:

34.21
The Queen Takes the Part of Peace
(A. L.)

34.22
Peace Concluded
(B. P.)

34.23
Peace Ratified in Heaven
(G. D.)

34.24
Time Discovers Truth
(A. L.)

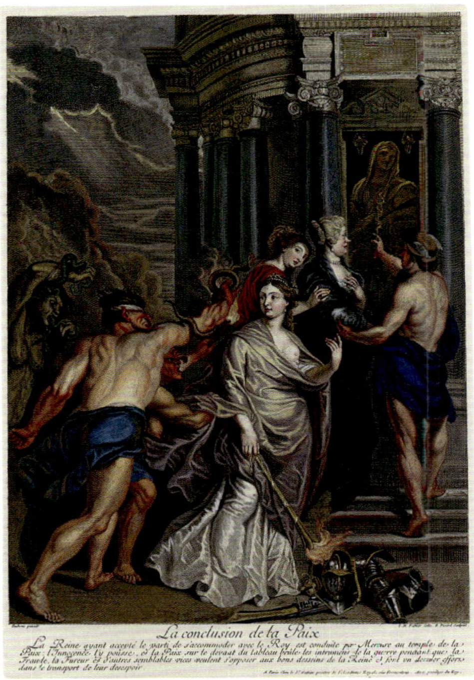

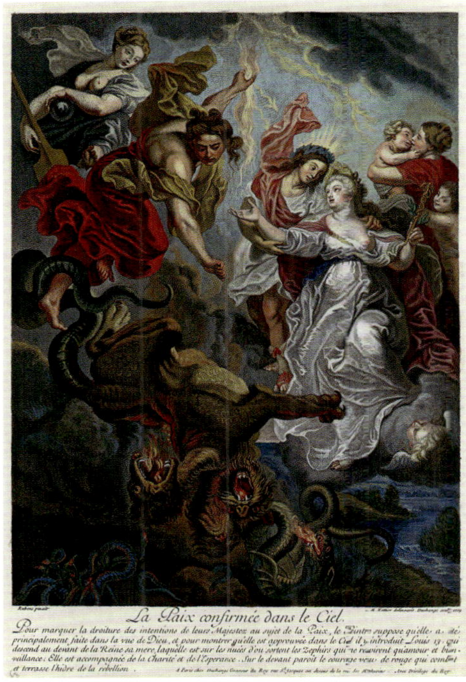

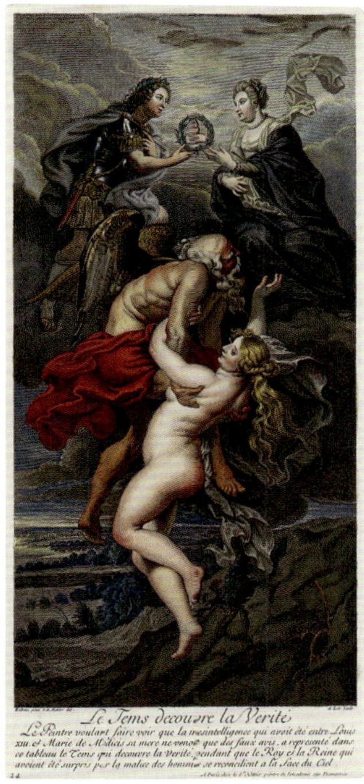

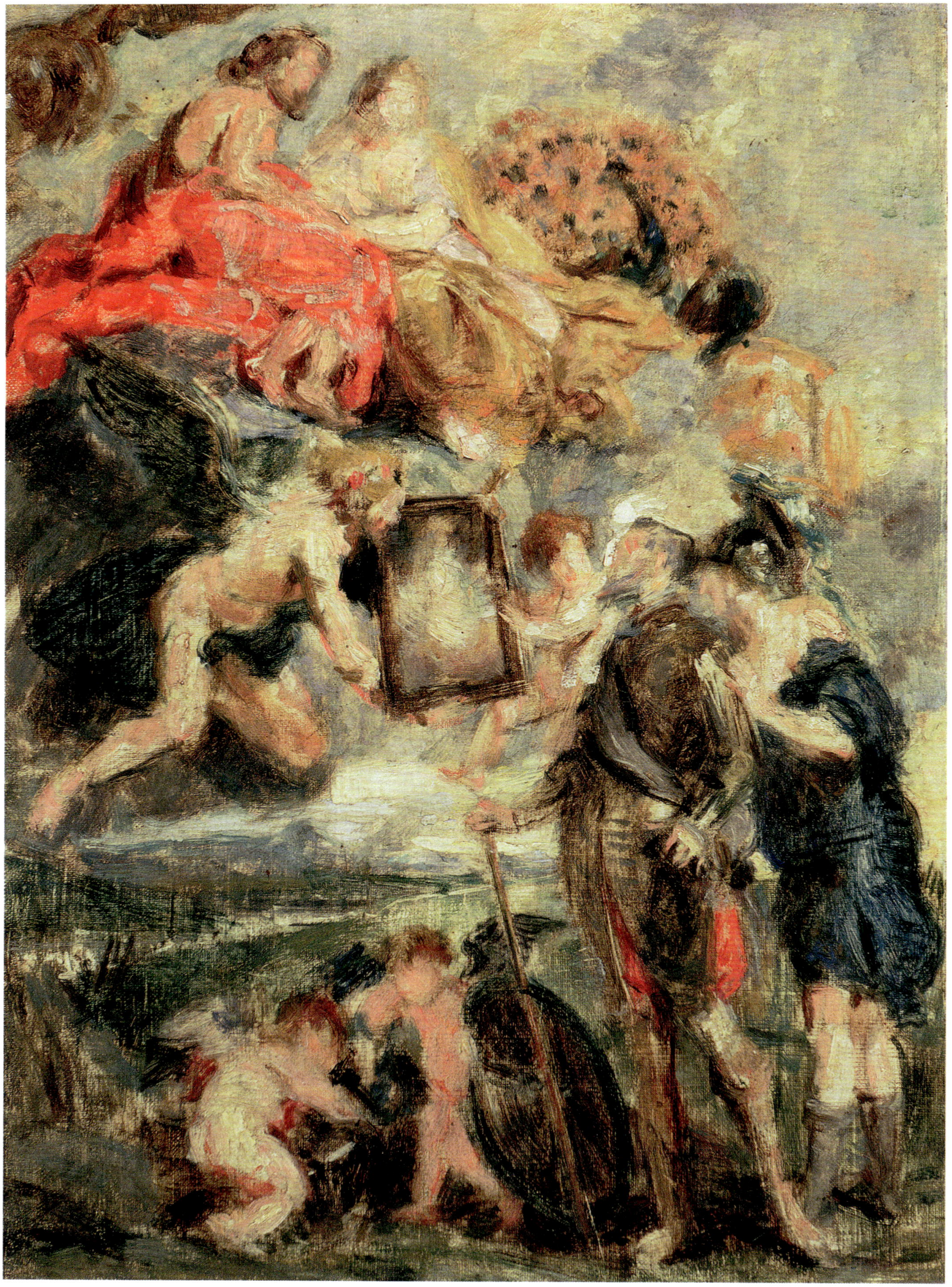

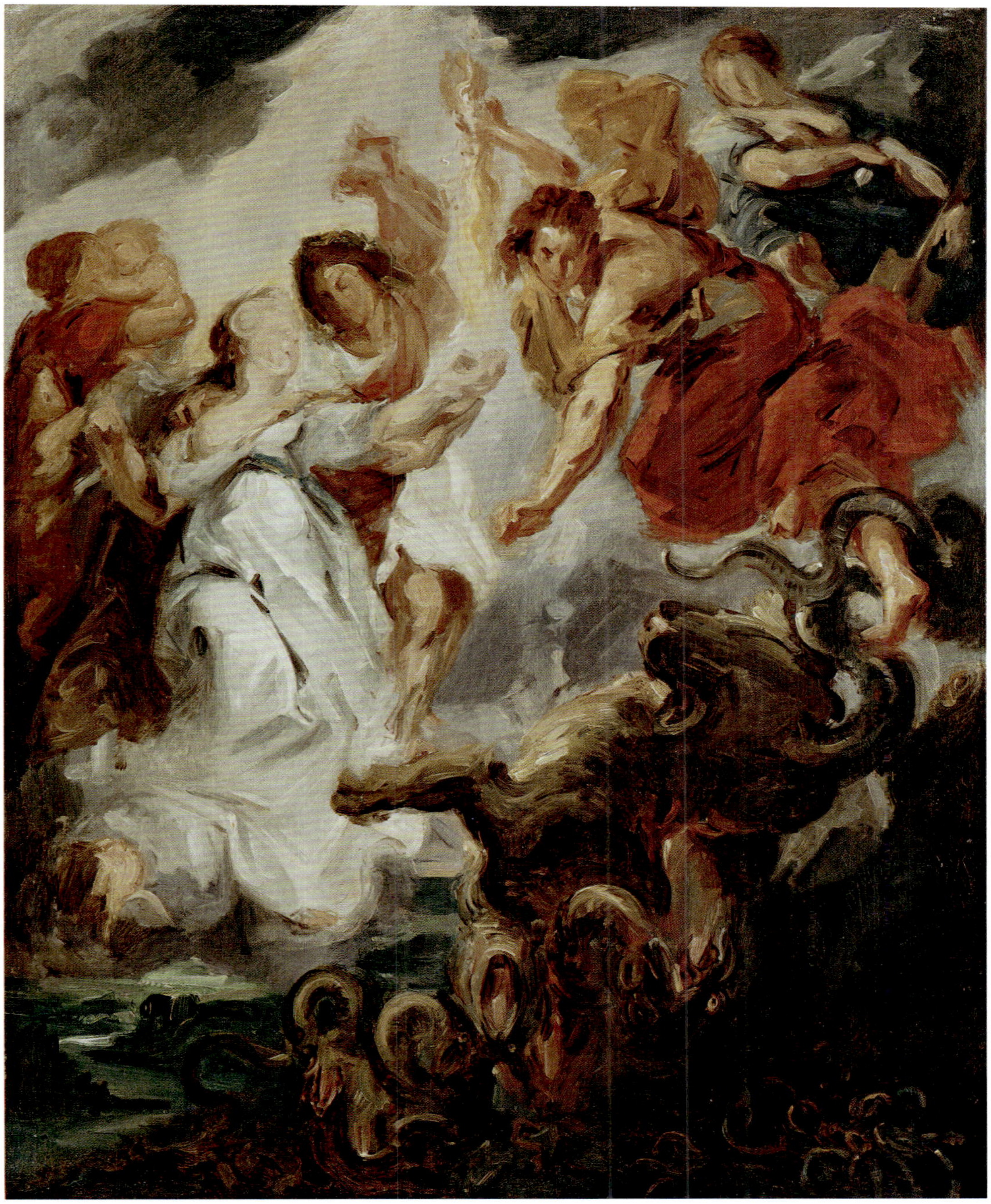

35

HENRI FANTIN-LATOUR (1836–1904)
Sketch (after Rubens's composition *The Presentation of the Portrait* in the Galerie Médicis) for *Homage to Rubens*, *c.* 1850–60
Oil on canvas, 40.5 x 30 cm
Southampton City Art Gallery, inv. 336

PROVENANCE: probably identifiable as the sketch in the possession of A. M. F. Bracquemond before 1911, then in the Galerie Georges Petit, Paris, in 1926; acquired by the museum in 1938 with the support of the Chipperfield Bequest Fund
SELECTED REFERENCES: Dubourg 1911, no. 368; Thuillier and Foucart 1967 (1969), p. 75; Ellis and Roe 2007, pp. 45 and 278

36

Attributed to
EUGÈNE DELACROIX (1798–1863)
Sketch after Rubens's composition in the Galerie Médicis *The Reconciliation of the Queen and Her Son*, 1828
Signed 'E. D.' on the frame
Oil on canvas, 62 x 51 cm
Wallraf-Richartz Museum and Fondation Corboud, Cologne, inv. 3182

PROVENANCE: Wildenstein & Co., New York, 1960; acquired for the museum in 1964
SELECTED REFERENCES: Keller 1965, pp. 423–25; Thuillier and Foucart 1967 (1969), p. 93 (with a suggested attribution to Louis Mettling, 1847–1904); White 1967, pp. 37, 43, 49, no. 25 (before 1850); Johnson 1981, vol. 1, no. R21 (attribution to Delacroix rejected)

According to one of the two contracts relating to the decorations in the Palais du Luxembourg (26 February 1622),[1] Rubens had undertaken to execute 'de sa propre main' ('by his own hand') all the figures in the paintings projected to adorn the two parallel galleries in the Queen Mother's palace in Paris. In the part that had already been completed (the west wing) the contract specified that the artist would paint the 24 pictures for the Galerie Médicis. In the other gallery, which was not 'encore faicte' ('yet made') in the east wing, the artist undertook to represent: 'all the battles of the late King Henri the Great, the encounters he had had, his battles, captures and the sieges laid to towns with the triumphs of the said victories depicted in the fashion of the triumphs of the Romans following the specifications which will be given to him by his Maj.y.' Rubens did not begin to sketch out the compositions in posthumous celebration of the late king of France until the winter of 1627–28, the work on the second gallery being somewhat behindhand. One of the strangest aspects of Rubens's partial fulfilment of the 1622 contract, work that was to continue over about a decade, is the lack of resolution among the French (including Richelieu, who was remarkably well informed) about how to dismiss a person who was so harmful to France's immediate interests, and whose diplomatic activities had made him the subject of strict surveillance from 1624 onwards.[2] Once Rubens had returned from England (March 1630), where to the fury of the French he had taken part successfully in efforts to re-establish Anglo-Spanish diplomatic relations, he took up his brushes again. The painter may have had mixed feelings about Henri IV, who had always

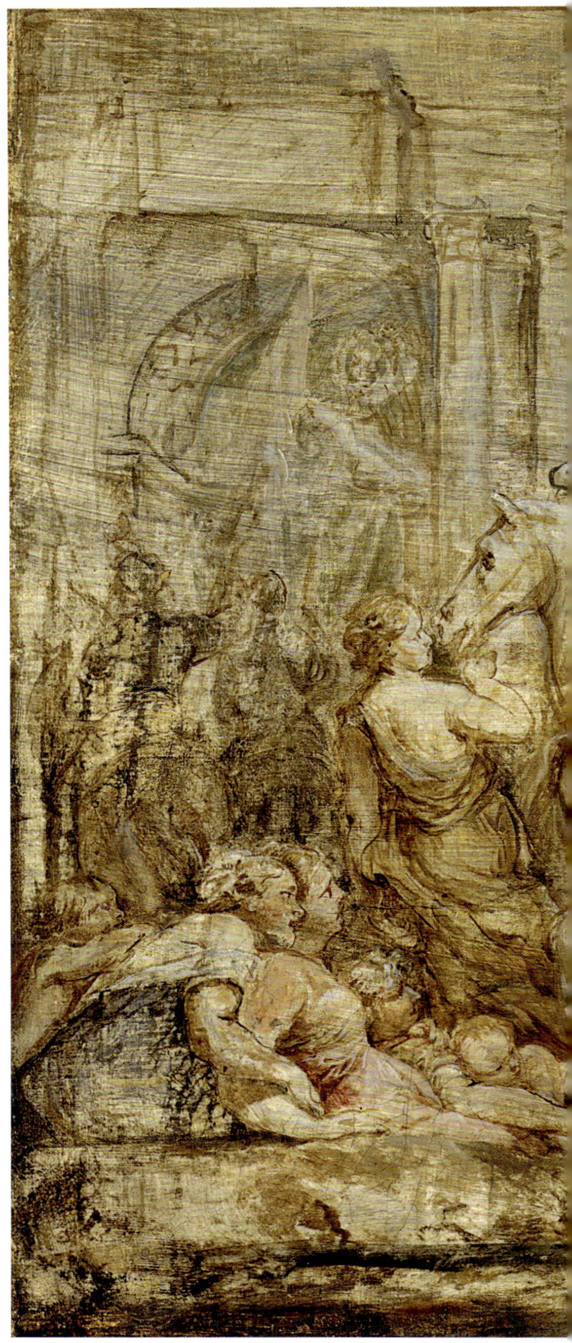

37

PETER PAUL RUBENS (1577–1640)
Sketch for *The Triumph of Henri IV*, 1630
Oil on panel, 49.5 x 83.5 cm
Lent by The Metropolitan Museum of Art, New York, inv. 42.187. Rogers Fund, 1942

PROVENANCE: in the collection of 4th Earl of Darnley, Cobham Hall, Kent, 1815; by descent to 8th Earl of Darnley, until 1909–10; Colnaghi, London, 1910, sold to Knoedler; Knoedler, New York, 1910–11, sold to John W. Simpson (d. 1920), New York; Mrs John W. Simpson (Kate Seney), New York, from 1920 to 1942; sold to the museum through Knoedler in 1943 (Rogers Fund)
SELECTED REFERENCES: Jost 1964, p. 205, no. 80; Florence 1977, no. 94; Held 1980, vol. 1, no. 85; Liedtke 1984, vol. 1, pp. 156–63; Jaffé 1989, no. 958; Madrid 1999, no. 27; Van Hout 2001A, pp. 29, 39, no. 42

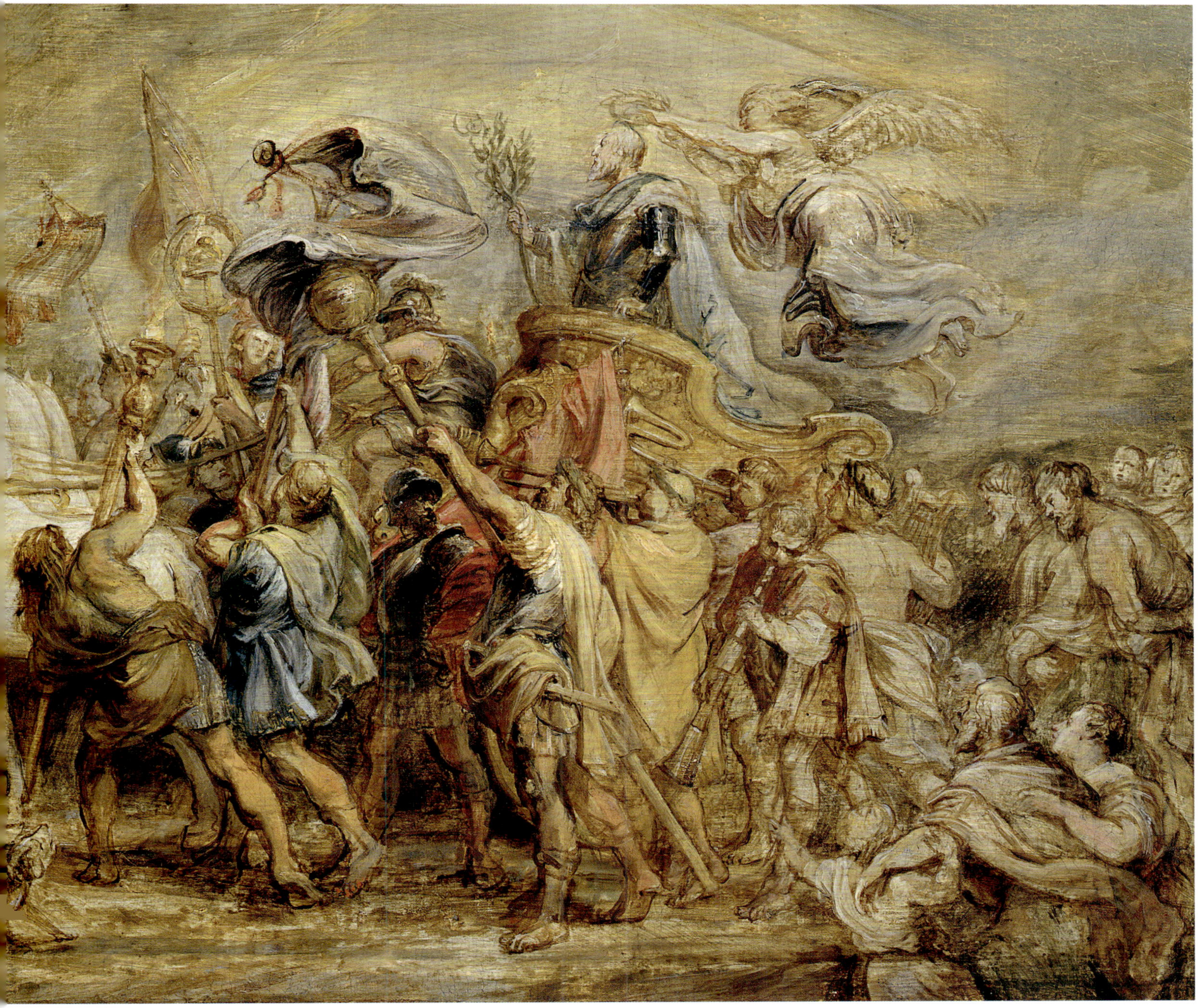

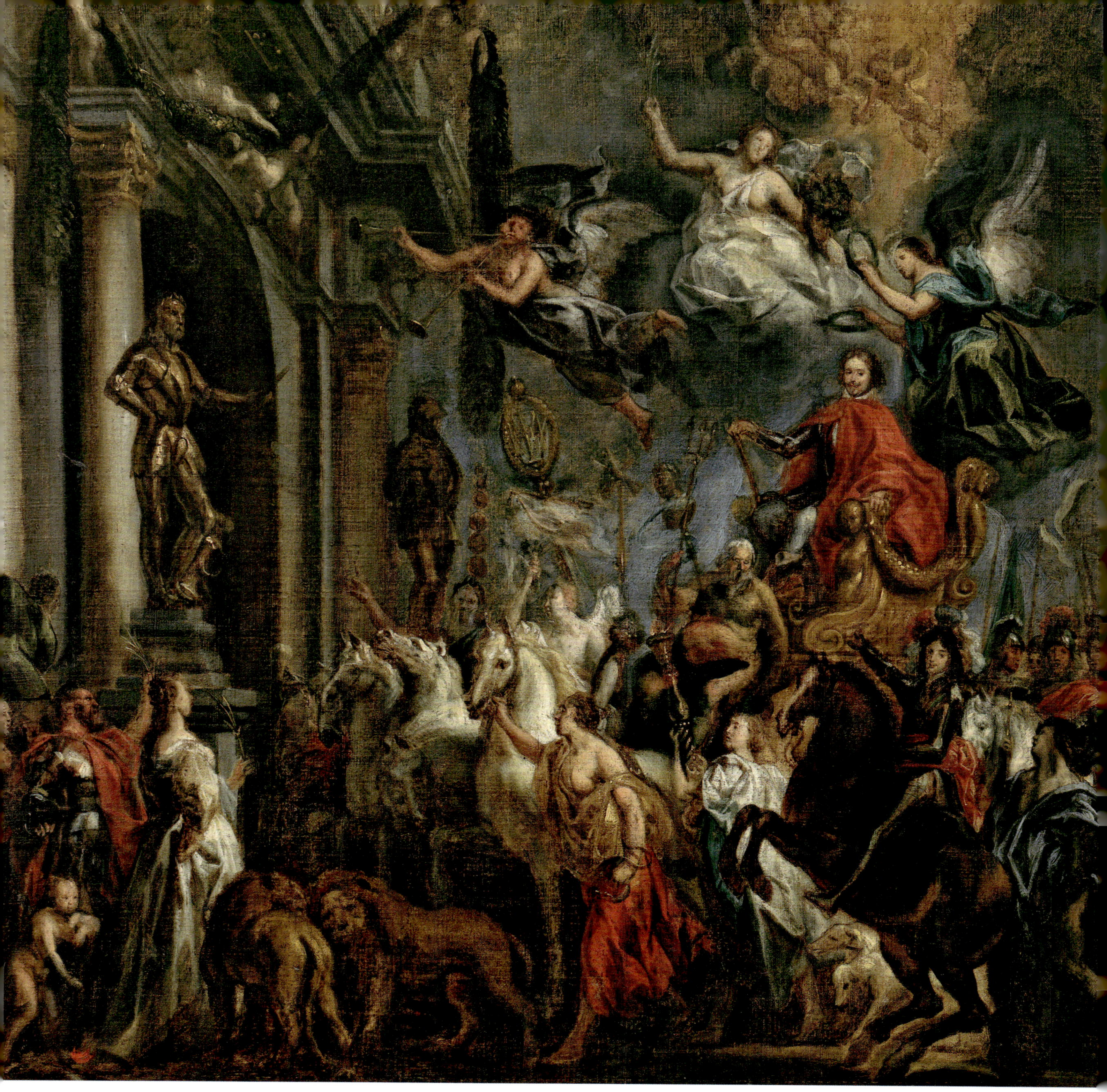

38

THEODOOR VAN THULDEN (1606–1669)
Sketch for *Allegory of William III Bidding Farewell to His Grandmother, Amalia van Solms, as He Leaves to Enter the Service of the State*, 1661
Oil on canvas, 115 x 97 cm
On long-term loan to Het Noordbrabants Museum, 's-Hertogenbosch, inv. SKA 4654. Lent by Rijksmuseum, Amsterdam

PROVENANCE: Galerie Sanct Lucas, Vienna, 1937; sold to a private purchaser (Klosterneuburg, near Vienna), March 1942; Galerie Sanct Lucas, Vienna, 1946; sold anonymously (Dorotheum, Vienna), 12 March 1974 and following days (no. 136, acquired for the museum for 22,404 florins)
SELECTED REFERENCES: Hairs 1965, no. 60; Van Thiel 1976, p. 538; Strasbourg 1991, no. 72; 's Hertogenbosch 2000, pp. 89–91, no. 47

39

JACOB JORDAENS (1593–1678)
Sketch for *The Triumph of Frederick Henry*, *c.* 1650–51
Signed on the reverse, centre: *J. JOR*
Oil on canvas, 116 x 126 cm
Royal Museum of Fine Arts Antwerp, inv. 799

PROVENANCE: in the collection of H. Weck; sold at the Weck sale, Drouot, Paris, 30 April 1900, no. 28 (bought by Féral); acquired from E. de Koninck, Brussels, in 1901
SELECTED REFERENCES: Ottawa 1968, no. 100; Antwerp 1978, no. 28; Peter-Raupp 1980, pp. 154–63; d'Hulst 1982, p. 233 and p. 317, no. 2; Rotterdam 1983, no. 19; Antwerp 1993, no. A82; The Hague 1997, no. 14; Paris 2013, no. III-12

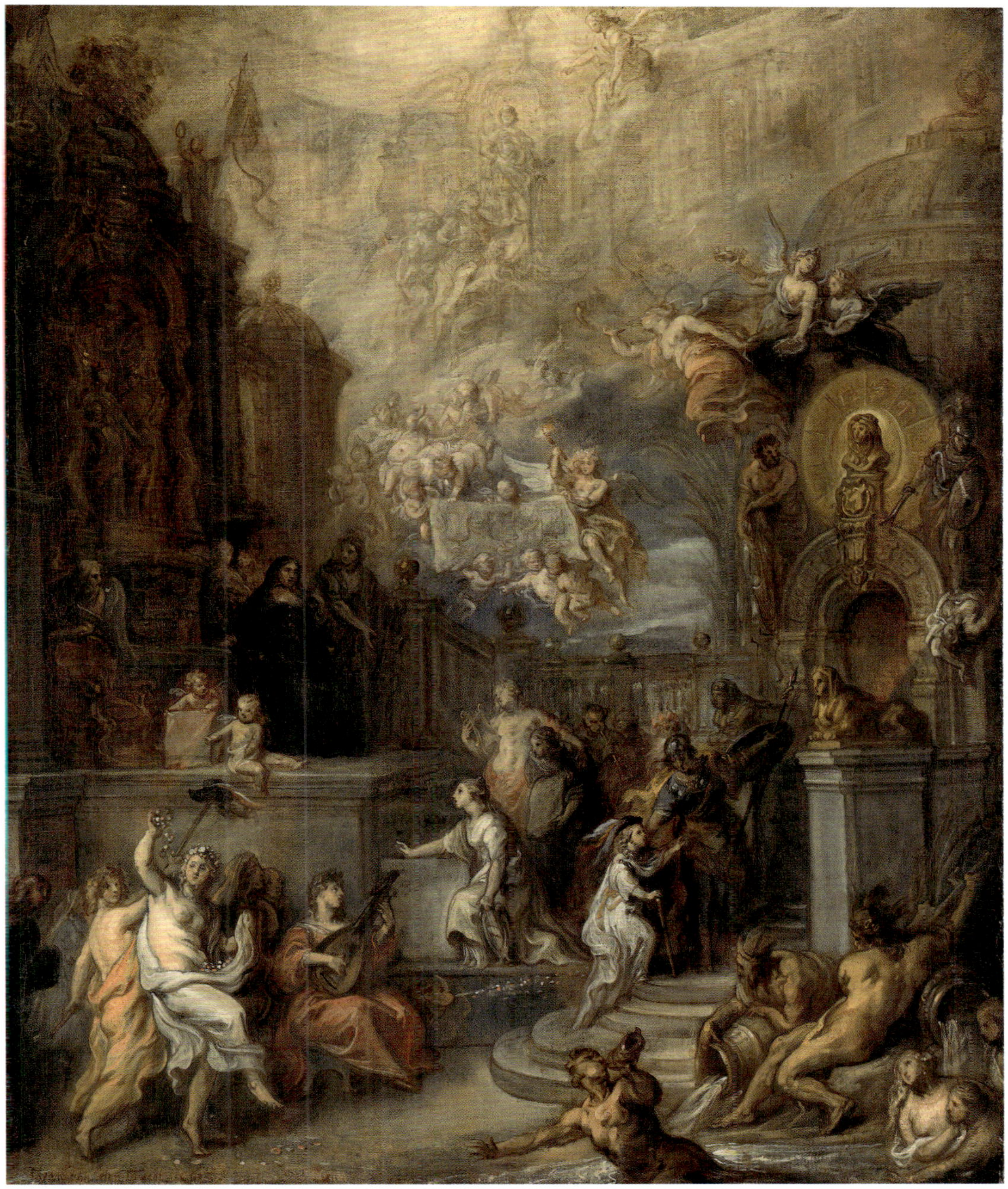

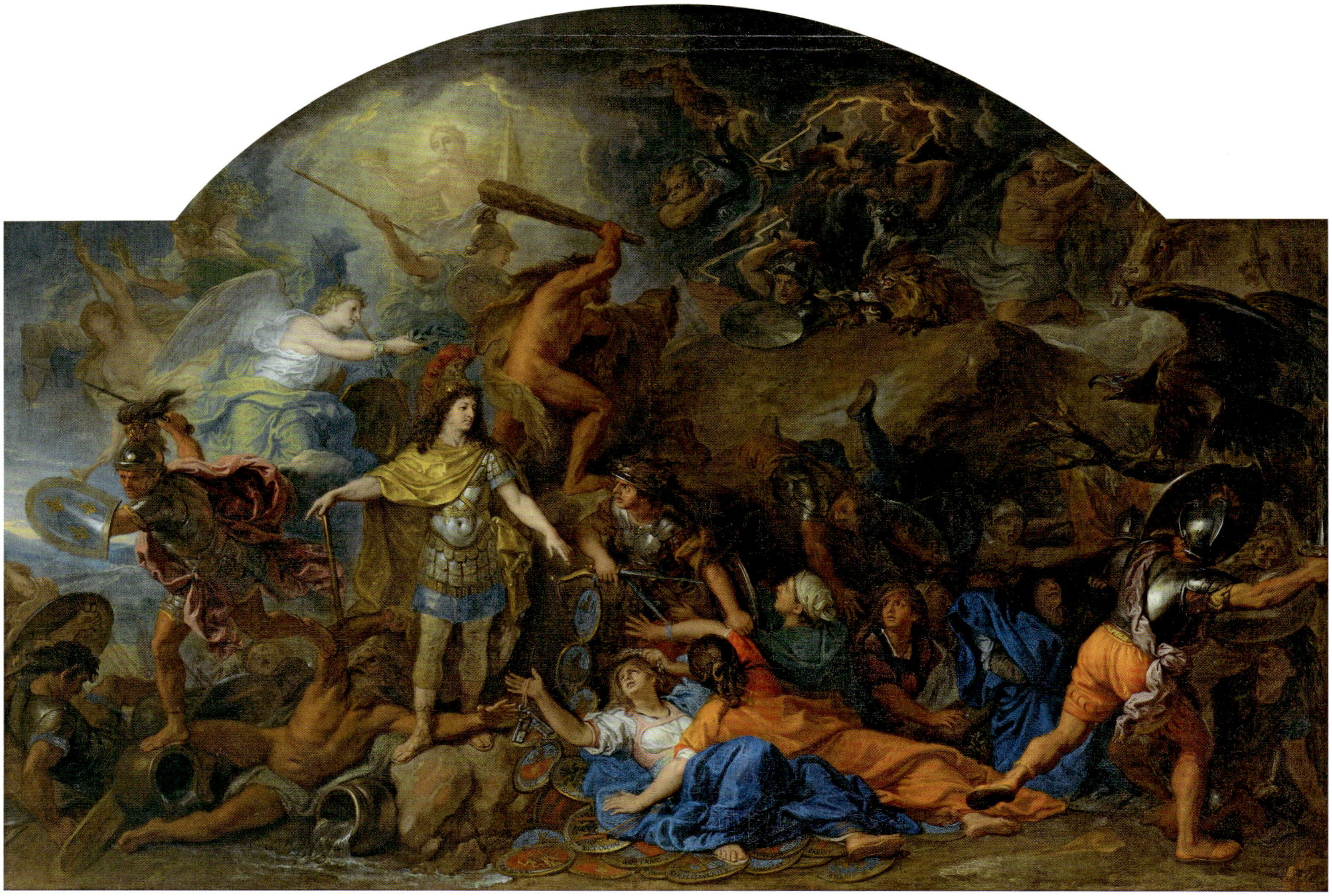

40

CHARLES LE BRUN (1619–1690)
Sketch for *The Second Conquest of the Franche-Comté, 1674*, 1679–84
Oil on canvas, 95 x 140 cm
Musée National des Châteaux de Versailles et de Trianon, inv. MV 6360

PROVENANCE: the sketch is related to one of the large compositions on the ceiling in the Galerie des Glaces in Versailles; the artist's workshop; entered the royal collection (1690); listed in inventories of the royal collections between 1706 and 1722; in the Louvre in 1785; seized during the French Revolution; deposited at the Château de Versailles in 1884; restored in 2006
SELECTED REFERENCES: Jouin 1889, p. 444; Versailles 1963, p. 109 and no. 40; Lille 1968, no. 4; Constans 1995, vol. 2, no. 3142; Bajou 1998, pp. 180–81; Versailles 2002, no. 7

encouraged the Dutch to make war in the Spanish Netherlands, the country of Rubens,[3] but he must also have felt a sense of relief at the prospect of depicting a life that was genuinely heroic, which fed his poetic genius[4] (and which did not demand the same degree of dissimulation that had been required to depict the much less dazzling life of Marie de Médicis). Rubens would undoubtedly have completed a series of masterpieces in the second gallery of the Palais du Luxembourg if his patron, Marie de Médicis, had not met her downfall during the Day of the Dupes (November 1630), which resulted in her permanent exile in July 1631.

Although the Galerie Henri IV remained to a large extent unfinished, its programme has given rise to all sorts of conjecture.[5] According to the contract of 1622, its climax was to be the monumental *Triumph of Henri IV*, which was to occupy one end of the gallery; for this Rubens produced at least four preparatory sketches between 1628 and 1630.[6] This series of *bozzetti* and *modelli* (terminating in the New York sketch, cat. 37) allows us to follow Rubens's 'apologetic' language as far as the large unfinished painting (*c.* 1630) now in the Uffizi in Florence, a work that performs an extraordinary synthesis: a series of antique models mingled with figures from Italian, French

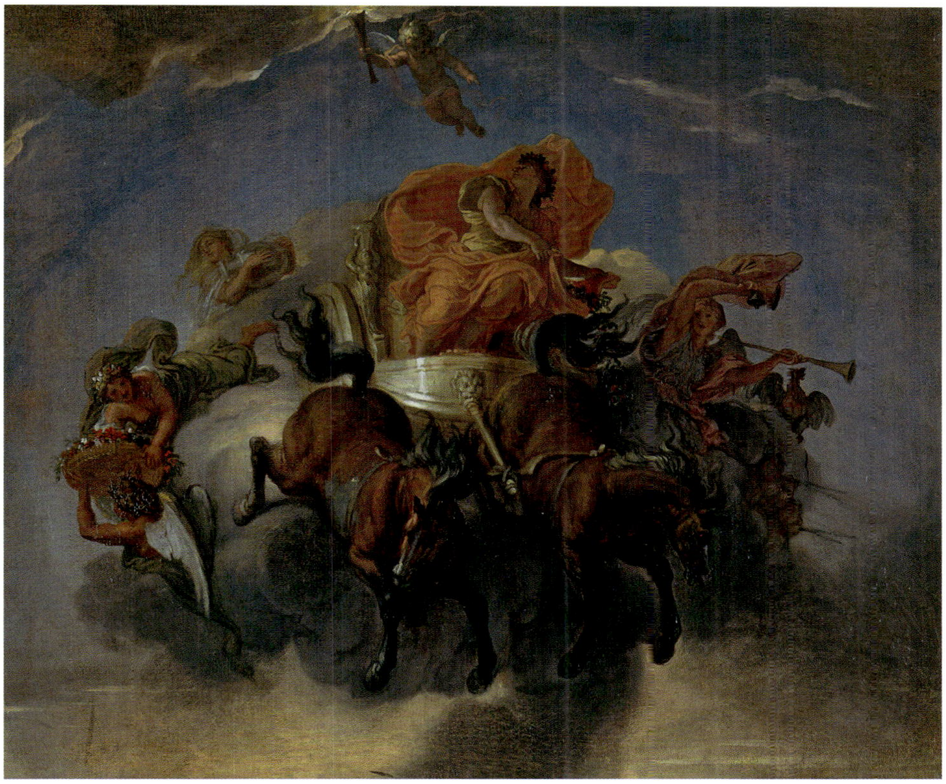

41

CHARLES LE BRUN (1619–1690)
Sketch for *Aurora on Her Chariot*, *c.* 1672
Oil on canvas, 67 x 82 cm
Private collection, Paris

PROVENANCE: preparatory sketch for the central section of the decoration in the cupola of the Pavillon de l'Aurore, Domaine de Sceaux, the property of Jean-Baptiste Colbert (1619–1683); in the sale of Jean-Baptiste Pierre Lebrun, Paris, 11 April 1791, lot 185
SELECTED REFERENCES: Dupont 1958, p. 70; Sceaux 2000, pp. 112–13

and Northern precedents. To regard this as the apogee of triumphal painting of the modern period is surely no exaggeration.

The rhetoric of Rubens's triumph found its most skilled heir in the person of Jacob Jordaens, who from about 1617 onwards often worked with Rubens himself. In the early 1650s he participated in the posthumous celebration of the life of the Stadhouder Frederick Henry (d. 1647) at the Huis ten Bosch on the outskirts of The Hague. Prepared in a series of oil sketches (three, including cat. 39, have survived), this immense triumph depicting the Prince of Orange (dated 1652) surrounded by a host of allegorical figures certainly offers recognisable similarities with some of Rubens's compositions, especially those designed to celebrate the 'joyous entry'[7] into Antwerp of the Cardinal-Infante Ferdinand in 1635 (see cat. 51) – a cycle with which Jordaens was closely associated. For the large painting at the Huis ten Bosch, Jordaens seems to have been inspired particularly by the *Triumph of the Cardinal-Infante* (1634–35; Galleria degli Uffizi, Florence),[8] which, in many respects, is a vertical adaptation of the Henri IV triumph. Theodoor van Thulden betrays a high degree of familiarity with the apologetic art of Rubens but, ten years later, is less successful at the seamless blending of allegorical and historical figures. His *Allegory of William III*, which exists today only as an oil sketch (cat. 38), nevertheless is strongly evocative of Rubens's great eulogistic cycles, in particular *The Death of Henri IV and the Proclamation of the Regency* (see cat. 34.14), one of the large paintings in the Galerie Médicis.[9]

A comprehensive account of the influence of Rubens's work on the development of large decorative schemes, sacred and profane, in Europe

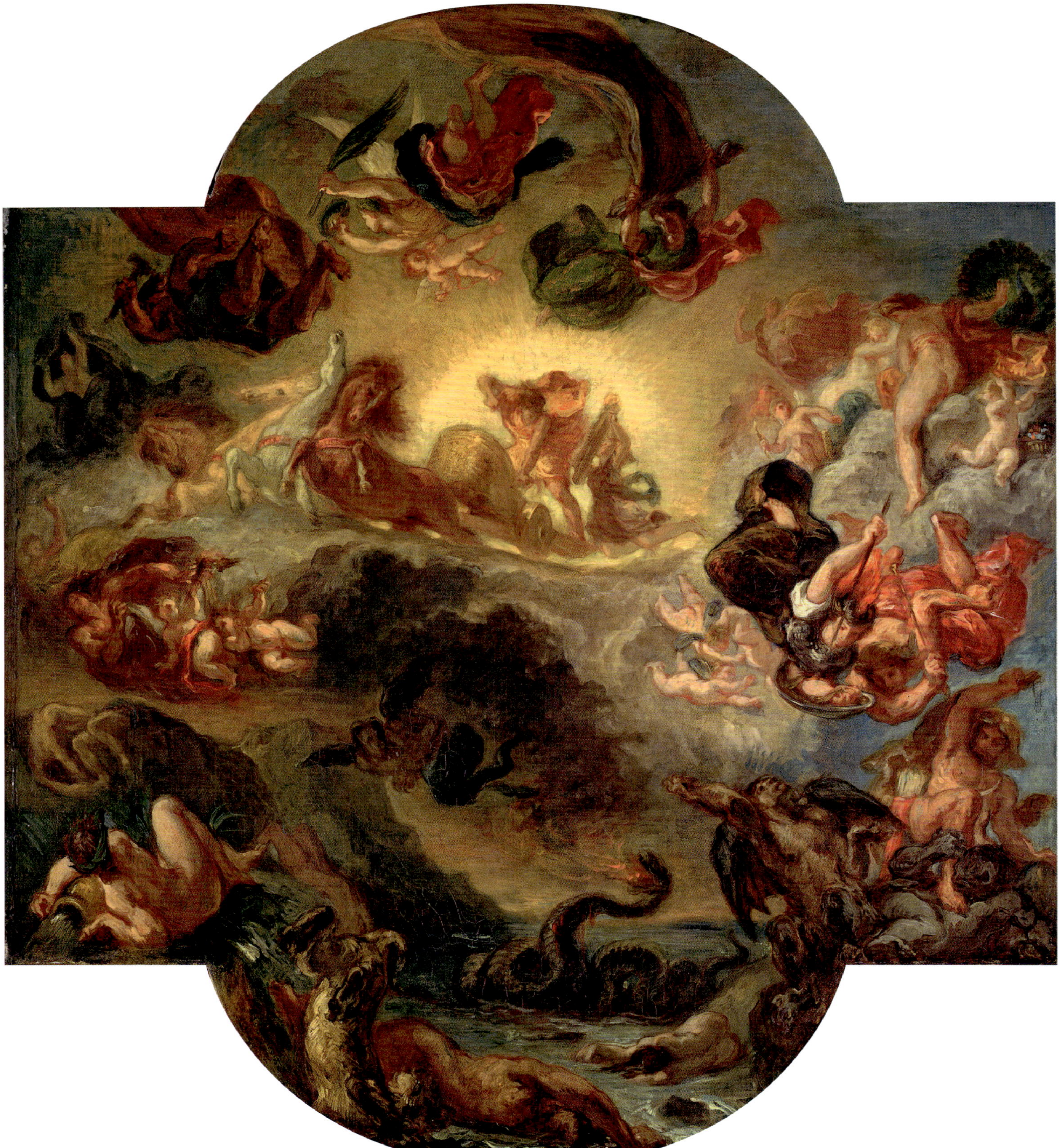

has yet to be written. In France this influence lurked for years behind strong prejudice in favour of the 'French genius', reputed to present perfect balance and symmetry. Charles Le Brun, 'first painter to the King', the great manipulator of pomp and ceremony for Louis XIV, in particular at Versailles (see cats 40 and 41), could be considered a case in point. He shared Rubens's extraordinary impetuosity and his unerring feeling for the paroxysmal moment. Le Brun seems to have been spurred on throughout his career by rivalry with the great Flemish artist and a spirit of emulation.[10] He was well acquainted with the art of Rubens (gaining this familiarity first through prints and engravings, but also through paintings by Rubens in France and tapestries produced after the master's designs). Le Brun often took as his subject episodes of fierce fighting, hunting scenes and large cycles (among them Rubens's *The Life of Constantine*, *Pompa introitus Ferdinandi* and *The Triumph of the Eucharist*), as well as representing the damned or rebel angels cast into hell as imagined by his predecessor. Such influences and subject-matter were common to other painters of the period who also worked on the interiors at Versailles, for example Gabriel Blanchard and Charles de La Fosse.[11]

When Delacroix was commissioned to complete the decorations in the Galerie d'Apollon in the Louvre in 1850 he was conscious that he was participating in the making of art history, as well as following in the footsteps of the great painters who had made their names in the royal palaces, in particular Rubens and Le Brun. His large *The Triumph of Apollo* (see cat. 42) pays homage especially to Rubens. Before executing his great canvas, he had spent the summer of 1850 in Belgium meditating on the tempestuous vitality of Rubens's great religious paintings;[12] through Delacroix these were to remain a formidable influence on the great French decorative schemes of the mid-nineteenth century.

42

EUGÈNE DELACROIX (1798–1863)
The Triumph of Apollo (Apollo Vanquishing the Serpent Python), sketch for (or perhaps *riccordo* of) the decoration of the ceiling in the Galerie d'Apollon, Musée du Louvre, Paris, c. 1853. Signature of doubtful authenticity
Oil on canvas, 110 x 99.5 cm
Fondation E. G. Bührle Collection, Zurich, inv. 127

PROVENANCE: in the Delacroix sale, Paris, February 1864, lot 24; acquired for 5,150 francs by Cadart, the dealer; Georges Petit, Paris, 1873; in the collection of Baron Vitta, Paris; Marlborough Fine Art Ltd, London; acquired in London by Emil Bührle in 1951; in the Bührle Collection, Zurich, 1951–56, then presented by Emil Bührle's heirs to the Fondation E. G. Bührle Collection, Zurich, 1960
SELECTED REFERENCES: Zurich 1958, no. 115; Zurich 1987, no. 80; Johnson 1989, nos 576 and 577 (Delacroix and an assistant?); Copenhagen 2000, no. 26

At some point during the end of the 1620s or the beginning of the 1630s the Stuart court offered Rubens a fresh opportunity to display both his extraordinary skill at monumental decorative painting and his ability to handle allegory with circumspection (to the point of ambiguity). This time he was not required (as he had been in Paris) to produce 'wall decoration' that harked back to the age-old tradition of using tapestry to embellish the walls of castles and palaces; instead the commission required him to decorate the nine oval and rectangular panels in the ceiling of the state room in the palace at Whitehall, then the principal London residence of the monarchs of England.[1] Designed by Inigo Jones between 1619 and 1622 in the Palladian style – its first appearance in the British Isles – the 'Banqueting House' was not designed solely as a place for entertaining. The theme of the ceiling – the allegorical glorification of the reign of James I (1566–1625), predecessor and father of Charles I (1600–1649) – can be seen as the highly politicised use of a space in which the sovereign officiated at ceremonies and received foreign dignitaries.

The earliest plans relating to the great decorative scheme finally entrusted to Rubens were designed first and foremost to exalt the union – under the aegis of the first English king from the Scottish house of Stuart – of England and Scotland after centuries of hostility.[2] Although space was reserved for this theme, the final programme was organised around a large posthumous apotheosis of the monarch James I. This crucial scene was preceded in England by the breathtaking *Apotheosis* (sometimes *Glorification*) *of the Duke of Buckingham*, completed by the master from Antwerp at the same time as an equestrian portrait also of George Villiers, the Duke of Buckingham, in September 1627 for York House, the London residence of this favourite of the Stuarts. Both paintings, alas, were destroyed in 1949. With regard to the *Apotheosis*, the admirable oil sketch (*c.* 1625), now in the National Gallery, London, survives.[3] William Etty, himself a fervent admirer of the Flemish artist, appears to have made a copy of the sketch some time around 1830 (cat. 43).[4] Rubens made the acquaintance of Buckingham in May 1625 in Paris, where the Duke was attending the marriage by proxy of his master to the sister of Louis XIII. It was formerly supposed that the heroic *Apotheosis* in York House had been executed after the assassination of the Duke in 1628. Nowadays it is generally agreed that during his lifetime Buckingham had no objection to a depiction that showed him being transported heavenwards by Minerva and Mercury; a scene clearly executed in the style of the apotheosis recently painted in the Galerie Médicis to glorify the late Henri IV and to give visible confirmation to the idea of the transcendental nature of the sovereign at the height of the absolutist idea of monarchy.[5] Rubens's celebration of the reign of James I at Whitehall assumes a slightly sombre (and retrospectively ironic) aspect if we remember that Charles I, who was to defend the divine nature of royal rights and prerogatives even more determinedly than his father, was beheaded just outside the building on 30 January 1649, after having crossed the great hall decorated with the artist's aerial allegories (see cats 44 and 45).

Rather than the Palais du Luxembourg, where Rubens had distinguished himself for the greater glory of the mother-in-law of King Charles, it was more likely to have been the astounding decorative scheme he had

43

Attributed to
WILLIAM ETTY (1787–1849)
Sketch of *Apotheosis of the Duke of Buckingham*, *c.* 1825–35
Oil on panel, 24.1 x 24.1 cm
York Museums Trust (York Art Gallery), inv. YORAG 571

PROVENANCE: acquired by the museum in 1951
SELECTED REFERENCES: Farr 1958, no. 298; Martin 1972, no. 187, p. 150 (copies); Held 1980, vol. 1, as no. 291 (copies); York 2011, no. 52

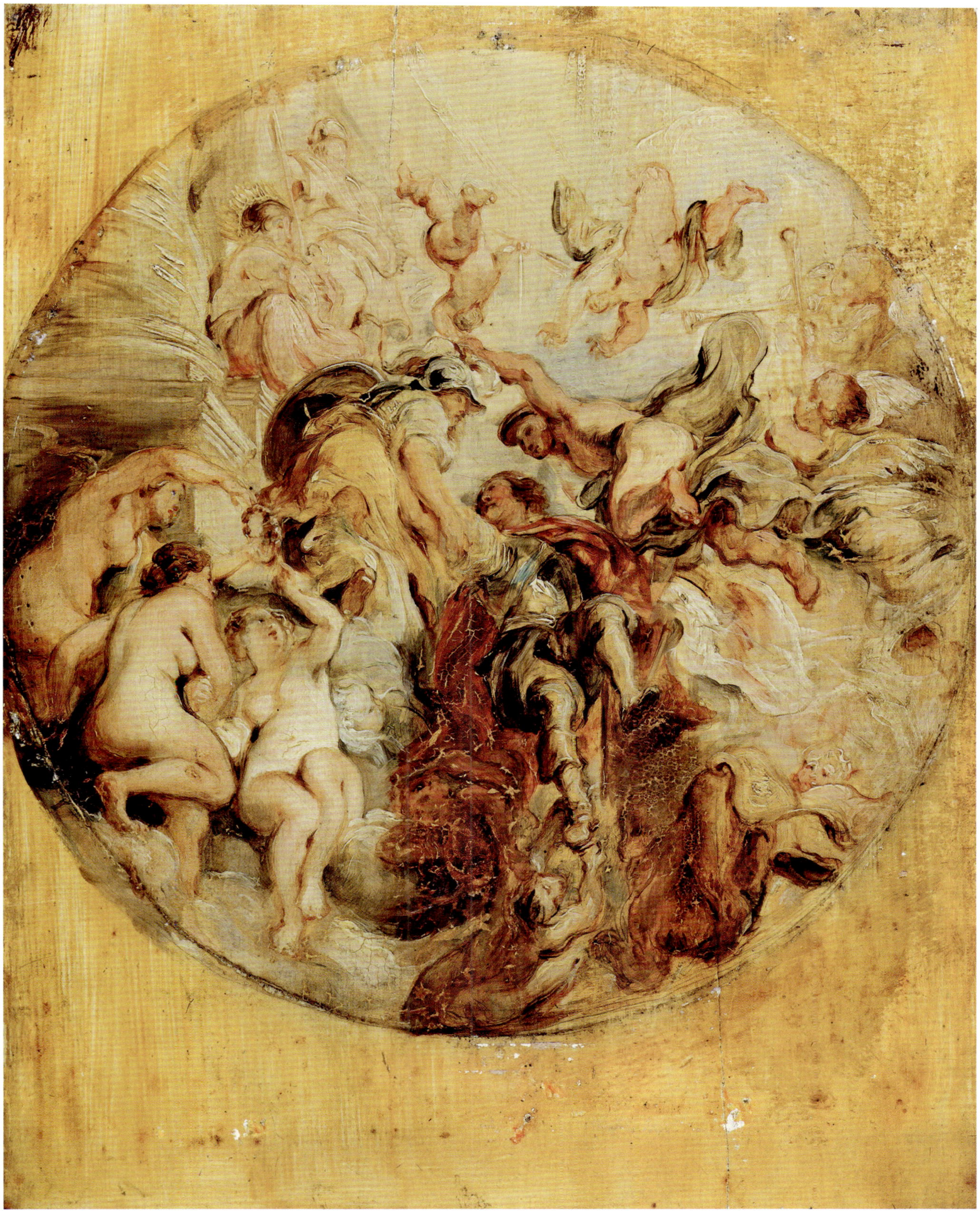

44

PETER PAUL RUBENS (1577-1640)
Sketch for *Prudence (Minerva) Overthrowing Ignorance (or Sedition)*, the oval composition occupying the northeast corner of the Banqueting House ceiling, 1632–33
Originally oil on panel (transferred to a canvas on a composite backing), 62.8 x 49 cm
Royal Museum of Fine Arts Antwerp, inv. 802

PROVENANCE: estate sale of the dealer Christianus Johannes Nieuwenhuys, Brussels, 4 May 1883, lot 18, bought for 7,000 francs by H. Le Roy; in the collection of De Potemkin, Brussels, 1893; in the possession of the dealer Lampe, Brussels, 1895; in the Valentin-Roussel (Roubaix) sale, Brussels, 14 June 1899, lot 26, bought by Delahaye for the museum
SELECTED REFERENCES: Held 1980, vol. 1, no. 142; Jaffé 1989, no. 1019; Martin 2005, vol. 1, no. 7b (with a comprehensive bibliography); Brussels 2007, no. 88

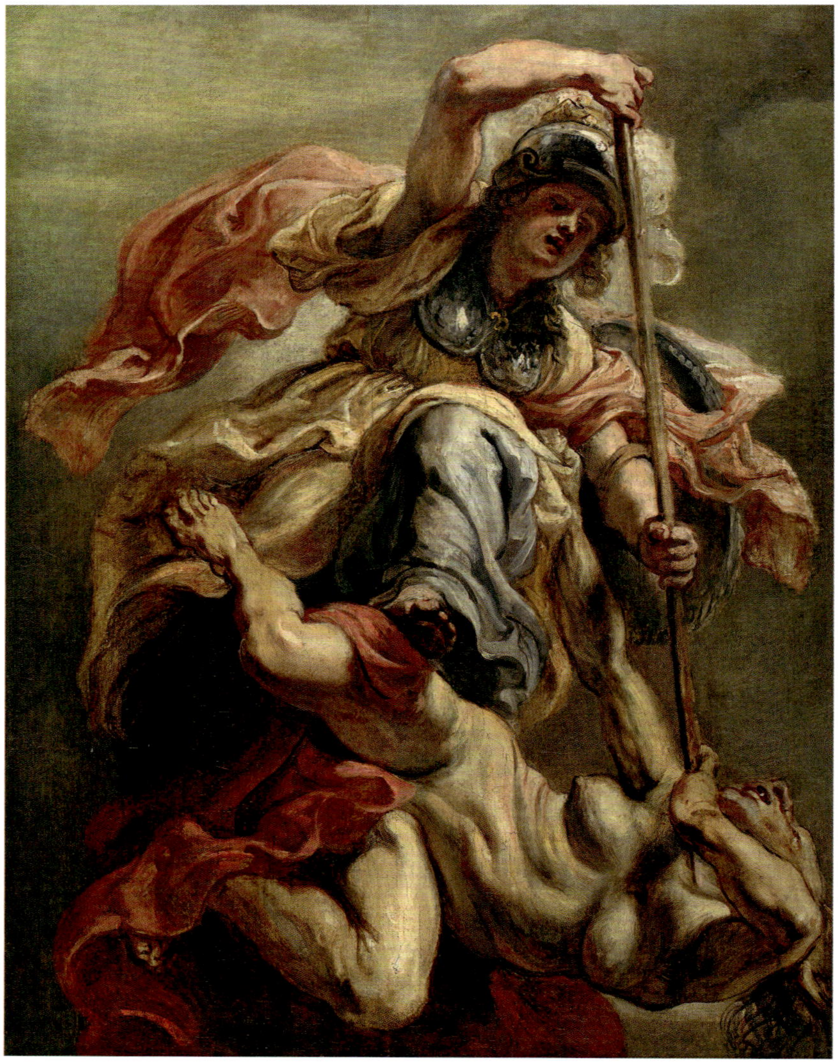

designed for the ceiling of Antwerp's Jesuit church (1620–21, destroyed in 1718), which had confirmed him as one of the most skilled artists of the day as far as decorated ceilings were concerned. The artistic scheme in the Jesuit church already possessed a strong neo-Venetian character, recalling the great compartmentalised ceilings in the churches and civic buildings of La Serenissima, particularly those painted by Veronese; the same character can be found in the Banqueting House in the division of the ceiling into three longitudinal axes, whose heavy framework was designed by Inigo Jones.

Rubens was introduced to the court of King Charles during the negotiations surrounding the resumption of diplomatic relations between England and Spain between 1629 and March 1630; he must certainly have grasped this opportunity to obtain the commission for a decorative scheme about which he had first been approached in 1621.[6] The grisaille oil sketch from Tate shown here (cat. 46), with the lower part allegedly containing a battle scene linked to the plan for the Galerie Henri IV, may date from this visit to London (or it may have preceded it). According to a *modus operandi* long promoted – unverifiable (although the

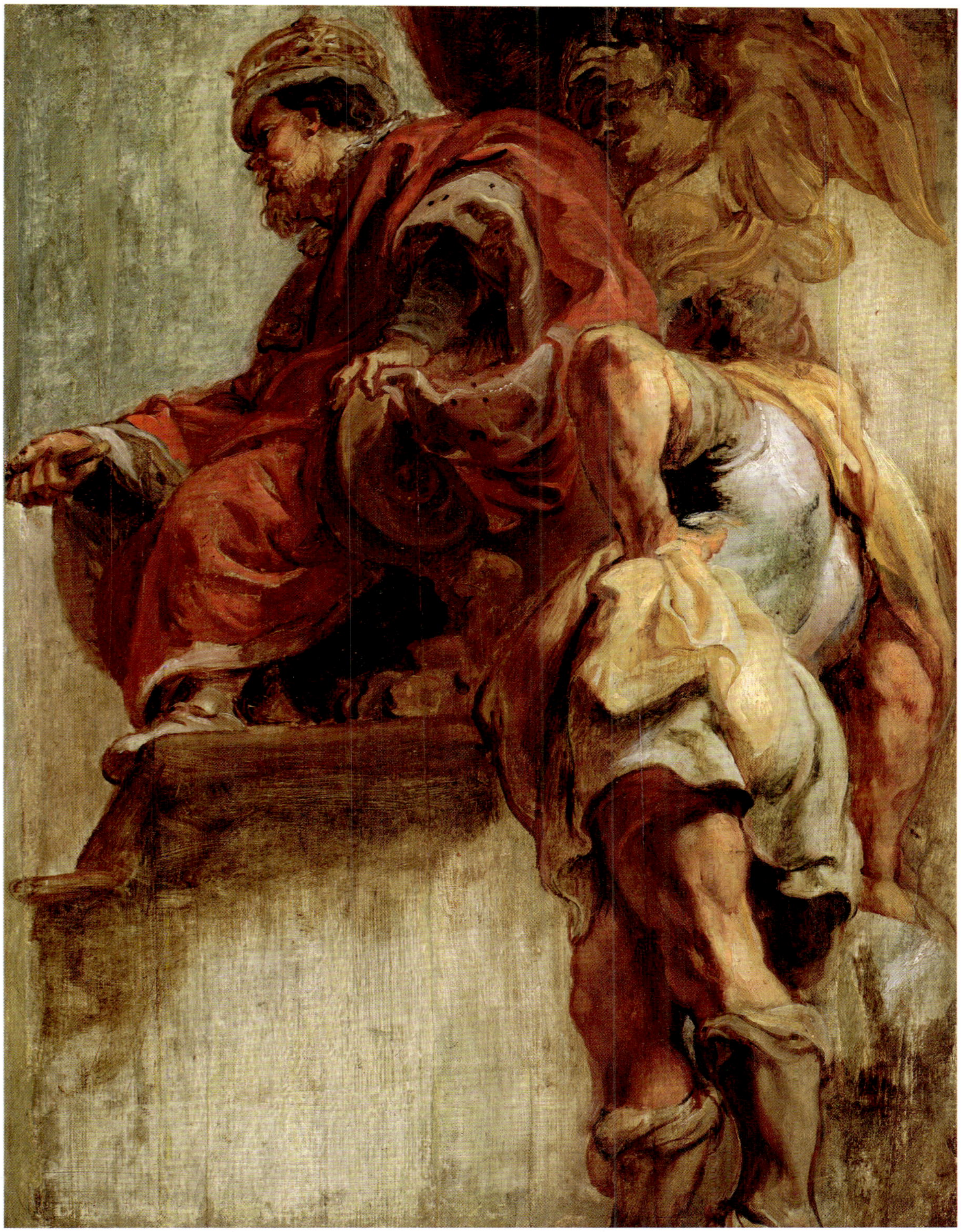

45

PETER PAUL RUBENS (1577–1640)
Study for *James I Uniting England and Scotland (James I on His Throne with a Guard)*, *c.* 1632–33
Oil on panel, 63.5 x 48.3 cm
Birmingham Museums and Art Gallery, inv. 1984 P 2
RA ONLY

PROVENANCE: estate sale of F. A. E. Bruyninex, canon and archdeacon of Antwerp Cathedral, Antwerp, 1 August 1791, lot 3, as 'Assuerus on his throne ...', bought for 8 florins by Mensaert; estate sales of Richard Cosway RA, London (Stanley), 19 May 1821, lot 71, and 9 March 1822, lot 67; bought by Colonel Th. H. Davies (d. 1846), Elmley Castle, Worcestershire; by descent to Lt Col. R. H. R. Davies (d. 1982); acquired by the museum in 1984
SELECTED REFERENCES: London 1972, no. 41; Held 1980, vol. 1, no. 138; Jaffé 1989, no. 1031; Martin 2005, vol. 1, no. 5f (with a comprehensive bibliography); Wood 2010B as no. 162

46

PETER PAUL RUBENS (1577–1640)
The Apotheosis of James I and other studies, 1628–30
Oil on panel, 95 x 63.1 cm
Tate, inv. T12919. Purchased with assistance from the National Heritage Memorial Fund, Tate Members, The Art Fund in memory of Sir Oliver Millar (with a contribution from the Wolfson Foundation), Viscount and Viscountess Hampden and Family, Monument Trust, Manny and Brigitta Davidson and the Family, and other donors 2008

PROVENANCE: may have been acquired in Rome by a syndicate consisting of Thomas Trevor, later 2nd Viscount Hampden (d. 1824), Motteux and O'Brien; sold anonymously (Viscount Hampden), Christie's, London, 31 May 1799 (no. 102, sold for 18 guineas); by descent to Mrs Humphrey Brand, Glynde Place, Sussex, then to her descendants; on loan to the National Gallery, London, from 1985; acquired by the National Gallery, 2008 (with financial support from, in particular, the National Heritage Memorial Fund, the Tate Members and The Art Fund) in memory of Sir Oliver Millar
SELECTED REFERENCES: London 1972, no. 39; Held 1980, vol. 1, no. 133; Jaffé 1989, no. 1003; Martin 2005, vol. 1, no. 1 (with a comprehensive bibliography); Brussels 2007, no. 85; London 2009, no. 13; Martin 2011, in particular pp. 100–06

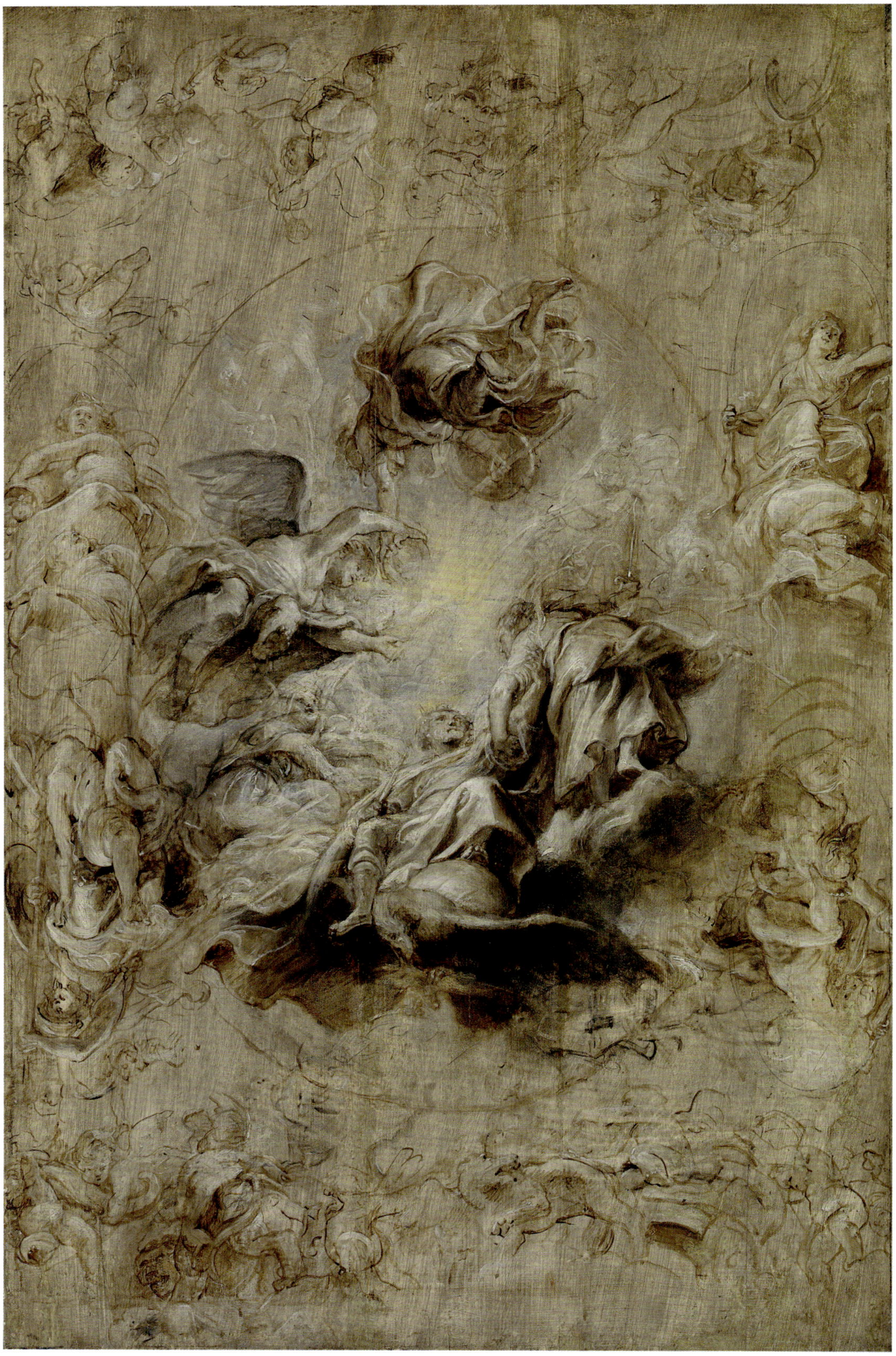

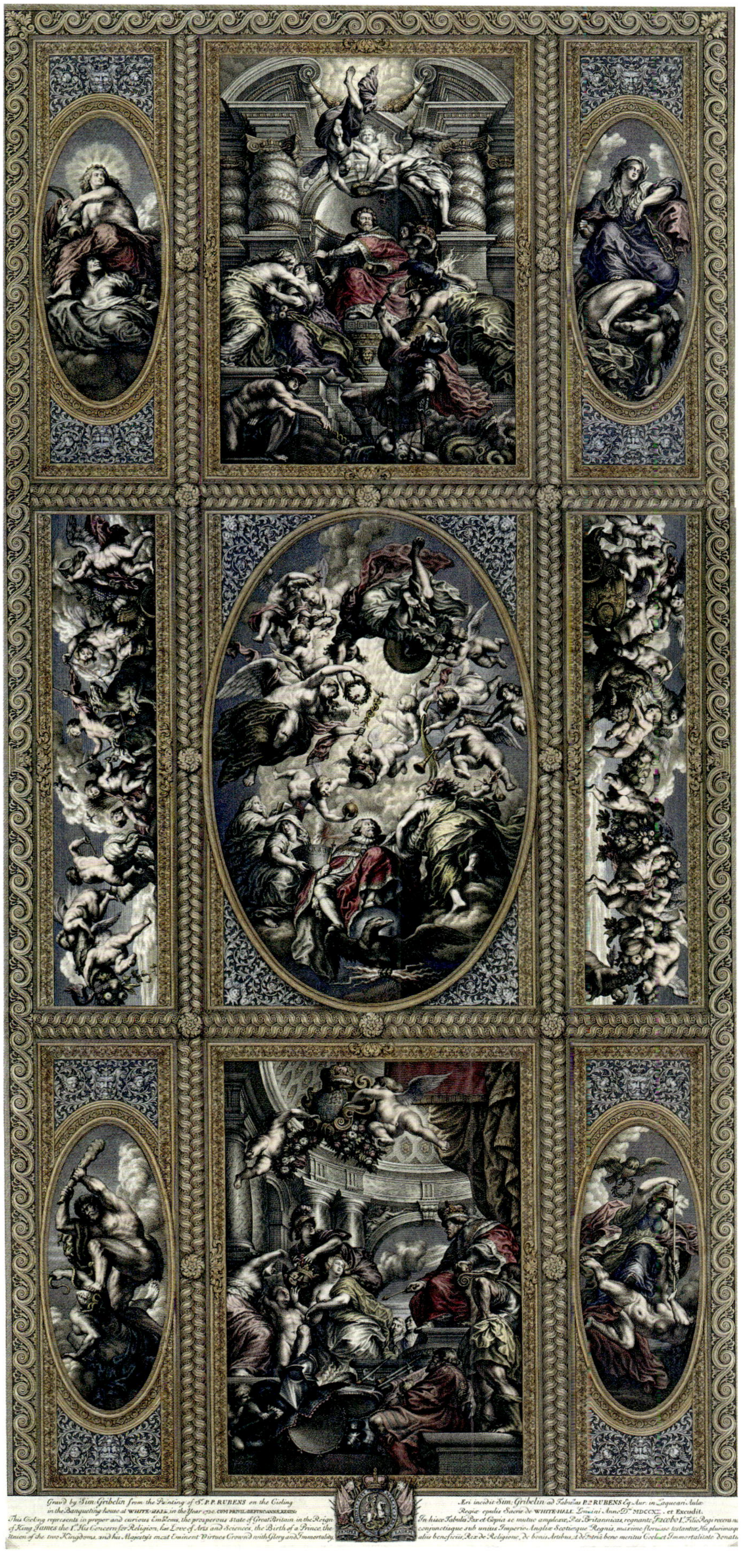

47

SIMON GRIBELIN THE ELDER (1661–1733)
The Ceiling of the Banqueting House in Whitehall, 1720
Hand-coloured engraving across three sheets: 31.7 x 46.4 cm, 31.7 x 46.4 cm and 32.7 x 46.4 cm
Royal Academy of Arts, London, inv. nos 03/2754–6

SELECTED REFERENCES:
Voorhelm Schneevoogt 1873, p. 143, no. 60; Rome 1977, nos 376–79; O'Connell 1985, pp. 31–33, 34, no. 10; Martin 2005, particularly vol. 2, pp. 333–35 (appendix VI)

48

LOUIS LAGUERRE (1663–1721)
Sketch for *The Ascension of Christ and the Incredulity of St Thomas*, 1689–93
Oil on canvas, 39 x 28 cm
Victoria and Albert Museum, London, inv. P.27-1949

PROVENANCE: design for a decorated ceiling in the chapel of Chatsworth House, Derbyshire, residence of the Earls (later Dukes) of Devonshire; in the collection of Sir Anthony Cope; sold at Eversley Manor, Hampshire, 14–15 July 1949, lot 355, as a sketch by Antonio Verrio, acquired by Einstein; entered the museum collection in the same year
SELECTED REFERENCES: Thompson 1949, pp. 40 and 135–38; Croft-Murray 1962, p. 251, no. 6; Daniels 1974, pp. 421–22

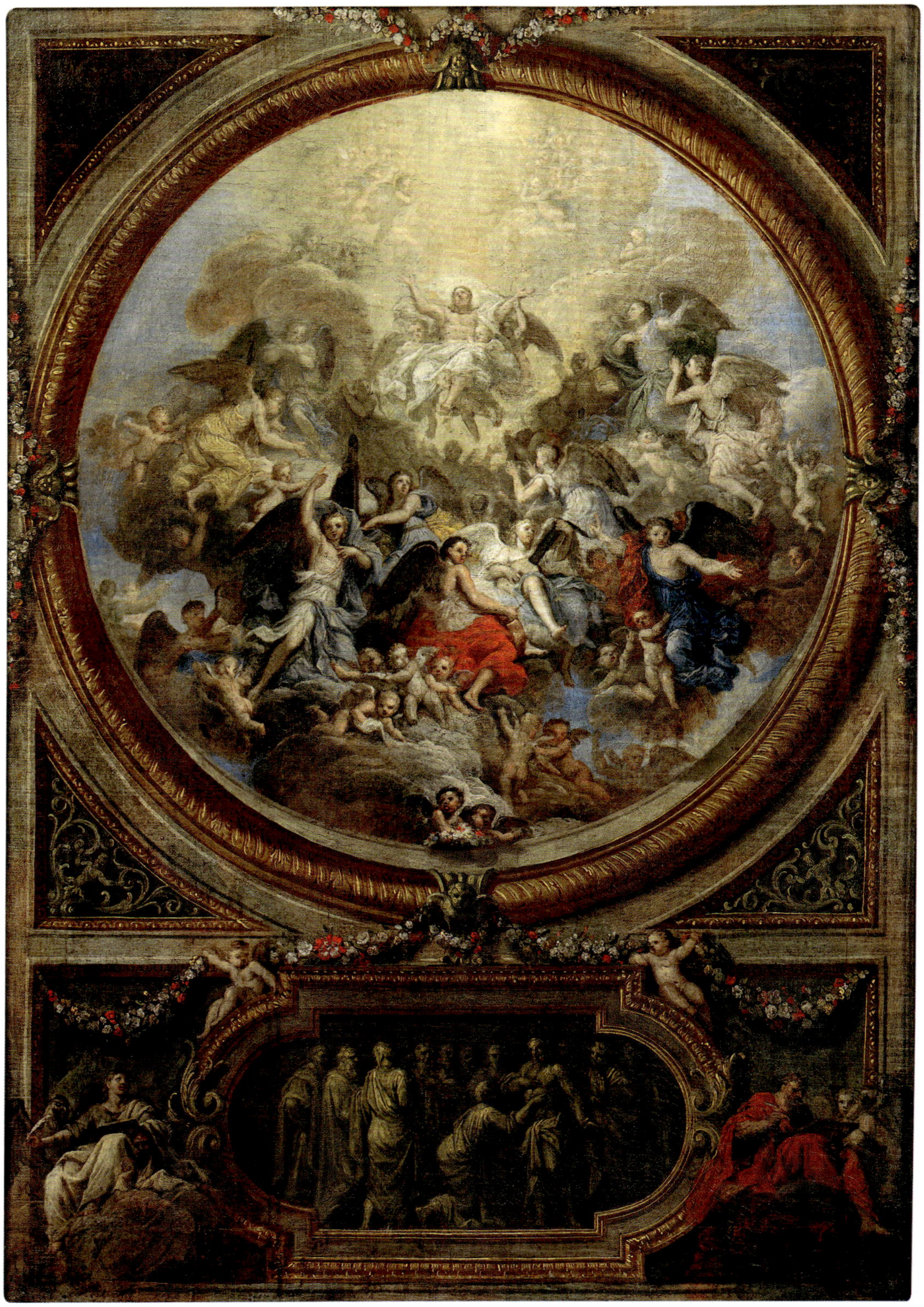

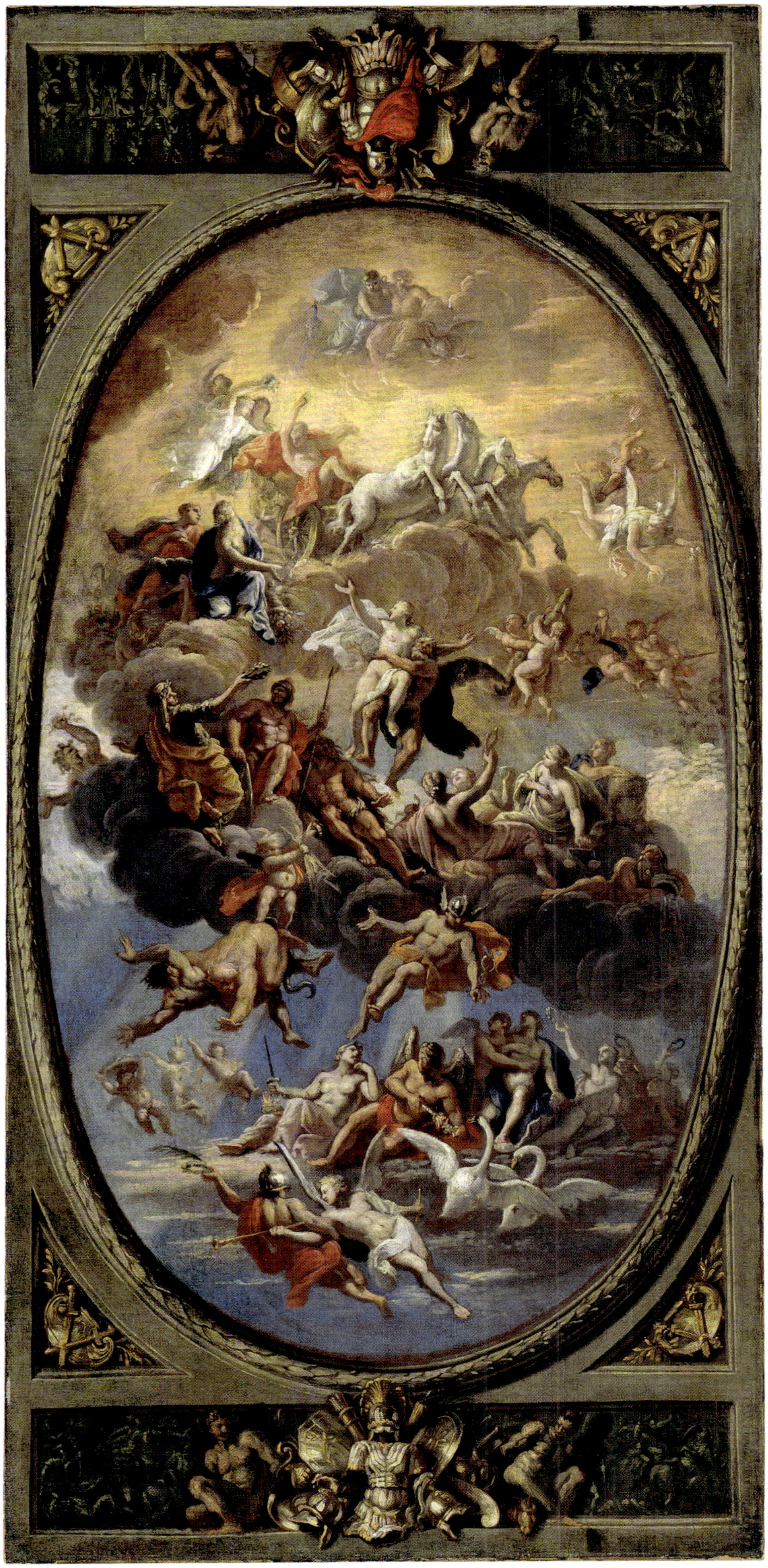

49

ANTONIO VERRIO (1636/39–1707)
Sketch for *The Assembly of the Gods*,
c. 1680–1700
Oil on canvas, 169.2 x 82.9 cm
Tate, inv. T00916. Purchased 1967

PROVENANCE: probably executed for the painted ceiling at Moor Park Hall, Hertfordshire; collection of John Scott, 1st Earl of Eldon (d. 1838); sold anonymously, Sotheby's, 22 February 1967, lot 43, as the work of James Thornhill, and acquired by Leger; bought from the Leger Galleries (Grant-in-Aid) in 1967
SELECTED REFERENCES: *The Tate Gallery Report 1967–68*, London, p. 52; Brett 2010, p. 90

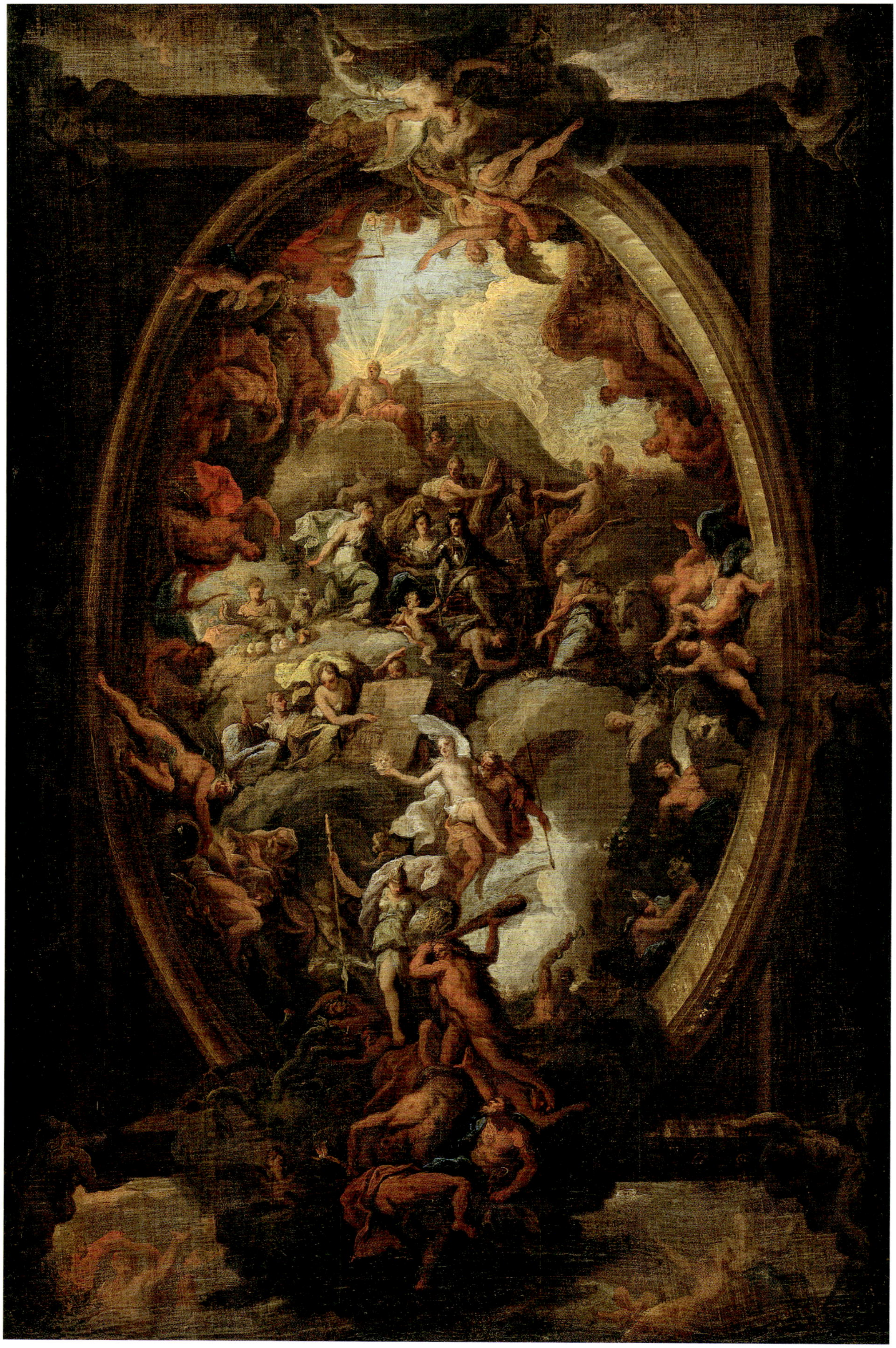

hypothesis based on the evidence of the artist Godfrey Kneller [1646–1723], who claimed that Jordaens assisted Rubens, is perfectly credible)[7] – collaborators worked from *modelli* provided by Rubens (at least ten of these are known). Completed in 1634, the vast canvases were finally installed in the palace in 1636, without the artist being present. This is the only one of Rubens's great schemes that can today be seen *in situ*.

The posterity of the Whitehall ceiling is not very clear. It does not seem to have had many descendants.[8] Spared by the fire that devastated the palace in 1698, the main hall designed by Inigo Jones captured the interest of the Stuart and Hanoverian monarchs in the early eighteenth century. Published in 1720 in print form (the copyright designed to protect the scheme goes back to the reign of Queen Anne, who died in 1714), the monumental reproductions (cat. 47) by the Frenchman Simon Gribelin the Elder testify to lively curiosity, as well as to the worldwide diffusion of the grand scheme.[9] Resonances of it can be discerned, hypothetically, in the work of the decorative painters of the Baroque period, for example the Italian artist Antonio Verrio (cat. 49), the Frenchmen Louis Chéron[10] and Louis Laguerre (cat. 48), and Sir James Thornhill in England (cat. 50); they worked successfully between the end of the seventeenth and the first quarter of the eighteenth centuries, producing grand schemes for the English monarchy, for the aristocracy or for institutions.[11] In certain respects these artists should be defined in relation to their predecessor during the reign of Charles I, but it must be stressed that, although dependent on earlier models, in particular on the great schemes at Versailles, they never emulated the type of perspective so generally favoured by the Flemish master. Rubens had set a precedent and created an impact with his ceiling figures; these seem to stand directly above the spectator's head, making violent foreshortening of perspective necessary.[12] This spectacular illusionist tradition of ceiling decoration was borrowed from the Venetian school of the Cinquecento, from Titian and Veronese, and also indebted to Correggio and the subsequent Bolognese school.[13] It was superbly handled by Rubens in the Jesuit church at Antwerp but challenged – and often superseded – in Europe by the technique known as *quadro riportato*. This consisted of ceiling panels composed in the manner of easel paintings, freed of the violently foreshortened figures and architecture that seemed to many onlookers tiring to the eye, ostentatious, almost unintelligible (and *risqué* as regards nudity).

Of course many intermediate solutions existed, and the sketches presented here bear witness to the hybridisation that improves the visual equilibrium of the figures to be found in the illusionist representations of Venice, of Rubens and of the Baroque artists of the seventeenth and eighteenth centuries. Such illusionist representations often present the onlooker with two focal points; they were not renowned for their geometrical rigour.[14] The 'apologetic' art of the reign of Louis XIV in France was influential also in England; in it, precision was sacrificed to *taste* rather than to *effect*, thus a system of empirical practice was established in which viewpoints were multiplied, and foreshortening that was too violent (and too unseemly) was banned.[15]

50

SIR JAMES THORNHILL (1675–1734)
Sketch for a ceiling painting *King William III and Queen Mary Presenting Europe with Peace and Liberty*, c. 1710
Oil on canvas, 96 x 66 cm
Victoria and Albert Museum, London, inv. 812-1877

PROVENANCE: preparatory study for the ceiling of the 'Painted Hall', Greenwich Hospital, London, designed by Christopher Wren (1632–1723); commissioned by the governors of the Royal Hospital for Seamen, Greenwich; acquired by the museum in 1877
SELECTED REFERENCES: *An explanation of the Painting*…, n.d., pp. 9 ff.; Croft-Murray 1962, p. 268, no. 16; Mayhew 1967, p. 13, no. 9; Held 1980, vol. 1, p. 281; Kaulbach 2004, p. 65; Martin 2005, vol. 1, p. 135; Ellis and Roe 2008, p. 287

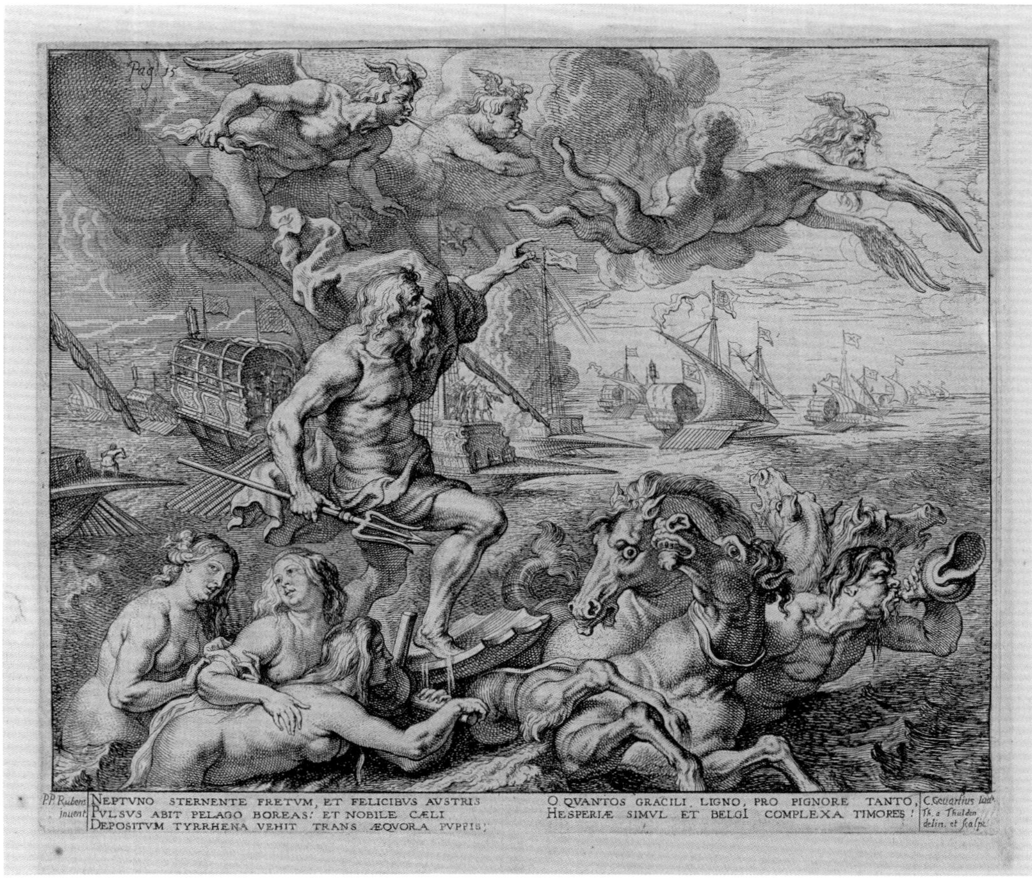

51

THEODOOR VAN THULDEN (1606–1669)
The Voyage of the Cardinal-Infante Ferdinand from Barcelona to Genoa in April 1633, with Neptune Calming the Waves (known as *Quos Ego*), *Pompa introitus Ferdinandi*, Antwerp, 1642, p. 15
Etching, 28 x 34.1 cm
Royal Museum of Fine Arts Antwerp, inv. 10722

PROVENANCE: engraved by Van Thulden (probably from one of his own drawings, *c.* 1635, British Museum, London) for *Pompa Introitus Honori Serenissimi Principis Ferdinandi* (published Antwerp, 1642); from the collection of Max Rooses (d. 1914)
SELECTED REFERENCES: Voorhelm Schneevoogt 1873, no. 27, 7; Martin 1972, no. 3; Rome 1977, no. 242

The task of designing the temporary decorations put up in Antwerp in 1634 for the ceremony to welcome Cardinal-Infante Ferdinand (1609–1641) fell mainly to Rubens. The younger brother of Philip IV of Spain, Ferdinand was the new Governor of the Spanish Netherlands. Weakened by illness but with his powers of invention intact, Rubens produced a series of detailed colour sketches, known as *modelli*. A battalion of painters (including Jordaens and Van Thulden), sculptors and joiners translated these into scenery and monumental triumphal arches.[1] Ferdinand's 'joyous entry' took place on 17 April 1635, and was testimony to the joy and relief felt by the city on the Scheldt river, as well as to the high expectations vested in the young prince by Antwerp – at that time caught in a stranglehold caused by the United Provinces blockading the Scheldt. To preserve the memory of the occasion, the town councillors of Antwerp paid for a monumental volume of reproductions, engraved by Van Thulden, of the decorations, with a commentary by J. G. Gevartius. This volume, entitled *Pompa Introitus Honori Serenissimi Principis Ferdinandi*, appeared only in 1642, after the death of the Cardinal-Infante (and two years after the death of Rubens).

The scene shown here, a depiction of Neptune calming the waves (cat. 51), is one of Rubens's best compositions; Rubens participated in the task of painting the great set piece (now in the Gemäldegalerie, Dresden), which was located at the left side of the scenery at the start of the welcoming display. The artist idealised

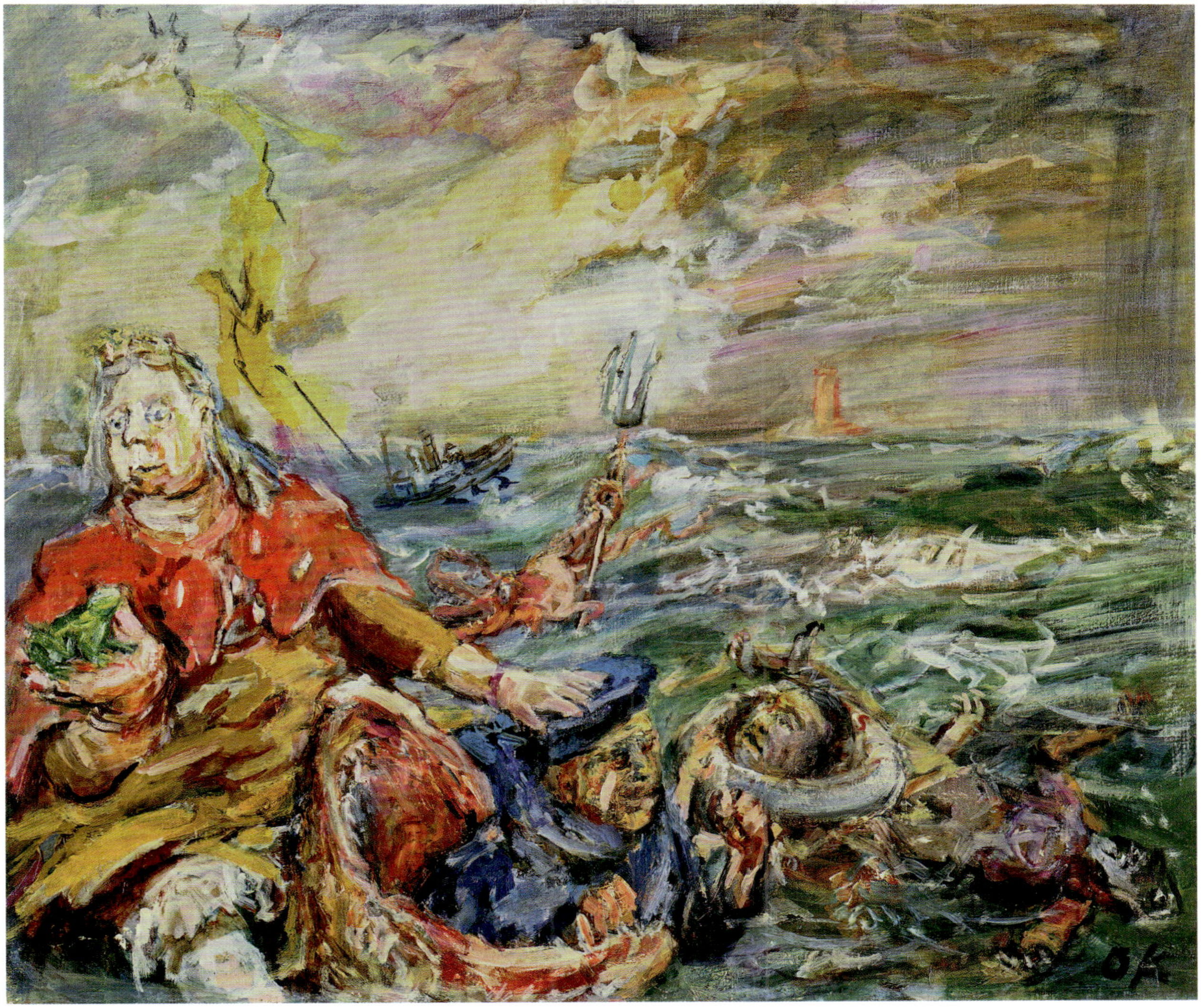

'Don Fernando's' perilous sea voyage by invoking a famous passage from Virgil's *Aeneid* (I.135), plus some well-known artistic precedents (including Raphael, Giulio Romano and Perino del Vaga).[2]

During the darkest hours of the twentieth century, Oskar Kokoschka painted his *Loreley* (cat. 52), the title a reference to the melancholy siren described by, among others, the poet Heinrich Heine. In the painting Kokoschka replaced Virgil's Neptune with Queen Victoria and in doing so he changed the allegorical eulogy of the prince into a bitter indictment of the waning British Empire, embodied in the figure of the deceased ruler. After the outbreak of war in 1939, the British government had decided on a policy of internment for 'enemy aliens'. From 1938 Kokoschka was resident in England (protected by his recently acquired Czech nationality), and in 1942 the Austrian artist took up the cudgels on behalf of the internees, several hundred of whom had perished in July 1940 when a ship taking them to Canada, the *Arandora Star*, was torpedoed by a U-boat and sank.

52

OSKAR KOKOSCHKA (1886–1980)
Loreley, 1942
Signed lower right 'O.K.'; on the reverse 'LORELEY – by O.K./1942'
Oil on canvas, 63.5 x 76.2 cm
Tate, inv. T05486. Presented by Mrs Olda Kokoschka, the artist's widow, in honour of the directorship of Sir Alan Bowness, 1988

PROVENANCE: donated in 1988 by the artist's widow, Olda Kokoschka ('in honour of the directorship of Sir Alan Bowness')
SELECTED REFERENCES: London 1986, no. 94; Los Angeles 1997, pp. 86–94 (especially pp. 88–89) and no. 84; Sultano and Werkner 2003, p. 177–79; Litti 2006, pp. 108–09; Vienna 2008, pp. 104–05, no. 27

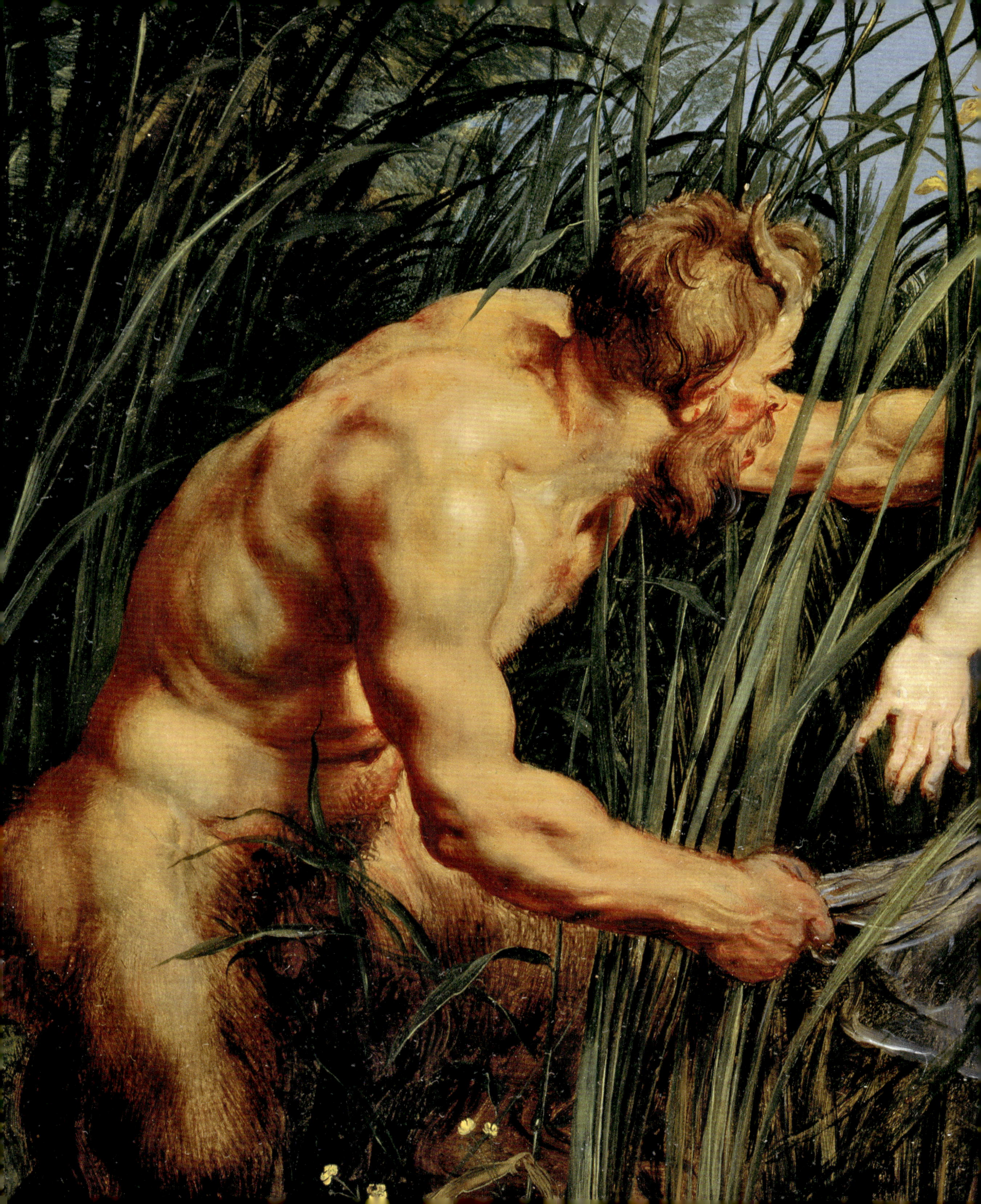

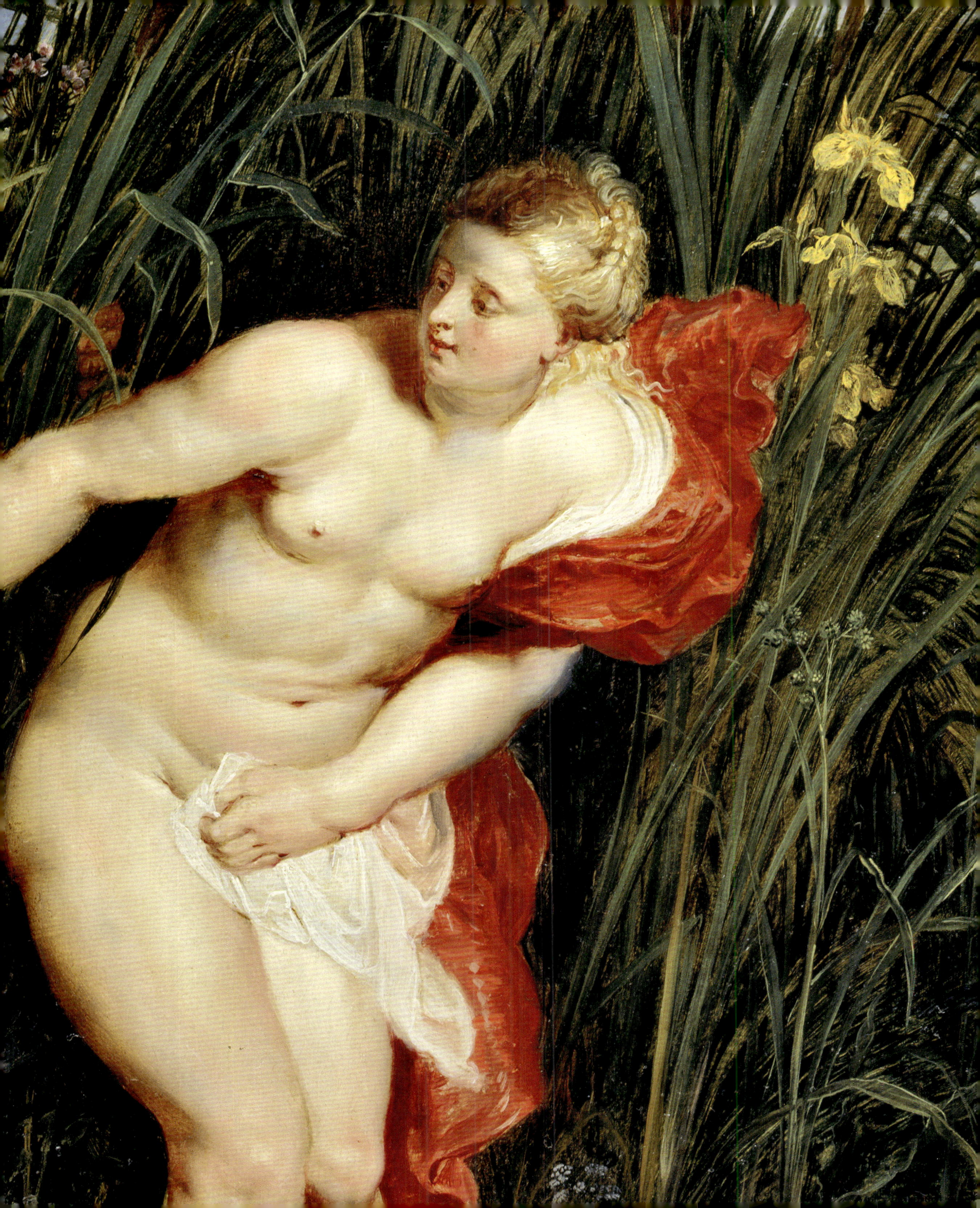

LUST

GERLINDE GRUBER

LUST, EROTICISM AND AMBIGUITY

The work of Peter Paul Rubens is often described as passionate and sensual, and as being charged with eroticism. As the philosopher Konrad Paul Liessmann recently concluded, although eroticism is obviously related to lust, desire and sensuality, its foundations lie more in the tension between the sexes than in actual sexual gratification.[1] The Flemish master gave many of his themes an erotic charge that, centuries later, still prompts artists to engage with his work.

In Ingmar Bergman's movie *The Silence* (fig. 18), for instance, the camera repeatedly returns to Rubens's *Nessus and Deianeira* (fig. 19). This painting, which exists in a number of versions,[2] portrays a mythological scene described by Ovid in his *Metamorphoses* (IX.101–33) in which the lust-driven centaur Nessus abducts Hercules' wife Deianeira. After the helpless victim has been carried across a river, she cries out in alarm to her husband, who shoots the centaur with an arrow, averting the impending rape. In Rubens's painting, the centaur has already been mortally wounded, but this is not immediately obvious to the viewer, as the arrow has struck the shadowed right side of the centaur's body. And there is considerable ambiguity in the connection between Deianeira and her abductor. She appears to be climbing up onto the centaur's back rather than down from it and away from Nessus's hand. There are echoes here of classical and Renaissance statues, but this does not in itself explain why Rubens selected such a pose.[3] Deianeira, to judge by her appearance, is neither terrified nor seeking help. In the centre of the painting the two figures are entangled in a single piece of

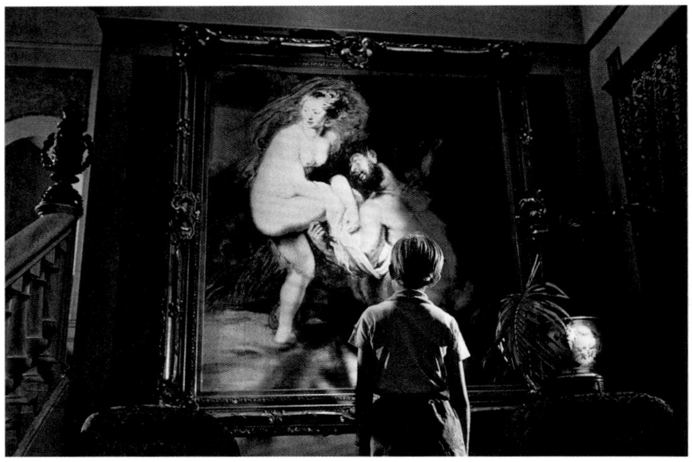

FIG. 18 Still from Ingmar Bergman's *The Silence* (1963)

white drapery, further emphasizing their physical closeness. Bergman also noted this ambiguity. His movie script offers a description of the painting: 'a fat, entirely naked lady, fighting with a man in hairy fur pants and with hooves in lieu of feet. The lady is very pink, and the dark brown man is covered with hair. On closer inspection the lady, to judge from her stupid smile, doesn't seem altogether displeased by his attentions.'[4]

Bergman uses the painting as a prelude to the increasing – also erotic – tensions between his own protagonists. His commentary, despite its refreshingly non-art-historical approach and complete disregard for the mythological background, illustrates the same point as this essay aims to make, namely that Rubens's ideals of beauty can be difficult to follow and are not always straightforward to read. The differentiated depiction of skin and skin tones clearly has an important part to play in the impact of this work. The skin of the female figure is a warm pink, a considerable contrast to the skin of her abductor and would-be rapist, which is dark brown and hirsute. And yet, on closer inspection, a much more complex and ambiguous narrative emerges, which attaches tension and excitement to this composition.

In what follows, we will explore the three aspects that have determined the reception of Rubens's paintings: his ideal of beauty, his depiction of skin, and the ambiguous nature of many of his compositions. This is, of course, not to relegate the complexity and virtuosity of his paintings, which have provided centuries of artists with a wide range of different points of departure for their own work and sources of inspiration. His tipsy, fleshy figures of Bacchus for example are so filled with life that to this day they shape our image of the sensuous revelries of the classical god of wine. In Lovis Corinth's *The Homecoming After the Bacchanalia* (fig. 20), for instance, there are still very clear traces of Rubens's *Drunken Silenus* (*c.* 1618–25; Alte Pinakothek, Munich); Corinth has mirrored the Silenus of Rubens, though he has also changed the mythic figure to suit his own visual language. Corinth takes away the drunken elegance: his Silenus stands with both feet on the ground, needing no support. Indeed, Silenus himself supports two drunken maenads, groping the breast of the figure to his left. Silenus' belly is here depicted as even larger than in Rubens's rendering and the emotion of the protagonists heavily overstated. The grotesqueness of drunkenness is paraded relentlessly before our eyes. Corinth thus both adapts the earlier image, and casts it in an ironic light.

Eroticism is hard to define; not only is it subjective, but it is also coloured by history, society and gender. Jan Białostocki, for instance, wrote about eroticism in Rubens's paintings, focusing above all on what we would nowadays describe as voyeurism (see pages 150–63), yet he denied any sensual sexuality in Titian's nudes, despite these being a source of inspiration for the erotic compositions of Rubens.[5]

Ovid comes to mind again, if we want to explore notions of eroticism in relationships between men and women in

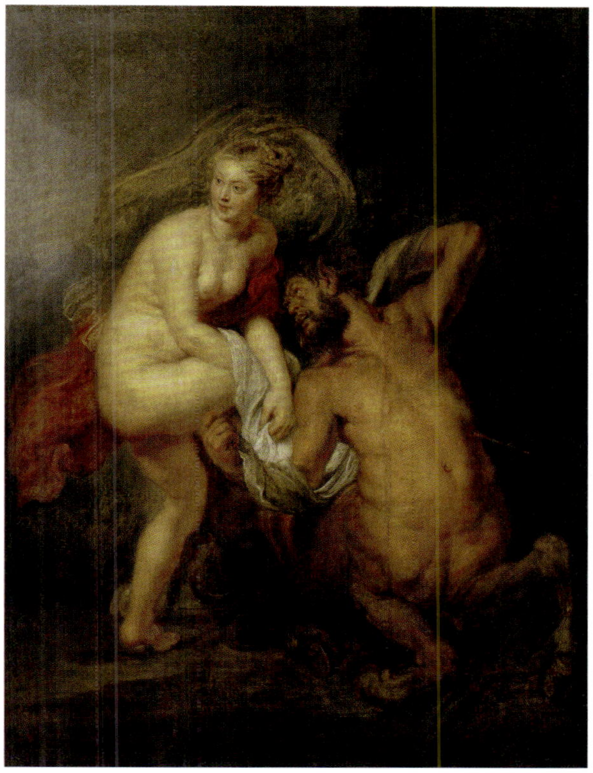

FIG. 19 Peter Paul Rubens and workshop, *Nessus and Deianeira*, *c.* 1630. Oil on canvas transferred to panel, 82 x 63.5 cm. State Hermitage Museum, St Petersburg

Rubens's day. In the poet's influential *The Art of Love*, an extended didactic elegy on love that was well known in the seventeenth century, the man takes on a highly active, dominant role – often to the point of aggression – while the woman is passive or even dismissive, although she secretly wishes to succumb. The ensuing potential for an eroticism tending towards violence in Rubens's painting has already been explored in some detail by scholars.[6] Besides the voyeuristic nature of the subjects in some of his paintings, contrasting depictions of sexuality have also been investigated,[7] as have many different kinds of love.[8] Particular importance is attached to the naked or only partially clad human body in erotic compositions; however, during the Baroque era male and female nudes were viewed very differently: it was above all the female figure that was imbued with an erotic charge, whereas male nudes were traditionally depicted as elevated, heroic figures.[9]

The erotic compositions of Rubens's time drew predominantly on mythological, literary and, to a lesser extent, biblical sources. Rubens had access to an especially rich repertoire of themes.[10] During his time in Italy he studied classical art and paintings from the Italian Renaissance by artists such as Raphael, Michelangelo, Giulio Romano and Titian, but also paintings by his contemporaries, such as Caravaggio and the Carracci brothers. This rich treasure trove of visual sources also included lascivious prints, as is evident from a drawing in the Rubens *cantoor* (a piece of furniture in which valuable papers and documents were kept; the term is sometimes used to refer to the private room where the *cantoor* stood).[11] Most of these *cantoor* drawings we know through copies by Willem Panneels, a member of Rubens's workshop who ran the studio in the master's absence; although it has been suggested that Rubens himself is the creator of this specific drawing.[12] The copy was made after a print of *Lot and His Daughters*, by Agostino Carracci, which was itself part of the so-called *Lascivie*. This series of prints with mythological and biblical subjects was made before 1595, and its erotic content was so unabashed that Pope

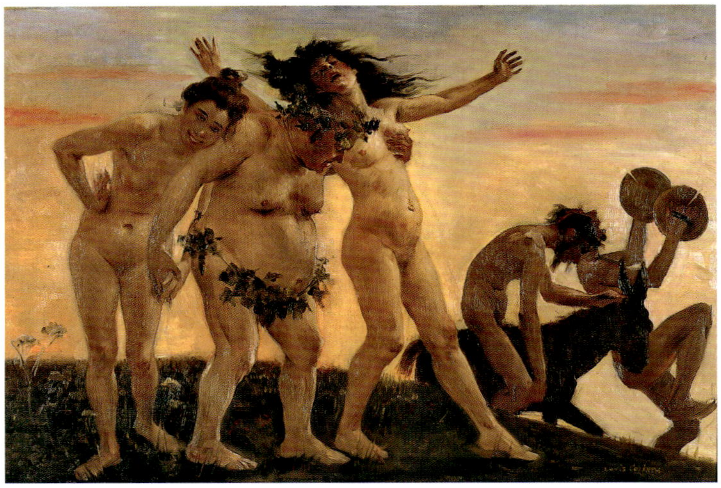

FIG. 20 Lovis Corinth, *The Homecoming After the Bacchanalia*, 1898. Oil on canvas, 60.5 x 90.5 cm. Von der Heydt-Museum, Wuppertal

Clement VIII specifically rebuked Carracci.[13] However, there are no such blatant depictions in compositions by Rubens, who almost always managed to conceal his protagonists' private parts; he was more than able to create erotic tension by other means. Rubens possessed the ability to portray the various emotions and states of mind of the figures in his compositions; he could also surprise the viewer with unusual details in their gestures and facial expressions, or by portraying them from an unexpected perspective.[14] One of his strategies was to create a sense of ambiguity – as in *Nessus and Deianeira* – in the nature of the relationship between his protagonists, which in turn greatly heightens the tension within their interaction.

BEAUTY, SKIN AND AMBIGUITY

Let us turn first, however, to Rubens's attitude to female beauty, which – as we saw earlier – Bergman in effect ridiculed. No other artist has depicted women as characteristically, or as famously, as Rubens. His preferred female body type has become a legend in its own right and to this day any reference to these figures calls to mind a powerful, voluptuous form: the Polish poet and Nobel Prize winner Wisława Szymborska has described them in one of her poems as examples of 'pumped-up corpulence'.[15]

The female nude has traditionally been regarded as the essence of an artist's work and the practice of judging an artist's overall qualities by his depictions of nudes goes back to antiquity. Rubens's contemporary René Descartes, for instance, regarded the female nude as the epitome of beauty, truth and virtue,[16] and several clients and customers explicitly asked for female figures in their paintings.[17] Cardinal-Infante Ferdinand of Spain, who complained in a letter to the Spanish King that the three goddesses in Rubens's *Judgement of Paris* of 1639 (now in the Prado, Madrid) were excessively naked, also added that the figure of Venus was a portrait of Rubens's own wife, who was the most beautiful woman in Flanders.[18] Rubens's female figures reflected the ideals of beauty of the time.

The figures in Rubens's paintings have a heightened, very immediate presence, which reinforces the narrative and conveys their various emotions all the more effectively. The viewer is drawn into the composition by the use of light and shade, by the figures' sheer physicality, by the brilliance of the colours, the pathos of certain gestures and the concentration of the narrative – all of which allow viewers to lose sense of any distance between themselves and the painting.[19] In the case of certain erotic subjects, viewers may even find themselves cast in the role of voyeur (cat. 66, for example).

Yet the vitality of these works may be only one of the reasons why some viewers, over the centuries, have reacted so emotionally and sometimes highly negatively to these paintings. Generally, those who have rejected Rubens's ideals of beauty have been (consciously or not) proponents of classicist art theory. The German archaeologist and art theorist Johann Joachim Winckelmann argued that Rubens had no sense of beauty or grace. In 1768 he wrote to Johann Karl Philipp, Count von Cobenzl (the Minister of State to Charles, Prince of Lorraine and Habsburg Governor of the Austrian Netherlands): 'I have come to the conclusion that Rubens is the glory of art, of his school, of his century and of all centuries to come; that one has to admire the fecundity of his imagination; that his draughtsmanship is flawless; that his draperies are magnificent, and that his work must surely be the great model for chiaroscuro, insofar as there is such an ideal; but it does seem to me that he has not paid due homage to the goddesses of beauty ... and the Graces.'[20]

Cobenzl answered with a reference to the strength of Rubens's use of colour and his compositions, adding that one could only properly become acquainted with his work in the Netherlands. Cobenzl concedes that it may be a mistake to portray such weighty female figures, but feels that Rubens can be excused because Flanders is a region 'where the fair sex is generally well nourished'.[21] Thus Rubens's portrayal of women comes to be regarded as typical for Flanders as a whole. In 1760 the French sculptor Etienne-Maurice Falconet had already made reference to 'some women painted by Rubens, who, despite their incorrect and Flemish appearance, will always seduce the viewer by the charm of their colouration'.[22]

As a consequence of such criticism as Winckelmann's, Rubens's women have repeatedly been described as 'fleshy'.[23] The German naturalist and travel writer Georg Forster commented on the women he had seen in paintings by Rubens on his trip to the Netherlands with Alexander von Humboldt in 1790. He described them as 'mountains of flesh ... inexpressibly repulsive'.[24] Negative descriptions of this kind, which were sometimes extended to include the character of the women too, continued until well into the twentieth century – witness Ingmar Bergman's reference to Deianeira's 'stupid smile'.[25]

However, Rubens himself could easily have referred to classical antiquity to justify the opulence of his female figures: Quintilian cited Homer, who was said to have preferred stronger female figures. He also reported that Zeuxis, one of the most

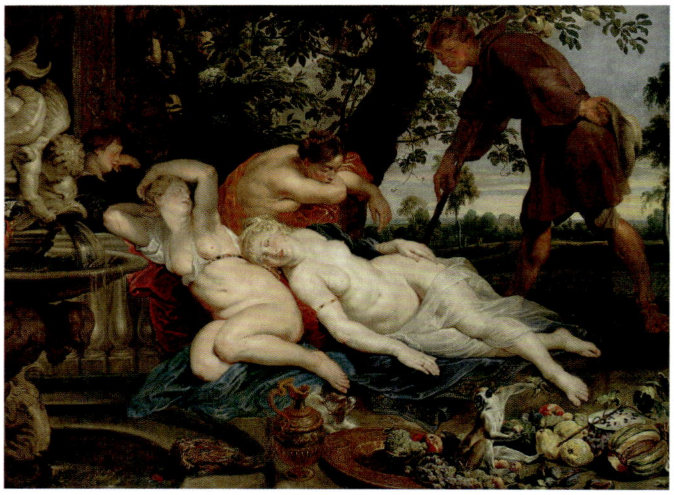

FIG. 21 Peter Paul Rubens, *Cimon and Iphigenia*, *c.* 1617. Oil on canvas, 208 x 282 cm. Kunsthistorisches Museum, Vienna

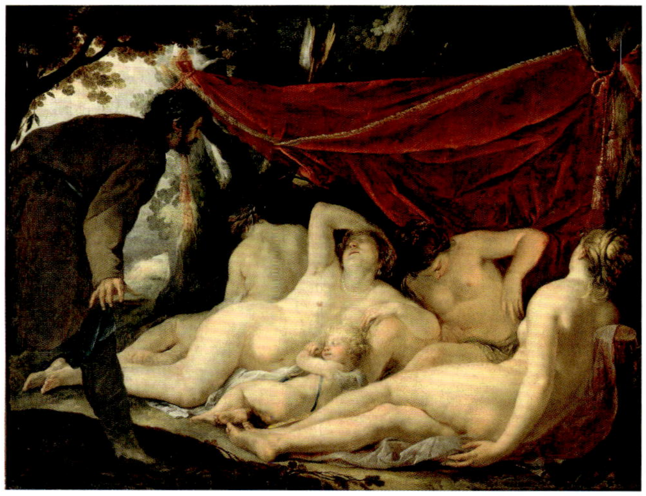

FIG. 22 Jacques Blanchard, *Venus and the Graces Surprised by a Mortal*, *c.* 1631–33. Oil on canvas, 170 x 218 cm. Musée du Louvre, Paris

renowned painters in antiquity, gave his figures fuller forms in order to make them appear more dignified and noble.[26]

The special effect of so many of the figures in Rubens's paintings is fundamentally due to his astonishing depiction of skin, which Bergman also instinctively alluded to in the lines cited at the beginning of this essay.[27] In his *Cimon and Iphigenia* (fig. 21), Rubens uses the skin tones of his protagonists to express a particular hierarchy.[28] The story of Cimon is the first novella told on the fifth day in *The Decameron*, Boccaccio's fourteenth-century *opus*. Reluctant to engage in education and thus living like a coarse peasant despite coming from a noble family, Cimon falls in love with the sleeping Iphigenia and henceforth resolves to fundamentally change his life. Iphigenia's body glows most brightly, it stands out against the naked bodies of her serving maids and almost clamours for the viewer's attention. In Boccaccio's account, Iphigenia, when she awakes, is initially anxious at the sight of the 'wild' (that is to say, uneducated) figure of Cimon. In Rubens's depiction of the same moment, however, her eyes are slightly open, her head is turned towards the viewer, and from the corner of one eye she is secretly able to glimpse Cimon, who is lost in wonder at the sight of her. Since Iphigenia does not move her head, Cimon is not aware that he is being observed. In that sense, Iphigenia's glance is just as voyeuristic as Cimon's gaze. Moreover, the position of Iphigenia's upper body – which seems to be turning towards Cimon, implying that she will submit to his advances – creates an ambiguity that noticeably reinforces the erotic tension between the two main figures.

Rubens's portrayals of sleeping female nudes draw on an Italian tradition going all the way back to the woodcuts illustrating the very popular *Hypnerotomachia Poliphili* of 1499, which started a practice that was taken up and developed by Giorgione and Titian. The Flemish master breathed new life into this tradition by lovingly depicting every curve and rounded outline in his female figures and imbuing them with a heightened presence in the process. The virtuoso technique that he used to paint these figures – applying transparent glazes and semi-opaque scumbles over an *imprimatura* – gives their skin a mother-of-pearl sheen, but also makes them appear more voluminous than Titian's figures and more striking visually.[29] In Rubens's own time they were already regarded as particularly sensuous, almost physically tangible. Skin represented by Rubens suggests warmth, smoothness and softness, all naturally regarded as erotic qualities by his own contemporaries.[30] It was also admired by artists who sought to replicate it in their own compositions: 'Watteau', wrote Friedrich Bayl, 'clad his curvaceous Gothic figures with finely tapered limbs and gently swelling bodies in the shimmering skin of Rubens's women.'[31] Something very similar could be said of the paintings of Boucher or Renoir, to name but two, even if they were pursuing very different ideals of beauty.

It is as though a large number of French painters discovered the achievements of the Cinquecento in Venice mostly through Rubens's eyes. In Jacques Blanchard's *Venus and the Graces Surprised by a Mortal* (fig. 22) the figure of the Grace on the right, seen from behind, seems to be a paraphrase of Rubens's Iphigenia, while the pose of the mortal, bent forwards as he gazes transfixed at these examples of female beauty, is not unrelated to that of Cimon. One is left wondering if Blanchard could already have known Rubens's *Cimon and Iphigenia* in the early 1630s.[32] When Rubens's painting was sold to the 1st Duke of Buckingham in either 1626 or 1627, Blanchard was in Venice, far away from Flanders. Although the smoothness and colouration of the skin in Blanchard's painting are more reminiscent of works by his contemporary Simon Vouet, it is hard to imagine *Venus and the Graces Surprised by a Mortal* coming about without the influence of Rubens, both in regard to its overall composition and in the deep, glowing red of the drapery in the trees.

In the second half of the seventeenth century the early art critic Roger de Piles published a number of texts in which he cited Rubens as the perfect artist and thus fuelled intense interest in the work of the Flemish master.[33] The ensuing

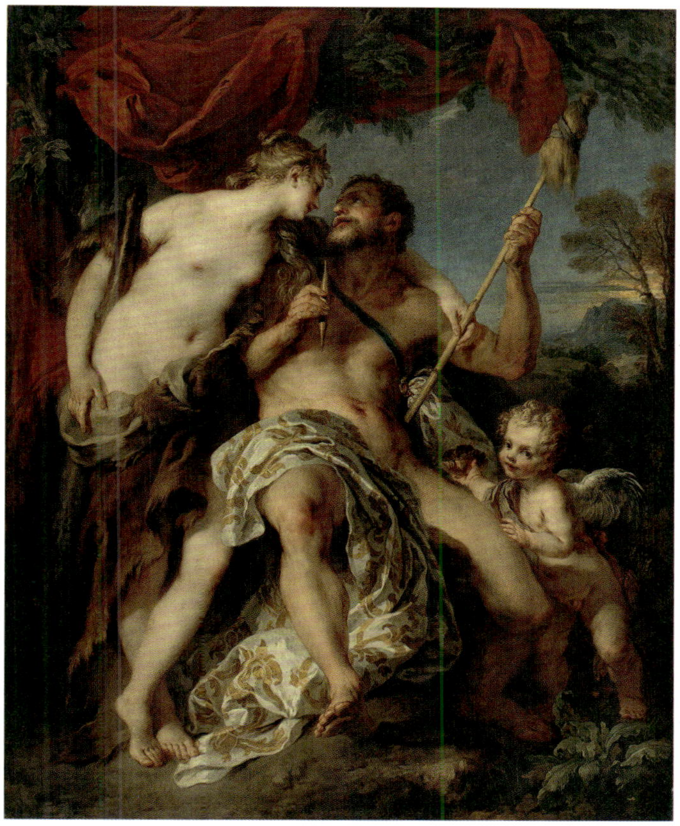

FIG. 23 François Lemoyne, *Hercules and Omphale*, 1724. Oil on canvas, 184 x 149 cm. Musée du Louvre, Paris

debate between Rubenists and Poussinists – simply put, between the primacy of colour or line – raged for some time. Charles-Antoine Coypel, for instance, who was famous for his history paintings, reported that his father Antoine had been criticised by his contemporaries because his paintings too obviously reflected their maker's boundless admiration for Rubens's use of colour, and so did not look entirely natural.[34] By the eighteenth century, artists already felt less inhibited about openly enjoying the sensuality of Rubens's handling of colour. François Lemoyne's *Hercules and Omphale* of 1724 (fig. 23) is clearly influenced both in its composition and distribution of light by the work of Rubens. The standing figure of Omphale is reminiscent of figures in Rubens's own depiction of *Hercules and Omphale* (*c.* 1606; Musée du Louvre, Paris) and also in his *The Return from War: Mars Disarmed by Venus* (*c.* 1610–12; J. Paul Getty Museum, Los Angeles). The colours in Lemoyne's composition are also clearly inspired by Rubens and contribute significantly to the erotic tension between the two figures.

But let us return to Ingmar Bergman's comment, that on closer inspection one no longer sees what one might have expected. A fine example of this is Rubens's portrait of Hélène Fourment, his second, and very young, wife (fig. 24). He called the work *Het Pelsken* ('the little fur') in his will and expressly left it to his widow. This stipulation would at least partly explain both how he dared to portray his own wife as a life-sized nude and how Hélène could allow herself to be painted in this pose: the painting was obviously created for private use. Although there is no mention of this painting between 1658, when it appears in Hélène's own will, and 1730, when it is listed in the imperial collection at Vienna, it is clear that the identity of the model was known, because it is already described in 1730 as a portrait of Rubens's wife.[35] From time to time, however, there does appear to have been some unease at the fact that this was a life-sized portrait of the naked figure of Hélène. In 1783, when the Swiss engraver and art dealer Christian von Mechel was reorganising the imperial gallery at Belvedere, he described the painting as 'a derobed woman, with a brown fur coat thrown lightly around her. The head is known to be a portrait of Hélène Formann, Rubens's second wife. Whole figure, life-size.'[36]

Mechel reduced the portrait to the head alone. Evidently he could not believe that a respected townswoman would have allowed herself to be depicted in this way, whereas Rubens's own contemporaries, such as the Cardinal-Infante, were much less troubled by the idea, as we have already seen. Later on, however, Mechel's successor and rival, the painter Joseph Roos, imagined how the painting might have come about, and thus influenced the reception of this portrait for the whole of the nineteenth century: 'She appears to be coming from her bath, clad only in a fur. In full life-size, on wood; in view of the skin tone and the brushwork it is on a par with any Titian.'[37]

Roos rightly identified the connection with Titian, whose *Girl in a Fur Coat* (*c.* 1535; Kunsthistorisches Museum, Vienna) is another example of the sensuous interaction of skin and fur, and was already present in the imperial gallery. However, he completely missed any other possible interpretations. It was not until the twentieth century that the complexity of this originally very private portrait came to be recognised.[38] Even today, new aspects of the work are still coming to light. The portrait of Hélène has been examined with regard to the reception of classical art, with regard to cultural history and in terms of gender politics, to name but a few of the approaches taken – and she still has the capacity to polarise opinion.[39]

Like a classical statue of Venus, Hélène's arms are wrapped around her body. Yet she gazes directly on the beholder. And whereas the classical pose of a *Venus pudica* is slightly bent forwards, in order to conceal herself, Hélène does not try to hide her breasts like her classical forerunner; on the contrary, she raises them up in the act of holding the fur coat in position to hide her lower body. Rubens advised young artists to study classical statues and then to breathe life into these figures.[40] In his portrait of Hélène, he achieved this with extraordinary success. He was clearly at pains to portray the movements of the soft tissue in her body, for instance above the knees and in her midriff. Recently Andreas Thielemann has even described Rubens as 'ruthlessly' rendering 'the misshapen body parts of his young wife'; yet the notion of 'ruthlessness' is not quite appropriate.[41] Even if Rubens was clearly interested in portraying the voluptuousness of Hélène's figure, he does so with an unfailing sense of the beauty of human skin: it shimmers, it looks soft and warm. I would prefer to reserve the term 'ruthless' for descriptions of works such as Lucian Freud's monumental nude portraits of Sue Tilley or Leigh Bowery,

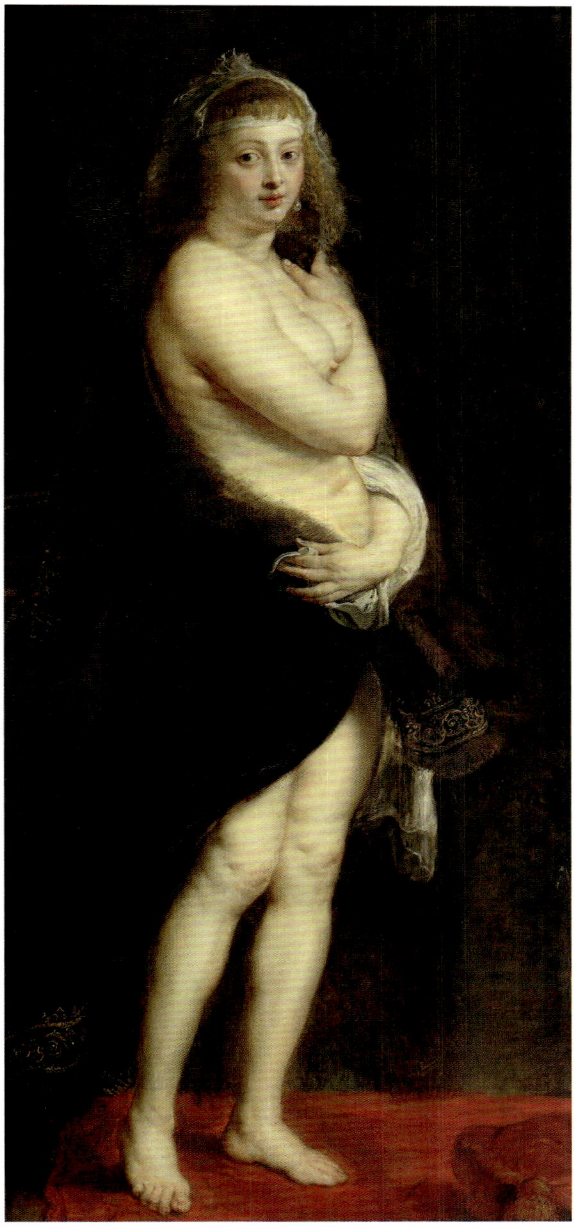

FIG. 24 Peter Paul Rubens, *Het Pelsken (The Little Fur) c.* 1638. Oil on panel, 176 x 83 cm. Kunsthistorisches Museum, Vienna

although Freud nevertheless also showed great respect for his models.[42] Despite using a completely different technique, Freud, like Rubens, wanted to use colour and paint to convey a sense of a real human being, stating: 'I want the paint to feel like flesh.'[43] Yet, whereas Freud's scrutiny of his sitters was always analytical and relatively cool, Rubens's renderings of his models always seem to allow for at least some degree of transfiguration.

Recently the erotic potential of the fur coat in the portrait of Hélène Fourment has been the subject of particular attention, furthermore the point has been made that the portrait contains various iconographic and artistic uncertainties.[44] It is not clear whether Hélène is on the point of completely covering herself up or of fully revealing herself to the beholder. It is this ambiguity that gives this painting its particular appeal. The various emotions that Rubens's protagonists are going through are often reflected in the appearance of their skin:[45] Hélène's cheeks are slightly rosy – it is up to the viewer to decide what the reason for this might be. And that is what Rubens toys with and conveys with such skill, which to this day makes his work so appealing and inspiring to artists and viewers alike.

53

PETER PAUL RUBENS (1577–1640)
Venus Frigida, 1614
Oil on panel, 145.1 x 185.6 cm
Inscription on the rock:
P.P.RVBENS.F.1.6.1.4.
Royal Museum of Fine Arts Antwerp, inv. 709

PROVENANCE: J. A. N. Peytier de Merchten, alderman of Antwerp; his widow, Am. M. T. Peeters; her daughter, G. Ch. J. de Knyff in 1791; her daughter Caroline de Knyff; bequeathed to Léonce de Knyff; sold on his death to Joseph Allard, Brussels; bought from whose heirs by the museum in 1881
SELECTED REFERENCES: Rooses 1886–92, vol. 2, no. 698, pp. 180–82; Burchard and d'Hulst 1963, vol. 1, pp. 105–6, no. 62; Dreier 1977, pp. 45–51; Renger 1981, pp. 115, 132; Cologne 2000, no. 23; Hamburg 2010, no. 10; Van Hout 2010, pp. 156–57; Westheider 2010, pp. 36–43; Heinen 2011, pp. 187–89

Venus crouches down on the ground, bending her beautiful body over in an effort to protect herself from the cold; Cupid sits curled up in front of her, also trying to ward off the chill air by making himself as small as possible. Venus has her back to the viewer, although her face is visible from the side as she rests her head on her right hand in a melancholy manner. Behind them Liber, portrayed as a satyr-like figure, holds a cornucopia filled with wheat, grapes and other items such as asparagus and artichokes, which were regarded in Rubens's day as aphrodisiacs. It is as though Liber, who is responsible for, among other things, the liberating effects of wine, is providing the means that will counteract the cold for Venus.

Rubens's painting (cat. 53) recalls a line by the Roman playwright Terence (*Eunuchus*, IV, v): 'sine Cerere et Libero friget Venus' ('without Ceres and Liber Venus grows cold') – love withers without food and drink. Erasmus elevated this line to the status of a proverb in his *Adagia* (1500), where he replaced Liber with the better-known god of wine, Bacchus.[1] The goddess is feeling the cold and is reacting very much in the manner of a mortal human being; in her pose and vulnerability she recalls depictions of the Old Testament figure of Susanna (cat. 66). Rubens took his inspiration for this image of the goddess of love from a classical statue of Venus crouching down as she bathes by Doidalsas of Bithynia (Royal Collection, on long term loan to the British Museum, London),[2] which in all likelihood he knew from his time in Mantua.

This painting was posthumously altered: the original vertical format, which concentrated attention solely on the group of figures, was extended to create a horizontal format showing more of the landscape around the group.

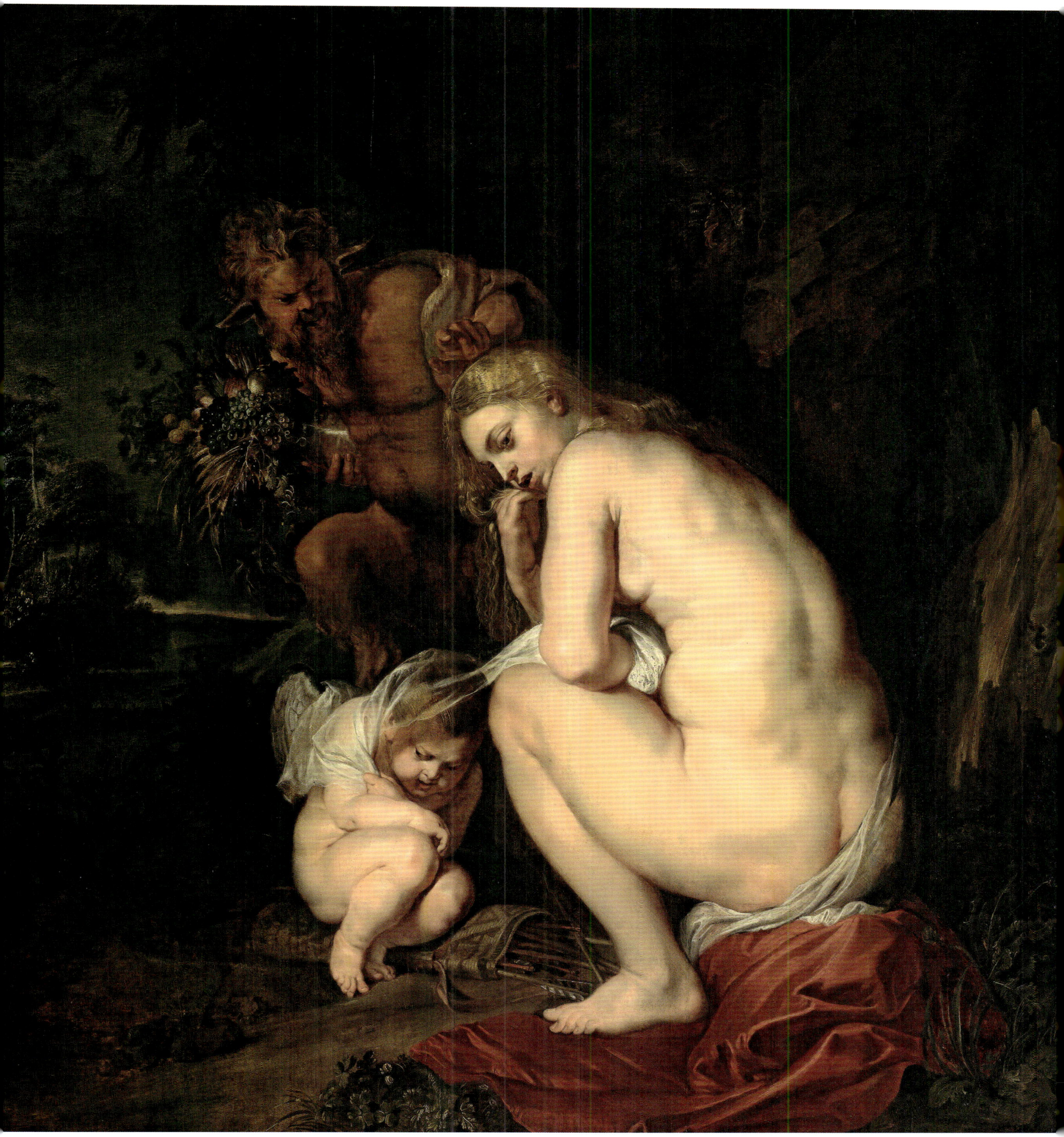

54

PETER PAUL RUBENS (1577–1640)
and workshop
Fortuna, 1636–37
Oil on canvas, 182.3 x 100.5 cm
Museo Nacional del Prado, Madrid, inv. P01674

PROVENANCE: Spanish royal collection (Torre de la Parada, El Pardo, Madrid, first floor, 1747, no. 19; Museo Nacional del Prado, Madrid, Academia, Sala Reservada, 1827, no. 68)
SELECTED REFERENCES: Rooses 1886–92, vol. 3, p. 18, no. 522; Panofsky 1966, pp. 309, 322; Alpers 1971, no. 23; Bonn 1999, no. 11

This painting (cat. 54) is dominated by the nude female figure who fills one diagonal of the composition almost entirely. With her right foot on an orb and both hands clasping a piece of grey fabric that billows out behind her like a sail, she appears almost to be running across the surface of the waves. Her pink stole enhances the mother-of-pearl gleam of her skin. While the sky to the left is streaked with the rosy light of approaching dawn or its afterglow, the sky and the sea to the right are in the grip of a raging storm.

The goddess was long taken to be Venus because the inventory compiled in 1700 of the Torre de la Parada, the royal hunting lodge near Madrid, records the painting as having been hung in immediate proximity to Vulcan, the husband of Venus – both figures are part of the decorative scheme created by Rubens for the Torre. However, the unstable orb beneath her feet clearly indicates that this is the goddess Fortuna.

Rubens created the painting with the help of assistants in his workshop; it is a reworking of an image from Alciato's *Emblemata* of 1600,[1] to which his attention was drawn by prints by artists such as Jan Harmensz. Muller.[2] Muller also depicted a female figure, on an orb, with a billowing sail; to the right a storm is developing while everything to the left is safe and calm. Characteristically Rubens concentrates in his version on the very sensual figure of the goddess, whose insecure footing draws less attention than the dynamic physicality of her movements. This dynamism is matched by the energetic brushwork of the menacing right-hand side of the painting.

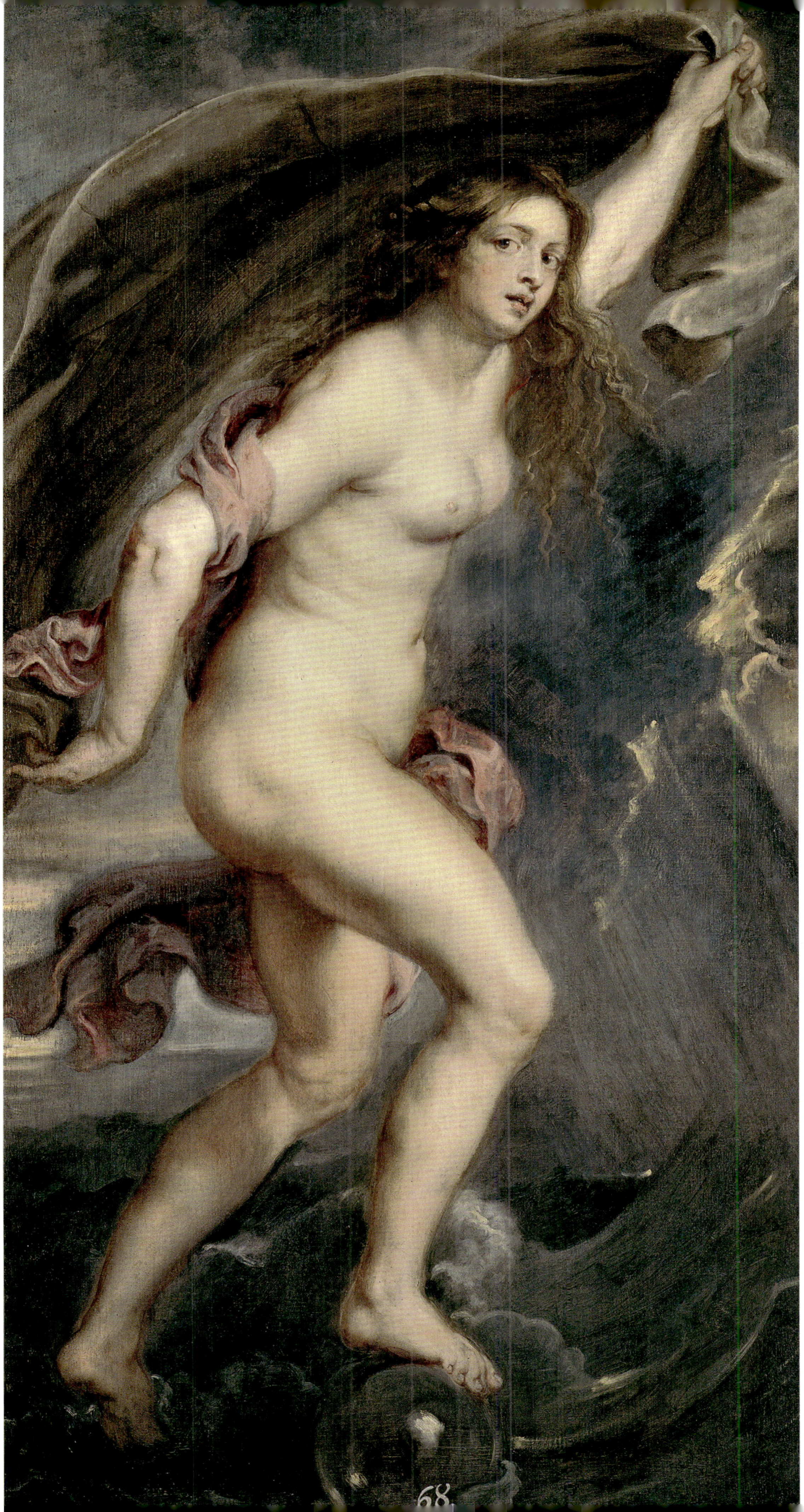
68

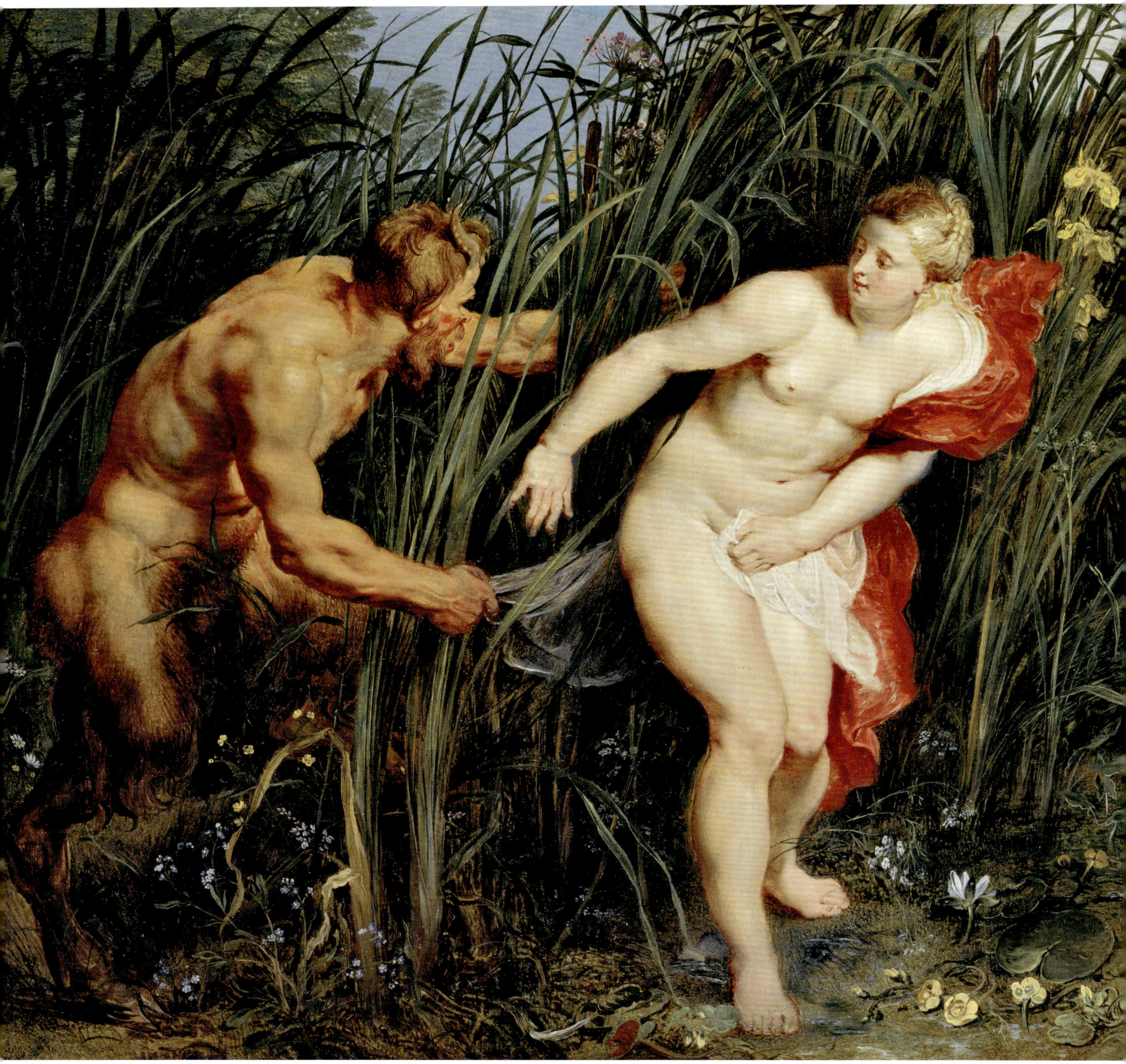

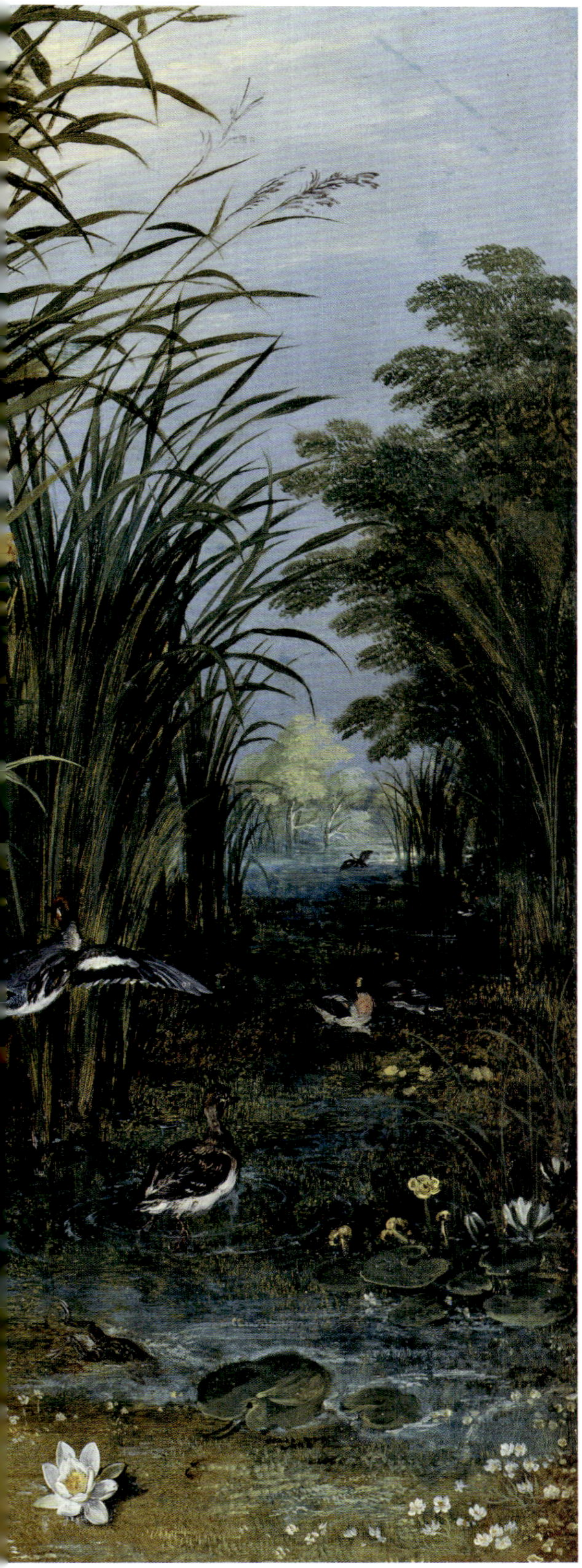

In Ovid's *Metamorphoses* (I.689–711) Mercury tells the story of the god Pan and the nymph Syrinx, a handmaiden to the virgin goddess Diana. While trying to escape the attentions of Pan, Syrinx found herself at the edge of the River Ladon and begged her sisters in the river to help her. They came to her aid by turning her into a reed just as Pan, thinking he had triumphed, reached out to grasp her. On hearing the tenderly plaintive sound of the wind in the reeds, he joined together unequal lengths of reed with wax and thus created the first pan pipes, or syrinx.

The figures in this exquisite cabinet painting (cat. 55) were painted by Rubens and the luxuriant, detailed landscape by Jan Brueghel the Elder. Rubens took inspiration for his virginal Syrinx from the classical pose of the *Venus pudica*, albeit re-creating her in a much more animated posture; after all, the figures here are seen in the last moments of the pursuit.[1] Syrinx, leaning forwards, does not use her right hand to conceal her breasts, as in many variations of the *Venus pudica*, but to ward off Pan, trying to keep him away from her – despite the fact that he is already grasping her drapery. However, her distinctive pose is somewhat at odds with her facial expression, which shows no fear or desperation and thus introduces an element of ambiguity into the scene. Pan, half-man and half-goat, was always portrayed as a particularly lustful nature-god, and Rubens subtly underlines the earthiness of his character by matching the colour of his animal hindquarters to the brown of the ground on which he stands. Syrinx, on the other hand, stands out very clearly against the background.

The flowering plants that are dotted around the protagonists seem to provide an additional commentary on the events

55

PETER PAUL RUBENS (1577–1640) and **JAN BRUEGHEL THE ELDER (1568–1625)**
Pan and Syrinx, *c.* 1617
Oil on panel, 40 x 61 cm
Museumslandschaft Hessen Kassel,
inv. GK 1229

PROVENANCE: sold 1626/27 by Jan Breughel the Younger (?); Suzanna Doublet-Huygens sale, The Hague, 6 November 1725, lot 35; Adriaan Bout sale, The Hague, 11 August 1733, lot 39; Hendrick van Heteren collection, The Hague; acquired by Wilhelm VIII of Hessen-Kassel, 1747; in 1813 taken to Paris by Jérôme Bonaparte, King of Westphalia, 1807–13; Musée Napoléon, Paris, 1814; Alphonse Giroux sale, Paris, 11–12 February 1851, lot 159; F. Kleinberger (art dealer), Paris, *c.* 1930; private collection, London, *c.* 1934; Sotheby's, London, 14 June 1961, lot 36 (from the collection of Mrs R. Makower); Waddingham; Liechtenstein, Fostcria Collection; Christie's, London, 23 June 1965, lot 31; Christie's, London, 23 March 1973, lot 27; Sotheby's, London, 12 July 2001, lot 29; Bremen, Galerie Neuse; acquired 2002
SELECTED REFERENCES: Rooses 1886–92, vol. 3, pp. 138–39, no. 660; Ertz 1979, pp. 417–18, no. 384; Kassel 2004, no. 18; Lange 2004, pp. 41–58; Van Mulders 2004, pp. 73–77; Vander Auwera 2004, p. 81; Los Angeles 2006, no. 5; Jakumeit-Pietschmann 2010, pp. 142–63; Ertz 2008–10, vol. 2, no. 386; Brussels 2012, no. 33

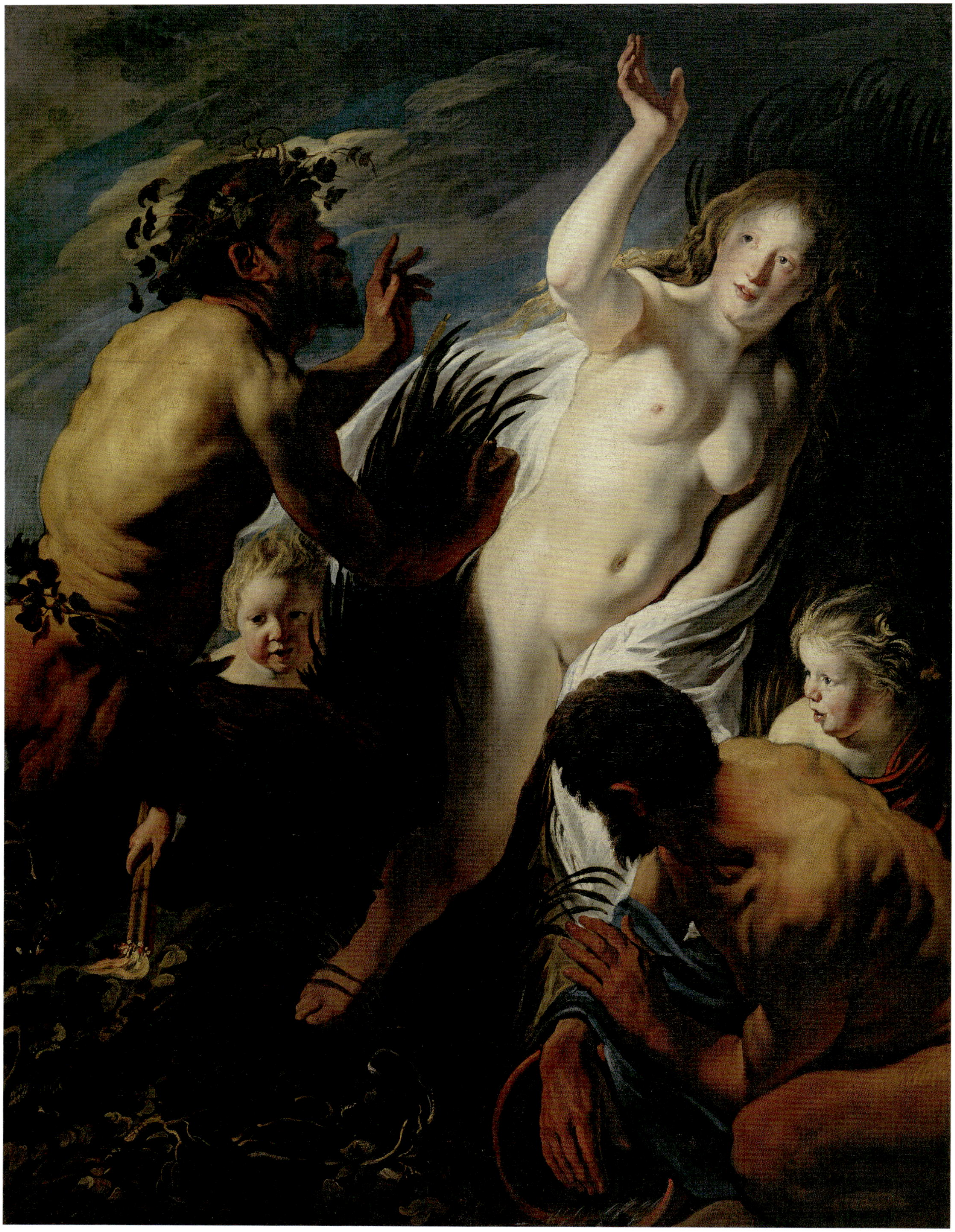

that are unfolding. Close to Syrinx there is a tall yellow iris, traditionally associated with the chaste modesty of the Virgin Mary; immediately in front of Pan there is a forget-me-not, anticipating the lasting impression that will be left by the nymph. Every time the faun plays his pan pipes, he will remember Syrinx.[2]

Jacob Jordaens's version of the theme (cat. 56) was presumably intended at least to rival the painting by Rubens,[3] although Jordaens's figures are not full length and his composition also includes the figure of the river god Ladon crouching in front of Syrinx. The god Pan, with his caprine legs, is shown with an erection, and Jordaens draws attention to this by directing towards it the gaze of both cupids and the river god.[4]

This scene has allusions to two notable emblems: the down-turned torch in one cupid's hand can be read as a reference to the adage 'Quod nutrit, extinguit', illustrated in Otto van Veen's polyglot *Amorum Emblemata* of 1608, which included an English translation, 'Loue killed by his owne nouriture':

The torche is by the wax
maintayned whyle it burnes,
But turned vpsyde-down it straight
goes out & dyes,
Right so by Cupids heat the louer
lyues lykewyse,
But thereby is hee kild,
when it contrarie turnes.[5]

Meanwhile, the cool, marble-smooth body of Syrinx might be read as an allusion to 'Frigida accendit', a motto illustrated in the emblem book of 1594 by Scipione Bargagli, which suggests that it is precisely the coldness of the *innamorata* that can kindle the flames of love.[6]

56

JACOB JORDAENS (1593–1678)
Pan and Syrinx, *c.* 1620
Oil on canvas, 173 x 136 cm
Musées royaux des Beaux-Arts de Belgique, Brussels, inv. 3292

PROVENANCE: J. St Hensé (art dealer), London; acquired 1895
SELECTED REFERENCES: Rooses 1906, pp. 48–49, p. 53; d'Hulst 1982, pp. 106, 111, no. 60; Antwerp 1993, no. A18; Kassel 2004, no. 20; Jakumeit-Pietschmann 2010, pp. 142–63; Brussels 2012, no. 32

It was Rubens who decisively shaped our image of Silenus, foster-father and mentor to Bacchus (Ovid, *Metamorphoses*, XI.99), by repeatedly casting him as the hero of his large-format paintings.[1] Rubens's own image of Silenus was informed by a classical marble statue (now in the Staatliche Skulpturensammlung, Dresden) that he studied in Italy and drew from a number of different angles.[2] In these drawings Silenus has a relatively muscular upper body. In his paintings and engravings Rubens creates a more realistic character – livelier than the marble figure but also weightier. With a bald crown, a full beard and a snub nose, Rubens's Silenus appears always old, corpulent and inebriated. His features would have called to mind the images that people had of Socrates in Rubens's day (Plato, *Symposium*, 215B–216C),[3] with the result that Silenus would also, by association, be credited with philosophical wisdom. In addition to this, Rubens is known to have had in his possession an antique intaglio (engraved gem) representing 'Socrates in the figure of Silenus'.[4] As he did so often, Rubens here merges an array of classical allusions in a composition of his own invention.

Christoffel Jegher's woodcut (cat. 57) is after a composition especially created for this purpose by Rubens.[5] Silenus, rather unsteady on his feet, is supported by a satyr and a faun. However, the perspective, looking slightly upwards towards the figure, gives him a certain dignity and points to his stoic intentions: widely recognised as a sage, Silenus takes advantage of the intoxicating properties of wine as an opportunity for rumination and meditation.[6]

The *Drunken Silenus Supported by Satyrs* (cat. 58) from Rubens's workshop – and in all probability painted by Van Dyck – portrays Bacchus' mentor in all his bodily splendour and gives a sense of why Rubens's portrayals of Silenus were so successful: although he is somewhat stouter than his classical forebear and his musculature is no longer identifiable under the layers of fat, his skin has a gleam that gives it a certain beauty, even if this may not always have been appreciated because of the opulent plumpness of his figure. Alpers has suggested that Silenus' skin in paintings by Rubens is, disturbingly, more like that of a mature woman.[7] As it happens, Rubens himself comments in his treatise on the human body (of which only copies survive) that the musculature should not be apparent in female figures.[8] Yet in Silenus case, this may simply be the outcome of the artist's desire to achieve a natural, lifelike effect: layers of fat make it impossible to see any muscles.

A similarly ambiguous indication of female or effeminate attributes is present in the *March of Silenus* (cat. 59)[9] by Jean-Antoine Watteau.[10] It is possible that the artist was influenced by the painting of Silenus (now attributed to Van Dyck) in the collection of the Duke of Orléans (1674–1723) at the time. However, Watteau treats his source of inspiration with considerable freedom. His Silenus, without a beard, appears younger; the figure supporting him from behind is grasping his chest rather than his fleshy midriff, and the accompanying bacchantes are grouped very differently around him. There also seems to be a greater air of merriment and abandon than in the London painting. Watteau repeatedly returned to the work of Rubens, studying not only his paintings – above all the Médicis cycle, which was in the Palais du Luxembourg at the time (see cat. 34) – but also his drawings, which he was able to consult in the large collection of the connoisseur Pierre Crozat (1661–1740).

57

CHRISTOFFEL JEGHER (1596–1652/53)
Drunken Silenus, *c.* 1635
Woodcut, 44.3 x 33.8 cm
Royal Museum of Fine Arts Antwerp, inv. 1138

PROVENANCE: the collection of Max Rooses, donated to the museum in 1900
SELECTED REFERENCES: Hollstein 1949–2010, vol. 9, p. 188; Renger 1975, pp. 177–78; Braunschweig 2004, no. 9; Van Hout 2004, pp. 96–98

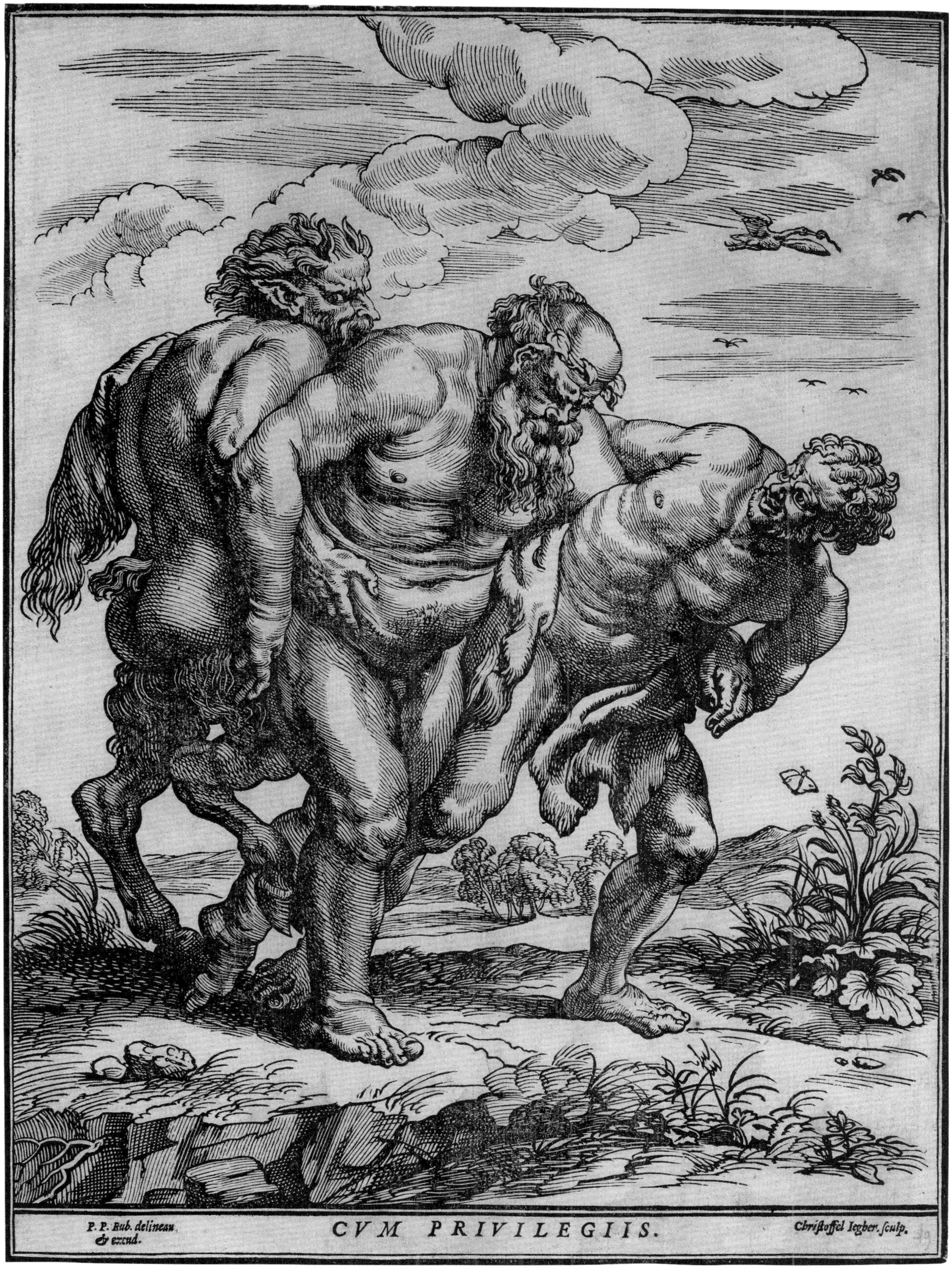
P. P. Rub. delineau.
& excud.
CVM PRIVILEGIIS.
Christoffel Iegher. sculp.

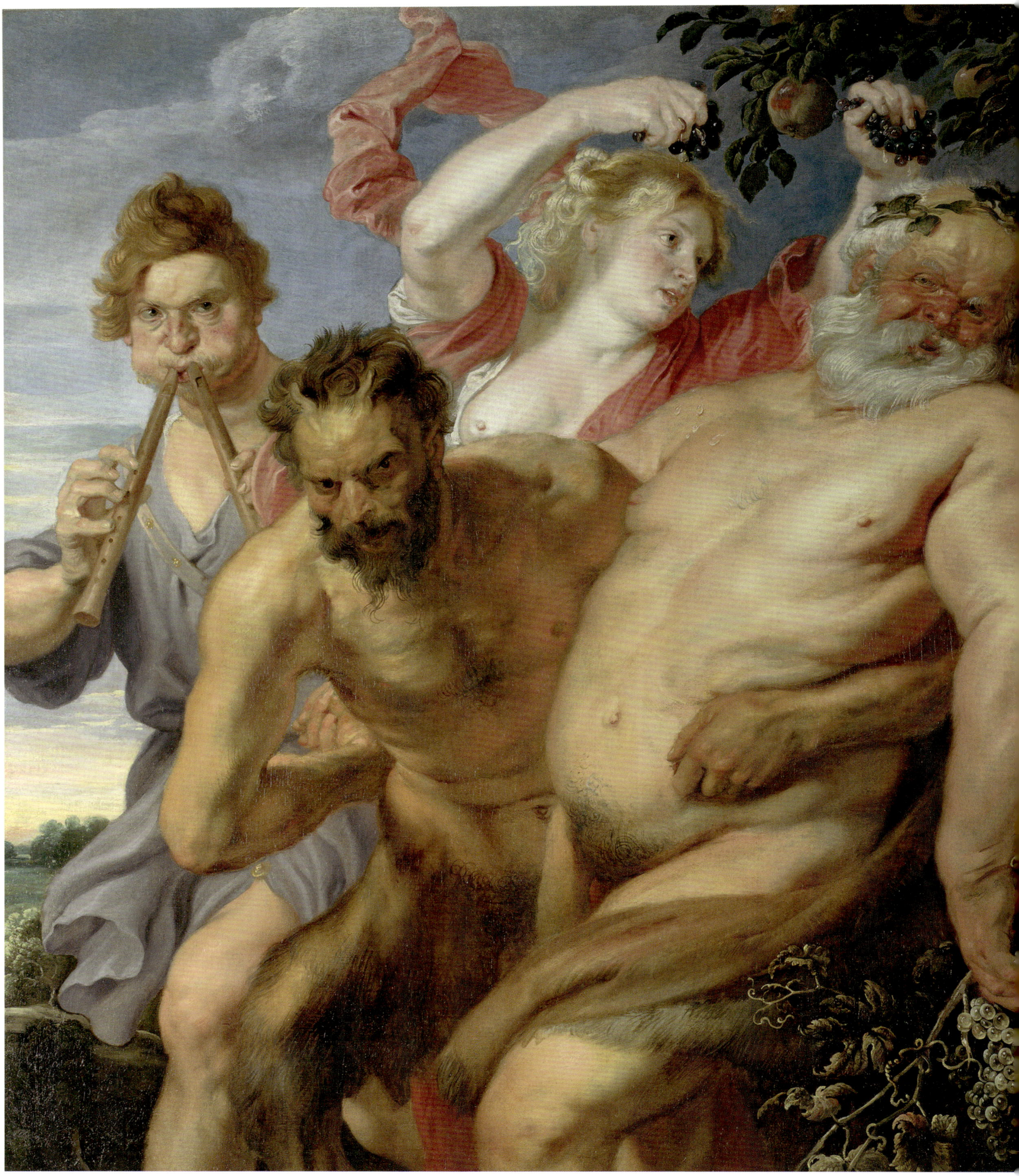

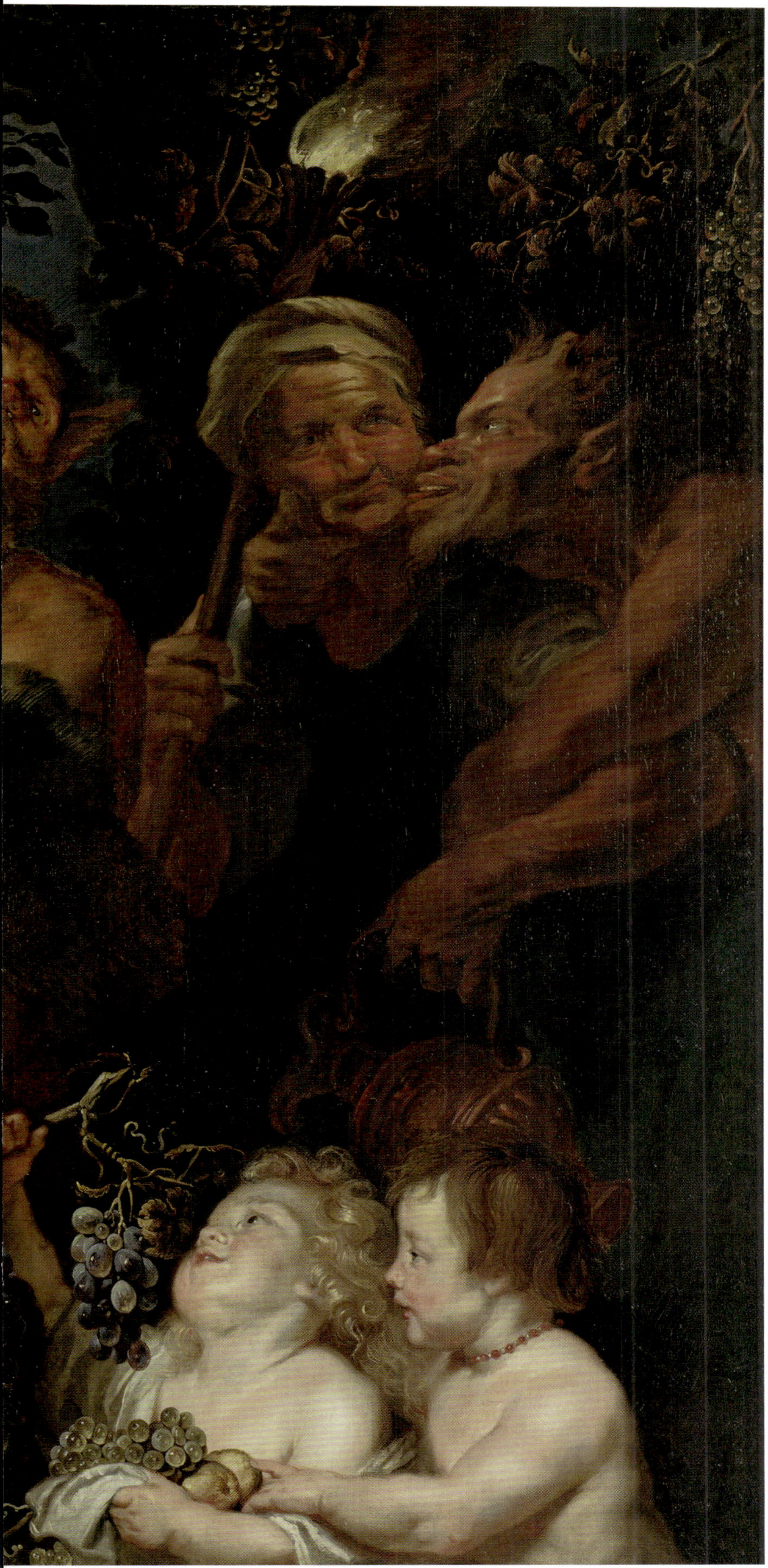

58

Attributed to
SIR ANTHONY VAN DYCK (1599–1641)
Drunken Silenus Supported by Satyrs, *c.* 1620
Oil on canvas, 133.5 x 197 cm
The National Gallery, London, inv. NG 853. Bought 1871

PROVENANCE: probably the collection of Lucas van Uffel (d. 1637), Venice; perhaps collection of Arnold Horebeek, Antwerp, from whom bought, through the agency of the dealers Picart and Musson, by the Duke of Richelieu, 1676; perhaps collection of Philippe II of Bourbon, Ducke of Orléans (1674–1723), Paris; probably collection of Dutartre, Paris 1780 or 1784; Dutartre sale, Paris 19 March 1804, lot. 16; collection of Lucien Bonaparte, 1812; Prince Lucien Bonaparte sale, by private contract, 14 May 1816, lot. 62; collection of Chevalier Bonnemaison, Paris, 1824; Chevalier Féréol Bonnemaison sale, Paris, 2 April 1827, lot. 72; sold by John Smith to the Rt. Hon. Robert Peel (later Sir Robert Peel, 2nd Baronet), 1827; purchased 1871
SELECTED REFERENCES: Martin 1970, pp. 217–25; Alpers 1995, pp. 106, 133, pl. 102; Keith 1999, pp. 96–104; Braunschweig 2004, no. 10

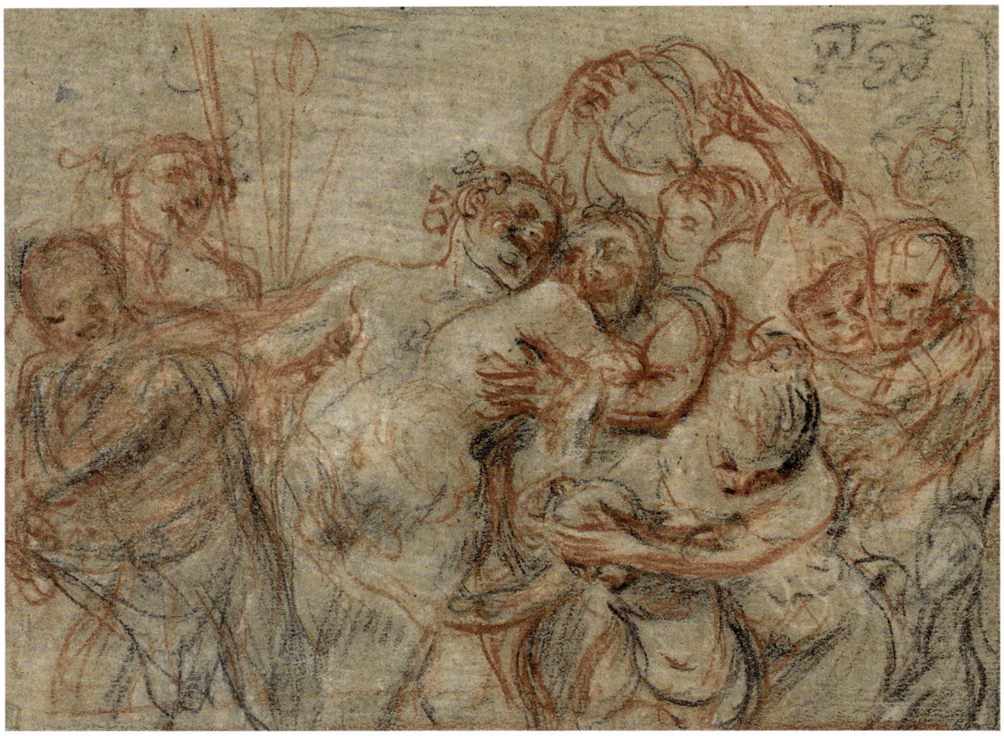

59

JEAN-ANTOINE WATTEAU (1684–1721)
The March of Silenus, c. 1715–16
Black, red and white chalk on paper, 15.6 x 21.1 cm
National Gallery of Art, Washington DC, inv. 1991.22.1.a. Gift of Mr and Mrs Paul Shepard Morgan to honour Margaret Morgan Grasselli, Curator of Old Master Drawings, and in honour of the 50th Anniversary of the National Gallery of Art, 1991

PROVENANCE: De Wailly, Paris; Hôtel Drouot, Paris, 17–18 February 1853, lot 159; Baron Louis-Auguste de Schwiter (1805–1889) (Lugt 1768), his sale, Hôtel Drouot, Paris, 20–21 April 1883, lot 174; Henri Michel-Lévy, his sale, Galerie Georges Petit, Paris, 12–13 May 1919, lot 135; Mme Piez, Paris, by 1957; Colnaghi, London, 1959, no. 41; private collection, Great Britain; Sotheby's, Monte Carlo, 11 February 1979, lot 51; Gift of Mr and Mrs Paul Shepard Morgan to honour Margaret Morgan Grasselli, Curator of Old Master Drawings, and in Honour of the 50th Anniversary of the National Gallery of Art
SELECTED REFERENCES: Parker and Mathey 1957, vol. 1, no. 259; Washington 1984, no. 131; Grasselli 1987, pp. 189-191, no. 13; Alpers 1995, p. 136, pl. 108; Rosenberg and Prat 1996, vol. 3, R. 838; Roland Michel 1998, r. 838; Grasselli 2001, p. 331

A drawing by Rubens (held by the British Museum) after the classical sculpture of Silenus now in Dresden served as the point of departure for the c. 1615 *Bacchanal* owned by the Pushkin Museum in Moscow; this was engraved (reversing the image) by Pieter Claesz. Soutman (cat. 60). In this scene of revelry the tipsy central figure is supported by a female and a male satyr, assisted by a black female musician with a tambourine; more satyresses recline on the ground. One of them is suckling two infants. Satyrs sport in the woods, where there is also a wildcat or tiger. The composition in Moscow is listed as a bacchanal with Silenus, and the inscription on the engraving also names Silenus. Yet this print has always been referred to as an image of 'Bacchus'.[11] Although it is sometimes difficult to distinguish Silenus from Bacchus, the close connection between this print and another painting by Rubens appears to confirm this figure's identity as Silenus: in the Alte Pinakothek in Munich some very similar revellers are grouped around an intoxicated Silenus.[12] This scene has been linked to a passage in Ovid's *Metamorphoses*, where we hear how Silenus was found by Phrygians and taken to their king, Midas, who celebrated his arrival for ten days before returning him to Bacchus (*Metamorphoses*, XI.90–99). Yet it has to be said that members of the entourage around this figure are clearly not Phrygian peasants.

A bacchanalian feast is surely the subject of the small panel in the Fitzwilliam Museum in Cambridge (cat. 61), with its group of mythological figures seated around a table in a woodland setting. Their more than relaxed poses suggest that considerable amounts of wine have already been consumed, although not a single wine glass is to be seen. The table is bedecked with a tablecloth, but otherwise entirely empty. The figure in the left foreground with his foot on a water amphora can be identified from this attribute as a river

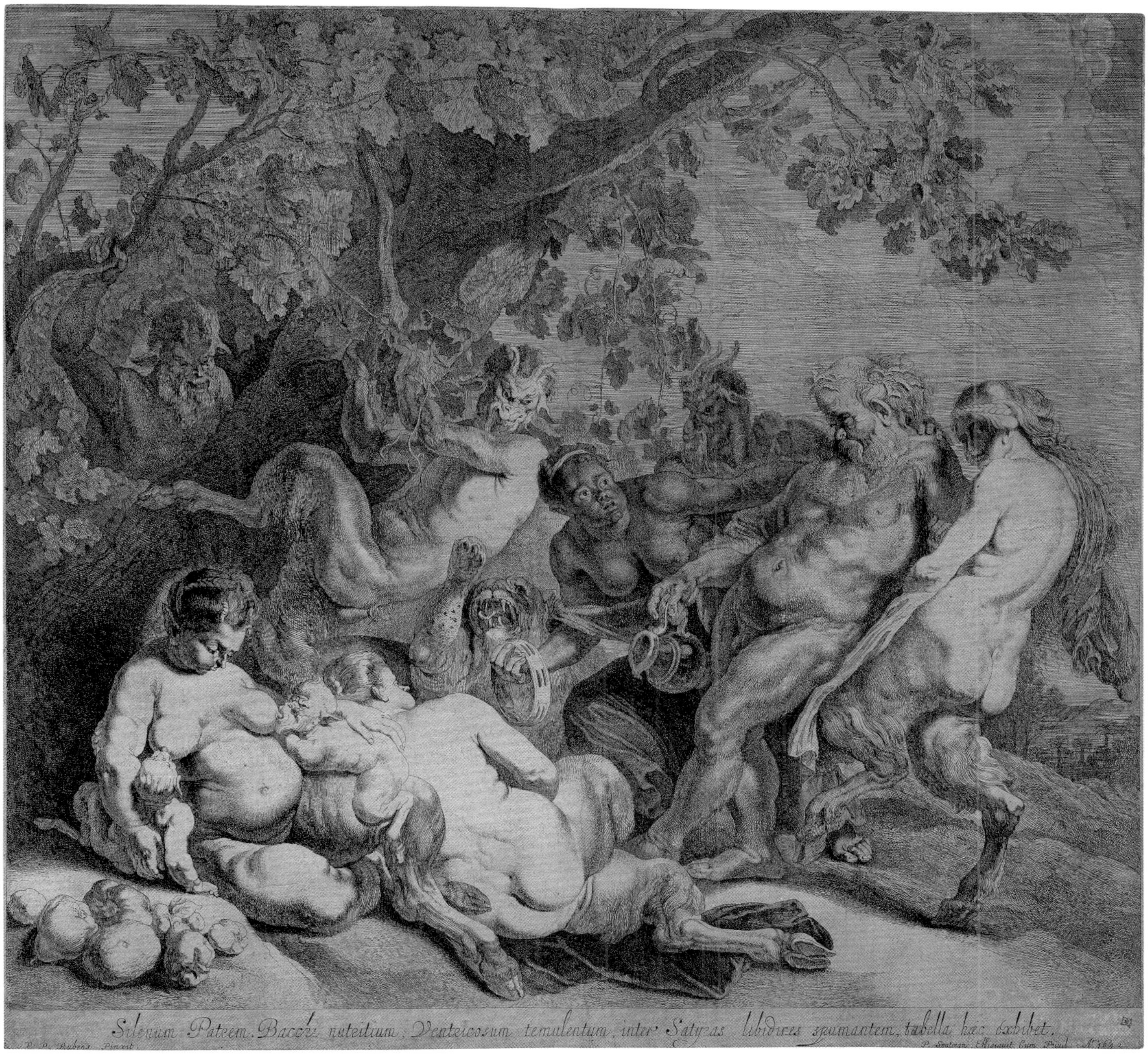

60

PIETER CLAESZ. SOUTMAN (c. 1580–1657)
Bacchanal, 1642
Engraving and etching, 44.8 x 49.5 cm
Royal Museum of Fine Arts Antwerp, 10529

PROVENANCE: the collection of Max Rooses, donated to the museum in 1900
SELECTED REFERENCES: Schneevogt 1873, pp. 134–35; Hollstein 1949–2010, vol. 27, p. 230, no. 15; Antwerp 1993, no. 75; Barrett 2012, no. Pr-41

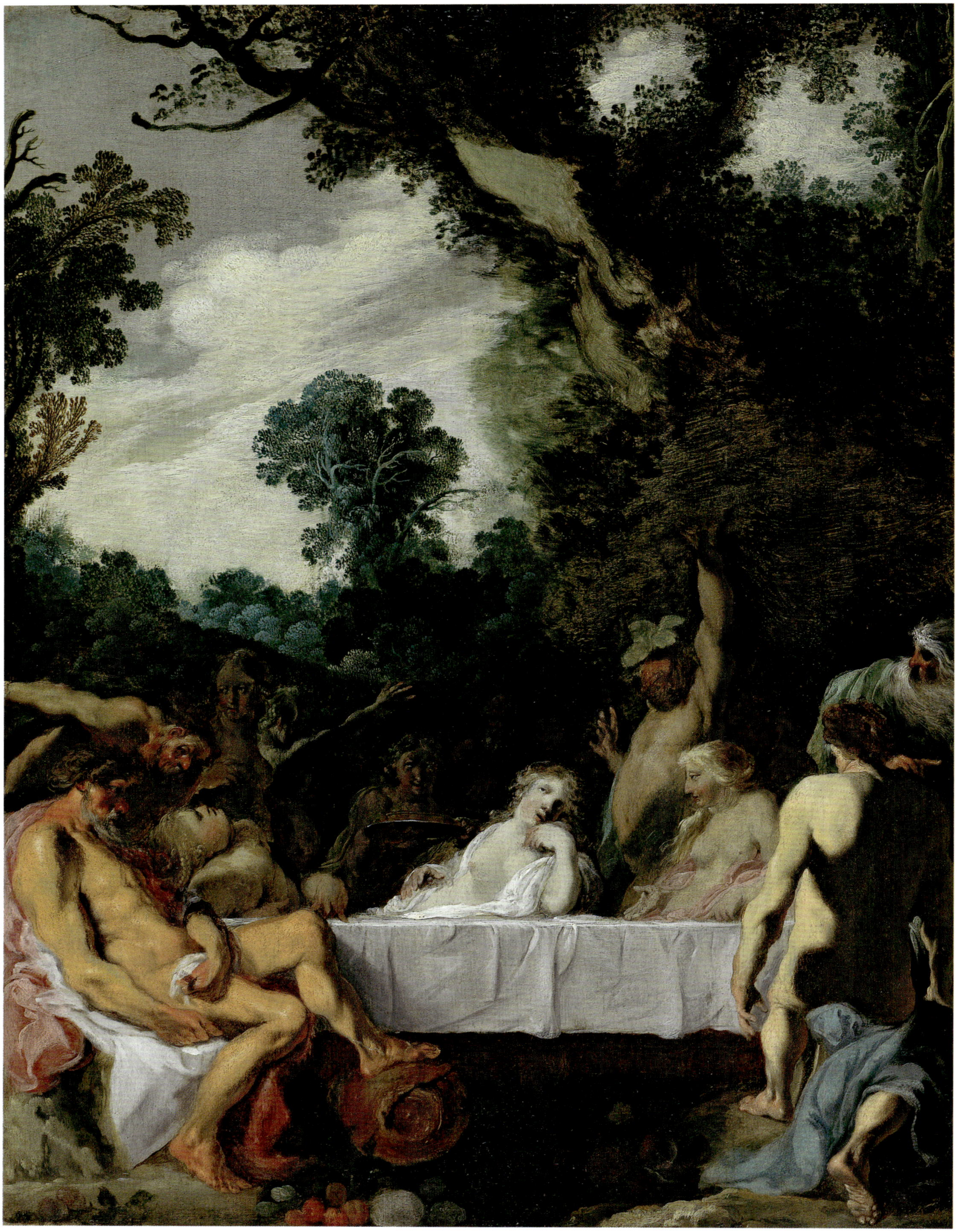

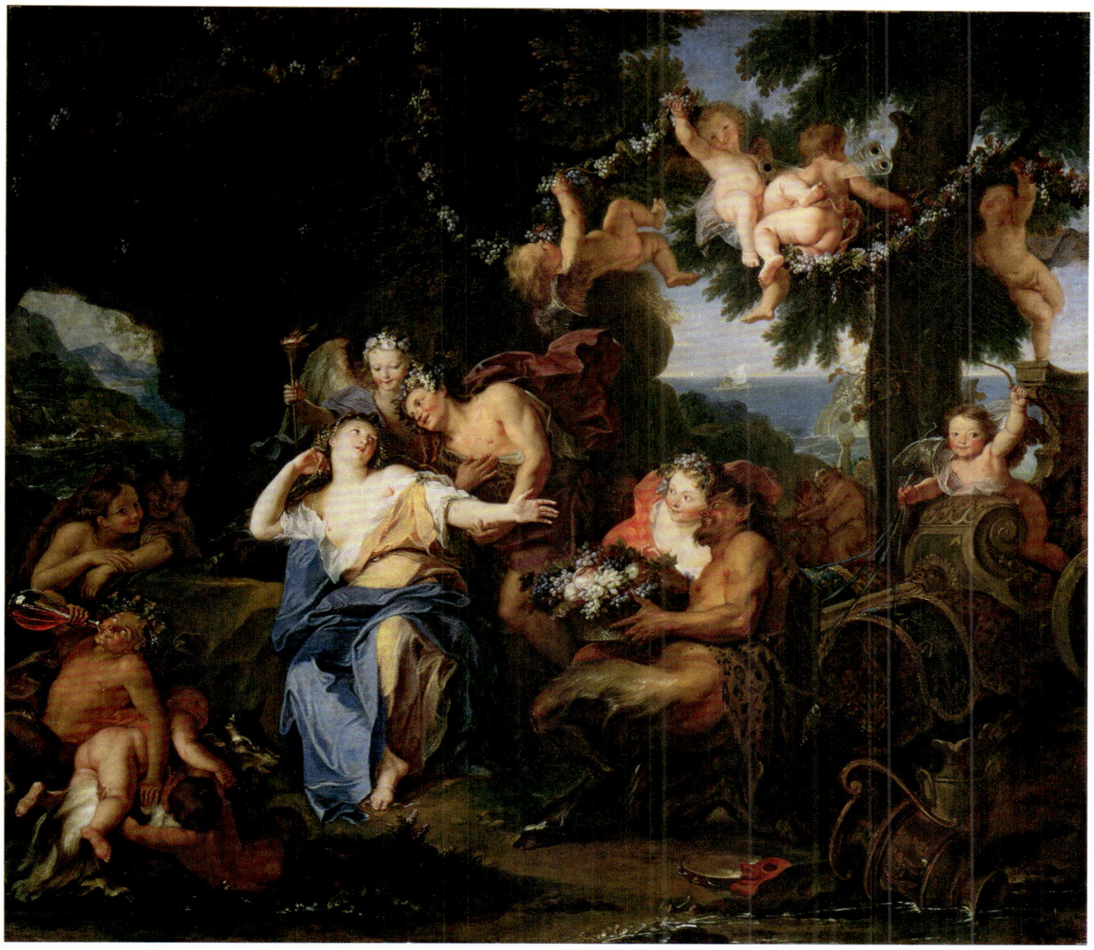

62

ANTOINE COYPEL (1661-1722)
Bacchus and Ariadne on the Isle of Naxos, *c.* 1693
Oil on canvas, 73 x 85.5 cm
Philadelphia Museum of Art, inv. 1990-54-1. Purchased with funds (by exchange) from the bequest of Edna M. Welsh and the gift of Mrs R. Barclay Scull, 1990

PROVENANCE: painted in 1693 for Philippe I, Duke of Orléans (1640–1701), brother of King Louis XIV, and placed in his picture cabinet at the Château de Saint-Cloud; Prince Philippe François de Rubempré, Brussels; sale, Cabinet de Rubempré, Brussels, 11 April 1765, lot 111; purchased by Deroy, buying for Basan (probably the dealer Pierre-François Basan, 1723–1797), Paris; Gerret Braamcamp (1699–1771), Amsterdam, as of 1766; possibly Frederick II of Prussia (1712–1786) or the Prussian royal collections; with Dr Nicholaas Beets, Antwerp, as of 1925; private collection, Basel, 1952; possibly Countess Clavel, Lugano; Christie's, Monaco, 15 June 1990, lot 50; purchased for the Philadelphia Museum of Art with funds (by exchange) from the bequest of Edna M. Welsh and gift of Mrs. R. Barclay Scull, 1990
SELECTED REFERENCES: Garnier 1989, pp. 19–21, no. 49; Paris 1991, no. 8; Mérot 1994, p. 296; Zirpolo 2010, p. 387; Gustin Gomez 2011, pp. 146, 179–80

61

JOHANN LISS (c. 1597-1631)
A Bacchanalian Feast, *c.* 1617
Oil on panel, 34.2 x 27.3 cm
Lent by the Syndics of the Fitzwilliam Museum, Cambridge, inv. PD 100-1978. Purchased with the Cunliffe Fund with contributions from the Art Fund and the Victoria and Albert Museum Purchase Grant Fund

PROVENANCE: 'AG' anonymous eighteenth- or nineteenth-century collector; with J. Weitzner, New York, 1956; 1959 Mrs Loewenstein; Christie's, London, 8 July 1977, lot 104, bought Colnaghi, London; purchased 1978 with help from the Cunliffe Fund with contributions from the National Art Collections Fund and the Victoria and Albert Museum Grant in Aid
SELECTED REFERENCES: Steinbart 1959, pp. 203–04, no. 1; *Fitzwilliam Museum, Cambridge, The Annual Reports*, 16, 1978; Klessmann 1999, p. 153 (as not Liss)

god. In the right foreground a naked man kneels, his back to the viewer; the female figures, partly clothed in pieces of drapery, could be either nymphs or maenads. The work's attribution to Johann Liss has been disputed by Rüdiger Klessmann.[13] The figures suggest the artist had studied the *bozzetti* of Rubens, such as the *Two Nymphs with a River God*, now in the Museum of Western and Oriental Art, Kiev.[14] Whereas the protagonists appear to have been painted quickly and almost in the manner of a sketch, the landscape – above all the foliage in the trees – has been executed in remarkable detail, which suggests that the work as a whole is not in fact a sketch.

The themes associated with Bacchus also include the love story between Ariadne and the god of wine himself, in which he is generally portrayed as a young man. Ariadne had arrived on Naxos with her beloved Theseus, but he stole away and left her while she was asleep. Bacchus fell in love with her and married her. In Antoine Coypel's account of this subject (cat. 62) the ship taking Theseus away is still visible on the horizon and Ariadne, turning towards Bacchus, has still not fully recovered from her pain. Yet the overall atmosphere of the painting is one of playful merriment; Hymen, standing behind Bacchus and Ariadne, has already lit their wedding torch. The literary inspiration for this scene is again found in the work of Ovid (*Metamorphoses*, VIII.174–83; *The Art of Love*, I.529–64). Coypel had studied the work of Rubens so thoroughly in the 1680s and early 1690s that his *Democritus* was even taken to be the work of Rubens.[15] In *Bacchus and Ariadne on the Isle of Naxos* he demonstrates, with playful ease, his knowledge of the work of other artists, too, such as Titian, Poussin and Van Dyck. Rubens's influence is particularly apparent in the depiction of the satyrs and nymphs, as well as in the warm colouration of the composition as a whole.[16]

When Honoré Daumier, who variously engaged with the art of the Old Masters around 1850, drew his *Drunken Silenus* (cat. 63), he took his lead from Rubens's paintings and prints. Rubens's influence is apparent in the way that the corpulent figure is drawn, yet Daumier's Silenus does not have the facial features of Socrates – neither a snub nose nor a beard. Daumier's intoxicated figure has a much greater resemblance to Dr Louis-Désiré Véron, a supporter of Louis-Napoleon (first President of the French Republic and soon to be Napoleon III, Emperor of the French), which gives this seemingly neo-Baroque composition a political undertone.[17] In order that the protagonist should still also be recognised as Silenus – and perhaps as an additional barb – there is to the left of the composition a donkey, proverbially lustful creatures and traditionally the mount of Bacchus' wise teacher.[18] Daumier exhibited this painterly drawing in the Salon of 1851, together with another homage to Rubens, his *Women Pursued by Satyrs* (cat. 82). Daumier's contemporaries noted his admiration of Rubens: in 1860 Edmond and Jules de Goncourt called him 'the prodigal son of Rubens'.[19]

Besides satyrs, centaurs (half-man and half-horse – another hybrid creature in Greek mythology) were also regarded as particularly lascivious and lustful; it is probably no coincidence that they too were purported to have a taste for large quantities of wine. Jean-Honoré Fragonard made two drawings after *Nessus and Deianeira* (fig. 19), which is attributed to Rubens and his workshop.[20]

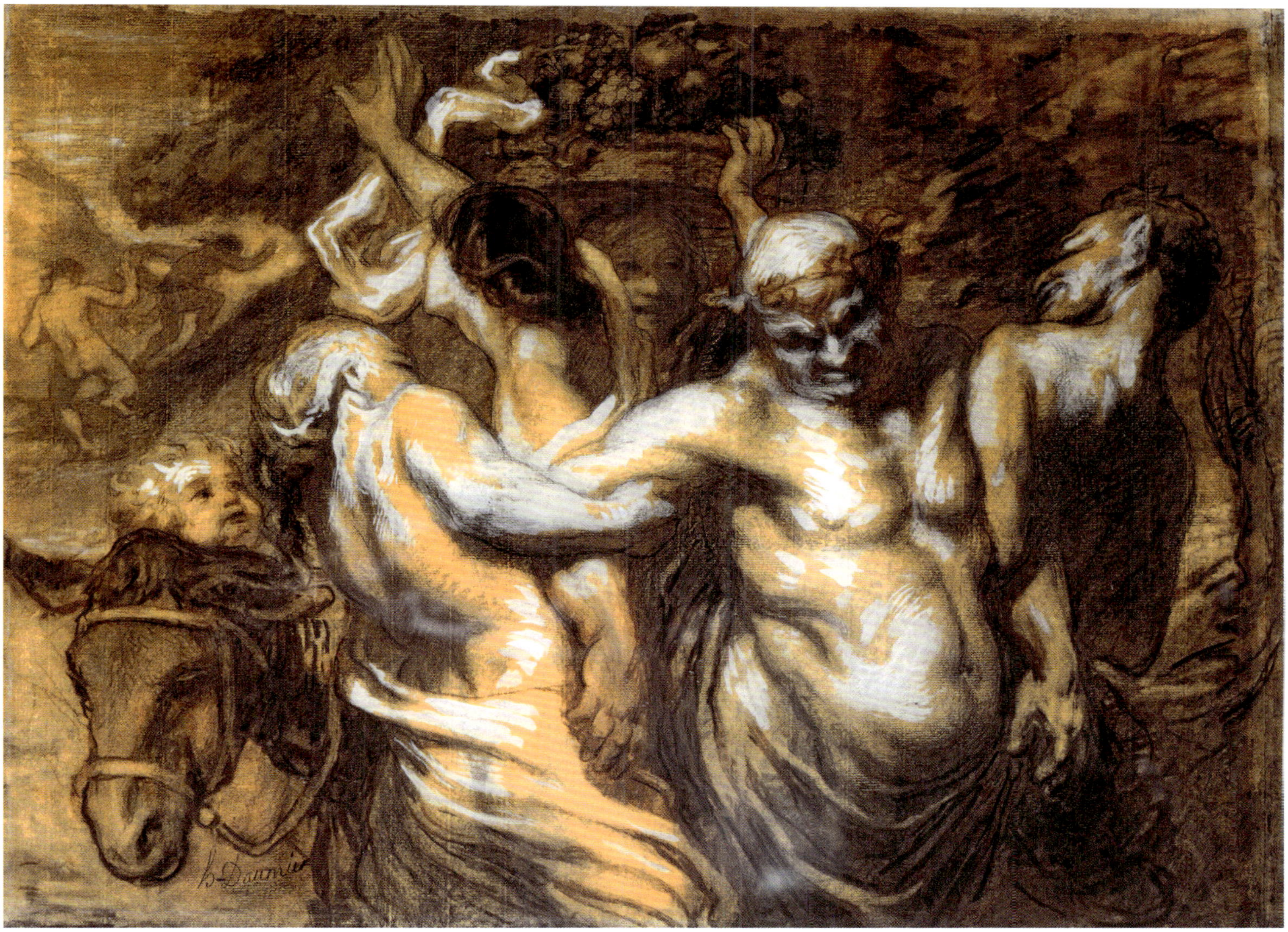

63

HONORÉ DAUMIER (1808–1879)
Drunken Silenus, 1850
Charcoal, brown chalk, sepia wash and white gouache on orange-tinted paper, 43 x 61 cm
Musée des Beaux-Arts, Calais, inv. 51.70

PROVENANCE: State purchase from the artist, 1863
SELECTED REFERENCES: Larkin 1966, p. 87; Maison 1968, no. 762; Frankfurt 1992, pp. 34–35, no. 86, pp. 111–12, 237, 255; Laughton 1996, pp. 29–31; Paris 2013, pp. 52, 55, no. 20

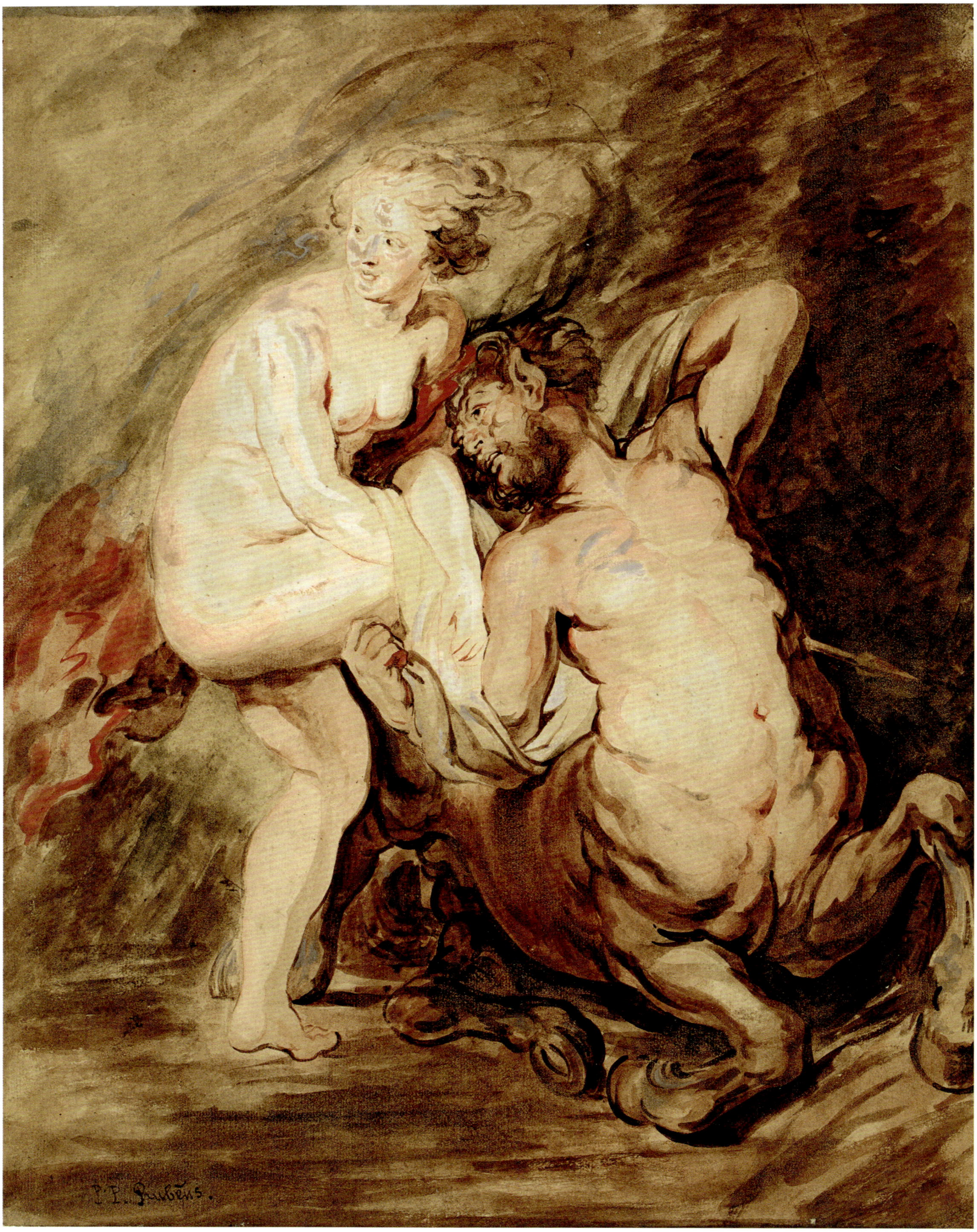
P. P. Rubens.

Fragonard had probably seen the painting in Paris when it was in the collection of the art dealer Jean-Baptiste-Pierre Le Brun. Included here is his drawing from the British Museum (cat. 64); the Paris drawing is part of the collection of the Musée du Louvre. The centaur Nessus helped Deianeira to cross the River Euenos, and then tried to abduct her. When Deianeira's husband Hercules heard her cries, he shot Nessus with an arrow poisoned with the venomous blood of the Lernaean hydra (killed by Hercules in his second labour). Before Nessus died, he gave Deianeira his blood-soaked shirt, saying that it would reinvigorate any waning love (Ovid, *Metamorphoses*, IX.101–33). Deianeira later found herself plagued by jealousy and gave the shirt to her husband; however, Nessus had lied, and Hercules died in torment from the ill-effects of the poisoned blood on the shirt.

In this scene, Nessus has already been struck down by Hercules' arrow; his yearning, agonised gaze is fixed on Deianeira's breasts. He has the pointed ears of a satyr – yet another indication of his lascivious, libidinous intentions. Deianeira, looking backwards, dismounts from the centaur's back, yet it appears more as though she is stepping upwards. In the Paris drawing, evidently the first of the two versions, Fragonard adheres quite closely to Rubens's painting and portrays Deianeira with a calm, friendly expression. Nothing hints at the trials she has just survived. In the London version her movement backwards is more dynamic, which in turn makes her facial expression harder to read. Fragonard thus heightens the potential erotic tension that was already implicit in Rubens's painting. And since the deadly arrow is all but hidden in the shadows, the viewer's attention is primarily drawn to the close bodily contact between the two protagonists.

Fragonard often copied paintings by Rubens. However, his two versions of *Nessus and Deianeira* are notable for a technique that is a rarity in Fragonard's copies after the Old Masters:[21] the brown wash and dark blue watercolour paint do not entirely cover the cream-coloured paper, which is used to create highlights in places. Like the colouration, this extremely economical approach calls to mind oil sketches by Rubens, to whom the Paris drawing was in fact attributed up until 1933.[22]

64

JEAN-HONORÉ FRAGONARD (1732–1806)
Nessus and Deianeira, *c.* 1778
Watercolour on paper, 42.6 x 34.1 cm
On loan from the British Museum, London, inv. 1933,0211.3. Presented by the Art Fund 1933

PROVENANCE: donated 1933 by the National Art Collections Fund
SELECTED REFERENCES: Parker 1933, p. 105; Ananoff 1963, vol. 2, no. 1104, p. 189; Paris 1987 no. 217, p. 448, no. 1; Raux 2005, p. 139; Raux 2007, pp. 21–22

The biblical story of Susanna and the Elders tells how two lascivious old men spy on the devout wife of Joachim and are so fascinated by her beauty that they are overcome with lust (Daniel XIII, 1–65, from the biblical Apocrypha). They try to force her to commit adultery by threatening to claim they had caught her in *flagrante delicto* with a young man. Susanna remains steadfast, is publicly charged and prays to God for help. It is only through the intervention of the young prophet Daniel, who insists that the witnesses should be questioned separately, that the elders' duplicity comes to light. Ultimately the elders are condemned to death.

Since the Renaissance, Susanna has been portrayed as beautiful and seductive, yet also chaste and modest. In depictions of Susanna artists frequently drew on the iconography of Venus, meaning – in the words of Daniela Hammer-Tugendhat – that 'the symbol of chastity became a desirable goddess of love'.[1] In antiquity, when Praxiteles sculpted his Venus (now lost) he was particularly successful in his representation of a similar ambivalence: the goddess of love was shown standing, modestly trying to cover herself with her hands.

When Rubens created his version of *Susanna and the Elders*, which was engraved by Vorsterman in 1620 (cat. 66), he chose the same pose that he had used for his *Venus Frigida* (cat. 53), which is in turn derived from an antique sculpture of a 'crouching' Venus, depicting the goddess of love bathing. But Rubens's figure is noticeably more curled up and thus appears all the more anxious to retain her modesty.

Rubens's Susanna, threatened by the elders, looks towards the viewer, searching for help. However, the viewer is in fact the beneficiary of the old men's importunate actions: by wrenching the stole away from Susanna, they reveal her body to the viewer, who unwittingly also becomes a voyeur and in this instant sees more than the actual perpetrators. Vorsterman's engraving, which was presumably made after a lost original by Rubens, bears a dedication to the Dutch poet Anna Roemers Visscher (1584–1651), who had probably been introduced to Rubens by his first wife Isabella Brant.[2] Visscher remained unmarried for a long time in order to care for her father, and is lauded in the dedication as the epitome of chastity. But that was only one side of the coin. The work's buyer, Dudley Carleton, 1st Viscount Dorchester (1573–1651), felt that Susanna had to be so outstandingly beautiful for the elders to fall in love with her.[3] Rubens himself described the subject-matter as a *galanteria*: a work neither sacred nor profane.[4] It is clear that in Rubens's day there were those who focused on – and perhaps re-enacted – the elders' lustful spying while others preferred a moralising interpretation of this libidinous scene.[5]

By contrast, the woodcut by Christoffel Jegher (cat. 65) is based on a painting by Rubens that still exists in two versions: one is in St Petersburg, the other is in Turin.[6] In this somewhat later composition, Susanna is under even greater pressure: the two elders are on either side of her and she is endeavouring to keep herself covered with her right hand as she tries to fend off the bald elder with her left.

Particularly in the early days of his artistic career, Manet repeatedly engaged, in a very original manner, with compositions by Rubens, as for instance in *Fishing* (cat. 128), or in a preparatory study (cat. 67) for his *Surprised Nymph* of 1861 (Museo Nacional de Bellas

65

CHRISTOFFEL JEGHER (1596–1652/53)
Susanna and the Elders, c. 1633
Woodcut, 44 x 58 cm
Royal Museum of Fine Arts Antwerp, inv. 11134

PROVENANCE: the collection of Max Rooses, donated to the museum in 1900
SELECTED REFERENCES: Nagler 1835–52, vol. 6, pp. 435–46; Kramm 1857–64, vol. 3, p. 807; Wurzbach 1906–11, vol. 1, p. 753; Hollstein 1949–2010, vol. 9, no. 1; Della Pergola 1967, pp. 11–12; McGrath 1984, pp. 81, 82, 84; d'Hulste and Vandenven 1989, p. 217; Van Hout 2004, pp. 94–96

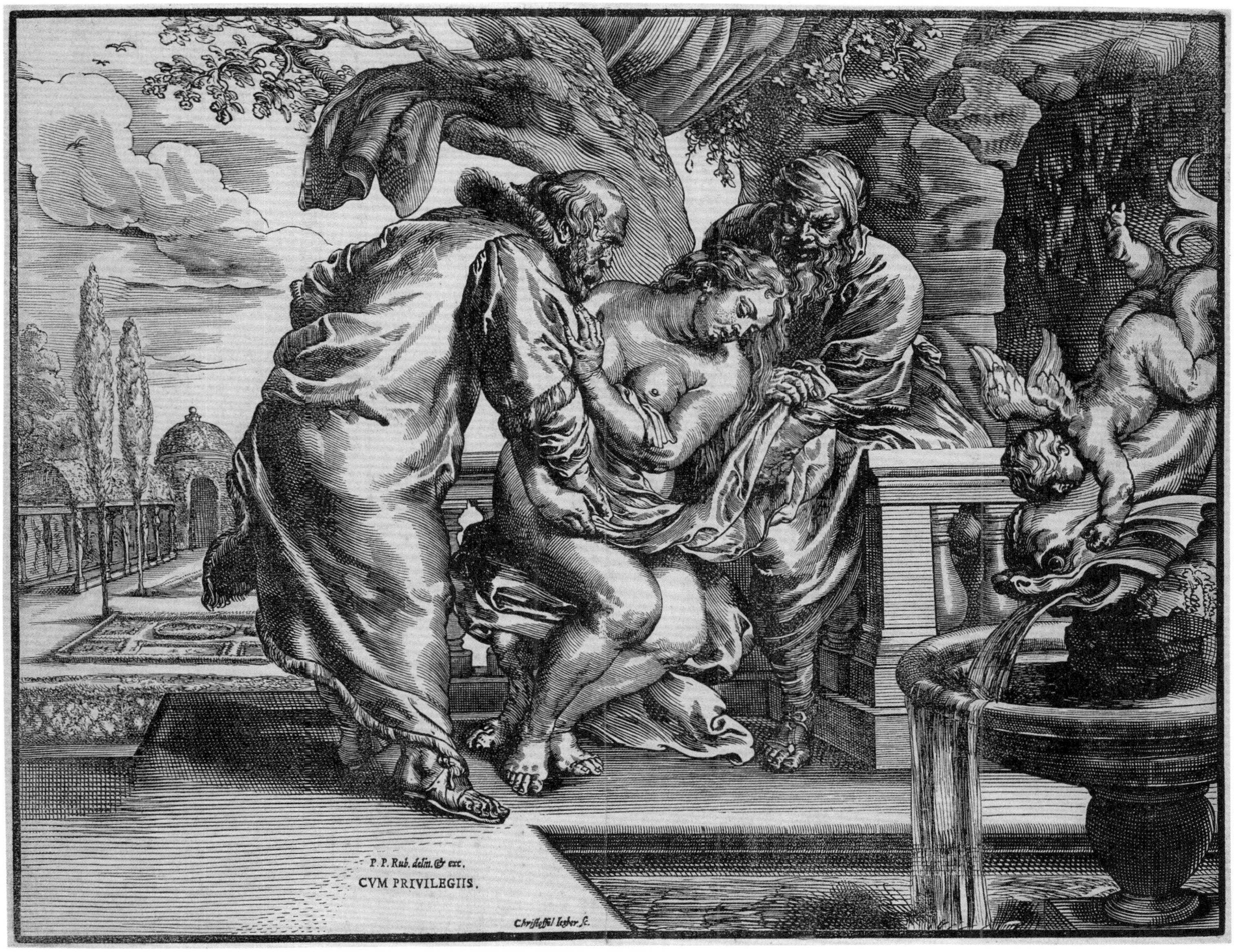

P. P. Rub. delin. & exc.
CVM PRIVILEGIIS.
Christoffel Iegher sc.

66

LUCAS VORSTERMAN THE ELDER (1595–1675)
Susanna and the Elders, 1620
Engraving, 39.6 x 27.8 cm
Royal Museum of Fine Arts Antwerp, inv. 10151

PROVENANCE: the collection of Max Rooses, donated to the museum in 1900
SELECTED REFERENCES: Hollstein 1949–2010, vol. 43, no. 4; Della Pergola 1967, pp. 14–15; Op de Beeck 1973, pp. 209–11; Rome 1977, no. 122, no. 3; McGrath 1984, pp. 81–85; Pohlen 1985, no. 40; d'Hulst and Vandenven 1989, pp. 211–13; McGrath 1997, vol. 1, pp. 49–50; Van Hout 2004, p. 48 2001, pp. 81–85, 87, no. 39; Paris 2011, pp. 28, 99–100, no. 57; Seta 2013, p. 54

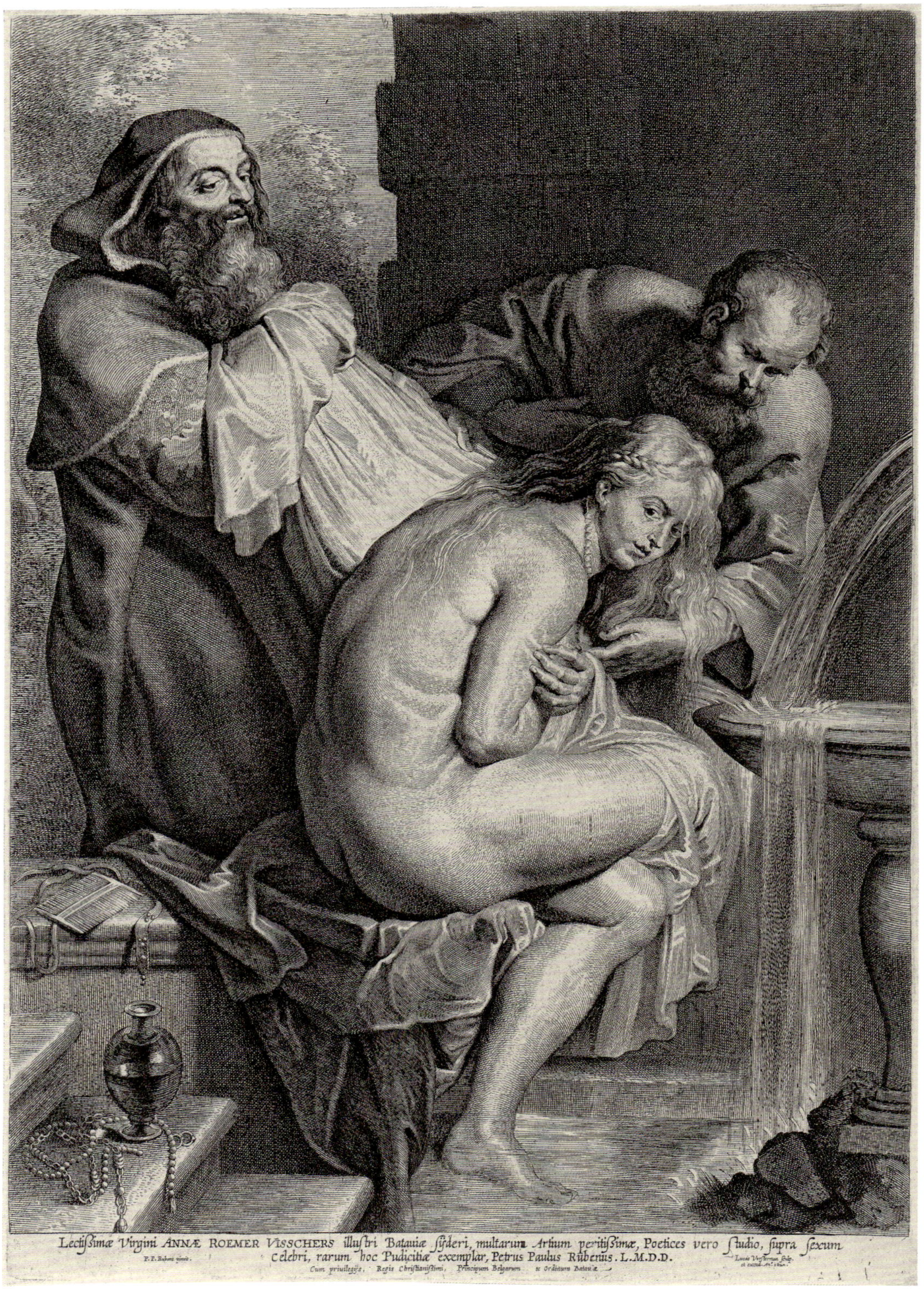

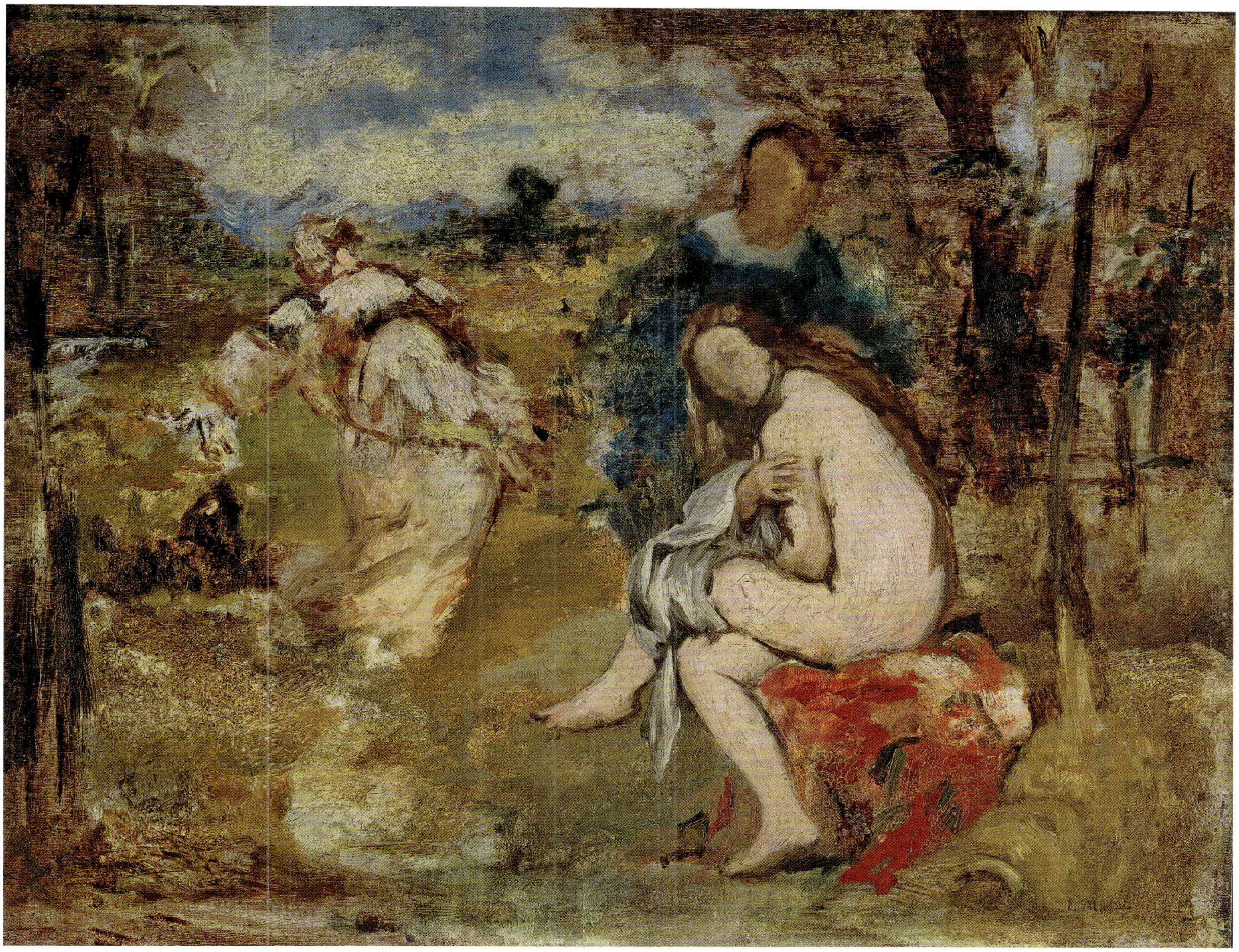

Artes, Buenos Aires). Although Manet had initially painted *Surprised Nymph* in a large, horizontal format, he later cut it down to create a vertical format, depicting a nude female figure in a landscape. Manet, who gave his nude what has been described as 'a more Rubensian fleshiness',[7] selected the pose of Rubens's figure of the bathing Susanna (in the version by Vorsterman) but changed the meaning of the scene.[8] By painting out a serving girl and adding a satyr, he turned the bather into a nymph. The satyr was in fact removed after Manet's death.[9] And there was yet another twist to the tale: the model for Manet's female nude, Suzanne Leenhoff, later became his wife. In the pose of the biblical heroine, with whom she shares her name, Suzanne was initially portrayed as a bather but was then subsequently cast as nymph. Despite the changes Manet made in the painting, Suzanne remains under the voyeuristic gaze of the viewer.[10]

67

ÉDOUARD MANET (1832–1883)
Study for *Surprised Nymph*, *c.* 1860
Oil on canvas, 35.5 x 46 cm
Inscribed bottom right
(by Suzanne Manet): E. Manet
The National Museum of Art, Architecture and Design, Oslo, inv. 1182

PROVENANCE: Suzanne Manet; sale 1884, no. 18, (?) bought by Léon Leenhoff; 1st Prince de Wagram; George Bernheim; purchased for the museum in 1918 by the Society of Friends of the Museum of Oslo
SELECTED REFERENCES: Duret 1902, p. 25; Krauss 1967, p. 622, no. 20; Della Pergola 1967, p. 10; Paris 1983, no. 20; Wilson-Bareau 1986, pp. 26–36; Locke 2001, pp. 81–85, 87, no. 39; Paris 2011, pp. 28, 99–100, no. 57; Seta 2013, p. 54

In a number of compositions Rubens created voyeuristic scenes, and these notably influenced certain later artists. The atmosphere of voyeurism is derived partly from literary sources – be these classical or modern[1] – and partly from his sensuous rendition of the subject-matter. The beholder's eye is deceived, and he or she is seduced into becoming an interested, no-longer distanced viewer who relishes the illusion the painter has set up.[2]

In *The Hermit and the Sleeping Angelica* (cat. 68) Rubens portrays a scene from *Orlando Furioso* (VIII.29–50) by Ludovico Ariosto (1477–1533). An old hermit falls in love with the beautiful Angelica; in order to abduct her to a desolate island, he bewitches her horse. When she resists his advances he gives her a magic potion to drink, so that she will fall asleep and he can admire her beauty and touch her at his leisure. This is precisely the moment depicted by Rubens: the old hermit is on the point of revealing her naked body by removing the last veil. Angelica, defenceless, is exposed to his gaze – and to that of the viewer. The demon at her head symbolises the dark magic the hermit has employed. The scene is dominated by Angelica's beauty and the lively, shimmering glow of her skin, which stands out sensuously against the red velvet cloak and the white cushion. The old man, by comparison, appears weak and dully coloured. Ultimately in Ariosto's tale the wizened hermit has to admit to his age: he lacks the manly prowess to inflict any greater injury on Angelica.

Van Dyck's *Jupiter and Antiope* contains probably one of the earliest female nudes in an *œuvre* that does not in fact contain many mythological subjects. The myth of Jupiter, who adopts the form of a satyr to approach the unsuspecting Antiope as she sleeps, has no more than a passing mention in Ovid's *Metamorphoses* (VI.110–11) and no location is named in the text. In Strabo's *Geography*, Antiope is the daughter of Nycteus, King of Thebes,[3] whereas others claimed the river god Asopus as her father.[4] Having been overcome by Jupiter, Antiope subsequently gave birth to the twins Amphion and Zethus.

Two versions of Van Dyck's composition have survived; the main differences between them lie within the details. At the far left edge of the painting that is now in Ghent (cat. 70) there is a voluminous, violet curtain, which occupies considerably more space than the equivalent green curtain in the Cologne painting (cat. 69). It is likely that both paintings were made when Van Dyck was working in Rubens's studio.

It has variously been suggested[5] that Van Dyck based his painting either on Rubens's *The Hermit and the Sleeping Angelica*[6] or on his *Cimon and Iphigenia* (fig. 21) – now both in the Kunsthistorisches Museum, Vienna – the subject of the latter taken from Giovanni Boccaccio's *Decameron*.[7] And it is true that there is a strong similarity in the pose of the female figures. However, the chronology of the works in question – *Angelica* was painted in 1626–28, *Cimon and Iphigenia* was made around 1617 and the two paintings by Van Dyck were made around 1618 – suggests that the figure of Rubens's Iphigenia was the source for Van Dyck's own creation (despite the fact that Angelica's pose and the position of her head correspond closely to those of Antiope). In all likelihood an engraving of the 1592 painting *Jupiter and Antiope,* sometimes entitled *Venus and a Satyr*, by Annibale Carracci will also have had some influence on Van Dyck's composition.

68

PETER PAUL RUBENS (1577–1640)
The Hermit and the Sleeping Angelica, 1626–28
Oil on panel, 43 x 66 cm
Kunsthistorisches Museum, Vienna, Gemäldegalerie, inv. 692

PROVENANCE: probably from Rubens's estate; probably already around 1663 in the imperial collection in Prague; imperial collection, Prague 1685; collection of Albert von Sachsen-Teschen, Pressburg Castle (Brastislava) 1781; Imperial Gallery Vienna 1781
SELECTED REFERENCES: Rooses 1886–92, vol. 4, no. 872; Vienna 1977, no. 42; Bialostocki 1985, pp. 189–91; Vienna 2005, no. 71; Heinen 2006, pp. 83–84

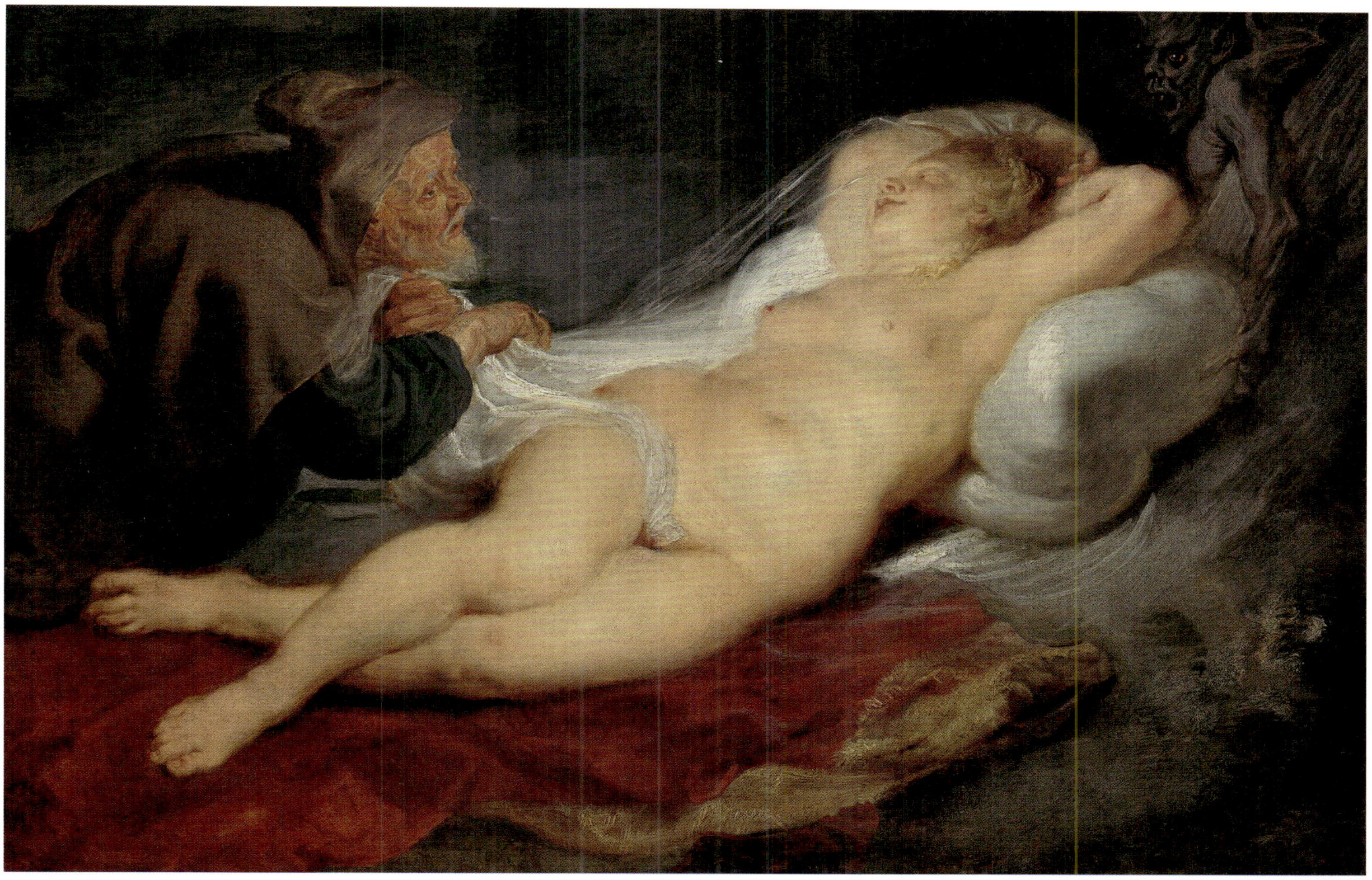

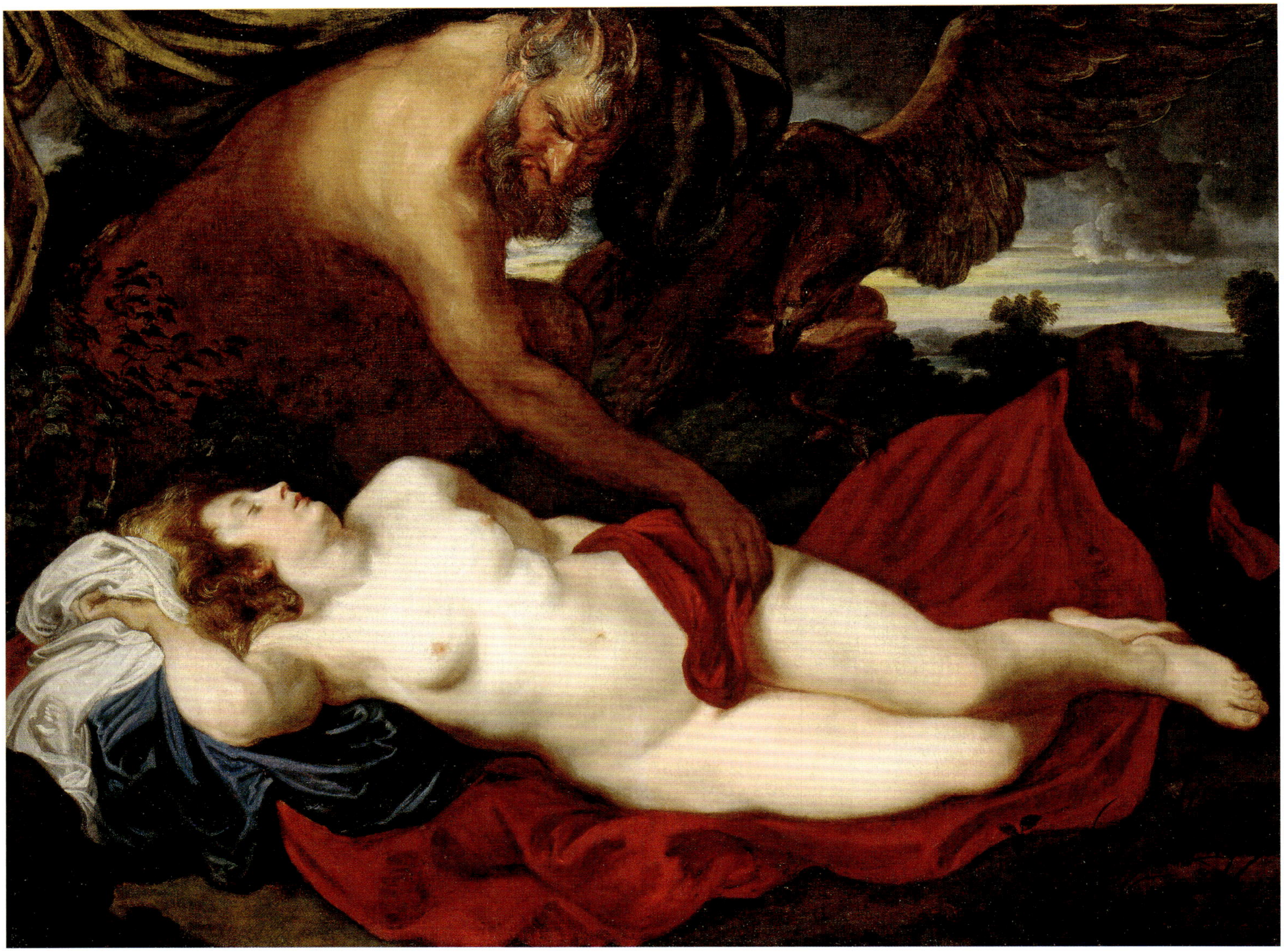

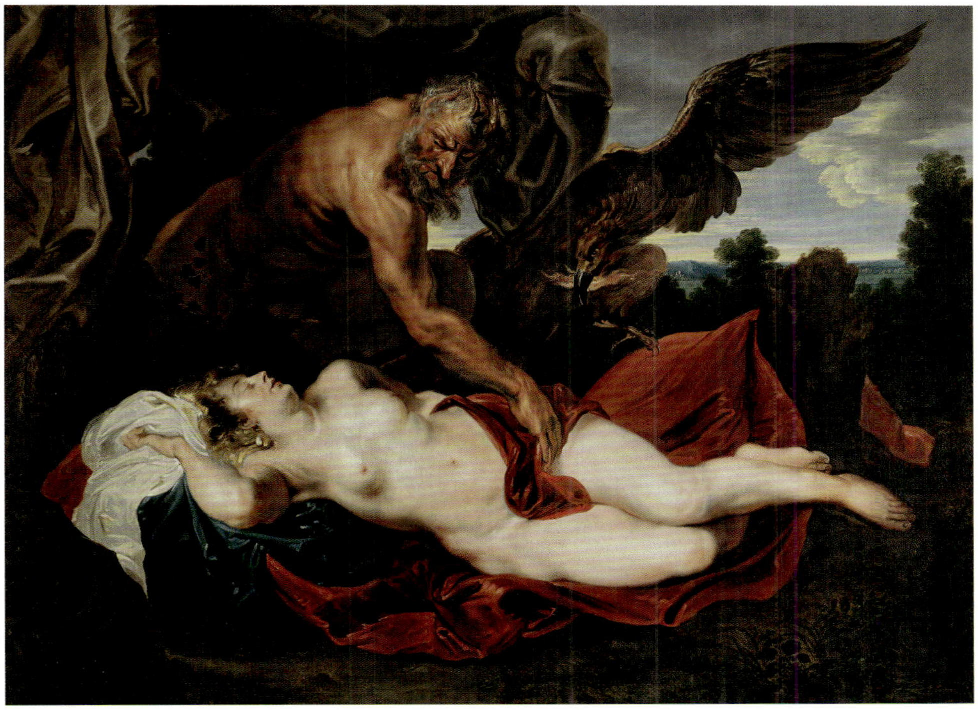

69

SIR ANTHONY VAN DYCK (1599–1641)
Jupiter and Antiope, *c.* 1618
Oil on canvas, 150 x 206 cm
Wallraf-Richartz Museum and Fondation Corboud, Cologne, inv. 278
BOZAR ONLY

PROVENANCE: Rubens's estate, 1640 (?); Madame Bosschaert collection (?); sale of the collection of Jean-Baptiste Grimberghs, Brussels, 1716, lot 23 (?); Benjamin van der Gucht, Christie's, London, 14 March 1788, lot 63 (?); 1809, collection of George William Coventry, 6th Earl of Coventry; 1900, Edward F. Pye Smith; 1928; Von Frey, Paris; 1929, Galerie Heinemann, Munich; 1931, Galerie Hansen, Lucerne; bought in 1938 by Antiquariat Karl Haberstock for the unrealised 'Führermuseum', Linz; deposited in 1965 by the Federal Republic of Germany in the Wallraf-Richartz-Museum
SELECTED REFERENCES: Antwerp 2004, no. 28; Barnes et al. 2004, no. I.81; Madrid 2012, no. 7

70

SIR ANTHONY VAN DYCK (1599–1641)
Jupiter and Antiope, *c.* 1620
Oil on canvas, 150 x 206 cm
Museum voor Schone Kunsten, Ghent, inv. 1900.D
RA ONLY

PROVENANCE: acquired by the Friends of the Museum from Desprets and Colnaghi, London, in 1900 (then attributed to Jacob Jordaens) and given by them to the museum
SELECTED REFERENCES: Ghent 1988, p. 54; Barnes et al. 2004, no. I.82; Cassel 2010–11, p. 82

Rubens admired Van Dyck's painting, and it seems that he owned one or other of the two versions: in the inventory of his estate is the first in a group of works by modern (contemporary) masters: 'L'Histoire d'Antiope & Iupiter transformé en Satyre, du Cheualier van Dyck'. It is significant, with regard to the ambiguity of the subject-matter, that the English version of the inventory describes this painting as 'A naked Venus, with a Satyre, by van dyke, vppon cloth'.[8]

Most artists who engaged with the story of Jupiter and Antiope took the opportunity to portray a female figure whose nakedness is revealed by a male viewer. By depicting Jupiter as a satyr, male desire is explained away as the lascivious nature of the satyr or faun. This allows the artist to indulge in explicit eroticism, since the perpetrator is a mythological creature and not a mortal man.[9] Jupiter's symbol of power, an eagle with a bundle of bolts of lightning, is a clear signal in Van Dyck's paintings that this is no ordinary satyr; however, it looks as though Jupiter and the eagle share the same urge to throw themselves onto Antiope. The mythological satyr or faun was an earthbound, natural creature and, by association, Jupiter and Antiope are also bound by earthy desires and at home in the landscape where Antiope is discovered asleep.

Fiona Healy has recently suggested that Van Dyck's *Jupiter and Antiope* may have been intended as a response to Rubens's *Cimon and Iphigenia*: the noble Cimon refuses to engage in any form of study and consequently has to live his life in the country. Only the sight of Iphigenia inspires him to improve his level of education so that he may be worthy of her. However, Rubens portrays Cimon as an uncouth peasant.

71

Attributed to
WILLEM BASSE (1613–1672)
Jupiter and Antiope, 1628–48
Etching, 12.5 x 17 cm
On long-term loan to Rijksmuseum, Amsterdam, inv. RP-P-H-O-48. Lent by Rijksakademie van Beeldende Kunsten

PROVENANCE: acquired 1816
SELECTED REFERENCES: Antwerp 1999, p. 336, no. 6; Turner and Depauw 2002, vol. 8, p. 144, no. 621; Barnes et al. 2004, p. 82

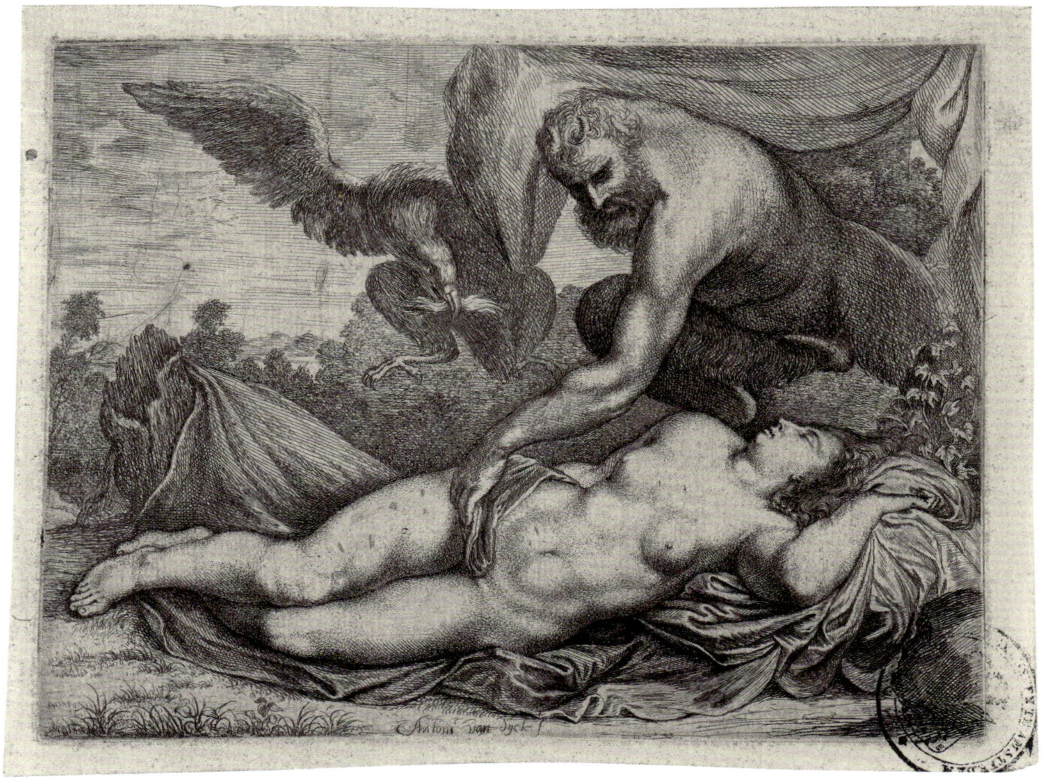

Anyone familiar with Boccaccio's tale knows the transformation Cimon is to undergo. That transformation, in Healy's view, symbolises the capacity of love to instigate change, whereas Van Dyck's *Jupiter and Antiope*, in her opinion, merely represents the gratification of one being's sexual appetite.[10]

It is hard to be sure nowadays just how explicit Van Dyck was in his depiction of Jupiter's sexual desire. In both paintings shadows and twigs obscure any clear view of Jupiter's lower body. In the engraving of this composition attributed to Willem Basse (cat. 71) an erect penis is clearly visible, but one has to exercise caution in making any assumptions, on this basis, about the original painting by Van Dyck. For, traditionally – in the modern era, too – erotic scenes could be rendered much more explicitly in drawings or prints than in paintings, for paintings were not nearly so well suited to private enjoyment as prints, which could be safely stored away in a drawer. Nevertheless, Jordaens does not seem to have censored his own work in his painting of *Pan and Syrinx* (cat. 56), proving that even in paintings, artists are sometimes quite explicit (although it is hard to imagine the same being true of Van Dyck).

Unlike Van Dyck, Rembrandt – in his etching of 1659 (cat. 72) – places his Antiope in a down bed. He takes a fundamentally different approach in other respects, too. A much older-looking Jupiter tentatively steals up on the sleeping woman. The sense of imminent physical violence, so palpable in Van Dyck's paintings, is all but absent here; an air of doubt surrounds the potency of this supreme god.[11] Rembrandt includes none of Jupiter's traditional attributes of power in this print, which was to be one of his last. Although the pose of the female nude is reminiscent of the figure in Annibale Carracci's engraving, it has

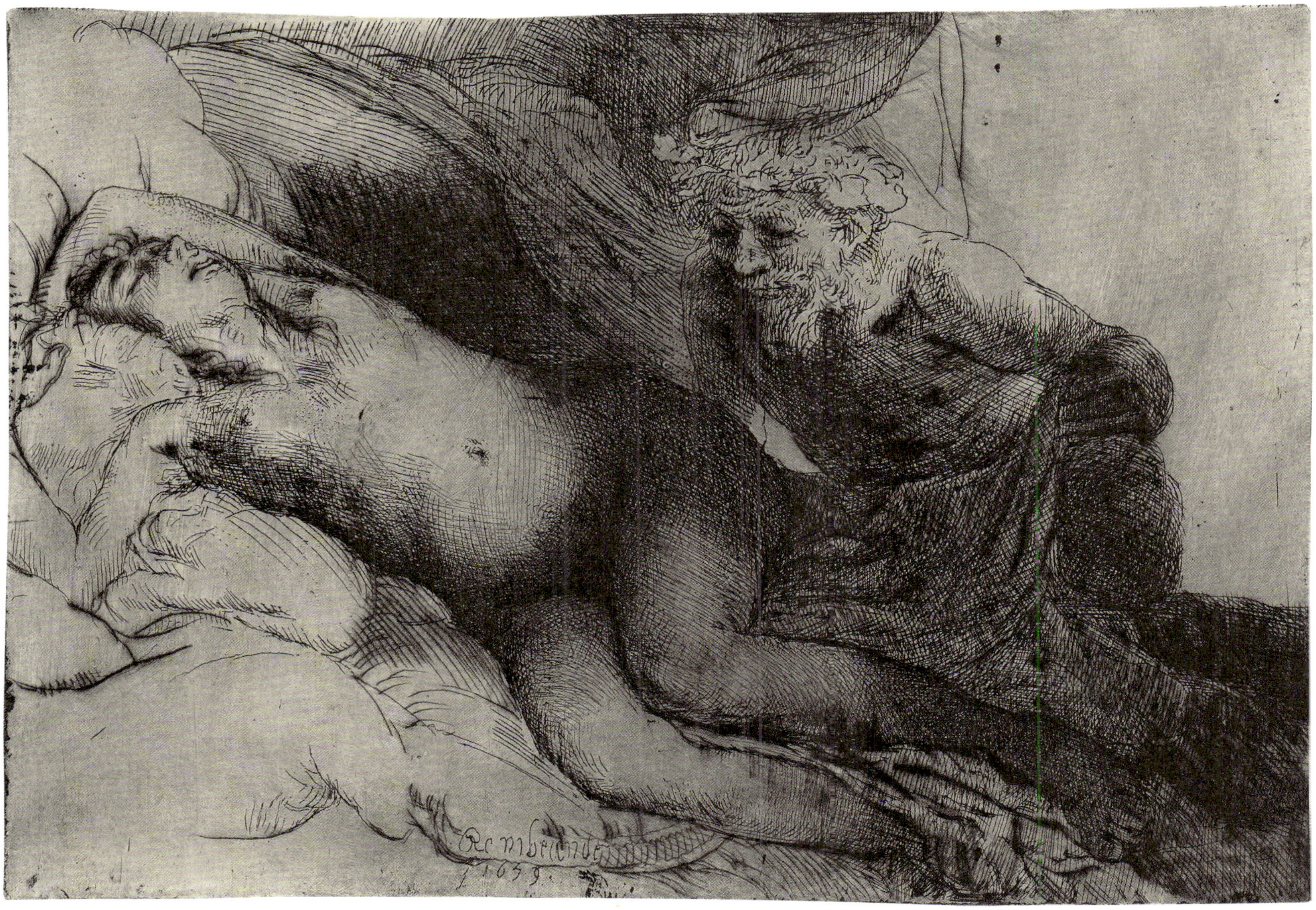

72

REMBRANDT VAN RIJN (1606–1669)
Jupiter and Antiope (the larger plate), 1659
Etching, 13.9 x 20.5 cm
Rijksmuseum, Amsterdam, inv. RB-P-1961-1112. Mr and Mrs De Bruijn-van der Leeuw Bequest, Muri

PROVENANCE: 1961, legacy of Mr and Ms De Bruijn-van der Leeuw
SELECTED REFERENCES White and Boon 1969, no. 203.I; Hinterding et al. 2000, p. 90; Boston 2003, no. 98; Springer 2008, p. 85, no. 63; Hammer-Tugendhat 2009, pp. 149–50, 154–5, no. 76

73

PABLO PICASSO (1881–1973)
Faun Uncovering a Sleeping Woman, 12 June 1936
Etching and aquatint on laid paper, 34 x 44 cm
Museo Nacional Centro de Arte Reina Sofía, Madrid, inv. AD01991

PROVENANCE: purchased in 2001
SELECTED REFERENCES: Dallas 1983, no. 99; Baer 1986, vol. 3, pp. 93–98; Bottinelli 2004; London 2004, pp. 88–90, 92; Springer 2008, p. 187, no. 194; Hammer-Tugendhat 2009, p. 35, no. 16

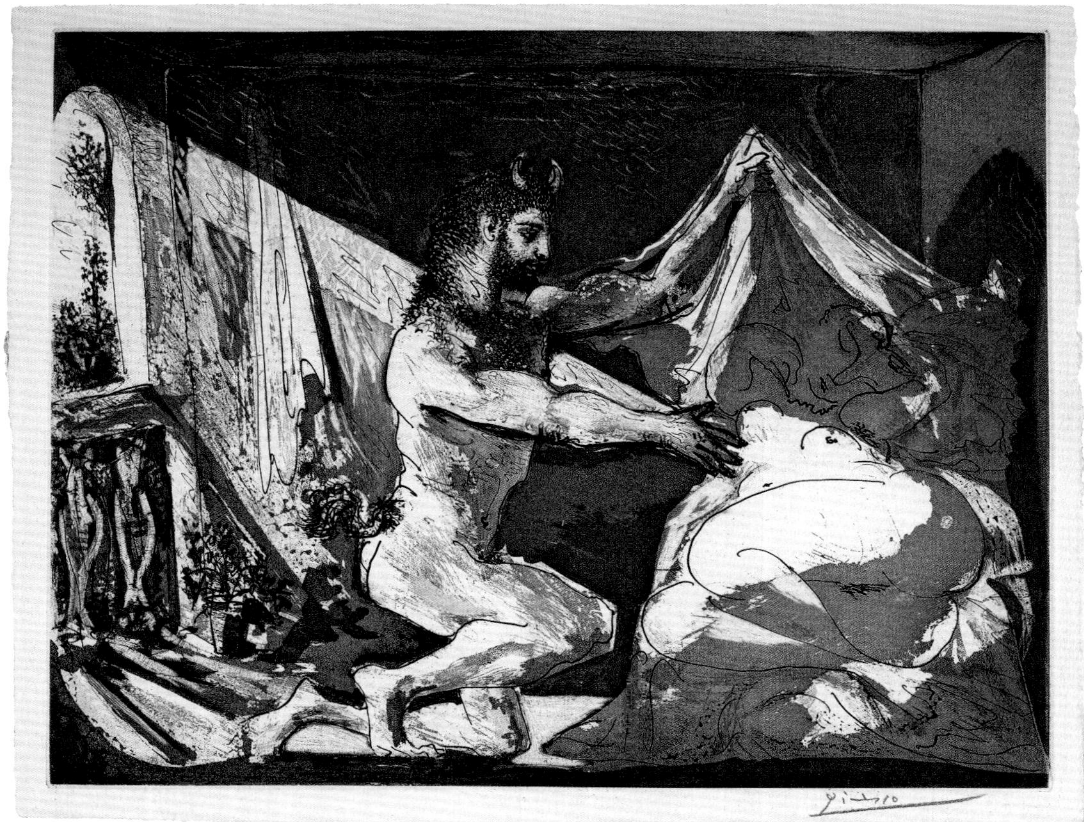

also been suggested that it may be based on Correggio's female nude in his *Venus, Cupid and Satyr* (1624; Musée du Louvre, Paris).[12] Yet Rembrandt's Antiope, with her daringly foreshortened facial features, seems more closely related to the figure of Angelica in Rubens's *Hermit with Sleeping Angelica* (cat. 68). Perhaps Rembrandt also took inspiration for his interpretation of Jupiter from Rubens's hermit, who even having administered a magic potion will never attain the object of his desire.

In the sequence of voyeuristic compositions influenced by Rubens, Jean-Antoine Watteau came up with a particularly original response: in his painting *Nymph and Satyr* (cat. 74; also known as *Jupiter and Antiope*), no doubt intended as a *sopraporta*, Antiope is so relaxed as she sleeps that her left arm dangles freely downwards. The satyr, who has just climbed up the embankment, uncovers the unsuspecting Antiope and is clearly delighted at the sight of her naked beauty, which has so excited him that he is already licking his lips in anticipation – a touch already present in Van Dyck's versions of the subject. The extent to which these figures can conclusively be identified as Jupiter and Antiope, as opposed to Venus and a satyr, or just a nymph and a satyr, has been and remains a cause for controversy. However, Watteau was evidently quite free in his treatments of mythological themes and in his day both Correggio's *Venus, Cupid and Satyr* (*c.* 1528) and Titian's *Pardo Venus* (*c.* 1535; both Musée du Louvre, Paris) were interpreted as Jupiter and Antiope.[13]

Even during his own lifetime Watteau's use of colour was already being compared to that of Rubens.[14] Watteau made a close study of Rubens's cycle for Marie de Médicis in the Palais du Luxembourg (see cat. 34) and for a time he lived in the home of Pierre Crozat

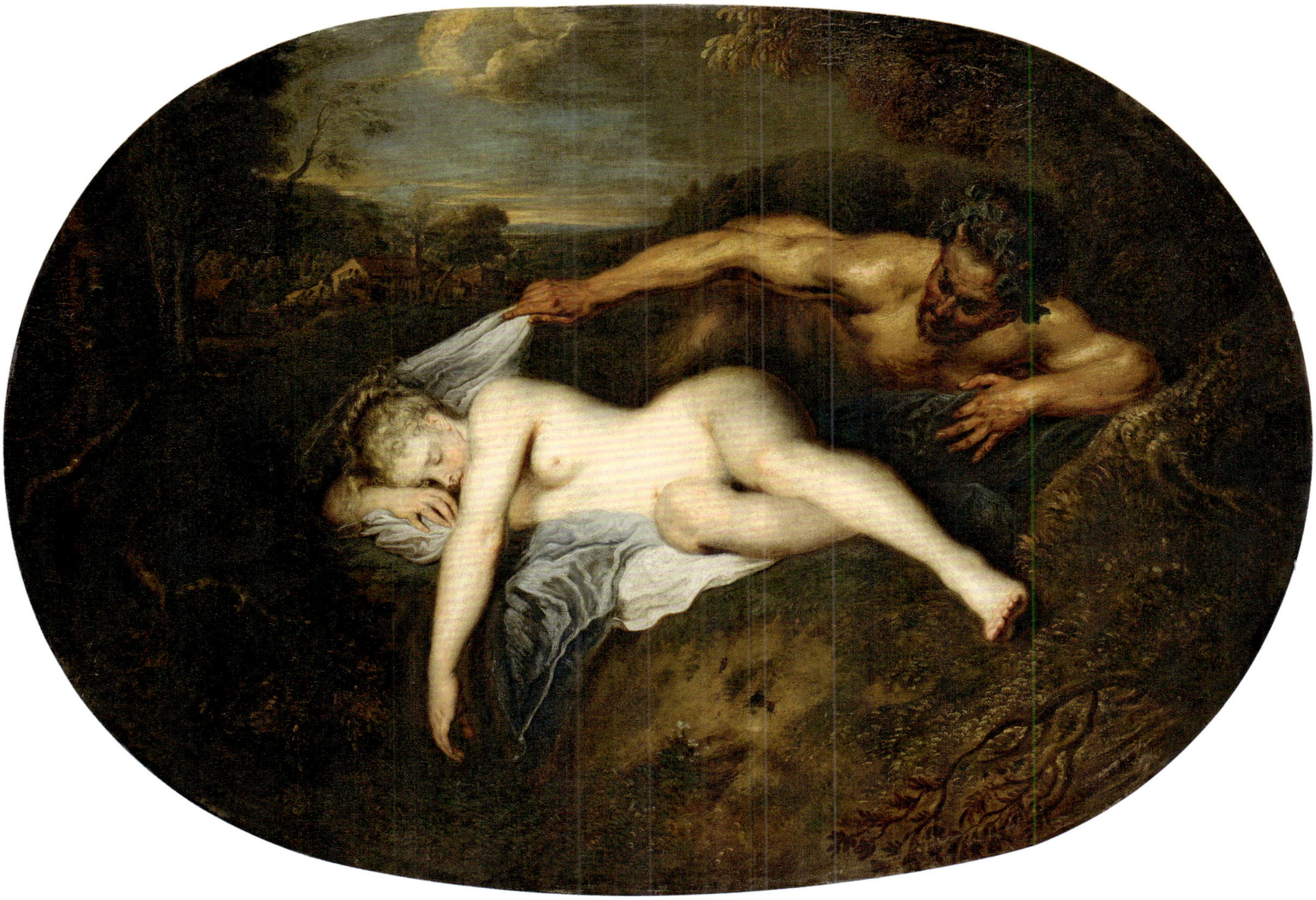

74

JEAN-ANTOINE WATTEAU (1684–1721)
Nymph and Satyr, or *Jupiter and Antiope*, 1715
Oil on canvas, 73.5 x 107.5 cm
Musée du Louvre, Paris, Département des Peintures, inv. M.I. 1129

PROVENANCE: Léopold-Philippe-Charles-Joseph, Duke of Arenberg (1690–1754) (?); Théodore Patureau, 'membre honoraire de l'Académie royale d'Anvers', his sale, Paris, 20–21 April 1857, lot 63; James de Rothschild (?), his sale, Paris, 9–11 March 1868, lot 44; Dr Louis La Caze (1768–1869); Louvre, La Caze Bequest 1869
SELECTED REFERENCES: Washington 1984, no. 36; Paris 1991, no. 14; Börsch-Supan 2007, p. 98, no. 89

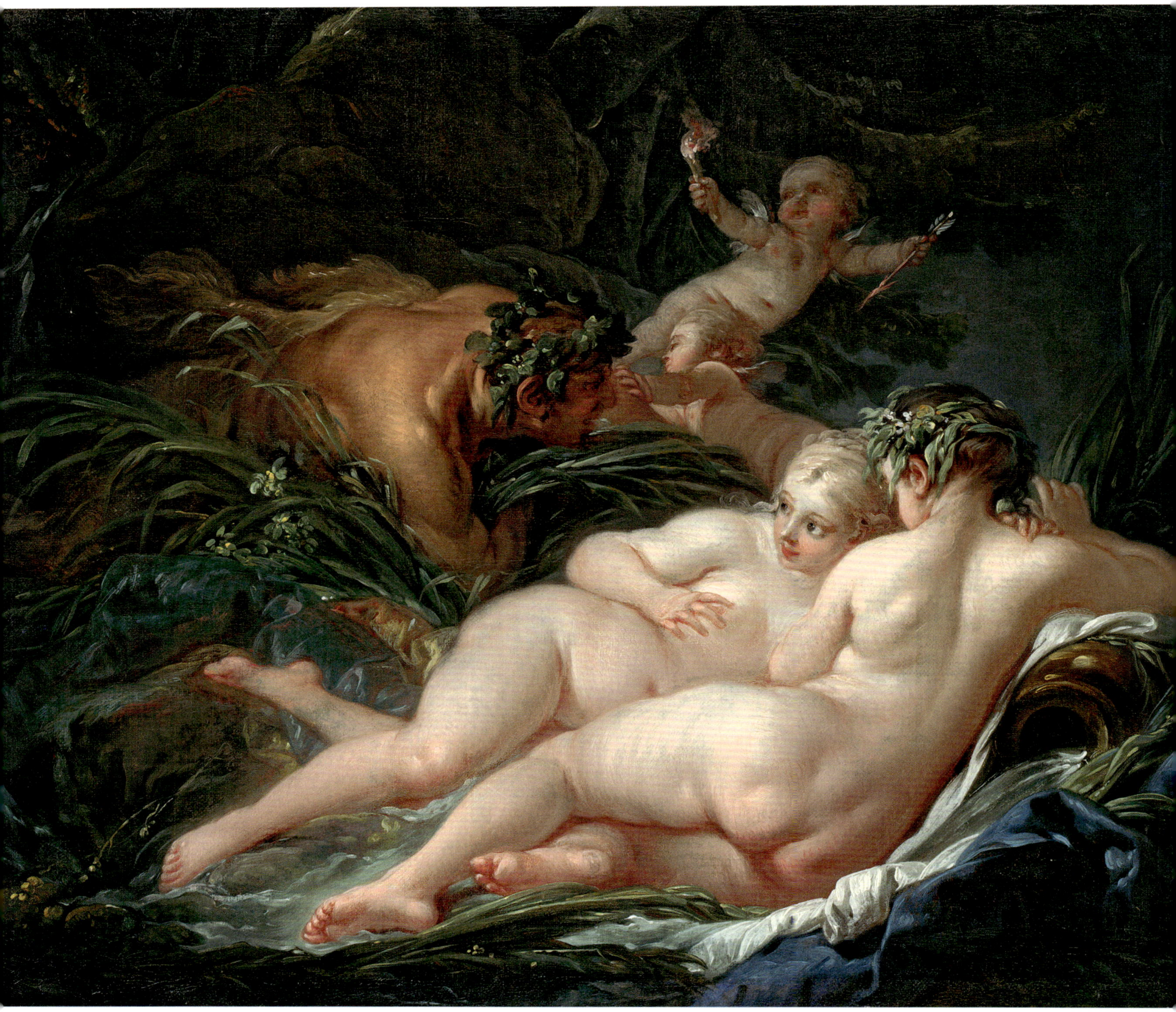

(1661–1740), whose astounding collection of drawings also contained works by Rubens and Van Dyck. The royal collection in Paris, which was already home to Rubens's *A Flemish Kermis* (fig. 58), provided yet another opportunity for Watteau to study works by the master. However, it was not only Rubens's use of colour that preoccupied Watteau; it appears that Rubens's notion of the enlivening of stone[15] (derived from his own study of classical works) was considered by Watteau when he re-created his memorable Antiope as a reclining statue adorning a fountain in *Elysian Fields* (*c.* 1719; Wallace Collection, London).

The last in this sequence of prints is Picasso's *Faun Uncovering a Sleeping Woman* (cat. 73), which continues the tradition of voyeuristic scenes in the guise of mythological events. Picasso's version of the theme is seen in a work in the group that is now known as the Vollard Suite, which is named after Ambroise Vollard (1866–1939), the first art dealer to handle Picasso's work. Picasso was commissioned by Vollard to create a group of one hundred etchings (made between 1930 and 1937) in exchange for a number of paintings.

Scholars have repeatedly cited Rembrandt's *Jupiter and Antiope* (cat. 72) as the model for Picasso's etching. Yet Picasso's faun is already reaching for the breast of the slumbering beauty, who seems to shift luxuriantly in her sleep. In addition to this, Picasso's faun exhibits a taut bodily strength befitting his youth and has nothing in common with Rembrandt's aged Jupiter. The faun and the sleeping woman in this etching have often been read as Picasso himself and his lover and muse Marie-Thérèse Walter.

François Boucher's *Pan and Syrinx* (cat. 75) completes this series of female nudes reclining in the open air, although in Boucher's painting there are two naked female figures. This was a completely new visual interpretation of the traditional story of Syrinx (as seen in cats 55 and 56). Surprisingly, Syrinx is not shown fleeing Pan, rather she has already reached a water-nymph sister. The River Ladon is present only in the form of an amphora with water pouring from it. In order to save Syrinx from the unwelcome attentions of Pan, the water nymph will transform her into a reed, which Pan will take, with other reeds, to make his pan pipes (Ovid, *Metamorphoses* I.694–95). The presence of two female figures in the same painting allowed Boucher to portray both the front and the back view of a sensual female body. As such (and in combination with their very naturalistic appearance), these two figures can be seen as developments of the naiads in Rubens's Médicis cycle: in the scene where Marie de Médicis is shown disembarking at Marseilles (see cat. 34.9) there are three naiads in the foreground who were to leave an indelible impression on French painting.[16]

75

FRANÇOIS BOUCHER (1703–1770)
Pan and Syrinx, 1759
Oil on canvas, 32.4 x 41.9 cm
The National Gallery, London, inv. NG 1090. Presented by Mrs Robert Hollond, 1880

PROVENANCE: Armand-Pierre-François de Chastre de Billy, his sale, Paris, 15–19 November 1784, lot 48, purchased by Quesnot (?) for 651 livres; M. Godefrouy, his sale, Paris, 15 November 1785, lot 45; Charles de Wailly (?) (1730–1798), his sale, Paris, 24 November 1788, lot 50; Pau de Saint-Martin (?), his sale, Paris, 2 October 1820, lot 77; Robert Hollond by *c.* 1840; bequeathed to the National Gallery in 1880 by Mrs Robert Hollond, entered the collection in 1885 after her death
SELECTED REFERENCES: Ananoff and Wildenstein 1980, no. 547; Washington 1984, no. 36; Paris 1989, pp. 25–26; Paris 1991, no. 50; Leppert 1996, pp. 223–29

76

JEAN-BAPTISTE CARPEAUX (1827–1875)
Crouching Flora, 1870
Oil on canvas, 60.8 x 49.8 cm
Musée des Beaux-Arts de Valenciennes, inv. P.46.1.324

PROVENANCE: collection of Mme J.-B. Carpeaux; 1906, bought by the city of Valenciennes
SELECTED REFERENCES: Jamot 1908, vol. 2, p. 180; Paris 1955–56, no. 230; Paris 1975, no. 267; Valenciennes 1978, no. 30; Valenciennes 1999, no. 17, pp. 46, 87, 147

During the Renaissance and Baroque periods, the depiction of naked human figures was primarily associated with biblical episodes, such as the Fall of Man, Susanna and the Elders, and the Last Judgement, or mythological subjects, such as Diana and Callisto, Venus bathing, or Syrinx.[1] However, this changed slowly during the eighteenth century. On the one hand, the depiction of these and similar themes became ever less rigorous, with the result that they were often no longer clearly identifiable; on the other, with the advent of genre painting, everyday activities such as bathing provided opportunities for artists to portray nudes. Images of the human nude in a natural setting retained their appeal, regardless of how the subject-matter arose.

The renowned sculptor and painter Jean-Baptiste Carpeaux admired Rubens. In 1864 he copied Rubens's *Martyrdom of St Stephen* in Valenciennes (today in the Musée des Beaux-Arts) and transformed the altar painting into a *bozzetto*; he also studied works by Rubens in the Louvre and in the Uffizi. Rubens's influence is particularly apparent in Carpeaux's paintings, but his sculptures also owe much to the master. In 1882, not long after his death, Carpeaux was already being aptly described in the following terms: 'Carpeaux was the Rubens of marble and stone. It is as though the flesh were alive.'[2]

Carpeaux's *Crouching Flora* (cat. 76) is closely related to an eponymous sculpture made for the art market and executed in various materials – marble, bronze and terracotta.[3] The painting has generally been regarded as a preparatory study for the sculpture, but Patrick Ramade has suggested it is a *ricordo*,[4] on the basis that Carpeaux made paintings of his most famous works and kept these in his collection. In this crouching figure of a young woman, Carpeaux developed an idea that he had first realised in a multi-figure relief for the Pavillon de Flore at the Louvre in response to a commission from Napoleon III (fig. 3). The pose of the goddess of spring and flowers echoes a classical statue of Venus that had also been a source of inspiration for Rubens (see his *Venus Frigida*, cat. 53), and Carpeaux's painterly, free, extremely expressive application of paint is in itself very reminiscent of the work of Rubens.

When Narcisse-Virgilio Diaz de la Peña embarked on landscapes with pastoral scenes he sought to emulate Françoise Boucher's lightness of touch in his depiction of human lust and desire.[5] The great success he enjoyed with erotic themes in natural settings encouraged him to go on exploring scenes of this kind throughout his life.[6] Diaz's painting of *Nymphs and Satyrs*, now in Cambridge (cat. 77), seems to transport these mythical beings into the forest of Fontainebleau, a location to which he frequently returned in his paintings.[7] Like Rubens, Diaz uses colour rather than outlines to define individual figures. The only distinct, expressive outline – of the kind used by Rubens in his oil sketches – delineates the right-hand side of the satyr bearing the nymph aloft on his shoulder: it calls to mind the outline on Rubens's figure of Triton in his oil sketch *Nereid and Triton* (*c.* 1636; Museum Boijmans Van Beuningen, Rotterdam), which was in fact on display in a private collection in the south of France in the nineteenth century.[8] The scene in Diaz's painting recalls bacchanals in paintings by Rubens, although it is not directly related to any single composition in particular. Vincent van Gogh, commenting on an oil sketch by Diaz, compared his work to that of Rubens, and concluded that they 'were

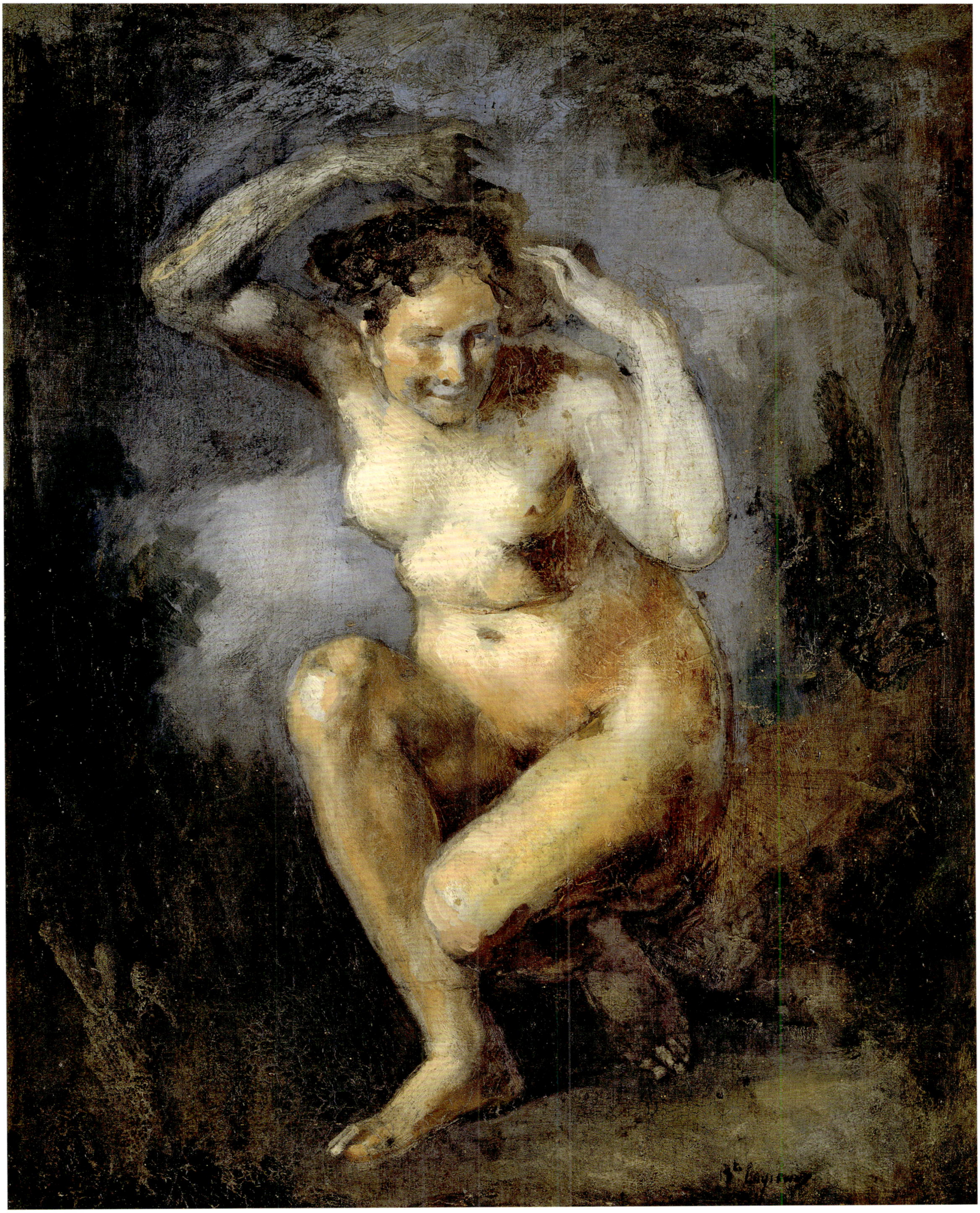

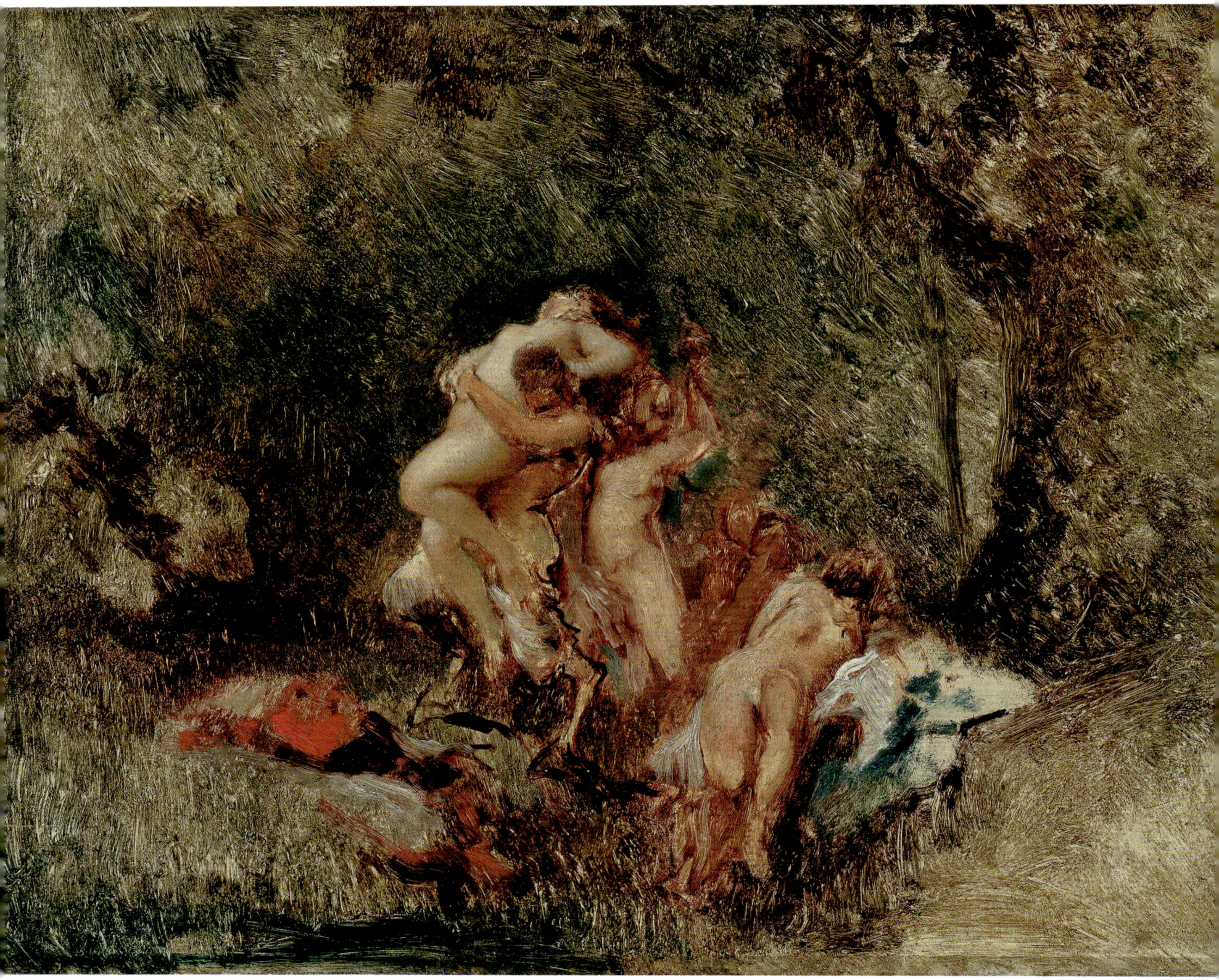

by no means the same, but the belief that the colour expresses the form when it's in its place and in its context – that they do have in common.'[9]

Auguste Renoir frequently returned to re-examine the work of Rubens: between 1860 and 1864 he copied Rubens's portrait of *Hélène Fourment with Her Son Francis* in the Louvre, and his late *Judgement of Paris* (1908; private collection) is clearly influenced by Rubens's painting of the same subject in the Prado (*c.* 1638). During his career Renoir absorbed various ideas from the work of his Flemish predecessor, but the red thread running through Renoir's work is the glow he achieves in his skin tones, which can only have resulted from his study of the shimmering light in Rubens's depictions of skin. This is very apparent in Renoir's *Bather with Long Hair* (cat. 78). The bather's body and surroundings are flooded with light and warm sunshine. She is not aware of being observed and fills the canvas with a memorable presence and physicality that recall many of Rubens's female figures. Renoir drew inspiration here from Rubens's paint techniques: he admired the other's ability to create glowing skin tones by means of his translucent brushwork: 'One day, in the Louvre, I noticed that Rubens had achieved more sense of values with a simple scumble than I had been able to do with all my thick layers of paint,'[10] and he strove to achieve the same effect in his own paintings. Renoir's female figure is portrayed by means of colour alone and the hues are closely related to those used by Rubens. At the same time Renoir gives his *Bather with Long Hair* an innocence and lightness worthy of work by his eighteenth-century role models: Watteau, Boucher and Fragonard.

Something similar may also be seen in his *Studies of Pierre Renoir, His Mother Aline Charigot, Nudes, and Landscape* (cat. 79). To the right is Renoir's future wife, Aline, wearing a hat; his son Pierre is pictured on the left, both waking and asleep. But of particular interest in the present context are Renoir's studies of reclining and seated nude female figures that are clearly connected to the landscape in some way. With the exception of the standing nude all the others are preparatory studies for his *Bathers in the Forest* (1897; Barnes Foundation, Merion) – even if the seated female figure putting up her hair was ultimately realised facing the other way. All the skin tones gleam in what could be described as a modern translation of Rubens's glowing skins. In Renoir's view, womanhood was closely tied to nature and fertility.[11] His very conservative views regarding these matters were clearly not in the spirit of the struggle for women's rights that was already under way in his time.[12]

Paul Cézanne's *Three Bathers* (cat. 80) of 1875 is just one of a large number of works depicting female bathers in natural settings; a theme with a rich tradition, and one to which Cézanne repeatedly returned.[13] It has been suggested that Cézanne was remembering his own youth – when he used to go swimming in the River Arc with friends – rather than evoking mythological scenarios.[14] In his female nudes Cézanne reduces the human body to patches of colour. He had studied Rubens's Marie de Médicis cycle (see cat. 34) and mainly made drawings of nude figures that were, as far as possible, full length and portrayed as figures in motion.[15] He also seems to have studied a drawing attributed to Lucas Vorsterman

77

NARCISSE-VIRGILIO DIAZ DE LA PEÑA (1807–1876)
Nymphs and Satyrs, 1870
Oil on panel, 30.2 x 40.6 cm
Lent by the Syndics of the Fitzwilliam Museum, Cambridge, inv. PD.134-1985

PROVENANCE: collection Everard, sale at Goupil & Cie, Paris; collection E. Chouanard, 1914; private collection, New York; Parke-Bernet, New York, 11 May 1955; with the Hazlitt Gallery, from whom acquired by John Tillotson, 1972; bequeathed to the museum, 1984
SELECTED REFERENCES: Cambridge 1985, no. 11; Miquel and Miquel 2006, vol. 2, no. 2426

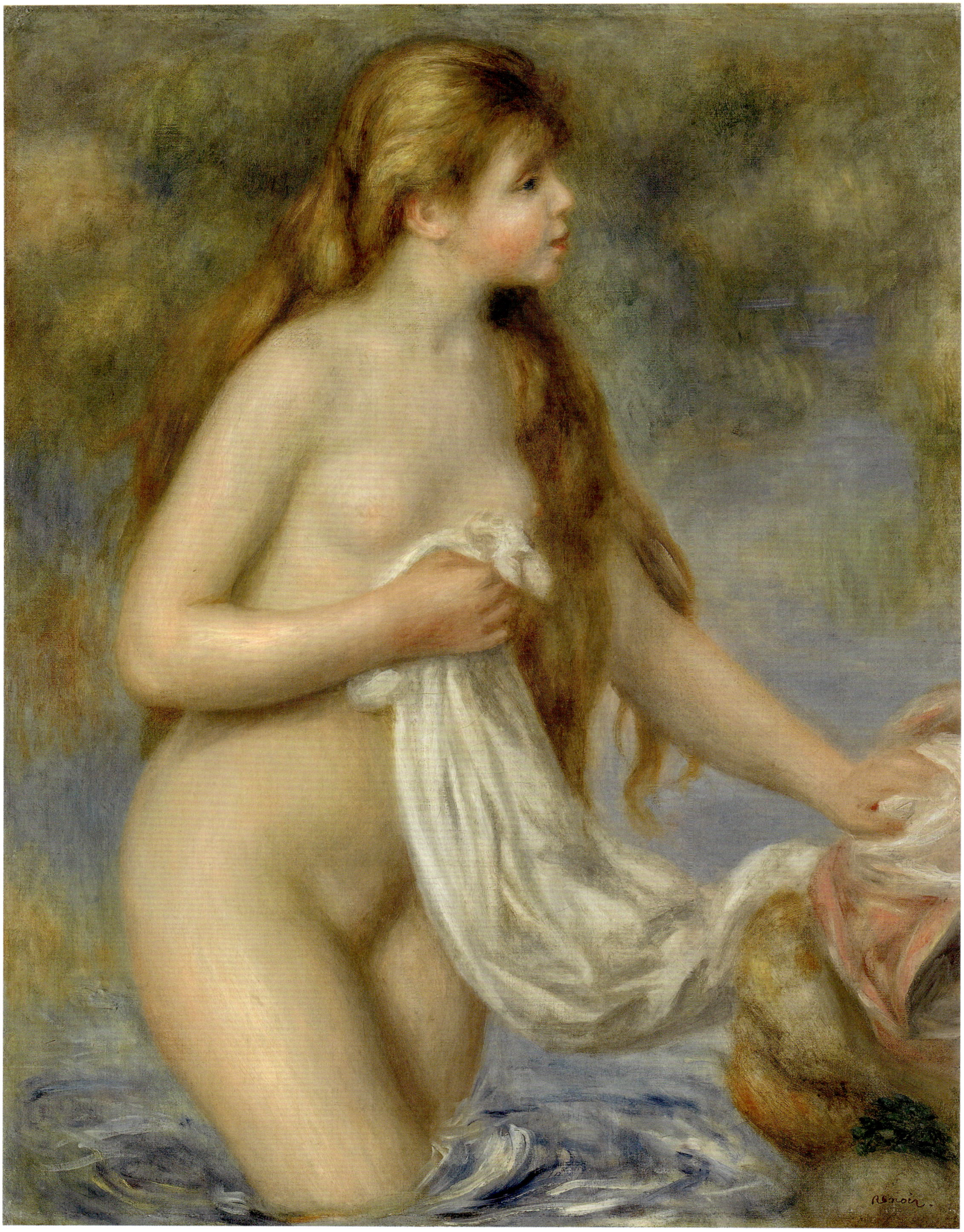
Renoir.

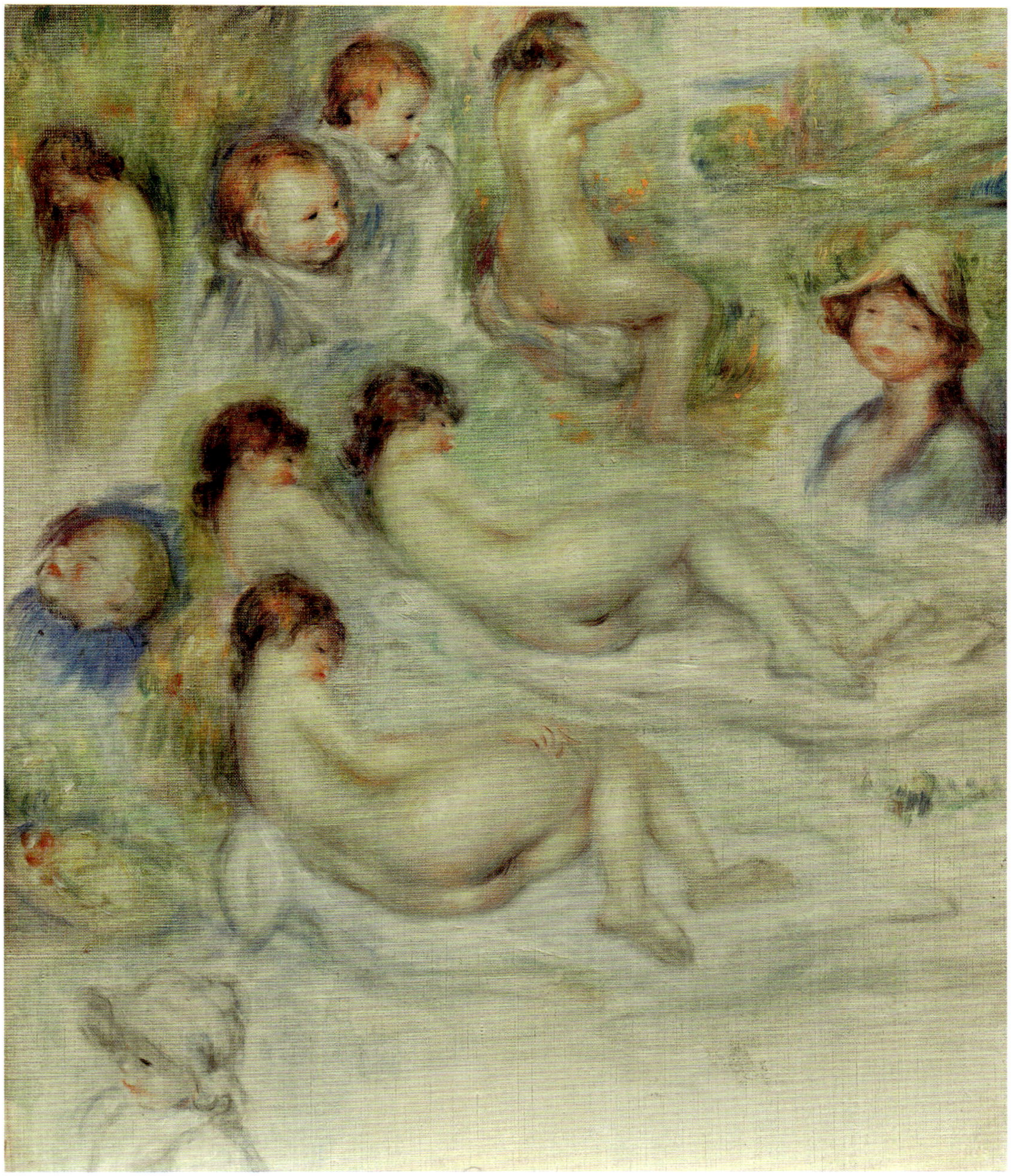

78

AUGUSTE RENOIR (1841–1919)
Bather with Long Hair, *c*. 1895
Oil on canvas, 82 x 65 cm
Musée de l'Orangerie, Paris, inv.
RF 1963–23. Collection Jean Walter
et Paul Guillaume
RA ONLY

PROVENANCE: 1896, bought by Paul Durand-Ruel from Renoir; 1911, Oscar Schmitz, Dresden; collection of Jean Walter and Paul Guillaume
SELECTED REFERENCES: Walter and Guillaume 1966, no. 26; Paris 1983, pp. 194–95; London 1985, no. 92; Néret 2009, pp. 329, 336; Dauberville 2007–12, vol. 3, no. 2451

79

AUGUSTE RENOIR (1841–1919)
Studies of Pierre Renoir, His Mother Aline Charigot, Nudes, and Landscape, 1885–86
Oil on canvas, 46.1 x 38.2 cm
The Art Institute of Chicago, inv. 1983.1.
Restricted gift of the Phillips Family Collection

PROVENANCE: probably Dr Prat, Renoir's physician at Cagnes; Mr and Mrs Lazarus Phillips, Montreal, bought through John Rewald in Paris in France in October 1958 (according to Ivan E. Phillips's letter of 27 April 1982); by descent to the Phillips family, Montreal; given to the Art Institute, 1983
SELECTED REFERENCES: New York 1958, no. 55; Tokyo 1985, no. 36; Chicago 1997, pp. 66–68, no. 19

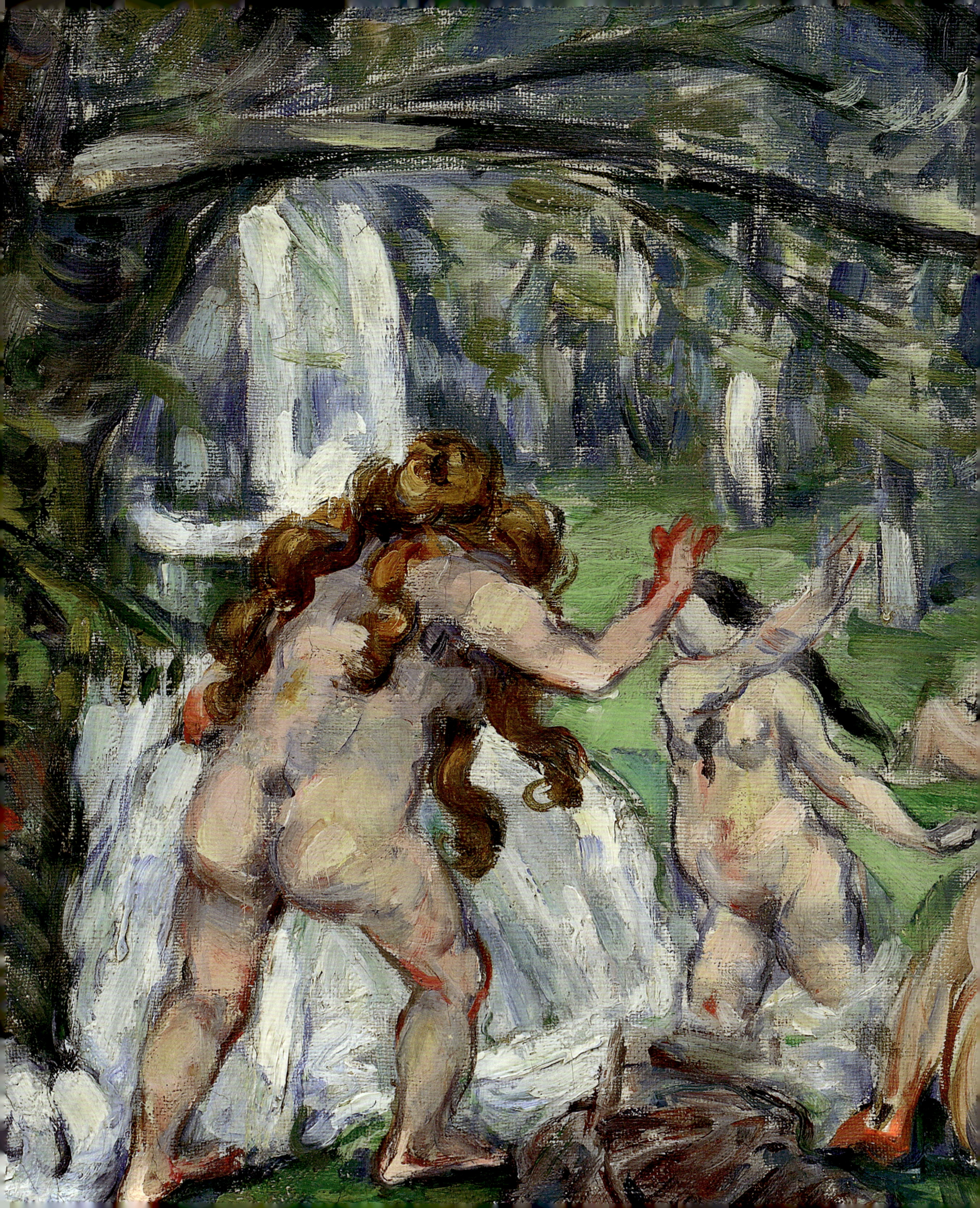

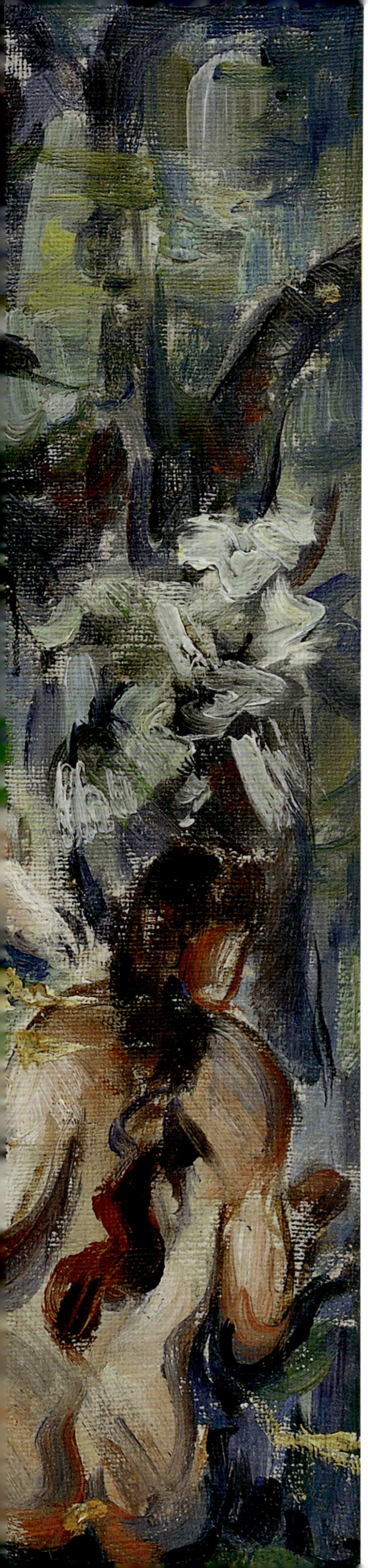

(1595–1675) for an engraving after Rubens's *Hero and Leander* (Musée du Louvre, Paris, Département des Arts graphiques), again singling out the poses of full figures.[16] It seems he was fascinated by the way that Rubens depicted human beings on the move and situated them in their surroundings; at the same time, he did not ignore Rubens's use of colour. Cézanne's *Three Bathers* is memorable for the sheer strength of the figures and for his willingness to countenance 'ugliness': the figure with reddish-blonde hair, rushing towards the water, does not conform to any classical ideals of beauty. At the same time, the hues in the skin of all three bathers recall those used by Rubens – above all in the occasional tinges of blue in combination with glowing, red outlines.

80

PAUL CÉZANNE (1839–1906)
Three Bathers, *c.* 1875
Oil on canvas, 30.5 x 33 cm
Private collection

PROVENANCE: Ambroise Vollard, Paris; Paul Rosenberg, Paris; Marlborough Galleries, London; 1960, bought by Henry Moore, Hertfordshire, England; Mary Moore; Henry Moore Foundation; private collection
SELECTED REFERENCES: Venturi 1936, vol. 1, no. 267; Basel 1989, no. 23, pp. 142, 144, 148, 297–99; Krumrine 1992, p. 584; Rewald 1996, vol. 1, no. 361

In his *Women Pursued by Satyrs* of 1850 (cat. 82), Honoré Daumier focuses on the flight of the two tipsy-looking women, while the two satyrs in the shadowy woods positively melt into their surroundings. The body of the woman wearing orange bends sharply backwards, as though the very gaze of the satyrs had struck her like a bullet in her back. Often, Daumier's somewhat corpulent female figures have been associated with the work of Rubens and unjustifiably dismissed as vulgar by critics such as Charles-Philippe de Chennevières.[1] Daumier did indeed make a detailed study of works by Rubens and copied, for instance, *A Flemish Kermis* (fig. 58) – then, as now, in the Musée du Louvre, Paris.[2] The strong red contours of the female figures, which cause them to stand out all the more against the green, are reminiscent of certain instances in paintings by Rubens, who often showed red fabrics casting a red glow on naked skin. And there are also precedents in Rubens's work for Daumier's symphony in orange, red and yellow – witness Iphigenia's companions in *Cimon and Iphigenia* (fig. 21), who are seen against red and orange fabrics. Yet, with his highly expressive brushwork and more lurid hues, Daumier transports his scene into modernity. The somewhat repetitive pink, blue and green brush strokes in the meadow were apparently added later by Daumier in order to reinforce the memorable colourist look of this painting.[3]

In October 1870, following his return from Paris, Wilhelm Leibl 'copied' Rubens's *Pastoral Scene* in the Alte Pinakothek in Munich. Using a smaller format, Leibl 'translated' Rubens's composition into the language of the Dutch Baroque painter Frans Hals (1582/83–1666), in other words, he did not attempt to replicate Rubens's sophisticated use of washes but instead concentrated on the expressivity and dynamism of his brushwork. These swift, sketch-like brush strokes suggest that Leibl may have made this painting (cat. 81) purely for his own ends, as a study. He was clearly fascinated by the way that the two figures intertwine. The landscape is barely present and other details, such as the bagpipes, are in fact no longer identifiable. Yet the coquettish smile of the shepherdess is certainly derived from Rubens. And that she is not unwilling to accept the man's advances is perfectly clear in both paintings.

The figures in this scene are presumably Corydon and Sylvia. The pastoral poet Theocritus cast Corydon as a cowherd, whereas in Virgil's *Eclogues* he was a shepherd; whatever the case, they were well known in Rubens's day as a frivolous couple.[4] Corydon passionately entreats Sylvia to succumb to him; her disinclination to repel him is accentuated by the unmistakable linking of their legs, which Leibl evidently found very appealing.

CAT. 82 *(detail)*

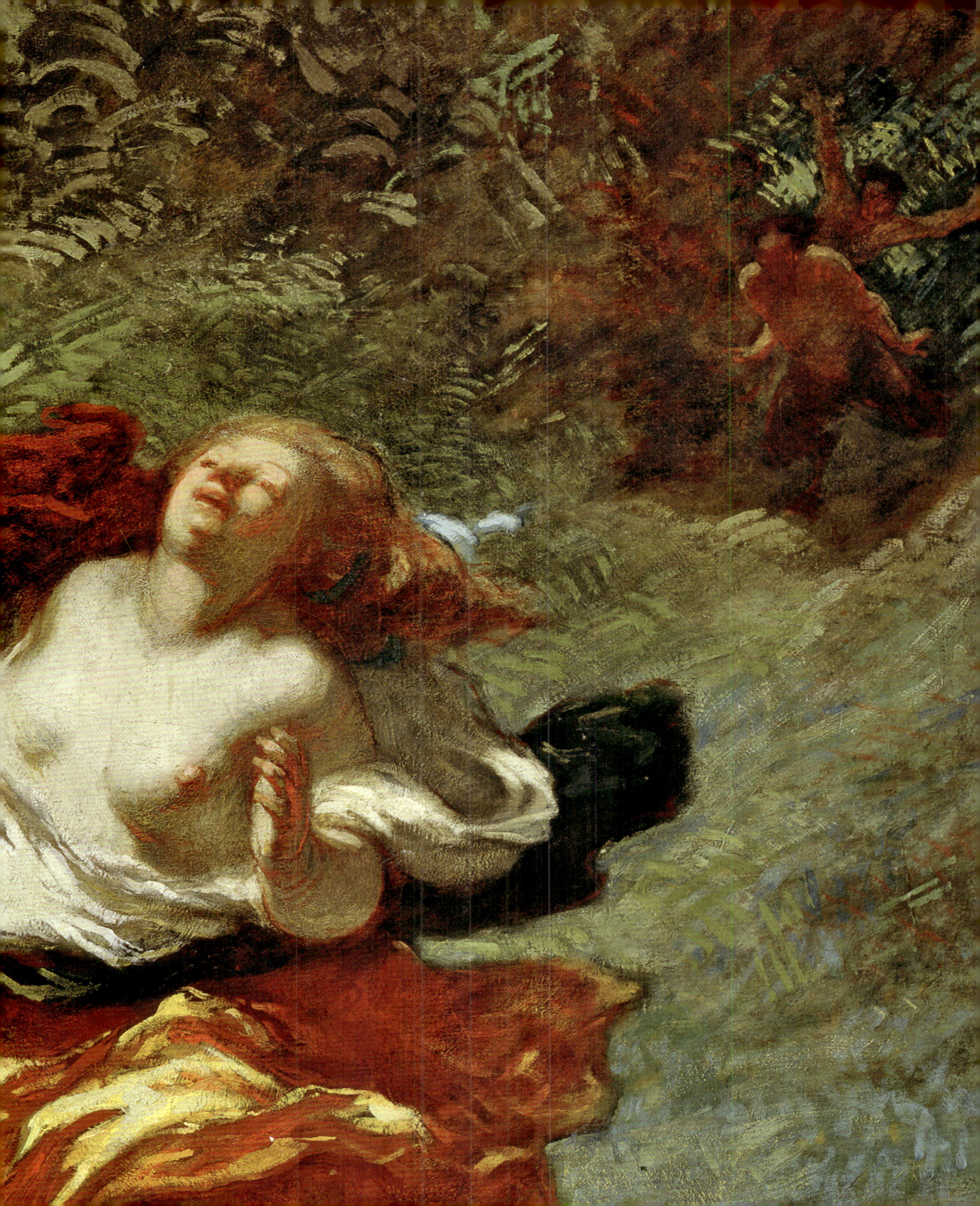

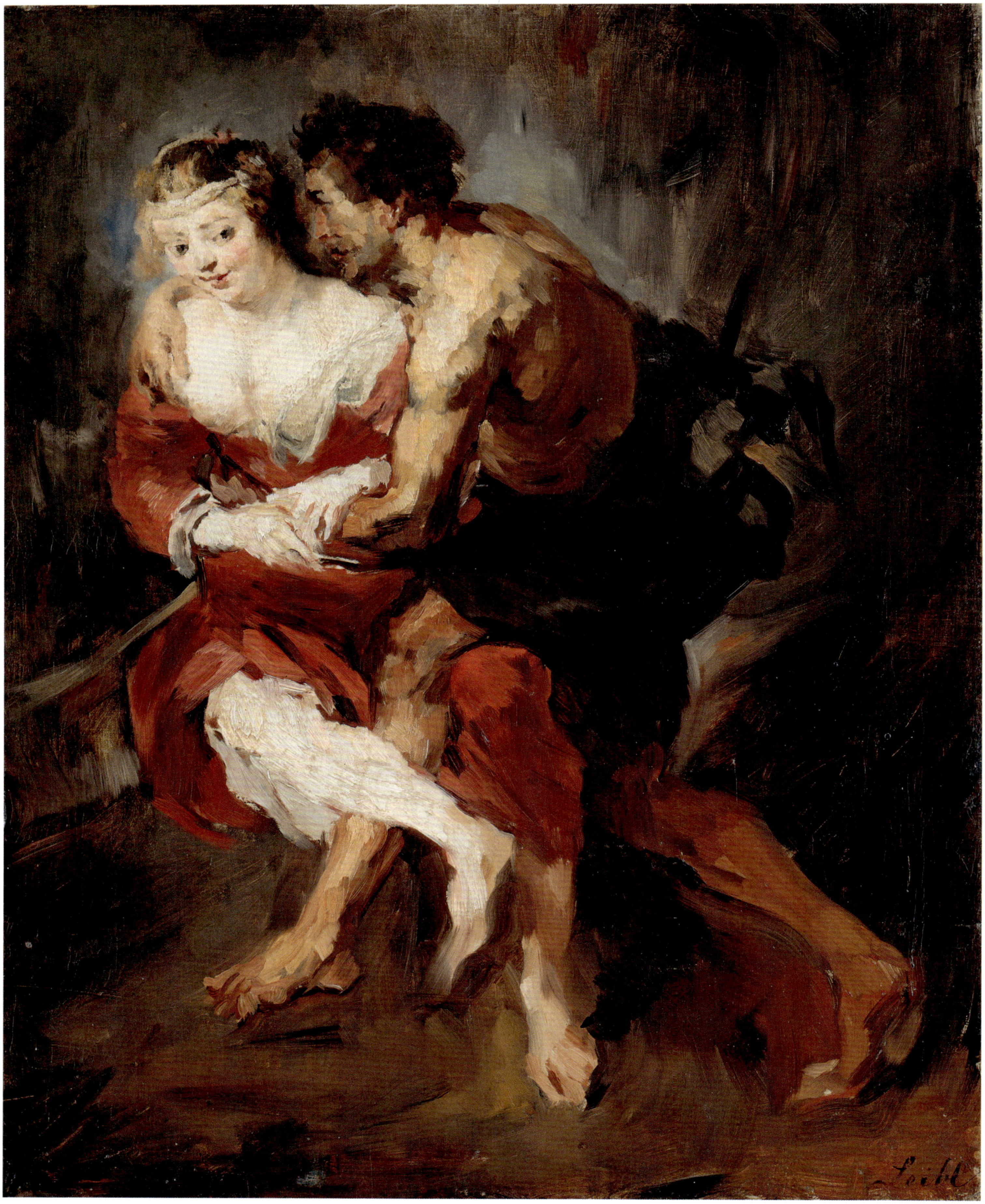
Leibl

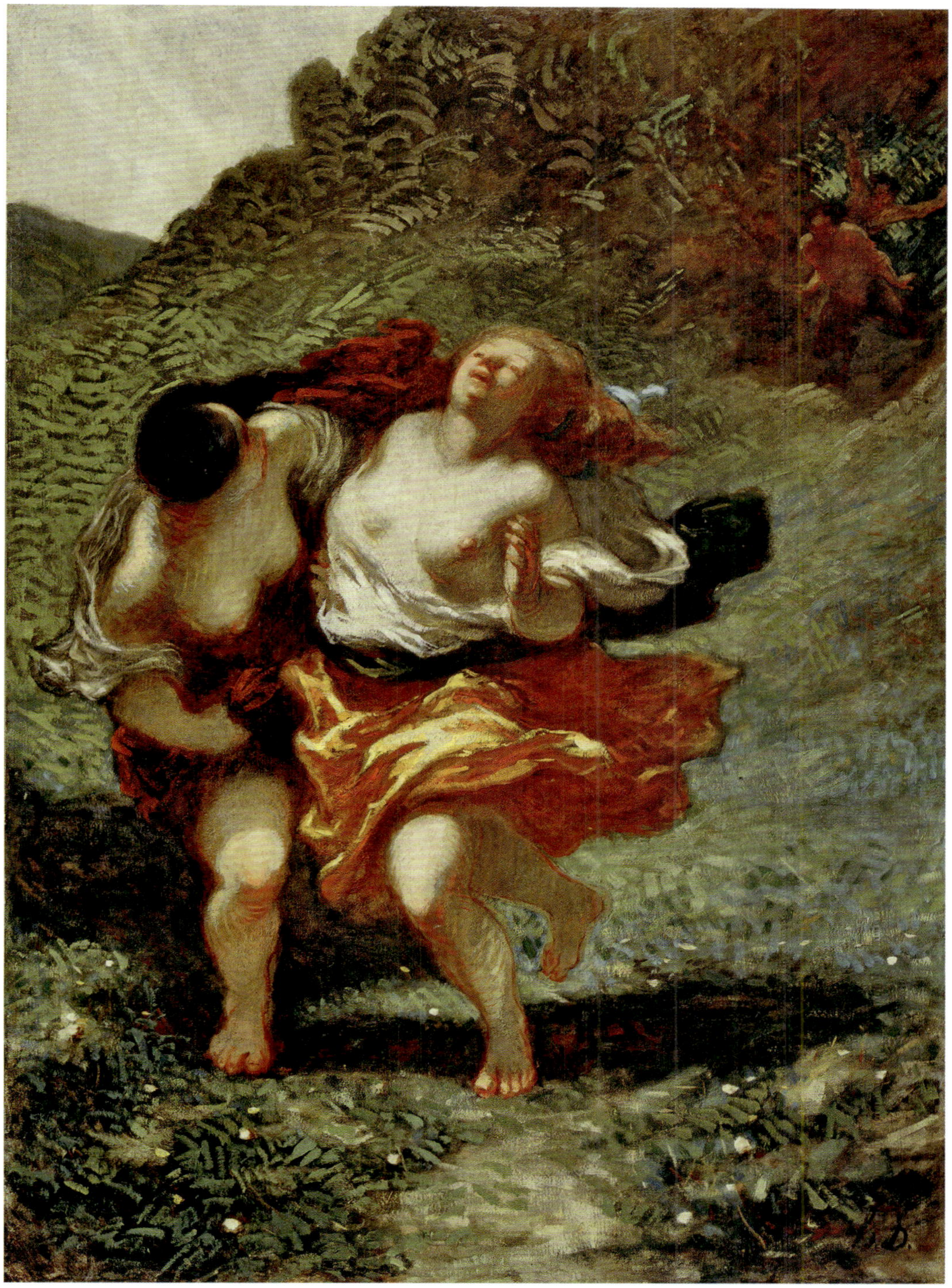

81

WILHELM LEIBL (1844–1900)
Pastoral Scene, 1870
Oil on canvas, 82.5 x 68.5 cm
Signed lower right: Leibl
Neue Pinakothek, Munich, inv. 9262.
Bayerische Staatsgemäldesammlungen

PROVENANCE: purchased from a Munich art dealer in 1925
SELECTED REFERENCES: Mayer 1925, pp. 279–80; Munich 1981, p. 188; Ruhmer 1984, p. 73; Munich 1994, no. 57; Stukenbrock 1994, p. 116

82

HONORÉ DAUMIER (1808–1879)
Women Pursued by Satyrs, 1850
(with later additions by the artist)
Oil on canvas, 129.3 x 97 cm
The Montreal Museum of Fine Arts, inv. 1945.880. Adeline Van Horne Bequest

PROVENANCE: Salon de 1850–51, no. 726; Wisseling Collection, Amsterdam; W. van Horne Collection, Montreal, 1910; bequest of Miss Adeline van Horne, 1945
SELECTED REFERENCES: Adhémar 1954, no. 56; Montreal 1960, p. 101; Maison 1967–68, no. I-32; Laughton 1996, pp. 30–31; Cabanne 1999, pp. 58–59; Ottawa 1999, no. 126; Lampert 2013, p. 18, no. 4

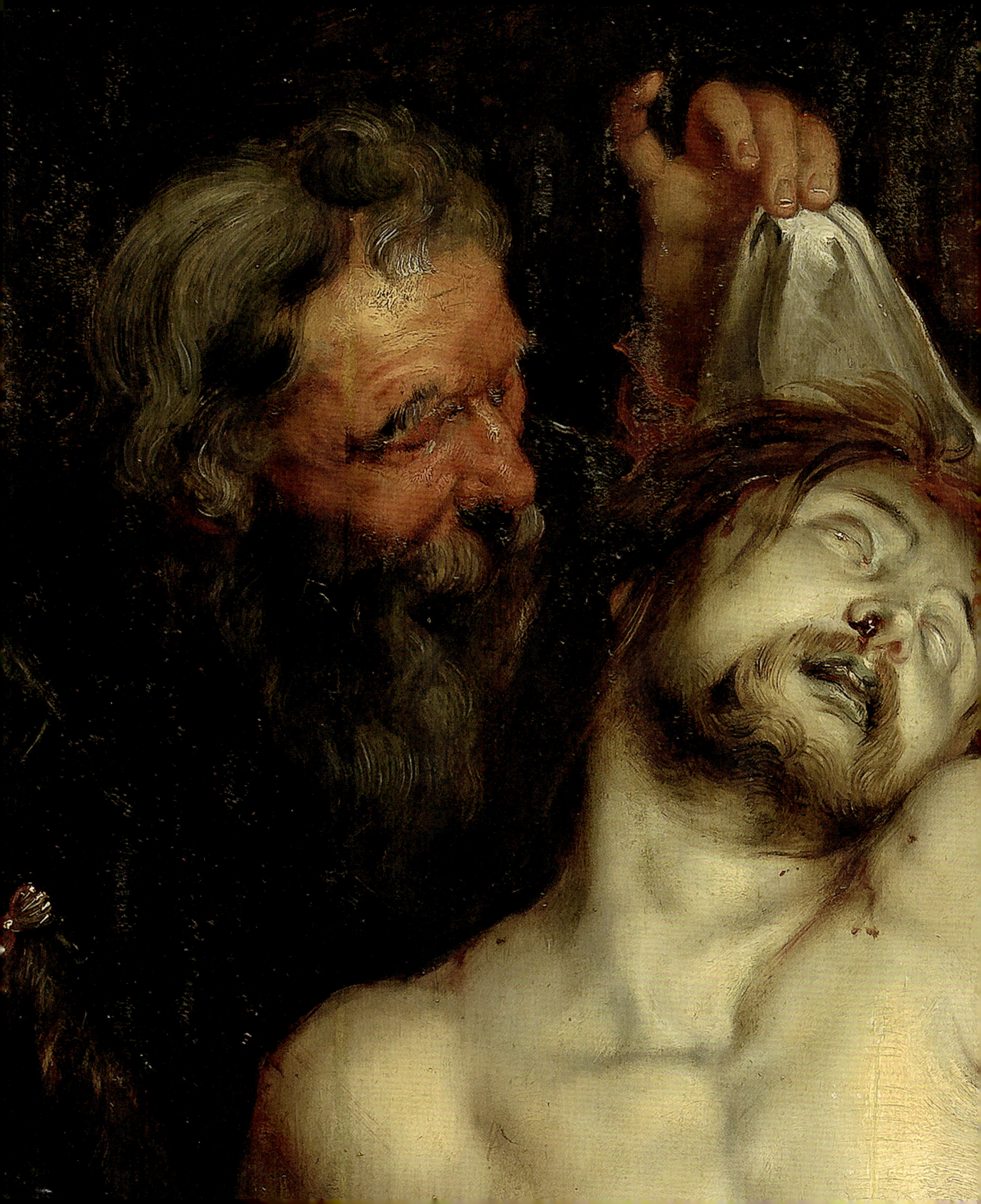

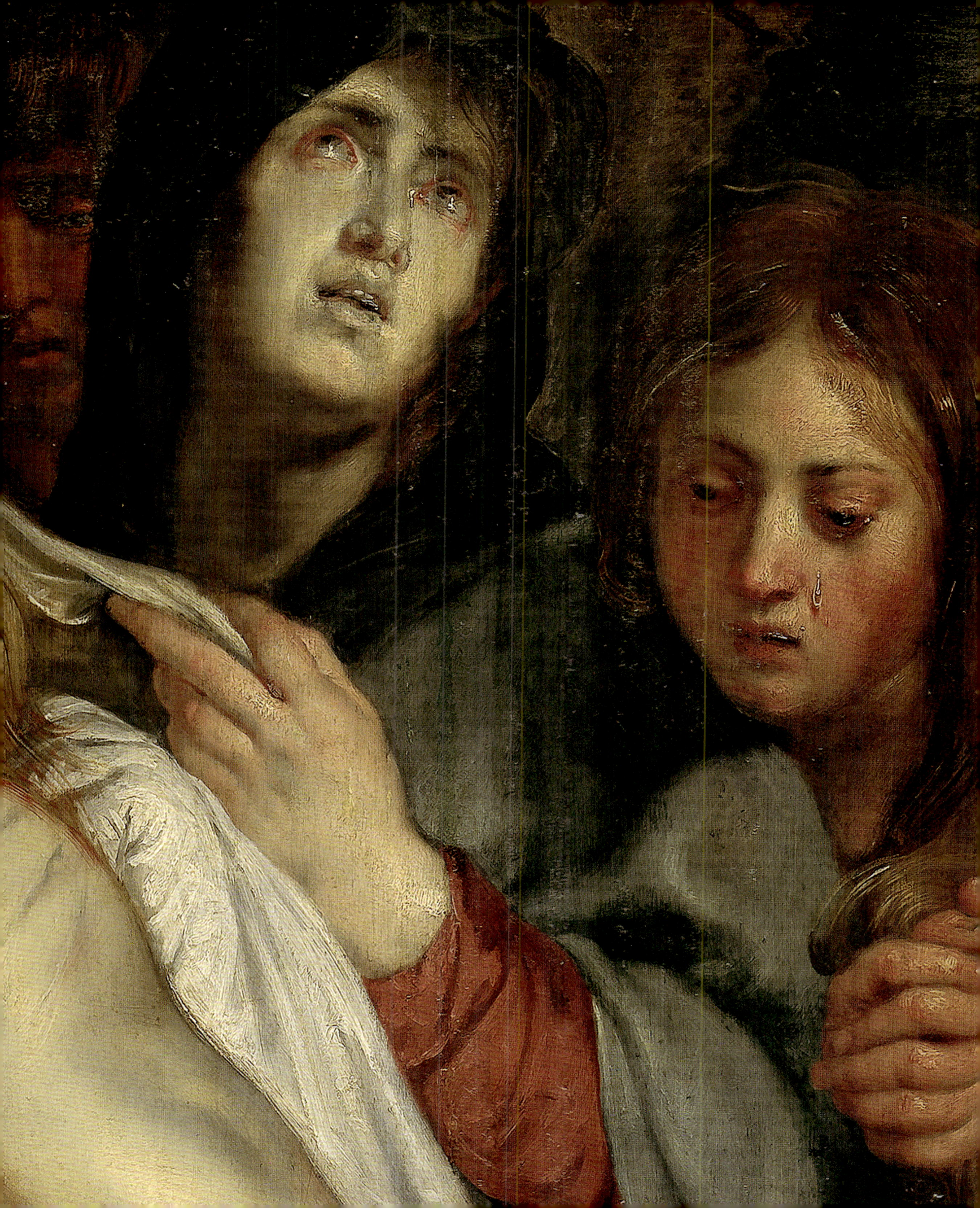

COMPASSION

ARTURO GALANSINO

Rubens, one of the most influential religious painters of all time, is revered for his intense drama and pathos, his fecundity and his enormous range. He was born to Protestant parents at a time of bitter religious strife, in an area that was at the centre of the conflict, yet he was converted and remained an ardent Roman Catholic all his life. It is difficult to be sure at what stage his personal faith began to influence his artistic choices, but the religious sensibility borne out of the Counter-Reformation undoubtedly influenced his style.

The iconoclasm of the Protestant rebellion in Flanders, from 1566 to 1585, brought about the destruction of a huge number of religious works of art that were deemed to be idolatrous. With the return of some provinces to Spanish rule, the archdukes Albert and Isabella took upon themselves the task of restoring Catholic ceremonial decoration in religious institutions, providing commissions for a large number of altarpieces to the younger generation of local artists.

The main aim of the new iconography of the Counter-Reformation was to move the spectator to compassion and to inspire faith. Religious subjects, in particular representations of martyrdom, grew increasingly declamatory, monumental and gruesome. After returning to his native land from Italy in 1608, Rubens, at work on a series of large altarpieces, became part of an artistic *reconquista* – an adjunct to the religious and political re-conquest – conducted through spiritual subject-matter. As one of Paul Claudel's characters in *The Satin Slipper* (1929) says: 'Rubens is the person who will save Flanders for Christianity against heresy. What is beautiful creates unity, what is beautiful emanates from God, what creates unity and emanates from God can to my mind only be called Catholic.'[1]

The young artist had made his mark as a religious painter in Italy with a number of important commissions, including the Roman altarpieces for Santa Croce in Gerusalemme (now in the cathedral of Notre-Dame-du-Puy, Grasse) and the Chiesa Nuova; the *Adoration of the Shepherds* (Pinacoteca Civica, Fermo) with its impressive light effects; and, in the Jesuit church in Genoa, the *Circumcision*, whose impressive appearance influenced the development of local painting by seventeenth- and early eighteenth-century artists such as Gioacchino Assereto, Gregorio de' Ferrari and Giovan Benedetto Castiglione. Rubens's long stay in Italy helped forge his visual language – a stunning synthesis of the classical forms of Roman antiquity, the colours of Venetian painting, the power of Michelangelo and the dramatic chiaroscuro of Caravaggio – and furnished him with the wherewithal to create an almost boundless repertory of invention, quotation and figurative experiments. Eugène Delacroix commented, on the subject of Rubens's *Elevation of the Cross* (fig. 25): 'He was steeped in sublime works, and one cannot say that he imitated.'[2]

Even before Rubens returned to Flanders many churches had been decorated with grisly scenes of martyrdom, graphically depicted in the altarpieces of Marten de Vos the Elder, Frans Pourbus the Elder, Ambrosius Francken the Elder and Otto van Veen.[3] These were precursors of the alarmingly expressive altarpieces painted by Rubens, whose own innovative style, combined with the new sensibility of the Counter-Reformation,

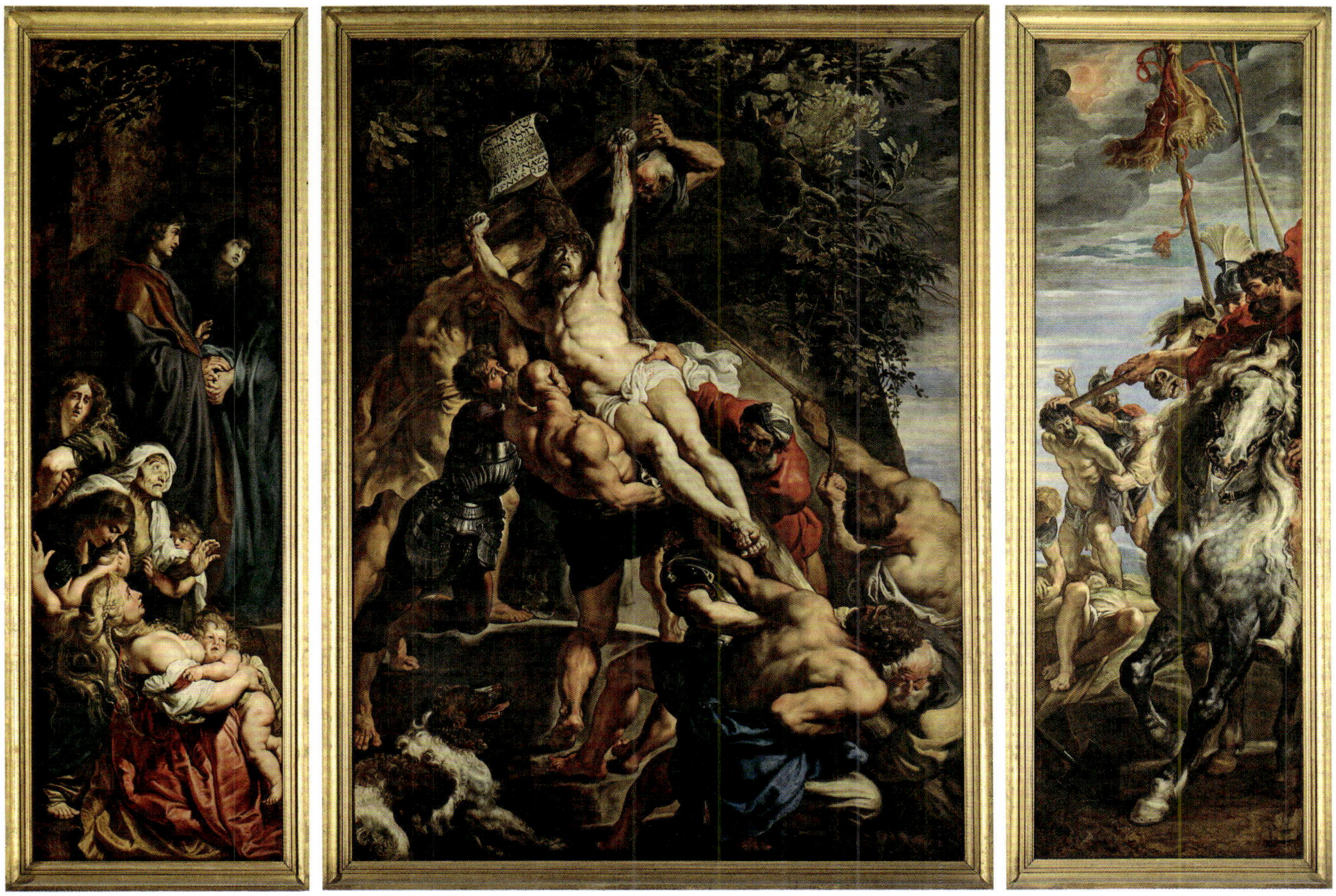

FIG. 25 Peter Paul Rubens, *Elevation of the Cross*, 1613. Oil on panel, 460 x 340 cm. Cathedral Church of Our Lady, Antwerp

seems to have borne quite different fruit and provided other models to the painters of successive generations.

Testimony to the extraordinary creative energy and the renown of Rubens's religious painting can be found in the work of the classicist Giovanni Pietro Bellori, who records in *Le vite de' pittori, scultori, et architetti modern* (Rome, 1672) how, thanks to his speed and his talent, Rubens filled the churches of Flanders with altarpieces, and how his compositions were reproduced and copied via prints and engravings. The spread of Rubens's religious works through engravings was literally global, a significant new phenomenon. Besides being collected and providing inspiration to artists throughout Europe, Rubens's prints were used at the far ends of the known world by missionaries in their evangelical work, sometimes also inspiring works of art in distant lands, as evidenced by the Chinese dish (cat. 83) whose design was based on the engraving of the *Coup de Lance* (cat. 84). The missionaries' choice reflects the expressive potency and strength of Rubens's religious imagery, the visual equivalent of the imagery used in Jesuit rhetoric. Rubens enjoyed a special relationship with the Society of Jesus, working for them on several occasions, in particular on the decorations for the ceiling of the Jesuit church in Antwerp. This church, the first to be dedicated to St Ignatius Loyola, the founder of the order, burnt down in 1718;[4] all that remains of the largest religious decorative scheme ever undertaken by Rubens are some sketches *di sotto in sù* ('looking up from beneath'), depicting saints as well as scenes from the Old Testament and the New Testament (see cat. 98).

The diffusion of engravings after Rubens's religious subjects beyond the confines of Europe provided one source for Mexico's rich style of Baroque painting. Sixteenth- and early seventeenth-century artists such as Sebastian López de Arteaga, José Juárez and Juan Correa made use of such engravings, reinterpreting them in a neo-Hispanic manner. Above all, the Mexican artist Cristóbal de Villalpando (fig. 4) had skill enough to rival the sublime power of the originals, although he had never seen them in the flesh. The work of these Latin American painters was influenced by Rubens's deep-rooted affinity for Iberian culture, an influence especially strengthened by his sojourns in Madrid, his works for Philip IV, and the presence of a large number of pictures from Rubens's own collection on the walls of the King's gallery. Spanish painters rarely travelled at this time, so the King's masterpieces fulfilled a fundamental role in their training as artists.[5] Obviously prints of Rubens's work were widely available in Spain too, and in 1638 the first Rubens engraving was printed in Spain – the work of Pedro Rodríguez, based on the pre-existing print of the *Martyrdom of St Lawrence*.[6] The court painter Francisco Rizi (1614–1685), a pupil of Vicente Carducho and in his turn the teacher of Claudio Coello (cat. 95), was the first real 'translator' of Rubens's personal language into Spanish – he was called 'the new Rubens' by the seventeenth-century commentator José García Hidalgo.[7] The epithet was attached to him because of his eclectic use of prints of Rubens's religious paintings as sources of inspiration, as can be seen for example in his *Martyrdom of St Peter* (1655; Church of St Peter, Fuente el Saz). In similar fashion, even Bartolomé Esteban Murillo (1618–1682), a painter not given to dramatic, violent atmospherics, freely translated Rubens's compositions into the vaporous style of Seville, as demonstrated in his slightly sickly altarpiece of the

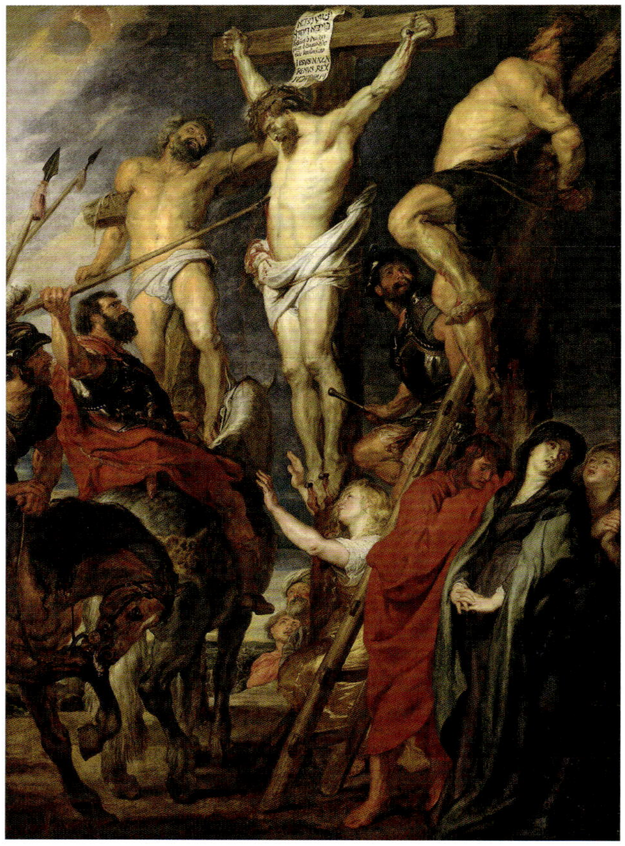

FIG. 26 Peter Paul Rubens, *Coup de Lance*, 1620. Oil on panel, 429 x 311 cm. Royal Museum of Fine Arts Antwerp

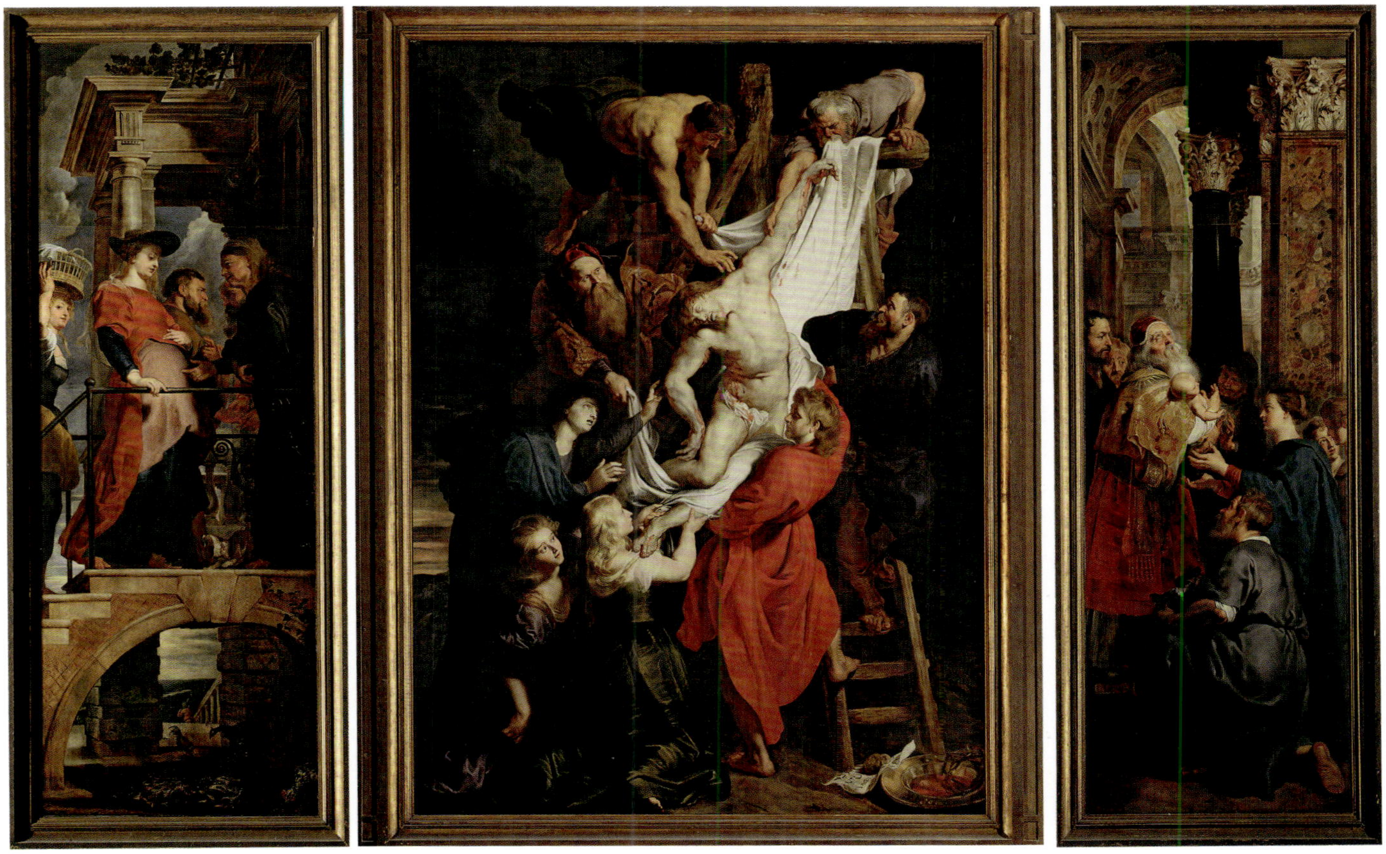

FIG. 27 Peter Paul Rubens, *Descent from the Cross*, 1614. Oil on panel, 421 x 311 cm. Cathedral Church of Our Lady, Antwerp

Martyrdom of St Andrew (1675–80; Museo Nacional del Prado, Madrid), which was inspired by Rubens's altarpiece in the church of the hospital of San Andrés de los Flamencos, Madrid.[8]

The altarpieces painted by Rubens after his return to Antwerp in 1608 conform to the rules regarding the production of religious images laid down by the Council of Trent. These new Counter-Reformation regulations demanded the inclusion of New Testament scenes in the central compartment of a polyptych, with subjects connected to the life of Christ or the Virgin Mary; the usual stories of saints were often relegated to the side compartments. Scenes of the Passion were the most favoured in this new religious vocabulary. Monumental altarpieces such as the *Elevation of the Cross*, the *Coup de Lance* (fig. 26) and the *Descent from the Cross* (fig. 27) provide the clearest examples of the religious language introduced by Rubens. In this heart-rending series of images, poised somewhere between realism and artifice, the classical proportions of Christ's body

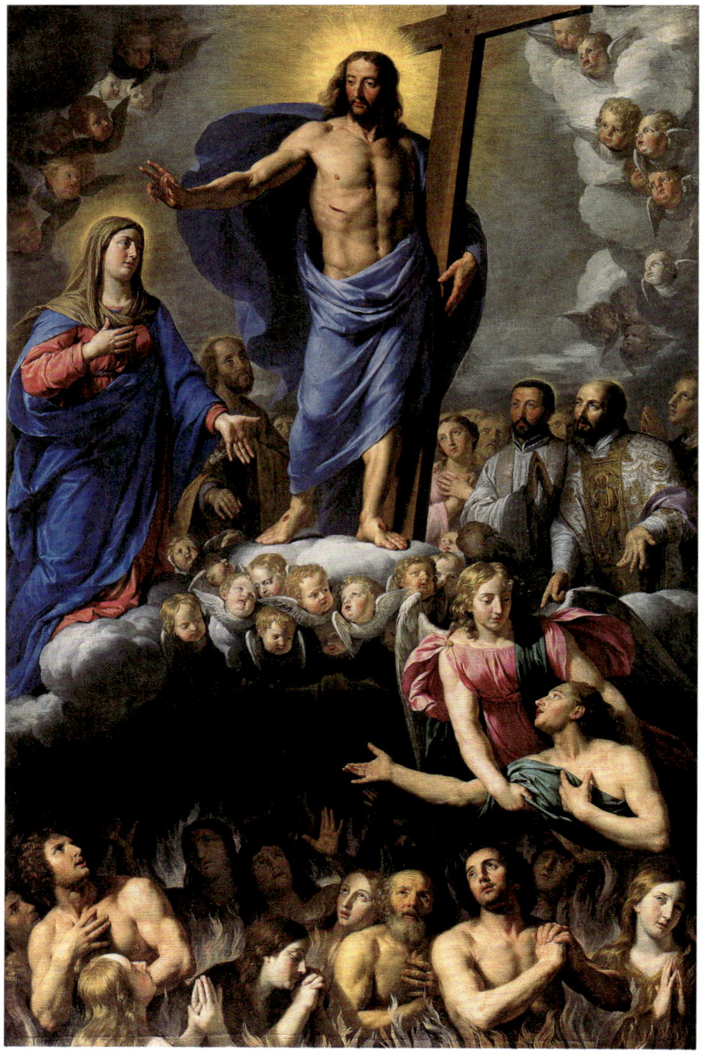

FIG. 28 Philippe de Champaigne, *Christ Among the Souls in Purgatory*, 1625–74. Oil on canvas, 384 x 255 cm. Musée des Augustins, Toulouse

are contorted into macabre postures, and we are not spared the grimmest details. All these religious masterpieces were gathered together, with many others, in Paris in the Louvre from 1794 to 1815 when Napoleon's plundering brought a large number of Rubens's greatest religious works to the new 'universal' museum; the works of art were thereafter dispersed to various museums, and not all of them restored to the places where they belonged. The multi-volume guidebook to the Galerie du Musée Napoléon by Joseph Lavallée describes this exceptional haul of the religious works of Rubens; among the usual praise for the master's use of colour and criticism of some examples of carelessness in his drawing, the author stresses the paintings' emotional impact and naturalism.[9] This group of images served as a training ground for young painters, and it is very likely that without Napoleon's plundered works of art, the nineteenth-century French revival of interest in the achievements of Rubens would not have taken place. A whole generation of artists born around the 1790s – including Théodore Géricault and above all Eugène Delacroix, encouraged by the example of Antoine-Jean Gros – became champions of Rubens, reclaiming his legacy. In their Romantic view the Flemish painter was no longer the gentleman-artist admired during the *grand siècle*; nor was he the cultivated humanist and collector of antiquities; nor was he even the international diplomat, treated as an equal by the great and the good. Rubens became instead the visionary genius, precursor of the painting frenzy that seized the post-Revolutionary generations; the sublime demiurge capable of transcending academic regulations: the 'Homer of painting', as Delacroix was to term him.

We have Delacroix to thank for having given prominence to the work of Rubens as a model for modern painting, in particular in France where, notwithstanding the classicism inherent in painting from Poussin to Ingres, a vestige of taste that was favourable to Rubens can be detected, even before the *querelle du coloris*. Over the seventeenth and the eighteenth centuries,

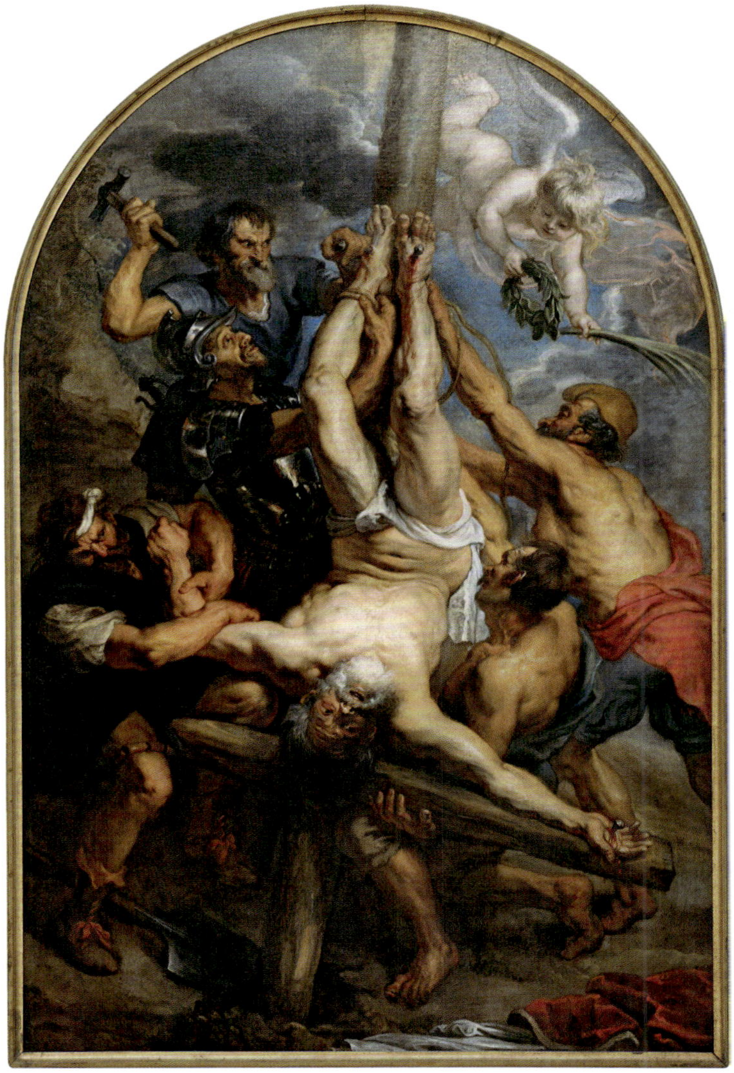

FIG. 29 Peter Paul Rubens, *The Crucifixion of St Peter*, *c.* 1638. Oil on canvas, 310 x 170 cm. Church of St Peter, Cologne

Rubens's example played a considerable role in transporting French painting beyond the typically rationalist boundaries, towards expressiveness and colour, making him the father of the rococo (as personified by Boucher and Fragonard), and an important point of reference even for a Neoclassical artist such as Jacques-Louis David.

It is true that the success of Rubens's religious visual language was limited during his lifetime. When, towards the end of the 1660s, the kingdom of France annexed a number of the northern provinces that were so generously stocked with altarpieces by Rubens, French aesthetic opinion did not alter; the altarpieces remained unknown to the wider public until the eighteenth-century interventions of Antoine-Nicolas Dezallier d'Argenville and Jean-Baptiste Descamps.

The Attic style of Jacques Stella, Eustache Le Sueur or Laurent de La Hyre, in fashion in France towards the middle of the seventeenth century, was completely anti-Rubens, and the birth of the Académie in 1648 was characterised by a literary flowering that was also indifferent to Rubens until the reassessment by Roger de Piles in his *La Vie de Rubens* (1681). Despite this, thanks to the diffusion of the prints, echoes of Rubens's religious output could be found in France. One example is Philippe de Champaigne's altarpiece with *Christ Among the Souls in Purgatory* (fig. 28), whose composition was inspired by Rubens's *St Teresa of Ávila Interceding for Bernardino de Mendoza in Purgatory* (cat. 103) via the print by Boetius Adamsz. Bolswert.[10] Of particular interest are the *Crucifixion of St Peter* (Notre-Dame, Paris) by Sébastien Bourdon (an eclectic reworking of the *Elevation of the Cross* in Antwerp, following the print by Hans Witdoeck)[11] and the case of Charles Le Brun. Despite being one of Rubens's greatest detractors, Le Brun was inspired by Rubens in both his *Descent from the Cross* (*c.* 1680; Musée des Beaux-Arts de Rennes) and his *Martyrdom of St John the Evangelist* (1642; Saint-Nicolas du Chardonnet, Paris).[12] At the end of the century, and especially with the election of Charles de La Fosse to the presidency of the Académie, the perfect time for welcoming Rubens to France had arrived.[13] In 1719 it appears that the Abbé Dubos praised the *Coup de Lance* – probably known to him via Bolswert's print – thus transforming it into an iconic work of religious art, as well as a permanent fixture in art theory. With regard to religious painting at the beginning of the eighteenth century, Jean Jouvenet was the artist most fruitfully engaged with the language of Rubens.[14] His monumental scenes from the life of Christ, painted for the church of Saint-Martin-des-Champs, Paris, in particular the *Expulsion from the Temple* (1706; Musée des Beaux-Arts de Lyon), translate Rubens's language into something more austere, lacking interest in flesh, colour or in the contortions of the human body, and with no more than a hint of violence of expression. A drawing by Jouvenet now in the Louvre displays a familiarity with the very violent *Crucifixion of St Peter* (fig. 29), probably approached via a sketch by Rubens (*c.* 1640; Kunstmuseum Basel, Kupferstichkabinett).[15] This sketch, at one time in the collection of Pierre Crozat, may also have influenced Jean-Antoine Watteau, as is possibly evidenced by a drawing in the Nationalmuseum, Stockholm, sometimes attributed to him.[16] The frequent inclusion of Watteau in this exhibition tells us that Rubens's sacred works made an impression on individuals with a culturally very diverse range of sensibilities, including for example the sculptor Etienne-Maurice Falconet, the favourite of Madame de Pompadour, who, writing to his friend Diderot, described the *Descent from the Cross* as the most frightening painting he had ever seen, the physical expression of the power of art.[17]

Rubens's sublime compositions also attracted the attention of some of the finest minds of the English Enlightenment, as the sketch by Thomas Gainsborough (cat. 90), taken from the print by Vorsterman (cat. 87), demonstrates.[18] The attraction Rubens's bold expressiveness exerted on the artists of the eighteenth century can clearly be detected also in the *Miracle of the Sufferers from St Anthony's Fire* (Saint-Roch, Paris), the masterpiece of Gabriel-François Doyen, a pupil of Carle Van Loo. When the painting was presented in Paris at the Salon of 1767 Diderot declared it to be a plagiarism of Rubens's *Miracles of St Francis Xavier* (1617–18; Kunsthistorisches Museum, Vienna).[19]

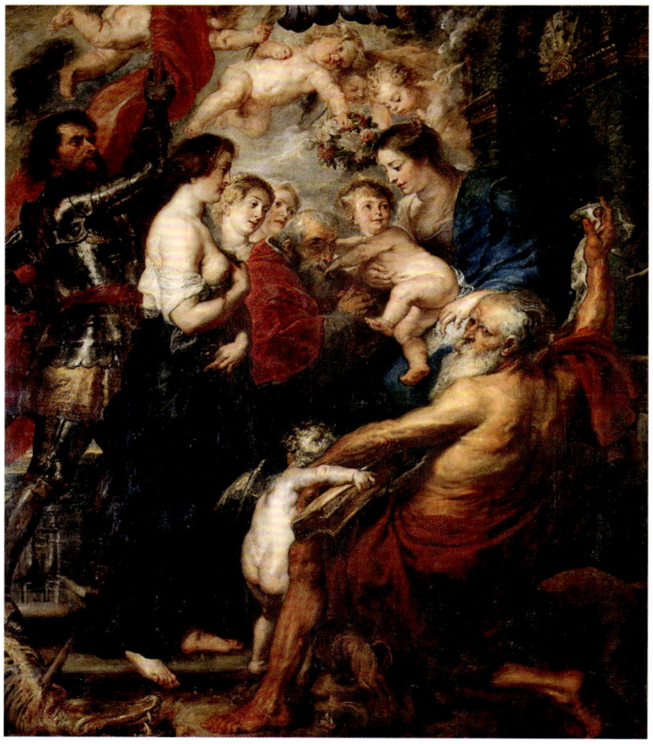

FIG. 30 Peter Paul Rubens, *Madonna and Child with Saints*, 1634. Oil on panel, 211 x 195 cm. Church of St James, Antwerp

Even a painter as little attracted to religious art as Jean-Honoré Fragonard could be influenced by Rubens's sacred works. His academic *Coresus and Callirhoe* (1765; Musée du Louvre, Paris) was inspired by Rubens's *Miracles of St Ignatius* (1618–19; Kunsthistorisches Museum, Vienna), seen by him in the Jesuit church in Genoa. Furthermore the artist seems to have drawn quite a number of Rubenesque pieces, including the altarpiece above Rubens's tomb (fig. 30; Fragonard's drawing is cat. 100), known through a print.[20]

Even more representative is the case of David, an artist who could not be further removed from the world of Rubens, but who also owes a debt to the Flemish painter. David's books of drawings reflect the journey to Flanders he made early on in his career, while they also suggest that he studied some of Rubens's religious works via engravings.[26] The great Neoclassical artist rediscovered the passion and expressiveness of Rubens's art just at the moment in history when the return to antiquity and the *beau idéal* were in the air, closing the Enlightenment and opening the Romantic period under the auspices of Rubens.

Among Rubens's admirers in the new era we find Géricault, inspired by the *Descent from the Cross* seen in the Louvre when he was younger; however, his brief career makes it difficult to evaluate to what degree he was influenced by Rubens's religious works.[21] His follower Delacroix, a truly fervent admirer of Rubens, seems to have visited Flanders twice, in about 1838 and again in 1850. He went in search of the work of his chosen master and to revisit the religious masterpieces he had once seen at the Musée Napoléon. In Rubens he found the model for the uninhibitedly tragic religious painting that Baudelaire liked so much and that made Delacroix – as critic Paul Mantz termed him – 'the painter of sorrow'.[22] Delacroix's travels attest to the fundamental part Rubens played in his career as a spur to thoughtful reflection as well as a source of inspiration. This is illustrated by his careful study of the central compartment of the *Christ on the Straw* (cat. 91), used in the composition of his *Pietà* (cat. 92), and the drawings and annotated description he made in 1850, while viewing the *Coup de Lance*. The latter had already been a source of inspiration, via an engraved version (cat. 84), for *Christ Between Two Thieves* (1835; Musée de la Cohue, Vannes); it was reinterpreted several times (cat. 85) before he painted his *Christ on the Cross*, presented at the Salon of 1847 (Walters Art Gallery, Baltimore). The *Elevation of the Cross* provoked 'extreme emotion' in him, and comparing it with *The Raft of the Medusa* (1819; Musée du Louvre, Paris) by his master Géricault caused him to rediscover its greatness: 'When I see this art, Géricault grows greater in my eyes: he divined this force and his work is in no respect inferior to what is here.'[23]

In the eighteenth and nineteenth centuries it was not just French artists who undertook pilgrimages in the name of Rubens. Sir Joshua Reynolds, the first president of the Royal Academy of Arts in London, went to Flanders in 1781 with the sole aim of seeing the work of Rubens. In his *Discourses*, written a few years earlier, Rubens had come second to the great artists of the Italian Renaissance; after seeing the altarpieces in Antwerp, Ghent and Bruges, Reynolds's 'estimation of his genius of course raised'. In his travel diary too we find notes on the *Coup de Lance*, the most complete and laudatory description of any one painting; notes on the *Elevation*, 'one of his best and animated compositions'; and notes on the *Descent*, which disappoints him somewhat because of its poor state of conservation. A pilgrimage to the tomb of the Flemish artist was something that Reynolds could not miss, and there he entertained himself by colouring in an engraving of the altarpiece (cat. 101), a late work by Rubens that still adorns the altar.[24] A few years later David Wilkie, another Royal Academician, followed in his footsteps (cat. 102).

Although Anglican religious sensibilities do not seem to have been disturbed by the Baroque impetus of Rubens's art – he was too deeply embedded in English culture – in the German Protestant world Rubens's turbulent religious scenes did not elicit only plaudits. The eighteenth-century German traveller, scholar and revolutionary Georg Forster, infused with Neoclassical theory, inveighed against the rhetorical and theatrical afflatus of Rubens's religious art, claiming to 'feel nothing' when confronted by the imposing *Descent*.[25]

A passionate admirer of Gothic art, he expressed scathing criticism of the *Assumption of the Virgin* (1626; Cathedral Church of Our Lady, Antwerp) and the powerful *Crucifixion of St Peter* in Cologne; the latter, an important example of the art of Rubens on German soil, was described by the eighteenth-century Romantic writer and friend of Goethe, Johann Heinrich Merck, as one of the 'few pieces where so many aspects of art are united in such an exquisite manner, that can withstand the most rigorous critical eye with such ease and leave such a sense of satisfaction', praising the figures for the 'immense depth of understanding in the diverse poses, garments and local colours'.[26] Forster's uncompromising rejection of Rubens's spectacular rhetoric was probably based on his progressive view of mankind, imbued with Enlightenment theory; it may have been the overlap between aesthetics and morals that prevented him praising the Flemish artist's compositions.

Other, similar reactions to the art of Rubens share Forster's rationalist rejection of different manifestations of religious sensibility, which were connected to the spirituality of suffering and appreciated by a post-Romantic, decadent culture. At the beginning of the twentieth century Joris-Karl Huysmans, in the middle of a spiritual crisis that led him to embrace the Roman Catholic faith, called Rubens's religious paintings the 'shame of Flanders', contrasting them unfavourably with the primitive purity of the *Virgin and Child* of the master of Flémalle (Städel Museum, Frankfurt).[27] Almost twenty years earlier, in a letter to his brother Theo, Vincent van Gogh expressed similar difficulties in respect of Rubens and his religious work; the master's painting is described as 'superficial, hollow, bombastic [...] like Giulio Romano and even worse fellows of the decadence'.[28]

Van Gogh's view is not entirely negative however, it is ambiguous and problematic, alternating between scorn and enthusiasm. Perhaps Van Gogh recognised the greatness of the Flemish artist at every level – inventive, technical, formal, poetic – but found him too far removed from his own tormented soul: grandiose in his depiction of energy, drama, joy and eroticism, weak in his representation of true compassion. 'Nothing moves me less than Rubens when it comes to the expression of human sorrow,' he wrote to his brother.[29] When he studied the huge altarpieces in Antwerp, Van Gogh found the well-muscled male figures in the *Elevation of the Cross* 'absurd [...] from the standpoint of modern analysis of human passions and emotions', but at the same time he adored the *Descent from the Cross*, in particular the weeping women (even though he found Rubens's rendering of her tears no more moving than 'the tears of a pretty tart'). Those female figures, with their noble, somewhat classical forms, reincarnations of classical

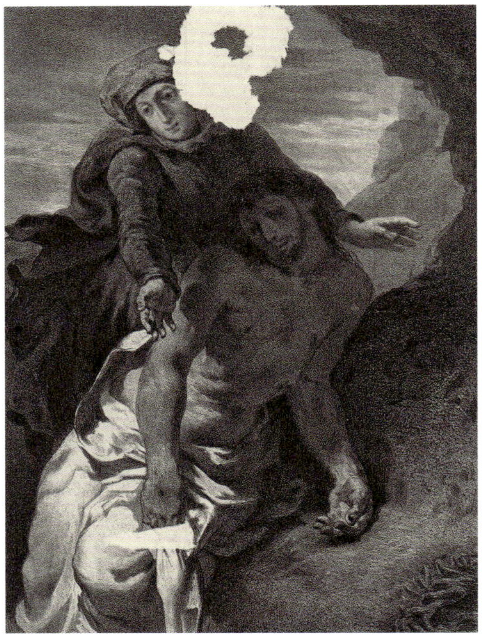

FIG. 31 Célestin François Nanteuil-Leboeuf, after Eugène Delacroix, *Pietà*, *c.* 1850. Lithograph, 21.7 x 16.7 cm. Van Gogh Museum, Amsterdam

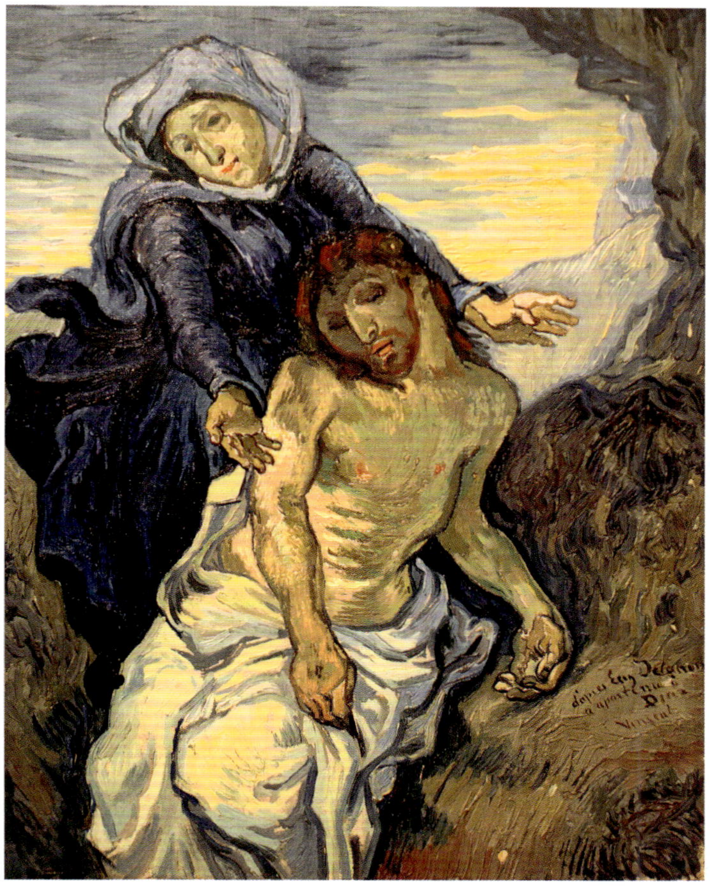

FIG. 32 Vincent van Gogh, *Pietà*, 1889. Oil on canvas, 42 x 34 cm. Vatican Museums, Vatican City

and Renaissance models, did not possess the human quality to be found in a religious painting by Rembrandt or Delacroix.

Most of all, the symphonic palette of Delacroix was to Van Gogh the conscious link between his own unquiet temperament and the Baroque art of Rubens. From a letter to his sister Wilhelmina, written from the asylum at Saint-Rémy-de-Provence in 1889, we know that Van Gogh, having recovered his health, was painting copies of works by Delacroix.[30] These included a version of the *Pietà* (fig. 32),[31] painted from an engraving by Célestin François Nanteuil-Leboeuf (fig. 31) that his brother Theo had sent him. As we have seen, the Flemish master's *Christ on the Straw* had in fact been used as a point of departure by the French painter for his own *Pietà*.[32] This protracted derivation typifies the role of Delacroix as a mediator between Van Gogh's pure, yearning spirituality and the hugely sophisticated, spectacular religious scenes painted by Rubens. The subject-matter of the *Pietà*, identified by critics as a 'Christological' self-portrait of the artist, is an exception in Van Gogh's output.[33] In spite of the fact that he was the son of a pastor and had been active as a preacher in his youth, his faith, as a Protestant, was aniconic. This work is Van Gogh's strongest point of contact with the Catholic iconic tradition. The contact also belongs to a significant degree to the extraordinary visual heritage of the religious paintings of Rubens.

The Gospel of John relates the moment during the crucifixion when Pilate's soldiers hasten the death of Jesus and the two thieves being crucified alongside Him: 'Then came the soldiers, and brake the legs of the first, and of the other which was crucified with Him. But when they came to Jesus, and saw that He was dead already, they brake not His legs. But one of the soldiers with a spear pierced His side, and forthwith came there out blood and water' (John XIX, 32–34). It is not known whether Rubens chose to focus on this particularly charged moment for his painting, which was to be placed above the high altar of the Franciscan Church of the Minor Friars in Antwerp, or whether the subject was dictated by his patron Nicolaas Rockox, Antwerp's burgomaster. Be that as it may, the 1620 commission resulted in one of Rubens's boldest compositions (fig. 26) and attracted widespread praise. In a publication relating to the monastery, the Flemish theologian Antonius Sanderus (1586–1644) wrote that Rubens had surpassed himself, with 'scarcely anything to match it'.[1] Sir Joshua Reynolds (1723–1792) marvelled at the master's powers of invention and his ability to heighten the drama of the scene with such arresting motifs as the thief convulsed in agony as one of the executioners attempts to fracture his limbs, causing one of his feet to tear free of the nail. Reynolds also admired Rubens's varied arrangement of the crucified figures and their contrasting attitudes, as well as the expressions of

83

UNKNOWN ARTIST, QING DYNASTY (1644–1911/12)
Porcelain dish with illustration after *Coup de Lance*, *c.* 1720–30
Porcelain, diameter 28.5 cm
Royal Museum of Fine Arts Antwerp, inv. 5160

PROVENANCE: brought to Europe from China by the Dutch East India Company in the eighteenth century; purchased by the museum from Jorge Welsh Gallery, London, in 2011
SELECTED REFERENCES: Van de Velde and Van Hout 2013, p. 64

84

BOETIUS ADAMSZ. BOLSWERT (c. 1580–1633)
Coup de Lance, 1631
Engraving, 62.3 x 44.7 cm
Royal Museum of Fine Arts Antwerp, inv. 10302

PROVENANCE: the collection of Max Rooses, donated to the museum in 1900
SELECTED REFERENCES: Voorhelm Schneevoogt, p. 48, no. 333; Van den Wijngaert 1940, no. 30; Holstein, vol. 3, p. 72, no. 7; Rome 1977, p. 37, no. 49; Providence 1975, p. 60; London 1977, p. 120, no. 161; Judson 2000, p. 142, no. 117

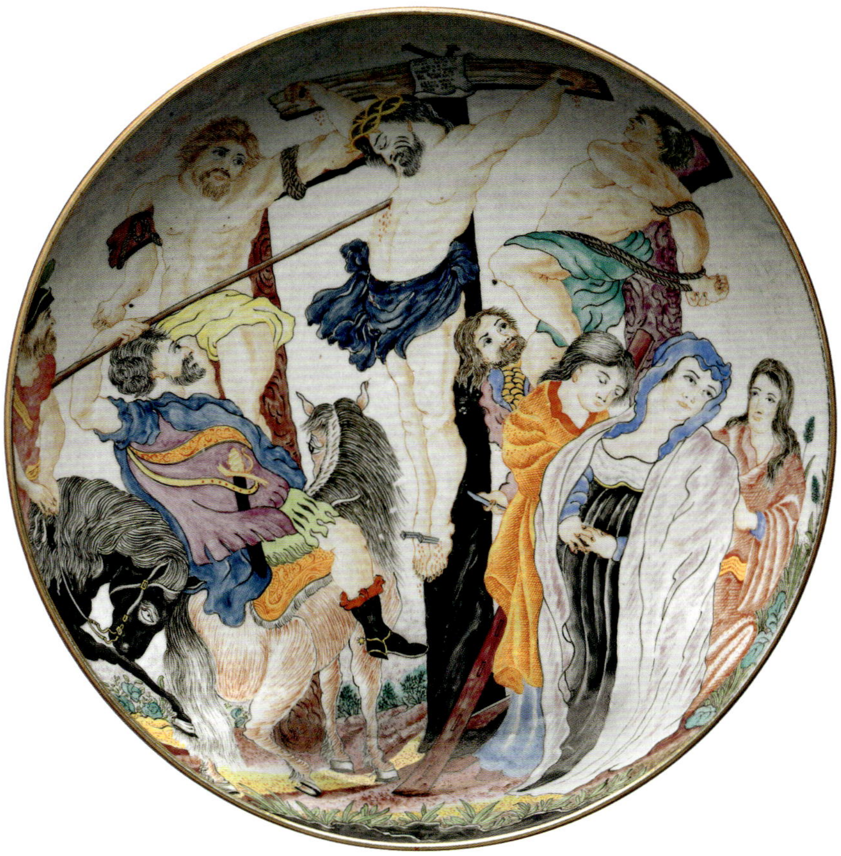

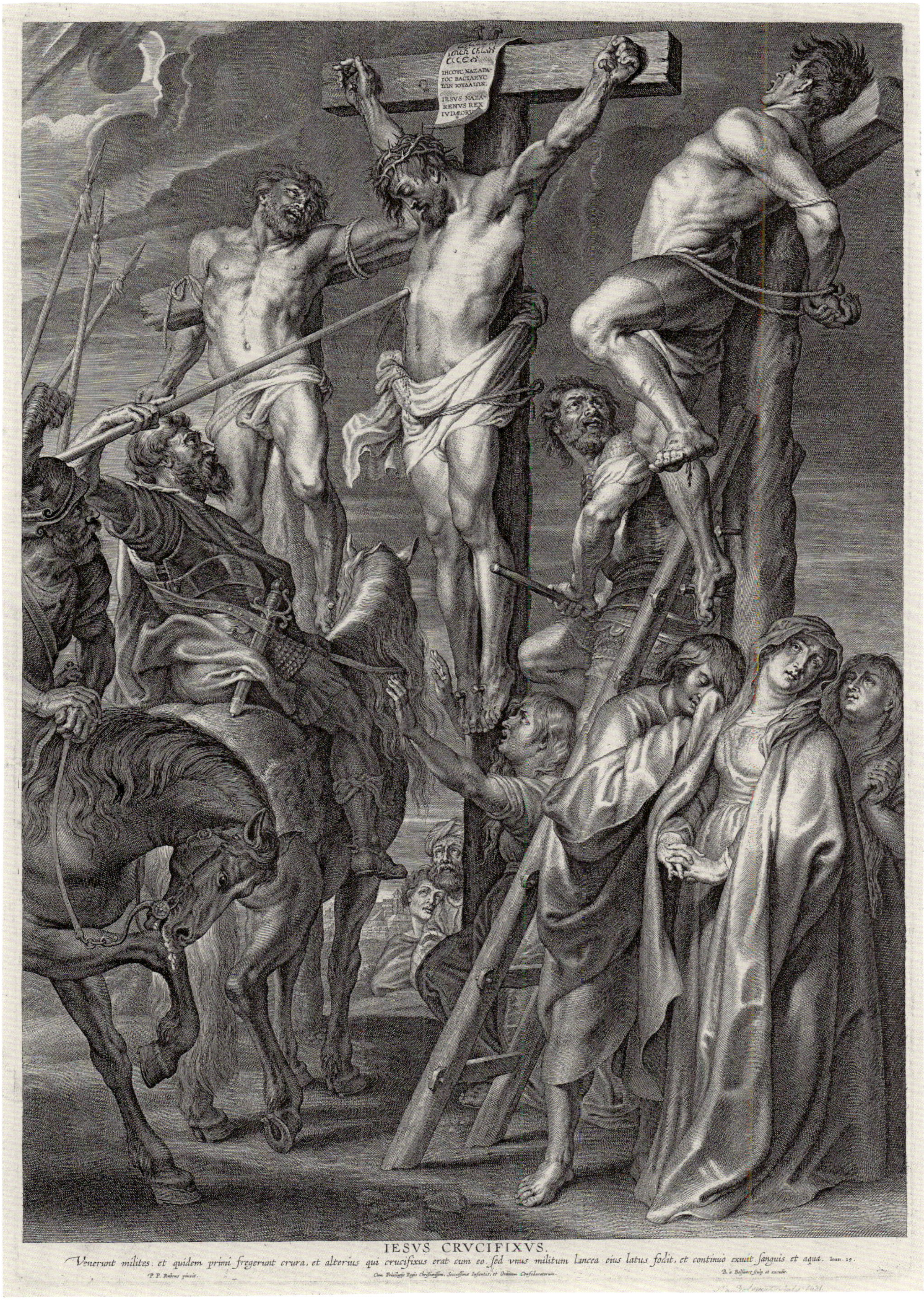
IESVS CRVCIFIXVS.
Venerunt milites: et quidem primi fregerunt crura, et alterius qui crucifixus erat cum eo. sed vnus militum lancea eius latus fodit, et continuò exiuit sanguis et aqua. Ioan. 19.
P. P. Rubens pinxit.
B. à Bolswert sculp. et excudit.

85

EUGÈNE DELACROIX (1798-1863)
Sketch for *Crucifixion*, 1846
Oil on panel, 37 x 25 cm
Museum Boijmans Van Beuningen, Rotterdam, inv. 2625

PROVENANCE: sold by Delacroix to Paul Meurice (1818–1905); by descent to Mme Albert Clemenceau-Meurice; V. Bloch; acquired by the museum in 1961 with the support of Vereniging Rembrandt
SELECTED REFERENCES: Juynboll 1961, pp. 2–11; Rotterdam 1963, p. 38; Harald Szeemann, Lee Johnson and George Sand, *Eugène Delacroix*, Madrid, 1988, no. 42; Sérullaz 1971, p. 52, no. 6; Johnson 1981–86, vol 3., p. 219, no. 432

sorrow and resignation of St John and the three Marys.[2] Earlier, Jean-Baptiste Descamps (1715–1791) had praised the way the Roman soldiers on horseback complete the composition, adding to its 'prodigious' overall effect.[3]

Wishing to disseminate his work, Rubens called on Boetius Adamsz. Bolswert. A drawing (now in the British Museum, London) was made after the painting, and contains some revisions, most notably the way Christ's loincloth spreads out and flutters in the wind – an early compositional idea.[4] Bolswert most skilfully translated this *modello* into print in 1631 (cat. 84). The figures are clearly modelled and the scene's emotional intensity is reinforced by the juxtaposition of light and dark effects, which broadly mirror Rubens's grey and brown washes with white heightening in the drawn preparatory design.

Bolswert's print circulated as far as China, probably travelling with the Catholic missionaries who established themselves there for a short period. Sometime during the reign of Kangxi, fourth Emperor of the Qing Dynasty, around 1720–30, it was reproduced by a painter on a dish made in Jingdezhen, China's porcelain capital. It is likely this dish (cat. 83) was used by the Jesuits in their proselytising efforts as a powerful reminder of Christ's sacrifice for the salvation of mankind. Note the colours, which are uncommon in European Christian imagery, and the Chinese appearance of the biblical figures.

Rubens's *Coup de Lance* continued to exert an influence on artists well into the nineteenth century. Closer to home, Eugène Delacroix, an apparent agnostic who nevertheless upheld the values of Christianity and was animated by a profound spirituality, had very sympathetically portrayed the subject of Christ on the cross several times between 1846 and the end of his life. Five drawings, a pastel and a painting are derived from Rubens's *Coup de Lance* (fig. 26),[5] which the artist saw in Antwerp during his stay there in August 1850. 'A young man who was making a copy of the great "Christ on the Cross" lent me his ladder and I was able to see the picture in a different light. It is of his finest period,' he recalls in his journal.[6] Delacroix proceeds to analyse the canvas, noting Rubens's brilliant use of colour, light and shade.

In the dazzling Rotterdam oil sketch (cat. 85), Delacroix singled out the figure of Christ, who radiates light in dramatic contrast with the dark, stormy sky. The sketch is a preparatory work for the painting (also executed in 1846) now conserved at the Walters Art Gallery, Baltimore. There the onlookers in the lower-left foreground – one of whom points towards Christ – and the two soldiers riding towards Christ with billowing banners from the right can more clearly be seen. The picture was exhibited at the Salon in 1847 and prompted the art critic Théophile Thoré-Bürger to liken it to 'Rubens's most beautiful' crucifixions.[7]

Rubens's *Coup de Lance* also attracted the attention of Sir Edwin Landseer. In 1840, then at the peak of his career, Landseer suffered a nervous breakdown and travelled in August to Europe as a

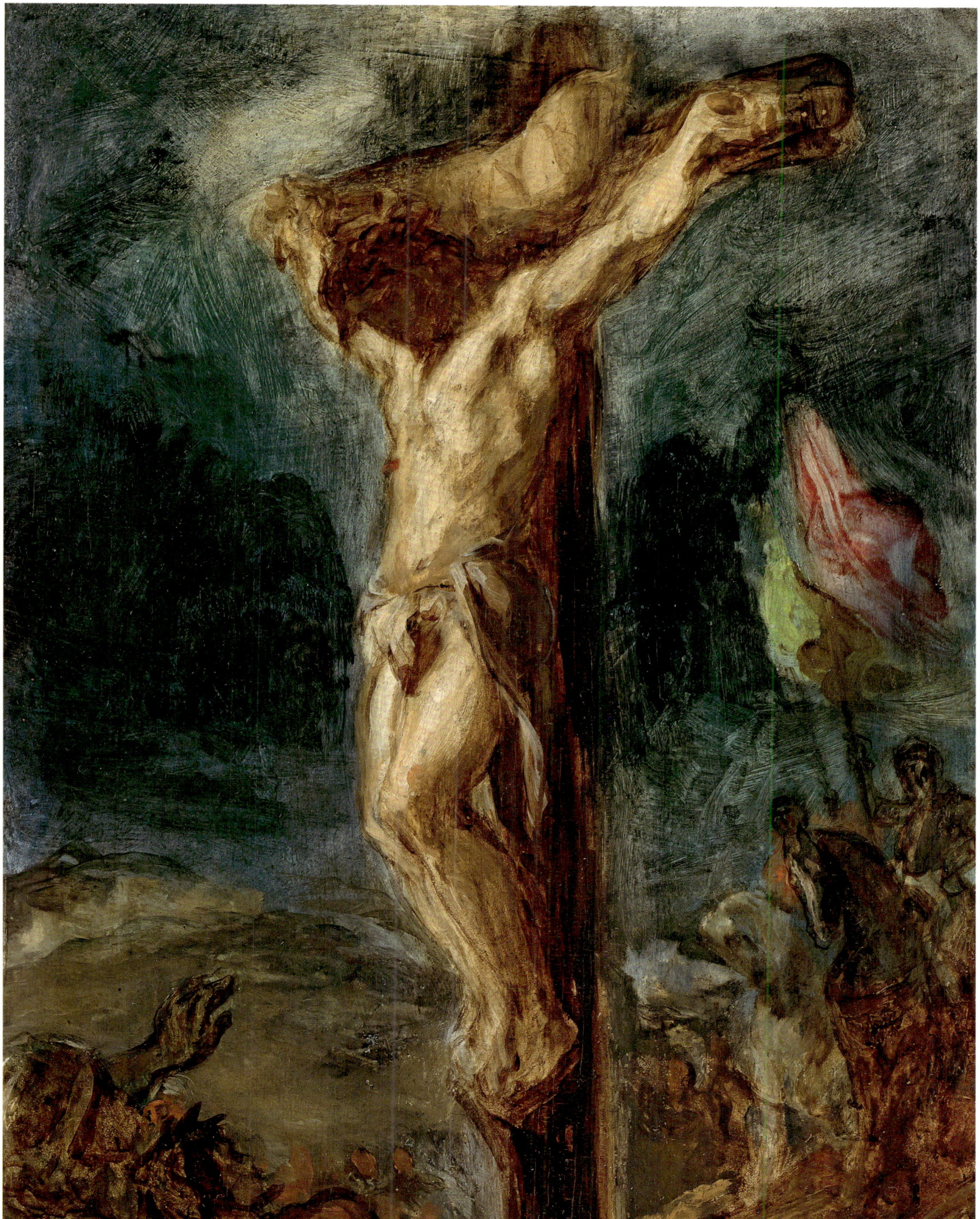

form of therapy. His trip took him along the Rhine to Cologne and Geneva, and on his way he stopped in Belgium, where he made copies of the head and torso of Christ (cat. 86) and the thieves in Rubens's *Coup de Lance* in the Royal Museum of Fine Arts Antwerp. Landseer must have been intensely moved by the master's crucifixion scene, especially considering his sombre state of mind at the time. Drawn softly and primarily in white chalk with some heightening, Christ emerges from the blue-grey paper like a ghostly vision; nevertheless the figure is modelled with realism and subtlety. Delicate touches of red indicate Christ's bleeding wounds and Landseer accentuates the Saviour's greyish complexion to draw attention to his face, the locus of emotion. He renders the pathos and beauty of Rubens's Christ in a manner that can only be seen as a tribute to the master. KP

86

SIR EDWIN LANDSEER (1802–1873)
Christ on the Cross, 1840
Black, red and white chalks
on blue-grey paper, 44.4 x 29.8 cm
The Royal Collection, RCIN 17333

PROVENANCE: presented to Queen Victoria by the artist's family, 1874
SELECTED REFERENCES: Millar 1995, vol. 1, p. 529, no. 3,232; Clayton 2004, p. 153, no. 61

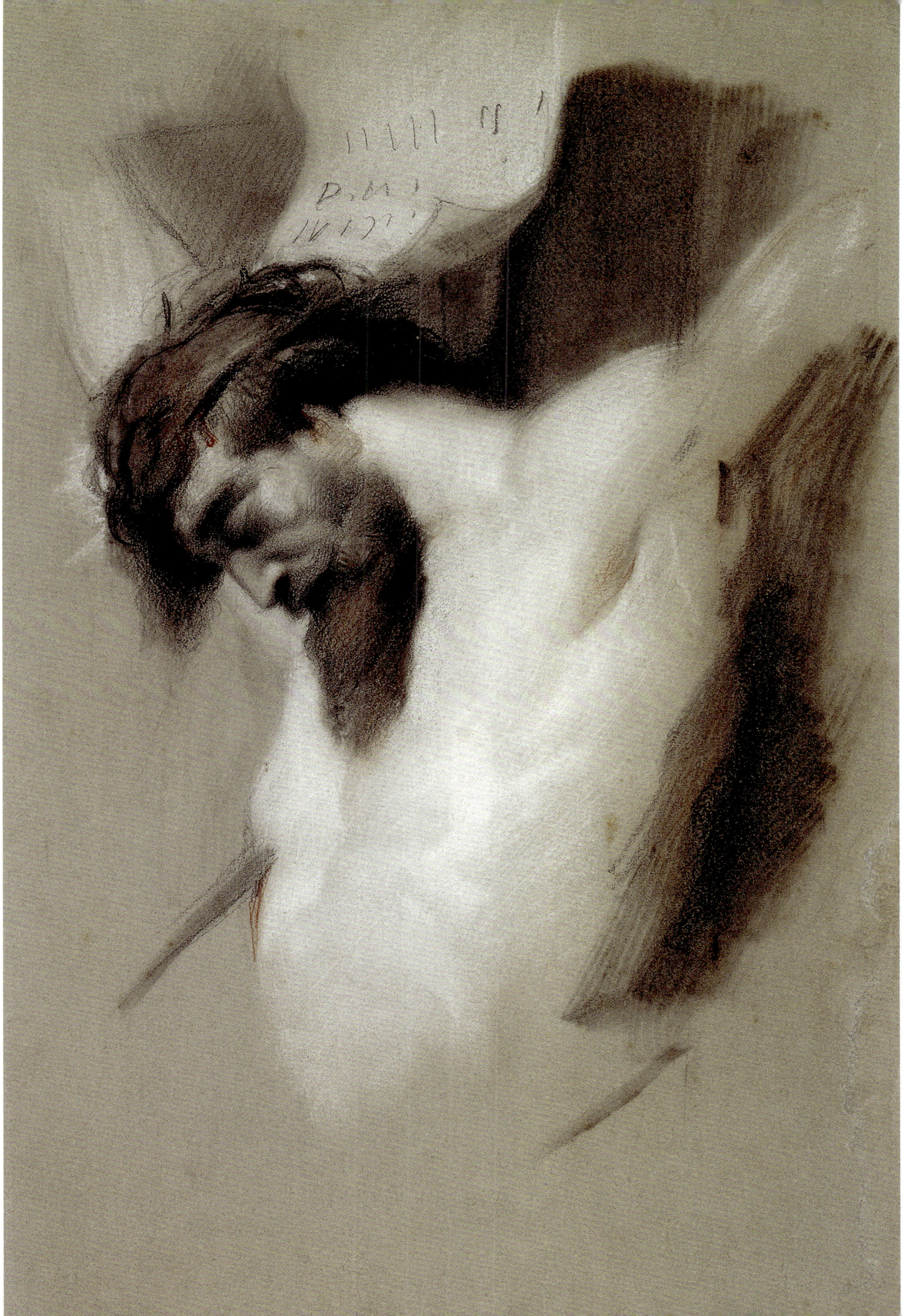

On 17 July 1611, Rubens received a commission from Antwerp's guild of arquebusiers to paint a triptych for their altar dedicated to St Christopher in the city's cathedral; the result, with its famous centrepiece, the *Descent from the Cross* (fig. 27), can still be admired there today. It took Rubens almost three years to complete the work,[1] and he entrusted Lucas Vorsterman with creating an engraving of the central panel (cat. 87). Aptly named 'le peintre au burin' by Joachim von Sandrart the Elder for his ability to render fine tone and subtle transitions between light and shadow, Vorsterman mustered all his skill to reproduce Rubens's virtuoso composition. As Nico Van Hout notes, the printmaker has carefully conveyed Christ's body and the clothes of the nearby figures by means of circular hatchings and stippling. However, this has the unwitting effect of evening out the elements of the composition rather than accentuating the pale figure of Christ and the luminous white shroud of the Rubens original.[2] The print is nevertheless notable for its monumentality and plasticity, and ranks as one of Vorsterman's most accomplished engravings after the master.

Made in 1620, Vorsterman's print was seen by artists across Europe, including Rembrandt, who never left Holland but had access to the work of his elder contemporary through these reproductions. Aged 25 when he established himself in Amsterdam, Rembrandt soon became engaged with an important commission from Frederick Henry, Prince of Orange, for a series of scenes of the life of Christ. Of these, *Christ on the Cross* (1631; Le Mas d'Agenais parish church) and *Descent from the Cross* (1632–33; Alte Pinakothek, Munich), both painted in a period described as his most baroque, were directly inspired by Rubens. The etching made after Rembrandt's *Descent from the Cross* (cat. 88) seems to have been executed largely by Jan Joris van Vliet under the Dutch master's supervision.[3] Clearly, Rembrandt was most interested in Rubens's dramatic and concentrated composition, which in his work takes on a pared-down, pyramidal structure and is theatrically illuminated by strong shafts of light. Only one helper leans over the cross and holds Christ's shroud, not with his teeth but with his right hand. The limp body of the Saviour is unidealised and His followers are likewise portrayed in a realistic manner, which results in a less rhetorical and heroic work yet one that is equally powerful and perfectly suited to private devotion.

Two centuries later Delacroix was privileged to see Rubens's painting *in situ* on one of the trips he made to Belgium in about 1838 and 1850. In a quick pen drawing (cat. 89) he captured Christ's lifeless body held by the loosely sketched figures of St John and Mary Magdalene, giving the group a more vertical accent. Here the artist must have been attracted to Rubens's beautiful rendition of the Son of God and the pathos of His pose, a brilliant adaptation of Italian and antique precedents by the seventeenth-century artist. Delacroix, who was aware of Sir Joshua Reynolds's writings on art, would undoubtedly have concurred with the British artist that Christ was 'most correctly drawn ... in an attitude of the utmost difficulty to execute', and that 'the hanging of the head on his shoulder, and the falling of the body on one side, gives such an appearance of the heaviness of death that nothing can exceed'.[4] Yet at the same time Christ's body appears weightless, as is evident from the relative ease with which He seems

87

LUCAS VORSTERMAN THE ELDER (1595–1675)
Descent from the Cross, 1620
Engraving, 57.5 x 43.3 cm
On loan from the British Museum, London, inv. 1841,0809.2

PROVENANCE: bequeathed by William Fawkener
SELECTED REFERENCES: Hymans, p. 81ff., no. 34; Voorhelm Schneevoogt 1873, p. 49, no. 342; Rooses 1886–92, p. 105ff.; Van den Wijngaert 1940, no. 718; Providence 1975, no. 16; Hollstein 1949–2010, vol. 31 no. 2; Van Hout 2004, pp. 46–47

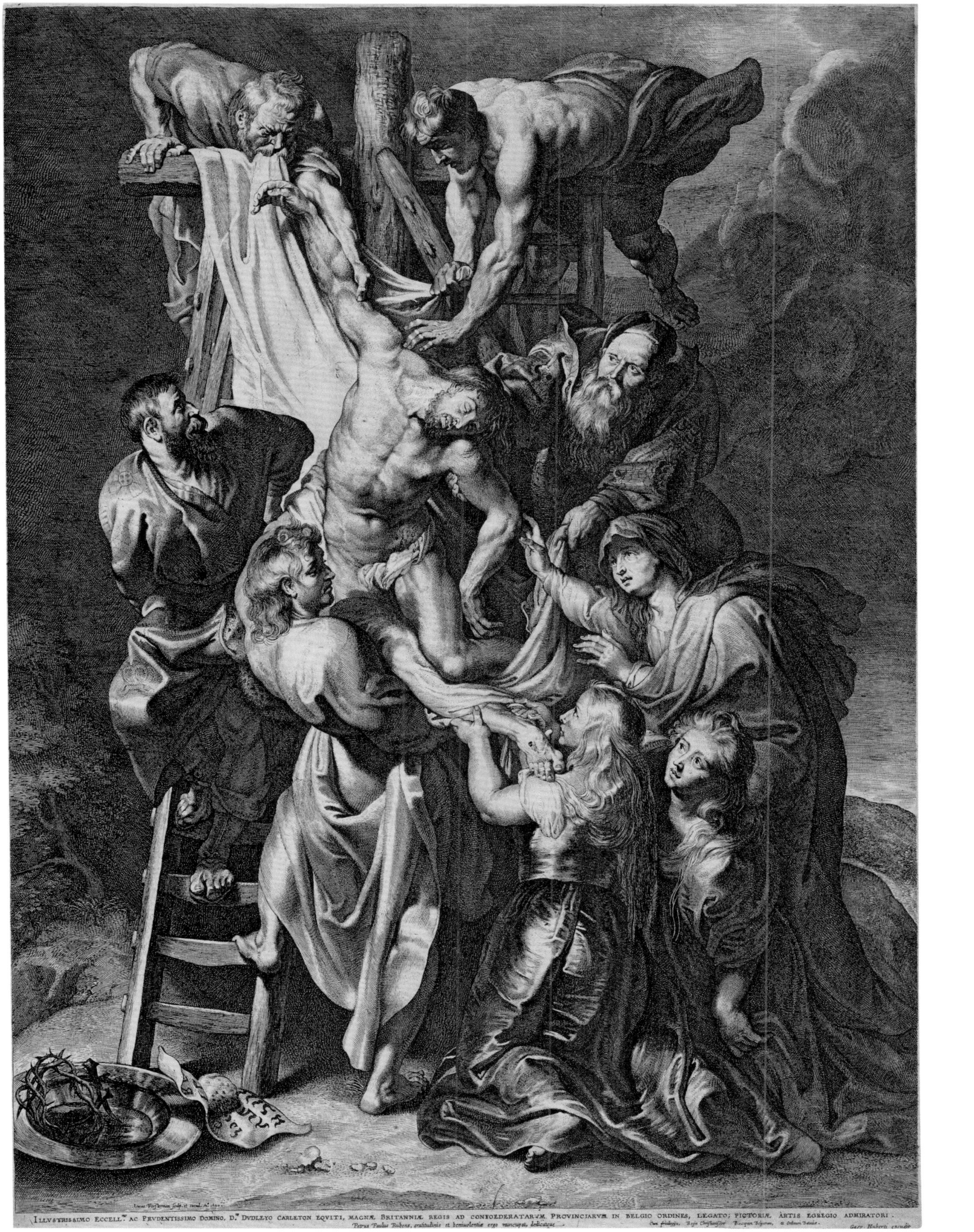
ILLVSTRISSIMO ECCELL.MO AC PRVDENTISSIMO DOMINO, D.NO DVDLEYO CARLETON EQVITI, MAGNÆ BRITANNIÆ REGIS AD CONFOEDERATARVM PROVINCIARVM IN BELGIO ORDINES, LEGATO; PICTORIÆ ARTIS EGREGIO ADMIRATORI.
Petrus Paulus Rubens, gratitudinis et beniuolentiæ ergo nuncupat, dedicatque.
Gasp. Huberti excudit

88

JAN JORIS VAN VLIET (c. 1610–c. 1635) and **REMBRANDT VAN RIJN (1606–1669)**
Descent from the Cross (second state), 1633
Etching, 52.7 x 40.7 cm
Rijksmuseum, Amsterdam, inv. RP-P-1961-1197A. Mr and Mrs De Bruijn-van der Leeuw Bequest, Muri

PROVENANCE: bequeathed by Sir Hans Sloane, 1753
SELECTED REFERENCES: Hind 1923, vol. 2, no. 103; White and Boon 1969, vol. 2, no. 81; Hinterding 2000, nos 22 and 23; Schama 1999, pp. 291–93

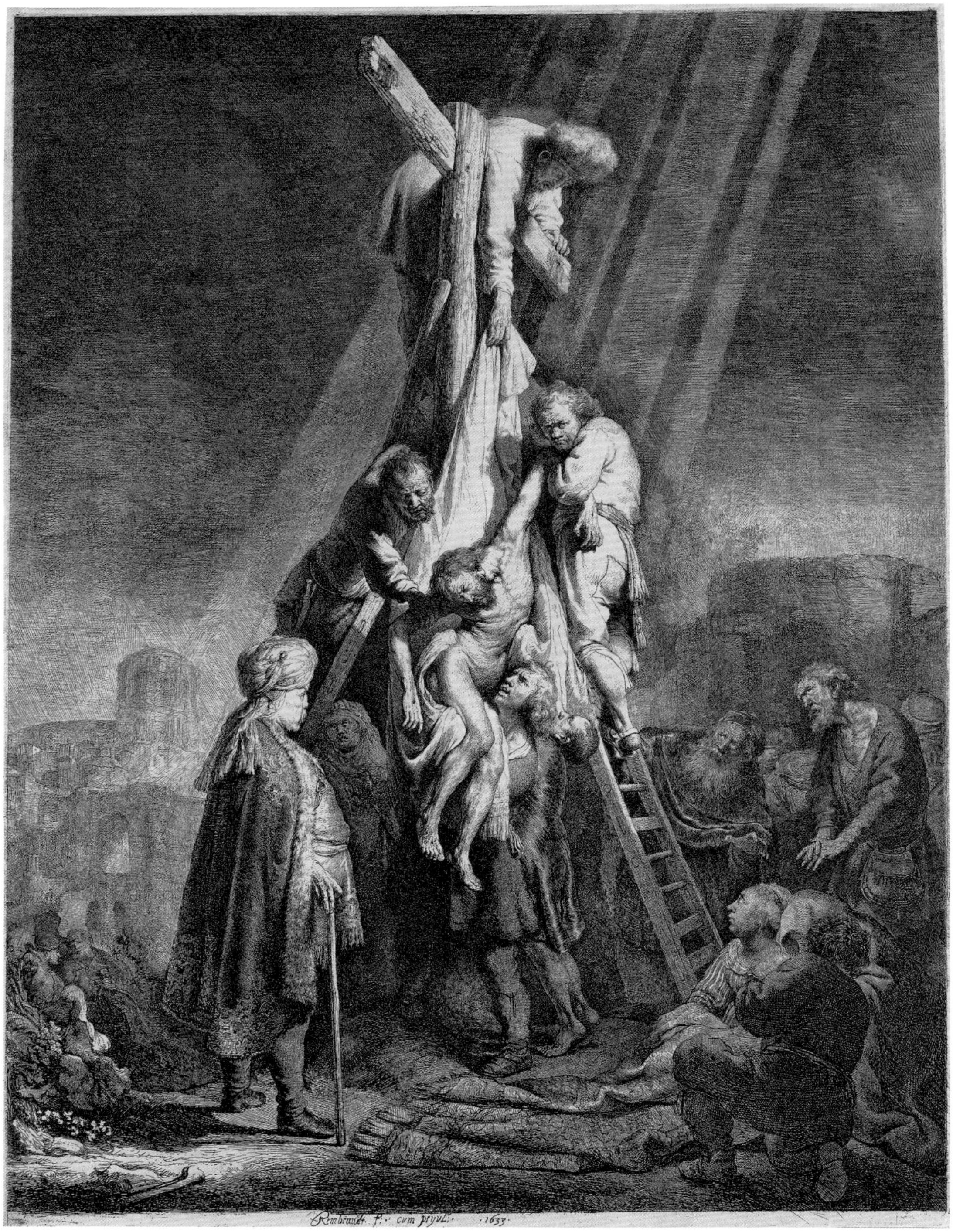

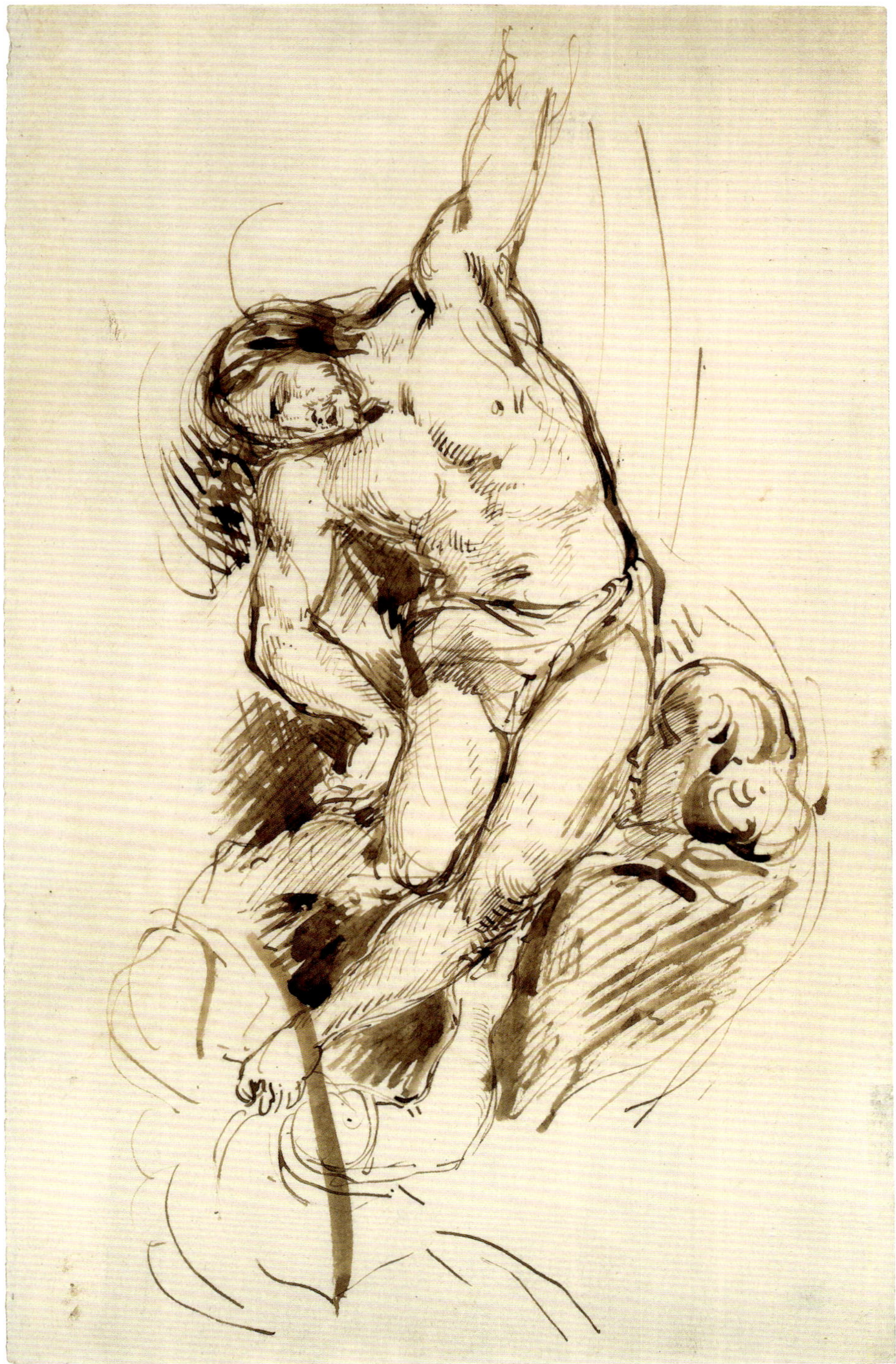

89

EUGÈNE DELACROIX (1798–1863)
Sketch after *Descent from the Cross*, *c.* 1838
Pen and brown ink on paper, 32.2 x 21.1 cm
Museum Boijmans Van Beuningen, Rotterdam, Koenigs Collection, inv. F II 84

PROVENANCE: F. Koenigs; donated to the museum by D. G. Van Beuningen in 1940
SELECTED REFERENCES: Mongan 1962, vol. 3, pp. 738–39; Amsterdam 1964, no. 158; Sérullaz 1998, no. 84; Karlsruhe 2003–04, no. 138, pp. 263–64

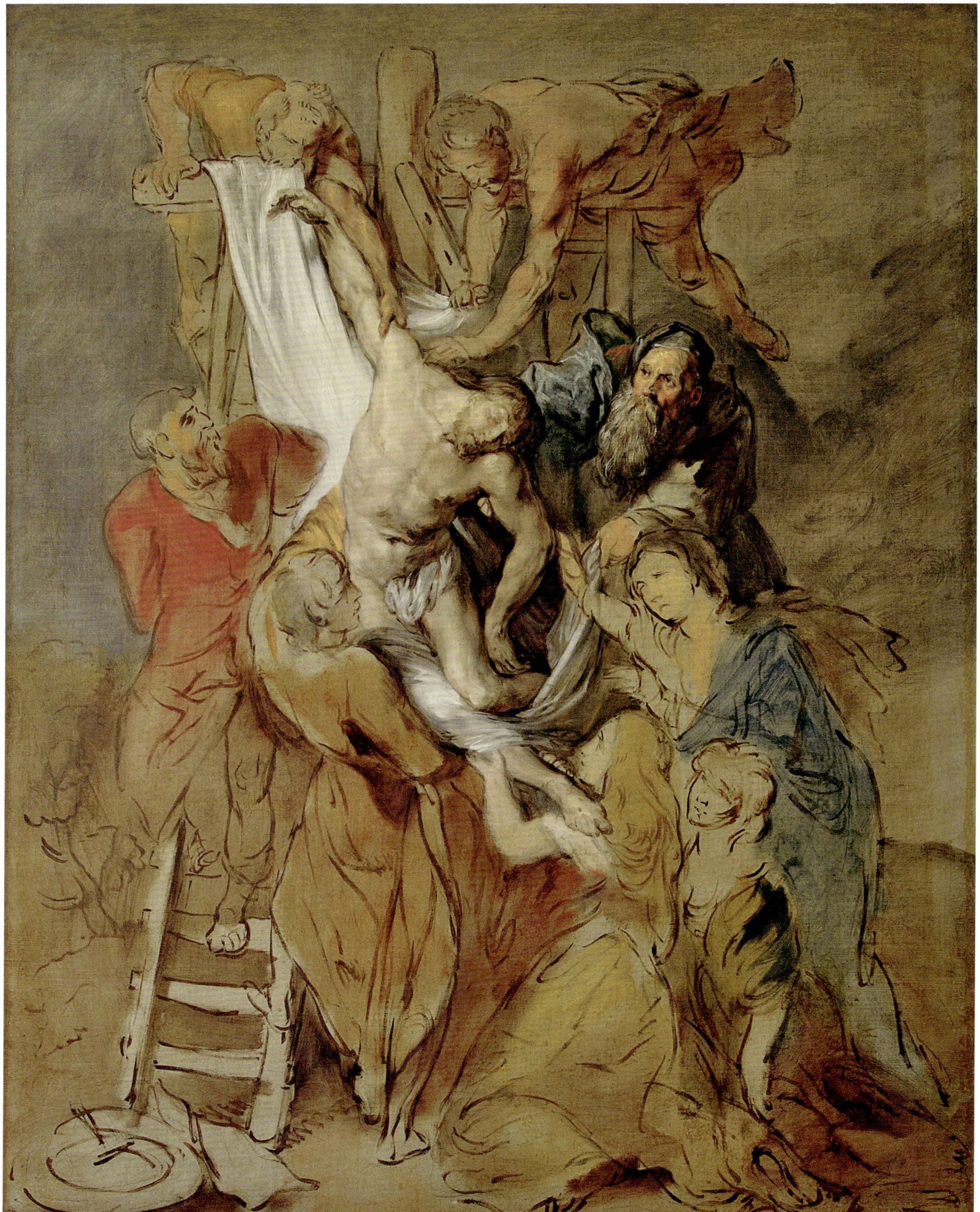

to be supported, a technical feat that Delacroix emulates in his drawing.

In England, Rubens's altarpiece was available both through print and the master's painted *modello*; this is now in the collection of the Courtauld Institute of Art Gallery, London, but during the lifetime of Gainsborough it was at Corsham Court, not far from Bath, where the artist had moved in 1759. Although Gainsborough is likely to have seen the work there, it is most probable that he looked at Vorsterman's engraving when undertaking a large copy of the work in oil. Indeed the scene is presented in reverse, as in the print, and includes details absent from the *modello*.[5] Gainsborough's oil sketch (cat. 90) is unfinished and bears all the hallmarks of an exercise in composition. The artist must have been impressed by the unity of Rubens's design, which the master achieved by grouping the figures tightly along three loose parallel diagonals, those on the left and right harmoniously counterbalancing each other as their gazes and gestures all converge on Christ, who takes centre stage. KP

90

THOMAS GAINSBOROUGH (1727–1788)
Sketch after *Descent from the Cross*, 1766–69
Oil on canvas, 125.5 x 101.5 cm
Gainsborough's House, Sudbury, inv. 1998.126

PROVENANCE: Mrs Gainsborough's sale, Christie's, London, 11 April 1797, lot 63, bought by J. W. Steers; his sale, Christie's, London, 3 June 1826, lot 52, bought Bond; W. R. G. Bond, Tyneham House, Dorset, by 1935; his anonymous sale, Sotheby's, London, 30 April 1947, lot 149, withdrawn; re-offered, Sotheby's, London, 25 June 1947, lot 22, bought Sinclair; Hon. Michael Astor by 1950; purchased in 1998 with grants from the Heritage Lottery Fund, the bequest of Miss Dorothy Elmer, the MGC/Victoria and Albert Museum Purchase Grant Fund and the National Art Collections Fund, through Suffolk County Council
SELECTED REFERENCES: Waterhouse 1966, no. 125; Hayes 1975, no. 52; London 1980, no. 107; Providence 1975, no. 63; Belsey 2002, no. 9

Rubens's *Christ on the Straw* (cat. 91) depicts the moment immediately following the descent from the cross. Quietly emotive, it is perhaps the artist's most poignant depiction of the Lamentation. In the central panel a rugged old man, probably Joseph of Arimathea, supports the body of the Saviour, which he helped carry to the stone block to be washed and anointed before burial. Christ's mother gazes towards Heaven, her eyes reddened by grief as she prepares to cover her son. On either side of the Virgin, St John and Mary Magdalene, shown in prayer, stare mournfully at the Saviour. The left wing portrays the young Virgin and the Infant Christ, who apprehensively considers his fate. In the right wing St John the Evangelist holds the book of Revelation and looks up towards an eagle, symbol of his inspiration. The triptych was commissioned as an epitaph by Maria Maes after the death in 1617 of her husband, the Antwerp merchant Jan Michielsen. It stood above his tomb in the Cathedral Church of Our Lady, a holy reminder of the body laid to rest beneath.[1]

Again, the aesthetic power of Rubens's conception did not escape Sir Joshua Reynolds when he visited the Antwerp Museum in 1781. He refers to it in his journal as 'one of his [Rubens's] most careful pictures; the characters … of a higher style of beauty than usual', in particular the Virgin and Christ, whose colouring is 'of a most beautiful and delicate pearly tint'.[2] Neither was Delacroix immune to the work's poignancy, as a moving, freely rendered study in pen, ink and wash conserved at the Musée du Louvre, Paris, attests. The drawing was probably executed during the trip the artist made to the Netherlands

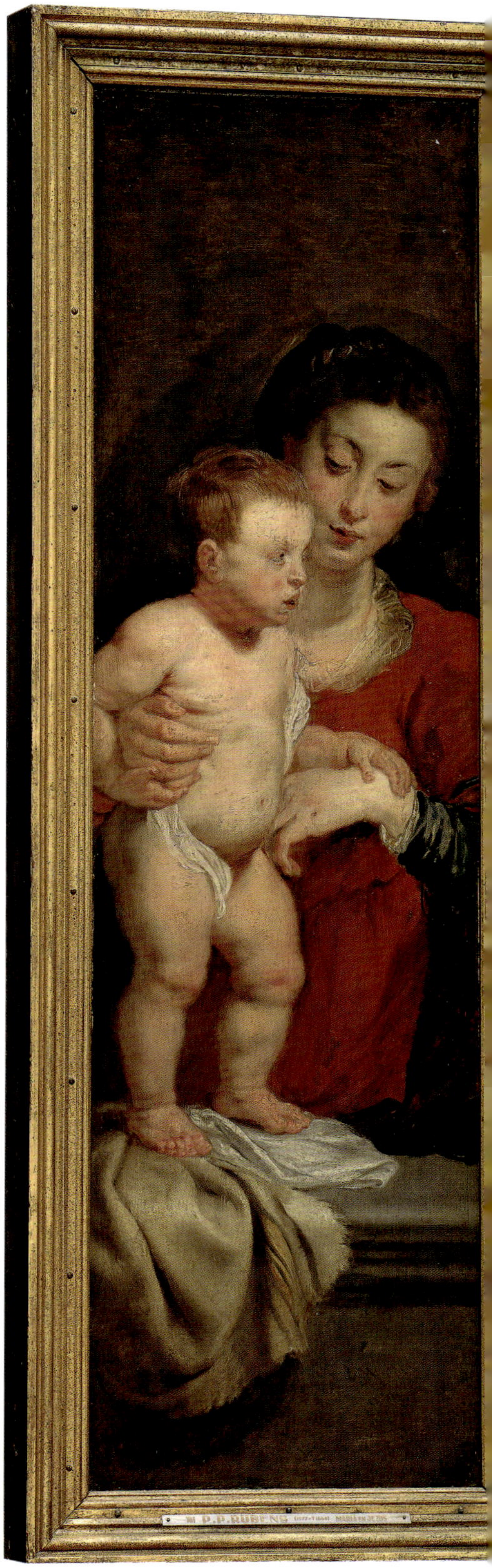

91

PETER PAUL RUBENS (1577–1640)
Christ on the Straw, 1617–18
Oil on panel, central panel: 138 x 98 cm
Royal Museum of Fine Arts Antwerp, inv. 300-304

PROVENANCE: Cathedral Church of Our Lady, Antwerp; in Paris from 1794 to 1815; part of the museum's founding collection
SELECTED REFERENCES: Eisler 1967, pp. 43–77; Jaffé 1972, pp. 107–14; Wuyts 1991, pp. 61–86; Reynolds 1996, pp. 38–40; Judson 2000, no. 64; Jacobs 2009, pp. 302–24; Van Hout and Balis 2012, pp. 142–43

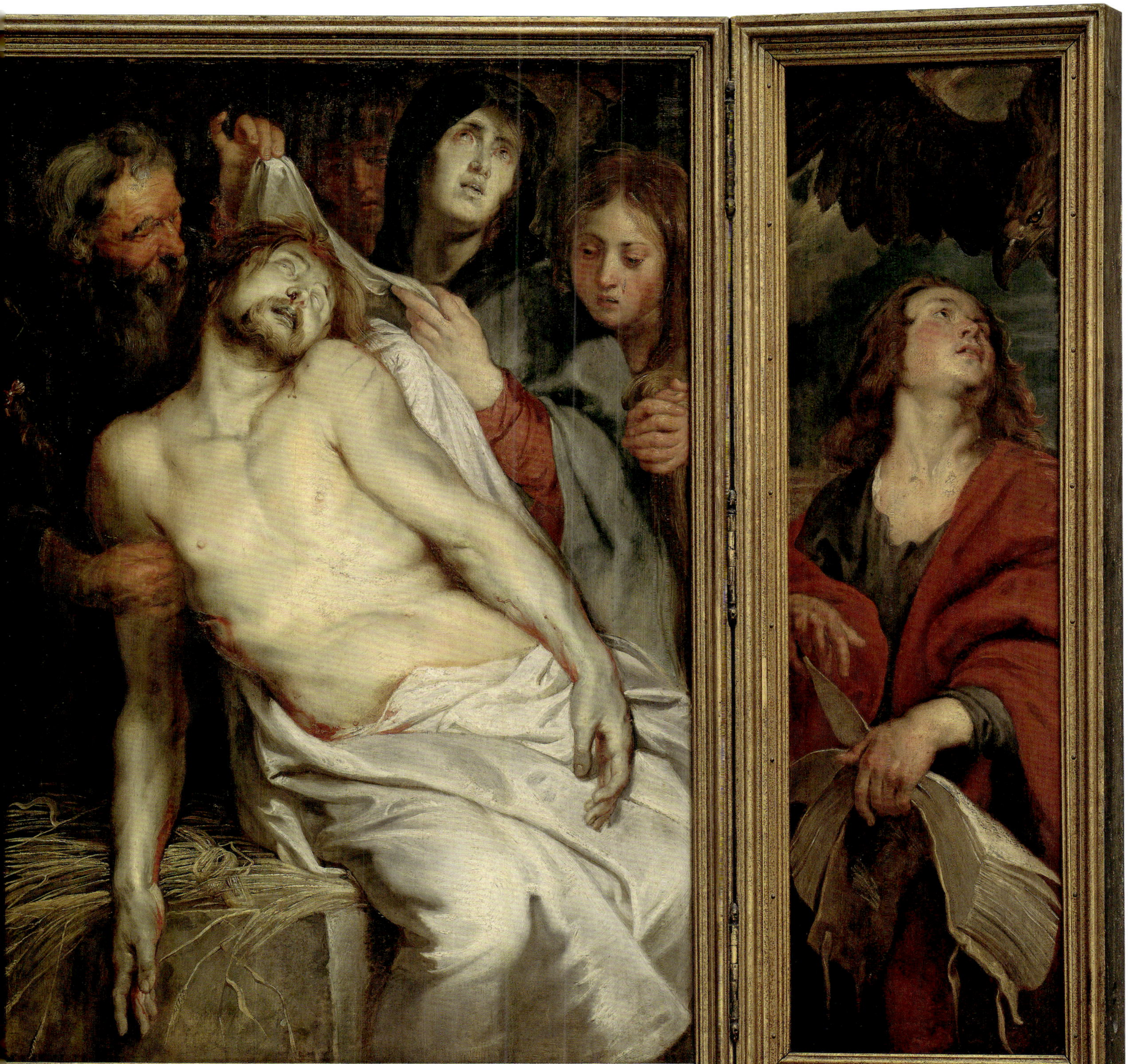

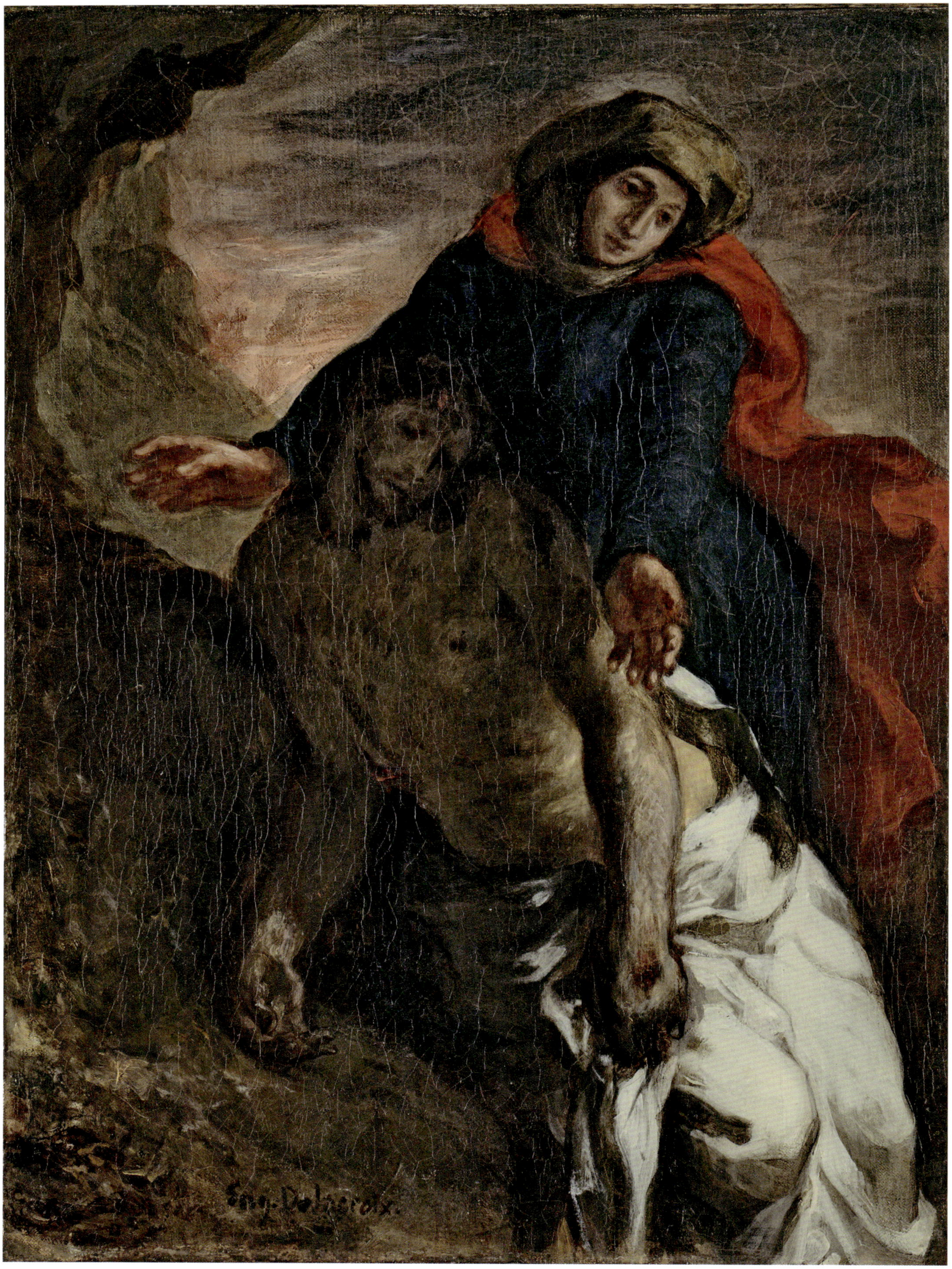
Eug. Delacroix.

with his lover Marie-Elizabeth Boulanger in September 1839, stopping in Antwerp on the way.

Delacroix went on to make a full, painted copy of Rubens's triptych, which closely echoes the model except that Delacroix swapped the left and right wings (the copy is now in a private collection).[3] In the Oslo canvas presented here (cat. 92), he retained only the figures of Christ and the Virgin Mary, which he freely interpreted and placed in a different setting. Van Gogh gives a vivid description of the work, noting its emotional force, which is enhanced by Delacroix's expressive use of colour, in a letter to his sister Wilhelmina written from Saint-Rémy-de-Provence in the autumn of 1889: 'The Delacroix is a Pietà, i.e. a dead Christ with the Mater Dolorosa. The exhausted corpse lies bent forward on its left side at the entrance to a cave, its hands outstretched, and the woman stands behind. It's an evening after the storm, and this desolate, blue-clad figure stands out – its flowing clothes blown about by the wind – against a sky in which violet clouds fringed with gold are floating. In a great gesture of despair she too is stretching out her empty arms'.[4]

Apparently, Van Gogh did not realise when he painted two copies (one of which is show as fig. 32) of Delacroix's *Pietà* – with reference to a *c.* 1850 lithograph by Célestin François Nanteuil-Leboeuf (fig. 31) – that the French painter's work was based on Rubens's invention. This seems a surprising notion, because Van Gogh had visited Antwerp and seen many works by the master there, including *Christ on the Straw*, which he refers to in his letters in passing. KP

92

EUGÈNE DELACROIX (1798-1863)
Pietà, *c.* 1850
Oil on canvas, 35 x 27 cm
The National Museum of Art, Architecture and Design, Oslo, inv. NG.M.01179

PROVENANCE: Diaz, by 1855, possibly acquired directly from the artist *c.* 1850; Paul Tesse, by 1864; Elisabeth, Queen consort of Romania, by 1889, d. 1916; donated to the National Museum of Art, Architecture and Design, Oslo, by the Friends of the Gallery, 1917
SELECTED REFERENCES: Ehrlich White 1967, pp. 38–39 and 43–44; Oslo 1973, no. 496, pp. 211–13; Johnson 1986, no. 443; Paris 1986, no. 6; Zurich and Frankfurt 1987, pp. 178–79; Copenhagen 2000, no. 19; Milan 2006, pp. 13–15; Vincent van Gogh, letter 804

Rubens's *Virgin and Child Enthroned with Saints* is widely recognised as one of his finest non-narrative religious scenes. Commissioned from Antwerp's Augustinian friars to glorify their cathedral church dedicated to Our Lady and All the Saints, the monumental canvas took up its position on the high altar in 1628. The challenge was how best to depict in *sacra conversazione* the great number of patron saints of the religious brotherhoods associated with the church. Taking Titian's *Pesaro Madonna* (1519–26; church of Santa Maria Gloriosa dei Frari, Venice) as a starting point, Rubens surpassed himself, elaborating his ideas in various drawings and oil sketches, including the present one from Berlin (cat. 93), whose design is reflected in the final painting in almost every detail. Most impressive are the great sweep of the composition and the figures' seamless sequence of varied and beautiful attitudes. Beginning with the Augustinian Friar Nicholas of Tolentino (who is depicted in the completed commission holding a loaf of bread) in the lower right, they are brilliantly organised around the pedestal to form a circular, ascending movement ending with the Holy Family. The richness of Rubens's palette and the freedom of his execution show the dazzling way in which he had assimilated the pictorial qualities of Venetian painting into his own style, which he was soon to have a further opportunity to develop. Indeed, a few weeks after the installation of his *Virgin and Child Enthroned with Saints*, Rubens departed on a diplomatic mission to Spain, where he was to encounter Titian's *poesie* paintings in the royal collection.

Rubens 'executed many great works for the king of Spain and other noblemen, earning him no less fame, so that his name was on everyone's lips', wrote Joachim von Sandrart in his short biography of the artist, first published in 1675.[1] The German painter and art historian had met Rubens in Utrecht and escorted him on an artistic voyage through Holland at the request of Sandrart's then master Gerrit van Honthorst. Sandrart appears to have visited Antwerp a couple of decades later, in 1645; the *Deposition* and *Assumption of the Virgin* he painted soon after for Würzburg Cathedral (1647; destroyed 1945) were visibly modelled on Rubens's paintings of the same subjects in Antwerp's Cathedral Church of Our Lady.[2] It is very likely that Sandrart would also have seen Rubens's *Virgin and Child Enthroned with Saints* during his stay in the Flemish city.[3] For its overall design, Sandrart's warm red chalk drawing of the *Enthroned Virgin and Child Adored by Saints* now at the Metropolitan Museum (cat. 94) is based both on Titian's *Pesaro Madonna* and Rubens's work, although Sandrart's figures are somewhat more classically arranged than those in the Antwerp altarpiece. The work reveals Sandrart's interest in evolving complex religious compositions alongside those of the masters he admired, at a time when altar painting had become the mainstay of his output.

An autograph copy of the *Virgin and Child Enthroned with Saints* was in Rubens's possession until it entered the collection of Philip IV of Spain soon after the artist's death in 1640. The work seems in turn to have served as a principal model for Claudio Coello's *Virgin and Child Adored by St Louis, King of France* (cat. 95), which was painted for Don Luis Faurés, a member of the personal guard of Mariana of Austria, Queen of Spain. Coello borrowed key motifs from Rubens's composition, adapting them for the purpose of his own iconography and

93

PETER PAUL RUBENS (1577–1640)
Sketch for *Virgin and Child Enthroned with Saints*, *c.* 1628
Oil on panel, 80.3 x 55.3 cm
Gemäldegalerie, Staatliche Museen zu Berlin, inv. 780
RA ONLY

PROVENANCE: in the royal collection at the Schloss Sanssouci, Potsdam
SELECTED REFERENCES: Van de Velde 1977, pp. 221–34; Held 1980, pp. 519–22, no. 385; Reynolds 1996, pp. 55–63; Van Hout and Balis 2012, pp. 74–75 (ill. 119), 83, 154–55

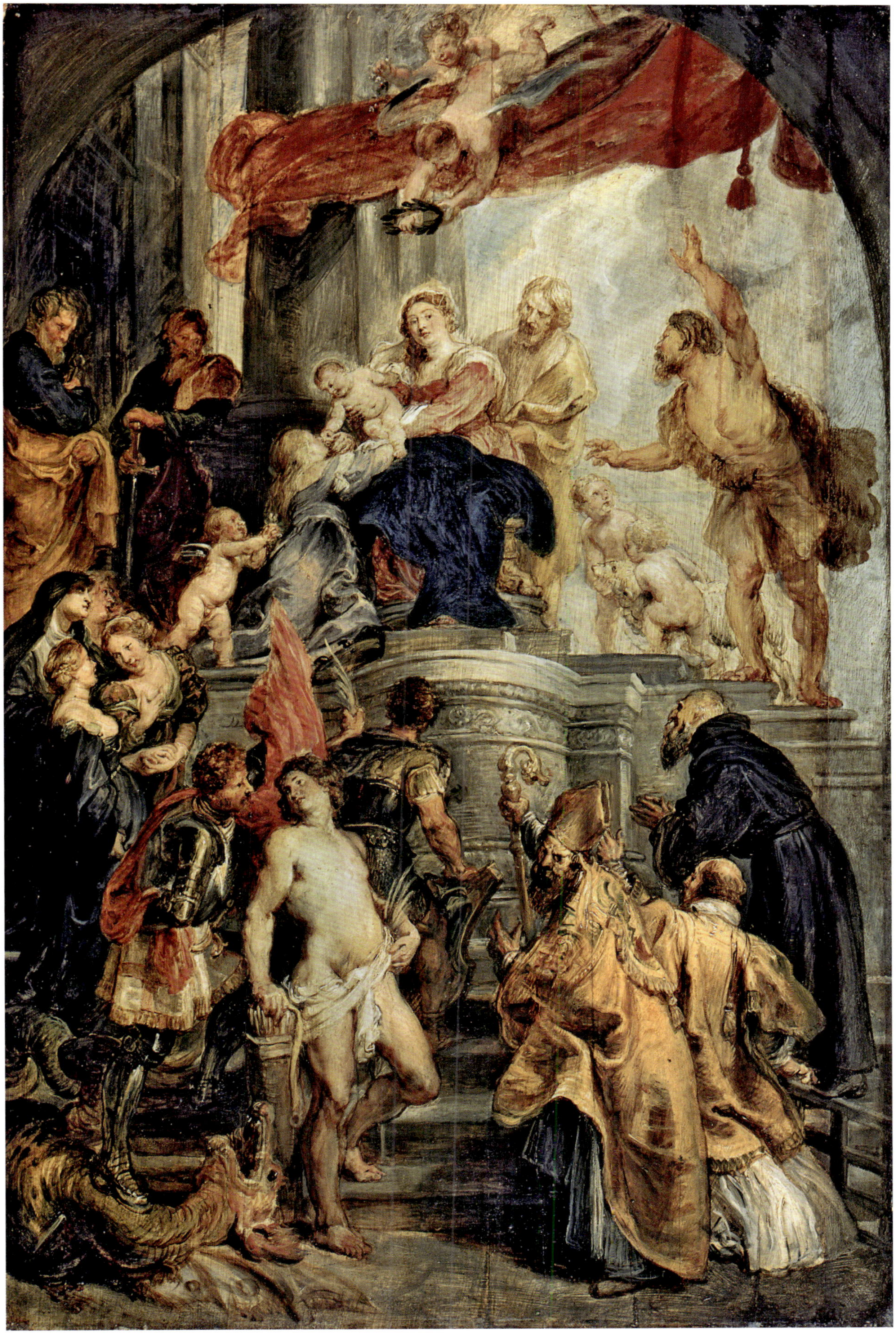

94

JOACHIM VON SANDRART THE ELDER (1606–1688)
Enthroned Virgin and Child Adored by Saints, c. 1665–75
Red chalk on paper, 31.9 x 20.2 cm
Lent by The Metropolitan Museum of Art, New York, inv. 2005.491. Van Day Truex Fund, 2005

PROVENANCE: Lutz Riester, Freiburg; purchased with the support of the Van Day Truex Fund, 2005
SELECTED REFERENCES: Wood 2005, pp. 17–19, pp. 34–55; Pietralata 2011, no. 392; New York 2012, no. 98

95

CLAUDIO COELLO (1642–1693)
Virgin and Child Adored by St Louis, King of France, 1675–68
Oil on canvas, 229 x 249 cm
Museo Nacional del Prado, Madrid, inv. P00661

PROVENANCE: Collection Don Luis Faurés, Madrid; Collection Marqués de la Ensenada, Madrid; royal collections, Madrid from 1794
SELECTED REFERENCES: Sullivan 1986, pp. 54–55, 114–16, no. P15; Rogelio Buendía 1994, p. 154, p. 155; Madrid 2011, p. 246, no. 661

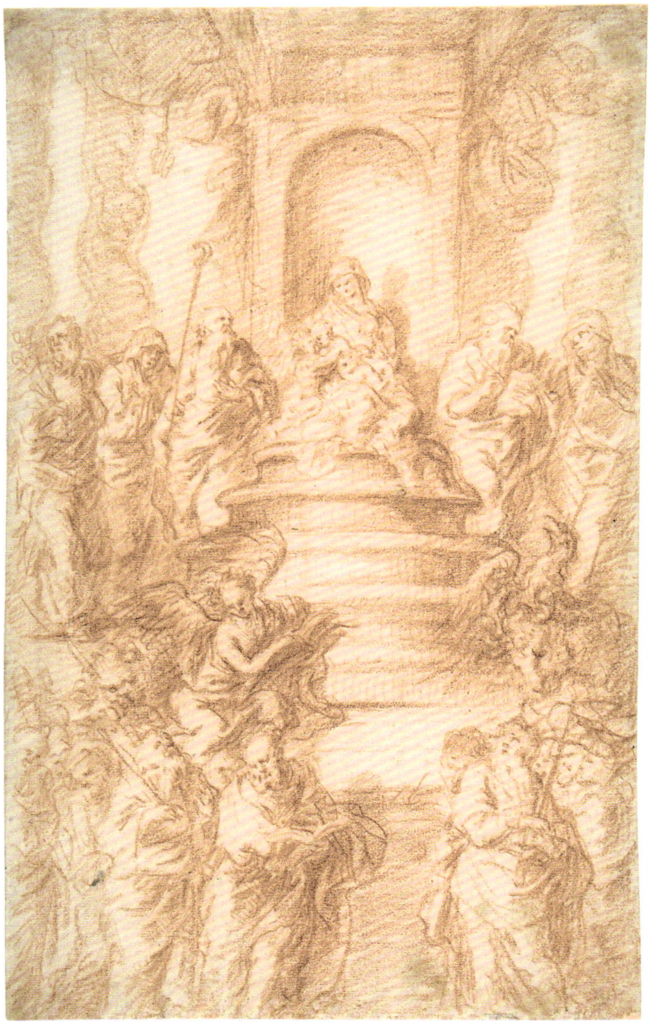

storytelling. The forward movement, extended right arm and profile view of King Louis kneeling in front of the Virgin are strongly reminiscent of the figure of St John the Baptist in Rubens's altarpiece, down to such details as the parting of the hair and beard. Similarly the stance and gesture of the young John the Baptist, who in the left foreground of Coello's work draws the viewer in, recall the angel proffering a rose towards the Infant in Rubens's *Virgin and Child Enthroned with Saints*. The Spanish artist's Virgin is framed in the same way by further sacred figures, and seated at the top of steps in a comparably grand and classical architectural setting, complete with a billowing red curtain and exuberant flying putti. Coello has also adopted Rubens's sumptuous range of saturated golds, reds and blues mixed with cooler colours, giving his dynamic and complex composition a markedly Northern feel. KP

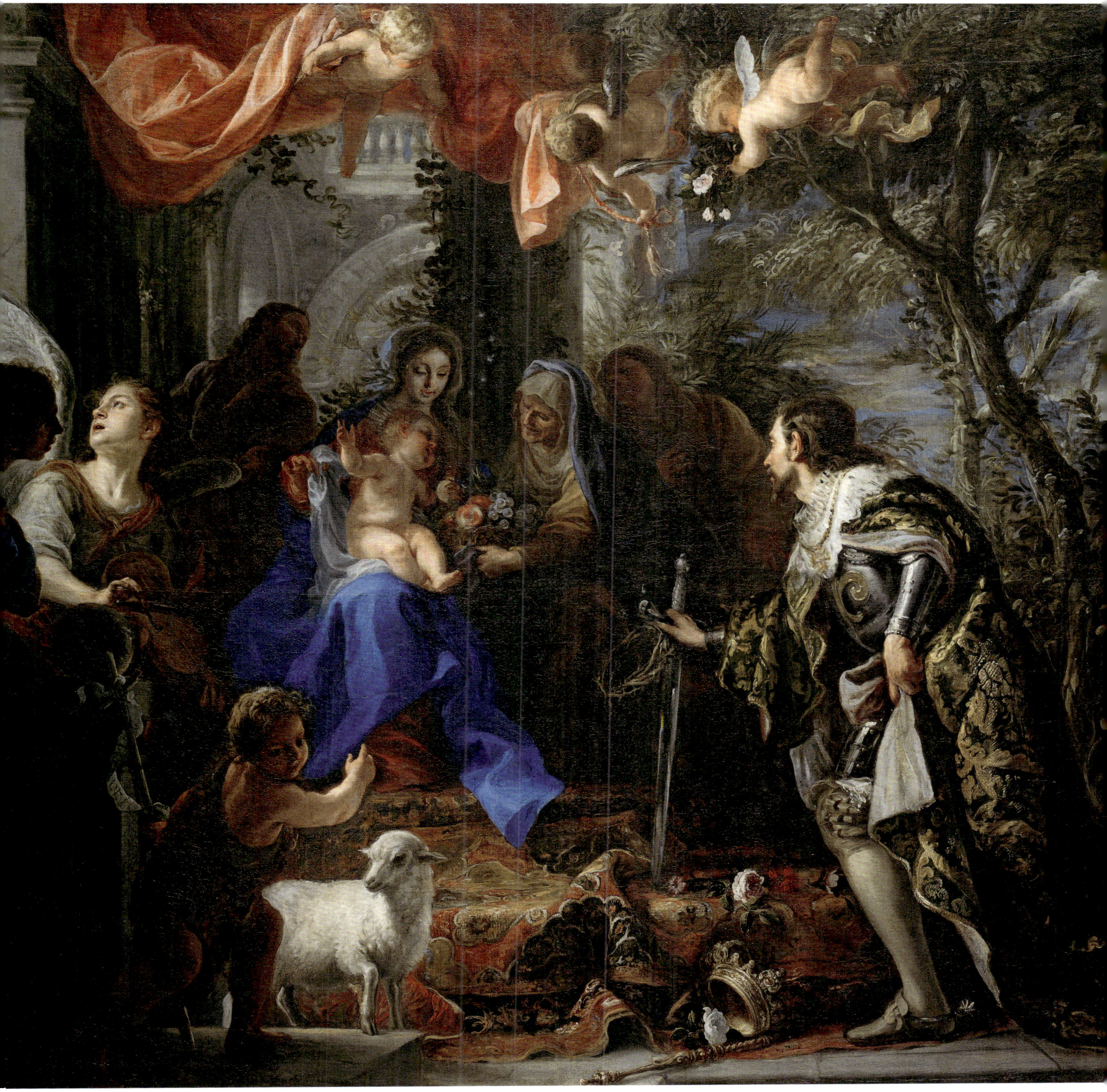

96

SCHELTE ADAMSZ. BOLSWERT (c. 1586–1659)
Conversion of St Paul, 1650–70
Engraving, 44.7 x 60.6 cm
Royal Museum of Fine Arts Antwerp, inv. 10461

PROVENANCE: the collection of Max Rooses, donated to the museum in 1900
SELECTED REFERENCES: Voorhelm Schneevoogt 1873, no. 63.468; Rome 1977, p. 35, no. 51; Antwerp and Amsterdam 1999–2000, p. 367; on the lost painting: Freedberg 1984, no. 31, pp. 123–28, no. 74 and Jaffé 1989, no. 149

Although succinct, the account of the conversion of St Paul in the Acts of the Apostles (IX, 1–9) offered artists great dramatic potential. Following Christ's resurrection, the Roman soldier Saul was travelling with his men to Damascus to arrest Christians when, en route, they were suddenly surrounded by a divine light. Struck blind, Saul fell to the ground and heard the voice of the Lord say: 'Saul, why persecutest thou me?' Soon afterwards Saul converted to Christianity and became known as the Apostle Paul. For his own treatment of the subject Rubens naturally looked at previous and contemporary Italian examples. But what is most fascinating is the way he used the same vocabulary and tense, compressed structure that he had deployed in his battle and hunting scenes for the depiction of this religious theme.

Rubens's last painting of the conversion of St Paul was destroyed in 1945 and is presented here in Bolswert's splendid engraving (cat. 96).[1] The rearing horses and struggling armoured and turbaned figures are dramatically portrayed with great contrasts of light and shade, as in Rubens's earlier *Tiger, Lion and Leopard Hunt* (cat. 1), *The Battle of the Amazons* (fig. 7) and *The Defeat of Sennacherib* (*c.* 1616; Alte Pinakothek, Munich; see cat. 17). Amid the chaos lies the future St Paul, arms outstretched to Christ who is bursting from the tumultuous heavens.

Rubens's *Conversion* is thought to have been commissioned by Władysław IV of Poland and was known to the rest of Europe through reproductive prints by engravers including Bolswert, François Ragot the Elder (1638–1670) and Gaspar Huberti (1619–1684). In Spain such prints were the inspiration for Murillo's *Conversion of St Paul* (cat. 97), the companion piece to his *Martyrdom of St Andrew* (1675–82; Museo Nacional del Prado, Madrid), itself indebted to Rubens's painting of the subject made for the Hospital de San Andrés de los Flamencos in Madrid, which Murillo would have seen during his stay in the city in 1658. Unused to depicting dramatic religious compositions, Murillo must have found Rubens's conception particularly successful since he produced a variant of it. The horse from which Saul has been thrown; Saul's pose, with his right leg not fully dismounted; the muscular figure helping him to his feet; his frightened companion; the standard-bearer behind; even the barking dog – all are largely identical to those in the Flemish prototype; however, Murillo has tempered Rubens's baroque exuberance. Although Murillo's work is theatrical, the mounted and rearing horses dominating the background of Rubens's painting are absent. In true Sevillian fashion Murillo divides the celestial and terrestrial realms clearly, suggesting the former primarily in luminous golden tones and the latter with darker colours. The whole is executed in the artist's signature soft style, a contrast to Rubens's harder-edged composition. KP

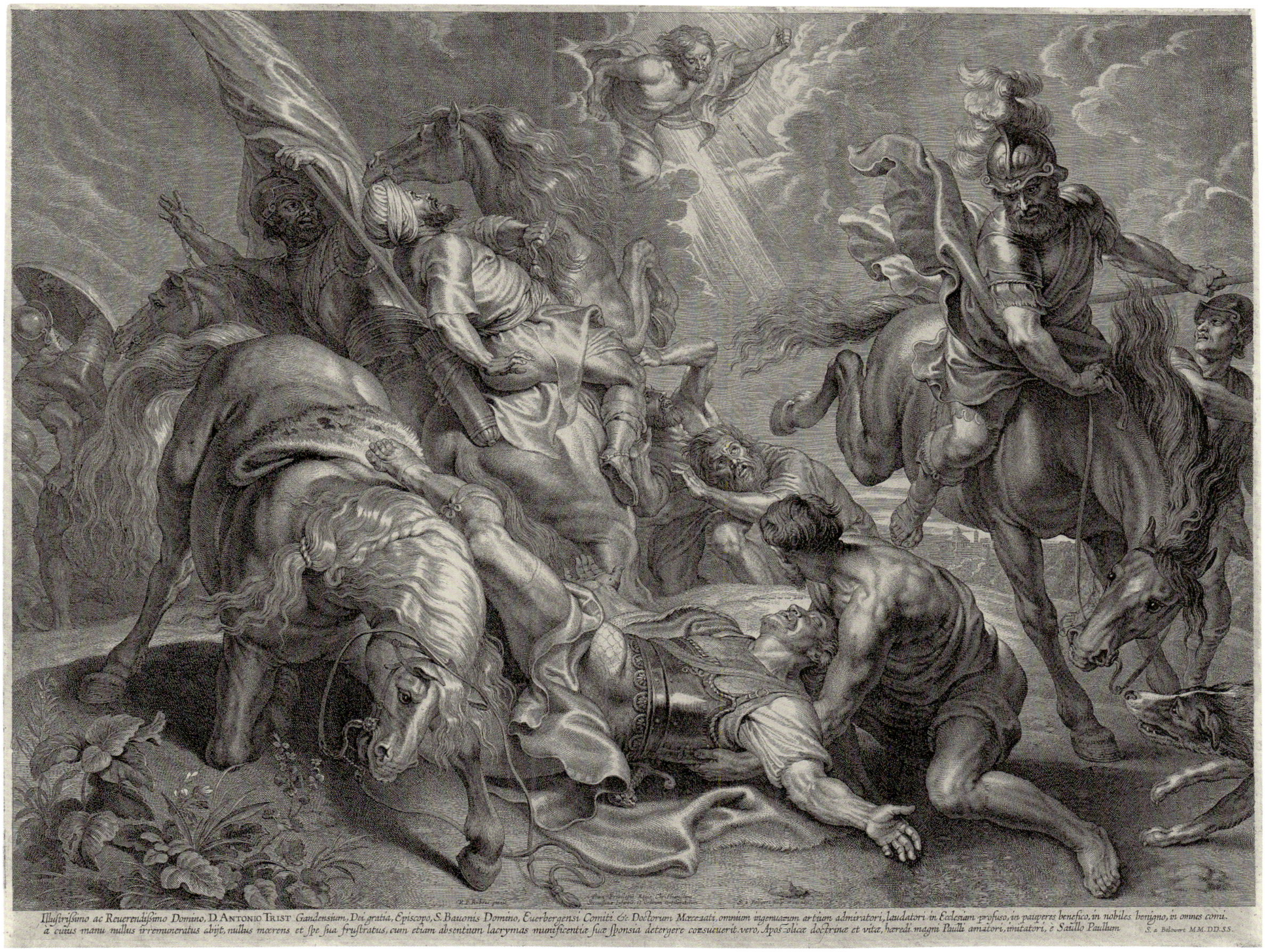
Illustrissimo ac Reuerendissimo Domino, D. ANTONIO TRIST Gandensium, Dei gratia, Episcopo, S. Bauonis Domino, Euerbergensi Comiti. &c. Doctorum Mæcenati, omnium ingenuarum artium admiratori, laudatori in Ecclesiam profuso, in pauperes benefico, in nobiles benigno, in omnes comi.
à cuius manu nullus irremuneratus abijt, nullus mœrens et spe sua frustratus, cum etiam absentium lacrymas munificentiæ suæ sponsia detergere consueuerit. vero, Apostolicæ doctrinæ et vitæ, hæredi magni Paulli amatori, imitatori, è Saullo Paullum
S. a Bolswert MM.DD.SS.

97

BARTOLOMÉ ESTEBAN MURILLO (1617–1682)
Conversion of St Paul, 1675–82
Oil on canvas, 125 x 169 cm
Museo Nacional del Prado, Madrid, inv. P00984

PROVENANCE: acquired by Charles IV; Palacio Real de Aranjuez, Madrid, 1814; Museo Nacional del Prado, 1819
SELECTED REFERENCES: Gaya Nuño 1978, no. 284; Iñiguez 1981, vol. 2, no. 363; Madrid and London 1982–83, p. 194, no. 92; Valdivieso 1990, pp. 198–99; Valdivieso 2010, pp. 202–04, 508, no. 345; Madrid 2011, pp. 210–11, no. 984

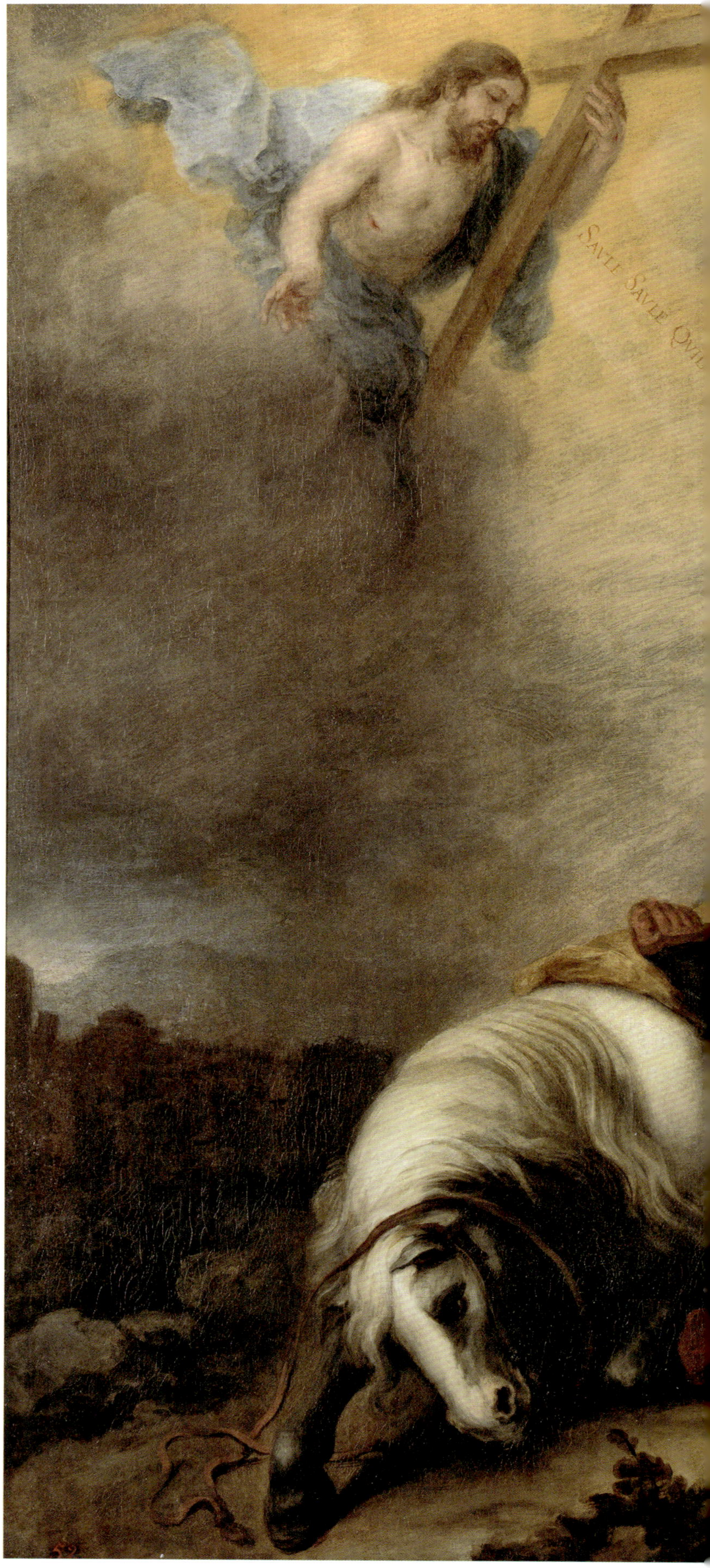

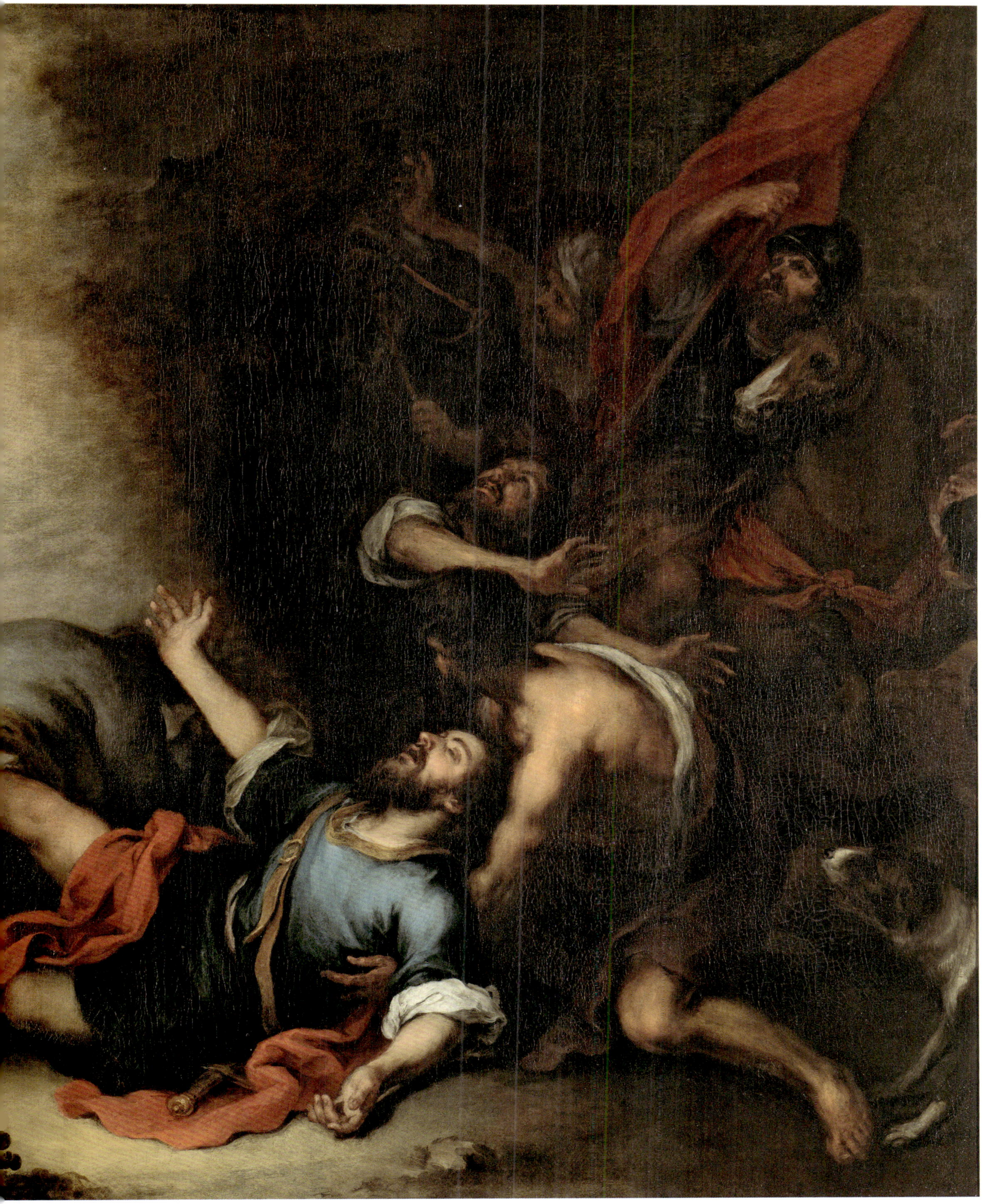

The building of Antwerp's Jesuit church in the new Italianate style provided Rubens with his first opportunity to execute ceiling decorations on an ambitious scale. In 1620 the artist agreed to design a cycle of paintings for the ceiling compartments in the aisle galleries. The upper level was to show biblical subjects while the lower level was to depict 16 saints. It was to be executed by Van Dyck and other assistants, and touched up by Rubens as required.

The church, noted for its sumptuousness and the magisterial handling of its interior decoration, was struck by lightning in 1718, and Rubens's cycle irrevocably ruined. Fortuitously, 25 of his spirited *modelli* in oil survive.[1] Of these, *St Cecilia* (cat. 98) is one of the most delightful. The patron saint of music is framed by a line indicative of the final, oval shape of the canvas; she is depicted seated on a cloud and playing an organ powered by a lively putto. The saint looks heavenwards for divine inspiration as an angel holds a crown of flowers over her head, alluding to her martyrdom.

The scene is remarkable for its lightness and vitality, conveyed by Rubens's spontaneous and fluid brush strokes – particularly in the depiction of the swirling clouds and billowing drapery – and his exquisite juxtaposition of delicate greys, pinks and yellows.

Rubens's *modelli* served as teaching aids to the artists working in his studio and he must have referred to them when, following his success with the Jesuit church cycle, he received the commission for the decoration of the ceiling of London's Whitehall Palace, now the Banqueting House. After his death, the sketches in oil became valuable collectors'

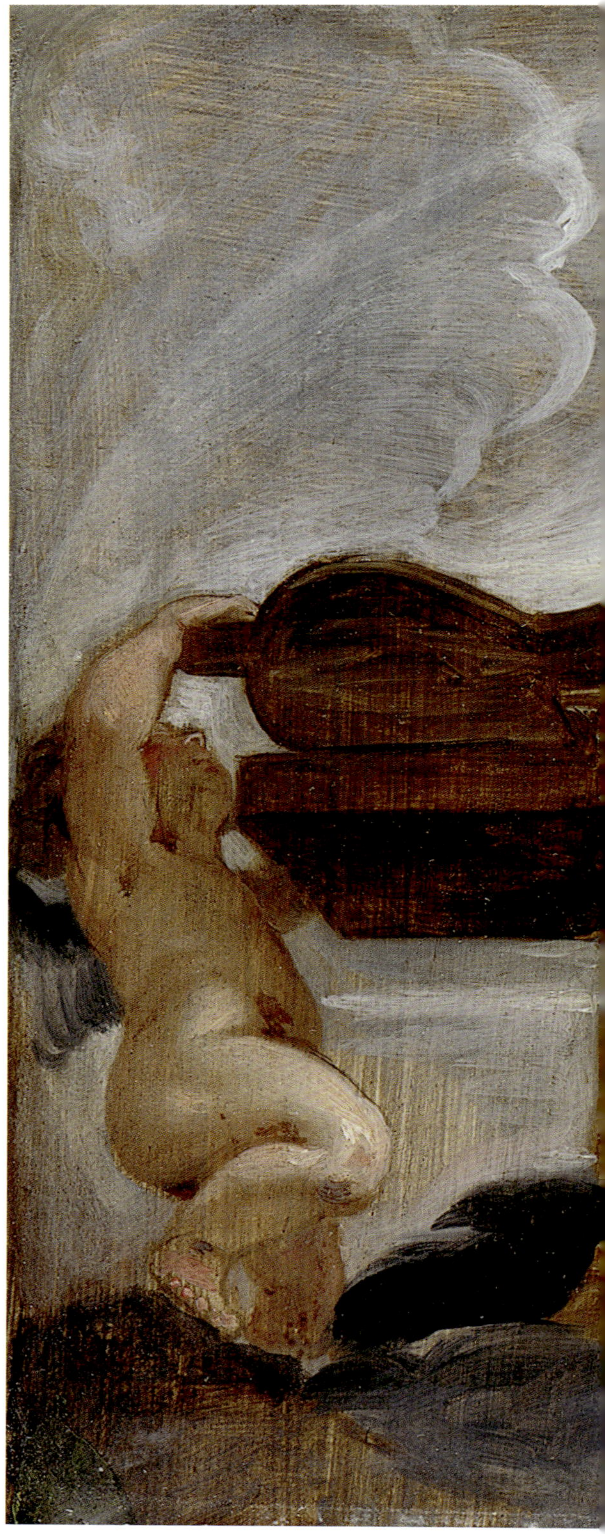

98

PETER PAUL RUBENS (1577–1640)
St Cecilia, 1620
Oil on panel, 27.5 x 43.4 cm
Akademie der bildenden Künste, Vienna, inv. 635

PROVENANCE: collection of Jacob de Wit (1695–1754); sale, Amsterdam, 10 March 1755; bought by Anthoni and Stephanus de Groot, The Hague; sale, The Hague, 10 March 1771; bought by Abelsz; collection of Anton Franz de Paula, Count Lamberg-Sprinzenstein (1740–1822), Vienna; donated by him to the Akademie der bildenden Künste, Vienna, 1821
SELECTED REFERENCES: Vienna 1961, p. 37, no. 35; Martin 1968, p. 134–35, no. 24b; Providence 1975; p. 12 (on the Jesuit church cycle); Held 1980, vol. 1, no. 32; White 1987, pp. 148–55 (on the Jesuit church cycle); Brussels 2002, pp. 192–97, no. 11

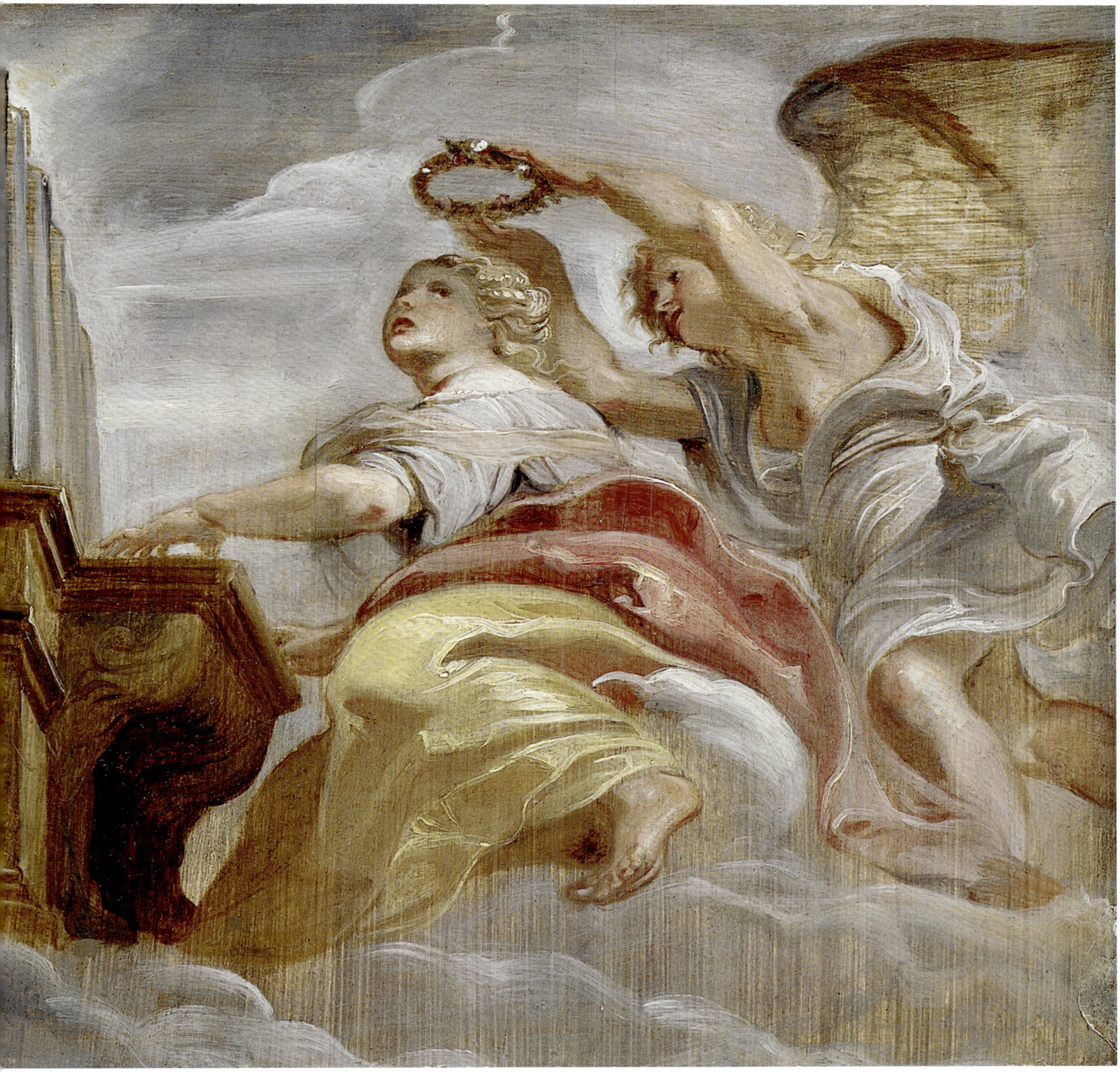

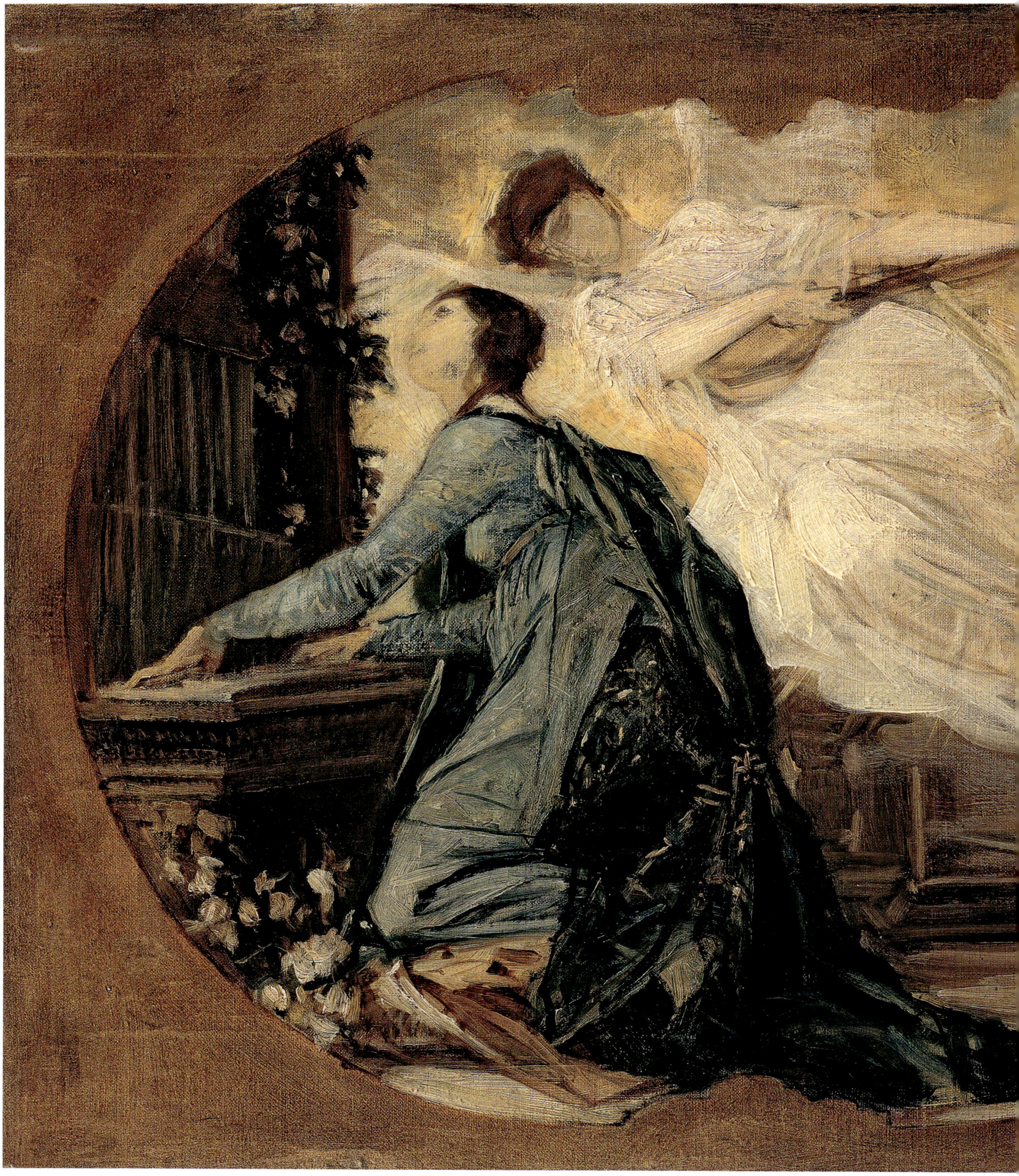

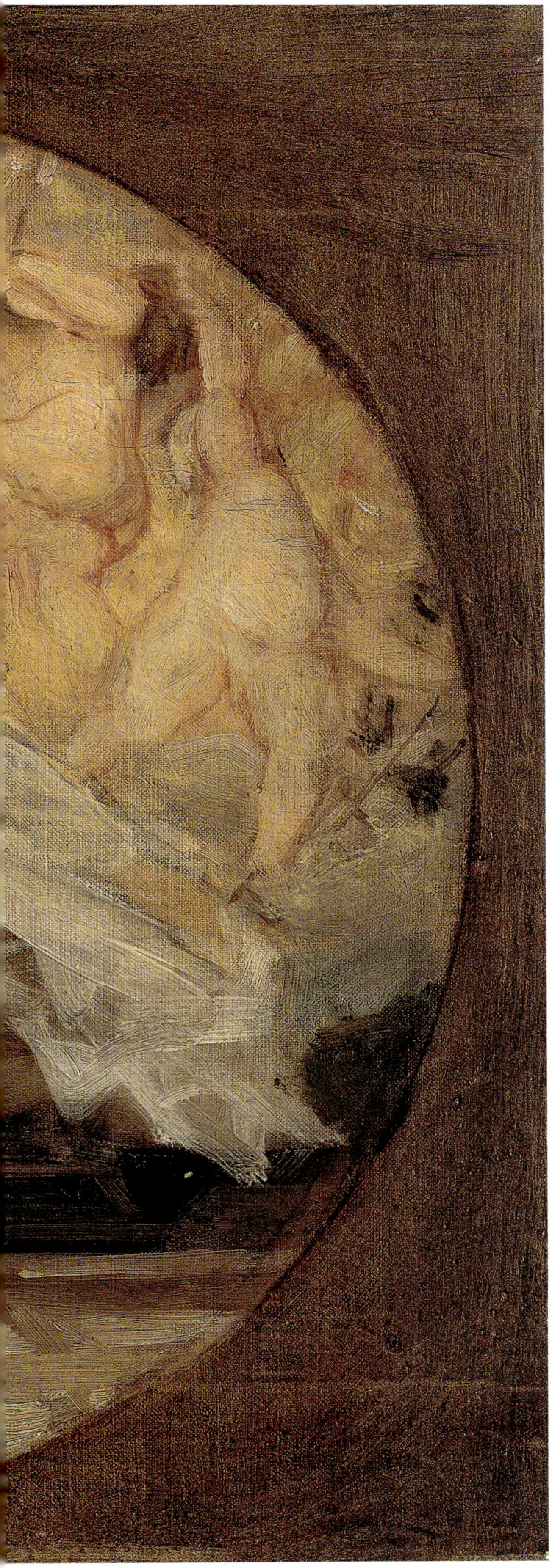

items.[2] *St Cecilia* was eventually acquired by Count Lamberg-Sprinzenstein and donated to the Vienna Akademie in 1821.

Gustav Klimt had just graduated from what is now the school of applied arts in Vienna when he undertook to paint three ceiling frescoes for the municipal theatre in Fiume (today Rijeka in Croatia). Among them was an allegory of music, also known as *St Cecilia*. Ferdinand Laufberger (1829–1881) and Hans Makart (1840–1884) have been cited as direct stylistic influences;[3] however, comparison with Rubens's *St Cecilia* suggests compellingly that Klimt had another principal model at hand when he proceeded with a study in oil (cat. 99) for his composition. Faced with the same testing problems of perspective and foreshortening inherent to ceiling decoration, and with the task of representing an identical subject in a similar oval format to Rubens's *modello*, it is not surprising that at this point in his career the young Klimt turned not only to his mentors but also to the Baroque master. The general composition and pose of Klimt's *St Cecilia*, who rests her fingers on the organ's keyboard, her face upturned while a musical angel accompanied by joyous putti hovers above her, surely refer to Rubens. KP

99

GUSTAV KLIMT (1862–1918)
St Cecilia, 1885
Oil on canvas, 38.5 x 50 cm
Österreichische Galerie Belvedere, Vienna, inv. 1459

PROVENANCE: the object was purchased from Kunsthandel H. O. Miethke, Vienna, in 1912
SELECTED REFERENCES: Frodl 1978–79, pp. 9–36; Munich, Berlin, London and New York 2007, p. 241; Natter 2012, p. 16 and p. 534, no. 41; Christina Bachl-Hofmann and Dagmar Diernberger in Vienna 2012, pp. 36–40, ill. p. 39

Rubens was buried in Antwerp on 2 June 1640 in the church of St James. A few years earlier, while suffering from ill health and evidently considering his own mortality, he had painted a *Madonna and Child with Saints* (fig. 30) to adorn his own tomb. In 1644 the work was placed above the altar in the funerary chapel erected by his family, where it remains to this day. In the eighteenth century the painting, one of Rubens's most lyrical, could be viewed not only in Antwerp but also by a select few through a studio copy at the Palazzo Balbi in Genoa. This is where Fragonard encountered the work when, after his period as a *pensionnaire* at the French academy in Rome, he was taken on a trip around Italy by Jean-Claude Richard, Abbé de Saint-Non (1727–1791). An art lover and friend of artists, Saint-Non had employed the young Fragonard to make drawings after the most important works of art in Italy with the intention of turning them into aquatints for his planned guide to the nation's treasures. Undoubtedly sharing Saint-Non's view that Rubens was 'as much a Poet as a great Painter',[1] Fragonard made 25 drawn copies after Rubens during the course of his career.[2] The present example (cat. 100), executed in black chalk, captures the tenderness of Rubens's *Madonna and Child with Saints* while softening its realism.

Sir Joshua Reynolds saw Rubens's original *in situ* during his visit to Antwerp in 1781; he is known to have spent long hours in the churches of the Flemish city, studying, analysing and frequently returning to Rubens's paintings.[3] Testimony to his interest in Rubens's *Madonna and Child with Saints* are both his laudatory assessment in his diary of one particular aspect of the canvas and his annotated and retouched counterproof of Rombout Eynhoudts's etching after the work (cat. 101). 'For effects of colours this yields to none of Rubens's works,' he exclaimed, adding that the painting was 'as bright as if the sun shone on it' and 'well worth the studying ... to a painter who wishes to become a colourist, or learn the art of producing a brilliant effect'. Reynolds clearly followed his own recommendations since he not only made a note on his counterproof of the range of tones in Rubens's painting (including 'black as possible / all the rest warm / The pope crimson') but also reworked it in red chalk and brown washes, and in so doing effectively translated its main colour contrasts.

David Wilkie had read Reynolds's *A Journey to Flanders and Holland* and had already appreciated Rubens's ability as a colourist in the Galerie Médicis at the Palais du Luxembourg by the time he stopped in Antwerp for a day in September 1816.[4] There he visited the museum and cathedral, and in a letter to his brother commented on the magnificence of Rubens's works.[5] Following in Reynolds's footsteps, he painted a watercolour after Rubens's altarpiece in the church of St James (cat. 102), which reflects the altarpiece's warm hues. He also took care to record the painting's architectural surroundings. KP

100

JEAN-HONORÉ FRAGONARD (1732–1806)
Virgin and Child with Saints, 1761
Black chalk on paper, 27.5 x 20 cm
On loan from the British Museum, London, inv. 1936,0509.46. Presented by Mrs Spencer Whatley, 1936

PROVENANCE: Sir Samuel Rush Meyrick; the Meyrick family; from whom inherited by Mrs Spencer Whatley; by whom donated to the British Museum in 1936
SELECTED REFERENCES: Anahoff 1968, no. 1795; Senior 1936, pp. 5–9; Paris 1987, pp. 118–20, 178–82; Rosenberg and Brejon de Lavergnée 1986, pp. 237–50, no. 339; Barcelona 2006, pp. 203–05

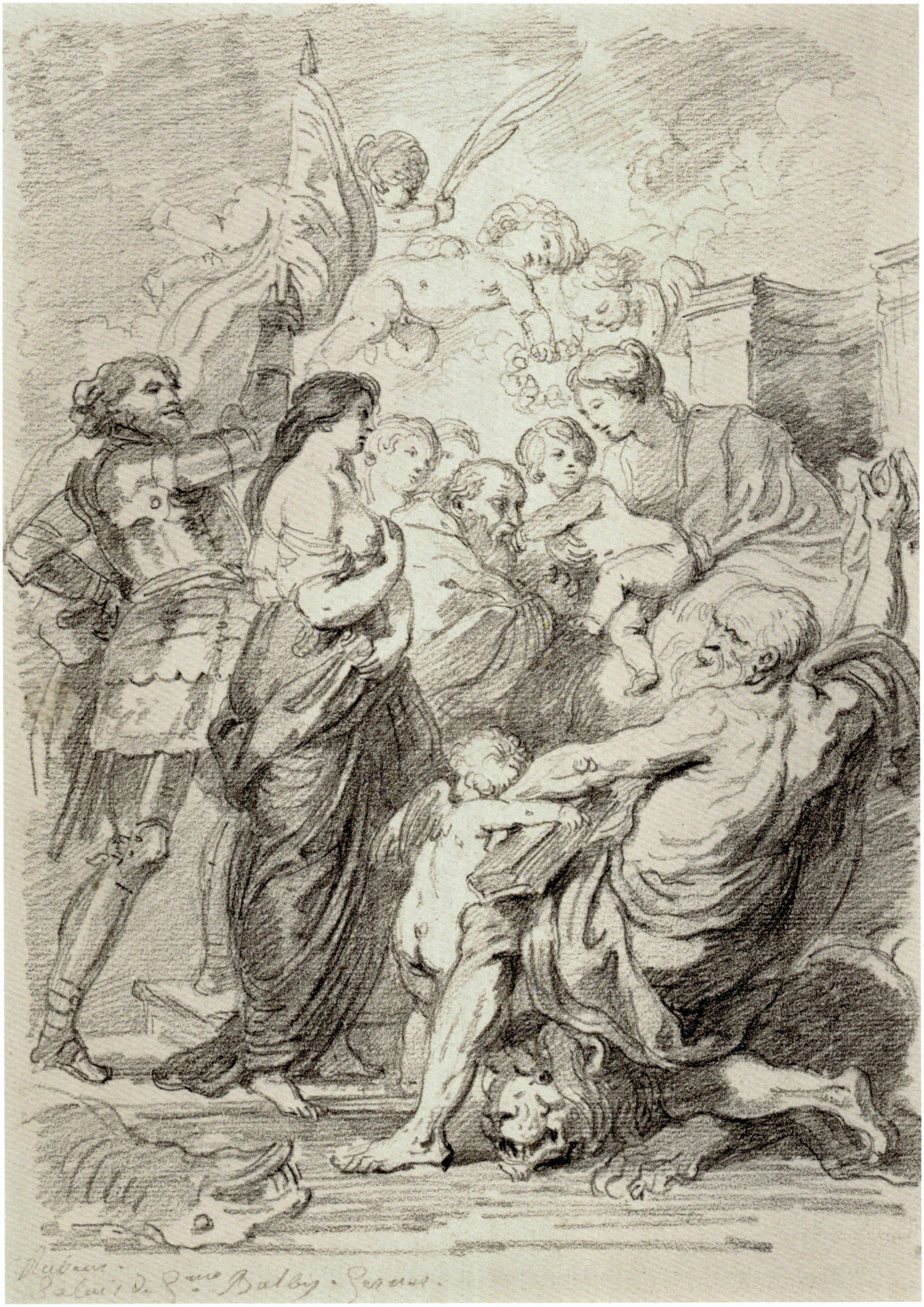

101

SIR JOSHUA REYNOLDS (1723–1792)
etching by **ROMBOUT EYNHOUDTS (1614–1679/80)**
Sacra Conversazione with St Bonaventura and St George, retouched *c.* 1781
Red chalk and brown wash over counterproof of etching, 34.7 x 25.2 cm
On loan from the British Museum, London, inv. 1885,0509.1578

PROVENANCE: Sir Joshua Reynolds (Lugt 2364, verso); sold 12 March 1798, as part of lot 640: '4 [prints] from Rubens, retouched by Sir Joshua Reynolds, with remarks on the margin', Harry Phillips, London; Sir Lawrence Thomas (1769–1830, Lugt 2446); Christie's, London, 12 December 1884, lot 217, bought by William Russell (1800–1884); from whom purchased by the museum through Alphonse Wyatt Thibaudeau in 1884
SELECTED REFERENCES: Voorhelm Schneevoogt 1873, p. 70, no. 49; Binyon 1902, p. 198, no. 11; Hollstein 1949–2010, vol. 6, p. 206; Perini 1988, p. 162; Reynolds 1996, pp. 76–77; Plymouth 2009–10, no. 83

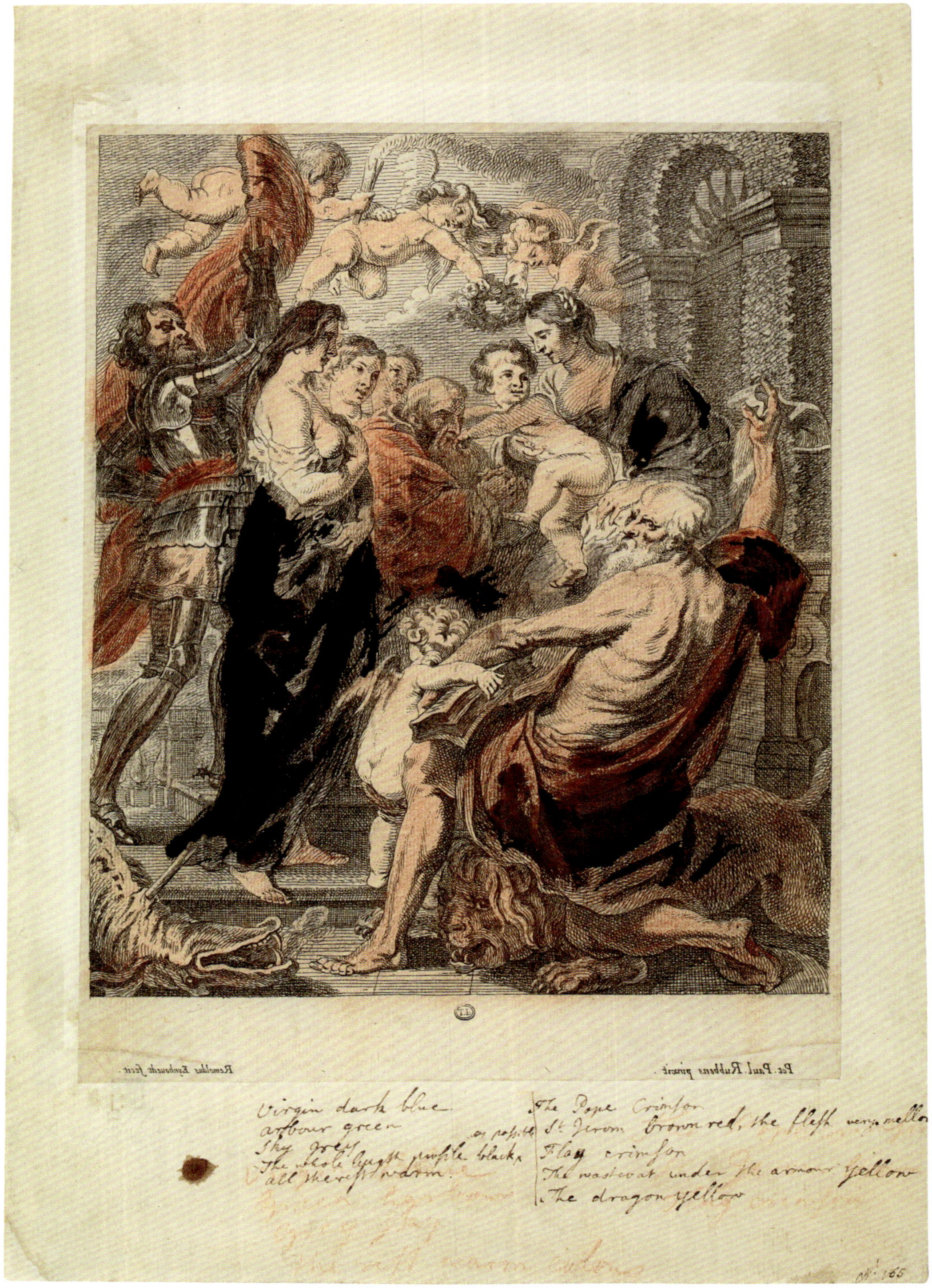

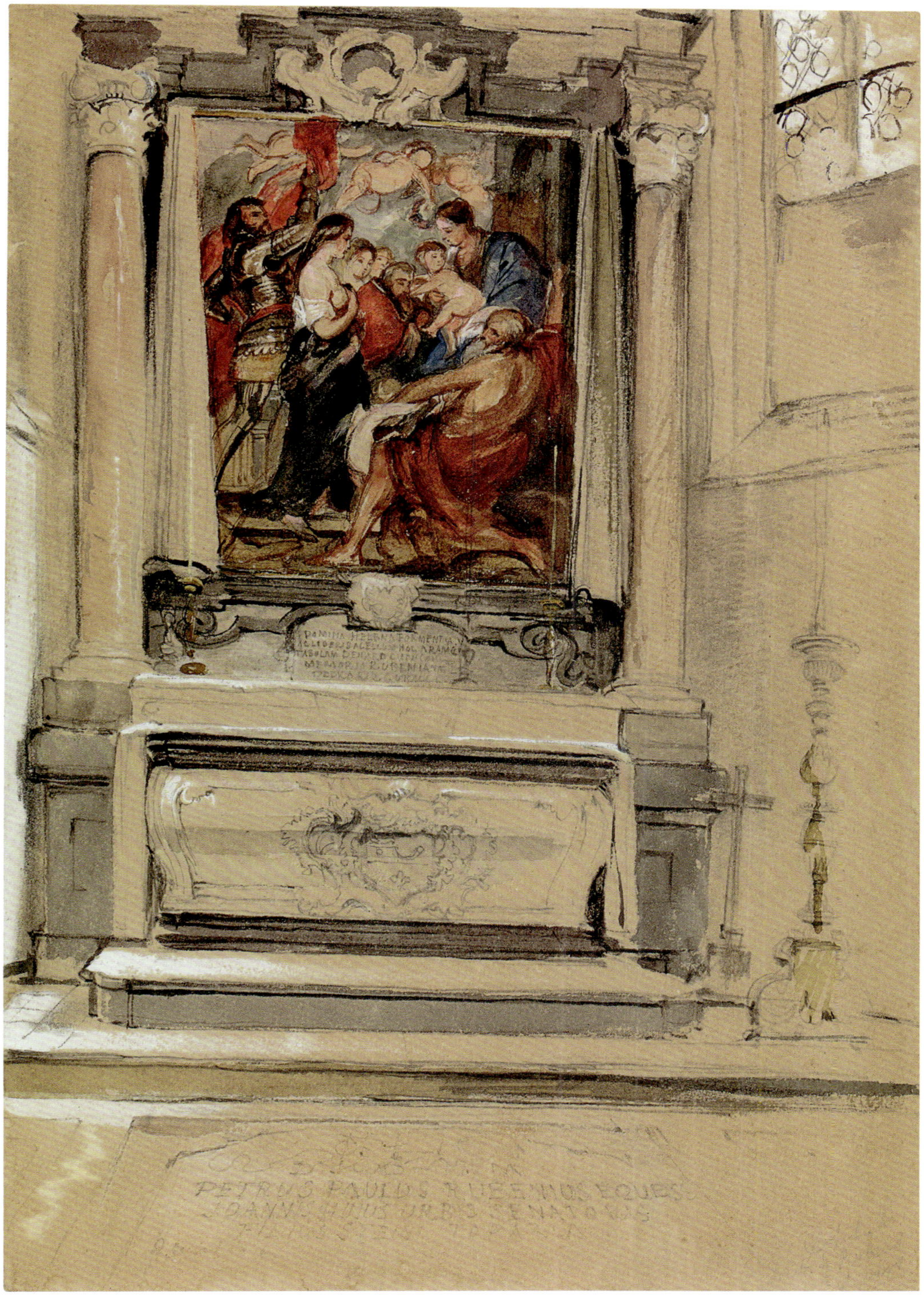

102

DAVID WILKIE (1837-1887)
Rubens's Tomb and Altarpiece in the Sint-Jacobskerk in Antwerp, c. 1816
Watercolour and graphite on buff paper, 37 x 26.5 cm
On loan from the British Museum, London, inv. 1865,0708.146

PROVENANCE: purchased from Alphonse Wyatt Thibaudeau in 1865
SELECTED REFERENCES: Cunningham 1843, vol. 1, pp. 440–41 and 442–44; St Andrews 1985, pp. 30–35, no. 21

In the early 1630s Rubens painted an altarpiece (cat. 104) depicting St Teresa of Ávila (1515–1582) interceding for Bernardino de Mendoza in Purgatory for the recently rebuilt church of the Discalced Carmelites at Antwerp. Mendoza, a wealthy young Spaniard and the brother of Ávila's bishop, had offered his house and garden near Valladolid so that the Carmelite nun Teresa could found a convent there. Soon afterwards, however, he died without receiving the last rites, meaning his soul would be consigned to Purgatory. The Lord revealed to Sister Teresa that Mendoza's soul would be saved if she arranged for a Mass to be said for him in the convent's chapel. Teresa proceeded with its construction and during the service Christ appeared to her in a vision, announcing that Mendoza had been released from the flames of Purgatory. The Spaniard is shown being lifted to Heaven by an angel while one of his companions – who must remain in Purgatory – wrings his hands and another clutches her chest in despair.

The woman with long blonde hair caught the attention of Van Gogh on one of the several occasions he visited the museum in Antwerp, where the painting is now held. 'I'm utterly carried away, for instance, by his [Rubens's] way of drawing the features in a face with strokes of pure red [...] those heads *are so alive* [...] I probably don't look at the ones that are most generally admired. I look for fragments such as those blonde heads in St Theresa in Purgatory. I'm also looking for a blonde model just because of Rubens.'[1] By contrast, comparison between Rubens's altarpiece and Philippe de Champaigne's *Christ Among the Souls in Purgatory* (fig. 28) strongly suggests that the seventeenth-century French artist was inspired by the composition as a whole. KP

103

PETER PAUL RUBENS (1577–1640)
and workshop
St Teresa of Ávila Interceding for Bernardino de Mendoza in Purgatory, 1630–35
Oil on canvas, 194 x 139 cm
Royal Museum of Fine Arts Antwerp, inv. 299

PROVENANCE: Church of the Discalced Carmelites, Antwerp; in Paris, 1794–1815; museum founding collection
SELECTED REFERENCES: Rooses 1886–92, vol. 2, no. 493, pp. 351–54; Salinger 1949, vol. 8, no. 3, pp. 97–108; Vlieghe 1973, no. 155, pp. 166–68; Monballieu 1976–78, p. 166

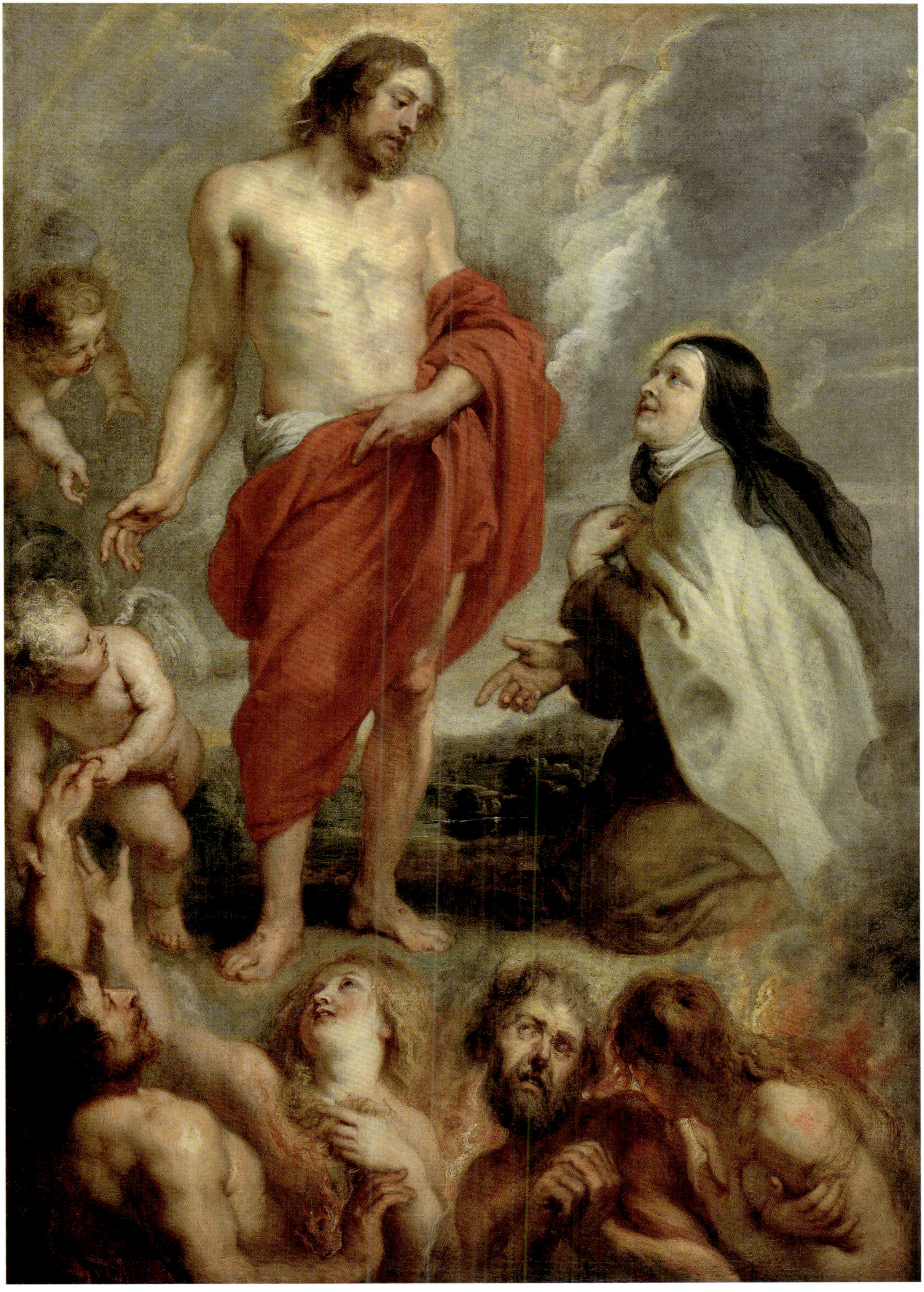

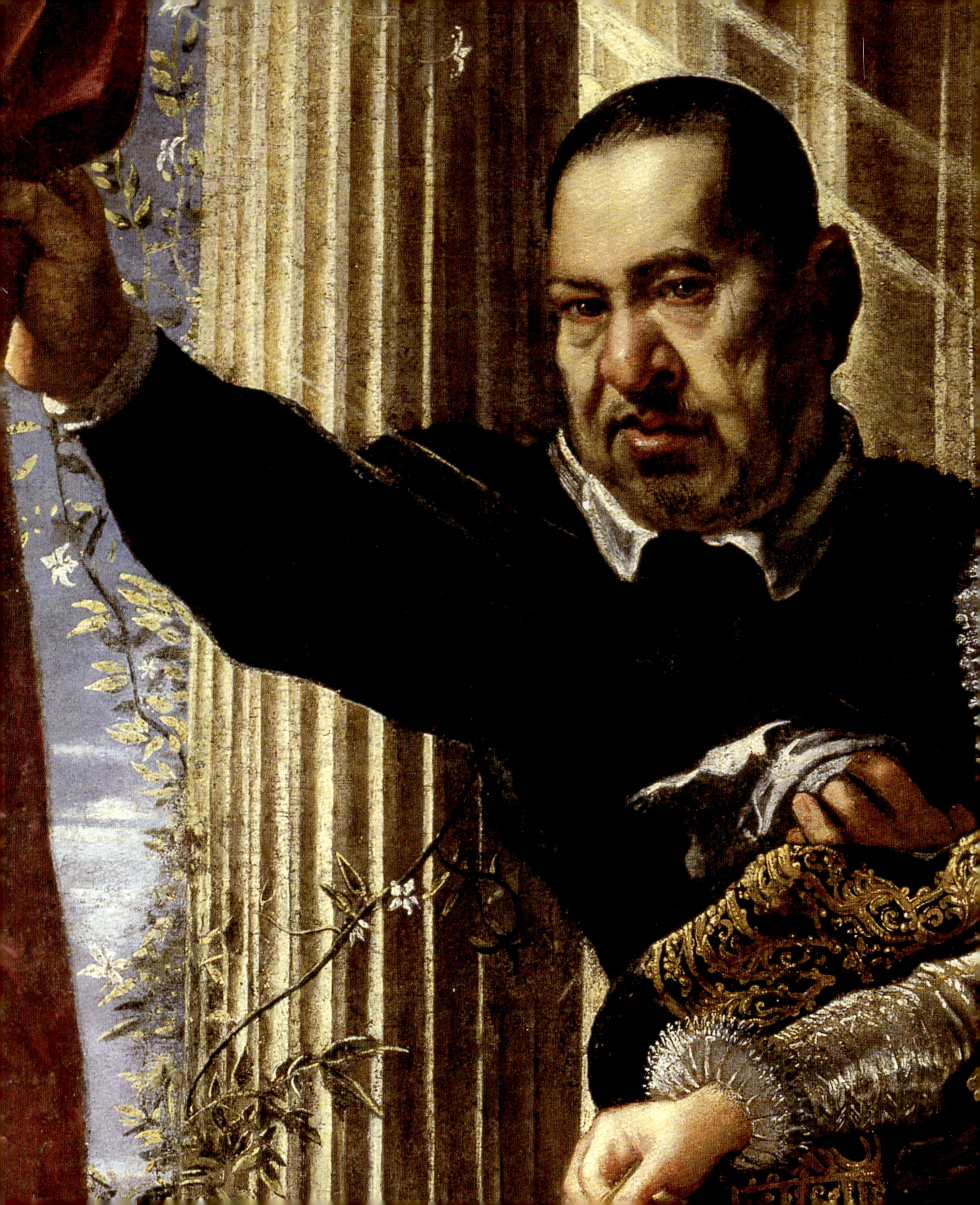

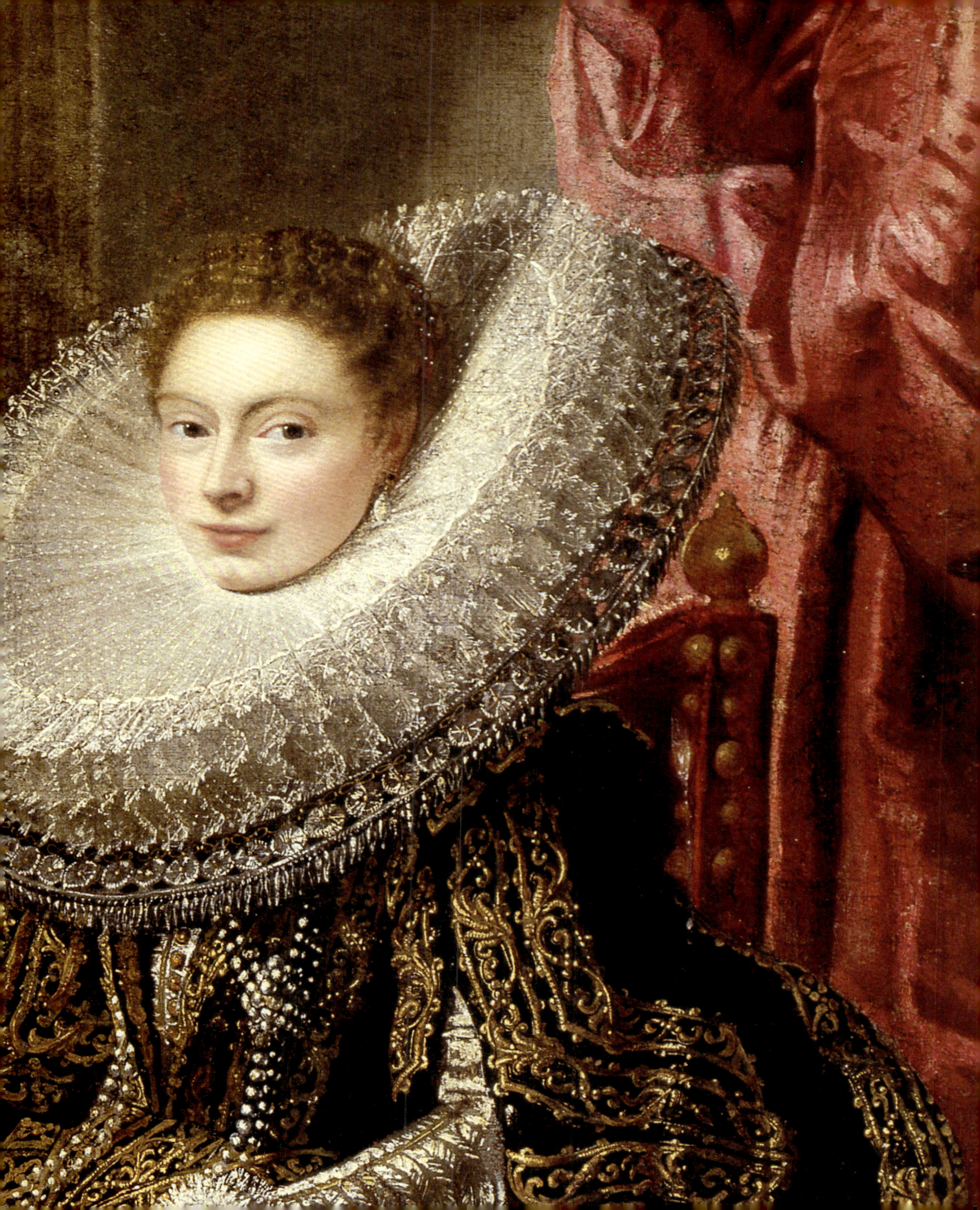

ELEGANCE

DAVID HOWARTH

Elegance is not an obvious characteristic of Rubens; his 'great mind', as Fuseli called it, was the antithesis of the art of cutting a figure.[1] Surely it must be what an anonymous catalogue called the 'chaste, correct and elegant' Van Dyck who deserves that epithet; knighted by Charles I for transforming the Elizabethan icon into the Stuart face. Van Dyck even inspired the Edwardian swagger portrait, though the meridian of his influence was the Georgian era, when such portraits as *A Genoese Noblewoman and Her Son* (cat. 105) set the tone for many a dynastic image. Van Dyck was preferred to Rubens, whose works were often thought to be his: indeed Rubens's *Portrait of Hélène Fourment* (fig. 39) was reproduced as a print after Van Dyck.[2] The melange of Rubens with Van Dyck created curious fusions: such as the marble busts of the two painters by Michael Rysbrack commissioned for Hagley Hall, Worcestershire, in 1747. Rysbrack conceived the two as mannered, languorous and effete: hardly appropriate for Rubens, who had always grasped life with both hands. Each painter wears 'Van Dyck costume', a sartorial invention which was to achieve its most elegant expression in Gainsborough's *Blue Boy*, a portrait of Jonathan Buttall (*c.* 1770; Huntington Library, San Marino, California). By grafting the elegance of Van Dyck to the naturalism of Rubens, these Rysbracks created a synthesis that reflected British perceptions of the time.

The relationship between Rubens and Van Dyck in life was turned upside down in Britain: Van Dyck became the master and Rubens the pupil. The *sprezzatura* of Rubens overstepped the boundaries of propriety, causing Sir Joshua Reynolds to sigh when delivering his fifth discourse to the students of the Royal Academy on 10 December 1775: 'Throughout the whole of his works, there is a proportionable want of that nicety of distinction and elegance of mind, which is required in the higher walks of painting.'[3] Reynolds, much to his own regret, never attained the 'higher walks', but as a vastly successful portraitist he always took the greatest interest in Rubens. It is the purpose of this essay to suggest the powerful influence of Rubens upon the trajectory of the British 'likeness'.

From the first, Rubens was consulted by Reynolds: his early work *Garrick Between Tragedy and Comedy* (1761; Waddesdon Manor, Aylesbury) owed more to an image such as the studio version of Rubens's *Drunken Silenus* (cat. 58) than to the usual source for conflict between our higher and lower nature, Annibale Carracci's *The Choice of Hercules*.[4] The congruence here shows Reynolds looking to Rubens even for the challenge of portraying this towering figure in the cultural life of London.

On the occasion of his first marriage, Rubens had painted the self-portrait with Isabella Brant (fig. 33). It was to this that Reynolds turned when commissioned by arguably the most interesting eighteenth-century Welsh patron of the arts, Sir Watkin Williams-Wynn, 4th Baronet. In 1769 Williams-Wynn was *en fête* and determined to celebrate his own marriage with a portrait (cat. 111).[5] The work is a poignant image of felicity; a state of harmony lamentably short-lived because

FIG. 33 Peter Paul Rubens, *Rubens and Isabella Brant in the Honeysuckle Bower*, 1609. Oil on canvas-covered panel, 178 x 136.5 cm. Alte Pinakothek, Munich

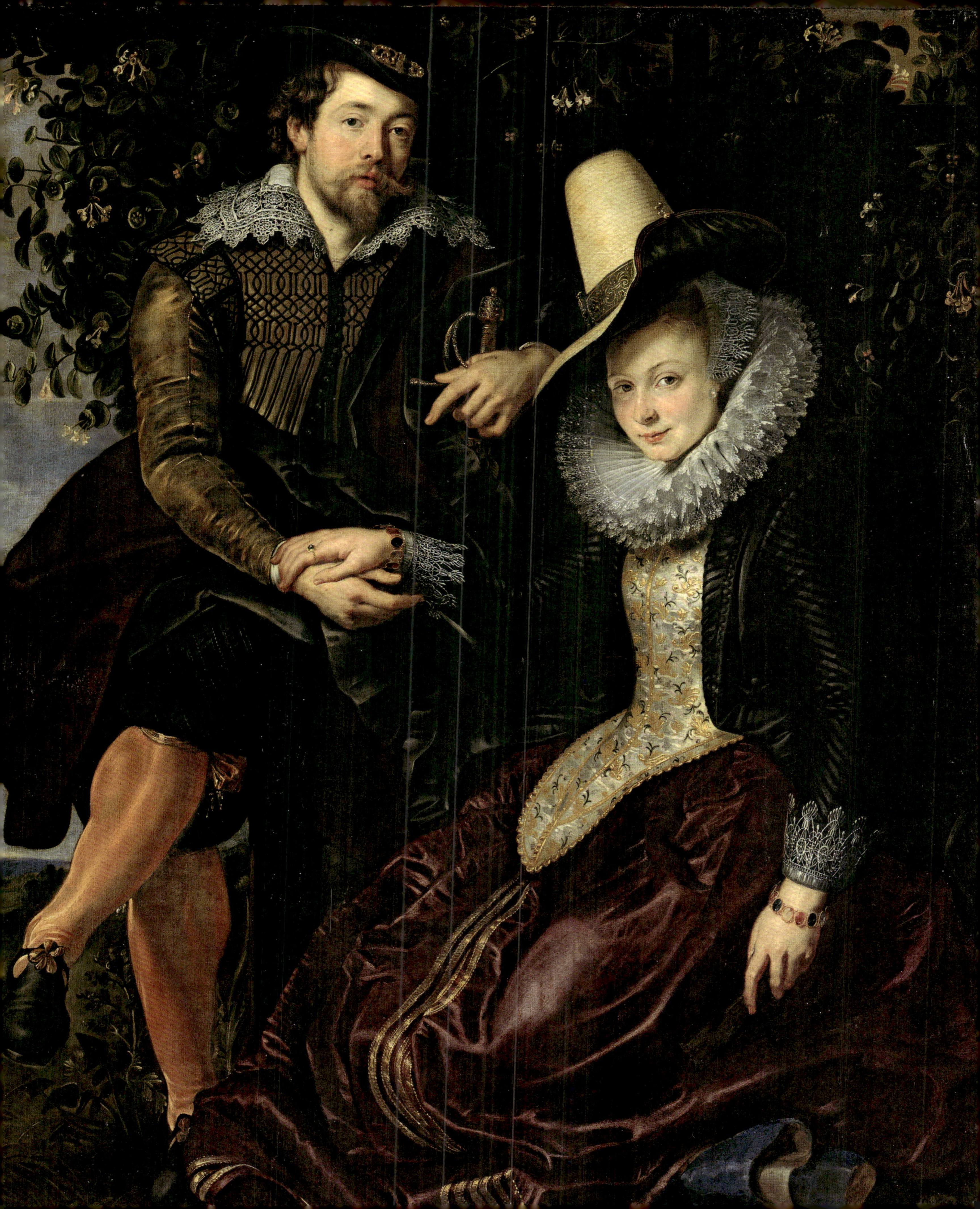

Lady Williams-Wynn died fifteen months after the portrait was painted. Sir Watkin's grief appears to have been barely more enduring, since he contrived a marriage the year after the death to the daughter of Lord Grenville, the erstwhile Prime Minister.

From the first, Reynolds was strongly drawn to the technique of Dutch painters. Unpremeditated in his love for the scumbling of Rembrandt, Reynolds studied assiduously the painterly technique of Rubens's *modelli*.[6] These fragile little panels, periodically recycled as old solutions to new challenges, had been the building blocks with which Rubens constructed his prodigious career.

A Rubens *modello* – apparently dashed off with enviable *sprezzatura* – was always of compelling interest to Reynolds, who would paint over two thousand likenesses and aspired to take society with the palette, as had Rubens in Spanish Antwerp. In time, Reynolds came to declare himself well able to carry off pastiches of the great master. These, he believed, would confound all but the most knowing of connoisseurs.[7]

But if the example of Rubens was especially important to Reynolds the public man, he took the measure of Rubens with a long brush: dependence was as intermittent as it was discreet.[8] One example is the pair of Dilettanti portraits (1777–79; Society of Dilettanti, London) that took as their point of departure Rubens's *Four Philosophers* (after 1611; Palazzo Pitti, Florence); a group Reynolds had much admired back in Florence in 1752.[9] Reynolds, too, was an avid collector of Rubens, valuing his *modelli* especially: *Apollo Bestowing Royal Liberality Suppresses Avarice* (1633–34; Courtauld Institute of Art Gallery, London) for the Whitehall Palace (now the Banqueting House) among them. This was derived from Michelangelo's Sistine ceiling, which at his Royal Academy lectures Reynolds would always extol as the most sublime creation in painting.

The debt of Reynolds to Rubens extended beyond the effect of portrait upon portrait, for he could deconsecrate an altarpiece as effortlessly as he could elevate an engraving: for instance in *Elizabeth Lamb, Viscountess Melbourne, with Her Son, Peniston* (cat. 118). Here elements from Rubens's *Virgin and Child with St Elizabeth and the Child Baptist* (*c.* 1635; Walker Art Gallery, Liverpool) were fused with prints such as Schelte Adamsz. Bolswert's *Madonna and Child*, after a Rubens painting once in the Walpole Collection. But then Reynolds may also have had a preliminary *bozzetto* to hand: on 14 July 1770 Lord Darnley, an old acquaintance who had sat for Reynolds in 1761, called at his studio. Darnley was not enquiring about another

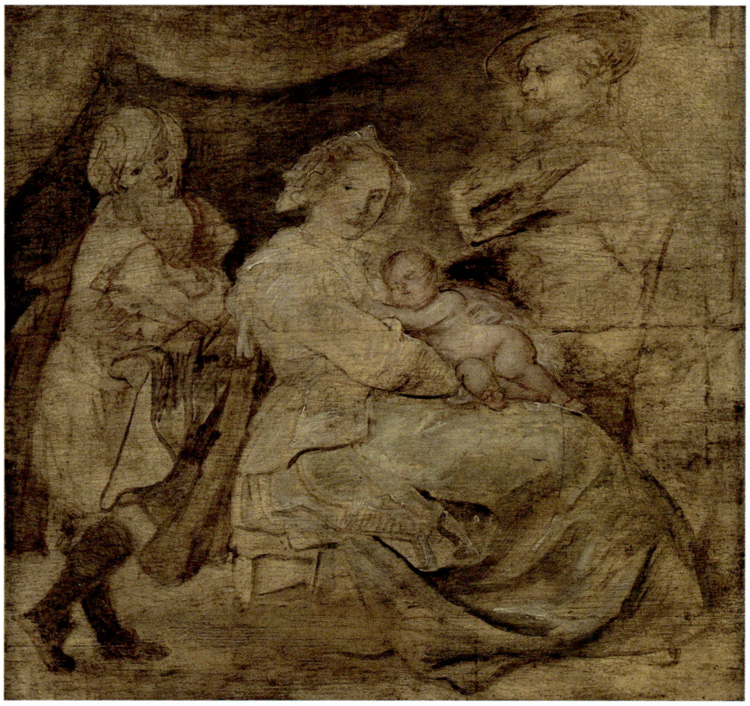

FIG. 34 Attributed to Peter Paul Rubens, *Sketch for a Portrait of a Family*, 1632–33. Oil on panel, 35.5 x 38.2 cm. Philadelphia Museum of Art

FIG. 35 Peter Paul Rubens, *Chapeau de Paille*, *c.* 1622–25. Oil on panel, 79 x 54.6 cm. The National Gallery, London

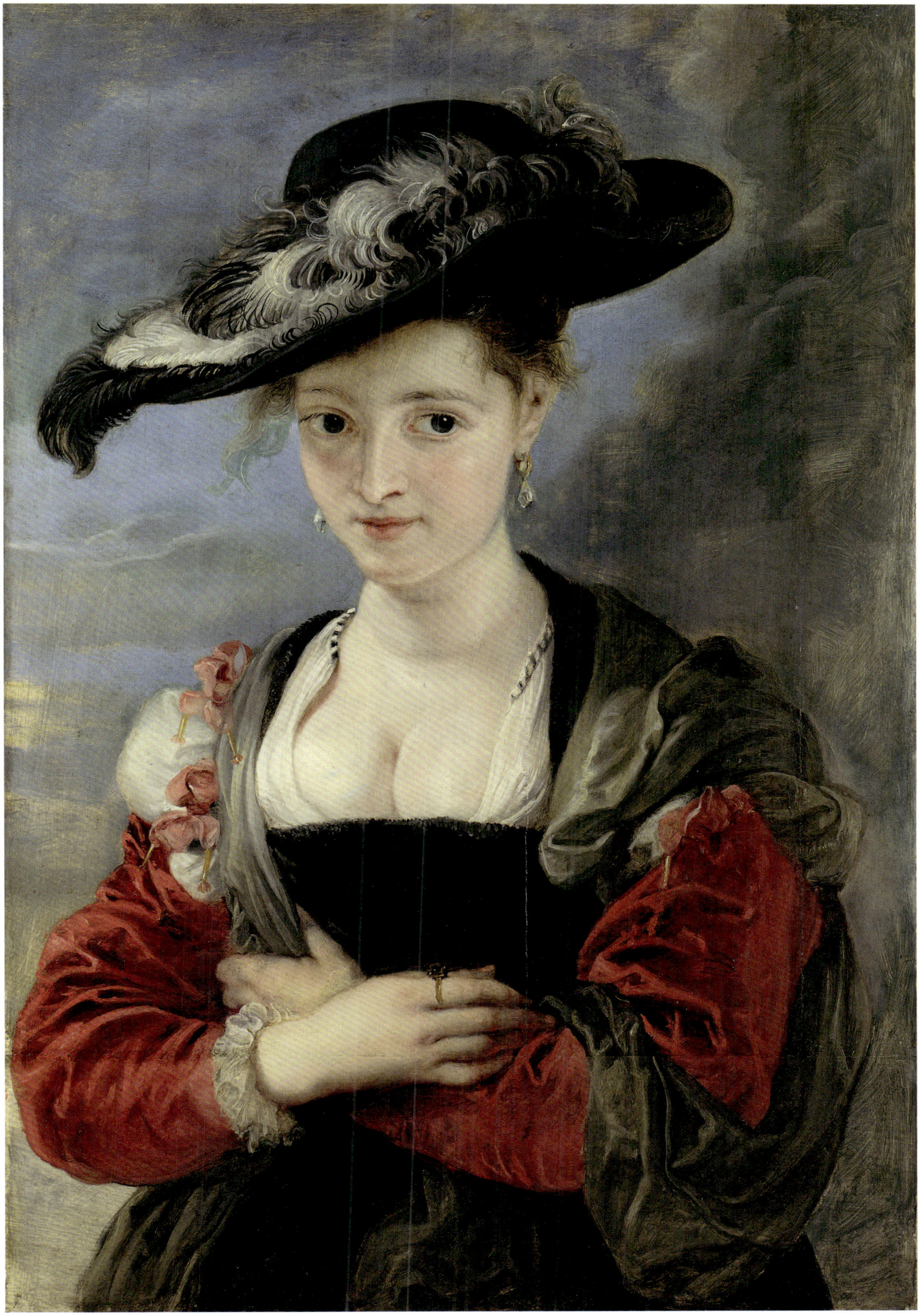

likeness. It appears that Reynolds knew a *bozzetto* thought to have been in Darnley's collection. Perhaps Darnley lent him the little panel, as certainly others were asked to lend theirs.[10] It is interesting too that Darnley visited Reynolds in July and the portrait of Melbourne was begun that November. The Darnley *bozzetto* (fig. 34) had been a first idea for a family portrait of, seemingly, Rubens and Hélène, with their offspring Nicolaas and Clara-Johanna. There are parallels between the *bozzetto* and Reynolds's Melbourne portrait. Furthermore, the wraith-like figure of Nicolaas was surely winsome inspiration for the difficult business of child portraiture. Nicolaas may have given Reynolds the idea for the pose of *Charles, Earl of Dalkeith* (1777; Bowhill, Selkirk). Such an elegant sprite, a mere will-o'-the-wisp, seems more Puck than peer.

Rubens was more powerfully present in Britain than anywhere except Flanders. In the High Victorian era, the indefatigable German scholar Dr Gustav Waagen made an inventory of British collections, only to discover paintings by Rubens and Van Dyck in unimagined profusion, divided between *palazzi* jostling for pre-eminence overlooking Hyde Park and baronial halls upon the blasted heaths of Scotland. Waagen's truffling turned up an astonishing 682 works divided between Rubens and Van Dyck: 262 for the former, 420 for the latter.[11] Even so, Waagen had looked only at the collections of the powerful, unaware of what may have been sequestered in the homes of brewers, aldermen or professors. But as if there were not enough Rubens on every side, Reynolds made not one but two visits to Flanders. These encounters were abundantly fruitful. His 1782 Waddesdon version of *Mary Robinson* betrays a debt to Rubens's *Portrait of Hélène Fourment*, which had been sold by Walpole just a few years before.[12] Reynolds turned to this because only the previous year he had made his first pilgrimage to the Southern Netherlands.

But what of the celebrated *Chapeau de Paille* (fig. 35)? Suddenly in 1823, and as if by a miracle, it arrived in London from Antwerp to a *grand éclat*. It is hard to convey the frenzy this caused, as if the French were now to sell to the English the *Mona Lisa*. Four thousand people had gawped at the painting by the fourth edition of a booklet, which was stiff with complacency about the English conquest of this Flemish national treasure. Sir Thomas Lawrence was duly smitten; as we see in his *Princess Mary, Duchess of Gloucester* (cat. 113): a synthesis of the *Chapeau de Paille* and Rubens's 1628 portrait of Sister Ana Dorotea, then in the collection of the Duke of Wellington at Apsley House (where it remains).[13] So struck indeed was Lawrence that his most beguiling masterpiece, *Julia, Lady Peel* (fig. 36), owes all to that famous straw hat.[14] But whereas Lady Peel's portrait surely stands as the most radiant and unmediated of all English tributes to Rubens, Lawrence often expressed reservations in public about a man he admired readily enough when behind his canvas. *Julia, Lady Peel* is partly a tribute to Sir Robert Peel, who had commissioned such an iridescent vision. A pre-eminent collector of Rubens, the future Prime Minister's appreciation of his wife's portrait scarcely outshone his relish for Rubens. Peel acquired the *Chapeau de Paille* after its public exhibition, an acquisition that helped gain for his collection the status of prime repository of Flemish painting in Britain. When the Peel Collection was eventually acquired for the National Gallery in 1871, it signally augmented the nation's holdings of the Northern schools.

But the *Chapeau* was no new discovery, either for the British or the French. Had the 'chevalier Reynholes' not been quite so mean, it might have come to London nearly forty years earlier, in 1785; three years after it had arrested the fast-moving Elisabeth-Louise Vigée-Lebrun in Antwerp. Reynolds, too, had been mightily impressed by the painting just the year before; although he was not apparently sufficiently captivated in 1785, when, at a second assignation, it was reported that he had had the chance to buy it but had baulked at the price.[15] If Reynolds did not possess the *Chapeau*, it possessed him. Once home and at his studio, he

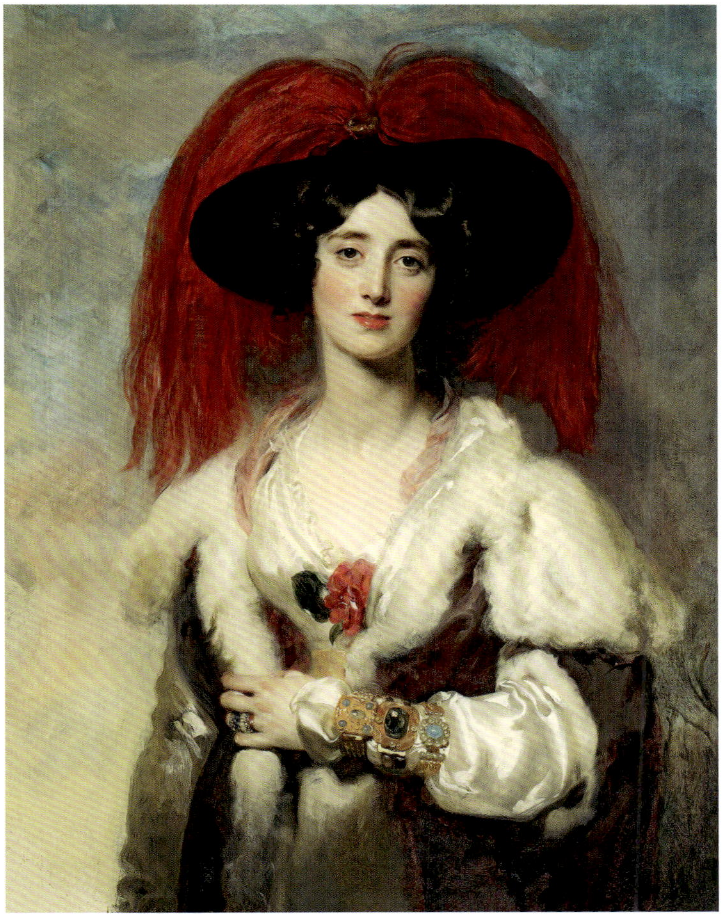

FIG. 36 Sir Thomas Lawrence, *Julia, Lady Peel*, 1827.
Oil on canvas, 90.8 x 70.8 cm. Frick Collection, New York

set to grafting the vision into his own compositions. In a letter now at Althorp, Northamptonshire, the Hon. Mrs Howe wrote breathlessly to her friend Georgiana, Countess Spencer, on Christmas Eve of the same year: 'Sir Joshua is about an excessive pretty [portrait] of Nanette [Anne Bingham] in a straw hat, and, as Rubens painted one which was called "the Chapeau de Paille" – this is to be called Sir Joshua's!!'[16] Interestingly to the modern eye, however, the painting does not at once betray the famous source here so confidently identified by Mrs Howe.

Vigée-Lebrun was a successful French painter for whom the purpose of portraiture was to give pleasure not insight. In Antwerp in 1782 she had seen the *Chapeau de Paille* as just the thing for a much-needed re-launch of her flagging career. She recalled her epiphany that same summer and in Brussels, where she painted a self-portrait which became the sensation of the 1783 Académie. An autograph replica followed (cat. 115), immediately judged to be either ravishing, bold, disarming, impertinent, or all four at once. The painting seems to have seduced half the French Académie. No less dramatically, it succeeded too in captivating the most powerful woman in France, Yolande-Martine-Gabrielle de Polastron, Duchess of Polignac. Both respected as a consummate courtier and maligned as a guileful courtesan, the Duchess understood the power of such a startling exercise in self-promotion, at once ordering her own variation upon the theme (cat. 116). But there are nice differences: the blush of eroticism suggested by the open lips and the emphasis on the bosom in the self-portrait came to be replaced by a degree of reticence more appropriate to one who was Gouvernante des enfants royaux. If it was a bold step for Vigée-Lebrun to discover herself in the way that she does in her self-portrait, hardly less striking is how the painter – serious student of Rubens that she was (and she was not serious about much!) departed from her source. Pigeon grey, cerulean blue, Seville orange, dusky plum; all serve to caress the sitter as they seduce the viewer. Such hues are derived from Vigée-Lebrun's admiration for the Bolognese school, whose representatives were exact contemporaries of Rubens: Guido Reni, Domenichino and Guercino especially. The ravishing tints were more likely to be found on a Meissen shepherdess than upon the dress of a Rubens matron.

It is tempting to think that the greater the degree of confusion as to what was a Rubens, the more influential Rubens became in his afterlife. Unhappily the hat in the *Chapeau* was found to be of felt not straw. But what matter? This much-loved painting became a peg upon which to hang a multitude of milliners' confections and thus helped create the 'fancy picture'. Nothing was more admired by French painters than Rubens's costume drama in 24 parts, the Marie de Médicis cycle (see cat. 34). These pictures, each the size of a church window, were unique; from its unveiling in the Palais du Luxembourg in Paris in 1625, the cycle provided an *encyclopédie* for French painters from Charles Le Brun to Paul Cézanne. An avid student had been Jean-Antoine Watteau, who was regularly admitted to the Luxembourg from 1708. Notwithstanding his adulation, Watteau did not transcribe these encounters directly, although his *fêtes galantes* would have been unthinkable without intense study of the women of the Médicis cycle.[17] Watteau's devotion to Rubens can be seen in his *trois crayons* drawings.[18] These declare him as the most sensitive of all who have made copies after Rubens: of the many counterpoints of Rubens's works, only Watteau's have been taken as originals.[19]

If Watteau's response was delicate, Jean-Honoré Fragonard's was robust. Take his *Young Woman with a Dog* (cat. 108): created fifty years after Watteau and as distant in intention as in time. Whereas Watteau plucks the lute, Fragonard blows the trumpet. It is almost certain that what scholars have taken to be a fantasy figure is actually a portrait of Marie-Emilie Coignet de Courson (1727–1806); evidently not a bluestocking but certainly a woman of real intellectual distinction.[20] If so, the picture cannot have been a *figure de fantaisie*.[21]

There is a conspiratorial air, about Mme Courson. Instead of holding up a mirror to see that accoutrements are in place before setting sail for the ball, pennants fluttering from every mast, she suspends from powerful wrists a wretched little dog as a *gourmande* might select her lobster. The animal exhibits the same discomfort as a baby obliged to say goodbye to its bathwater, while the sitter challenges us as she challenges herself, through the substitution of dog for mirror. By holding this timid little creature up to our scrutiny as well as hers, Marie-Emilie questions the life of hedonism into which she is bound by her ropes of pearl. But beneath the powder we see the pain: once she is divested of finery, she and we reflect that we are closer to the animal than is comfortable. Always a great

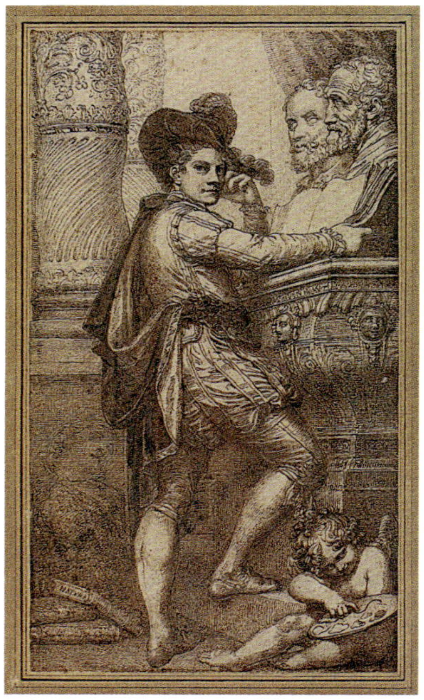

FIG. 37 Richard Cosway, *Self-portrait with Rubens and Michelangelo*, c. 1789. Pen and ink on paper laid on card, 24 x 13 cm. Fondazione Cosway, Lodi

painting, beneath the brassiness of Courson is a serious picture: although by all accounts, neither painter nor partygoer thought the fun should cease. Rouged chins, where silver, pink and grey render flesh uncommonly like boiled ham, are contrasted with molten pink and orange sleeves applied wet on wet. Brush strokes create a febrile vision of a Rubens *modello* thrown into chaos by overpainting as if furiously applied by Frans Hals. The sitter seems to have rummaged through the wardrobe of Rubens's Marie de Médicis and run off with her ruff. It is hard to tell whether the picture's wryness was Fragonard's arch tribute or a debunking of the 'master'; but then that is part of its sophistication.[22]

Masquerade was all the rage in Britain as in France and so the *beau monde* was much taken with a scholarly work by Thomas Jefferys. This appeared in four volumes in two publishing campaigns (1757 and 1772), and with the less than frivolous title: *A Collection of the Dresses of Different Nations, Ancient and Modern; particularly Old English Dresses. After the designs of Holbein, Vandyke, Hollar, and others.*[23] It was the first history of dress in English but it became a major source for masquerade and a guide to artists portraying historic exotica. No one learned more from it than Richard and Maria Cosway, whose careers were much influenced by a publication that would do for costume what Robert Adam's *Ruins of the Palace of the Emperor Diocletian at Spalatro in Dalmatia* (London, 1764) had done for interior decoration.

A portrait that would have been inconceivable without Jeffery's book is a work by Richard Cosway (cat. 109), a painting that pays its own tribute to the great, if insular, tradition of the English miniature. The portrait features the same Lady Melbourne as had been painted by Reynolds. She was a remarkable woman: Byron confessed her 'sagacious' and he was seldom one to rate women's minds highly. Lady Melbourne's intellect was something Cosway had overlooked until he thought more deeply and added the book.[24] Her couture is characteristic of an amalgam of antiquarian research and the English miniature; creating a soufflé of masquerade costume whipped up from the ingredients of the *Chapeau de Paille*.

Richard and Maria Cosway were a double act: Regency celebrities who today might have been chefs with their own television show, throwing parties no one could afford to miss. Richard was important as taste-maker. Intriguingly described by the great art critic William Hazlitt as 'Venus attired by the Graces',[25] Cosway was credited with creating George IV's liking for Flemish art, since the painter was 'wrapt up in Rubens', or so London's most canny dealer William Buchanan declared. Cosway was a devotee of Rubens because of what had always appealed about that painter to British artists; confined as they were by portraiture to the shrubberies rather than promenading upon what Reynolds had referred to as the 'higher walks'. They envied and admired Rubens in equal parts: for great painting certainly but also, hardly less importantly, for having been a great man – someone who had been able to move with as much facility through a palace as across a canvas. If Watteau had a uniquely responsive eye to Rubens, Cosway had the most rounded understanding. Unlike Reynolds, Cosway never felt Michelangelo was superior to Rubens; indeed a self-portrait (fig. 37) contains busts of the two artists alongside Cosway himself, leafing through a biography of Rubens. Cosway regarded Rubens as a way of life and was much taken with how, in the words of Reynolds, Rubens's figures seemed to have 'fed upon roses';[26] so much so that (as the devout hoarded relics of the saints) Cosway collected *Rubeniana*, including what he fondly believed was Rubens's paint box. This, more pyx than box, Cosway bequeathed to Lawrence as his apostolic successor in reverence for the artist.[27] Lawrence owed many triumphs to Rubens and he owned the greatest collection of Old Master drawings put together in Britain since the age of Charles I.[28] It was predictable that English artists fell for Rubens, the *beau idéal* of Castiglione's courtier. What was more, Rubens had painted a uniquely vivid autobiography in his portraits of himself and his family, so many of which then appeared to be set in England.

Rubens made more of an impact on painting in Britain than anyone, with the possible exception of Rembrandt; he did this through his own example and vicariously, through his pupil Van Dyck. Rubens had made giant leaps in portraiture, although he once professed to be bored by the whole business. He had taken Titian's ideas, and if not run, then strolled with them. Had you wanted to get moving with Titian you needed to bring along your own war horse; otherwise you came out a 'still'. But Rubens invented the movie in Genoa, where he first emerged as a great portraitist; such vivacity, a sense that something was afoot, was often deployed in later works in which the artist, arm in arm with Hélène, their children fluttering about like chicks, would take the air in their yard, or as Rubens liked to refer to it, if a little ambitiously, his 'Garden of the Hesperides'.

What captivated the British about Rubens was the way in which he had first given sitters *possession*. As Genoese *contessas* had once moved, so English countesses came to glide across their own lawns. Sitters felt not only that every prospect pleased – because they possessed them all – but also, and no less importantly, that others had to acknowledge what was so elegantly pencilled. Apparently Gainsborough declared upon his deathbed in 1788: 'We are all going to heaven and Van Dyke is of the company'; although in truth he owed more to Rubens than he had ever realized. Gainsborough's *Mr and Mrs William Hallett ('The Morning Walk')* (fig. 38), that summation of the career of Reynolds's great rival, amplifies an idea for the abandoned Henri IV cycle by Rubens, which was to have complemented the original cycle dedicated to Marie de Médicis. In 1777 there had appeared in England the *modello* for *The Wedding by Proxy of Marie de Médicis to King Henri IV*, a revelation that may have influenced the Hallett portrait. Maybe; maybe not. But what cannot be doubted is that all this began with Rubens – for whom indeed it must have been very heaven to sit.

FIG. 38 Thomas Gainsborough, *Mr and Mrs William Hallett ('The Morning Walk')*, 1785. Oil on canvas, 236.2 x 179.1 cm. The National Gallery, London

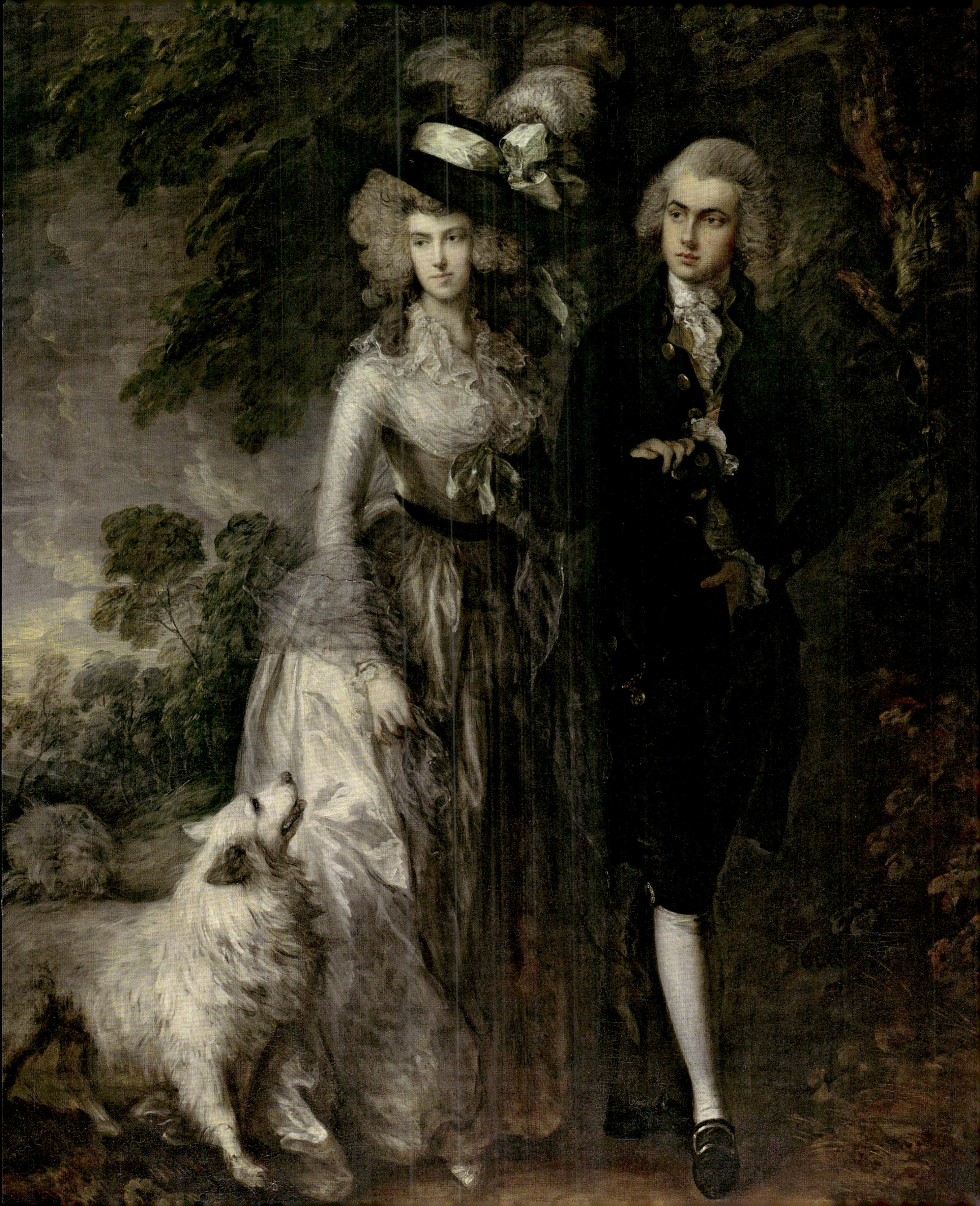

Variously identified, but perhaps a portrait of either Maria or Catarina Grimaldi,[1] a superlative painting by Rubens (cat. 104) was acquired by William Bankes of Kingston Lacy in Dorset in 1840 with another portrait of a woman who can be identified more confidently as Maria Serra-Pallavicino (*c.* 1606). The arrival of these two works, remarkable for being among Rubens's most powerful Genoese portraits, coincided with a pause in the influence Rubens and Van Dyck exerted on British portraiture as Regency extravagance gave way to Victorian sobriety. The 'Grimaldi' painting is Rubens's most striking double portrait. The two devices of extreme illusionism and the surreal *trompe-l'œil* of the dwarf drawing back the curtain, as if to reveal the Virgin, are reinforced by rays descending like the Holy Spirit at the Annunciation. This may have been an allusion to either the recent or the forthcoming marriage of the sitter and the hope in due course of an heir to the family fortune.[2] Such drama in portraiture is unparalleled in Rubens's *œuvre*. Rubens had looked at Bronzino (1503–1572): an influence detectable in facture and finish, overt realism, refulgent light and metallic reflection. Notwithstanding, this is a boldly individual tribute to power and money. Such idiosyncrasy may have been what Sir Joshua Reynolds (1723–1792) meant when he declared how Rubens had been ready to 'risk and to dare extraordinary attempts without a guide, abandoning himself to his own sensations, and depending upon them'.[3]

Van Dyck's sensitivity to the young is the highlight of his work (cat. 105). Cooler and more remote effects lend characteristic distance and station, appealing to Thomas Gainsborough (1727–1788) who adopted 'hauteur' in his portraits more frequently than did Reynolds.[4] Both Rubens and Van Dyck faced the challenge of integrating their figures; a difficulty neither has entirely overcome in these great portraits. In Rubens's 'beauty and the beast', the dwarf points up the prettiness of the woman but at the cost of disjunction. The scale and placement of the retainer is awkward; he appears to sprout from the arm of the chair in which Maria, luminescent and ethereal, quietly reposes, unaware of him. Could this be because he was an afterthought, a later interpolation when Rubens was well on his way with his composition? Maria's purity is further enhanced by the contrast between the soft and creased pouch of the dwarf's face and the luminous opal that is her head. A frond of honeysuckle describing the fluted column alludes to marital fidelity; a vigorous growth which after only three summers would become a bower in Rubens's own marriage picture of 1609. A fictive relief suspended as a tablet in the background above Maria's head, as yet undeciphered, surely refers to the virtues of the Grimaldi. If the noblewoman in the Van Dyck cannot see us because she is blind, a suggestion made by Boccardo in 1997,[5] then with innate tact, the painter may have been sacrificing unity to discretion. Reynolds was drawn to the lively dog, which he incorporated into his portrait of Mrs Elisha Mathew (1777; Museum of Fine Arts, Houston).[6]

CAT. 105 *(detail)*

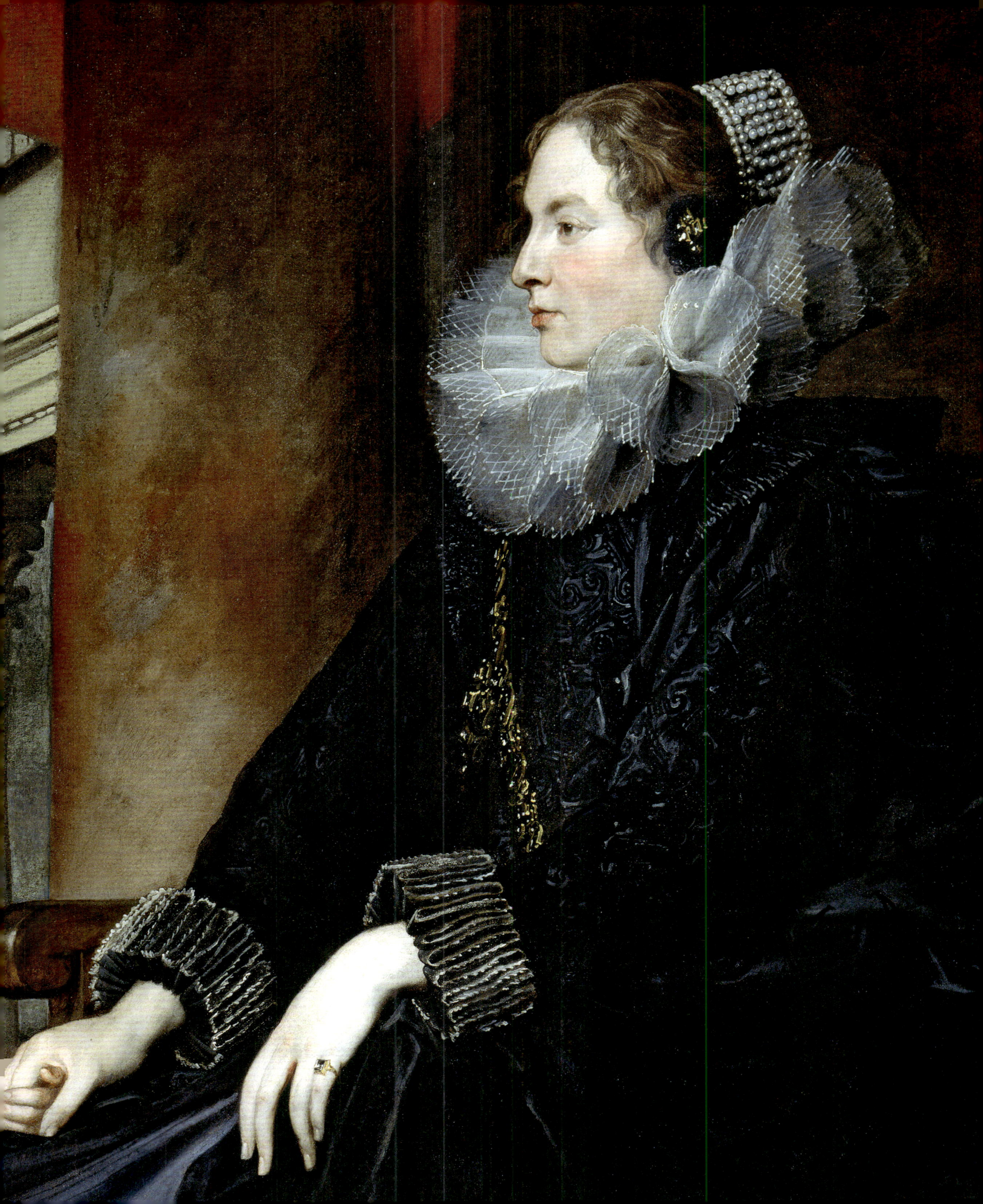

104

PETER PAUL RUBENS (1577–1640)
Portrait of Maria Grimaldi and Dwarf, *c.* 1606
Oil on canvas, 241 x 140 cm
Inscribed on the collar of the dog 'M^r AM'
Kingston Lacy, The Bankes Collection (The National Trust), Dorset, inv. 1257100/KLA/P/59

PROVENANCE: collection of Giovanbattista Grimaldi La Pietra (1780); acquired by William Bankes in Genoa in 1840; collection of the Bankes family until transferred to the National Trust in 1981
SELECTED REFERENCES: Jaffé 1977, p. 77 and no. 264; Jaffé 1989, no. 58; Lille 2004, no. 15

105

SIR ANTHONY VAN DYCK (1599–1641)
A Genoese Noblewoman and Her Son, *c.* 1626
Oil on canvas, 191.5 x 139.5 cm
National Gallery of Art, Washington DC, inv. 1942.9.91. Widener Collection

PROVENANCE: 2nd Earl of Warwick (at Warwick Castle by 1787); by descent to 5th Earl of Warwick (d. 1924); sold by Knoedler, Paris, *c.* 1915, to P. A. B. Widener, Philadelphia, 1909; Joseph Widener sold to National Gallery of Art, 1942
SELECTED REFERENCES: Genoa 1997, pp. 229–58; Antwerp 1999, no. 37; Barnes et al. 2004, no. II.74

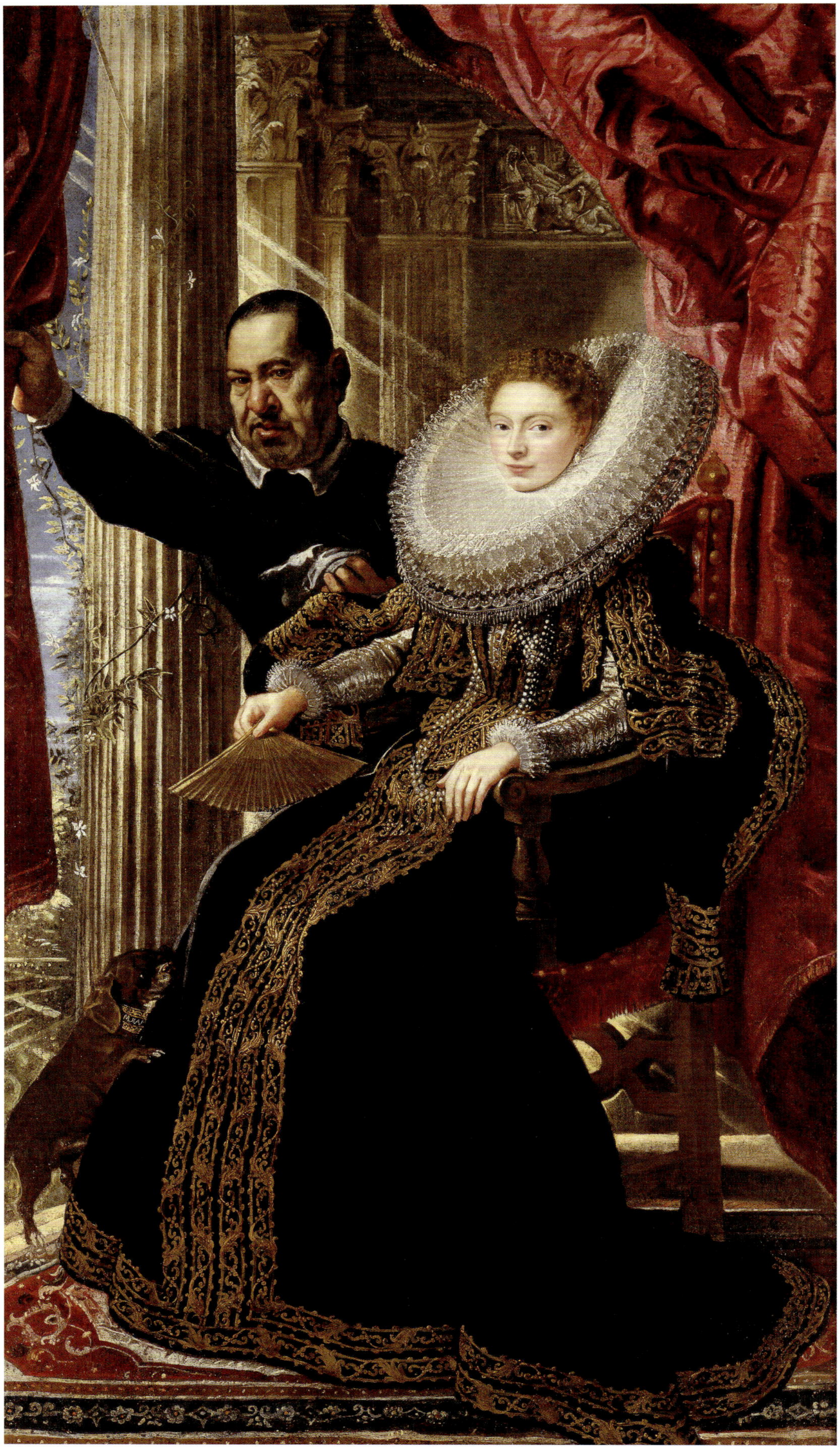

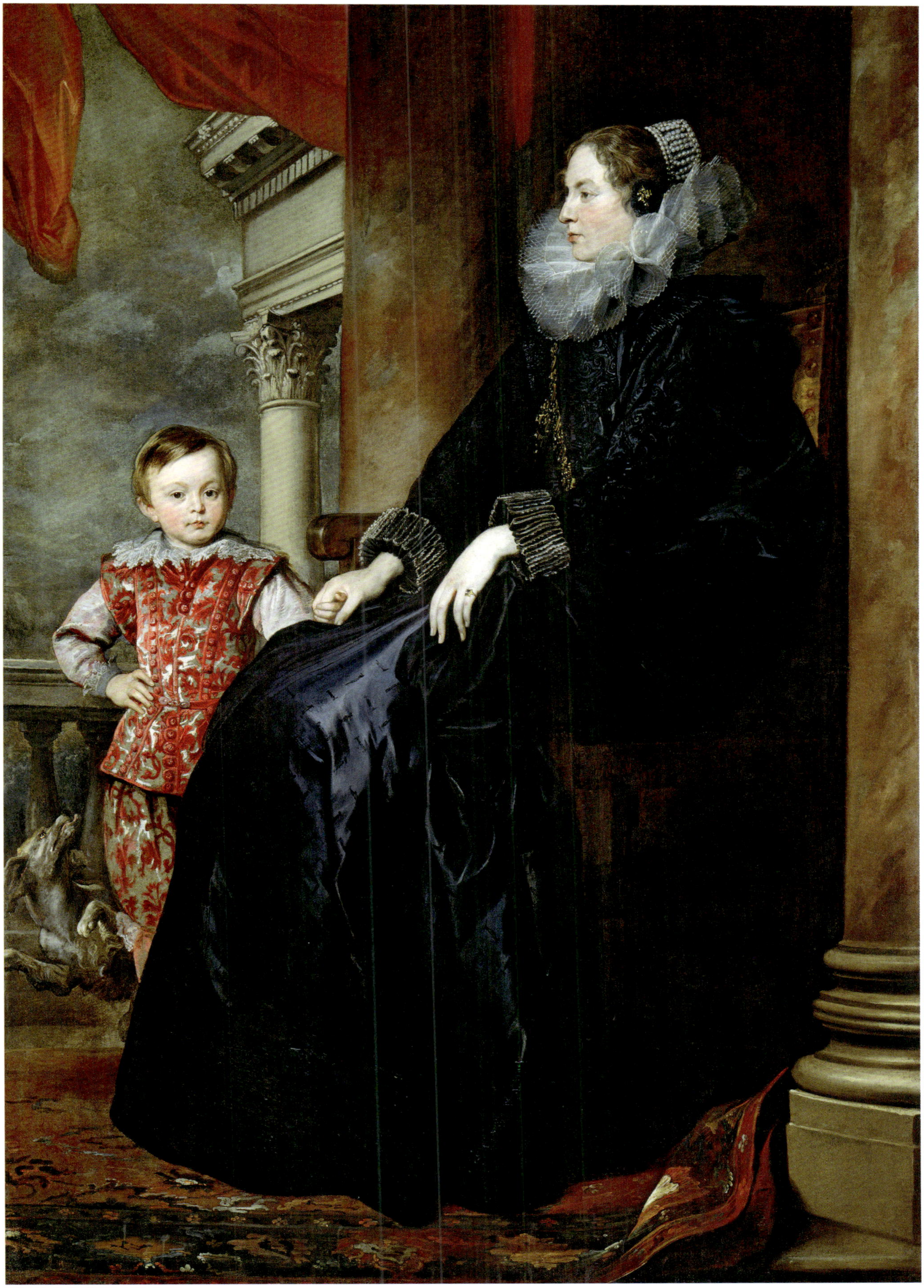

106

PETER PAUL RUBENS (1577–1640)
Portrait of a Woman, *c.* 1625–30
Oil on panel, four planks chamfered together, 86.8 x 59.3 cm, narrowing to 58.1 cm at the top
The Royal Collection, RCIN 400118
RA ONLY

PROVENANCE: Lunden Collection, Antwerp; Joseph van Havre Collection; 1818, sold by J.-M.-A.-J. van Havre to L. J. Nieuwenhuys for 12,500 francs as a portrait of 'Helena Fourment'; forwarded by Nieuwenhuys to John Smith, who offered the work to the Prince Regent, who bought it with gilt frame on 8 December 1818 for £840; Bow Room, Carlton House; Buckingham Palace, and then at Windsor
SELECTED REFERENCES: engraving by S. Smith for *The Royal Gallery of Pictures*, London, 1840, p. 27; Edinburgh and London 2007, no. 31; White 2007, no. 62

It is astonishing how many Rubens portraits were in England during the eighteenth century. There was an exceptional gathering at Blenheim Palace, Oxfordshire; Brussels having been inveigled into giving pictures by Rubens to the 1st Duke of Marlborough in 'gratitude' for his victories against the French in Flanders. Sir Joshua Reynolds was to have a twenty-year relationship with Blenheim (1757–77) and came to know these portraits intimately. Of the *Portrait of a Woman* (cat. 106), the Rubens scholar Christopher White records: 'Certain earlier writers did not accept the portrait as an original, but it is in fact a work of the highest quality throughout'; he considers the sitter to be 'conceivably' Elizabeth Fourment (b. 1609), younger sister of Susanna, and thus the portrait can be dated to the late 1620s.[1] The painting exactly reflected British interest in Rubens, especially a national prejudice for embroidering the 'story' told through Rubens's portraits of his family such as that most celebrated example the *Chapeau de Paille* (fig. 35). The *Portrait of a Woman* had been with the *Chapeau de Paille* when Reynolds saw it in 1781; perhaps, after noticing the latter, he observed that 'Its companion though equally well painted from not having the same advantage of dress receives no attention.'[2] This suggests how British taste often valued costume above character, and romance over reality.

Joseph van Havre may have taken the *Portrait of a Woman* to America, just before the establishment of the Napoleonic Kingdom of Holland (1806–10), to prevent the French from stealing it. G. H. Steuart noted in a 1853 letter to Sir William Stirling Maxwell that: 'This old Belgian gentleman [Van Havre] came to our country with his precious tulips and some of his valuable pictures at the time the French were about to invade the Netherlands. [...] I often saw as a boy *The Judgement of Paris*, and other celebrated pictures, [and] when (with the *Chapeau de Paille* that never crossed the Atlantic) [these] were afterwards sold for the benefit of the family – I recognised my old acquaintance, *The Judgement of Paris* – at the National Gallery but was unable to get a sight of the *Chapeau de Paille* at Sir Robert Peel's.'[3]

The appearance in London in 1818 of the *Portrait of a Woman* anticipated the arrival of the *Chapeau de Paille* by five years, making this a taster for connoisseurs whose appetite was whetted for the more famous 'sister'. For all its apparent spontaneity, the work features different preparatory grounds covering four separate planks chamfered together to make the panel, suggesting that it may have been composed in two campaigns. There are compelling resonances between Rubens's *Portrait of a Woman* and the Fragonard (cat. 108): the three-quarter length and the turn of the head for example.[4] But then no less mesmerising are the differences. The Rubens sitter seems to be well off but recognisably of the Flemish bourgeoisie, whereas Fragonard's model has been decked out with elements that create a medley from *de-luxe* appearances of Marie de Médicis.[5] Fragonard's sartorial detail is neither accurate nor respectful. A blue drape at bottom right droops like a collapsed curtain and recalls Marie's ermine robes, which are such an insistent presence in the Rubens cycle. Possibly subversive, this portrait has been seen as a projection of what some thought Fragonard's perversity in never seeking to be received at the Académie and in showing at the Salon de la Correspondance rather than the Salon. But Fragonard, like Watteau, had

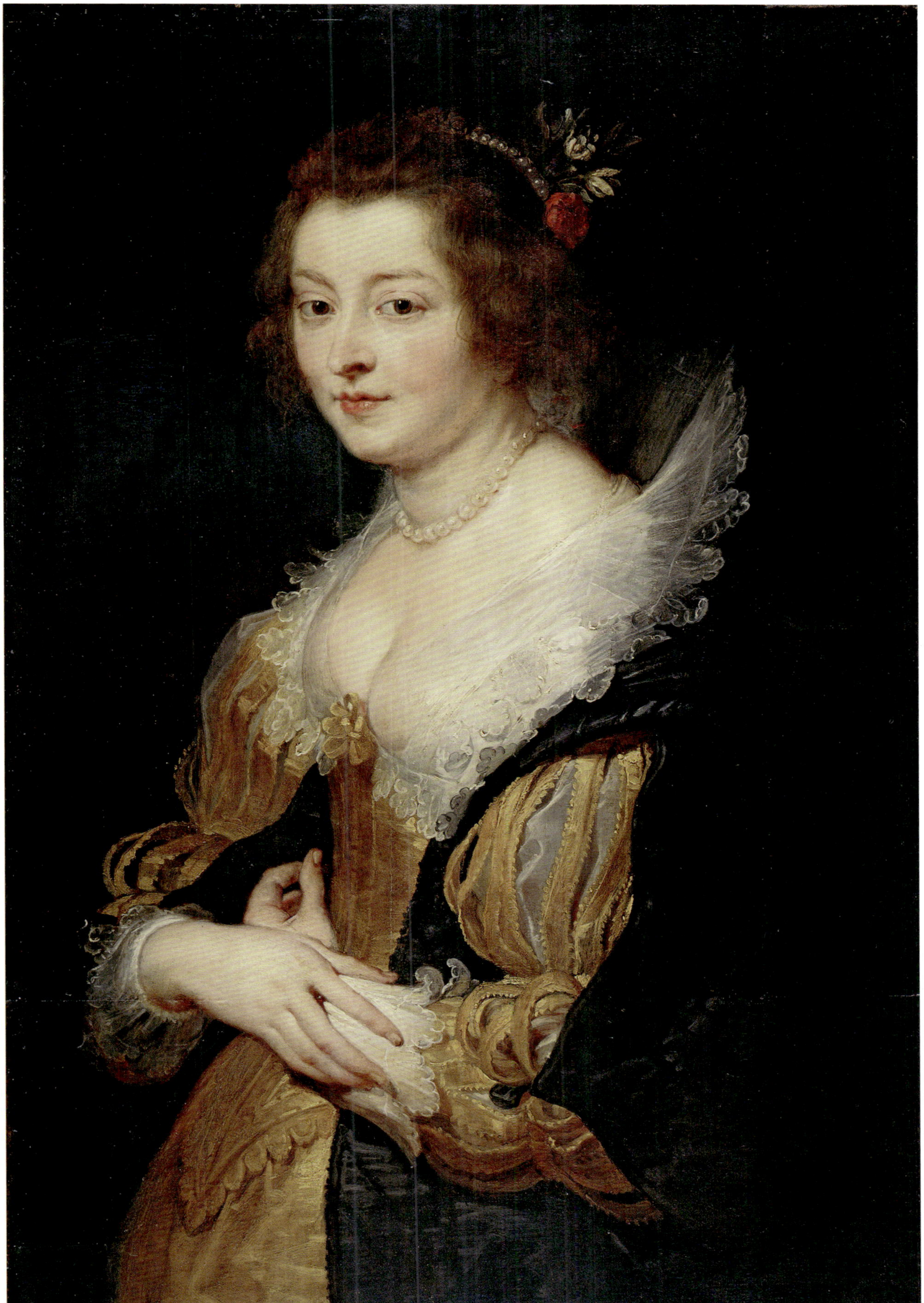

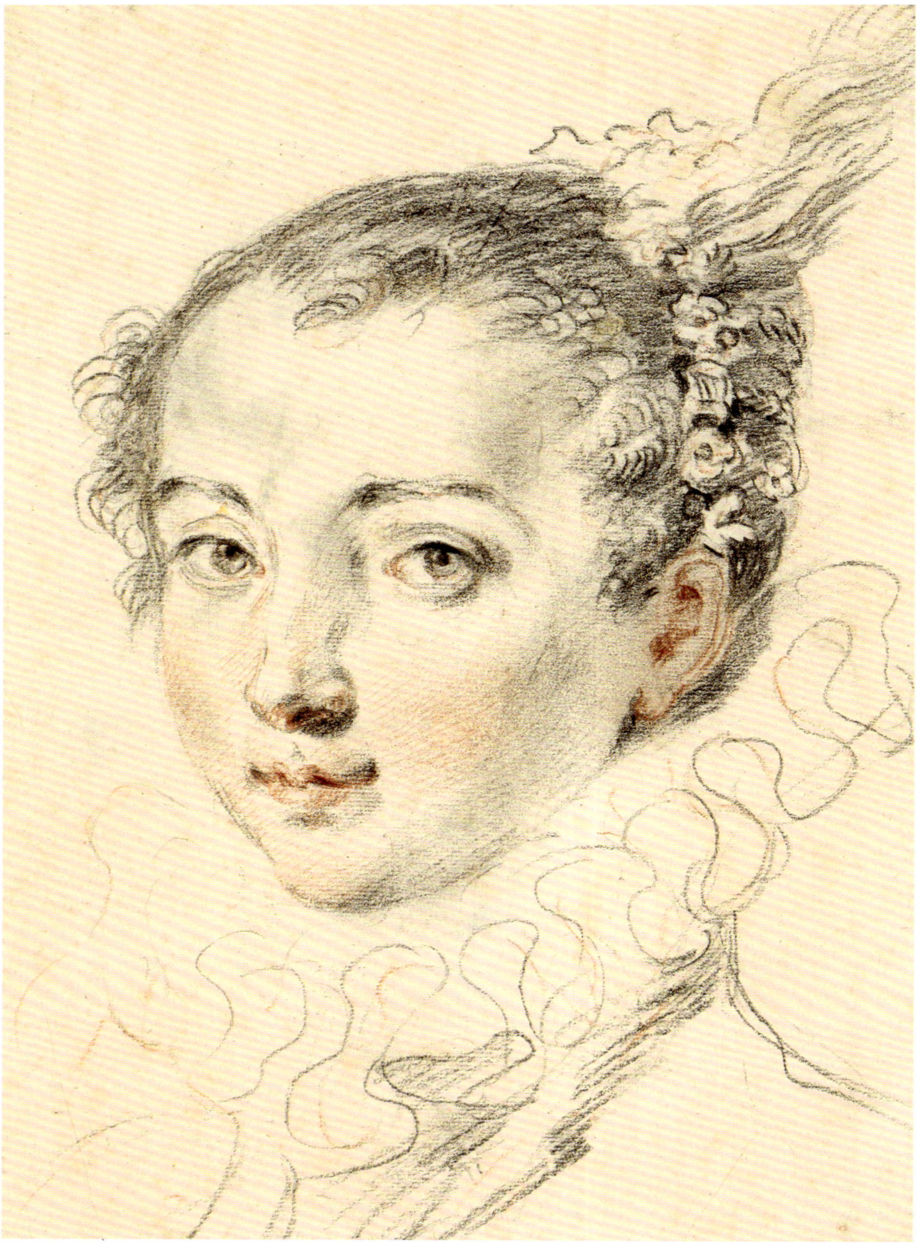

107

JEAN-ANTOINE WATTEAU (1684–1721)
Head of a Woman, c. 1716–17
Red and black chalk with stumping on cream paper, 31 x 22.8 cm
Museum Boijmans Van Beuningen, Rotterdam, Koenigs Collection, inv. FI 294

PROVENANCE: Mariette Collection (L.2097); E. Czeczowicka; F. Koenigs; D. G. van Beuningen; Boijmans van Beuningen
SELECTED REFERENCES: Parker and Mathey 1957, vol. 1, no. 290; Rosenberg and Prat 1996, vol. 1, no. 362

108

JEAN-HONORÉ FRAGONARD (1732–1806)
Young Woman with a Dog, c. 1769–79
Oil on canvas, 81.3 x 65.4 cm
Lent by The Metropolitan Museum of Art, New York, inv. 37.118. Fletcher Fund, 1937
RA ONLY

PROVENANCE: Marie Anne Eléonore de Grave; Cambis, Cambis-Alais and Siffrien des Isnards families, until sold to Eugène Feral prior to 1900; Mme Louis Burat estate sale, Paris, 17 June 1937, lot 3, for 1,450,000 francs to Seligmann, Rey & Co. for the Metropolitan Museum of Art
SELECTED REFERENCES: Paris 1987, no. 139; Percival 2012, pp. 19, 20–26, 32–36, 167, 224–25, 169–70; Blumenfeld 2013, pp. 18, 20, 22, 34, 59–60, 69, 71, nn. 35, 36

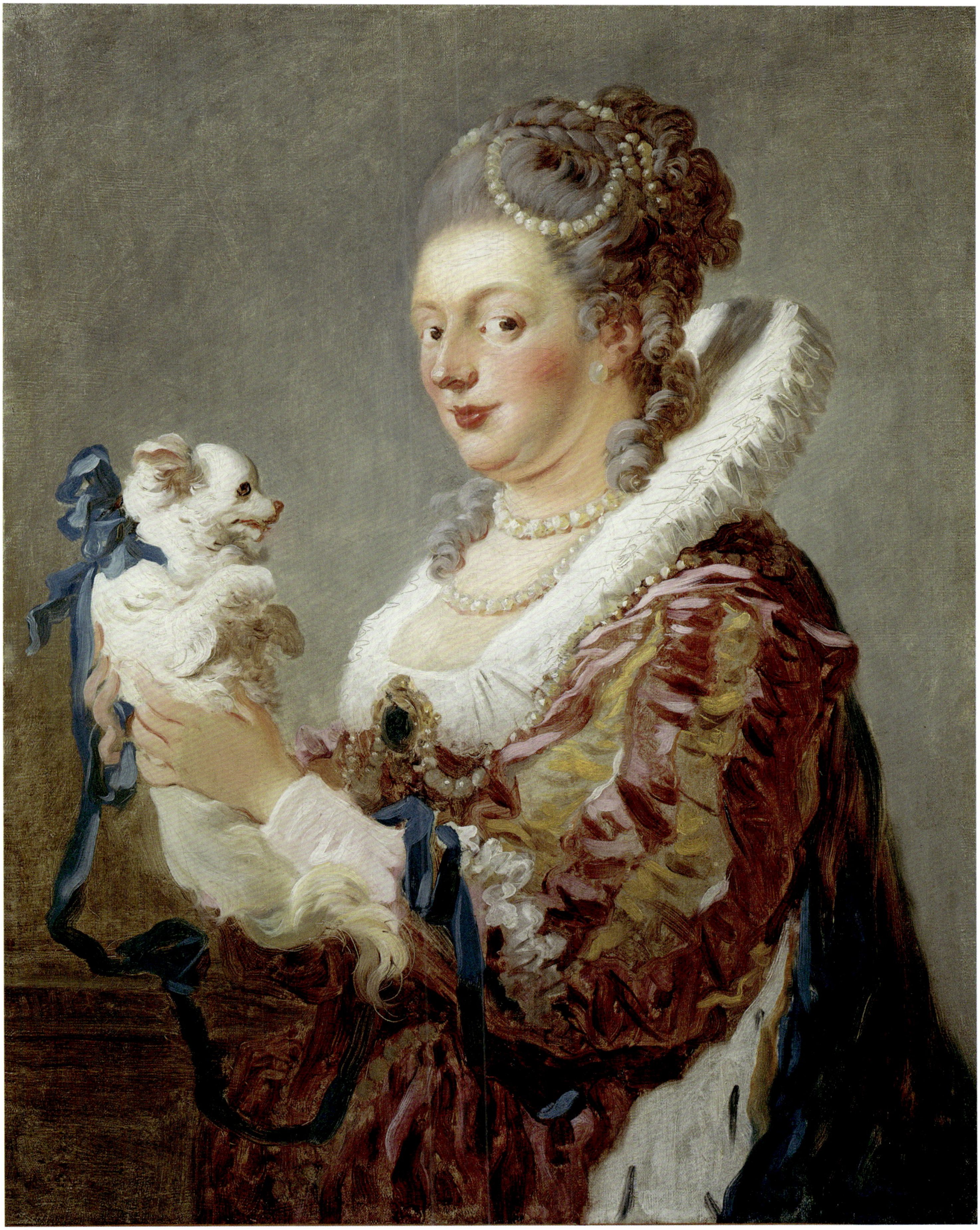

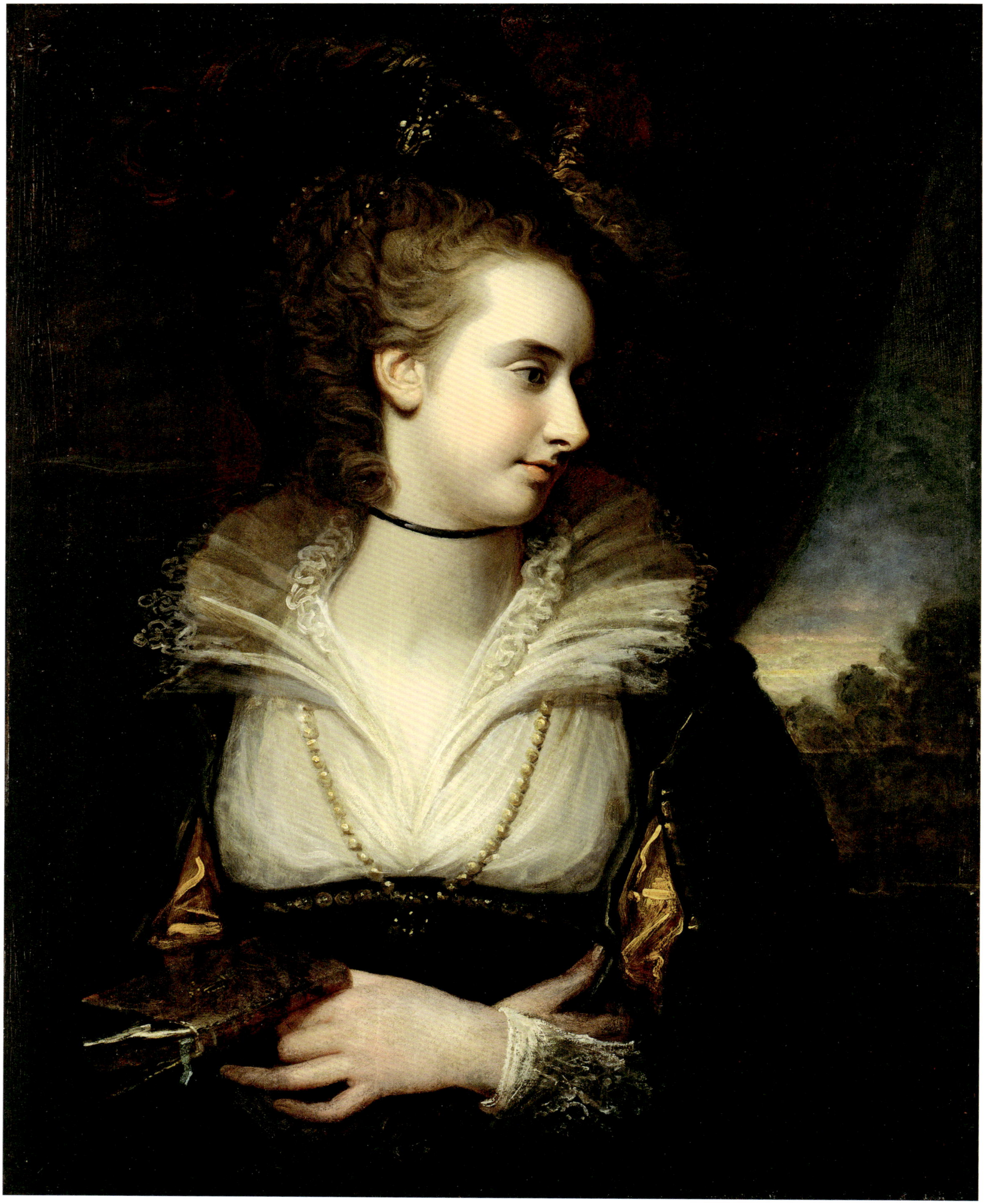

huge admiration for Rubens: Fragonard's drawing (*c.* 1765–68; Musée du Louvre, Paris) after Rubens's *The Crowning of St Catherine* (*c.* 1633–35; Toledo Museum of Art, Ohio) is nothing if not an exercise in humility. The Cosway of Lady Melbourne (cat. 109) has been dated to *c.* 1784 on the grounds of the probable age of the sitter and her then fashionable Jacobean fancy dress. This vision surely recalls the great English tradition of the miniature, but in a much larger format than had been customary in Tudor and Stuart England.

The Watteau (cat. 107) bears a resemblance to Van Dyck's Genoese *Marchesa Geronima Spinola* (*c.* 1624; Gemäldegalerie, Staatliche Museen zu Berlin), which suggests that the sitter may also have been from that city. Watteau's use of red, white and black chalks on one sheet is commonly referred to as his *trois crayons* technique, which approximates to Rubens's 'painted' drawings. An inscription by the celebrated collector Pierre-Jean Mariette (1694–1774) on the mount of the *Head of a Woman*, 'E Rubenio desumptum / opus / Ant. Watteau', reveals that Watteau's response to the Old Masters was sought after, especially by those who had known him. Jean de Jullienne (1686–1766) recorded that Watteau was 'excited by the beauties of the gallery in this palace [Luxembourg]' and 'often went to study the colouring and composition of this great master'.[6] As the art historian Egbert Haverkamp-Begemann has written: 'So masterfully could Watteau capture both the spirit and technique of Rubens's portrait drawings, that Gluck and Haberditzl who catalogued the master's drawings in 1928, not knowing this drawing, believed its counter-proof to be by Rubens's hand.'[7]

109

RICHARD COSWAY (1742-1821)
Elizabeth Milbanke, Viscountess Melbourne, *c.* 1784
Oil on panel, 76.4 x 63.0 cm
The Royal Collection, RCIN 400967

PROVENANCE: painted for George IV and in the Royal Collection since
SELECTED REFERENCES: Millar 1969, no. 716; Lloyd 1995, no. 30

110

SIR THOMAS LAWRENCE (1769–1830)
Philadelphia Hannah, 1st Viscountess Cremorne, 1789
Oil on canvas, 240.3 x 148 cm
Tate, inv. TO5466. Presented by the Patrons of British Art through the Friends of the Tate Gallery 1988

PROVENANCE: in the sitter's family until sold at Christie's, London, 15 April 1988; presented to the Tate by the Patrons of British Art, 1988
SELECTED REFERENCES: London 1980, no. 1; Levey 2005, pp. 78–79; London 2010, p. 88.

Philadelphia Hannah, 1st Viscountess Cremorne (cat. 110), has a critical position in the trajectory of Sir Thomas Lawrence's meteoric rise and glitteringly successful career. Although he was only 20 when he painted it, the portrait created the acclaim that he was to enjoy for the next forty years. It opened the portcullis of Windsor Castle, as the papers observed: 'It is Lady Cremorne's portrait and Lord Mulgrave's that introduced Mr Lawrence to paint the Queen.'[1] The great early Lawrence of Queen Charlotte (1789; The National Gallery, London) was the result. As has been perceptively remarked, the *Queen Charlotte* suggests a quite new departure both for Lawrence and for English portraiture;[2] the Queen's likeness a quite different take to that of Lady Cremorne, the latter the last of the ancient regime.

Queen Charlotte was described as a 'performance of which Vandyke himself would have been proud', as much perhaps for its novelty of conception as for its brilliance of execution.[3] When a boy, Lawrence had been taken to Corsham Court, Wiltshire, where he had seen outstanding works by Rubens and Van Dyck in the Methuen Collection.[4] Dress in the *Queen Charlotte* is a strong contrast to what might seem to be the widow's weeds donned by Lady Cremorne; however, in 1789 the viscountess was no widow but a newly married Quaker.[5] She was Philadelphia born and appropriately turned out, given that her grandfather was William Penn, an early proponent of the Society of Friends whose members were noted as much for the simplicity of their habit as for the sobriety of their lives. It would be ironical indeed if Lawrence had taken as his model Rubens's portraits of the Genoese plutocracy, many of whom were *arrivistes* whose rampant materialism and extravagance united a close-knit society in the pursuit of pleasure. But then Lady Cremorne is decidedly mid-Atlantic. Draped upon the plinth are the robes of a peeress, a note of splendour that might have raised an eyebrow in her native Philadelphia. She is firmly anchored by the ponderous pillar and red drape, the tassel acting as a finger post drawing attention to the luxuriance of material and colour as a contrast to the relative sobriety of her black dress. Lawrence's natural exuberance breaks out in the freely painted landscape, reminiscent of Titian's *poesie* for Philip II: well known in England during Lawrence's lifetime.

Sir Joshua Reynolds's 1769 commission (cat. 111), marking the first marriage of Sir Watkin Williams-Wynn, 4th Baronet, features the happy couple entwined around stage props like ivy on an oak, while all about them puffs the incense of rococo. A gallant air is evoked by the pretty masque costumes, the lace, bows, satin and silk of which serve to distract from the austerities of a backdrop that may reflect a scheme by James Byres for the patron's seat Wynnstay (a project that had threatened to become a vast Italian-style *palazzo* which would have dominated the Dee Valley). Sir Watkin is palpably no Greek hero, though his posture owes an unlikely debt to the *Farnese Hercules*. Where Hercules' club might have rested, we discover Lady Williams-Wynn, a gratifying conquest indeed: both immensely wealthy and the daughter of a duke. She perches under a vase, the serpentine lines of which duplicate an elegant figure as they subvert the rhetoric of a nude Hercules disporting himself in relief above her coiffure.[6]

A more sober prospect is Lawrence's portrait of Mrs Annesley and two of her children (cat. 112). Although the artist could work with astonishing

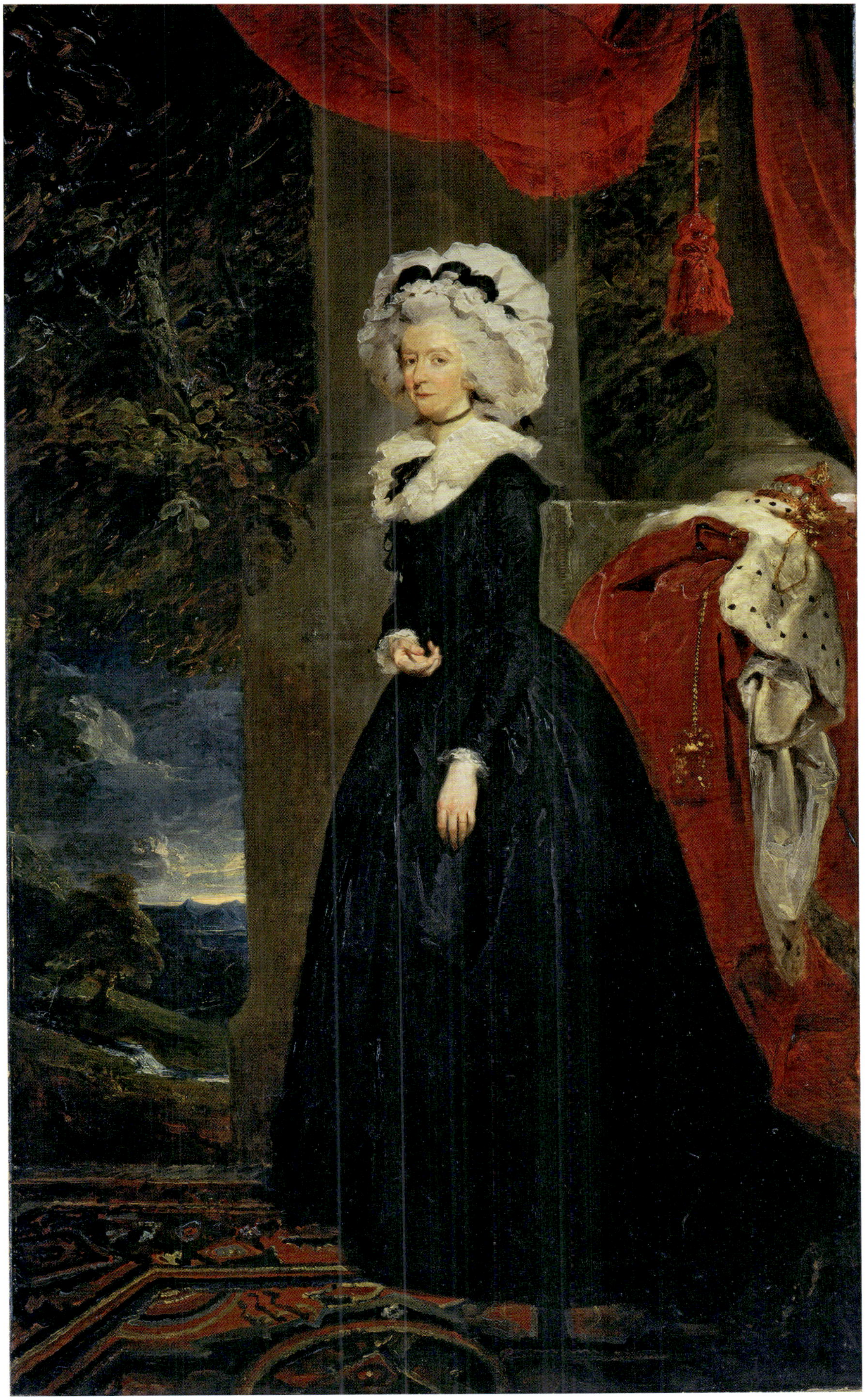

111

SIR JOSHUA REYNOLDS (1723–1792)
Sir Watkin Williams-Wynn and His Wife, Lady Henrietta, 1769
Oil on canvas, 253.5 x 167.4 cm
Ar fenthyg gan / Lent by Amgueddfa Cymru – National Museum Wales, Cardiff, inv. NMW A 12965
RA ONLY

PROVENANCE: painted for Sir Watkins Williams-Wynn, 4th Baronet, thence by descent until acquired with assistance from The Heritage Lottery Fund by the National Museum Wales by private treaty, 1998, negotiated by Agnew's
SELECTED REFERENCES:
MS notes by Ellis Waterhouse in his copy of A. Graves and W. V. Cronin, *A History of the Works of Sir Joshua Reynolds*, 4 vols, London, 1899–1901, (Paul Mellon Centre, London); Mannings and Postle 2000, no. 1947.

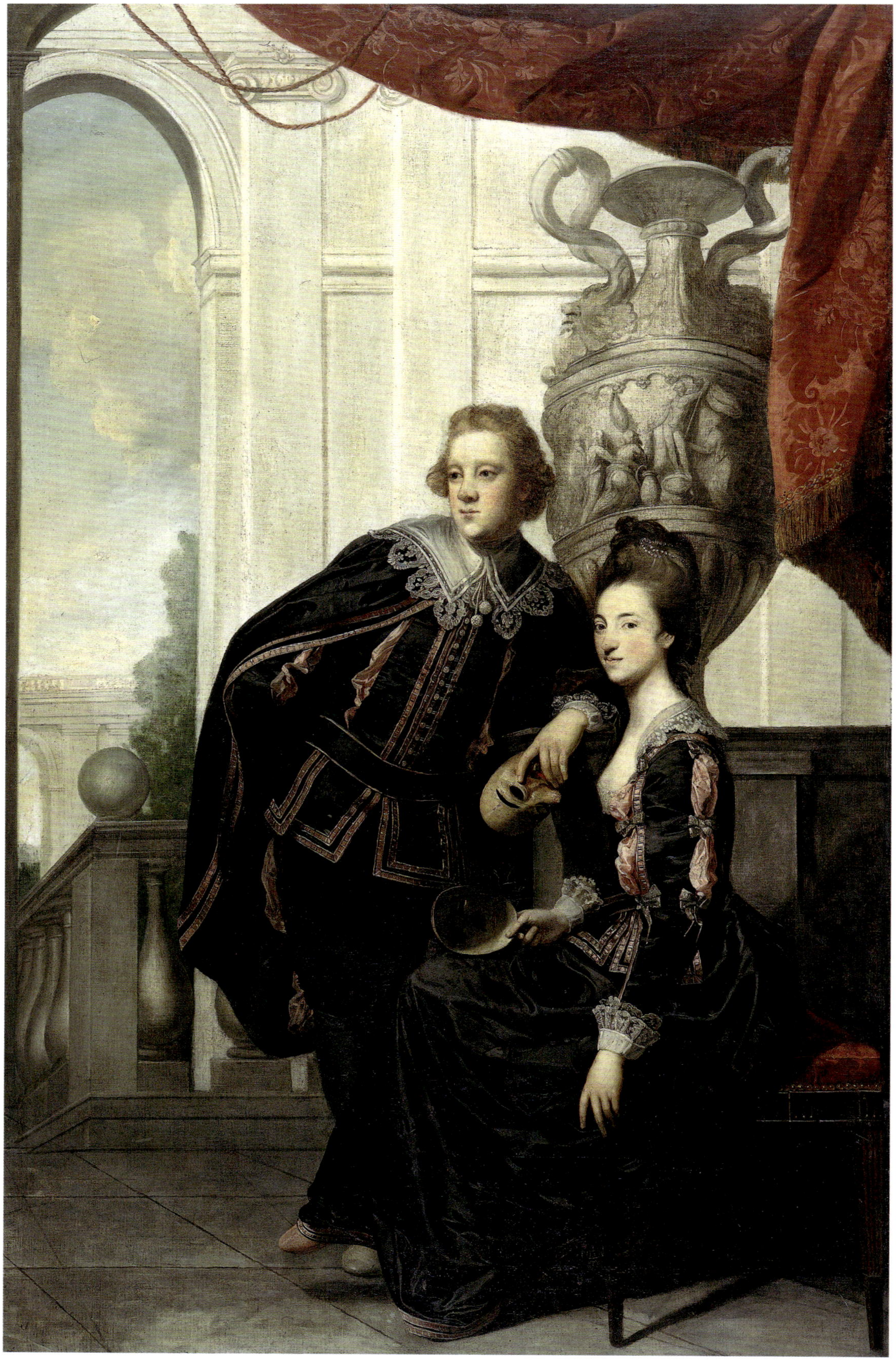

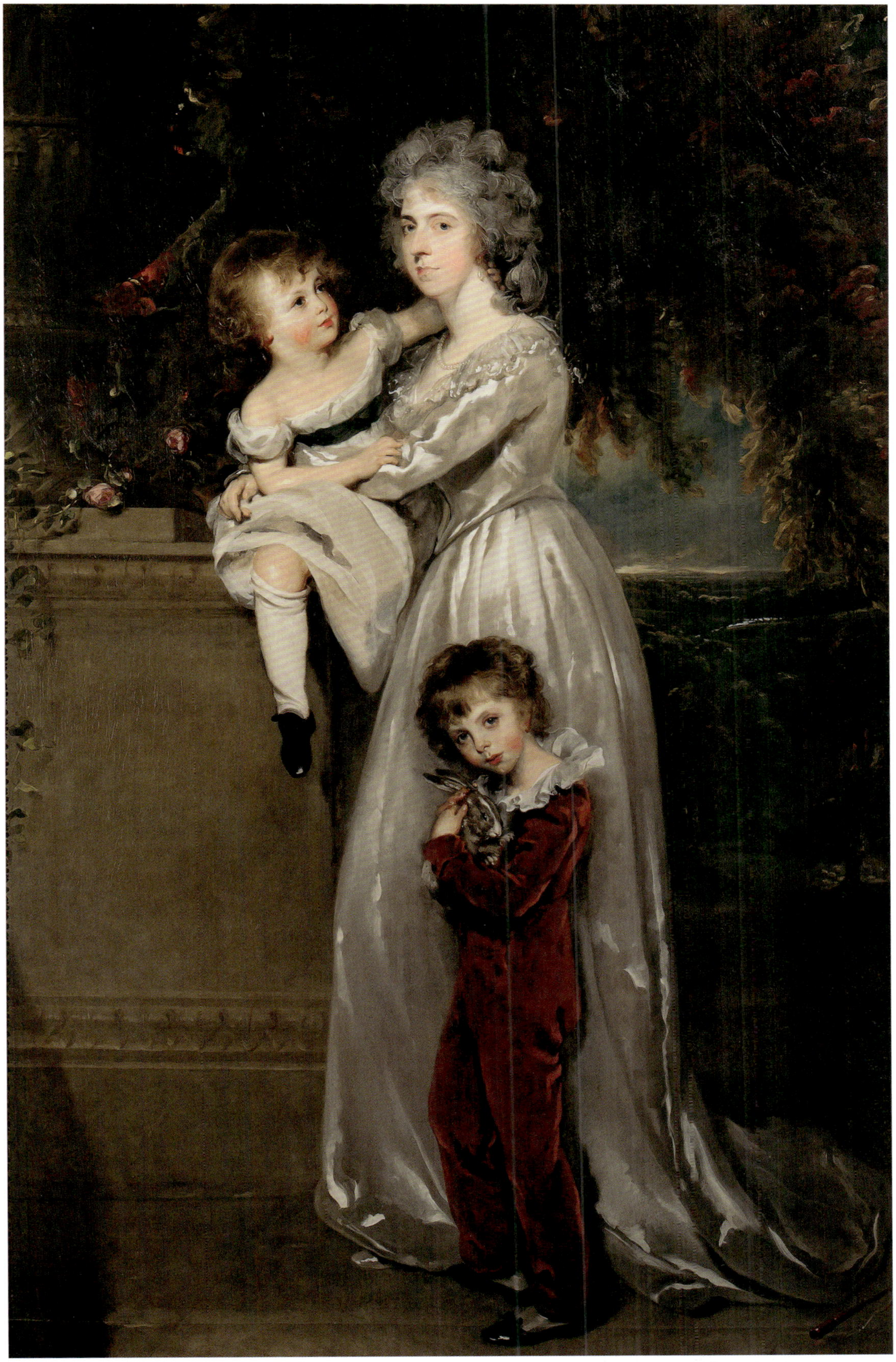

112

SIR THOMAS LAWRENCE (1769–1830)
Portrait of Mrs Arthur Annesley, with Two of Her Children, begun *c.* 1790 and left unfinished in the studio at Lawrence's death
Oil on canvas, 219.4 x 145.7 cm
Private collection, c/o Michael Tollemache Fine Art, London, inv. MFTA 1204

PROVENANCE: the sitter's family, thence by descent to the 12th Viscount Valentia, by whom sold to the Howard Young Galleries, New York, 1936; Mr and Mrs Walter O. Briggs, Detroit; G. W. Ritter, Detroit, by 1960; late G. W. Ritter, sale, Christie's, New York, 10 January 1980; private collection; sold Bonhams, London, 5 December 2007, lot 95 (£227,564); private collection
SELECTED REFERENCES: Garlick 1989, no. 36; Bonhams sale catalogue (as above)

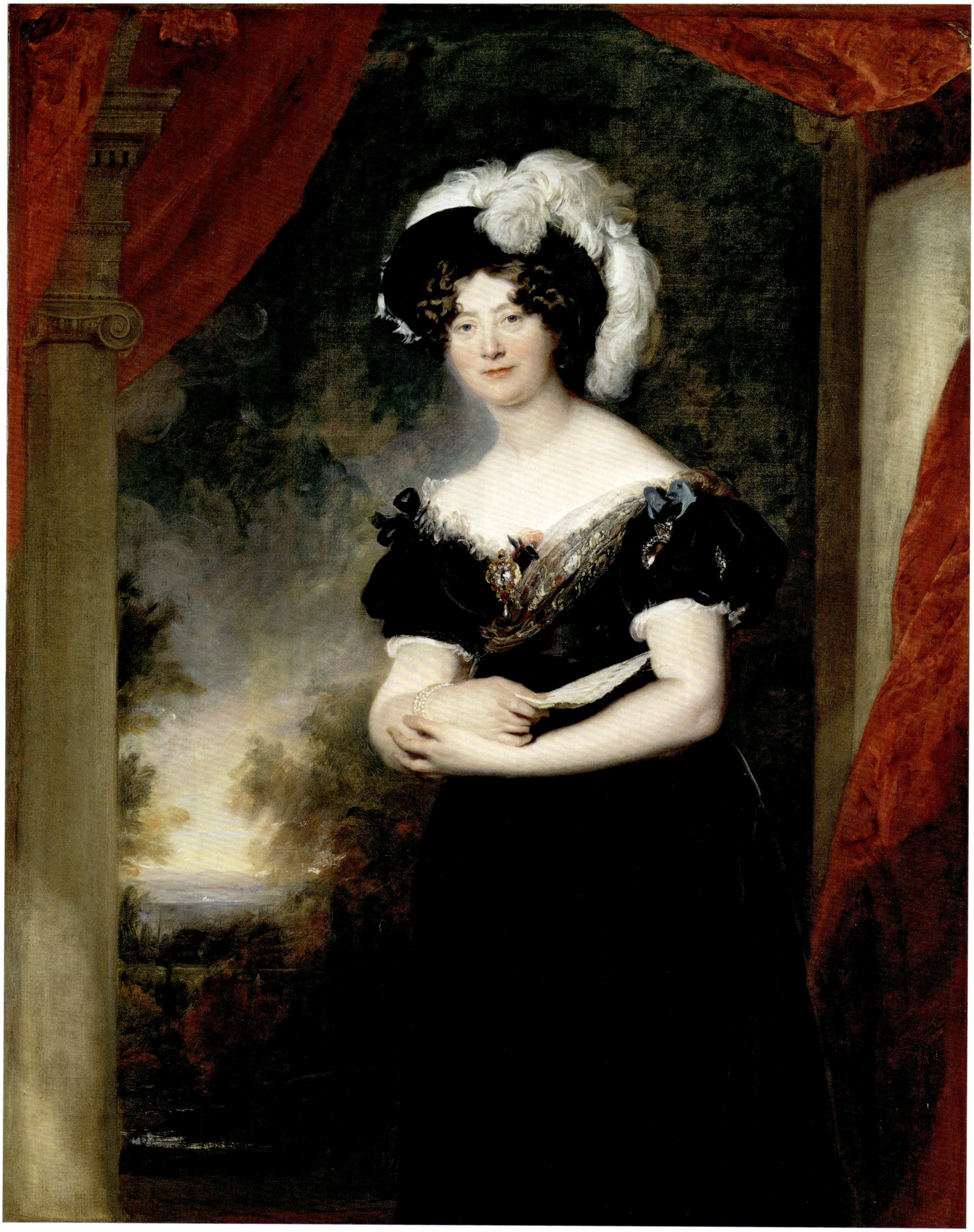

speed, at times he could be a master of procrastination. Indeed it may well be that he worked with unique sloth on this painting. It was but two-thirds complete when Lawrence died nearly forty years after the commission had been given. Why unfinished? It was one of a hundred likenesses in this condition discovered in his studio. Perhaps Lawrence had been less than scrupulous about the contract and his client simply dumped him and her picture. Lawrence had been commissioned in the early 1790s for a fee of 120 guineas, but when his bank manager interviewed him in February 1806, he gave the price as £147. It emerged that Lawrence had already received £73 10s.[7] It is uncertain which of Lady Annesley's ten children are present: though we can suppose that the mawkish boy in red clutching an understandably nervous rabbit is Arthur Annesley, heir to the title Viscount Valentia. Lawrence was childless but the tender and vulnerable portrait of Arthur suggests that this artist shared Van Dyck's capacity to enter into the imaginative world of children, though Van Dyck habitually lent his young sitters a gravitas beyond their years, as we may see in the Washington group shown earlier (cat. 105). Perhaps because of problems with the genesis of the Annesley portrait, Lawrence seems to have escaped gleefully into his full autumnal landscape of unusual abundance, reflecting perhaps his admiration for Van Dyck's watercolours of the English countryside, many of which Lawrence could have seen in Reynolds's collection and which, indeed, he could have acquired for himself at the Reynolds sale in March 1798.[8]

Princess Mary, Duchess of Gloucester (cat. 113) is certainly complemented by Lawrence's portrait of her sister Princess Sophia, which was finished the following year and is also in the Royal Collection. The later work has an affinity with some of the portraits Rubens painted in Genoa, such as *Veronica Spinola Doria* (*c.* 1607; Buscot Park, Faringdon).[9] The artist, or more probably George IV, that notable collector of Rubens, may have suggested that the likeness of his sister Princess Mary be related to Rubens's *Chapeau de Paille*, whose arrival just the year before no portraitist had dared to ignore. The sitter in the *Chapeau de Paille* (probably Susanna Fourment) is a picture of quiet serenity, the Lawrence all of a flutter. However if pressure was indeed brought to bear to make Lawrence still more *à la mode*, as if such a thing were possible, he seems to have put up some resistance. He created a hybrid from the *Chapeau*, Rubens's most celebrated portrait, and the more pious, if still pretty, image of a female Habsburg, *Sister Ana Dorotea* (1628; Apsley House, London). This was available to Lawrence since Wellington had stumbled upon the portrait after his great triumph at the battle of Vitoria and it had come to hang in his London house.[10] In the *Princess Mary*, we see royalty at its most amiable and approachable. Lawrence has his sitter hold a fan, a happy stroke of studied informality, while the feathers in her hat seem plucked from an ostrich rather than borrowed from the sober habit of a Flanders maid. A white halo and lustrous mahogany curls create a fussy albeit magnificent effect. Dress is central to the impact of all four portraits; however, the relative severity of Lady Cremorne, a reticence perhaps encouraged by this American sitter who was then unfamiliar with English social mores, makes her stand apart from the others, whose evident vitality is enhanced by lawn and cambric, silk and brocade.

113

SIR THOMAS LAWRENCE (1769–1830)
Princess Mary, Duchess of Gloucester, 1824
Oil on canvas, 141 x 111.8 cm
The Royal Collection, RCIN 403421

PROVENANCE: commissioned by George IV
SELECTED REFERENCES: Millar 1969, nos 879 and 880; Garlick 1989, no. 331B

114

LOUIS SAILLIAR (1748–c. 1795)
Helena Forman, 1783
Stipple etching, 57.2 x 39.5 cm
Royal Museum of Fine Arts Antwerp, inv. 10849

SELECTED REFERENCES: Dukelskaya and Moore 2002, pp. 216–17; Sampaio 2009, no. 16, p. 50; Houghton Hall 2013, pp. 70 and 138

115 *(overleaf, left)*

ELISABETH-LOUISE VIGÉE-LEBRUN (1755–1842)
Self-portrait in a Straw Hat, after 1782
Oil on canvas, 97.8 x 70.5 cm
The National Gallery, London, inv. NG 1653. Bought 1897
RA ONLY

PROVENANCE: sold by the executors of A. P. Pickering of 23 Queens Gardens, Hyde Park, London, through Messrs Mullett and Booker on 8 July 1897; bought by the National Gallery in early December 1897 from by J. T. Smith, dealer and curator of the Earl of Ellesmere's Bridgewater Gallery
SELECTED REFERENCES: Fare and Laget 1995, pp. 109–11; Sheriff 1995, pp. 455–88; Sheriff 1996, pp. 190–99, 202–03, 208–20; Perry 1999, pp.114–27; May 2005, pp. 41–42

116 *(overleaf, right)*

ELISABETH-LOUISE VIGÉE-LEBRUN (1755–1842)
Yolande-Martine-Gabrielle de Polastron, Duchess of Polignac, 1782
Oil on canvas, 92.2 x 73.3 cm
Musée National des Châteaux de Versailles et de Trianon, inv. MV 8971
BOZAR ONLY

PROVENANCE: thought to have been presented by Marie-Antoinette to the *maître de poste*; with his family until 1875, when left by descent to the Duke of Polignac; by *dation en paiement* in 1998 to the collection of the Château de Versailles et de Trianon
SELECTED REFERENCES: Forth Worth 1982; Paris 2008; Masseau 2009

The inspiration for this group is Rubens's *Portrait of Hélène Fourment* (fig. 39). Differences in the proportions between Sailliar's print (cat. 114) and the original could suggest that the Rubens was trimmed after the etcher worked. *Per contra*, the printmaker might have 'improved' the original with the amplitude of a more generous landscape. Sailliar ascribed his source as Van Dyck not Rubens. Michael Jaffé considered its starting point the Holbein full-length *Christina of Denmark, Duchess of Milan* (1538; The National Gallery, London).[1] The finished Rubens hung at Houghton Hall, Norfolk, home of Sir Robert Walpole and the finest collection of pictures in eighteenth-century Britain. It was an especially treasured item since William Kent designed a frame for it that featured a pearl motif and a frontispiece of a scallop shell and garland. The frame still graces the Cabinet Room at Houghton where Walpole had had it installed.[2] Sailliar's etching was published by England's leading entrepreneur of the print, John Boydell. The print is dated 1783, four years after Walpole's collection had been sold to Catherine the Great and taken to St Petersburg. The name 'Helena Forman', rather than 'Hélène Fourment', suggests how proprietorial the English had become over Rubens.

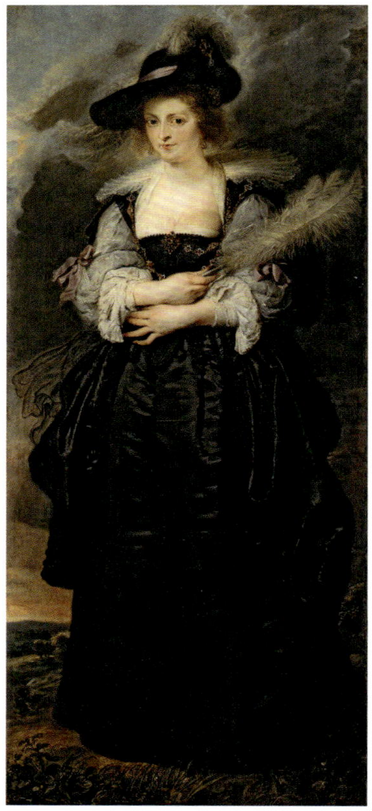

FIG. 39 Peter Paul Rubens, *Portrait of Hélène Fourment*, *c.* 1630–32. Oil on panel, 186 x 85 cm. Museu Calouste Gulbenkian, Lisbon, inv. 959

A memorable example of the genre and a piece of masterful self-promotion, Vigée-Lebrun's self-portrait (cat. 115) was acquired by the National Gallery in 1897, despite Alfred de Rothschild's claim that the picture was a copy of the prime original owned by his family. The work acquired is a duplicate, not a copy of a prime original; it was established as such only in 1985 after emerging from conservation, just as – after her exile following the French Revolution – Vigée-Lebrun herself had re-emerged no less triumphantly in French society in 1805.[3] Always copied and always enjoyed, the portrait is ever popular: a point of reference for feminists since it was mentioned in Simone de Beauvoir's celebrated *The Second Sex* (1949); frequently requested for exhibitions; and hardly less often to be seen in the press. The self-portrait, like its creator, is one of the great survivors.

In her portrait by Vigée-Lebrun (cat. 116), the Duchess of Polignac appears with studied informality. Although closely based upon the artist's own self-portrait, which had created such a sensation at the Académie, it is more reticent; certainly more appropriate for the Gouvernante des enfants royaux,

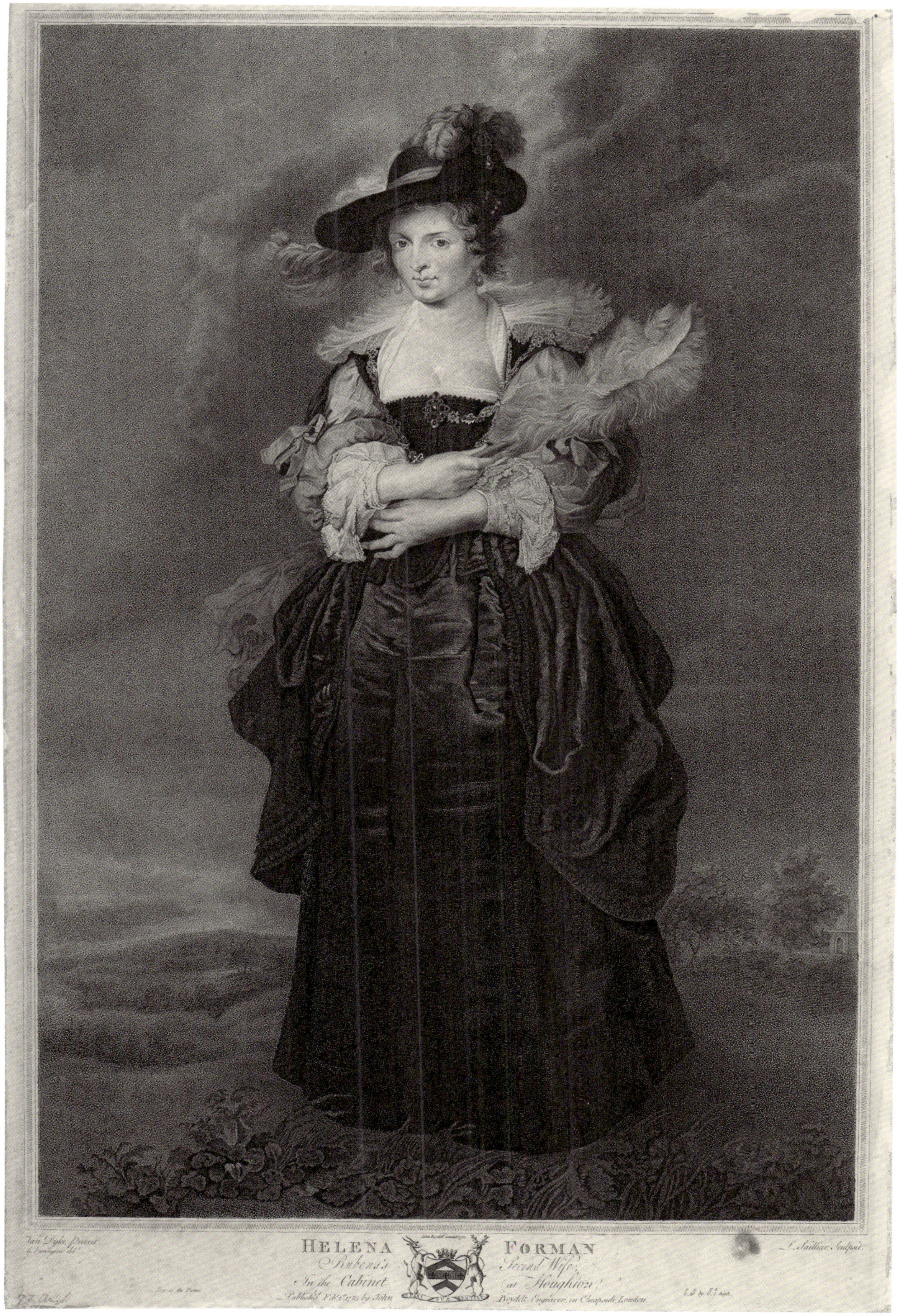
Van Dyke Pinxit.
G. Farington del.
HELENA FORMAN
Rubens's Second Wife,
In the Cabinet at Houghton.
Published Feb.y 1.st 1783 by John Boydell Engraver in Cheapside London.
L. Sailliar, Sculpsit.

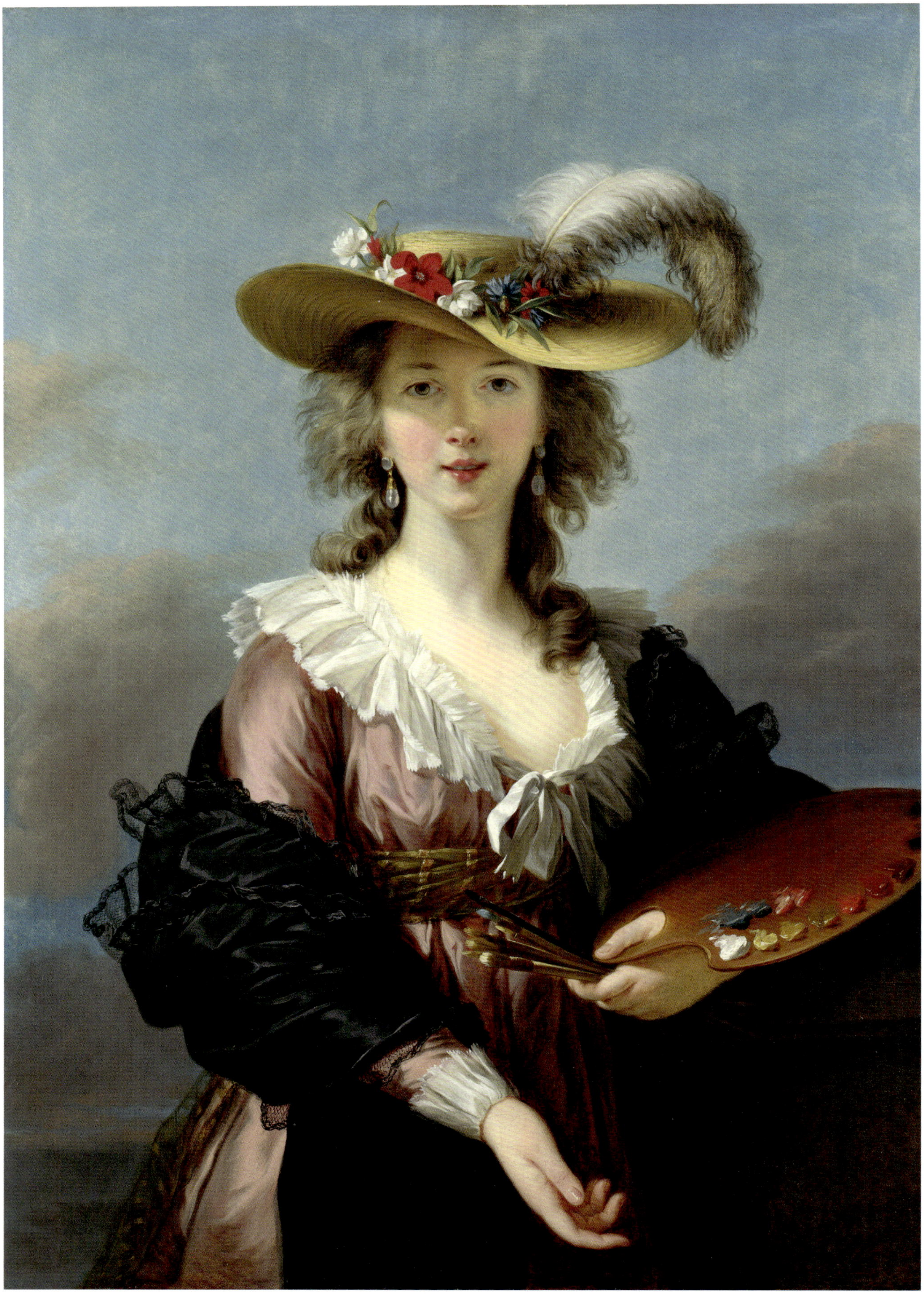

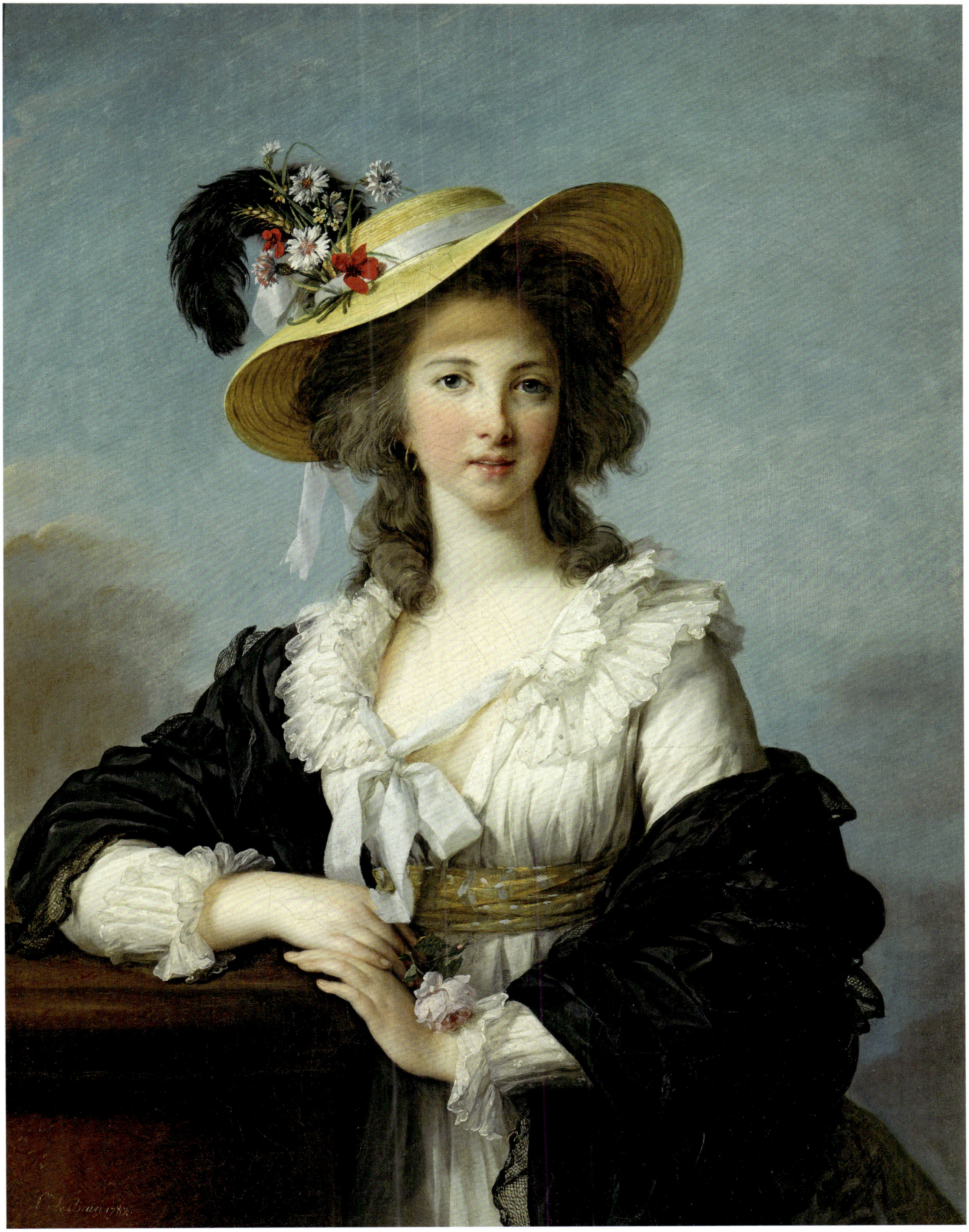

as the duchess was styled. The painting's provenance is of the highest romance; it is traditionally supposed to have been given by Marie-Antoinette to the *maître de poste* on 16 July 1789, to convince him to allow the duchess and her companions to race away, and thus escape the effects of the storming of the Bastille only two days before.[4]

It would be a mistake to discount the impact of the Maile (cat. 117). The text below the print proposes Susanna Lunden as a wife for Rubens; a presumption no contemporary document justifies, for in truth it was to be Susanna's younger sister Hélène who would eventually in 1630 become the second wife of the painter.[5] Scholars agree that at the time the original oil of Susanna (fig. 35; the starting point for the Maile print) was painted by Rubens (*c.* 1622–25), he was in fact blissfully happy with his first wife Isabella Brant, their lasting regard having been first immortalised in the so-called *Honeysuckle Bower* (fig. 33) of 1609. Who can say how such an assumption of an amorous entanglement between Rubens and someone he was indeed close to was ever contrived? Perhaps the answer is that this image comes out of Paris and Romanticism. Susanna has melting eyes, a complexion of porcelain perfection and a generous (if alarming) bosom, all making for a coy travesty of Rubens's generic 'woman'. The Rubens 'logo' of feathered hat adds a saucy air. Perhaps the print was issued when rumours began to circulate of a possible sale of the original portrait of Susanna, a work known fondly as the *Chapeau de Paille*. It would be five years before that lamentable sale was to take place. Shortly afterwards its English purchaser crowed about how his acquisition was, to Antwerp, the loss of something hitherto 'considered the idol of the city'.[6] This ridiculous mademoiselle, striving to be the new 'idol' of Antwerp, reflected the role of Rubens in depicting masquerade and historic costume, which had become a chief point of interest for admirers of Rubens since the growth of a taste for masquerade costume some fifty years before this print was published. The work of Cosway and others in the exhibition provides powerful testimony as to how Rubens's influence waxed towards the end of the eighteenth century, only to receive further impetus with the inception of Romanticism.

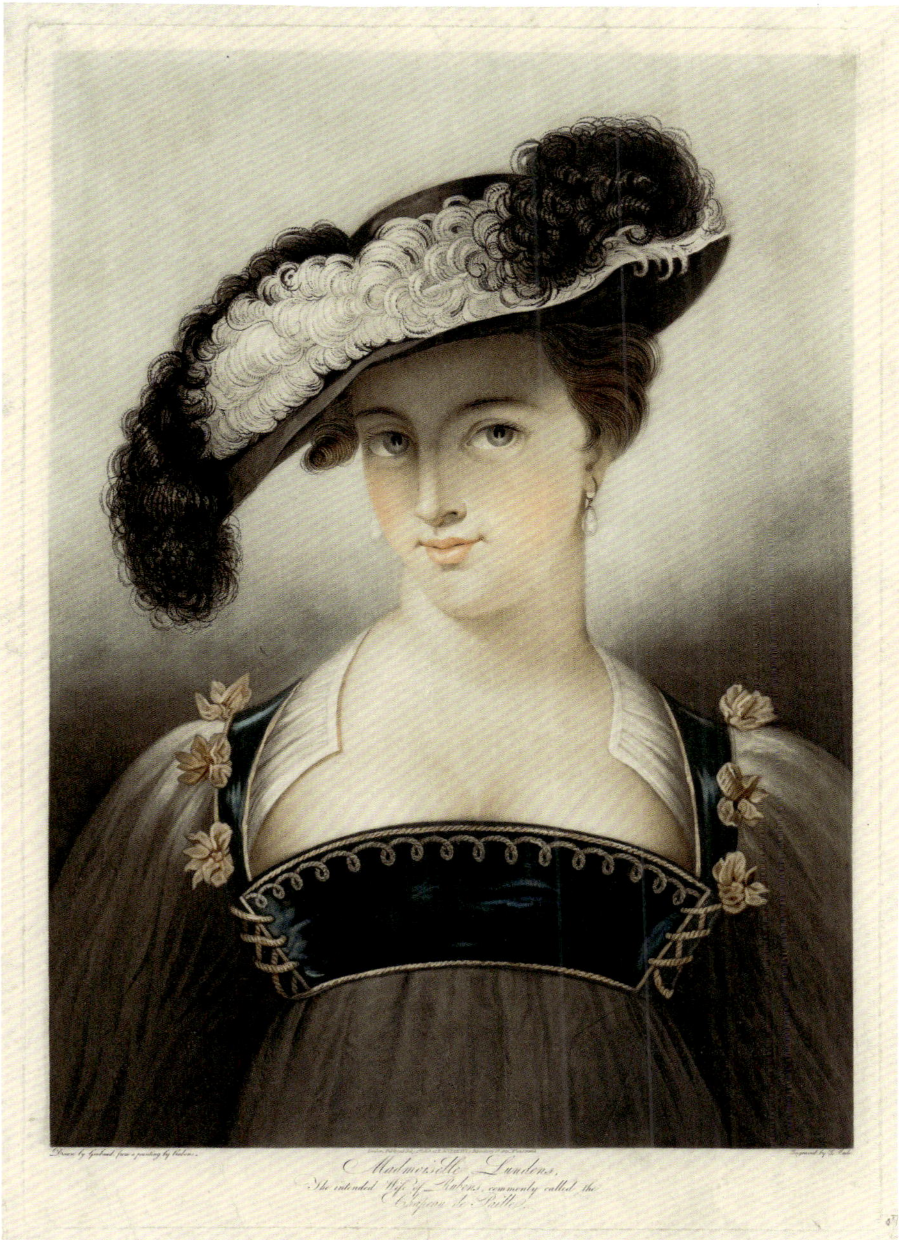

117

GEORGE MAILE (*fl.* 1808–24)
Mademoiselle Lundens, The intended Wife of Rubens, commonly called the Chapeau de Paille, 1818
Mezzotint, 60.5 x 42.0 cm
Royal Museum of Fine Arts Antwerp, inv. 10861

PROVENANCE: none published
SELECTED REFERENCES: Stanley 1823; Martin 1986, no. 852

An improbable but powerful influence on what might be termed the 'maternal' portraits of Reynolds were Rubens's relatively small-scale, domestic or portable altarpieces, of which there were many in Britain (those now at the Walker Art Gallery, Liverpool, and the Wallace Collection, London, among them). Reynolds began his Melbourne group (cat. 118) in November 1770. *The Virgin and Child with St Elizabeth and the Child Baptist* by Rubens (*c.* 1630–05; Walker Art Gallery, Liverpool) may have been the starting point. Rubens's various formal solutions to the presentation of the Holy Family – solutions that were lineal descendants from Titian for the most part – were much appreciated by English patron and connoisseur alike: the overt Catholicism of these altarpieces no impediment in Protestant England to appreciation of them as works of art. Many English copies and variations after such a subject by Rubens, as well as numerous prints, attest to this.[1] Part of Rubens's triumph was his success in transforming the sublime but sweet Madonnas of Raphael into appealing and believable family gatherings, humanising a Catholic 'Queen of Heaven' by endowing her with an accessible maternity; the resulting template qualifying as a source for many portraits of English families.

The type represented by the Liverpool Rubens was first cousin to *The Garden of Love* (cat. 130), a subject by Rubens widely accessible through the woodcuts of Christoffel Jegher (cat. 139) and, it should be noted, Rubens's most elegant contribution to the *fête champetre*; a genre that had begun with Giorgione, been expressed most suggestively by Jean-Antoine Watteau, and finally played out by Richard Cosway in the medium of print in 1784.[2] In one of only two etchings by Cosway, we see artist and wife seated in the garden of Schomberg House, Pall Mall. A black servant is serving them grapes; the whole evidently based upon close acquaintance with the sub-genre of Rubens and Hélène Fourment taking their ease.

In the Liverpool Holy Family the Madonna is notably disengaged, and in Reynolds's work, Lady Melbourne is barely more attentive to her child: the Mother of God sees the Atonement while the reputed mistress of a king hears our gossip. In the Reynolds a gymnastic son regards his crib, snug as an acorn cup, as climbing frame: the athleticism a conceit possibly taken from the cherubim of Rembrandt's *Holy Family* (1645; State Hermitage Museum, St Petersburg). The two children in the Rubens may have been modelled on the artist's sons; something Reynolds may well have spotted.

If the Melbourne group was indeed arranged after the altarpiece, there could be a political dimension here. The Rubens had long been in the possession of the Dukes of Devonshire, and theirs it was when the Devonshires and the Melbournes were passing upon the grand staircase of Whig politics: the former descending, the latter rising. The 4th Duke of Devonshire had been Prime Minister while William Lamb, younger brother of Peniston, was to be Queen Victoria's favourite premier. The connections between these two great families, whose houses and collections were well known to one another, had been reinforced when William Lamb contracted a disastrous marriage to a niece of the Duke of Devonshire. In the Devonshire altarpiece Rubens had used a portrait drawing of unsurpassed beauty for the head of the Virgin. Described in a recent exhibition catalogue as 'one of the most tender and sensitive of all Rubens's studies of women',[3] it would later be owned by Lawrence.[4]

118

SIR JOSHUA REYNOLDS (1723–1792)
Elizabeth Lamb, Viscountess Melbourne, with Her Son, Peniston, 1770–71
Oil on canvas, 236.2 x 114.7 cm
Trustees of the Firle Estate Settlement

PROVENANCE: by descent: Emily, a daughter of the 1st Viscount Melbourne, married 5th Earl Cowper; the picture hung at Brocket Hall, Hertfordshire, until the death of Lady Palmerston in 1869; afterwards in the possession of Lady Desborough (d. 1952) at Panshanger (demolished 1954); since at Firle Place
SELECTED REFERENCES: Held 1980, vol. 1, no. 296; Mannings and Postle 2000, vol. 2, no. 1080

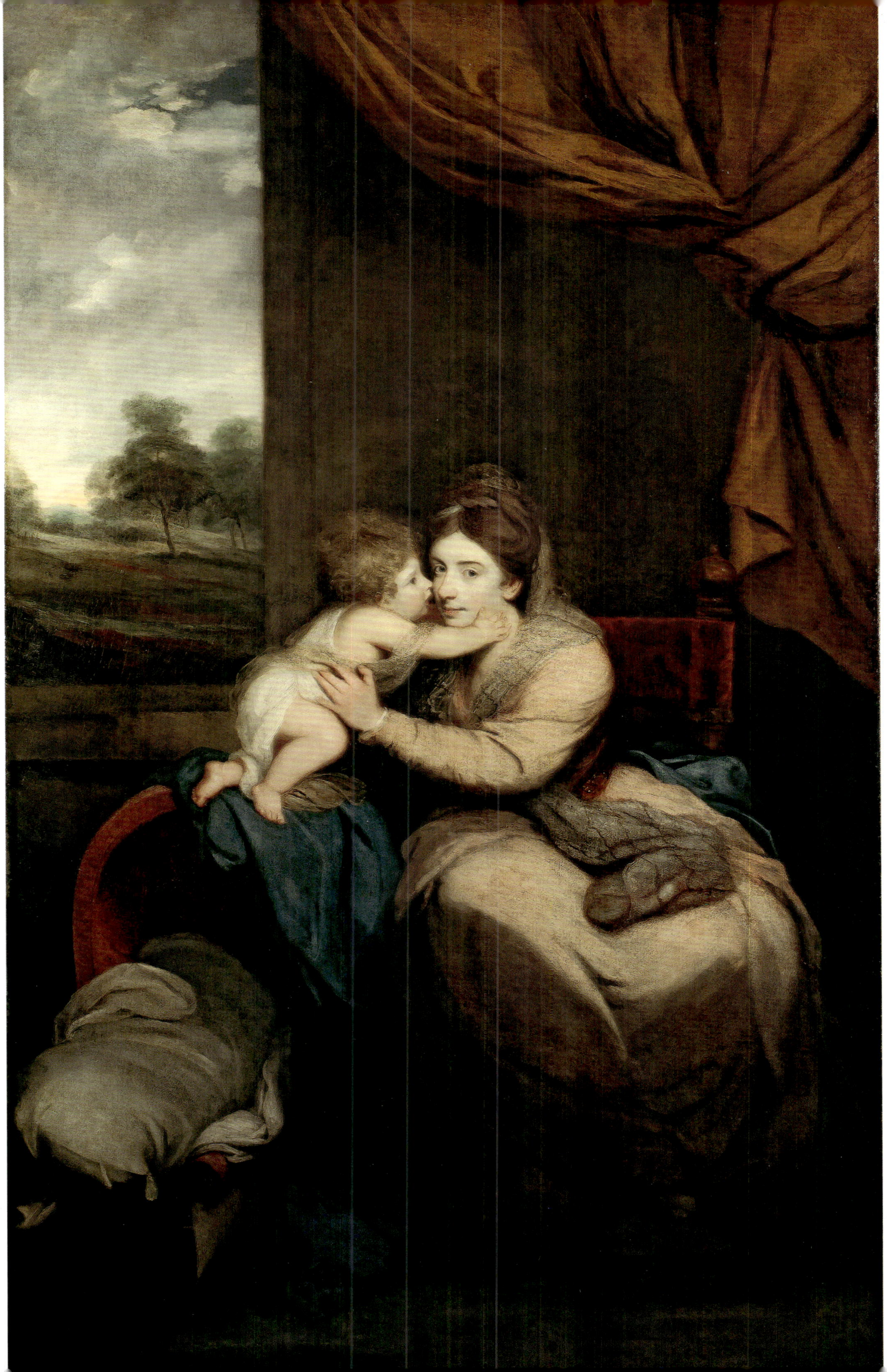

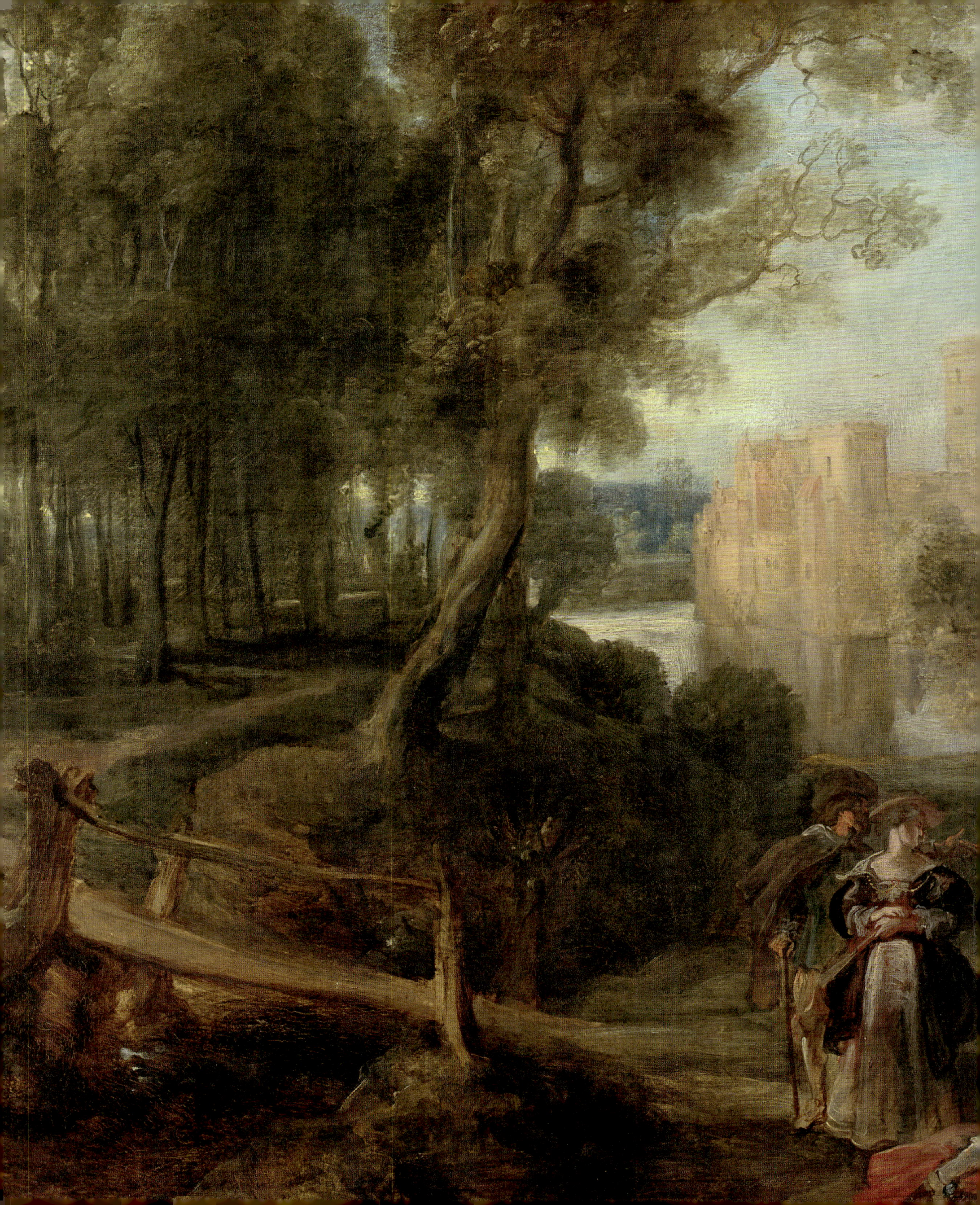

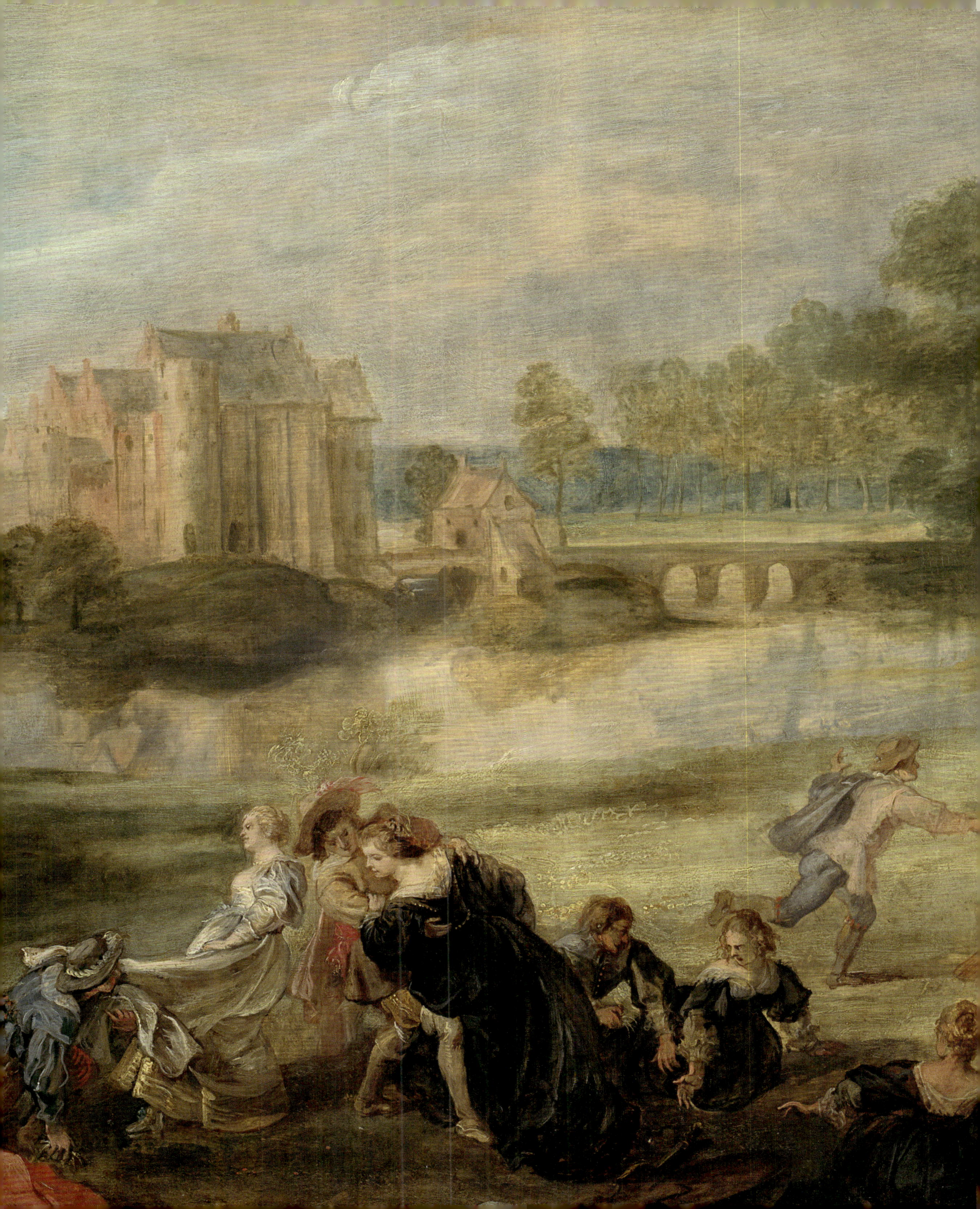

POETRY

TIM BARRINGER

EPIC TO PASTORAL

In the classical world, pastoral – the ancient Greek *Idylls* of Theocritus and the *Eclogues* of the Roman poet Virgil – stood as a modest, intimate alternative to the heroic modes of poetry. Where Virgil progressed from the gentle pastoral concerns of the *Eclogues* and *Georgics* in his youth to the heroic narrative of the *Aeneid* in his maturity, Peter Paul Rubens took the opposite path. Throughout his career a painter of grand allegories, religious and historical works, and portraits of monarchs and statesmen, Rubens only fully embraced the more modest forms of painting – landscape painting and rural genre – towards the end of his life.[1]

Theocritus set his poems in the hills of Sicily, whereas Virgil conjured up a pure, imaginary realm of the pastoral: Arcadia. The shepherds who inhabited this idyllic territory were not so much agricultural rustics as natural artists, poets and musicians with the leisure to express their feelings of love and loss. Their ideal world was conceived of as a contrast to the political and social pressures of Rome. For Rubens, the countryside and related forms of art-making offered a contrast with the anxieties of life as a courtier and diplomat, and an escape from the never-ending demands of his artistic patrons.

In 1935, William Empson described the pastoral as a form that 'puts the complex into the simple', and, notwithstanding their lyrical quality, Rubens's pastoral works are likewise richly layered with meaning and emotional import.[2] Rubens found his *locus amoenus*, or ideal place of pastoral repose, in the rural landscape of Brabant, particularly after he acquired there a splendid country seat, Het Steen, in 1635.[3] In a life of Rubens, based on conversations with the artist's nephew, Roger de Piles records that, at Het Steen, 'he would sometimes withdraw in solitude and there he enjoyed painting landscapes after Nature, since the countryside was delightful.'[4] The low-lying pastures and woodlands provided raw materials for ravishingly evocative works of art, from small studies made directly from nature to the grand, summative panoramas such as *A View of Het Steen in the Early Morning* (fig. 40). More robust pleasures were offered by the folk culture of the area, which Rubens celebrated in the bawdy, bucolic revelry of *A Flemish Kermis* (fig. 58 and see cat. 143).[5]

While the deeds of warriors in the field and matters of state occupied the writers of epic, the pastoral poet could turn to more tender feelings: love is, accordingly, a central preoccupation of the pastoral. In the last decade of his life, Rubens found renewed personal fulfilment after his second marriage in 1630, when the artist was 53 and his bride, Hélène Fourment, was a mere 16. 'I have taken a young wife of honest but middle-class family … one who would not blush to see me take my brushes in my hand,' he wrote in 1634.[6] The themes of nature and eroticism are woven together in Rubens's opulent late masterpiece, *The Garden of Love* (cat. 130). The painting celebrates the delights of youthful flirtation and declarations of love in an outdoor setting, recalling the garden dalliances of Shakespeare's suitors in *Much Ado About Nothing*, written about three decades earlier. Love's fictional garden contains architectural features akin to those of Rubens's townhouse in Antwerp. As in the famous *Concert Champêtre* of Titian (sometimes attributed to Giorgione) that Rubens would have

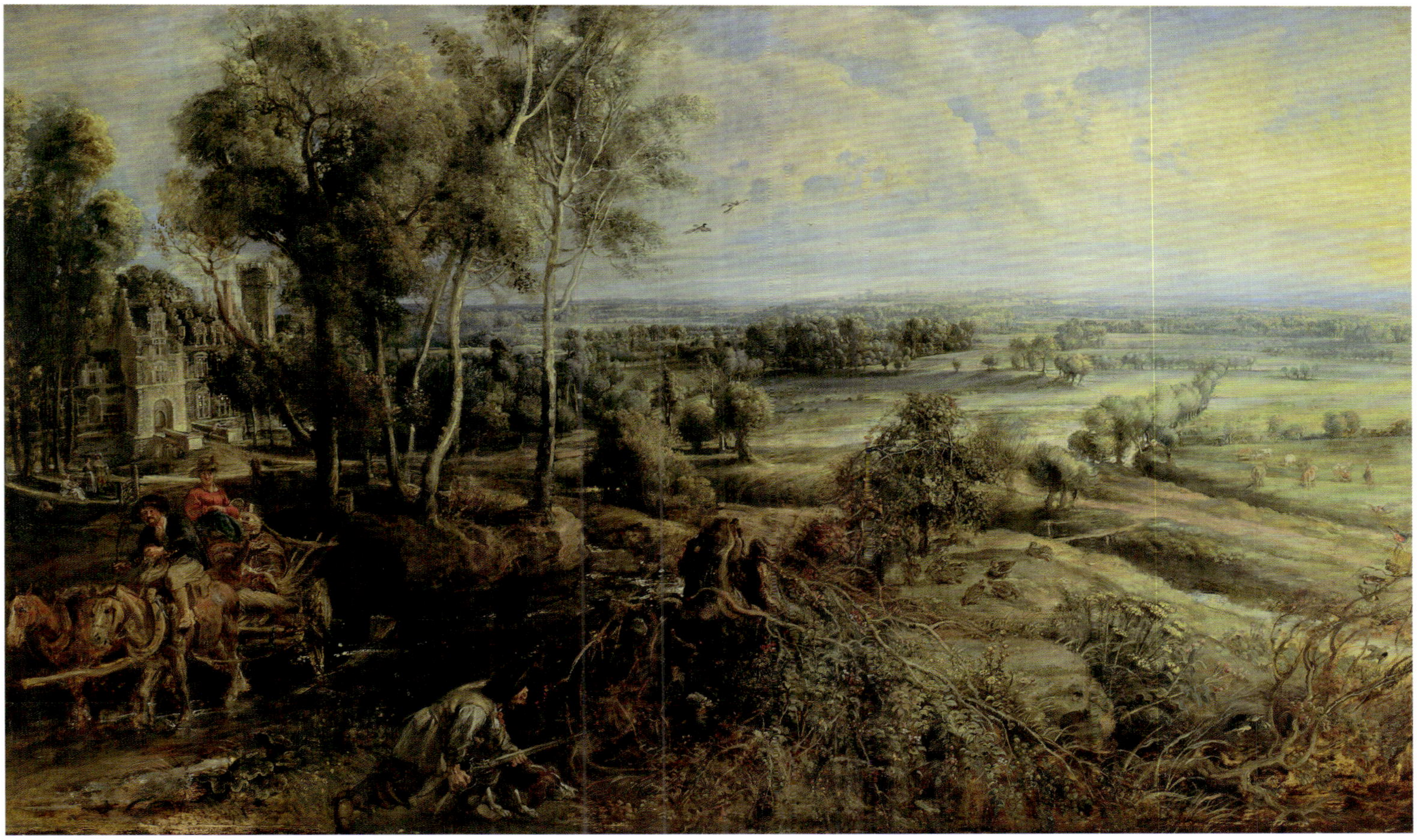

FIG. 40 Peter Paul Rubens, *A View of Het Steen in the Early Morning*, c. 1636. Oil on oak panel, 131.2 x 229.2 cm. The National Gallery, London

known in the French royal collection (fig. 41), in *The Garden of Love* the lavishly clad figures are disposed informally, some sitting on the grass. A fertile, natural landscape can be seen to the left. A successor to the *Concert Champêtre*, *The Garden of Love* is a tour de force of pastoral painting.

These late, poetic works of Rubens were widely admired in the centuries after his death. This final section traces two main currents in the response to the lyrical Rubens of the 1630s, revealing the many possibilities latent in the genre of the pastoral. In late eighteenth-century England, at the dawn of the industrial era, artists discovered in Rubens's landscapes an earthy, north-European naturalism that counterbalanced the dominant influence of Claude Lorrain's refined, but highly artificial, Italianate pastorals. Thomas Gainsborough and, later, John Constable, paid conscious and repeated homage to particular works of Rubens. The example of Rubens's landscapes in British collections, moreover, played a significant role in the quest of Constable, and his rival J. M. W. Turner, to raise the genre of landscape to new heights of expressive intensity in the era of Romanticism.

In France, a century earlier, around 1715, *The Garden of Love* (in the Spanish royal collection from 1666, but known in Paris through drawings, prints and painted copies) had worked its magic on the young painter Jean-Antoine Watteau. From Rubens's apotheosis of love among opulently attired young people in lavish gardens, Watteau fashioned the *fête galante*, a genre that, more than any other, has come to stand for the seductive elegance of the rococo. Sharing with Rubens the outdoor setting, Watteau, with light and fast-moving brushwork, created a distinctive playground of seemingly weightless figures of balletic elegance, whose motivations and desires remain mysterious.

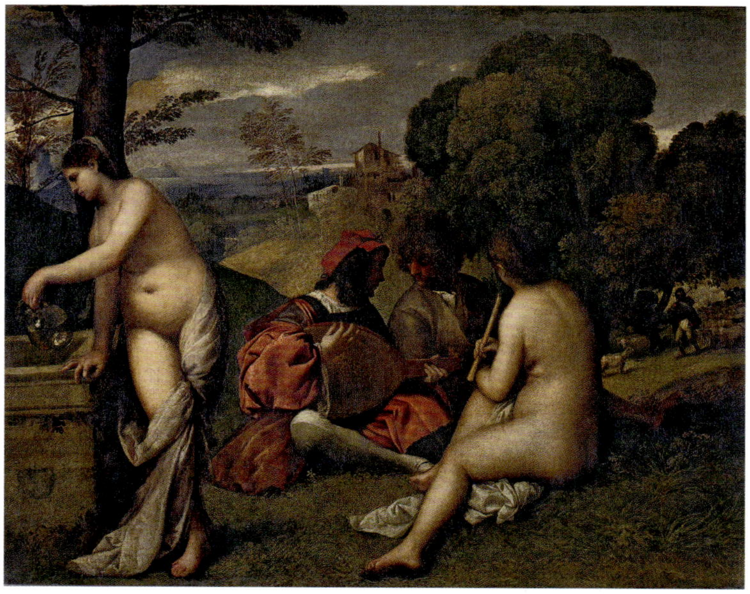

FIG. 41 Titian (or Giorgione), *Concert Champêtre*, *c.* 1510. Oil on canvas, 109 x 137 cm. Musée du Louvre, Paris

RUBENS IN ENGLAND

Rubens visited England in 1629–30 on a diplomatic mission that also produced a rich artistic legacy, including *Landscape with St George and the Dragon* (fig. 42), a painting made (so a contemporary noted in 1630) 'in honour of England and of our nation'.[7] The dragon-slaying narrative takes place against a sweeping landscape that seems to represent an idealised Thames Valley. It provided a powerful intimation of what English landscape painting could become. To the left can be seen buildings that suggest the Palace of Westminster and the Banqueting House in Whitehall, for which Rubens created magnificent allegorical ceiling paintings. The saint, who resembles Charles I, brings peace to the green and pleasant land. This painting returned with Rubens to Flanders but was brought back to England in 1634 by Endymion Porter and entered the Royal Collection. Sold under the Commonwealth, it was acquired by George IV in 1814, and arrived back in London at the very moment when landscape painting had, indeed, reached the apogee that Rubens's canvas had prophesied.

The *Discourses*, delivered by Sir Joshua Reynolds to the students and members of the Royal Academy between 1769

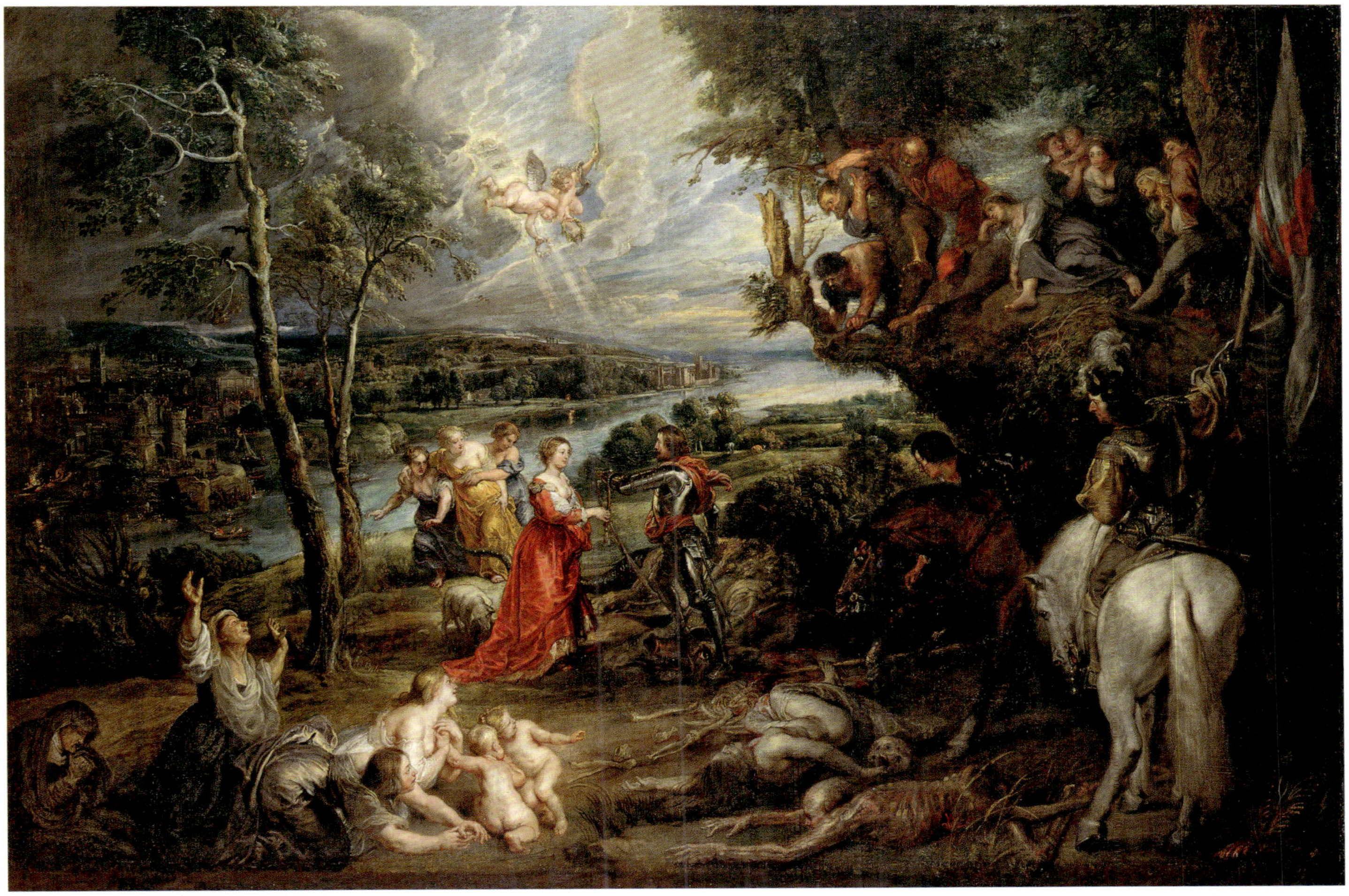

and 1790, articulate his understanding of the theory of art and his ambitions for art in Britain. Lauding the 'grand style' represented by Raphael and Michelangelo, he remained ambivalent about the position of Rubens: 'His figures have expression, and act with energy, but without simplicity or

FIG. 42 Peter Paul Rubens, *Landscape with St George and the Dragon*, *c.* 1630–35. Oil on canvas, 152.5 x 226.9 cm. The Royal Collection

dignity.'[8] Despite the 'luxurious harmony and brilliancy of his colouring', Rubens's work was, for Reynolds, marked by a 'careless, loose, and inaccurate style'.[9] Rubens's landscapes, on the other hand, were damned by association with the Dutch School, because of their 'locality' (meaning their interest in local topographical features): each, to Reynolds's eye, was merely a 'representation of an individual spot, and each in its kind a very faithful but very confined portrait'.[10] For Reynolds, the Dutch insistence on the particular details rendered painting a 'mechanical' exercise in representation, in contrast to the quest for universal truths that distinguished the liberal arts.

Reynolds did write with genuine affection about a work by Rubens in his own collection, the *Landscape with Moon and Stars* (fig. 43). This intensely evocative panel is a nocturne; the moon is reflected in the water and the scene embodies tranquillity and repose. Reynolds acknowledged that the Flemish painter had distorted the scene, making it lighter than moonlight could naturally be, because 'Rubens thought the eye should be satisfied in this case, above all other considerations: he might indeed have made it more natural, but it would have been at the expense of what he thought of much greater consequence, – the harmony proceeding from the contrast and variety of colours.'[11] When Reynolds visited the Low Countries and the Rhineland in 1781, allowing him to see more of Rubens's works, his critique of the history paintings softened, and his affection for the landscapes became more pronounced. 'There is an airiness and facility in the landscapes of Rubens', he conceded, such 'that a Painter would as soon wish to be the author of them, as those of Claude, or any other artist whatever'.[12]

THE NATURAL VISION

The naturalism and painterly quality of Rubens's late landscapes gave them special status in the eyes of landscape painters in England as the genre rose from nowhere to establish itself, by the late eighteenth century, as central to British art. Although the founding of the Royal Academy in 1768, under Reynolds, was the culmination of efforts to instigate an indigenous school of history painting, it was landscape and portraiture that soon dominated the Academy's exhibitions. In the British marketplace, pastoral outsold epic.

In his early days in Suffolk in the 1740s, Thomas Gainsborough conceived his landscapes after the manner of Dutch painters such as Jacob van Ruisdael (1628/29–1682) to the extent that he later wrote of them as 'my first imitations of little Dutch Landskips'.[13] Gainsborough probably also saw the work of Jan Siberechts (1627–*c.* 1703), a Flemish artist who had moved to England by 1674. Superbly fresh and textured with myriad details, Gainsborough's early landscapes transgressed the desire for generalisation and abstraction demanded by academic theory. Horace Walpole found in such work 'the drudging mimicry of nature's most uncomely coarseness'.[14]

Seeing Gainsborough's large, idyllic landscape *The Watering Place* (fig. 45) at the Royal Academy in 1777, however, Walpole noted: 'In the Style of Rubens, & by far the finest landscape ever painted in England & equal to the great masters.'[15] *The Watering Place* paid homage to Rubens's painting known by the same title (fig. 44), owned by George Montagu, 1st Duke of Montagu, from 1768. That year, Gainsborough urged David Garrick to 'call *upon any pretence* to see his Grace's landskip of Rubens'.[16] In Rubens's celebrated panel, dappled sunlight illuminates cattle and horses watering at a stream against the backdrop of a forest growing among rocky outcrops. Rubens luxuriates in the variety of vegetation, contrasting the dark greens of the foliage with the brilliance of the light on the sandy track in the foreground. Gainsborough's *The Watering Place* betrays clear similarities in the massing of the composition and the structuring of contrasts between sunshine and shade, foliage

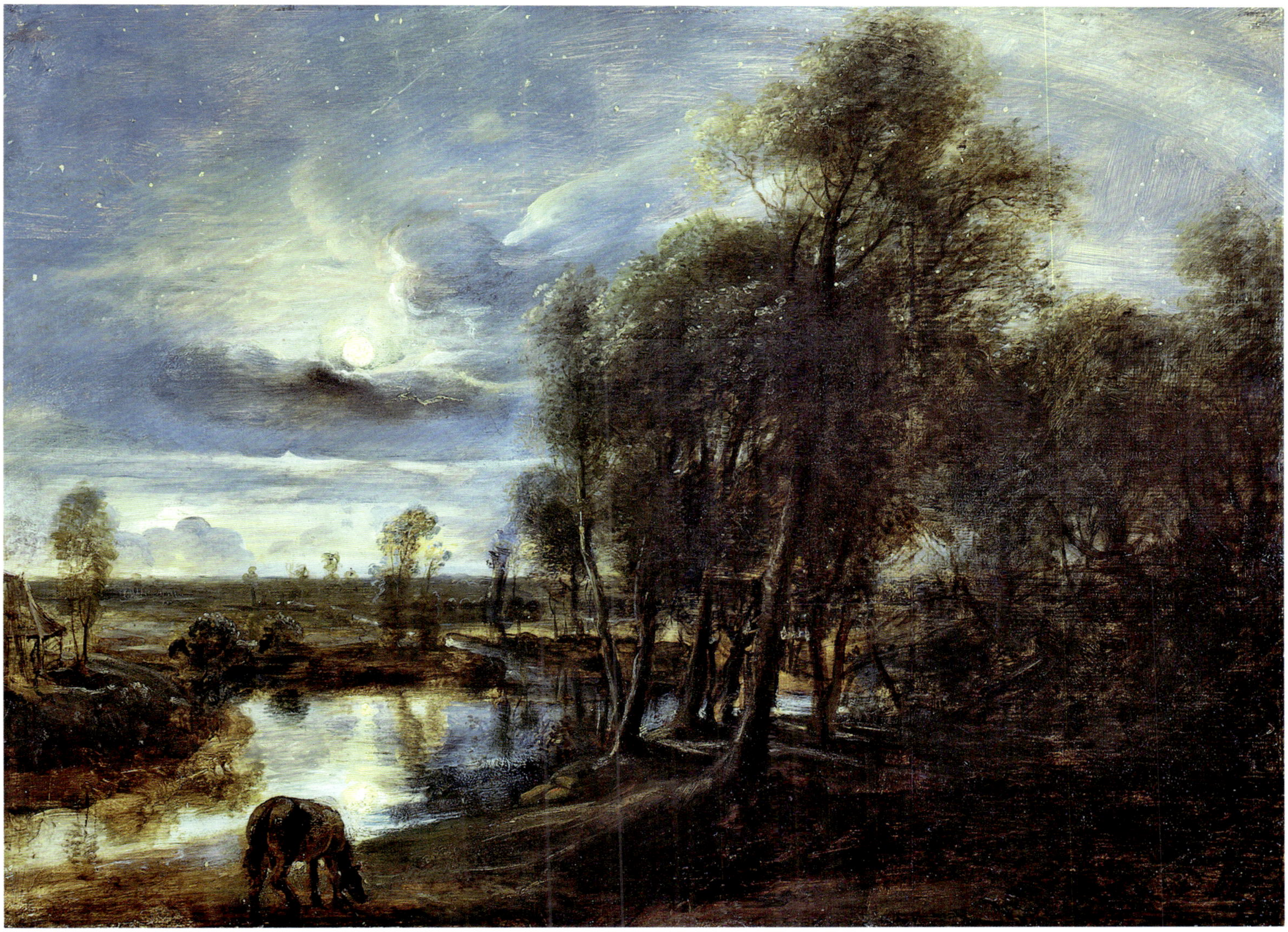

FIG. 43 Peter Paul Rubens, *Landscape with Moon and Stars*, 1637–38.
Oil on panel, 64 x 90 cm. Courtauld Institute of Art Gallery, London

and rocks. But the English painting seems further from real life than that of Rubens; Gainsborough's peasants recline in peace like the shepherd-poets of Virgil's *Eclogues*, eschewing the Bruegel-like rough and tumble of Rubens's rustics. Also to be found in the genealogy of Gainsborough's *The Watering Place* is a panel by Rubens, almost square in shape, *Evening Landscape with Timber Wagon* (cat. 121). Gainsborough likely saw this eloquent composition in the collection of John Pratt, 1st Marquess Camden (1759–1840). The richly textured portrayal of low sunshine through trees and the overall quality of rapturous elegy in Rubens's landscape find many echoes in Gainsborough's English idylls.

J. M. W. Turner, who was preoccupied with the pastoral throughout his life, much admired Gainsborough's 'full-toned depth of colour and a freedom of touch characteristically varied with the peculiarities of the vigorous foliage or of decaying nature'.[17] Yet he was surprisingly hostile to Rubens's landscapes, which share these very characteristics. In 1802, when a lull in the wars with France allowed Turner to see the Flemish master's celebrated *Landscape with Rainbow* (fig. 51) in Paris, the young Englishman declared Rubens to be 'ignorant of – natural effect'.[18] In a lecture delivered to the students of the Royal Academy in 1811, Turner acknowledged (in Reynoldsian vein) that, among Netherlandish artists, only Rubens and Rembrandt were able to raise nature 'above her commonalty'.[19] Turner found Rubens to be 'Master of every power of handicraft and mechanical excellence, from the lily of the field to animated nature', who, however, 'threw around his tints like a bunch of flowers'. (This, ironically, calls to mind the nineteenth-century American painter Thomas Cole's view of Turner's own work: 'rocks should not look like sugar candy nor ground like jelly'.)[20] Enthusiastic in his endorsement of the work of Poussin, Pier Franceso Mola and, above all, Claude, Turner considered Rubens to have scant regard

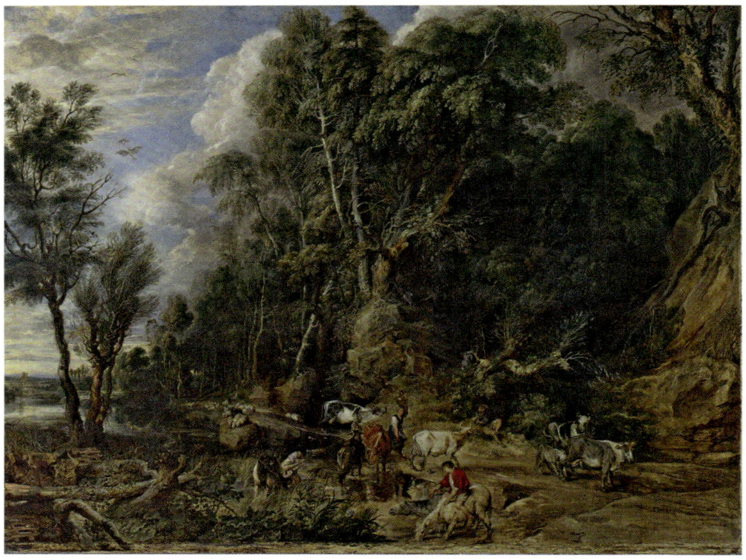

FIG. 44 Peter Paul Rubens, *The Watering Place*, *c*. 1615–22. Oil on oak panel, 99.4 x 135 cm. The National Gallery, London

for 'the simplicity, the truth, the beauty of pastoral nature'. Turner's paintings tell a different story: *The Forest of Bere* (cat. 126) is notable for its eloquent handling of the sunset; the deep shadows and glowing colours very clearly pay homage to Rubens – more so than to Cuyp or Claude, masters for whom Turner proclaimed his admiration.[21]

Like the last years of Rubens, the life of Turner's contemporary John Constable was divided between the town and country. Rubens, descended from a respected family in Antwerp, and resident in the city for much of his life from 1589, eventually purchased a rural estate. Constable, by contrast, was born in the Suffolk countryside, the son of a mill owner at East Bergholt, and moved only reluctantly to London in pursuit of his career as an artist. From 1819 to 1826 Constable

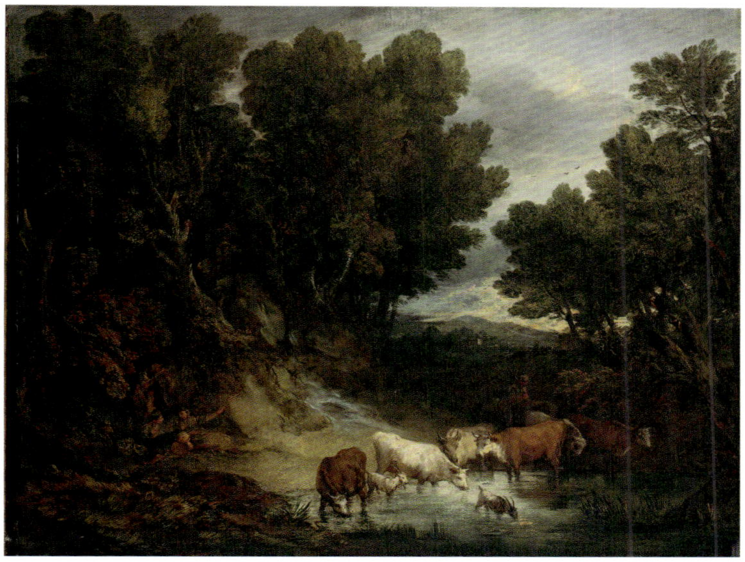

FIG. 45 Thomas Gainsborough, *The Watering Place*, before 1777. Oil on canvas, 147.3 x 180.3 cm. The National Gallery, London

spent the winters in the West End of London, and he usually summered in Hampstead. Only three miles north of central London, this outer suburb was attractive to the painter because of its extensive heath, a park with excellent views. Owing in part to the influence of his patron Sir George Beaumont, owner of *A View of Het Steen in the Early Morning*, Constable was profoundly influenced by the pastoralism of Rubens. In Hampstead he painted a series of works that, in richness of colour and faithful rendering of atmospheric effects, as well as in certain iconographic details, pay homage to the Flemish master. *Hampstead Heath, Branch Hill Pond* (cat. 123), bears comparison with the blustery prospect of Rubens's Brabant; and the prominence of the cart may allude to Rubens's celebrated *The Carters* (cat. 120), known to Constable through engravings. In a lecture given in 1833 in Hampstead, Constable avowed: 'In no other branch of art is Rubens greater than in landscape; the freshness and dewy light, the joyous and animated character which he has imparted to it, impressing on the level monotonous scenery of Flanders all the richness which belongs to its noblest features. Rubens delighted in phenomena – rainbows upon a stormy sky – bursts of sunshine – moonlight – meteors – and impetuous torrents mingling their sound with wind and wave.'[22]

Freshness of light; animated character; bursts of sunshine: these are phrases that well describe Constable's own major works and there is a degree of self-identification in these remarks. Even the characterisation of Flanders as 'monotonous' echoes the idea that Constable's Suffolk lacked the drama of popular sublime subject-matter such as the Alps or the Lake District. It was the brilliant light in his most celebrated composition, *The Hay Wain* (fig. 46; see also cat. 124), that so enraptured French artists and critics when the work was shown at the Paris Salon of 1824. The broad sweep of countryside, with extended views to the right, recalls the expansive example of *A View of Het Steen in the Early Morning*. Both works, executed on a grand scale, are paeans of praise to sites of personal association.

A self-conscious homage to Rubens can be found in Constable's deployment of the rainbow in one of his grandest compositions, a work with valedictory implications: *Salisbury Cathedral from the Meadows* (fig. 47). Constable told his biographer C. R. Leslie that in this painting could be found 'the fullest impression of the compass of his art'.[23] Constable knew Rubens's *The Rainbow Landscape* (*c.* 1636; Wallace Collection, London), which was in London from 1802, and the composition of *Landscape with Rainbow* was also widely known through copies. The inclusion of a rainbow at a late stage in the composition of *Salisbury Cathedral from the Meadows* suggests that Constable

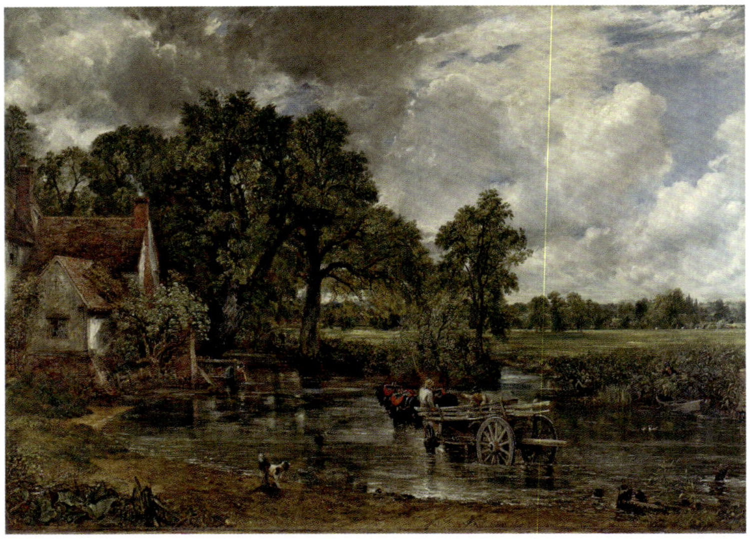

FIG. 46 John Constable, *The Hay Wain*, 1821. Oil on canvas, 130.2 x 185.4 cm. The National Gallery, London

wished, before this summative composition left his studio, to signal his association with Rubens.[24]

GARDEN OF LOVE TO FÊTE GALANTE

If the naturalism of Rubens's pastoral appealed to late eighteenth-century English painters, it was the lyrical eroticism of the late Rubens that decisively affected French art of a slightly earlier period, largely through the mercurial figure of Jean-Antoine Watteau. In *The Garden of Love* (cat. 130), Rubens provided a psychologically probing and physically opulent vision of courtship and flirtation. Five refined couples have come together, propelled by cupids, and the central group of young women – three graces in the latest fashions – turn their thoughts to love. The painting is notable for its combination of lovingly detailed contemporary dress with the allegorical adornments of flying cupids bearing attributes symbolising marriage (the yoke; the pair of doves). In this way, Rubens makes clear that the high-spirited gathering, vibrant with music and laughter, is not mere erotic play, but part of a courtship ritual devoted to the continuation of traditional family structures.

The son of a roofer in provincial Valenciennes (a town that was culturally closer to Flanders than to France, and whose jurisdiction was contested between the two powers), Watteau became the artist who, more than any other, thrilled French aristocratic patrons under the regency of the Duke of Orléans (which extended from 1715 to 1723). A crucial element in Watteau's transformation from the creator of the somewhat naive genre paintings and military tableaux of his early years into the painter of subtle and eloquent *fêtes galantes* was his exposure to the work of Rubens. Watteau's patron Pierre Crozat assembled a magnificent collection of Old Master drawings, containing some 320 works attributed to Rubens, and encouraged a circle of artists, including Watteau, to study them.[25] Watteau's surviving copies show him to have been keenly attentive to Rubens's manner, and yet able, however, to translate such vivacious drawings into his own distinctive idiom, just as Rubens had reinterpreted the Old Masters in his copies. Watteau's lucid drawings in chalk, particularly the studies of the female figure in contemporary dress, demonstrate close affinities with Rubens.

Most importantly for Watteau, Crozat owned the drawings (cat. 138), now in the Metropolitan Museum in New York, for Jegher's woodcut (cat. 139) of the revised composition of *The Garden of Love*.[26] A copy in oils also belonged to the Comtesse de Verrue, a significant collector of Watteau's work. Watteau's central innovation was to transform the baroque, courtly solidity of *The Garden of Love* into a new artistic genre,

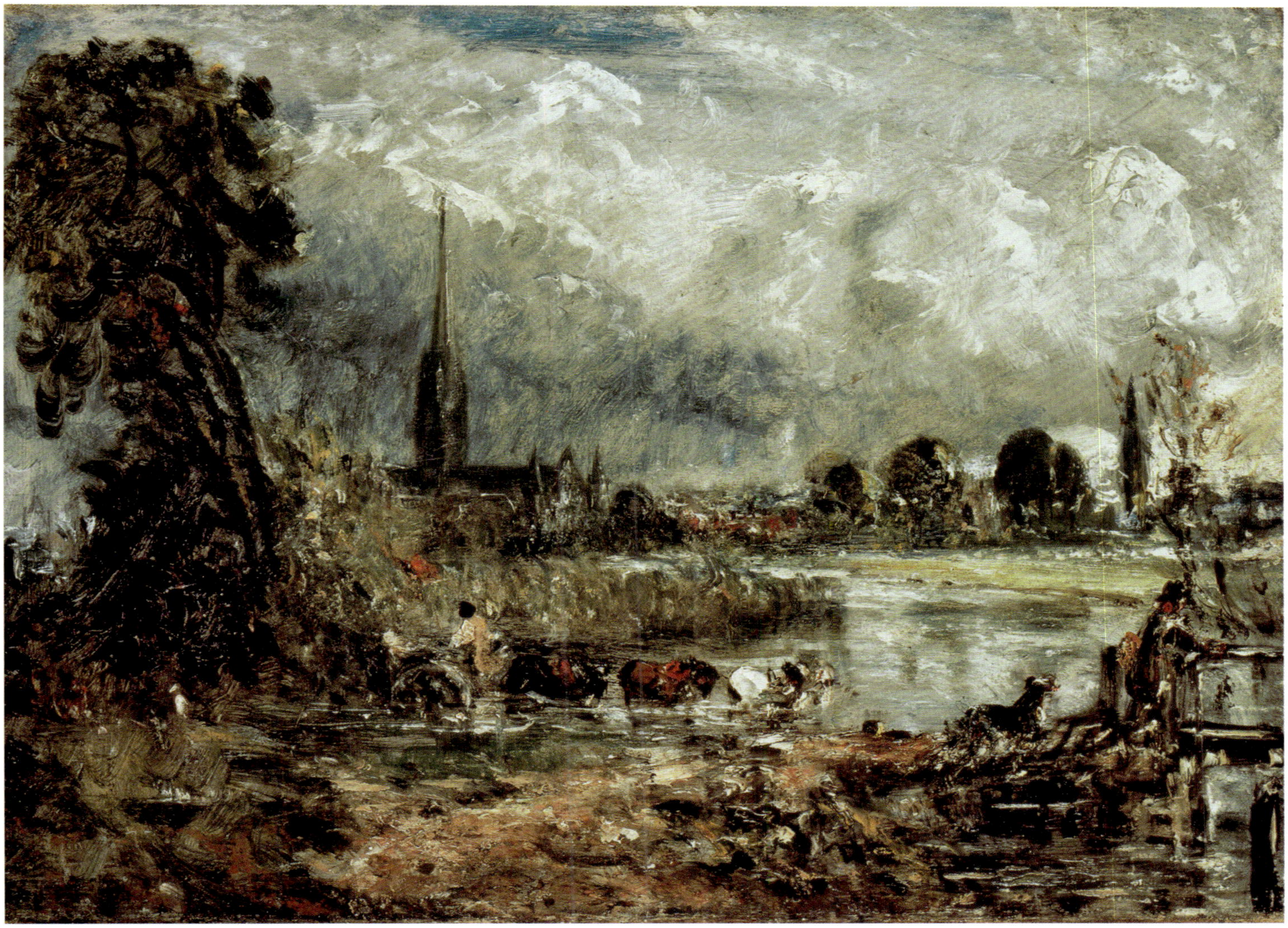

FIG. 47 John Constable, *Salisbury Cathedral from the Meadows*, 1831.
Oil on canvas, 151.8 x 189.9 cm. Tate, London (and partner institutions)

the *fête galante*, which explored the visual delights of costumed entertainments in the open air, complete with music, dance, theatrical performances and feasting.[27] The painted *fête galante* gained popularity in part because it enshrined a social practice beloved of the Parisian élite in the last years of the reign of Louis XIV. Balls took place outdoors, often at the summer home of a wealthy family, a *maison de plaisance* on the wooded outskirts of Paris. Crozat maintained such an establishment at Montmorency and Watteau's *The Pleasures of the Ball* (cat. 140) envisions the scene. These fashionable evening entertainments spawned a particular form of performative behaviour – witty and licentious, marked by charming conversation and flirtation. Although triviality and a lack of seriousness characterised the *fêtes*, an invitation to such an event signalled one's acceptance into established high society. Participants would often appear in fancy dress, sometimes costumed as peasants or characters from the *commedia dell'arte*. In Watteau's *fête-galante* paintings, as in the masquerades they depict, appearances are deceptive, emotions are complex; some genuine, some the product of theatrical artifice.

A quintessential example of Watteau's *fête-galante* compositions is *Pilgrimage to the Island of Cythera* (fig. 48), chosen by the artist to represent him in the collections of the Académie royale de peinture et de sculpture, to which body he submitted it as his reception piece. Watteau had been admitted to the ranks of the Académie on 30 June 1712, but by January 1717 he had still not deposited a work. On 9 January that year, the Académie 'requested the candidates to come and explain their delay [and] gave Sieur Watteau six months'.[28] Chastened, Watteau created *Pilgrimage to the Island of Cythera*, the largest canvas he was to produce. Its central conceit is simple: that it is human destiny to undertake the journey to an island of love. The interweaving of the bodies, and their amorous dynamism, surely demonstrates that Watteau had studied Rubens's *The Garden of Love* drawings in the Crozat collection. The gallants and fine ladies interact with the same physical and psychological intricacy as Rubens's figures, even if, more ethereal, they lack the sheer red-blooded solidity of the Flemish company. The long line of figures crossing the composition forms a graceful arabesque, moving across the canvas with a musical rise and fall marked by visual and psychological incident. The pilgrims have reached the island in a barge, a gilded rococo confection above which a group of cupids cavorts in the sky. In contrast to *The Garden of Love*, however, there is little sense that marriage will be the outcome of this journey to Cythera: it is an exploration of eroticism and dalliance rather than courtship leading ultimately to the securing of dynastic heirs.[29] Michael Levey caused consternation in 1961 by arguing, against the weight of accumulated tradition, but convincingly, that the 'real theme' of the painting was not the departure for the island of love, but the pilgrims sadly preparing to leave the island – another profound contrast with Rubens's garden, where cheerful courtiers are arriving.[30] Certainly, we are on Cythera. The sculptural bust of Venus, goddess of love, which can be seen on the right, has been decorated by the pilgrims. They now slowly turn to leave the enchanted isle and head for the barge. A lady in a mustard yellow dress looks back for one last, nostalgic, glimpse of the shrine of Venus.

Another work by Rubens assiduously observed by Watteau was *A Flemish Kermis* (fig. 58), in the French royal collection, which was brought from Versailles to Paris in 1706. *Couple Dancing* (cat. 144), in particular, imparts to the figures a rococo lightness of touch, even while retaining Rubens's Dionysian energy. Watteau incorporated these figures, with further modifications, into his painting *La Surprise* (cat. 145), transforming Rubens's hefty, tumbling Flemish rustics into a single, sculptural emblem of balletic poise. A new psychological

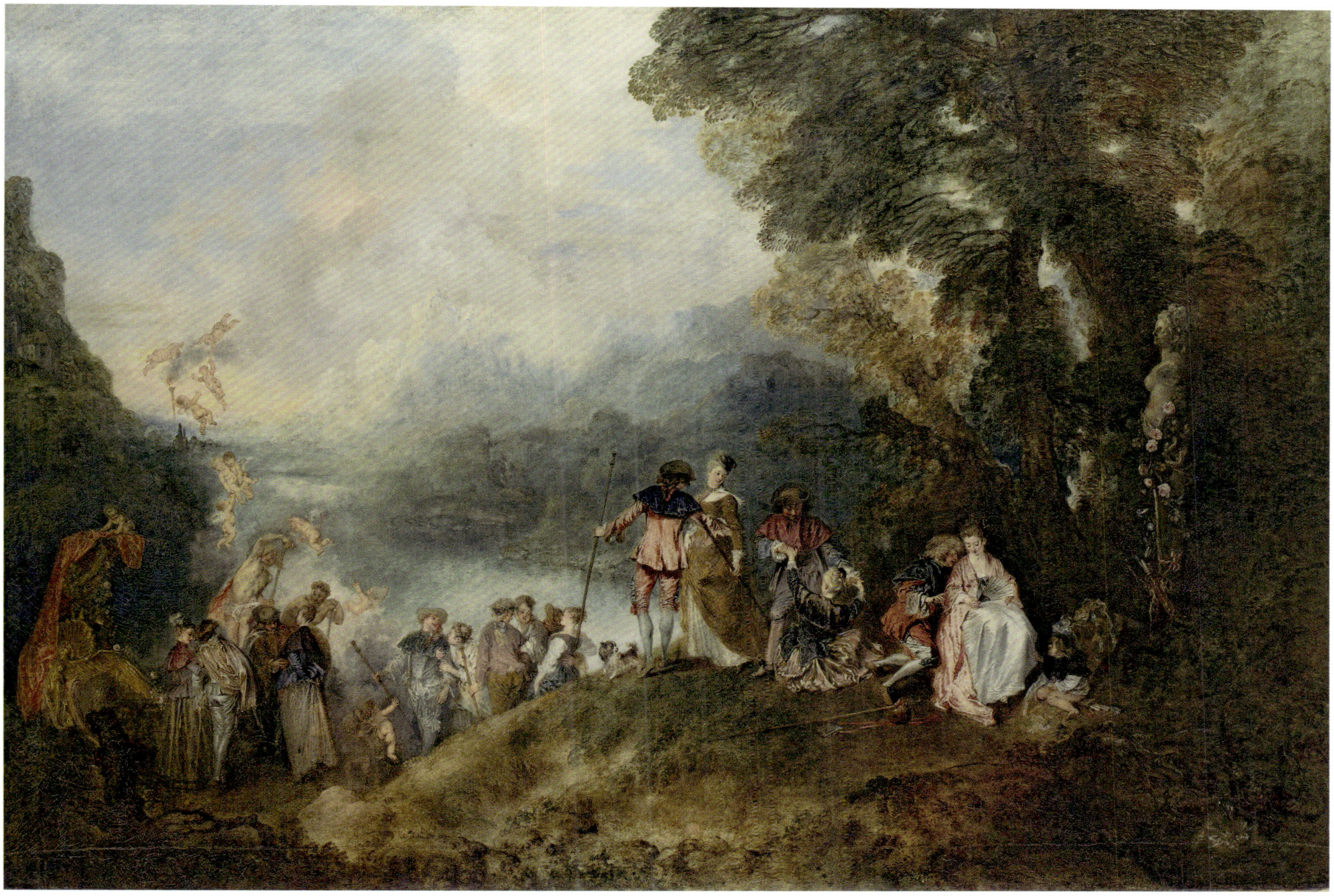

FIG. 48 Jean-Antoine Watteau, *Pilgrimage to the Island of Cythera*, 1717. Oil on canvas, 129 x 194 cm. Musée du Louvre, Paris

dimension emerges; clearly the young woman rejects her partner's advances, turning her face away, while his actions have acquired a sinister, invasive character. For Watteau, Rubens was a catalyst to a new, ambivalent and self-reflexive vision of the role and identity of art in relation to a society on the cusp of modernity.

AFTERWORD: RUBENS'S PASTORAL IN THE AGE OF MODERNISM

Just two centuries after Watteau sketched *Couple Dancing*, a startlingly different response to the same figures emerged in the work of the English painter Wyndham Lewis. Like Watteau, Lewis was drawn to the fashionable demi-monde of his day, and had been asked in 1912 to create a large painting for the entrance to the Cabaret Theatre Club, or Cave of the Golden Calf, an avant-garde nightclub opened in the West End of London by Frida Strindberg. The painting, entitled *Kermesse* and intensely provocative in both style and subject, is lost. No photograph of it survives, but a study (fig. 49) depicts a frenzied dance with two figures at its centre, alluding perhaps to the fashionable Apache Dance and also to the traditional carnivals the Lewis had observed in Brittany years earlier.[31] The title, and the central motif, are derived from Rubens's *A Flemish Kermis*, which Lewis had studied in the Louvre. Lewis claimed to dislike the way 'Rubens IMITATED Life – borrowed the colour of its crude blood, traced the sprawling and surging of its animal hulks' and particularly inveighed against the 'carnivorous Belgian bumpkins' of *A Flemish Kermis*.[32] Yet the primeval vigour of Rubens's painting, so suggestive to Watteau, had once again generated a powerful artistic response.

The wild, destructive energies of Lewis's Vorticist project did not survive the maelstrom of the First World War. After the mechanised carnage of 1914–18, the landscapes of

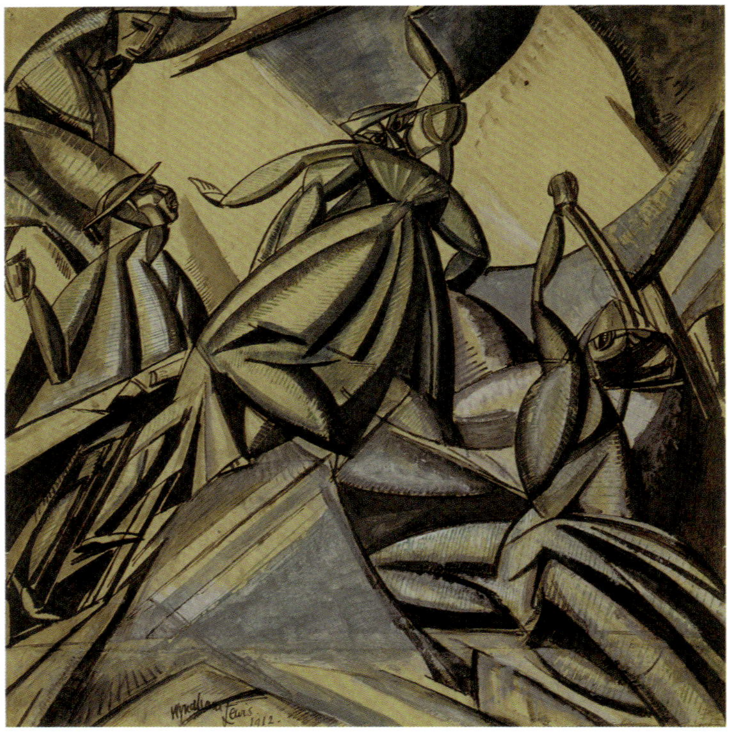

FIG. 49 Wyndham Lewis, study for *Kermesse*, 1912. Gouache, watercolour, pen and black ink, wash and graphite on medium, smooth, beige wove paper, 30.2 x 30.5 cm. Yale Center for British Art, New Haven. Paul Mellon Fund and Gift of Neil F. and Ivan E. Phillips in memory of their mother, Mrs Rosalie Phillips

Rubens on view in the National Gallery in London (*A View of Het Steen in the Early Morning* prime among them) appealed to a war-weary public and, because of their intimate relationship to Gainsborough and Constable, occupied a cherished place in the genealogy of British art. Visitors to the National Gallery were encouraged to see a family resemblance between *A View of Het Steen in the Early Morning* and Constable's *The Hay Wain*, and

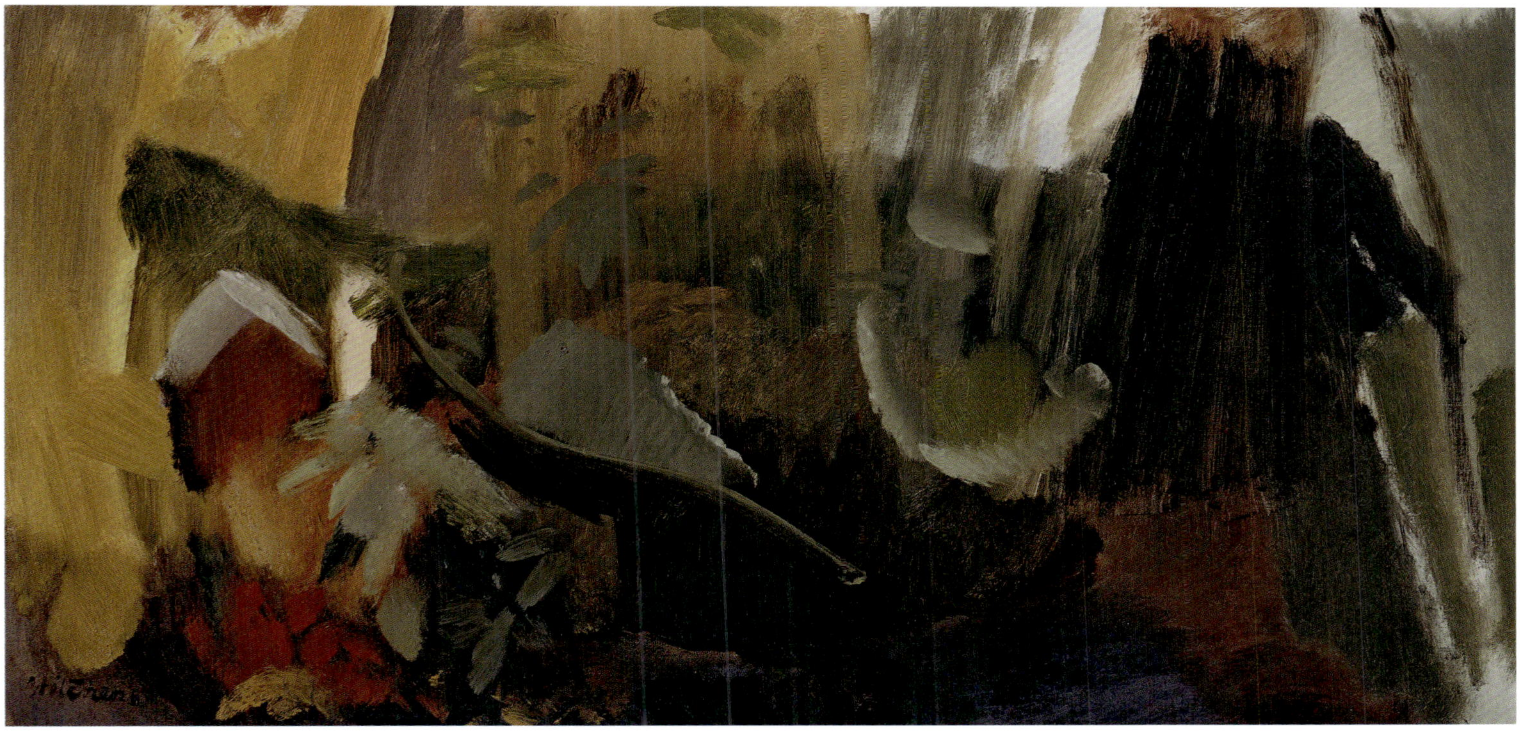

between Gainsborough's *The Watering Place* and similar pictures by Rubens.[33] Neo-Romantic artists of the inter-war years, such as John Piper, Graham Sutherland and Ivon Hitchens (fig. 50), deeply influenced by the European avant-gardes, turned back to the local, even insular, tradition of Gainsborough and Constable. The resulting works, often elegiac in tone and autumnal in shading, represent, once again, a turn from epic to pastoral, from global to local, from general to particular, re-enacting Rubens's own move from history painting to landscape in the last years of his life.

FIG. 50 Ivon Hitchens, *Autumn*, *c.* 1936–40. Oil on canvas, 52.1 x 104.8 cm. National Gallery of Canada, Ottawa

The *Landscape with Rainbow* (fig. 51), painted during the mid-1630s, marks Rubens's triumphant achievement of a synthesis between the traditions of the classical pastoral and a natural vision of landscape. The two swains beneath the tree to the left, each paired with a buxom shepherdess, are unmistakably derived from the literary tradition of Virgil's *Eclogues*: the semi-naked figure on the left is loosely derived from classical sculpture, while to the right of him sits the other swain, enjoying a moment of reverie between playing airs on the pan pipes. By contrast, another amorous couple in the centre foreground, who seem to have drained the contents of a substantial copper flask of beer or wine, belong more firmly to the present day. Their intertwined bodies and the flirtatious, if not lustful, set of the man's face suggest the erotic pleasures of Titian's *Concert Champêtre* (sometimes attributed to Giorgione; see fig. 41).[1]

The lofty mountains in the distance have no analogue in the Low Countries: Rubens seems to have derived them from a *c.* 1540 woodcut by Domenico Campagnola, *Landscape with Hurdy-gurdy Player*.[2] The scale and deployment of figures recall the pastorals of Annibale Carracci (1560–1609). These allusions to the cultured, southern-European world of classical poetry, and its analogues in Venetian painting in the circle of Titian, are balanced by the carefully elaborated flock of sheep, picked out in sunlight and occupying the centre of the composition. The livestock, the Flemish-looking farm buildings and village behind, the bridge and the weir all speak of patient observation in the farmlands of Brabant. Such is Rubens's mastery of chiaroscuro that the disparate elements of the composition fold together to create a compelling, indeed dramatic, totality. The picture is structured by the effects of bright sunlight and deep shadows, portending the arrival of a summer thunderstorm. The spectacular double rainbow appears where the two weather conditions meet in the distance.

In a slightly earlier version of the composition (early 1630s; State Hermitage Museum, St Petersburg), the farmland is less lavishly stocked and the figures are more sharply drawn. The rustic characters in the St Petersburg canvas seem to be neglecting their sheep, suggesting a moral critique of idleness; in the present version, however, the animals seem as content as their masters, well fed and placid, with only the sharply angled muzzle of the whippet-like sheepdog indicating any concern at the dramatic weather beyond.

The painterly and dramatic qualities of Rubens's rainbow landscapes exerted a powerful influence over British painters in the Romantic era. A panoramic scene of the Het Steen estate at harvest time, now known as *The Rainbow Landscape* (*c.* 1636; Wallace Collection, London) was in London from 1802, and widely admired. The upper third of the composition is dominated by a magnificent single rainbow. A dissenting opinion on Rubens was voiced by J. M. W. Turner, who studied *Landscape with Rainbow* in the Louvre in 1802. Finding it 'defective in light', the young English painter objected to 'the vivid Blue in the distance which is another instance of his distorting what he was ignorant of – natural effect'.[3]

Turner's contemporary and rival, John Constable, knew the Wallace Collection painting, which he saw in 1804, and almost certainly encountered the composition of the present work through an engraving entitled *Shepherds and Shepherdesses in a Rainbow Landscape*

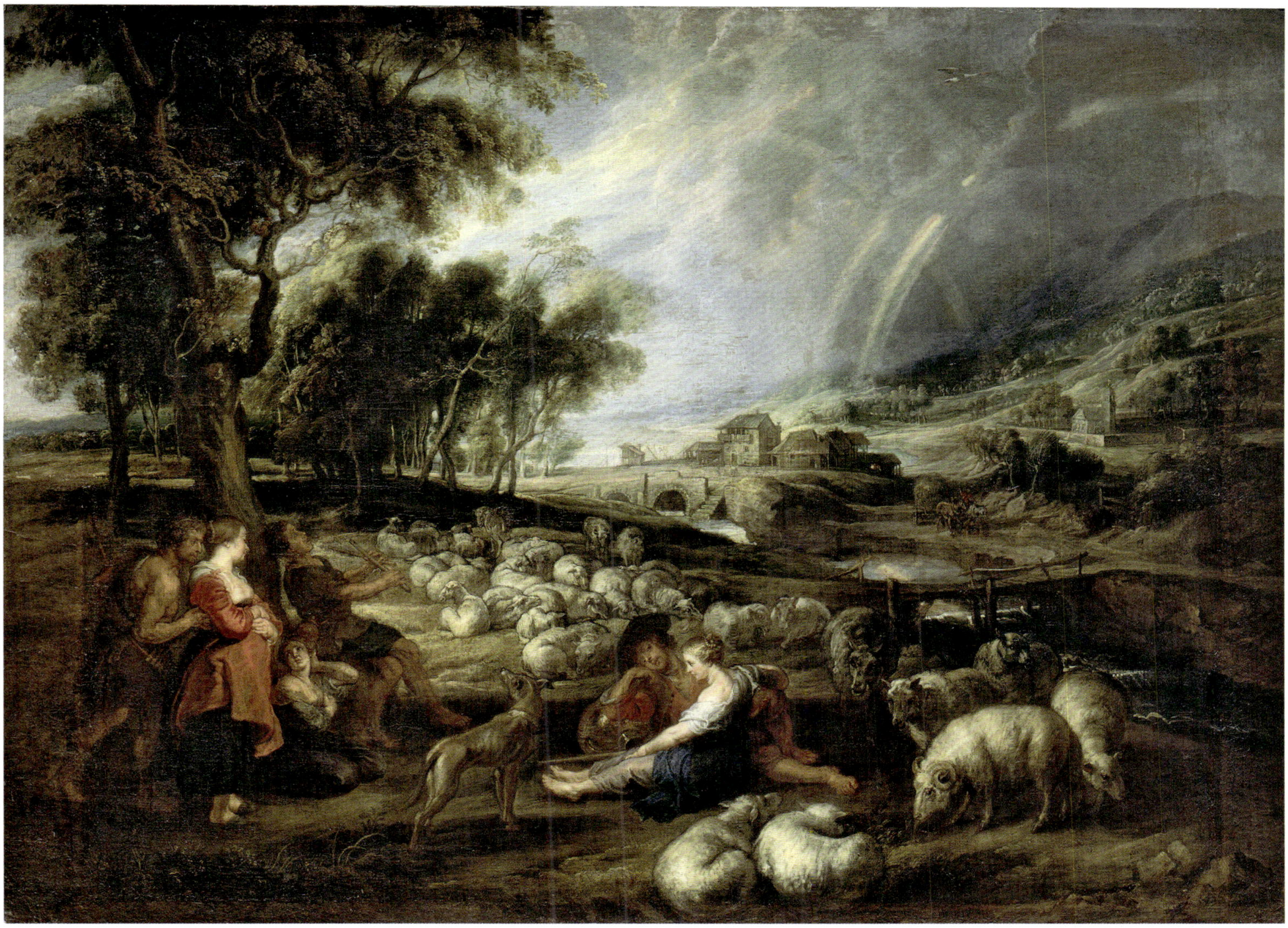

FIG. 51 Peter Paul Rubens, *Landscape with Rainbow*, mid-1630s, Oil on canvas, 123 x 172 cm. On long-term loan to Musée des Beaux-Arts de Valenciennes. Lent by Musée du Louvre, Paris

by Schelte Adamsz. Bolswert after the St Petersburg version of *Landscape with Rainbow*. The rainbow became an emblem of the Flemish painter, as Constable made clear in his third lecture at the Royal Academy: 'By the Rainbow of Rubens, I do not allude to a particular picture, for Rubens often introduced it.'[4] The rainbow emerged as a motif in perhaps the most ambitious and dramatic of all Constable's 'six-footers' (the exhibition pieces of the 1820s and 1830s that are his finest public utterances): *Salisbury Cathedral from the Meadows* of 1831 (fig. 47). It appeared once again in one of Constable's last, and most adventurous, paintings, perhaps as a valedictory homage to Rubens. The anodyne title, *Cottage at East Bergholt* (cat. 119), hardly prepares the viewer for the turbulence of this substantial sketch, largely created with a palette knife. An extra section of canvas, nine inches wide, was added at the right to facilitate the addition of the rainbow, which, here as in *Salisbury Cathedral from the Meadows*, was an inspired afterthought.

As a mill owner's son, Constable was well aware of the impact of storms on the process of harvesting. Under the rainbow to the right of the painting can be seen a row of reapers, battling against time – the very men he had depicted in far greater detail in *The Wheat Field* (1815–16; Sterling and Francine Clark Art Institute, Williamstown).[5] The kinetic frenzy of the brushwork reveals Constable's process: this studio work represents an intermediate phase between small sketches made on the spot, and a planned later version with much higher finish, destined for exhibition at the Royal Academy. This is no sketch from nature, but rather a palimpsest of themes from earlier works, including a drawing from 1817 and several works from the 1820s, all based on recollections of the village where he was born. In this case, Constable died before making a finished version for submission to the Royal Academy, so the English painter's last homage to the Rubensian rainbow remains at this raw, expressive stage. Both here and in *Salisbury Cathedral from the Meadows*, despite the turbulent darkness of the foreground, Constable gives us the very characteristics he saw in the landscapes of Rubens: 'dewy light and freshness, the departing shower, with the exhilaration of the returning sun'.[6] TB

119

JOHN CONSTABLE (1776–1837)
Cottage at East Bergholt, *c.* 1833
Oil on canvas, 87.5 x 112 cm
Lady Lever Art Gallery, Liverpool, inv. LL 3120

PROVENANCE: Henry Engelheart soon after 1834; (?) Sir John Charles Robinson; James Orrock, 1893; W. H. Lever, later Lord Leverhulme, 1904; by whom given to the Lady Lever Art Gallery, 1922
SELECTED REFERENCES: Parris, Fleming-Williams and Shields 1976, no. 329; Reynolds 1984, no. 36.20; Parris and Fleming-Williams 1991, no. 217, pp. 378–79

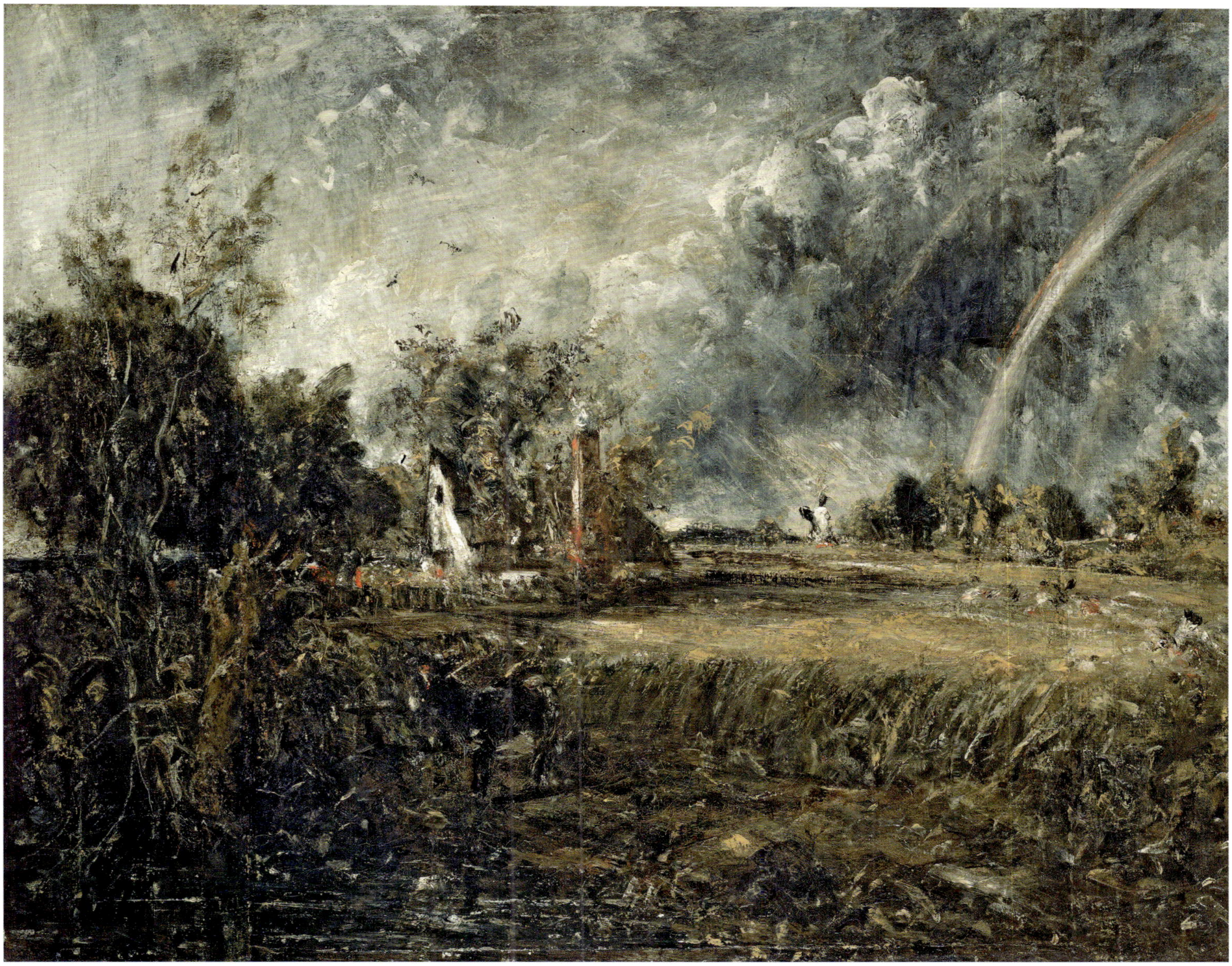

Replete with earthy tones and brimming with natural fecundity, *The Carters* (cat. 120) is an enigmatic composition that has prompted much scholarly discussion. In it Rubens is close to Netherlandish precedents. The strange natural phenomenon of the cleft in a rocky outcrop recalls fantastical hillsides in the work of Joachim Patinir, a Flemish sixteenth-century artist, which Rubens certainly knew.[1] The vigorously designed tree to the right suggests an acknowledgement of drawings and etchings of natural scenery by Rubens's contemporary Roelandt Savery.[2] Although many details are carefully observed from nature, the painting seems to demand allegorical interpretation. It juxtaposes a daylight pastoral landscape to the right, a nocturne with a rising moon where figures sit round a campfire to the left, and the massive outcrop of rock in the centre. To some this has suggested the allegory of mankind forced to choose between good and evil, while others have argued that it represents an unusual lighting effect observed from nature.[3] Lisa Vergara convincingly describes *The Carters* as a 'cosmological landscape', noting that Rubens pointedly includes the four elements – earth, air, water and fire – all seemingly held in balance.[4] In the microcosm surrounding the unfortunate carters, struggling to convey their heavy load across difficult terrain, are found all the elements of the macrocosm, the universe beyond. The painting represents both a specific country scene and the general principle of the harmonious relationship of all the parts of the universe.

Almost square in format, the panel *Evening Landscape with Timber Wagon* (cat. 121) is a smaller and more straightforward work probably painted some years after *The Carters*. Once

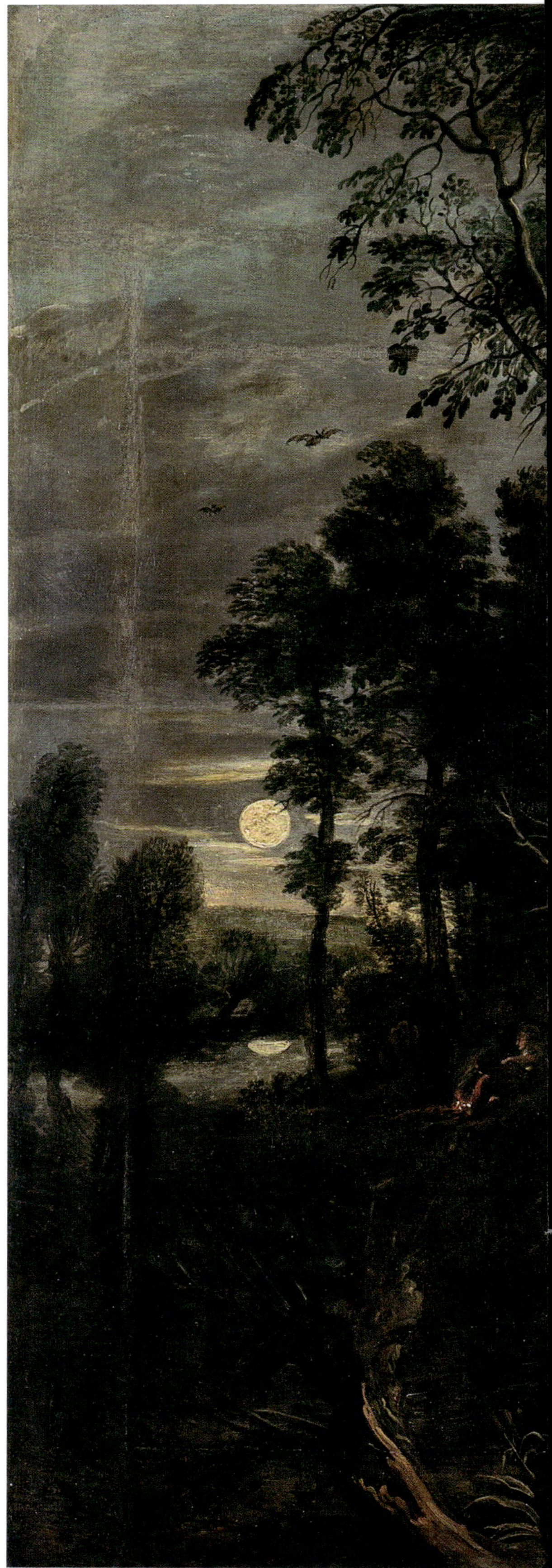

120

PETER PAUL RUBENS (1577–1640)
The Carters, *c.* 1629
Oil on canvas transferred from panel, 87 x 129 cm
State Hermitage Museum, St Petersburg, inv. GE 480

PROVENANCE: (?) Cardinal Mazarin, Paris, 1661; D. Potter, sale, The Hague, 19 May 1723, lot 144; 1st Earl of Cadogan; sale of Cadogan coll., London, 14–22 February 1726; Robert Walpole, 1st Earl of Orford, 1728 Arlington St, 1736 Downing St (Lady Walpole's Drawing Room), later Houghton Hall, Norfolk (Gallery); sold by George Walpole, 3rd Earl of Orford (1730–1791), to Catherine II, Empress of Russia, in 1779
SELECTED REFERENCES: Walpole 1762, p. 85; Evers 1942, p. 392; Evers 1943, p. 176; Adler 1982, no. 19; Vergara 1982, pp. 48–55; Brown 1996, pp. 49–51

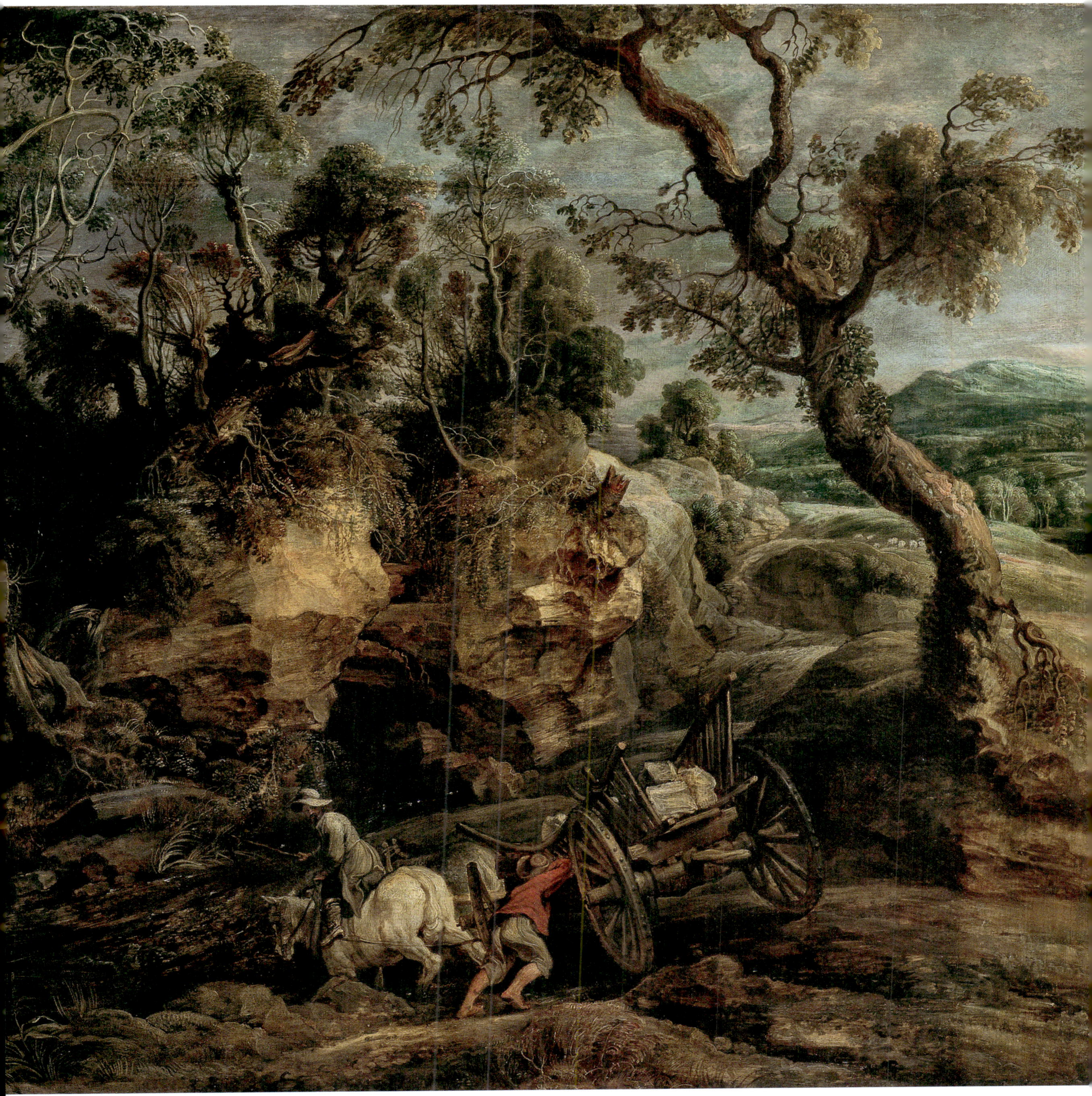

121

PETER PAUL RUBENS (1577–1640)
Evening Landscape with Timber Wagon, 1630–40
Oil on panel, 49.5 x 54.7 cm
Museum Boijmans Van Beuningen, Rotterdam, inv. 2514

PROVENANCE: John Jeffreys Pratt, 1st Marquess Camden, sale, Christie's, London, 4 March 1809, lot 102; George Pratt, 2nd Marquess Camden, sale, Christie's, London, 3 May 1856, lot 707; T. Baring, Earl of Northbrook; Frans Koenigs, Haarlem, 1928; D. G. van Beuningen, Vierhouten; Museum Boijmans Van Beuningen, 1955
SELECTED REFERENCES: Evers 1942, p. 392; Evers 1943, p. 176; Adler 1982, no. 19; Vergara 1982, pp. 48–55; Brown 1996, pp. 49–51

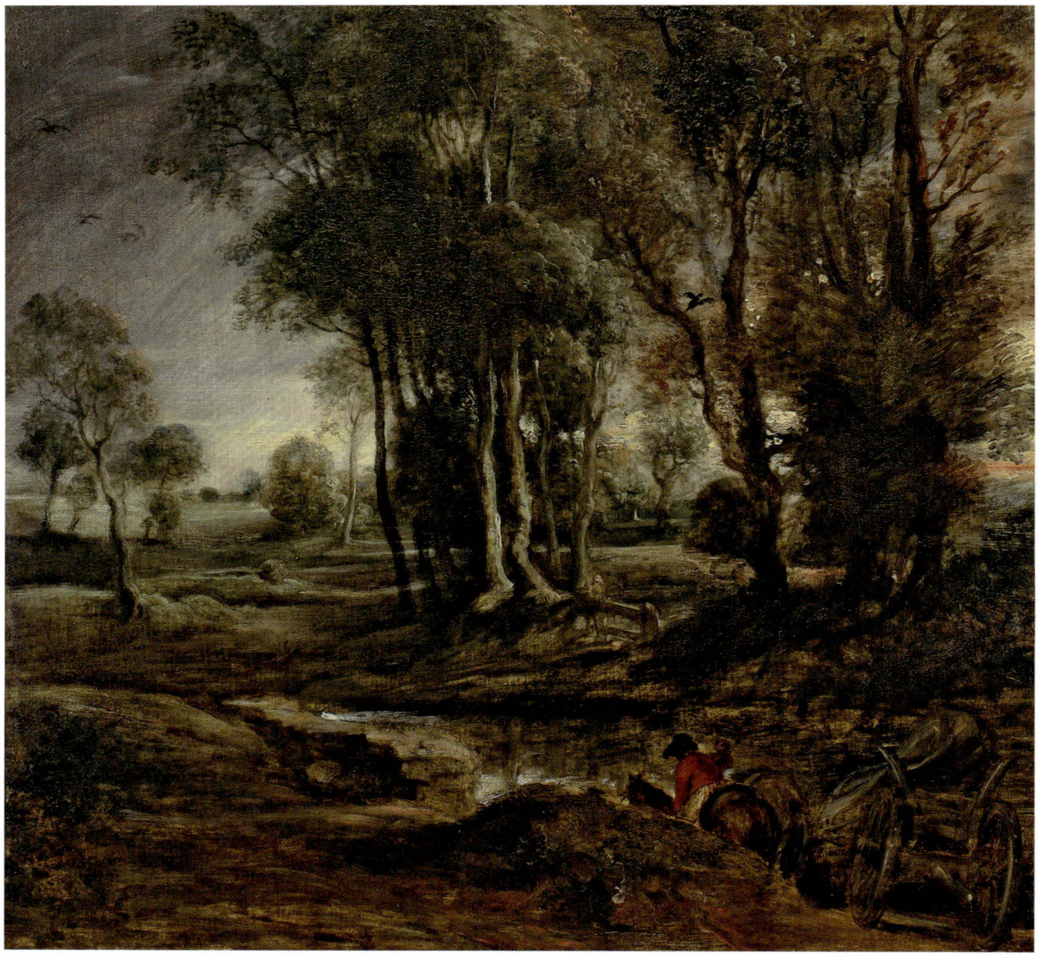

again the trundling wagon is set in the foreground negotiating uneven terrain. This later work (probably based on an unfinished sketch in oil and chalk at the National Gallery, London), is supremely evocative, catching the last embers of the setting sun through a group of trees. While providing ravishing pleasure for the eyes, Rubens also appeals to the other senses: birds are calling in the trees while others circle over the fields to the left; and the painting evokes the rich, bosky smells of a damp hedgerow in the late summer sun. The cosmological complexities of *The Carters* have been set aside and, nearing the end of his long life, Rubens seems simply to have enjoyed transcribing in richly layered oil paint the spectacular end of a warm day in the Brabant plains. Confident enough to leave large areas broadly brushed and with little detail, Rubens nonetheless notes the tiny studs on the wheels of the cart. The driver, a rough, georgic figure standing for the timeless labours of the countryside, seems oblivious to the chromatic display above his head.

The landscapes of Rubens were sought out by English patrons. *The Carters* seems to have been in the collection of Cardinal Mazarin, in Paris, by 1661; it passed through several hands before being purchased before 1728 by Robert Walpole, 1st Earl of Orford, who ultimately displayed it at Houghton Hall, his seat in Norfolk. Probably the best known of Rubens's landscapes in eighteenth-century England, *The Carters*

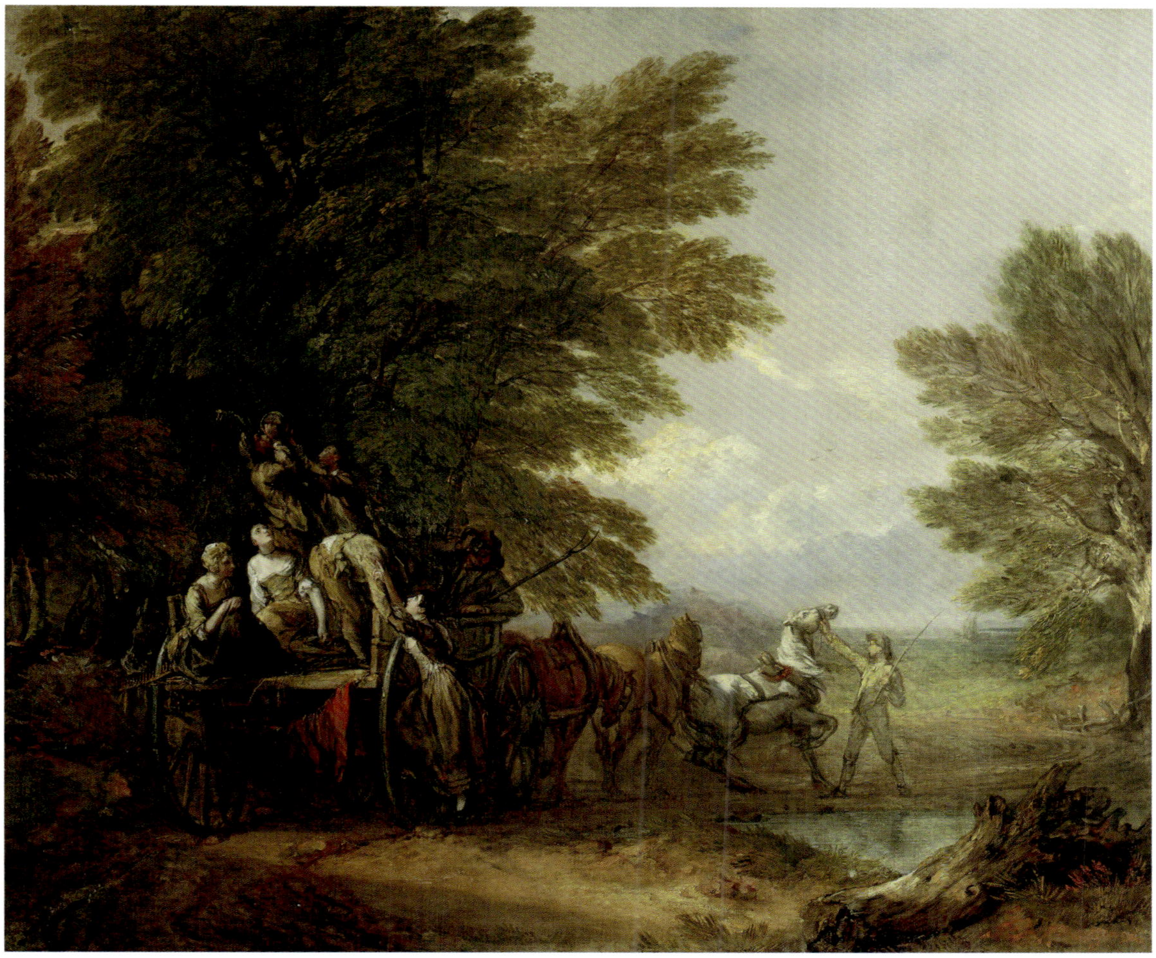

122

THOMAS GAINSBOROUGH (1727–1788)
The Harvest Wagon, 1767
Oil on canvas, 120.5 x 144.7 cm
The Barber Institute of Fine Arts, University of Birmingham, inv. 46.8. The Henry Barber Trust

PROVENANCE: presented by the artist to Walter Wiltshire, 1774; John Wiltshire sale, Christie's, London, 25 May 1867, lot 126; Sir Dudley Marjoribanks; Sir Samuel Montagu, 1904; Barber Institute, 1946
SELECTED REFERENCES: Hayes 1963, pp. 92–94; Pointon 1979, p. 49; Barrell 1980, pp. 59–62; Gordon 1981, p. 18; Hayes 1982, vol. 2, no. 88, pp. 427–30; Rosenthal 1999, pp. 210–14; Rosenthal and Myrone 2002, no. 43, pp. 108–09

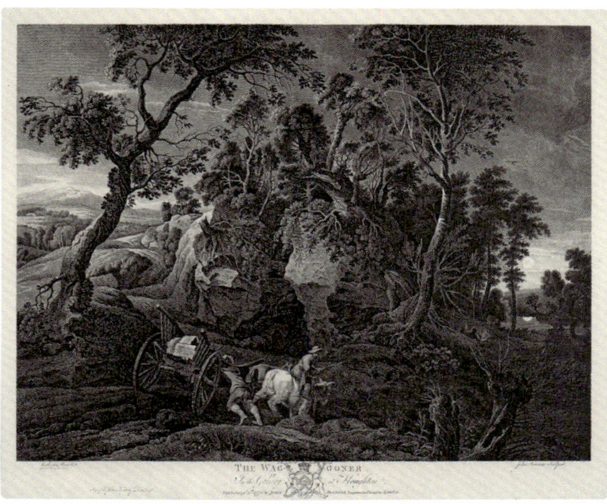

FIG. 52 John Browne, after Joseph Farington, *The Waggoner*, 1776. Engraving and etching on paper, 47.0 x 58.3 cm. Victoria and Albert Museum, London

mainstay of the collection at Houghton until it was sold to Catherine the Great for the Hermitage in 1779.[5] *The Carters* was published in the catalogue of the collection by Walpole's son Horace, and is discussed in the younger Walpole's *Anecdotes of Painting in England*.[6] Copies of the Houghton pictures, including Joseph Farington's chalk drawing after *The Carters* (then entitled *The Waggoner*), were exhibited at Boydell's Gallery from 1774.[7] Boydell commissioned a print after Farington's chalk copy from the distinguished etcher and engraver John Browne; it too was entitled *The Waggoner*, and was published in 1776 (fig. 52).

Evening Landscape with Timber Wagon was in various London collections throughout the nineteenth century, leaving for Holland only in 1928.[8] English landscape painters of the Romantic era, recognising scenery similar to their own, found special poignancy in this intimate work. Thomas Gainsborough may have seen *The Carters*, or a copy that was in the collection of Nuneham House, Oxfordshire;[9] he almost certainly saw the *Evening Landscape with Timber Wagon* when it was in the collection of John Pratt, 1st Marquess Camden, whom Gainsborough remembered 'with a degree of veneration' for 'patronage and favour' during his years in Bath.[10] Gainsborough would certainly have known Browne's engraving and perhaps also that made by Schelte Adamsz. Bolswert in the decade after the painting was completed. His works of the 1760s show a clear debt to Rubens's pastorals.

In *The Harvest Wagon*, completed in 1767 (cat. 122), Gainsborough paid explicit homage to Rubens, though perhaps to an unexpected work.[11] The figural group on the wagon is a sophisticated response to Rubens's *Descent from the Cross* (fig. 27) in Antwerp Cathedral which Gainsborough knew from a sketch in oils then at Corsham Court near Bath (now in the Courtauld Institute of Art Gallery, London), but also through the engraving of 1620 by Lucas Vorsterman. From these sources, Gainsborough prepared a copy in oil on canvas (cat. 90). Although it seems counter-intuitive to transform a sacred subject into a profane scene of rural merrymaking, there is a clear resemblance between the cluster of figures topped by a beer keg on the hay cart and the Antwerp composition. The energetic grouping and interaction of figures is quite unlike anything Gainsborough had achieved before. A second version of *The Harvest Wagon* painted years later in 1784–85 (fig. 53) declares an affiliation with *The Carters*, which is not obvious in the Barber canvas. The Ontario composition includes a mysterious rock formation, a figure to the side of the cart and a gnarled tree to the left. That these elements are reversed from Rubens's composition confirms that here Gainsborough was alluding to one of the engraved versions of *The Carters*.

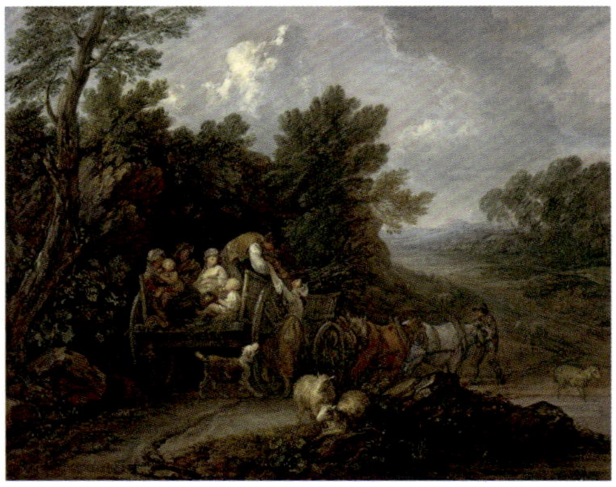

FIG.53 Thomas Gainsborough, *The Harvest Wagon*, 1784–85. Oil on canvas, 121.9 x 149.9 cm. Art Gallery of Ontario, Toronto

The Carters also resonated deeply with another, later, painter from East Anglia: John Constable. Constable's patron Sir George Beaumont was among Rubens's foremost admirers, and surely drew his protégé's attention to prints after the famous painting. More importantly, Beaumont owned the great *A View of Het Steen in the Early Morning* (fig. 40). Constable saw that work in 1804, two years after Beaumont acquired it. Although it was at Coleorton Hall, Beaumont's seat in Leicestershire, from 1808, Constable renewed his acquaintance with the painting when it was included in the British Institution's exhibition of Old Masters in 1815. He also painted a copy of *View of Het Steen* when he visited Coleorton in 1823, and it was available for study at the National Gallery after Beaumont's paintings entered the collection in 1826.

123

JOHN CONSTABLE (1776–1837)
Hampstead Heath, Branch Hill Pond, 1828
Oil on canvas, 59.6 x 77.6 cm
Victoria and Albert Museum, London, FA.35(o). Given by John Sheepshanks
RA ONLY

PROVENANCE: John Sheepshanks, before 1838; by whom given to the South Kensington (later Victoria and Albert) Museum, 1857
SELECTED REFERENCES: Parris, Fleming-Williams and Shields 1976, no. 254; Reynolds 1984, no. 28.2

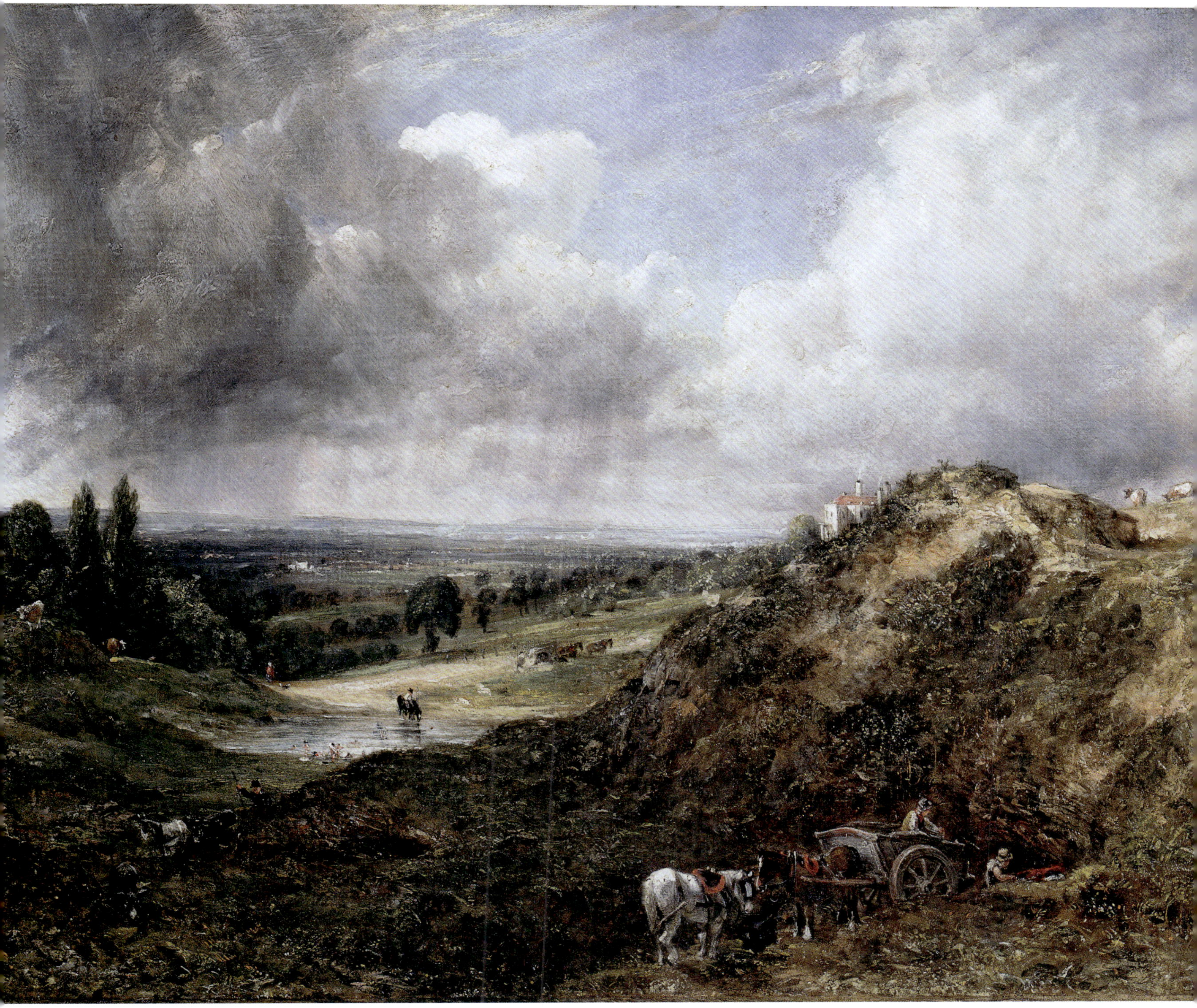

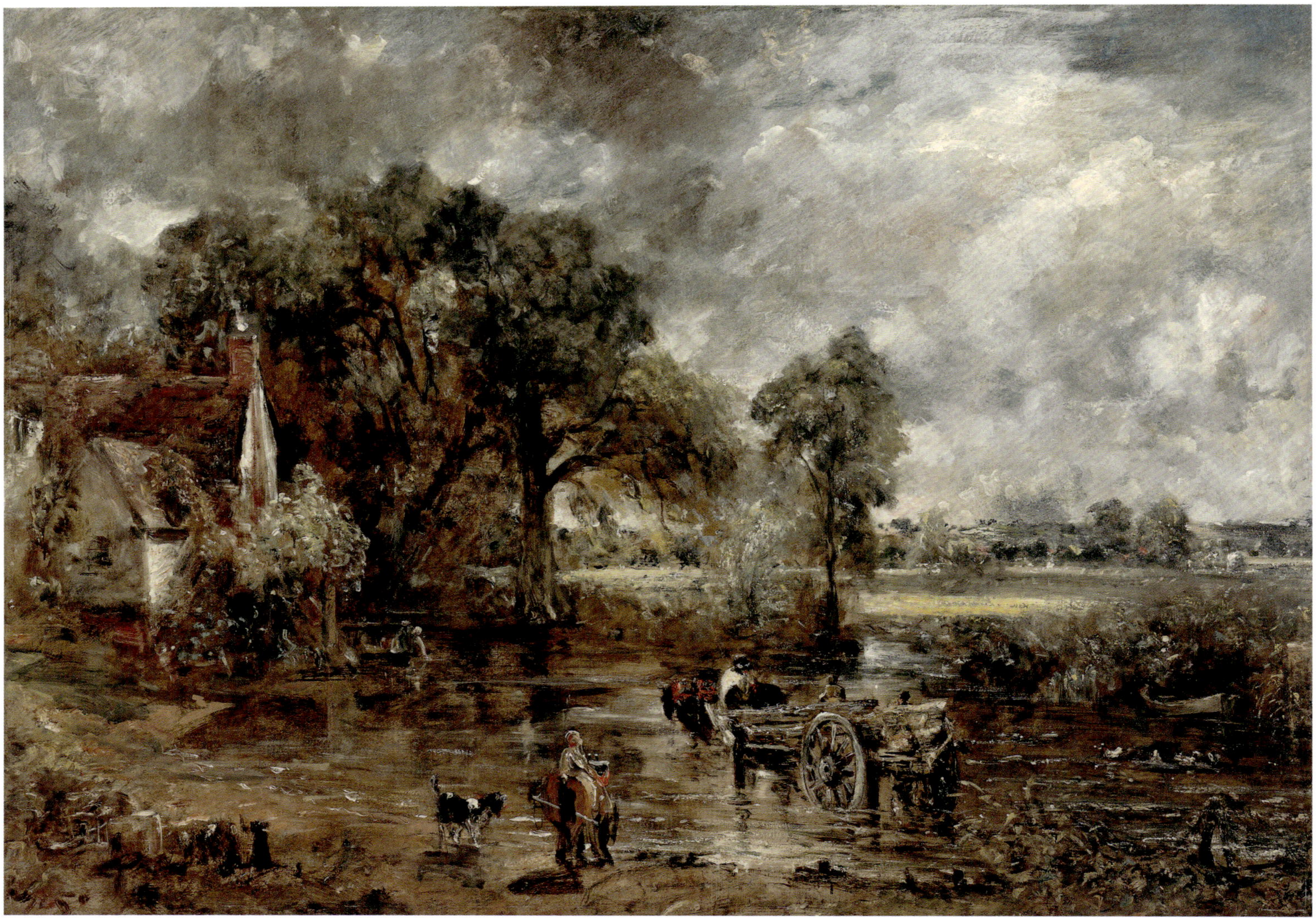

In 1819 Constable made a small oil sketch of Branch Hill Pond, Hampstead Heath, under a stormy sky (Victoria and Albert Museum, London), which established a composition that he was to explore repeatedly over the next decade.[12] The foreground motif of two men with a cart and horses was a recurring trope in Constable's work from 1814, when he made an oil sketch in East Bergholt that he incorporated into *The Stour Valley and Dedham Village* (1814–15; Museum of Fine Arts, Boston). The heavy, Suffolk cart here is being used for the transportation of manure from a 'dungle' to fertilise the fields; the carters in the finished painting of *Hampstead Heath, Branch Hill Pond* exhibited in 1828 (cat. 123) seem, likewise, to be filling their vehicle with loamy soil. To give prominence to such earthy subject-matter in the context of the Royal Academy's exhibitions was to announce a radical manifesto for a realist landscape painting rooted in Rubens's practices. Whether Constable's placid rural labourers constitute a self-conscious reference to Rubens's anguished rustics in *The Carters* is a matter for debate.

Perhaps the most Rubensian of all Constable's paintings is also his most celebrated: *The Hay Wain* (fig. 46), exhibited in 1821 as *Landscape: Noon*. Although he had sketched Willy Lott's house at East Bergholt numerous times, the composition of *The Hay Wain* is derived from a small oil sketch (12.5 x 18 cm) now in the Yale Center for British Art, New Haven. Following a practice established for *The White Horse* (1819; Frick Collection, New York), Constable then prepared a freely executed oil sketch virtually the same size as the finished work. The full-size sketch, exhibited here (cat. 124), shows Constable working out the masses of the composition, leaving large areas bereft of the myriad details that were to dazzle audiences seeing the final version when it was exhibited at the Royal Academy in 1821 and, to spectacular effect, at the Paris Salon of 1824: 'one felt the freshness ... one saw a luxuriant, verdant nature, without blackness, crudity of mannerisms', recalled the painter Paul Huet of his first sight of *The Hay Wain*.[13]

The Hay Wain combines the Rubensian motif of the carters stymied by the forces of nature with a sweeping composition ultimately paying homage to *A View of Het Steen in the Early Morning*. Successive stages of compositional planning saw Constable open up the vista to the right, just as Rubens delivers the viewer's eye to the horizon in his great panoramic landscape. There is a cart at the extreme left of the Het Steen composition, but *The Hay Wain* seems closer in spirit to *The Carters*. A hay wain was lighter and longer than the heavy vehicles used for moving soil or muck, and larger than the distinctive Netherlandish wagon in *The Carters* with its high, slatted sides. A hay wain had to move quickly to transport the dried grass at the perfect moment. If carting occurred too soon, or too late, the hay would rot and there would be no winter feed for the cattle. Constable carefully indicates the processes of haymaking in the right distance, where we can see white-shirted men at work in the fields. The carters in *The Hay Wain* are hurrying to collect the harvest, but they have paused, anxious perhaps about the depth of the water.[14] Mankind is not stretched to the limits that Rubens depicts in *The Carters*, but nature still has the upper hand. The sky, painted with Rubensian energy, indicates the

124

JOHN CONSTABLE (1776–1837)
Full-scale sketch for *The Hay Wain*, *c.* 1821
Oil on canvas, 137 x 188 cm
Victoria and Albert Museum, London, inv. 987-1888. Bequeathed by Henry Vaughan
RA ONLY

PROVENANCE: probably the artist's sale, Foster's, London, May 1838 (part of lot 38); D. T. White by *c.* 1854; Henry Vaughan by 1862; by whom bequeathed to the Victoria and Albert Museum, 1900
SELECTED REFERENCES: Parris, Fleming-Williams and Shields 1976, no. 190; Gage 1980, p. 250; Reynolds 1984, no. 21.2; Parris and Fleming-Williams 1991, p. 204

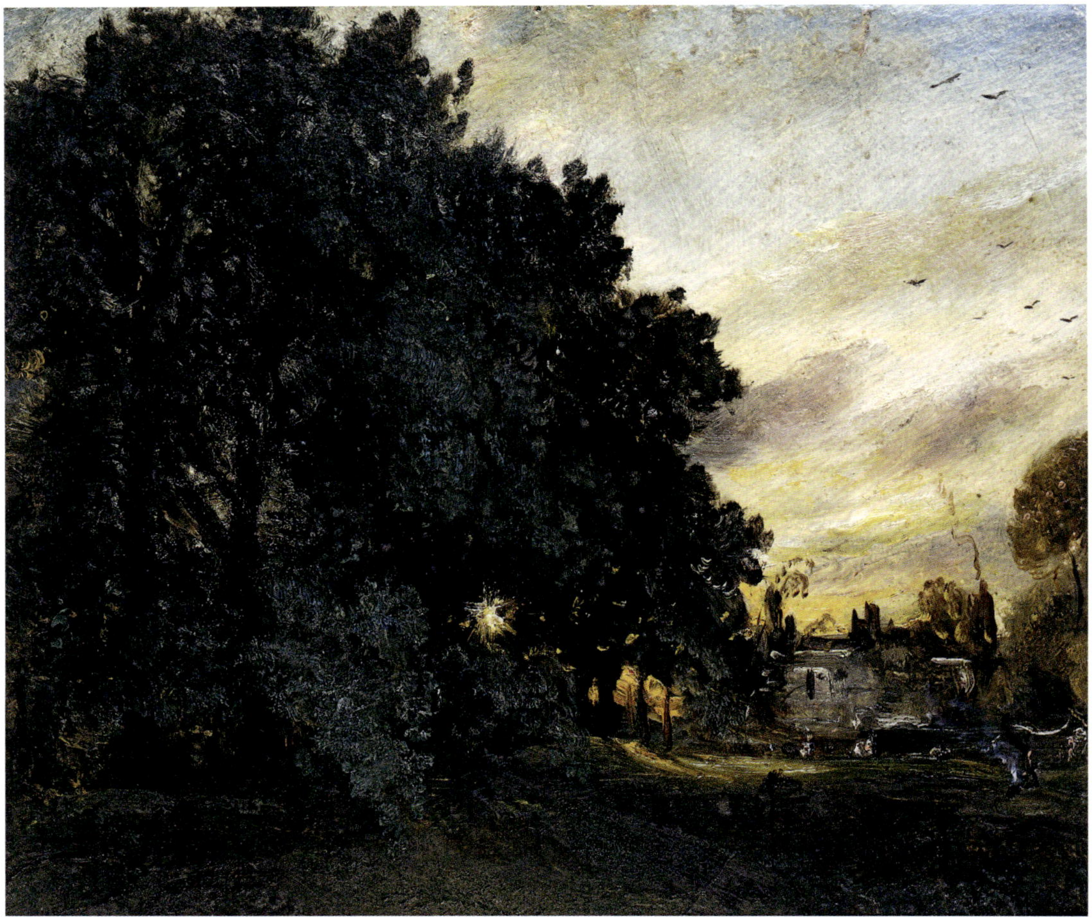

125

JOHN CONSTABLE (1776–1837)
Study of a House Among Trees: Evening, 1823
Oil on paper, 25.1 x 30.7 cm
Inscribed in pencil by the artist on the back Saturday Evg 4th Oct 1823
Victoria and Albert Museum, London, inv. 152-1888. Given by Isabel Constable, 1888
BOZAR ONLY

PROVENANCE: Isabel Constable; by whom given to the South Kensington (later Victoria and Albert) Museum in 1888
SELECTED REFERENCES: Reynolds 1984, no. 23.23

recent passage of a storm that has perhaps caused flooding.

It is quite possible that Constable also saw the *Evening Landscape with Timber Wagon* (cat. 121) when it was in the collection of Marquess Camden. One of Constable's most exquisite oil sketches from the Hampstead years, *Study of a House Among Trees: Evening* (cat. 125), shares a sense of revelation as the dying sun bursts through rich foliage just before disappearing over the horizon. Although two centuries separate the two works, the handling of oil paint is strikingly similar.

Constable's great rival J. M. W. Turner was less explicit in his admiration of Rubens, avowedly preferring the historical landscapes of Claude as an object of emulation. Nonetheless, many of his works bear the imprint of Rubens. *The Forest of Bere* (cat. 126), exhibited in 1808, was based on sketches Turner made in woodland north of Portsmouth, where he was to watch the return of the triumphant British fleet after the surrender of the Danish navy at Copenhagen in 1807. National identity is understood in much more intimate terms in this poetic interpretation of English woodlands at sunset.[15] An interest in local agricultural pursuits is shared with Rubens: individuals in the foreground here are removing the bark from chestnut branches, providing raw materials for the tanning industry. Turner's contemporary, the engraver John Landseer, admired this work and compared it favourably to the cattle paintings of the Dutch seventeenth-century artist Aelbert Cuyp.[16]

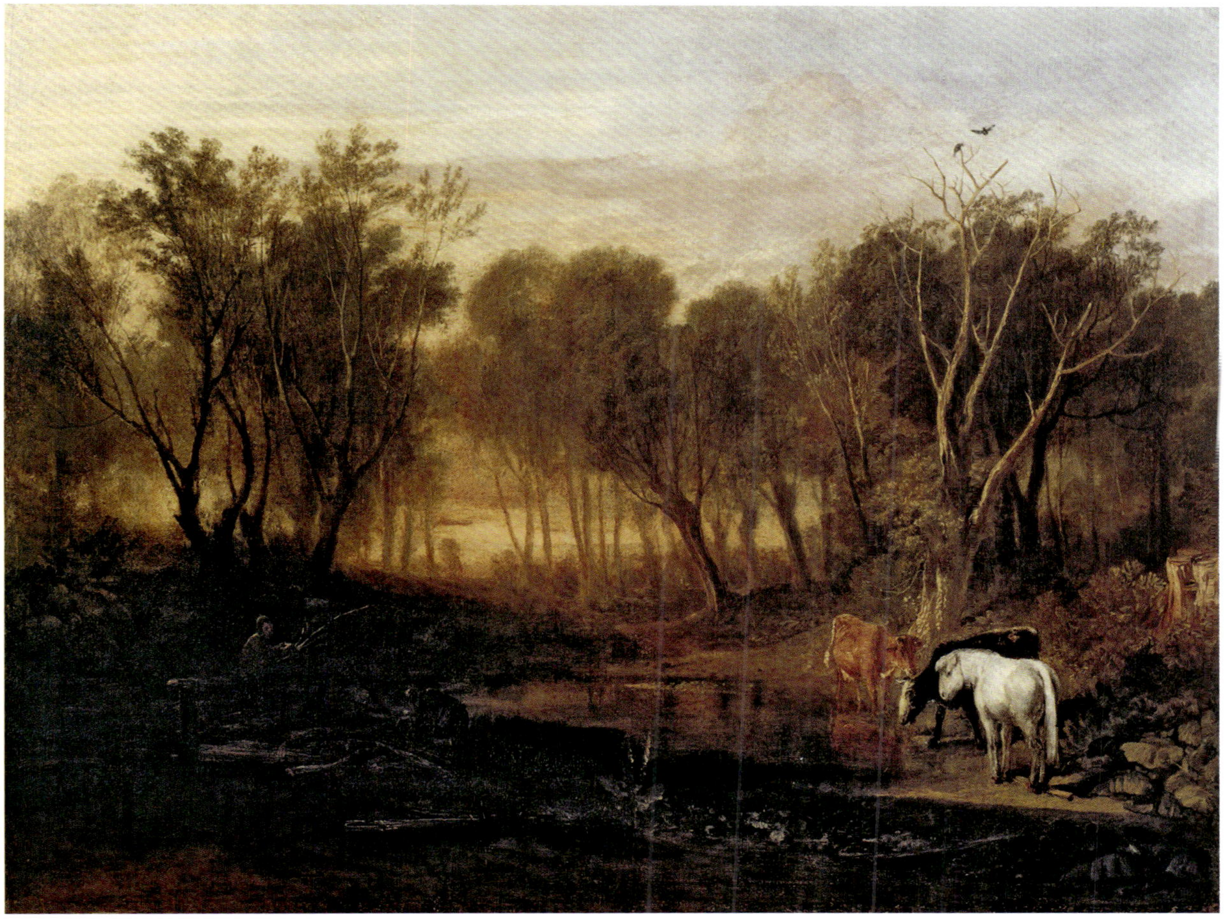

But the rich colour, the opulent impasto and the animated characterisation of the dying tree to the right place the work in close proximity to Rubens's *Evening Landscape with Timber Wagon*. TB

126

JOSEPH MALLORD WILLIAM TURNER (1775–1851)
The Forest of Bere, 1808
Oil on canvas, 89 x 119.5 cm
Tate. Accepted by HM Government in lieu of tax and allocated to the Tate Gallery, 1984. *In situ* at Petworth House

PROVENANCE: bought by Lord Egremont from Turner's gallery in 1808; by descent to the third Lord Leconfield who in 1947 conveyed Petworth to the National Trust; in 1957 the contents of the State Rooms were accepted by the Treasury in part-payment of death duties
SELECTED REFERENCES: Finberg 1961, pp. 146, 149, 469, no. 122; Herrmann 1975, pp. 19, 229; Joll 1977, p. 375; Butlin and Joll 1984, no. 77, vol. 1, pp. 58–59

Château in a Park (cat. 127), Rubens's idyll of genteel amusement in the grounds of a moated castle, is a distinctive contribution to a Flemish courtly tradition of paintings representing outdoor music, dancing, feasting and flirtation. A fine example of this tradition is David Vinckboons's *Merry Company in the Open Air* (*c.* 1610; Gemäldegalerie der Akademie der bildenden Künste, Vienna).[1]

Recent scholarship has rejected the identification of the castle setting with Rubens's own country estate, Het Steen, in Brabant. The building shown does not seem to relate to a particular place, but is rather a fantasy of a northern European moated and fortified manor.[2] Certainly Rubens appreciated the delights of a crenellated rural seat, and enjoyed the title of 'Lord of Steen' that accompanied ownership of his property. So perhaps we see here a fantastical rendering of his ideal country residence. Rubens's composition frames the castle between extensive areas of planted trees, which, on the right, form an avenue. A sizeable estate is indicated in the background, leading to a ridge of wooded hills. We are in the demesne of a noble of considerable means. The sky, unmistakably northern, is filled with cloud, but this seems to be an afternoon's rather than an evening's revelry.

This landscaped parkland sets the scene for merriment of a rather more dynamic nature than the gentrified flirtations of *The Garden of Love* (cat. 130), gesturing, indeed, towards the kind of physical interaction of the sexes found in the *Kermis* drawings (cat. 143). The refined couple at the left are reminiscent of the two entering from the same direction in *The Garden of Love*, and again some scholars have often taken this youthful duo for portraits of Rubens (then in his mid-fifties) and his young bride Hélène Fourment.[3] The gentleman gestures towards a group of three couples, artfully arranged by Rubens into a pyramidal form in the central foreground. The body language reveals that male efforts at seduction are being playfully rebuffed. Particularly effective is the sportive male figure who has thrown

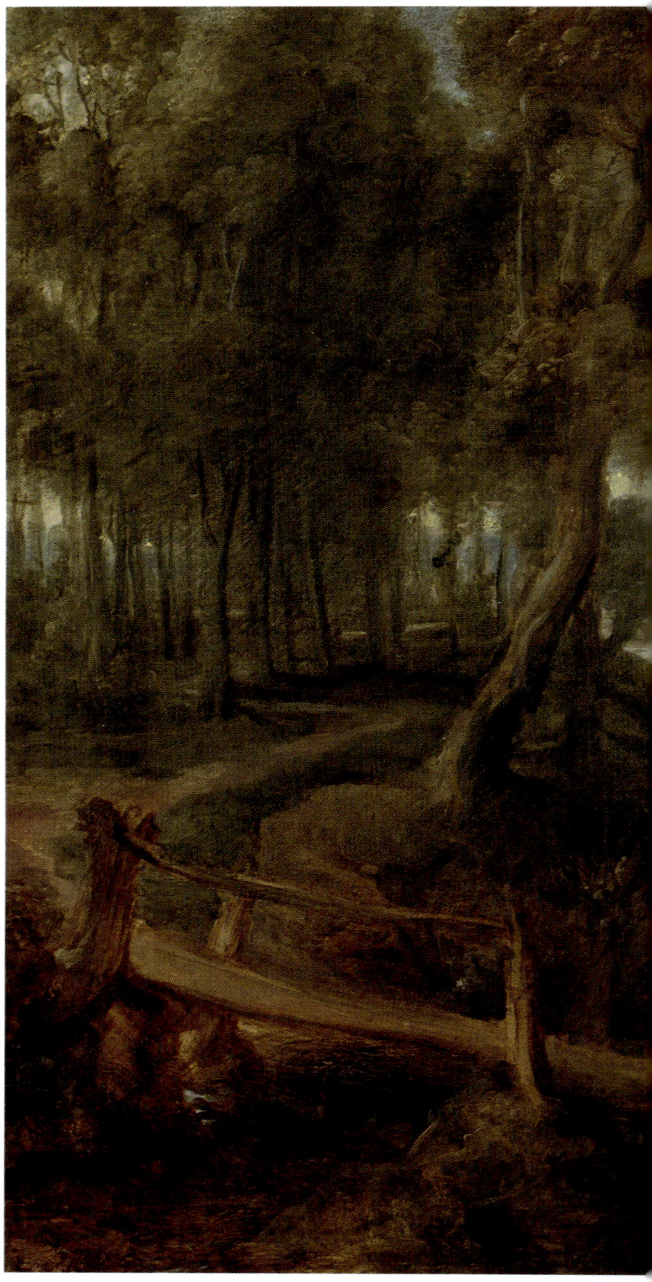

127

PETER PAUL RUBENS (1577–1640)
Château in a Park, *c.* 1632–35
Oil on panel, 52.5 x 97 cm
Kunsthistorisches Museum, Vienna, Gemäldegalerie, inv. 696

PROVENANCE: Imperial collection, Vienna, 1781
SELECTED REFERENCES: Vienna 1977, pp. 132–33; Adler 1982, no. 42; Vergara 1982, p. 66

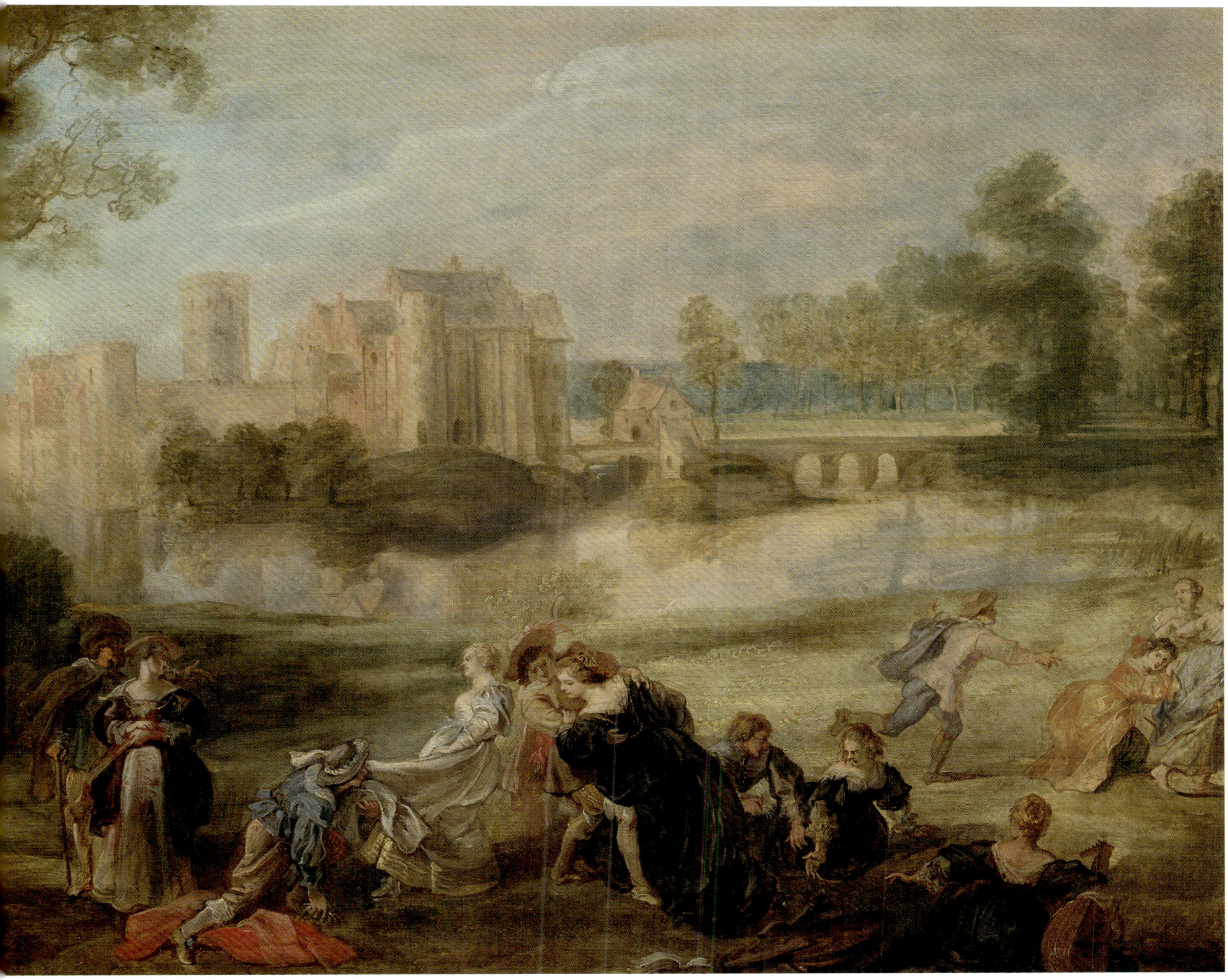

his red cloak to the floor in a dramatic gesture, and now evidently tries to lift the extensive skirts of his paramour, creating a superb baroque swirl of draperies. To the right of this group a female lutenist recoils from the scene. The prominence of this instrument recalls another scene of erotic revelry and music in an Arcadian setting, the famous *Concert Champêtre* by Titian (fig. 41), sometimes attributed to Giorgione, in the Louvre. Music is further represented by the discarded lute, tenor viol and music book of the couple who have just stood up. Further back, and towards the right margin, things are getting out of hand as a young man runs

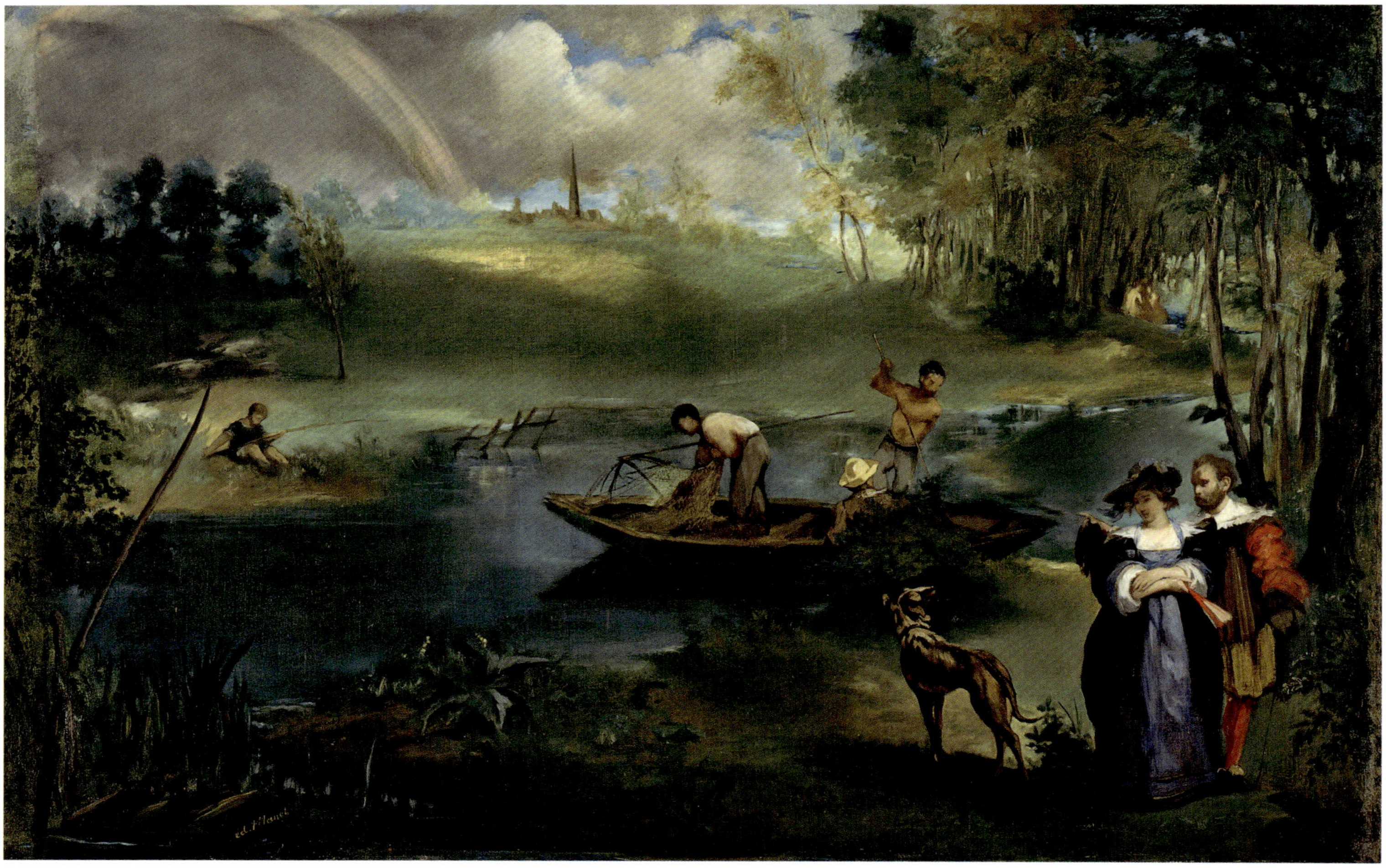

128

ÉDOUARD MANET (1832–1883)
Fishing, *c.* 1862–63
Oil on canvas, 76.8 x 123.2 cm
Lent by The Metropolitan Museum of Art, New York, inv. 57.10. Purchase, Mr and Mrs Richard J. Bernhard Gift, 1957

PROVENANCE: the artist, Paris (until d. 1883); his family and heirs (1883–85); the artist's widow, Suzanne Manet, Paris, 1885–97; Durand-Ruel, Paris, 1897–1950; Société Artistique George V, Paris, 1950–c. 1956; Sam Salz, New York, *c.* 1956–57; sold to the Metropolitan Museum of Art
SELECTED REFERENCES: Reff 1969, p. 46; Cachin and Moffett 1983, pp. 70–74, 330, 405, no. 12; Sutton 1993, pp. 94–95; Armstrong 2002, pp. 26–27, 305; Atlanta 2007, no. 51

at full tilt in pursuit of a maiden who cowers in the arms of a friend, warding him off.

This work has received less scholarly attention than most of Rubens's late paintings, but of all his works is the closest in spirit to Jean-Antoine Watteau's *fête-galante* imagery. Its provenance before 1783 is unknown and it is quite possible that Watteau saw the work or a copy, or an engraving after the work by Schelte Adamsz. Bolswert. Bolswert's print, however, imparts more grandeur to the landscape and understates the flirtations in the foreground.[4]

The painting became the central referent for a *jeu d'esprit* by Edouard

Manet, painted in about 1862–63, a provocative, unstable work notable for its eclectic borrowings and its resistance to interpretation. The work, now known as *Fishing* (cat. 128), is an act of homage to Rubens's landscapes that recalls an early episode in Manet's career. With his friend Antonin Proust, Manet visited the studio of Eugène Delacroix, who, Proust recalled 'received us most graciously ... inquiring as to our preferences and expressing his own: you should look at Rubens, emulate Rubens, copy Rubens. Rubens was his god.'[5] The rich colour palette and painterly quality of the foliage acknowledge the Flemish master as a forebear. In the distance, the rainbow clearly refers to Rubens's *Landscape with Rainbow* (fig. 51). The whippet-like dog has wandered into Manet's composition from the foreground of the same Flemish work. The overall composition of *Fishing*, with the foreground figures and the position of the river immediately behind them, calls to mind *Château in a Park*, though by paraphrase rather than direct quotation.

In *Fishing*, Manet himself and his mistress – and soon-to-be wife – Suzanne Leenhoff take the place of the figures traditionally believed to be Rubens and Hélène, suggesting perhaps that Manet wanted to partake of Rubens's iconography of connubial bliss. Manet playfully dresses himself and Suzanne in clothing of Rubens's era, despite the fact that every other element in the composition could belong to nineteenth-century Paris. This makes yet more explicit the parallels between the two bearded artists, separated in time by more than two centuries.

In the distance to the right are two naked female figures, classical bathers whose presence here hints at the controversy that was to greet *Luncheon On the Grass* (Musée d'Orsay, Paris) in 1863. The mysterious fishing boat has been the subject of scholarly speculation. A possible source for the figure of the bending fisherman has been found in Raphael's cartoon *The Miraculous Draught of Fishes* (*c.* 1515; Victoria and Albert Museum, London).[6]

The family drama unfolds as we examine the diminutive figure of Léon Leenhoff on the far shore. The paternity of Suzanne's son was a subject of uncertainty, although Manet believed himself to be the father. The painting has been dated to between late 1862 and 1863, in part because Manet had concealed the relationship with Suzanne from his father, who died in September 1862. The two were married in October 1863. This peculiar, neo-Baroque presentation of the Manet family brings to mind Rubens's celebrated group portrait of himself, Hélène and their son Frans (*c.* 1635; The Metropolitan Museum of Art, New York), although that work remained in England until 1884, when it passed to the Rothschild collection in Paris. In Rubens's group portrait, Frans's closeness to his mother is signified by reins, which she gently holds to prevent him from wandering. Manet's *Fishing*, in which Léon is placed at implausible distance, provides a striking contrast. TB

Throughout his career Rubens made and bought copies after both old and contemporary art.[1] He was indefatigable in absorbing the most diverse sources and in attempting to understand and improve upon old concepts. This makes Rubens not only a prince and a Homer among painters, but also an art historian. The most important reinterpretations painted by Rubens from Italian models are two copies after Titian: *The Worship of Venus* (1636–38; Nationalmuseum, Stockholm) and *The Andrians* (cat. 129). The subjects of these two paintings were taken from the *Imagines* (I.vi and I.xxv) by Philostratos the Elder, a French translation of which was purchased by Rubens on 25 May 1614. The book describes 64 mythological wall paintings in a villa outside Naples, including a representation of the Island of Andros, where Bacchus had created a river of wine. Crowned with leaves of oak and bryony, the Andrians in Titian's painting (fig. 54) sing and dance on the shore, while a river god reclines on a bed of vines. The bacchantes and satyrs welcome Bacchus' ship, which can be seen in the background as it moors at the island.

Titian created *The Worship of Venus* (Museo del Prado, Madrid) and *The Andrians* around 1518 for Alfonso d'Este, Duke of Ferrara. Together with other mythological works by Giovanni Bellini and Dosso Dossi, they decorated the *camerini* in the Castello Estense at Ferrara. However, it was not there that Rubens discovered the paintings, since Cardinal Pietro Aldobrandini had the pieces conveyed to Rome in 1598. In theory Rubens could have seen the canvases during his visits to the Eternal City in 1602–03 and 1605–08, but this is not very likely, because Titian's masterpieces do not resonate in Rubens's *œuvre* until the 1630s. That he did not see

129

PETER PAUL RUBENS (1577-1640)
The Andrians, after Titian, *c.* 1635
Oil on canvas, 200 x 215 cm
Nationalmuseum, Stockholm, inv. F I 84
BOZAR ONLY

PROVENANCE: in Rubens's possession until his death in 1640 (no. 82); bought before 1645 by Don Francisco de Rochas (Cardinal-Infante Ferdinand's ayuda de Cámara, or chamberlain) on the orders of Philip IV of Spain for 1,800 guilders; presumably identical with the anonymous copy, inventoried in the Sala de la antecámara in the Palacio Real de El Pardo in 1700; recorded in the Antecámara del infante don Luis de Borbón in the Palacio Nuevo in Madrid, 1772; moved, perhaps out of prudishness, to the Academia de San Fernando in 1816; possibly taken to Sweden by Field Marshal Bernadotte (later Karl XIV) in 1810 or to Paris by Joseph Bonaparte after 1814 and subsequently to Sweden by Bernadotte's wife, Désirée, in 1823; recorded in Bernadotte's possession in 1844; donated by Karl XV to the Nationalmuseum in 1865
SELECTED REFERENCES: Nordenfalk 1938, pp. 36–48; Tietze-Conrat 1949–50, pp. 435–36; Grossmann 1951, p. 25; Lohse Belkin 1987, pp. 76–79; Van Hout 2001B, pp. 15–17; Cavalli-Björkman in Munich 2009, pp. 251–54, no. 17; Cavalli-Björkman, Fryklund and Sydén 2010, no. 151; Wood 2010, no. 113

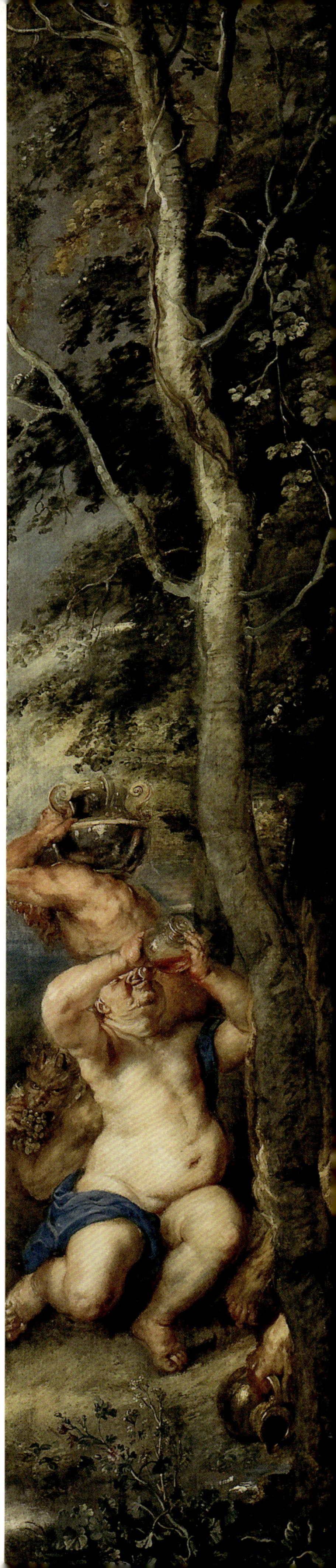

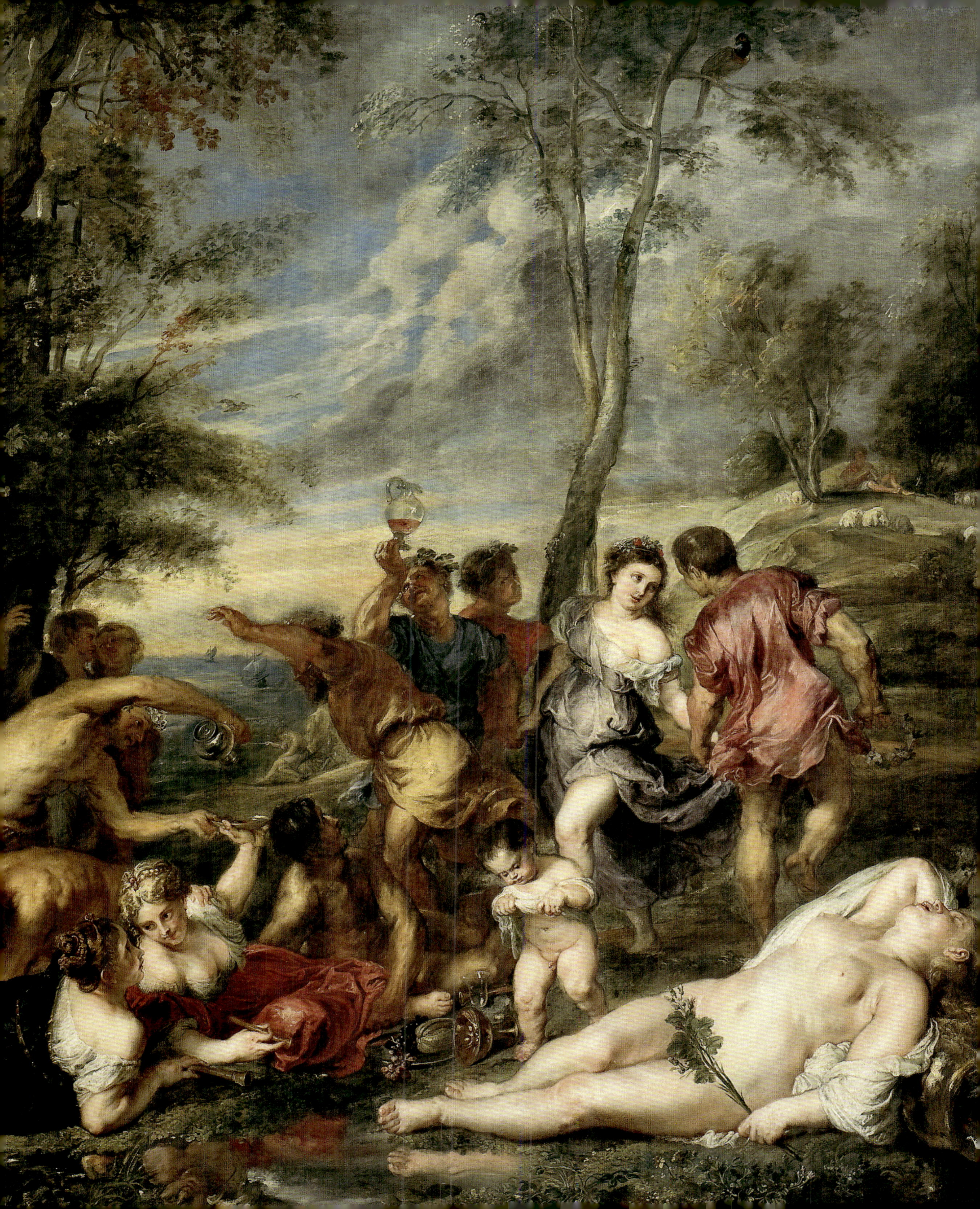

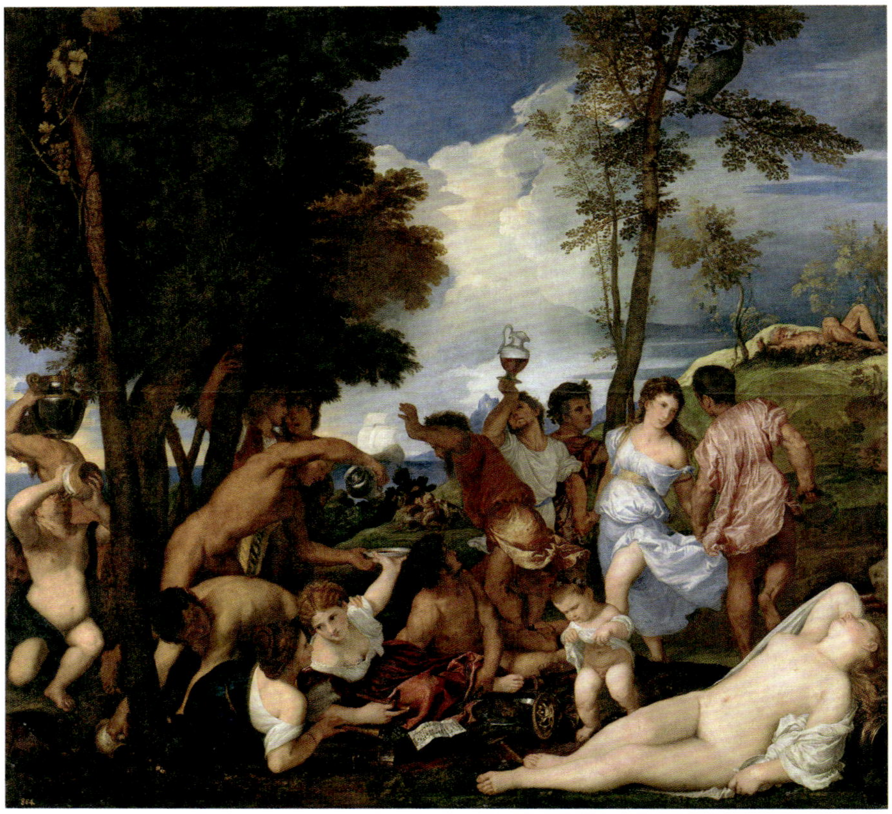

FIG. 54 Titian, *The Andrians*, *c.* 1518. Oil on canvas, 175 x 193 cm. Museo Nacional del Prado, Madrid

the works is unsurprising, for Roman art collections were rather inaccessible in those days – even for prominent visitors. Nor is it possible that Rubens saw Titian's paintings during his stay in Madrid in 1628–29, because the originals did not arrive in the Spanish capital until ten years later, when they were presented to Philip IV.

It has meanwhile been concluded that Rubens must have worked from copies made in Italy by Anthony van Dyck and brought by him in 1627 to Antwerp,[2] where they were admired at the Hanseatic House by Marie de Médicis in 1631.[3] Two other documents support this assumption: Van Dyck's Italian sketchbook contains a cursory chalk drawing of *The Andrians*,[4] and the 1696 inventory of the connoisseur Everhard Jabach lists a copy painted by Van Dyck after Titian.[5] Moreover, *The Andrians* is seen as a source of inspiration for *Amaryllis and Mirtillo* (fig. 55), a *poesia* that Van Dyck painted in the early 1630s for Frederick Hendrik of Orange that is now in the Schönborn Collection at Pommersfelden.[6] Jeremy Wood has suggested that this painting possibly stimulated Rubens to make the pendants now owned by the Nationalmuseum in Stockholm. Furthermore, Wood rightly points out the great impact these two compositions had on Rubens's own masterpiece, *The Garden of Love* (cat. 130).[7]

At any rate, it seems that Rubens painted his versions of *The Worship of Venus* and *The Andrians* for himself. Both canvases are listed in the inventory of his estate as originals and, as the

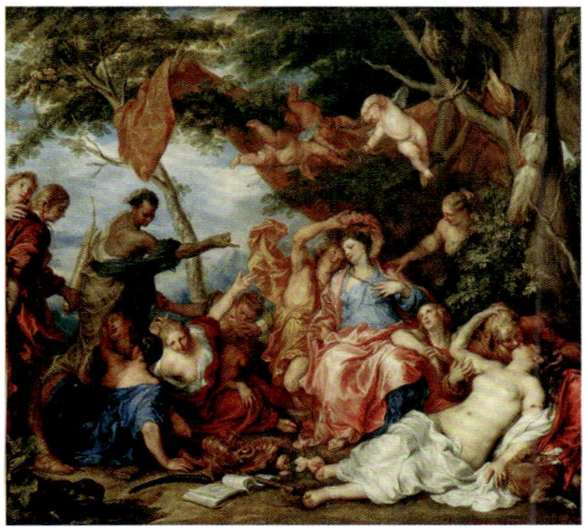

FIG. 55 Sir Anthony van Dyck, *Amaryllis and Mirtillo*, *c.* 1631. Oil on canvas, 123 x 137 cm. Kunstsammlungen Graf von Schönborn, Schloss Weissenstein, Pommersfelden

most expensive pieces, they fetched 1,800 guilders each. In fact, they differ from the originals in quite a few ways. For example, Rubens painted the river of wine in *The Andrians* as a clear brook, whose water turns to wine only at the moment of drinking. To visualise the transformation, he changed Silenus' earthenware jug, at the left, into a glass.[8] The wine-pourer, bending over to fill the drinking vessel of the woman in red, was changed by Rubens into Bacchus. In the right background Rubens exchanged Titian's reclining river god for a flute-playing shepherd beneath a tree. He also censured the child lifting its shirt to pee in the brook. The copy is larger than the original, whose dimensions are 175 x 193 cm; Rubens used the extra space at the bottom to paint several beautiful reflections in the water.

The Neoclassical court painter Anton Raphael Mengs considered the two copies by Rubens to be translations into the Flemish idiom, which succeeded in preserving the meaning of their examples but from which all grace had disappeared.[9] The copies can certainly be called translations, because Rubens painted in a manner completely different from Titian's. The transparent colours and the silvery tonality of Rubens's version of *The Andrians* clearly differ from the opaque paint layers and the sultry twilight of Titian's original. Rubens introduced blue-grey nuances to the flesh tones. By taking advantage of the grey *imprimatura* in the trees, the river and the contours of the figures, Rubens succeeded in creating atmosphere, depth and movement. He delighted in enlivening Titian's perfect composition by means of simplified, virtuoso brushwork – an exercise in painting technique with which he attempted to emulate his model.[10] In his version of *The Andrians*, Rubens exchanges the mystery of Titian for a refinement and evanescence that heralds the lyricism of the eighteenth century. NVH

The painting in the collection of the Prado now known as *The Garden of Love* (cat. 130) is the culminating version of a composition that occupied Rubens between about 1631 and 1635. The gestation of this work is complex and has been the subject of scholarly debate, but copies by other artists reveal that Rubens's original composition was substantially different from the final version exhibited here.[1] A group of nine surviving preparatory studies of individual figures in chalk, five of which are included here (cats 131–35), indicates the attention Rubens lavished on the work during its long evolution.

The Garden of Love remained in Rubens's own collection throughout his life and seems to have been painted for his own pleasure: most scholars agree on a date of *c.* 1635. It has been widely acclaimed as a masterpiece of Baroque painting and a consummate product of Rubens's last years. Keen, perhaps, to acquire widespread recognition for the composition, Rubens reworked it in two drawings (cat. 138), each based on half of the painting but with significant changes to the figures and the setting. These were in turn elaborated by another hand in preparation for a woodcut by Christoffel Jegher (cat. 139).

Rubens's deep admiration for Titian is clearly evident in *The Garden of Love*. The putti resemble the jovial inhabitants of the earlier artist's *The Worship of Venus* (1518–20; Museo Nacional del Prado, Madrid), of which Rubens made a copy in about 1635 (now in the Nationalmuseum, Stockholm), around the same time that he painted *The Garden of Love*.[2] The rich colour palette, the outdoor setting and the blend of music and flirtation also recall Titian's *Concert Champêtre* (fig. 41), sometimes attributed to Giorgione. The interlocking female figures and the

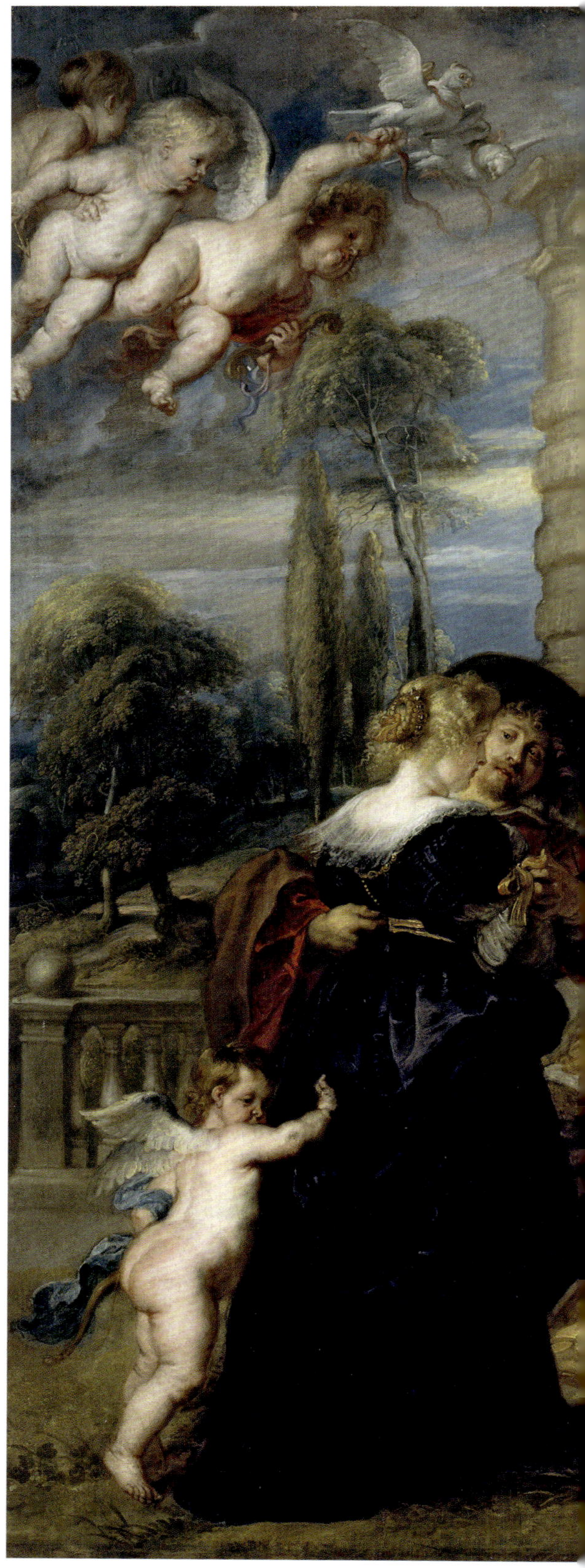

130

PETER PAUL RUBENS (1577–1640)
The Garden of Love, *c* 1635
Oil on canvas, 199 x 286 cm
Museo Nacional del Prado, Madrid, inv. P01690

PROVENANCE: Spanish royal collection from 1666
SELECTED REFERENCES: Glück 1920–21; Waterhouse 1950, pp. 199–202; Burchard 1963, pp. 428–32; Held 1980, vol. 1, p. 400; Vergara 1982, p. 52; White 1987, pp. 268–72; Goodman 1992; Díaz Padrón 1995, vol. 2, pp. 982–86; Belkin 1998, pp. 269–72, Vergara 1999, pp. 158, 160, 163

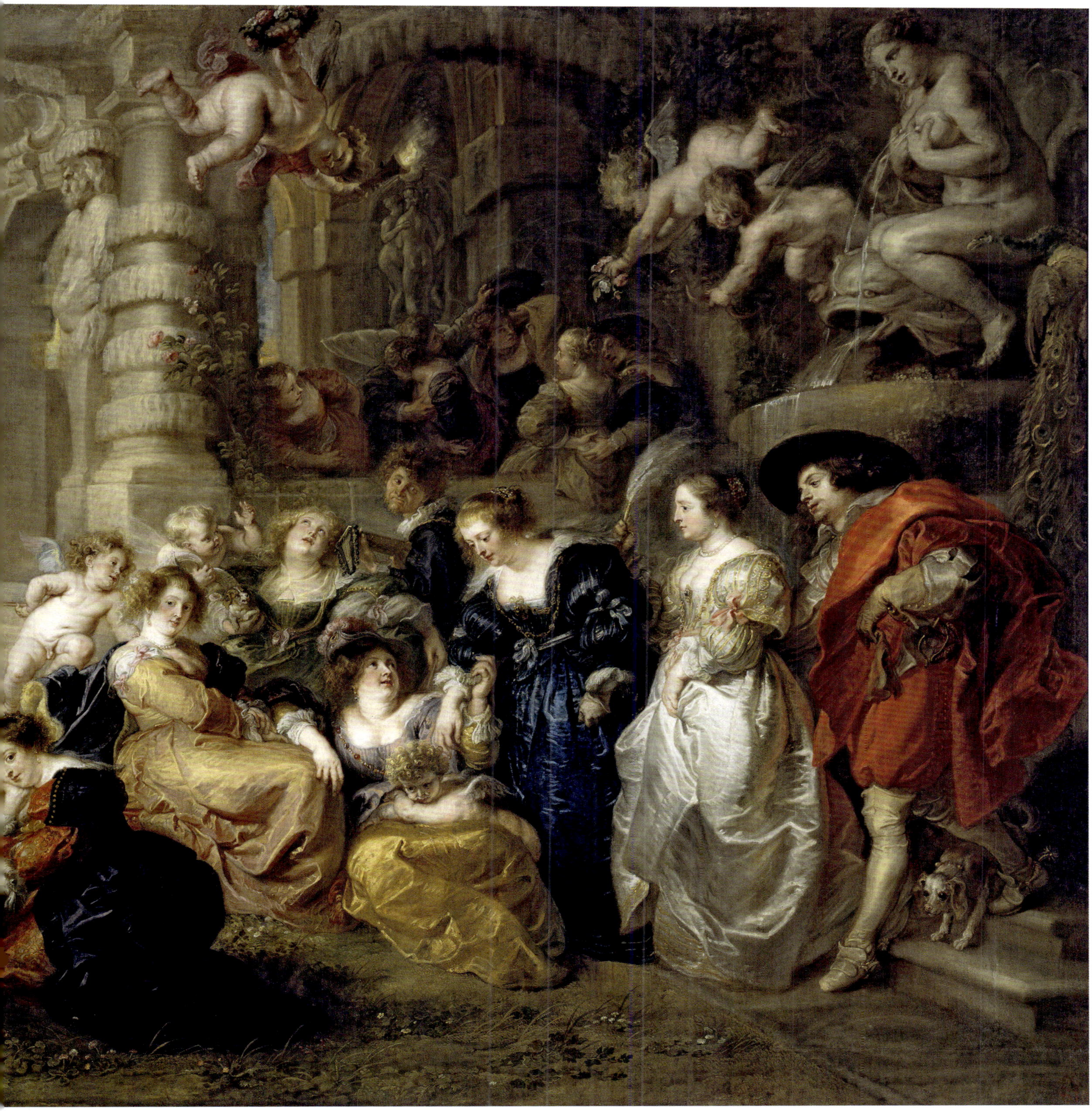

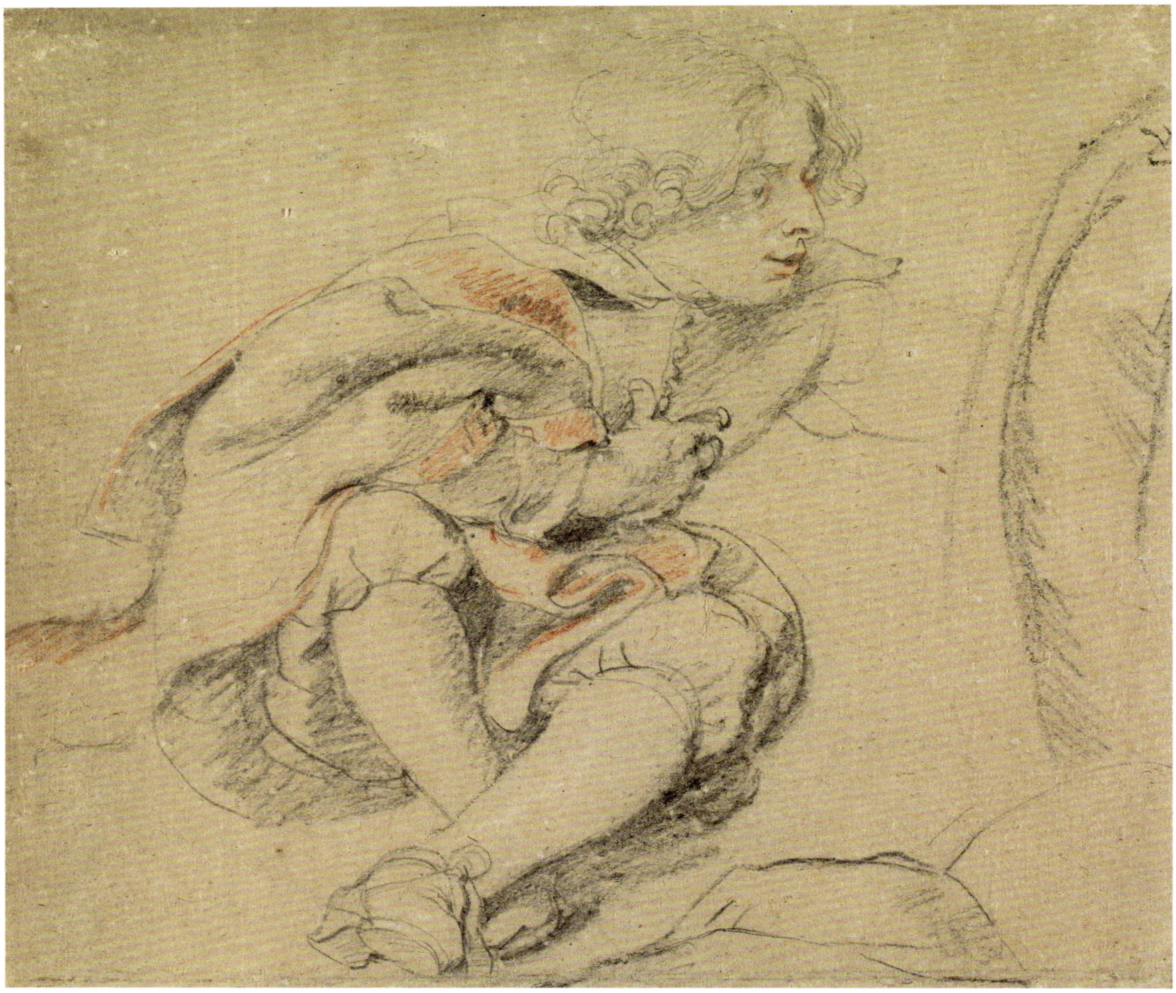

131

PETER PAUL RUBENS (1577–1640)
Seated Young Man, before 1635
Black and red chalks, with white heightening, on light brown paper, 32.2 x 30 cm
Amsterdam Museum, inv. TA 10302. Bequest of Carel Joseph Fodor

PROVENANCE: Sir Thomas Lawrence; King William II of the Netherlands; bought by Carel Joseph Fodor
SELECTED REFERENCES: Burchard and d'Hulst 1963, vol. 2, no. 185; Glang-Süberkrüb 1975, pp. 73–76; Díaz Padrón 1995, vol. 2, pp. 984–87

richness of tonality also echo Titian's *Diana and Actaeon* (1556–59; The National Gallery, London, and National Gallery of Scotland, Edinburgh), a work that Rubens copied.[3]

The Garden of Love is a wholehearted celebration of courtship and of love among the wealthy and fashionable citizens of Antwerp in Rubens's day. Five amorous couples, encouraged by cupids, have been drawn together in *The Garden of Love*, where they encounter a group of alluring young women. Presiding over the scene is a statue of Juno, goddess of marriage, seated on a dolphin, incorporated into an elaborate fountain and accompanied by her emblem, a peacock. The festivities are attended by flying putti, one of whom enters the composition at a dizzying angle carrying a burning torch and a crown of roses; another, to the upper left, bears a yoke – symbol of marriage – and a pair of doves. On the terrace of a richly decorated pavilion to the rear, containing a sculpture of the Three Graces, some more revellers are startled by a *jeu d'eau*, a garden feature in which unsuspecting guests were caught in light jets of water.

Despite the presence of winged cupids, supernatural beings that embody love itself, the painting is not a complex allegory. Rather it explores the multifarious effects of love on real people of Rubens's time. For many years, the figures on the left were identified as Rubens and his young wife. This

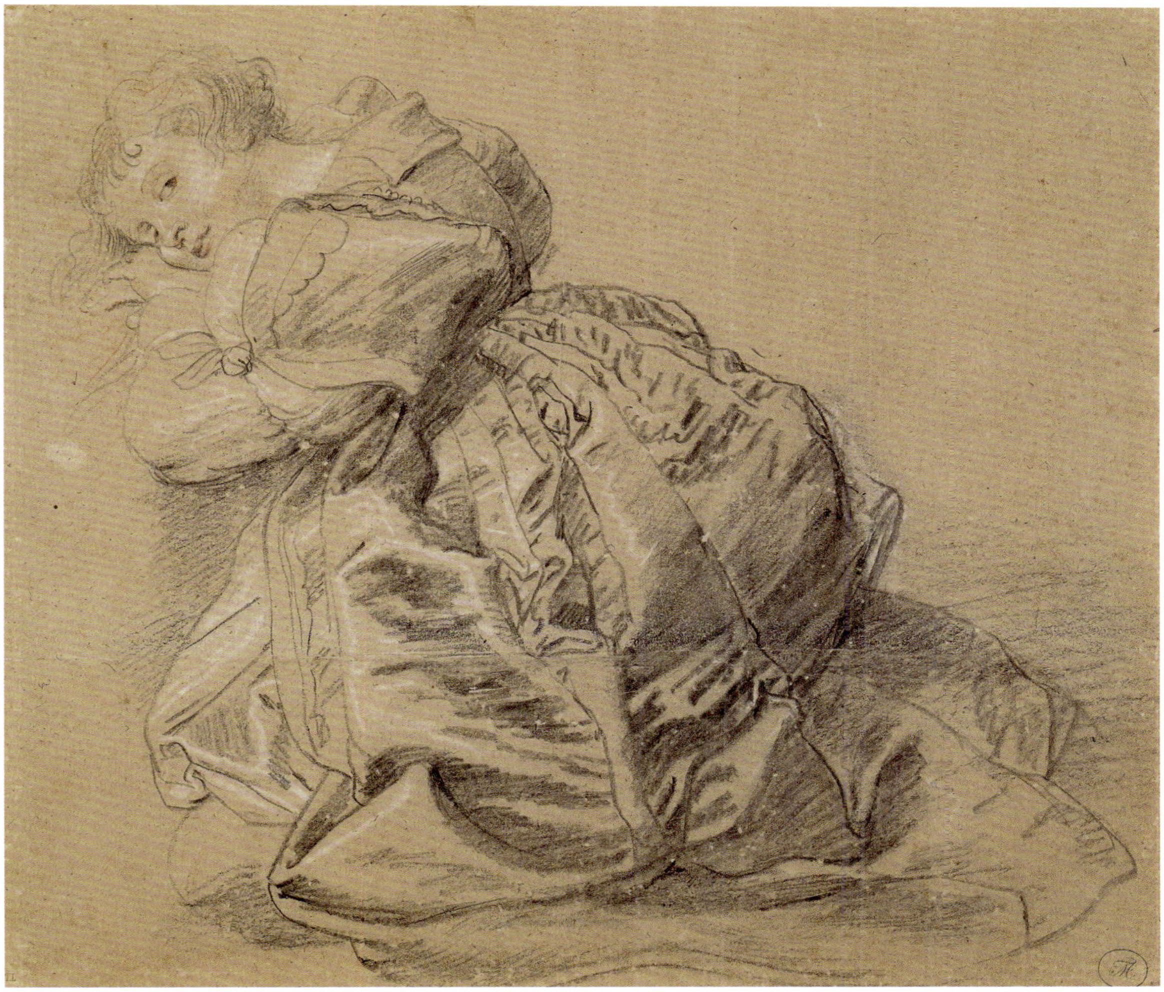

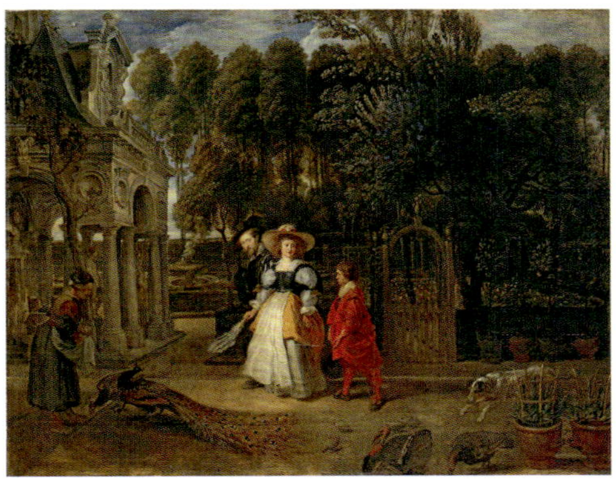

FIG. 56 Peter Paul Rubens and workshop, *Rubens with Hélène Fourment and Nicholas Rubens*, 1631. Oil on wood, 97.8 x 130.8 cm. Alte Pinakothek, Munich

identification is unconvincing, as neither the figures nor the setting betray so direct a referent. The youthful male, in particular, whose features can be seen more clearly in a study (cat. 133), bears little resemblance to the artist, by then in his mid-fifties. The elaborate, even bombastic architecture of the pavilion loosely resembles features of Rubens's own garden in Antwerp, as seen in a work of Rubens's studio, *Rubens with Hélène Fourment and Nicholas Rubens* (fig. 56).[4] Albeit indirectly, *The Garden of Love* surely expresses Rubens's delight in his familial and domestic circumstances, and in the social life he enjoyed as a wealthy and eminent citizen. The painting is a confection, an idyll affectionately crafted

132

PETER PAUL RUBENS (1577–1640)
Young Woman Kneeling, before 1635
Black and red chalk, with white heightening, on buff paper, 40.3 x 47.4 cm
Amsterdam Museum, inv. TA 10300. Bequest of Carel Joseph Fodor

PROVENANCE: Sir Thomas Lawrence; King William II of the Netherlands; bought by Carel Joseph Fodor
SELECTED REFERENCES: Burchard and d'Hulst 1963, vol. 2, no. 184; Glang-Süberkrüb 1975, pp. 73–76; Díaz Padrón 1995, vol. 2, pp. 984–87

133

PETER PAUL RUBENS (1577–1640)
Young Man Embracing a Young Woman, before 1635
Black and red chalks, with white heightening, on light brown paper, 32.2 x 30 cm
Amsterdam Museum, inv. TA 10301. Bequest of Carel Joseph Fodor

PROVENANCE: Thomas Hudson, London; Sir Thomas Lawrence, London; William II of the Netherlands; Carel Joseph Fodor
SELECTED REFERENCES: Held 1959, vol. 2, no. 120; Burchard and d'Hulst 1963, vol. 2, no. 181; Glang-Süberkrüb 1975, pp. 73–76; Held 1986, no. 209; Díaz Padrón 1995, vol. 2, pp. 985–87; New York 2005, pp. 256–60

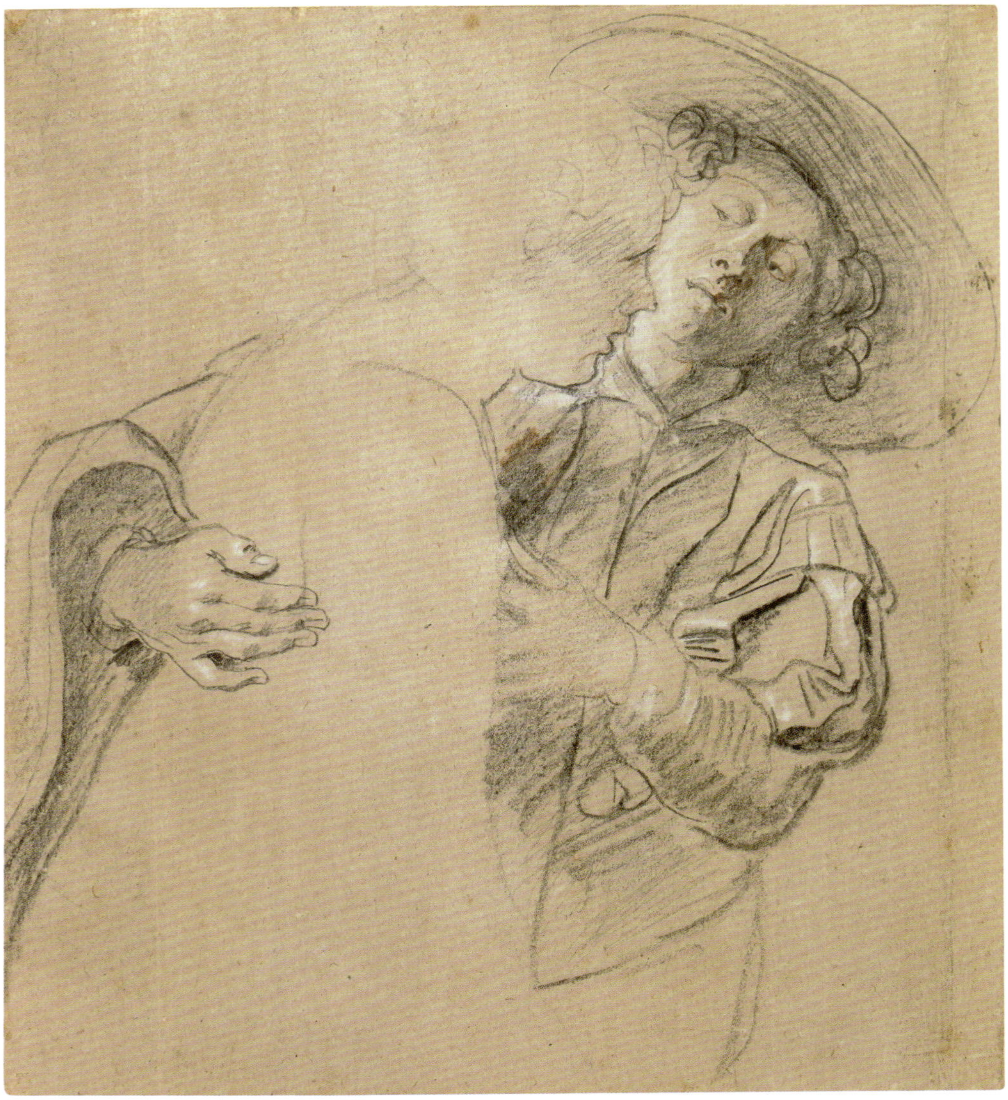

from the elements of everyday life, a celebration of youth, beauty and the delights of the body, with marriage as its happy conclusion.

Elise Goodman has persuasively argued that *The Garden of Love* is best entitled *Conversatie à la Mode*, as it was at the sale of Rubens's goods in 1645; it is a modern conversation piece.[5] There are eleven lavishly attired women and only six men, all players in a refined game of seduction. The scene represents a relaxed, *haut-bourgeois* code of behaviour, in contrast to the highly formalised court rituals of the period. The emphasis is on individual subjectivity, on love and desire, rather than on the creation of dynastic links through marriage. Some interactions are touching, such as the seated woman in the lower left who places her hand tenderly on the leg of her lover; others are more earthy, such as the man on the balcony who takes the opportunity to fondle the breast of one woman while playfully shielding another from the squirting water with his hat. Rubens draws particular attention to the sense of touch; couples grasp each other tenderly, hands entwine, and the image is replete with luxurious fabrics and opulent flesh.

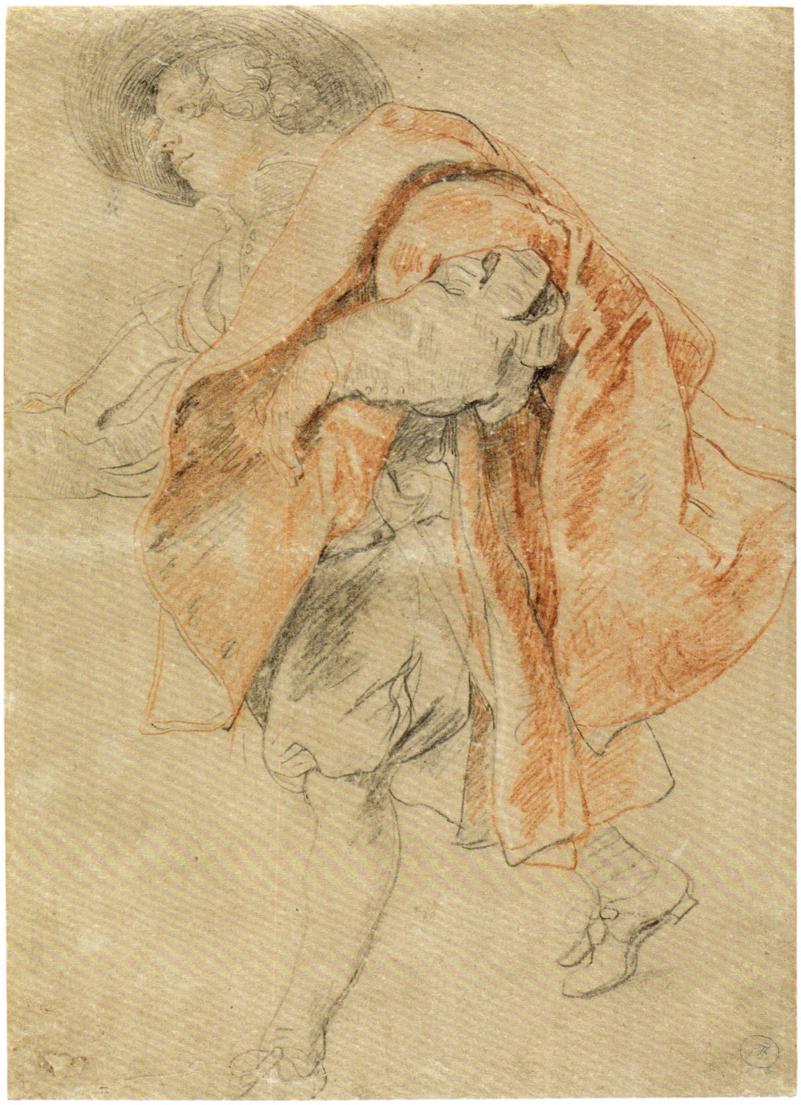

134

PETER PAUL RUBENS (1577–1640)
Young Man Descending Stairs, before 1635
Black and red chalks, with white heightening, on light brown paper, 56.1 x 41.5 cm
Amsterdam Museum, inv. TA 10299. Bequest of Carel Joseph Fodor

PROVENANCE: Thomas Hudson, London; Sir Thomas Lawrence, London; William II of the Netherlands; Carel Joseph Fodor
SELECTED REFERENCES: Held 1959, no. 119; Glang-Süberkrüb 1975, pp. 73–76; Held 1986, no. 209; Díaz Padrón 1995, vol. 2, pp. 985–87; New York 2005, pp. 256–60

Rubens pays loving attention to the details of attire, displaying his knowledge of the latest fashions. The woman who enters from the left, already in the arms of her beau, wears a high-waisted black-velvet garment known as a *robbe*, or overdress, intended to emphasise the curves of the female body, especially in motion. As Elise Goodman notes of the fashions of the period, as represented by Rubens: 'Mass was emphasised at the expense of line. All was round, fleshy, and sensuous ... the deep, funnel-shaped cuffs, the rounded, puffed sleeves, the curved *décolletage*, the bared breasts, the padded hips.'[6] The seated woman who gazes flirtatiously out at the viewer also wears a *robbe*, but Rubens reveals the rich red of the dress beneath, as well as her pale skin. The implied viewer – presumably male – is surely intended to linger over each detail of the painting, which, itself, becomes the object of desiring reverie.

Music was an essential component of outdoor entertainment. A lutenist wearing a ruff sits just above the centre of the composition, and the neck of the instrument is foreshortened to emphasise the movement of his left hand. He turns his head to his left, perhaps

135

PETER PAUL RUBENS (1577–1640)
Seated Young Woman with Raised Arms, *c.* 1631–32
Black and red chalks, with white heightening, on light brown paper, 40.6 x 50 cm
Kupferstichkabinett, Staatliche Museen zu Berlin, inv. KdZ 4003
RA ONLY

PROVENANCE: Jonathan Richardson Jr (1694–1771), London; Earl of Aylesford (1786–1859), London; acquired 1893
SELECTED REFERENCES: Burchard and d'Hulst 1963, vol. 2, no. 183; Glang-Süberkrüb 1975, pp. 73–76; Díaz Padrón 1995, vol. 2, pp. 984–87; New York 2005, pp. 256–60

136

PETER PAUL RUBENS (1577–1640)
Hagar in the Desert, *c.* 1630–32
Oil on panel, 71.5 x 72.6 cm
By Permission of the Trustees of Dulwich Picture Gallery, London, inv. DPG 131
RA ONLY

PROVENANCE: Sir Peter Francis Bourgeois; bequest to Dulwich College, 1811
SELECTED REFERENCES: d'Hulst and Vandenven 1989, no. 11; Jaffé 1989, no. 1,052

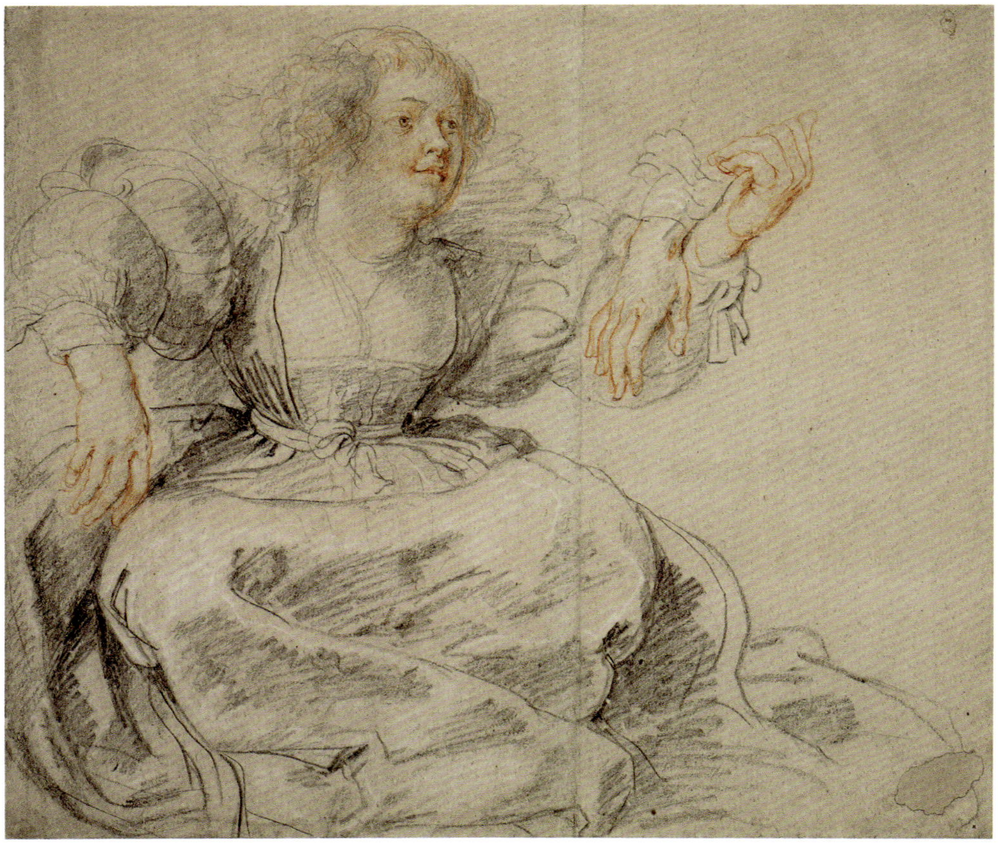

singing of love's melancholy rather than its joys. His presence suggests music's sensuous delights and its direct appeal to the emotions. A female figure to the immediate left of the musician is enraptured. She may be singing from a songbook held open by a little cupid to her right. Her eyes, however, turn away from the book and stare upwards to the heavens. Her ecstatic expression, which is often associated with St Cecilia, patron saint of music (as in Raphael's celebrated composition of 1514 in Bologna and Rubens's own, very late, work of *c.* 1640 in Berlin; see also cat. 98), here seems to suggest earthly, even carnal, delights (the little Hogarthian spaniel in her hand is a reminder of the physical world), rather than the heavenly music of the spheres that St Cecilia discerned.

Elements in *The Garden of Love* indicate Rubens's admiration for French culture, and particularly Parisian fashions in women's clothing and in literature. Rubens seems to have met the French poets Vincent Voiture and Tristan l'Hermitte, and he prepared a frontispiece for a work by the latter. Their work, like *The Garden of Love*, is notable for 'elegance, sensuality and playfulness'.[7] Rubens acquired the collected works of Théophile de Viau, published in 1624, whose libertine lifestyle and sensualist writings (such as *Parnasse satyrique*, 1622) eventually led to his banishment from Paris.[8] Yet despite his awareness of this socially transgressive literature, *The Garden of Love* ultimately celebrates marriage as the natural outcome of courtship.

Few preparatory drawings survive from the major works of the preceding decade: Rubens had tended to move directly to the medium of the oil sketch.

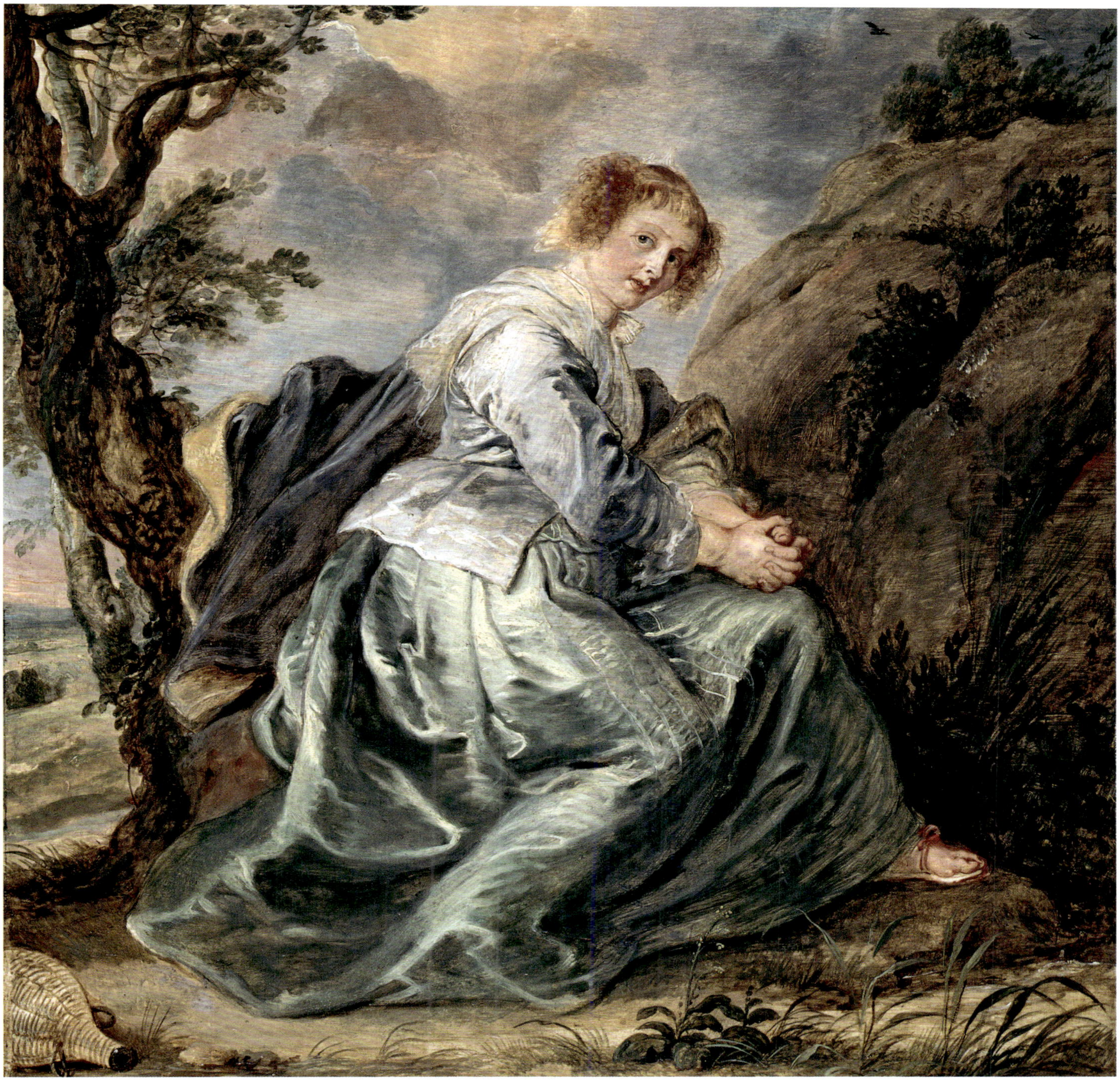

The survival of drawings for *The Garden of Love* seems to indicate that, in creating a painting for his own pleasure, and with the vital resource of time at his disposal, Rubens could enjoy immersing himself in the project.[9] The study of the young woman kneeling (cat. 132) to the left of the composition, is a masterly exposition of the volume of the body elaborated by opulent textiles. Her ardent companion, hand rhetorically positioned by his heart, seems almost weightless in a drawing (cat. 131) that reveals his full figure. Largely obscured in the Prado

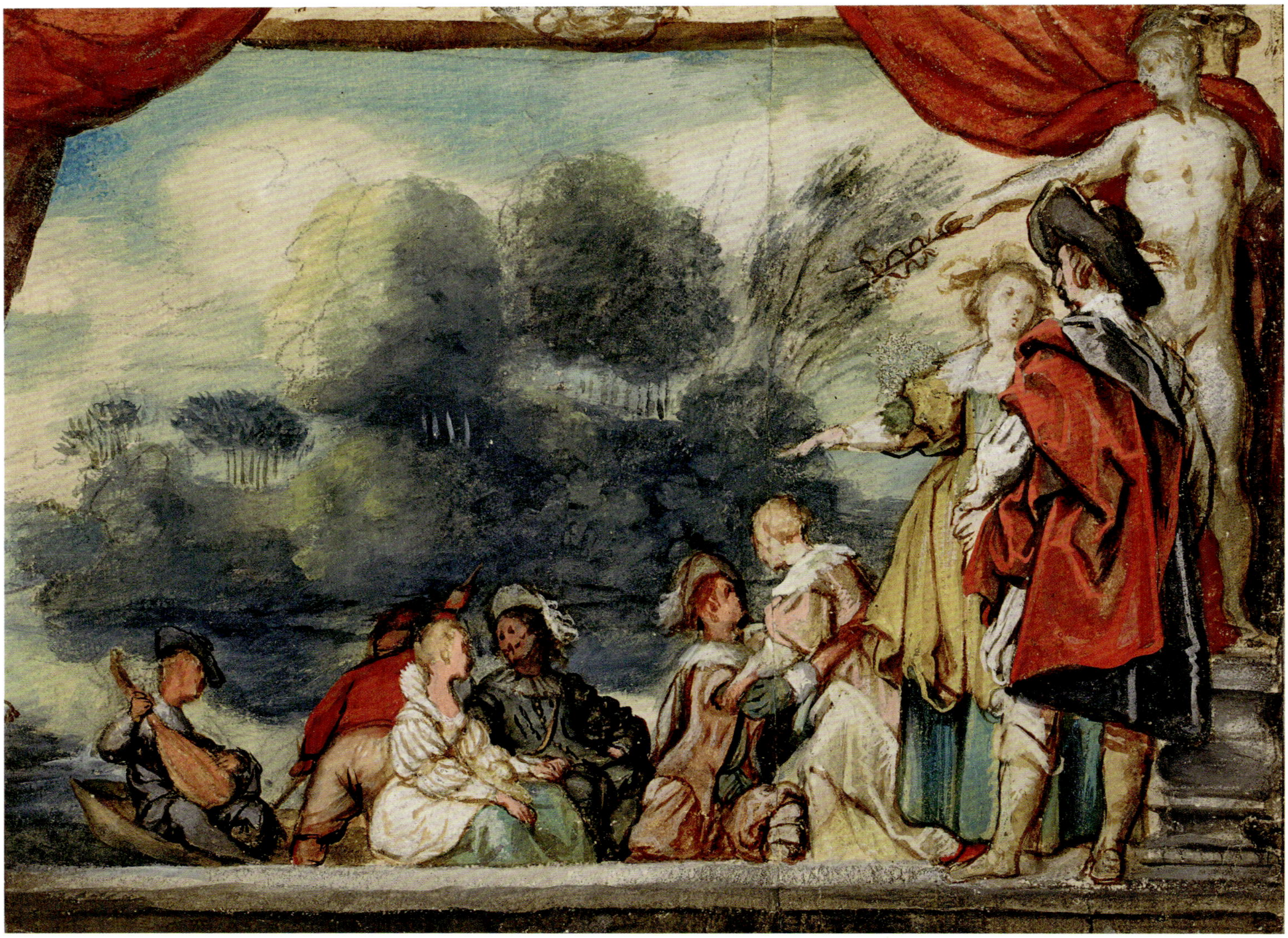

137

JACOB JORDAENS (1593–1678)
Boating Party, 1630–35
Watercolour and bodycolour, heightened with white (partially oxidised) over charcoal, on two conjoined sheets of paper, 28.1 x 38.1 cm
On loan from the British Museum, London, inv. 1885,0711.268

PROVENANCE: W. Russell (London, 1800–84); acquired by the British Museum, London, in 1885.
SELECTED REFERENCES: d'Hulst 1982, p. 312; Antwerp 1993, B27, p. 49

composition, this figure emerges more fully in the Metropolitan Museum's drawings for Jegher's woodcut. The study of the couple entering from the left (cat. 133) is significantly modified in the painting: the face is older and bearded. Yet the tenderness and concern of the male figure, so perfectly captured in the drawing, survive in the final composition. Most flamboyant is the splendid young man descending the stairs (cat. 134), a first study of the magnificent swirl of the gallant's red cloak. As can be seen from the extreme right of the Prado painting, the man's pantaloons eventually also acquired the vermilion hue.

The seated young woman with raised arms (cat. 135) relates to the ample figure positioned on the ground with a putto sprawled on her lap. The pose of the woman seated to her left, richly dressed in yellow, seems also to have fascinated Rubens. He reworked this figure in the small panel painting of *Hagar in the Desert* (cat. 136), changing her dress to a demure blue and subtly modifying her air of courtly ennui to one of anxiety and even despair. In a completely different narrative context, but still lavishly dressed, the figure becomes Hagar, who has fled into the arid wilderness with her son Ishmael. The panel seems to have been cut down and overpainted, obscuring the angel who appeared to Hagar and revealed that Ishmael would survive to become the founder of a great nation (Genesis XXI, 17–18). The original composition, seen in an engraving by Frans De Roy of *c.* 1750, included an angel in the sky behind Hagar's head and the figure of Ishmael in the middle distance on the far left.

The influence of *The Garden of Love* can clearly be seen in the work of Jacob Jordaens, a collaborator with Rubens over several decades. Many elements of Rubens's composition are subtly adapted in Jordaens's watercolour, *Boating Party* (cat. 137). As in *The Garden of Love*, a refined company is seen in a garden setting; here, however, they embark on a boat trip, accompanied by a lutenist. Once again a sculpture presides over the action, but this time it is Mercury who dominates proceedings. The lively interaction of opulently dressed, amorous figures and the couple entering from the right pay homage to Rubens's invention. It has been suggested that the composition was intended as a design for a tapestry, but there is no evidence that one was ever executed.[10] The later French painter Jean-Antoine Watteau was to take up the theme of the mysterious departure of a party of lovers on a boat trip in *Pilgrimage to the Island of Cythera* (fig. 48). TB

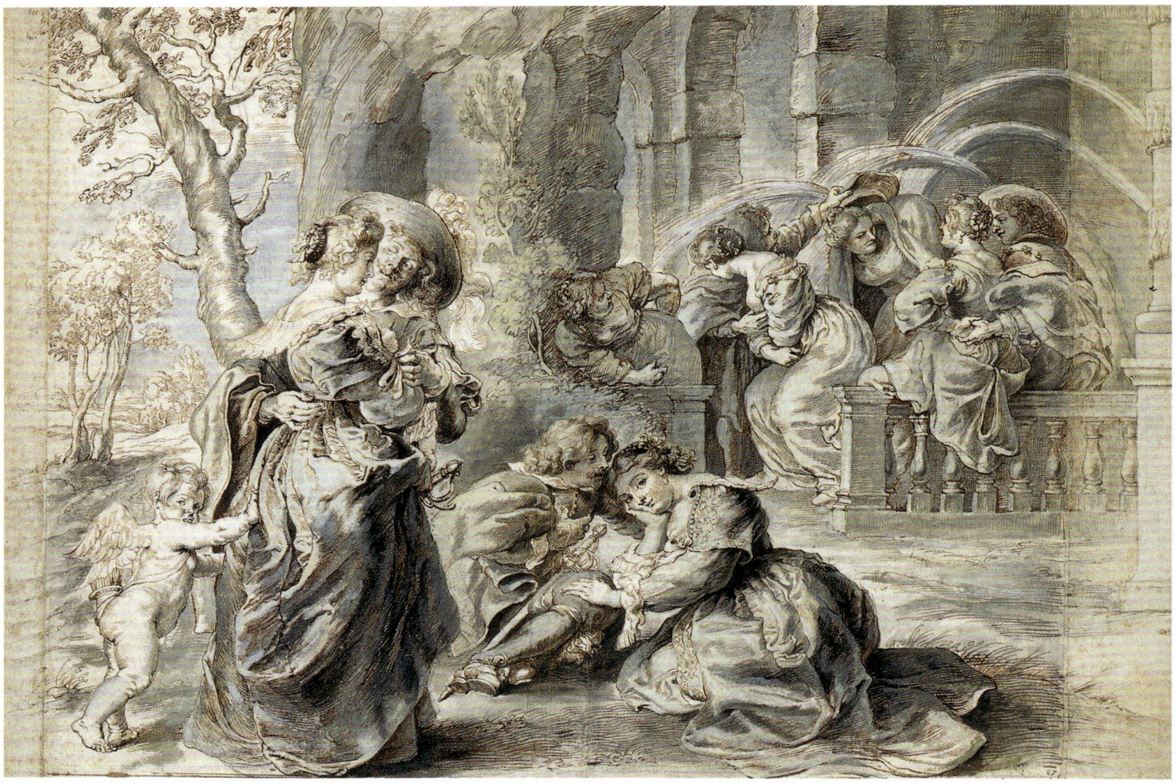

138.1–2

PETER PAUL RUBENS (1577–1640)
and assistant
The Garden of Love (left half),
c. 1633–35
Black chalk, pen and brown ink, probably brush and grey-green wash and dark brown ink, 46.3 x 70.5 cm
strip at left folded under 2.5 cm; 6.5 cm-wide strip added at right. Annotated in pen and brown ink at bottom: *Petrus Pauwlo Rubbens*; Crozat number added by Mariette, 27; at bottom of mount, 133
The Garden of Love (right half),
c. 1633–35
Black chalk, pen and brown ink, brush and greyish white and greenish gouache, with additions in brush and dark brown ink and wash, 47.6 x 70.6 cm
Annotated in pen and brown ink at bottom left: *Petrus Paolo Rubbens*, at centre 134
Lent by The Metropolitan Museum of Art, New York. inv. 58.96.1. Fletcher Fund, 1958

PROVENANCE: Johannes Philippus Happaert, Antwerp; Pierre Crozat, Paris; Pierre-Jean Mariette, Paris; Jan Gildemeester Jansz., Amsterdam; Hendrik van Eyl Sluter, Amsterdam; Heneage Finch, 5th Earl of Aylesford; Sir John Charles Robinson; William Hesketh Lever, 1st Viscount Leverhulme; Lady Lever Art Gallery, Port Sunlight; acquired by Metropolitan Museum of Art, 1958
SELECTED REFERENCES: Held 1959, vol. 1, no. 152; Bean 1962, pp. 166–67; Burchard and d'Hulst 1963, vol. 2, no. 180; Glang-Süberkrüb 1975, pp. 49–53, 73–76; Held 1986, nos 210, 211; Goodman 1992, pp. 73–83; Díaz Padrón 1995, vol. 2, pp. 985–87; New York 2005, nos 93–94

The two drawings (cat. 138), magnificent in scale and in elaboration of detail, are based on the Prado version of *The Garden of Love* (cat. 130), although they substantially modify the composition.[1] They are preparatory designs for two large woodcuts by Christoffel Jegher (cat. 139). Each of Jegher's woodcuts functions satisfactorily as a separate composition, but the two sheets join neatly to form a single, panoramic composition whose width is just over two and a half times its height. Only when the two halves are united does the full rhythmic exuberance of the work become apparent. In this robust form, the composition circulated widely.

Among Rubens's contemporaries, Jegher was the pre-eminent Flemish exponent of the woodcut, a form of printmaking that had reached its apogee the previous century. Although he had previously favoured engraving as a

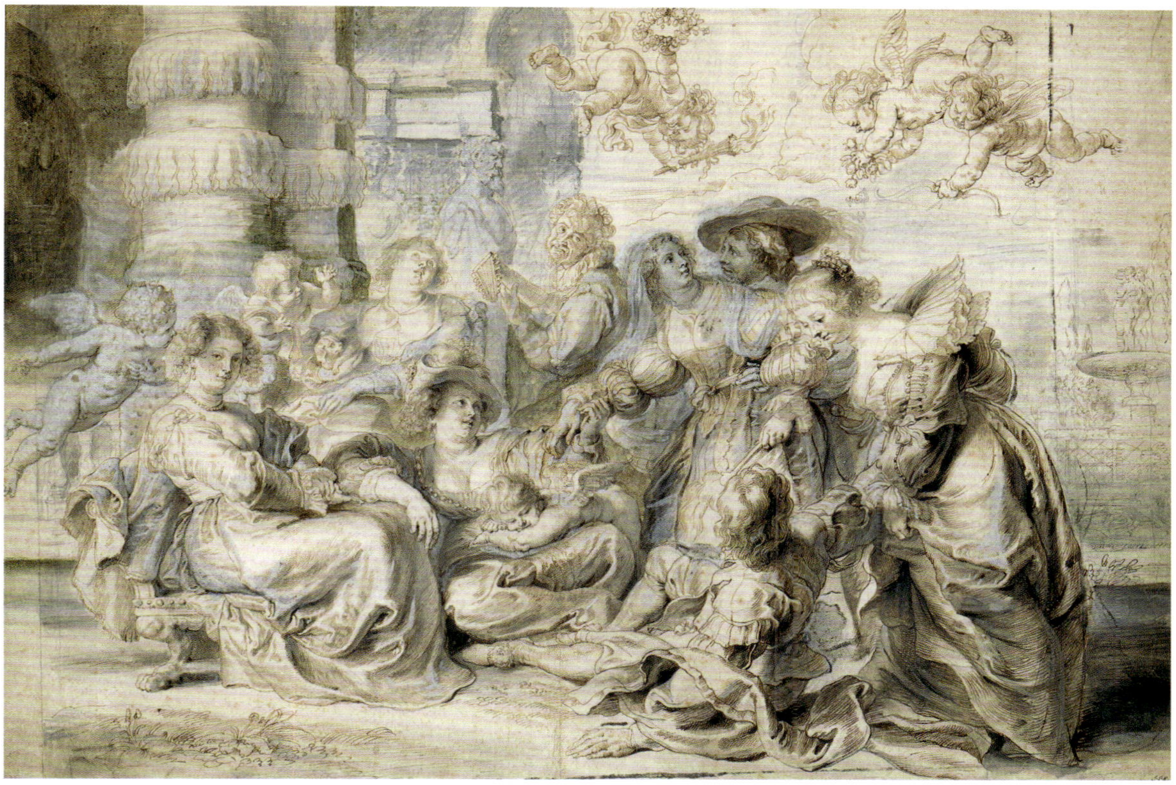

reproductive medium, Rubens clearly admired Jegher's work, since Rubens himself published all nine of the woodcuts made by Jegher after his work. Their period of close collaboration has been dated to 1633–35.[2]

The drawings in the Metropolitan Museum are complex objects with three distinct layers in different media.[3] The initial compositional outlines were laid down in black chalk. Scholars are agreed that Rubens himself must have been responsible for this underlying framework, which confidently re-grouped the figures from the painted version and made significant changes to the setting. Indeed, the inscription at the bottom margin of the left woodcut, 'P. P. Rub. delin.' ('Peter Paul Rubens drew it') makes this very claim. Although most of the chalk lines are obscured by subsequent work in ink and grey-green wash, their presence can be detected across the whole of both sheets.

The chalk outlines have been carefully elaborated in pen and brown ink by an expert hand. The line is marginally thicker and more confident in the left half. Details of costume, hair and foliage are rendered with precision and clarity – see, for example, the couple to the left: the gentleman fingers a fine ribbon tied into a bow, known as a 'little goose'.[4] (This detail is seen in the Prado version of the painting but not in the earlier version, represented by an early copy at Waddesdon Manor, Buckinghamshire.)

The subtle hatching of the pen drawing, in Christopher White's vivid summary, 'gave the printmaker the precise instructions he could follow in transferring the design to the woodblock ... [and] exchanges the fine hatching required for the intaglio print for the more open, weightier line of the woodcut'.[5] For all its refinement, this layer of pen drawing was clearly not completely satisfactory to Rubens, who has made

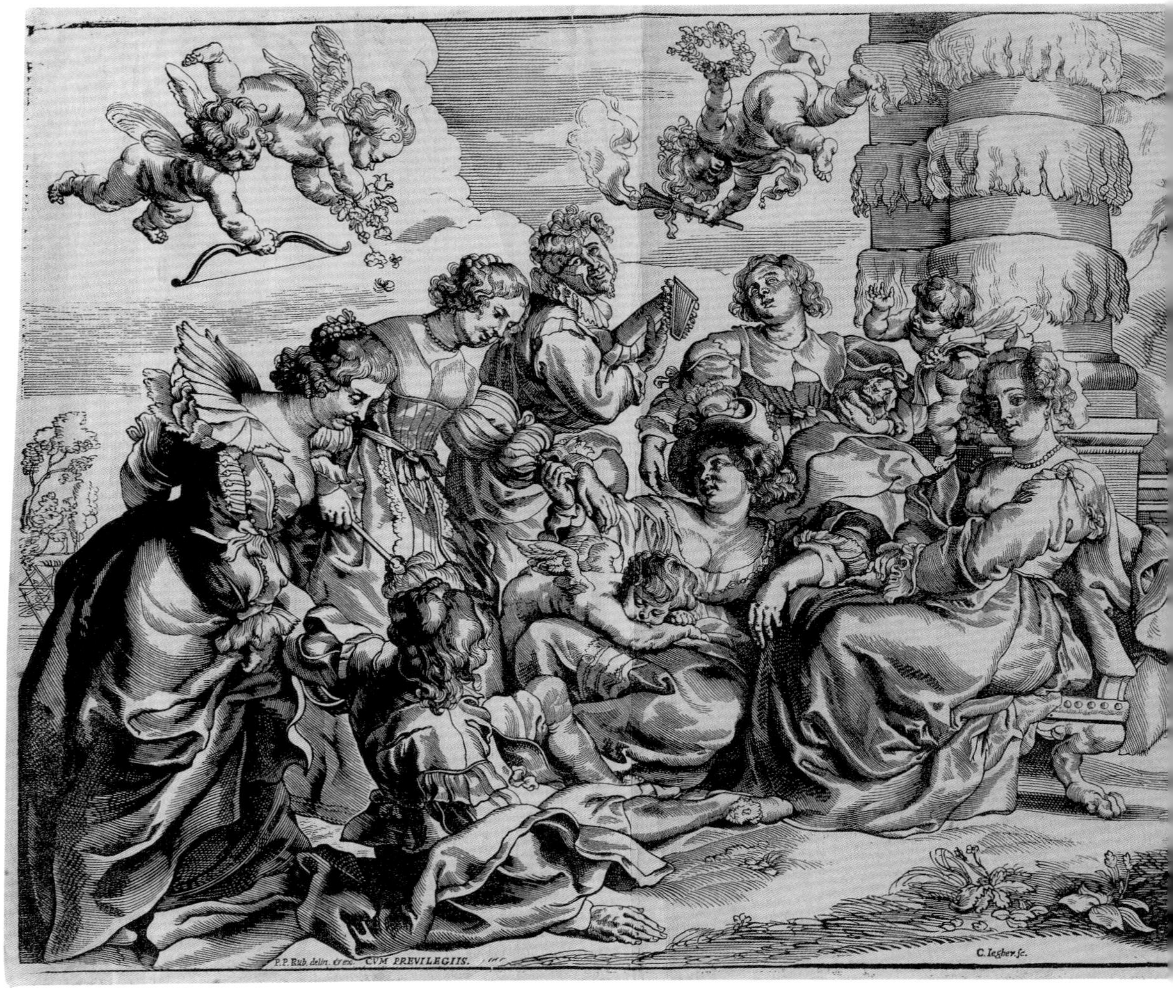

extensive corrections and changes in grey-green wash and pen, using much the same technique as he employed when altering the drawings of other artists in his own collection.[6] Stijn Alsteens has concluded on this basis that the pen drawing, lacking the confidence and certainty of Rubens's own hand, must belong to a studio assistant.[7]

The composition of the Metropolitan drawings is significantly modified from that of the painted version of *The Garden of Love* in the Prado. At the extreme left, behind the cupid who pushes an elegant couple towards the centre of the composition, the drawings present an open landscape where, in the painting, a balustrade intervenes. The revellers in the garden pavilion have migrated from centre-right to centre-left of the middle ground, and the spurting water emitting from the sculpture is far more apparent. The heavy, rusticated columns of the pavilion and the two grotesque guardian figures so clearly delineated in the painting have undergone a metamorphosis of almost Ovidian magnitude, becoming a natural rocky form, which now resembles the entrance to a grotto.

Many details from the drawings are omitted from the woodcut version, most significantly the architectural features in the background of the right sheet of the drawn version. A fountain clearly showing the Three Graces in the drawing (right sheet, extreme right) has

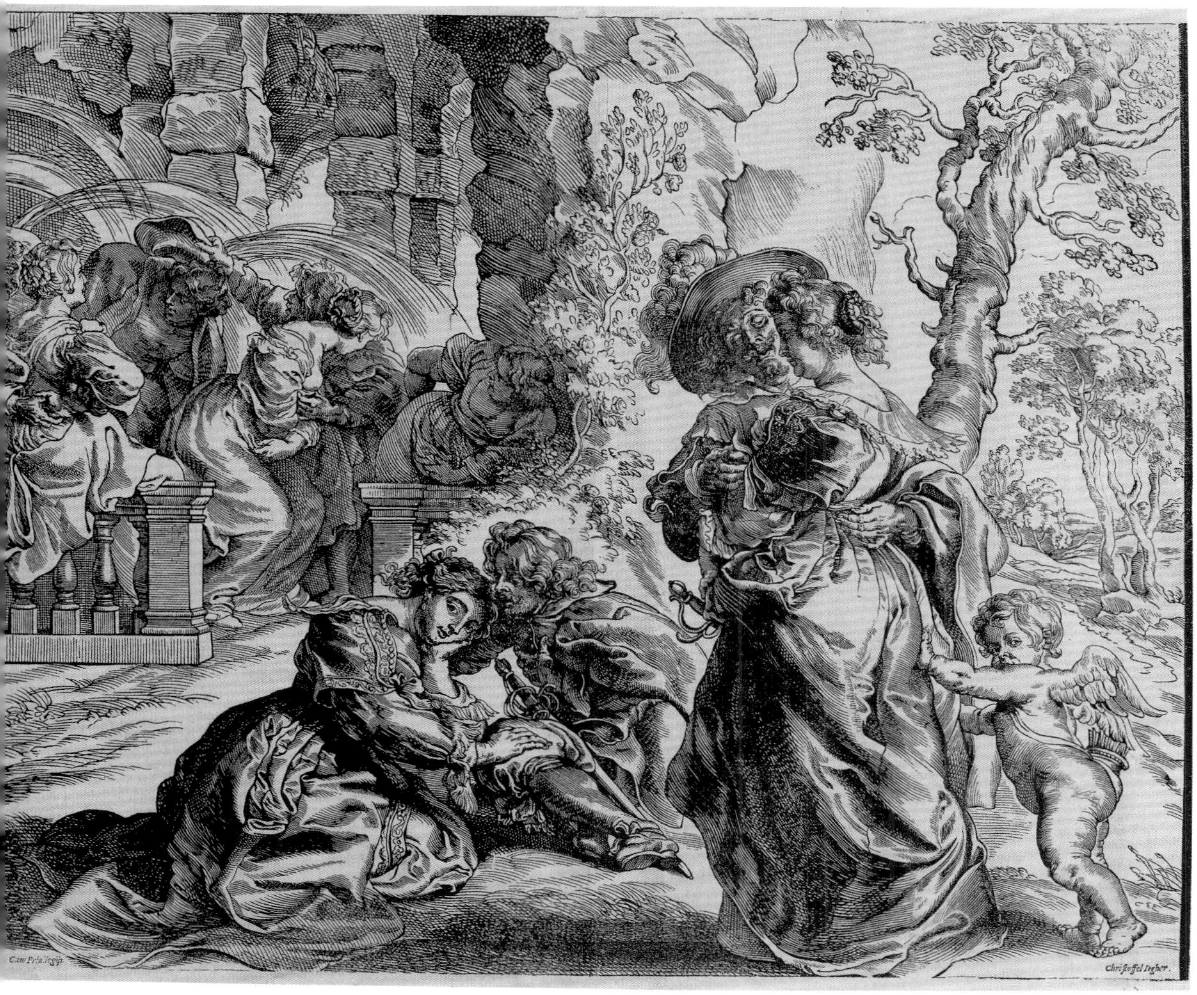

139

CHRISTOFFEL JEGHER (1596–1652/53)
The Garden of Love, *c.* 1635
Woodcut, two sheets,
each 46.2 x 120.2 cm
Royal Museum of Fine Arts Antwerp,
inv. 11140

SELECTED REFERENCES: Glang-Süberkrüb 1975, pp. 49–53, 73–76; Goodman 1992, pp. 73–83; Díaz Padrón 1995, vol. 2, pp. 985–87; New York 2005, pp. 262–63

metamorphosed into a tree (engraving, left sheet, extreme left). The robust nature of the woodcut medium also leads to a shift in character from the refinement of the drawings. Solidity and vigour overpower the gracious wit of the drawings.

The putto or cupid hovering by the ear of the seated lady to the left side of the right-hand sheet of the drawing, based on the figure in a gorgeous yellow dress at the centre of the Prado painting, adds a perplexing detail. This cupid, brought to three-dimensional prominence with wash and pen outlines in the drawing, presumably by Rubens himself, does not appear at all in the woodcut, where his heels would have straddled the joint between the two sheets. It seems unlikely that Rubens would have corrected the sheet after the prints were made; we can assume, then, that he expected this figure to appear in the woodcut. This excision was probably proposed by Jegher in order to simplify the margin of the composition. TB

In *The Pleasures of the Ball* (cat. 140), Jean-Antoine Watteau lays before us Parisian high society at play, indulging in the sort of entertainments he must have encountered at Montmorency, the imposing country house of the collector Pierre Crozat which the painter visited several times.[1] The elaborate gardens at Montmorency, represented in Watteau's painting *La Perspective* (*c.* 1714; Museum of Fine Arts, Boston), were graced with avenues of trees and grandiose architectural features. They made the perfect setting for musical evenings and masquerades. At these events, wealthy and influential Parisians would costume themselves as Pierrot, Harlequin and Columbine, characters from the Italian *commedia dell'arte*.

At such events, the well-to-do would mingle with actors and musicians, the kind of socially marginal characters with whom Watteau had spent his early adulthood. The adoption of disguises – a form of social cross-dressing – was a central aspect of these outdoor festivities. Julie Anne Plax has called attention to the 'paradoxical role of masquerade in the economy of élite self-definition'.[2] Only the rich and the leisured could afford to play with their identities. The figure dressed as Harlequin who dances to the centre left of the painting is typically mysterious; his facial expression gives nothing away. Is this prominent character a nobleman or financier in costume, or a poor performer from a travelling troupe? The face of a Pierrot, peeping over the crowd at the back, is mask-like and inscrutable. To the right, two men, seated beneath the musicians, wear ruffs, popular a century earlier: are they merely in fancy dress, or could this be a sly allusion to Rubens himself? Meanwhile, away from the social whirl, a servant of African descent peers down from a balustrade in the upper right, the very embodiment of alienation.

The Pleasures of the Ball is most likely an imaginary confection, based on observations Watteau made at many such events, daringly informal by the courtly standards of the day. Important for the present context is the natural way in which the figures interact: their bodies, some in movement, some seated, are all animated, and intertwine in a complex arabesque. This Watteau had learned from his study of Rubens's *The Garden of Love* drawings (cat. 138.1–2) and *A Flemish Kermis* in Paris (fig. 58).

The music is provided by a motley band of oboe and strings pushed up against the pillars to the right; the dancing seems improvised, even somewhat rustic (the dancing male figure resembles another in Watteau's painting *The Country Ball*, now in a private collection, a work that offers a gentle satire on rustic manners).[3] There is quite a crowd; 66 figures have been identified. They interact easily, flirt and gossip. There is much play with fans. Details of clothing, faces and hands are rendered with deft flashes of the brush, giving a brilliant effect. The evening light, however, dissolves the distant landscape into indistinctness, throwing a mysterious veil over the gardens such that we can only just discern couples walking and sitting by the elegant fountain.

The intimacy of the exchanges contrasts with the grandiosity of the architecture, the massive portico reminding us that these revellers are of high birth and fortune. The ringed columns make reference to the Palais du Luxembourg in Paris, designed in about 1615 by Salomon de Brosse for Rubens's great patron Marie de Médicis. Evidently Watteau was greatly concerned with the setting, since X-radiography examination

140

JEAN-ANTOINE WATTEAU (1684–1721)
The Pleasures of the Ball, 1715–17
Oil on canvas, 52.6 x 65.4 cm
By Permission of the Trustees of Dulwich Picture Gallery, London, inv. DPG 156

PROVENANCE: (?) François II de Boyer de Bandol; Claude Glucq; Louis Pasquier; Jean de Jullienne; Marquis de Montesquiou; Noel Desenfans; Sir Francis Bourgeois; by whom bequeathed to Dulwich College, 1811
SELECTED REFERENCES: Posner 1984, pp. 167–69; Washington 1984, pp. 367–72; Plax 2000, pp. 133–35; Ramade and Eidelberg 2004, p. 65; Mirzoeff 2006, p. 130; Raymond 2013, p. 168

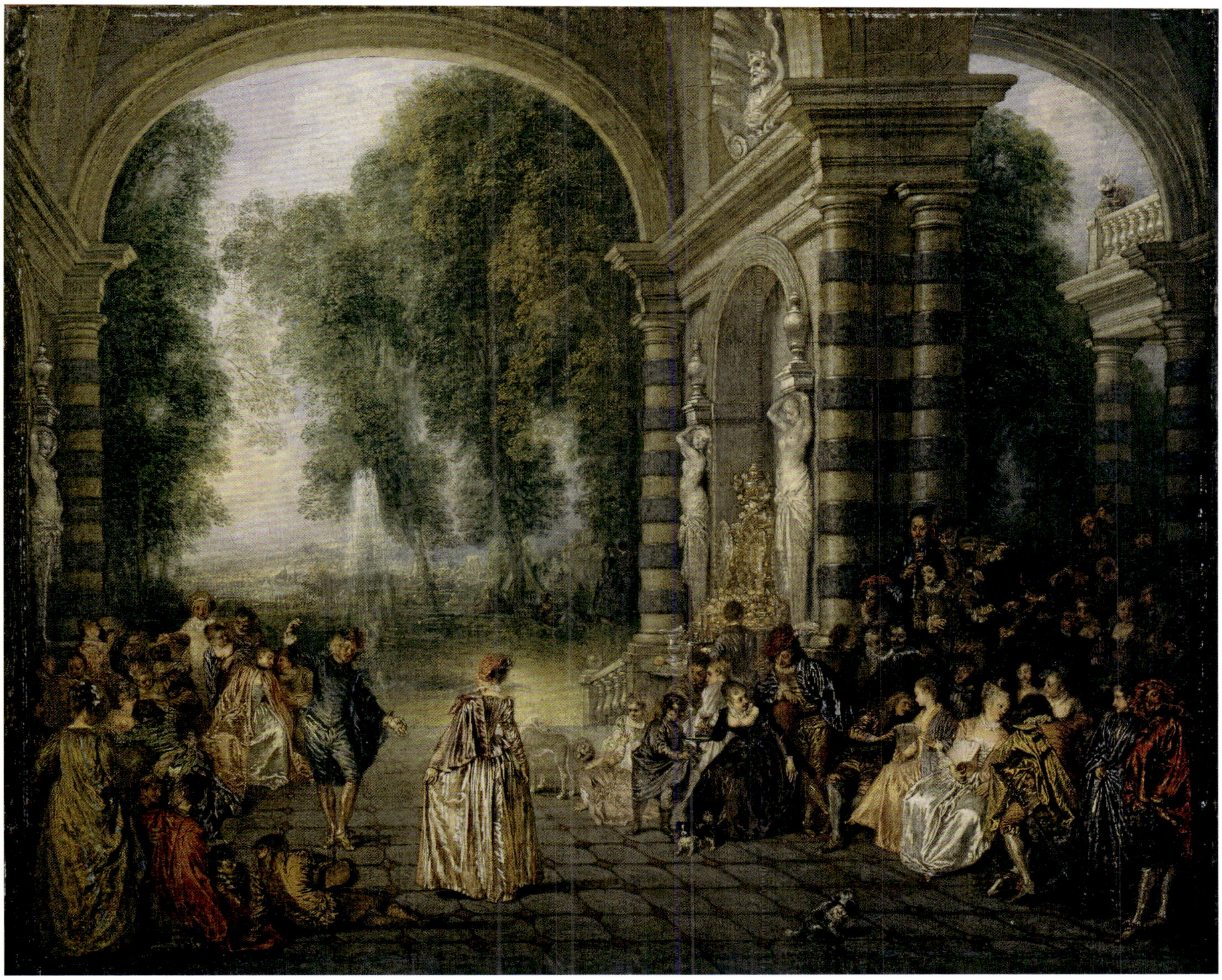

of the canvas has revealed that his original design was set in a colonnaded hall.[4] Between two slender and flirtatious caryatids is an outburst of gilded rococo ornament so opulent as to resemble a Hogarthian satire.

The Pleasures of the Ball was possibly painted for François II de Boyer de Bandol, president of the Parlement de Provence. In the early nineteenth century the work entered the collection of Dulwich College's Picture Gallery. John Constable thought the painting seemed to have been 'painted in honey: so mellow, so tender, so soft and so delicious'. Comparing it favourably to two masters he greatly admired, the landscape painter added: 'be satisfied if you touch but the hem of his garment, for this inscrutable and exquisite thing would vulgarise even Rubens and Paul Veronese'.[5] For William Hazlitt, Watteau 'might almost be said to breathe his figures and flowers onto the canvas – so fragile is their texture, so evanescent is his touch'.[6]

Jean-Antoine Watteau's technique as a draughtsman was acquired piecemeal, rather than through a standard academic training, in which study from the antique

141

JEAN-ANTOINE WATTEAU (1684–1721)
Studies of a Seated Woman and a Detail of Her Head and Shoulders, *c.* 1716
Red, black and white chalks on light-brown paper, 23.1 x 26.4 cm
Rijksmuseum, Amsterdam, inv. 692

PROVENANCE: Jacques Doucet; Charles Pardinel; François Coty; Fritz Mannheimer; Government of Holland, 1940; transferred to the Rijksmuseum, Amsterdam, 1953
SELECTED REFERENCES: Parker and Mathey 1957, vol. 2, no. 557; Posner 1984, pp. 237, 241; Roland Michel 1984, pp. 97–98; Washington 1984, p. 380; Rosenberg and Prat 1996, vol. 2, no. 476; Salomon 2010, pp. 50–52

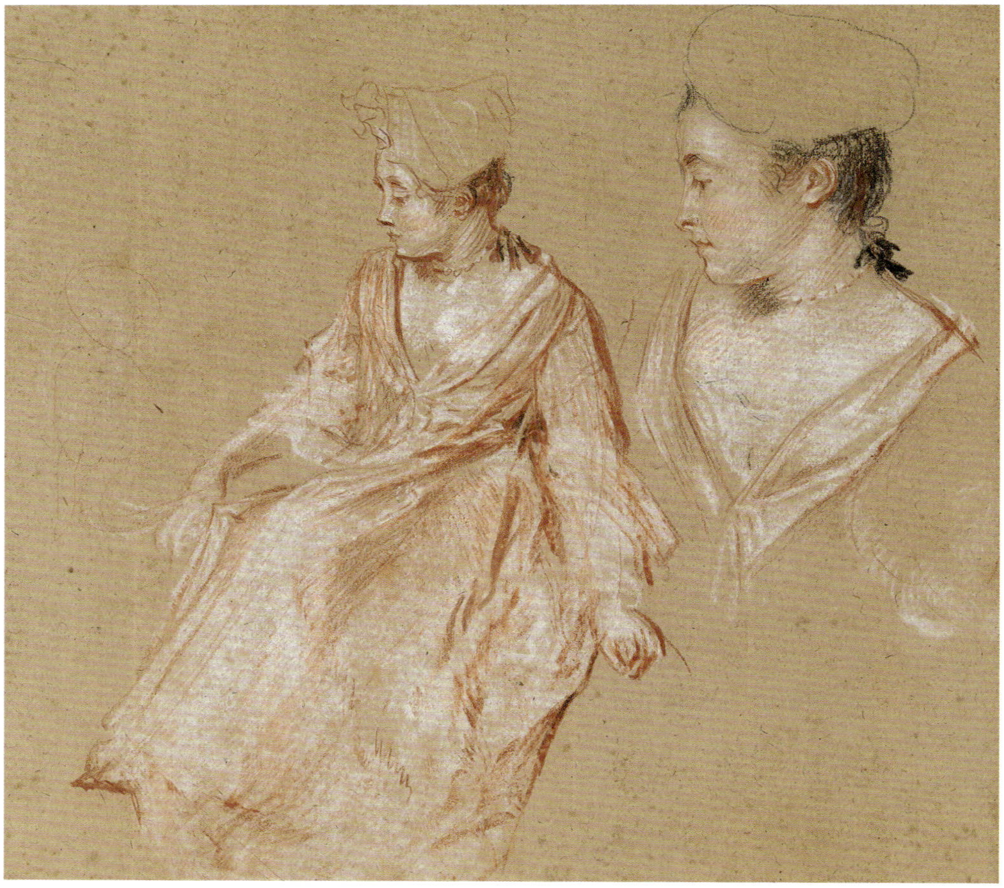

would precede working from life. He was profoundly affected by master drawings he studied in the Crozat collection. His mature drawings exhibit consummate mastery in the use of chalk, usually in three colours – red, white and black (the *trois crayons* technique) – on grey-brown paper. Comparison with sheets of multiple figures similarly composed and executed by Rubens reveals a distinct family resemblance – for example, in Rubens's seated young woman with raised arms (cat. 135) and Watteau's drawing of the same subject in the same medium (cat. 141). Unlike Rubens, however, Watteau seems not to have drawn in pen.[7]

Watteau clearly made studies of individuals in his circle, friends or servants; their faces recur through many sheets. These are not professional models who would sit for life classes at the Académie, nor do their poses follow standard arrangements suggested by classical sculpture. Rather, they have the look of everyday people going about their business – people, perhaps, such as the beautiful servant whom Antoine-Joseph Dezallier d'Argenville, author of a mid-eighteenth-century biography of Watteau, described the artist using as a model.[8] Watteau would begin with the deep red, or sanguine, chalk to delineate the face; black would follow with details of hair, clothing and jewellery. Finally, in white chalk he would draw in the collar line and add a shimmer to the highlights of the skin.

In many cases Watteau's drawings cannot be related to particular paintings and, indeed, were probably not intended as studies for a specific work; rather, they were storehouses of images for future

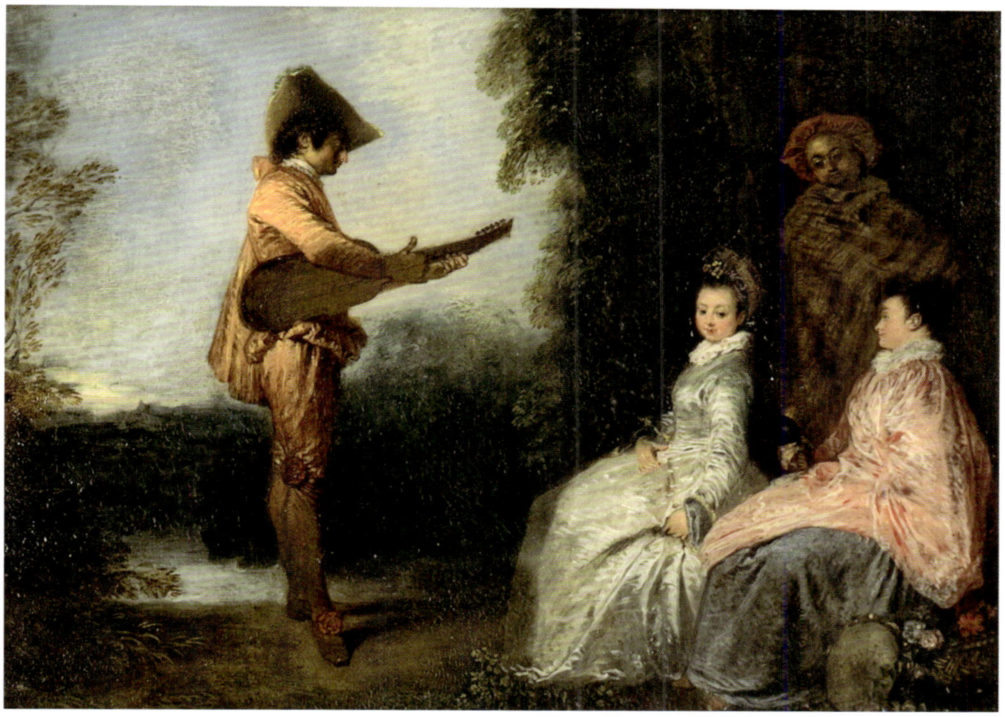

compositions.[9] The Count of Caylus (1692–1765) recalled that 'in general [Watteau] drew without any purpose .... When it took his fancy to paint a picture he resorted to his collection of studies, choosing such figures as suited him for the moment.'[10] The sheet of studies from the Petit Palais (cat. 142) can, however, be associated with several paintings. The man in profile at the lower left, to give one example, appears in the late version of his painting *The Enchanter* (fig. 57).

The sheet of *Studies of a Seated Woman and a Detail of Her Head and Shoulders* (cat. 141) is related to *Gallant Assembly* (*c.* 1718; Staatliche Museen zu Berlin) and *The Family* (1717–18; private collection).[11] Unusually, we can tentatively ascribe a name to the sitter. Posner identifies her as Mme Le Bouc-Santussan on the basis that *The Family* has been established, from a description in an inventory of 1777, as a portrait of the goldsmith Jean Le Bouc-Santussan, his wife and young son. For Posner, this work is 'a private conceit', in which a family portrait is concealed

FIG. 57 Jean-Antoine Watteau, *The Enchanter*, after 1718. Oil on copper, 19 x 26 cm. Brodick Castle, Isle of Arran (National Trust for Scotland)

within what seems to be a conversation piece.[12] Certainly the drawing makes every effort to convey a likeness of the female figure, adding a second study of the head in which her distinctive profile is more fully captured. TB

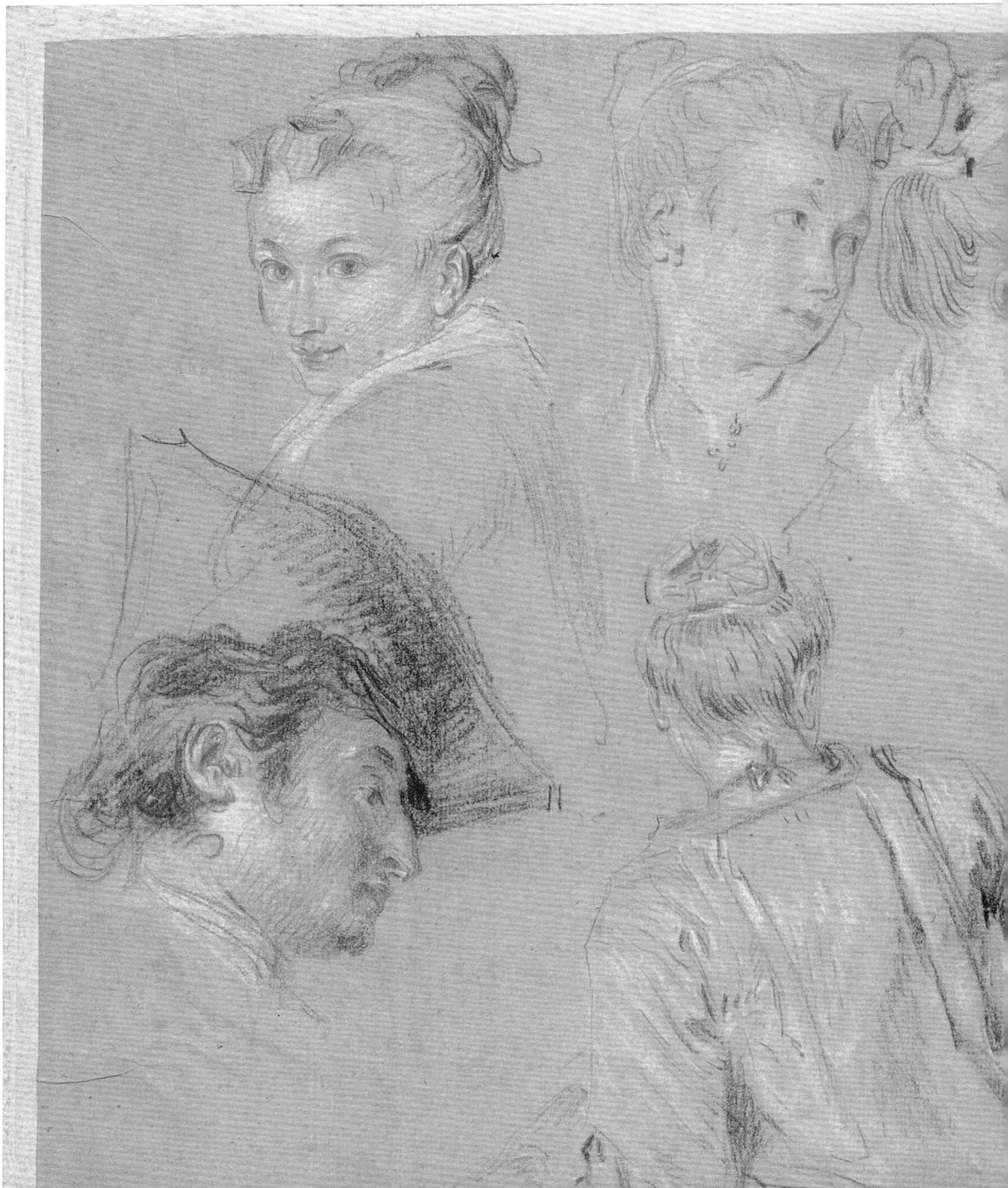

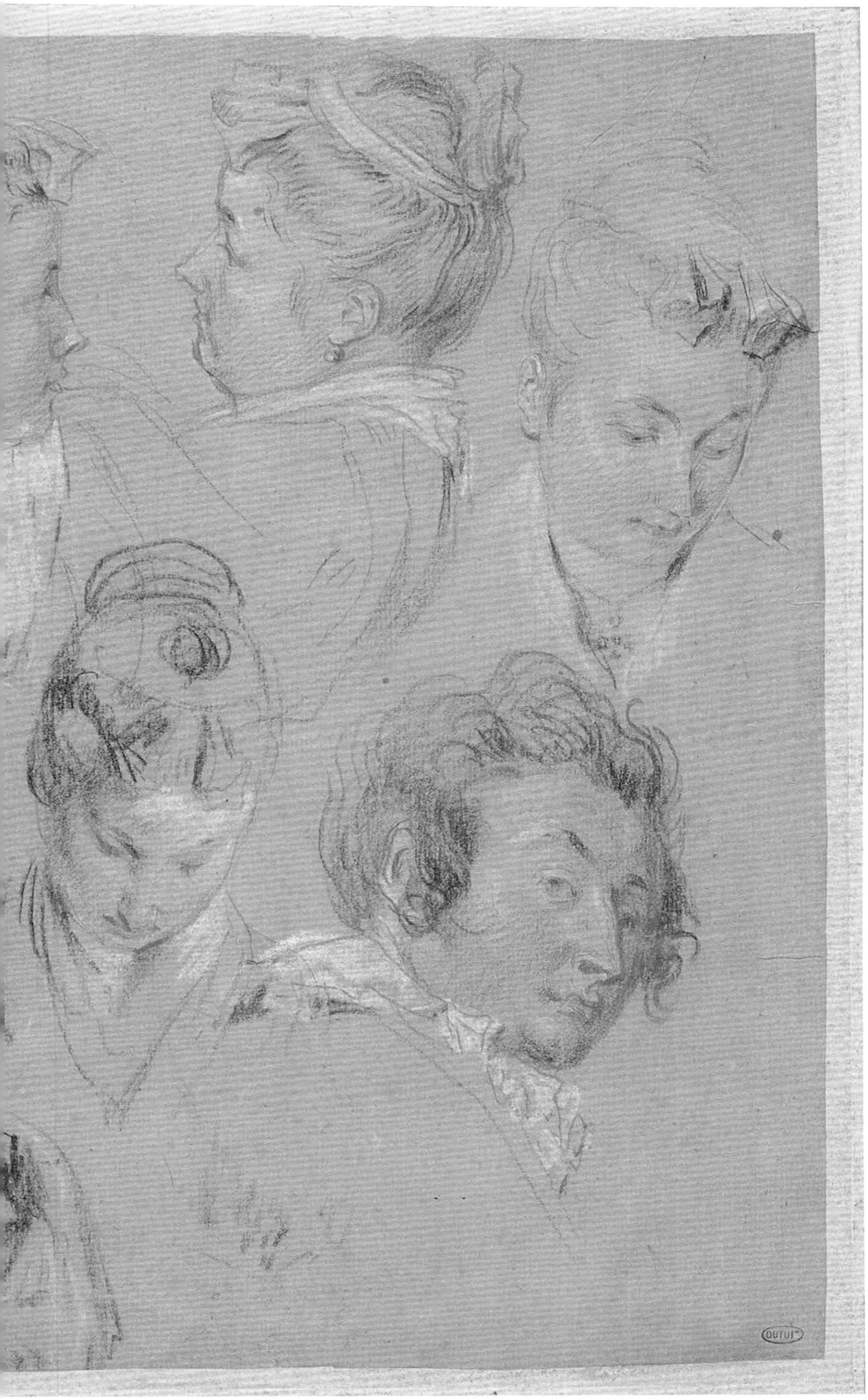

142

JEAN-ANTOINE WATTEAU
(1684–1721)
Sheet of Studies Showing Nine Heads,
c. 1717–18
Red, black and white chalk on yellowish grey paper, 27.0 x 42.0 cm
Musée du Petit Palais, Paris,
inv. DDUT 972
BOZAR ONLY

PROVENANCE: (?) Jean de Jullienne; Edouard Guichardot; M. Rutter; Auguste Dutuit; acquired by the Petit Palais, 1895
SELECTED REFERENCES: Parker and Mathey 1957, vol. 2, no. 731; Washington 1984, pp. 284–86, 382–83; Roland Michel 1987, pp. 120, 123

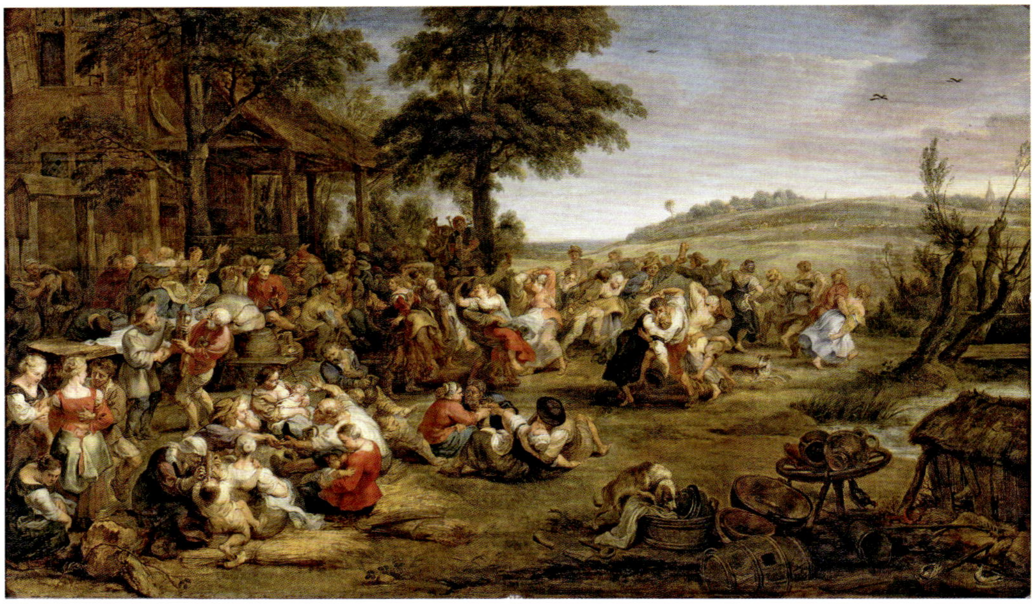

FIG. 58 Peter Paul Rubens, *A Flemish Kermis*, mid-1630s. Oil on wood, 149 x 261 cm. Musée du Louvre, Paris

Rubens's riotous painting *A Flemish Kermis* (fig. 58) is a celebration of Flemish folk culture and a homage to Pieter Bruegel the Elder. Rubens owned at least twelve paintings by Bruegel and more by Adriaen Brouwer, another Flemish artist identified with genre scenes of rustic interiors. The scene depicted seems to be a village festival connected with the patronal saint's day of the local church. Against the tranquil setting of a pastoral landscape and village buildings, a splendid orgy of music, dancing, feasting and drunkenness is taking place.

In preparation for the painting, Rubens created one of the most remarkable of all his sheets of drawings (cat. 143). A multitude of small figures initially set down in chalk have been in places redrawn with firm strokes of the pen. On the verso, from the upper-right corner, figures tumble down, feasting, brawling, chatting at trestle tables and, in at least one case, passing out drunk on the ground. Towards the bottom left, a man buys a foaming stein of ale, while another looks on, leaning on the wheel of a wagon. Despite the profusion of incident and observation, Rubens notes in writing that 'beggars ... roses [and] children' are missing.[1] He also jotted down memoranda about the colours of the peasants' clothing. The festivities are observed from above, as if from the gallery of an inn, a viewpoint familiar from Pieter Bruegel the Elder's works, such as the drawing *Kermis at Hoboken* (1559; Courtauld Institute of Art Gallery, London).

On the recto are figures of even greater interest: seventeen couples are shown dancing with unbridled vigour and passion. Some were drawn initially in chalk, but when reworking the group in ink, Rubens seems to have been inspired by the different medium to experiment with the potential of the complex positions of the peasants' bodies. In creating a sequence of dynamic couples he uncannily anticipates the interest of modernist artists in the body in motion in the era of photography and film. The sheet

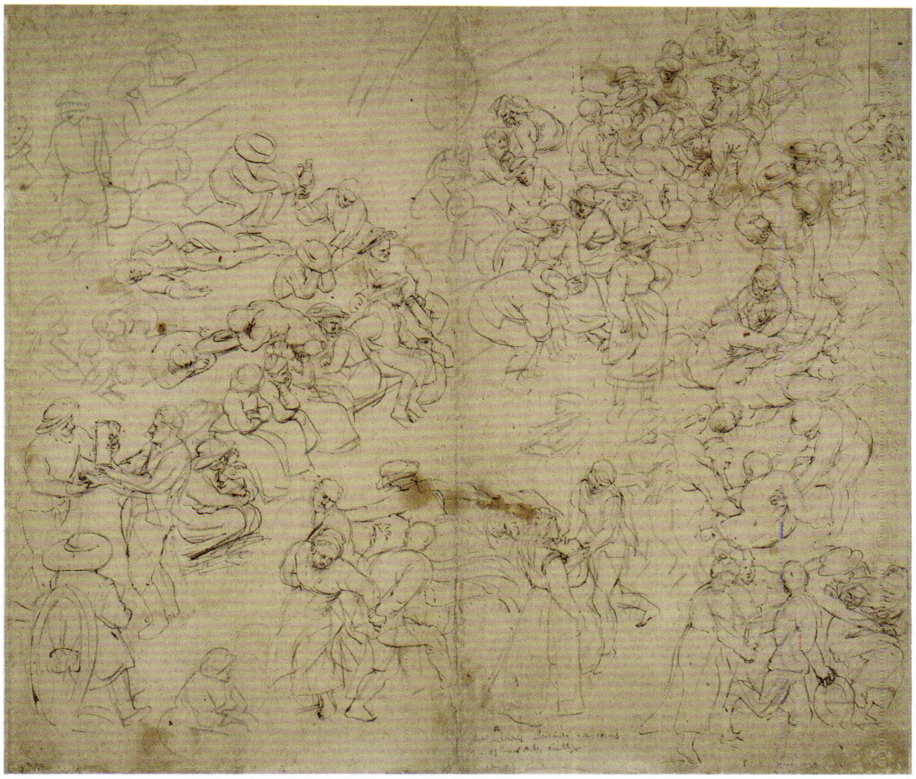

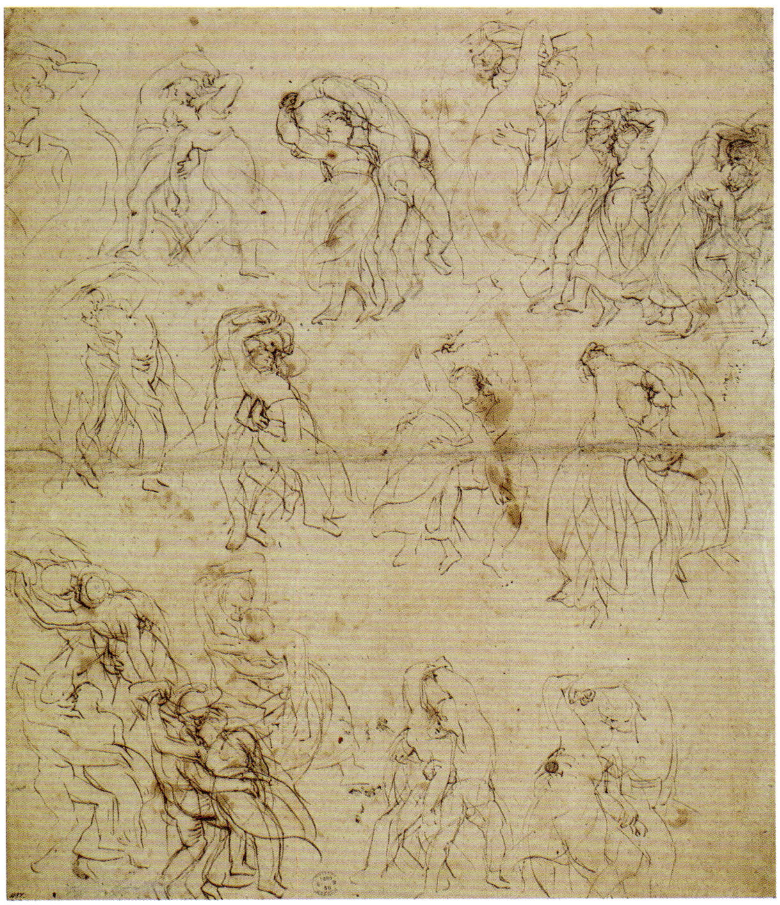

43.1–2

PETER PAUL RUBENS (1577–1640)
Studies for *A Flemish Kermis*, *c.* 1630–36
Verso: various studies for dancers, drinkers, onlookers and revellers; pen and dark brown ink over preliminary drawing in black chalk,
Recto: seventeen studies of dancing peasants; brown chalk and pen and brown ink (and a few traces of red chalk)
59.5 x 51.2 cm
On loan from the British Museum, London, inv. 1885,0509.50

PROVENANCE: Jonathan Richardson Sr; Sir Thomas Lawrence; Samuel Woodburn; Alphonse Wyatt Thibaudeau; William Russell
SELECTED REFERENCES: Held 1959, vol. 1, no. 57; Burchard and d'Hulst 1963, vol. 2, no. 150; London 1977, no. 178; Held 1986, nos 193, 194

144

JEAN-ANTOINE WATTEAU (1684–1721)
Couple Dancing, c. 1714
Red chalk on paper, 21.9 x 14.4 cm
Musée des Arts Décoratifs, Paris, inv. 1991.22.1a
RA ONLY

PROVENANCE: Marquis de Cavalière; Baron Louis-Auguste de Schwiter; H. E. Perrin; given to the Union Centrale des Arts Décoratifs; presented to the Musée des Arts Décoratifs, 1909
SELECTED REFERENCES: Parker and Mathey 1957, vol. 1, no. 279; Posner 1984, pp. 68–69; Rosenberg and Prat 1996, vol. 1, no. 245; Glorieux 2004, p. 47; Glorieux 2011, pp. 204–05; Raymond 2013, p. 118

145

JEAN-ANTOINE WATTEAU (1684–1721)
La Surprise: A Couple Embracing While a Figure Dressed as Mezzetin Tunes a Guitar, 1718–19
Oil on panel, 36.8 x 29.2 cm
Private collection

PROVENANCE: Nicolas Henin, Paris (1691–1724); Jean de Jullienne, Paris in 1731; Ange-Laurent de La Live de Jully, Paris (in 1764); François-Michel Harenc de Presle, Paris (in 1792); Citoyen M. Robit until 1801; Lady Murray until 1848
SELECTED REFERENCES: Rosenberg and Prat 1996, vol. 1, pp. 392–93, no. 245, vol. 2, pp. 762–63, no. 459; New York 2009, no. 11, pp. 42–44

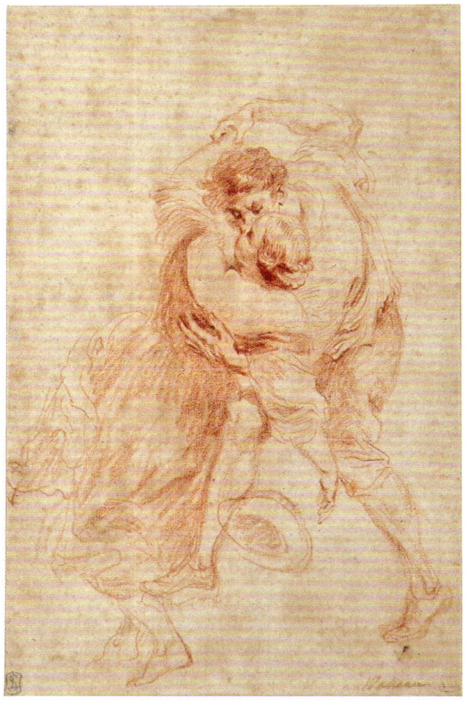

of drawings is overt in its celebration of the earthy sexuality of the dance: the couples are joined together at the lips, their solid bodies pivoting in motion around this nodal point.

The presence of Rubens's oil painting *A Flemish Kermis* in France's royal collection allowed Watteau the chance to study and copy a work that explicitly celebrated the folk culture of Watteau's – as well as Rubens's – Flemish homeland. On one sheet (cat. 146), Watteau made a measured annotation of some of the relatively static figures to the left of the composition, but far more significant was the drawing *Couple Dancing* (cat. 144), probably made in 1714. In this significant work, he used sanguine (red chalk) alone, creating a compositional unit that was to become a profound generative force in his work. The figures appear in the right middle ground of Rubens's tableau (recto), their strong, youthful bodies bound together in a Bernini-like outburst of energy. The man's hat falls to the floor; his strong left hand supports the woman, while his right hand grasps her left wrist as they corkscrew around in frenzied clockwise motion. Watteau depicted the dancers, in JoLynn Edwards's words, 'with rapid strokes, open contours and loose modelling that re-enact the swinging movement of the figures'.[2] As Edwards notes, Watteau established a 'pivotal focus' in the man's hair and the low neckline of the back of the woman's dress, effecting a metamorphosis from the Dionysian baroque dynamism of the original figures into the more graceful dances of the *fête galante*.

In *La Surprise* (cat. 145), Watteau paid double homage to Rubens. The couple embracing on the left are derived from *A Flemish Kermis*, of which, as we have seen, Watteau had made an energetic yet delicate drawing. These two, perhaps in fancy dress, perhaps theatrical performers, seem to have been possessed by sudden and uncontrollable desire, and embrace passionately. The guitarist, tuning his instrument, starts in surprise at the dramatic turn of events. Watteau adapts the heavy peasant dance of Rubens's original, reworking it with more genteel personalia in an Arcadian setting. The position of the man's body is hard to comprehend; seemingly seated (unlike Rubens's dancers), his balance is precarious. He holds his partner in a static pose in contrast to the rapid movement of the Flemish peasant. His grasp of the lady's pale wrist is gentler than that of Rubens's boor. The interplay of forms has taken on a quality of rococo lightness.

Elements of emotional, even moral, ambiguity creep into the image on close examination. The lady appears to turn her face a little towards the viewer, leaving the impassioned suitor to kiss only her cheek. The lover has sinister long fingernails, far more so than the guitarist (who, as he is not using a plectrum, might be expected to need them). The lover's eyes and pointed nose give him

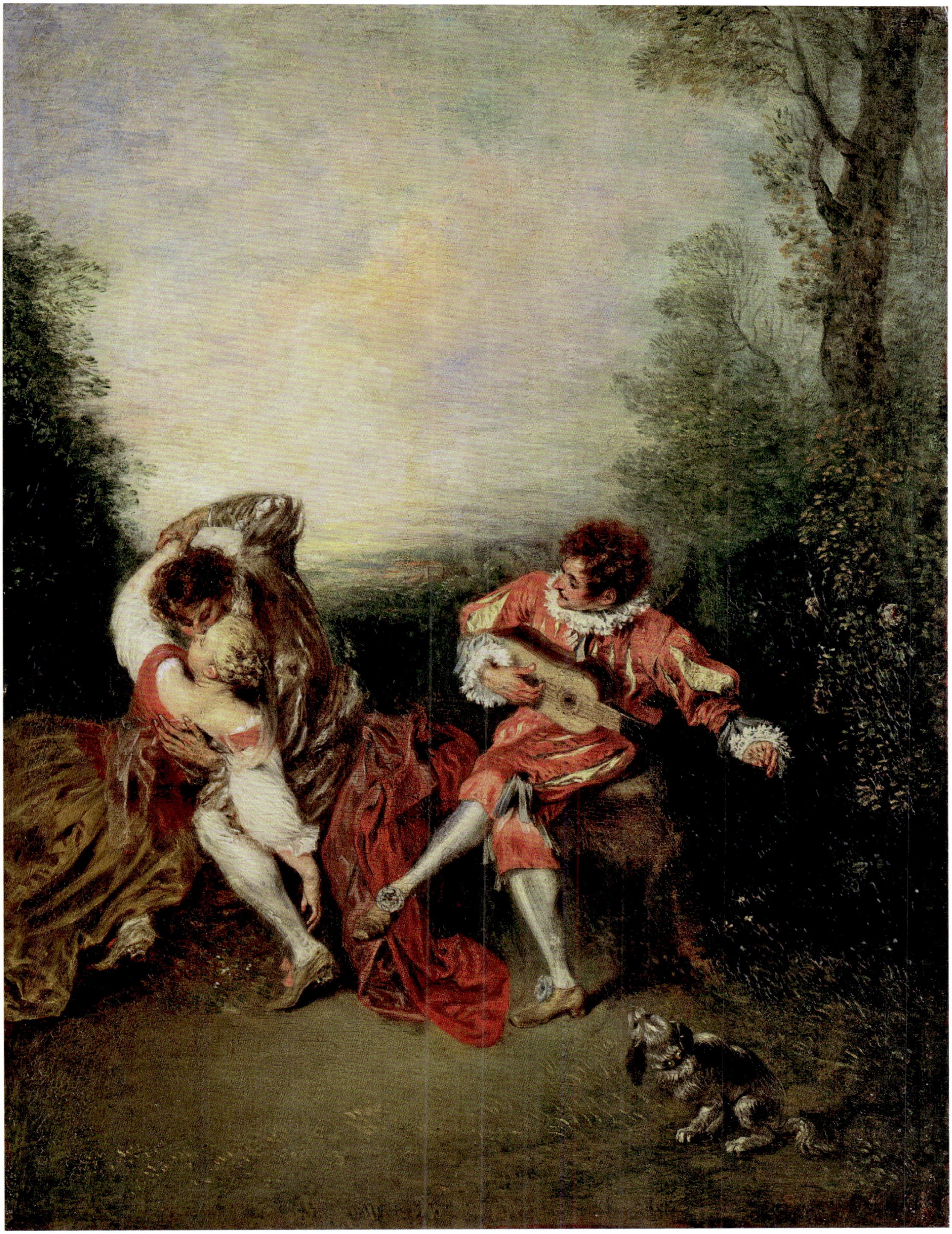

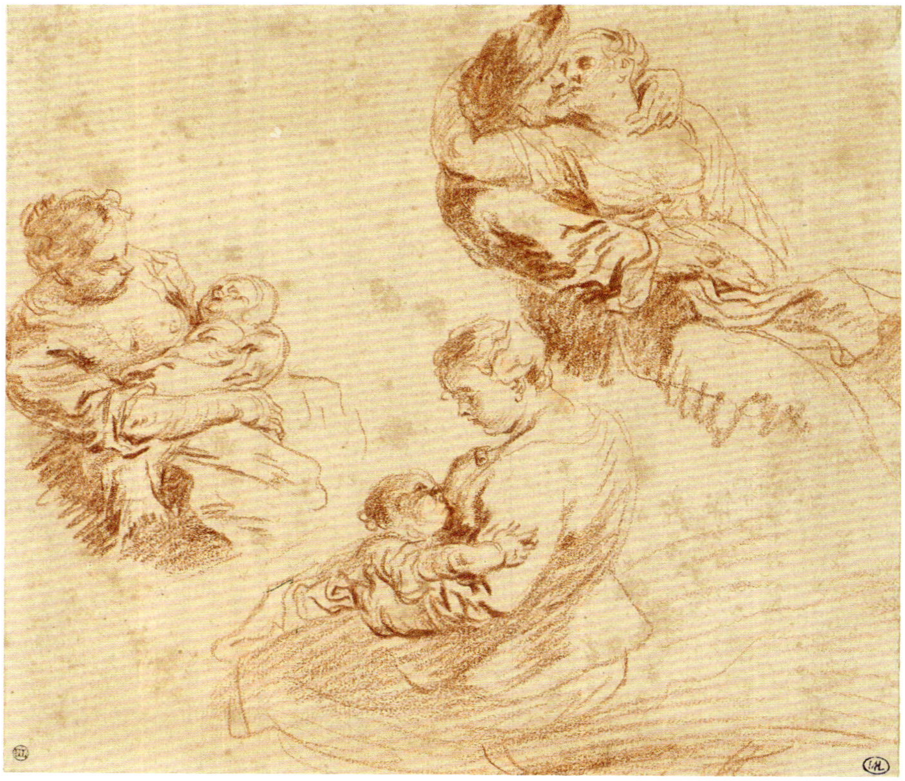

146

JEAN-ANTOINE WATTEAU (1684–1721)
A Pair of Lovers and Two Women with Their Children, c. 1715–17
Red chalk on paper, 17 x 19.8 cm
Musée du Louvre, Paris, Département des Arts graphiques, inv. RF 776
BOZAR ONLY

PROVENANCE: Aimé Charles Horace His de la Salle; given to the Louvre in 1878
SELECTED REFERENCES: Parker and Mathey 1957, vol. 1, p. 261; Banks 1977, pp. 224, 290; Roland Michel 1984, p. 145; Moureau and Morgan Grasselli 1987, p. 249, n. 22; Rosenberg and Prat 1996, vol. 2, no. 426

a decidedly sinister, even vampiric, quality, quite at odds with the honest rough and tumble of *A Flemish Kermis*. The lady, perhaps, is more surprised than anyone.

The figure of the guitarist, traditionally identified as Mezzetin, is a character from the *commedia dell'arte*, a form of vernacular musical theatre that was fashionable in all classes of Parisian society. Mezzetin, a musician, was a duplicitous character often involved in crime and deception; but he was also disappointed in love. The costume appears in many of Watteau's works and was almost certainly kept in his studio. Mezzetin alone, playing the same guitar, is the subject of a canvas from the same date as *La Surprise* (and held at the Metropolitan Museum of Art, New York).

The comical small dog in the foreground of *La Surprise* seems to have been derived, paradoxically, from a far grander source than the couple: it has migrated from the foreground of the wedding in Rubens's Marie de Médicis cycle (see cat. 34.8). In Rubens's painting, the startled animal stands as a comical contrast to the spectacular grandeur of the solemn rite being enacted behind. In Watteau's work, the position of the dog is reversed in what is surely a humorous gesture.

The panel was originally in the collection of Nicolas Henin, Councillor to the King of France and a friend of the artist. It was believed to be lost until its rediscovery in an English collection in 2007, which provided a major addition to Watteau's surviving *œuvre*. TB

ENDNOTES

INTRODUCTION
NICO VAN HOUT
I am indebted to Duncan Bull, Herwig Todts, Friso Lammertse and Adri Verburg for stimulating talks on this subject and their comments on both the introduction, and the chapter on Violence that follows it.

PAGES 16-21

1 De Piles 1699, p. 402: 'Aucun Peintre n'a traîté di doctement ni si clairement que Rubens les Sujets Allégoriques: & comme l'Allégorie est une éspéce de langage, & que par consequent elle doit être autorisée par l'usage, & entenduë de plusieurs, il y a introduit seulement les symbols que les Médailles & les autres Monuments de l'Antiquité ont rendus familiers, du moins entre les Savans.'
2 Schaffer 2007, pp. 36–37.
3 *The Fall of the Rebel Angels* (1842) measures 1,153 x 793 cm, *The Triumph of Christ* (1848) 625 x 1,104 cm and *A Great of the World* (1860) 918 x 680 cm. See Namur 2007.
4 Eiselein 1825, p. 145: 'Rubens hat nach der unerschöpflichen Fruchtbarkeit seines Geistes wie Homer gedichtet: er ist reich bis zur Verschwendung: er hat das Wunderbare wie jener gesucht, überhaupt wie ein dichterischer und allgemeiner Maler, und insbesondere was Komposition und Licht und Schatten betrifft.'
5 Baudelaire 1992, p. 162: 'Un des caractères principaux du grand peintre est l'universalité. – Ainsi le poète épique, Homère ou Dante, sait faire également bien une idylle, un récit, un discours, une description, une ode, etc. De même, Rubens, s'il peint des fruits, peindra des fruits plus beaux qu'un specialiste quelconque.' The comparison also holds true for Eugène Delacroix; see Delacroix 1996, p. 627.
6 Taine 1869, p. 63: '... il a sous sa main toute la nature humaine, sauf la plus haute cime. C'est pourquoi son invention est la plus vaste qu'on ait vue et comprend tout les types, cardinaux italiens, empereurs romains, seigneurs contemporains, bourgeois, paysans, vachères, avec les diversités innombrables que le jeu des focus naturelles imprime aux creatures, et plus de quinze cents tableaux ne suffisent pas à l'épuiser.'
7 London 2005; Brussels 2007.
8 Artists who collected Rubens's drawings include Prosper Henry Lankrink, Jan Boeckhorst, Erasmus Quellinus II, Joachim von Sandrart, Matthäus Merian II, Jonathan Richardson I, Jacob de Wit, Thomas Hudson and Sir Thomas Lawrence (see New York 2005). Rembrandt, Sir Joshua Reynolds and Léon Bonnat owned paintings and oil sketches by the master.
9 Providence 1975.
10 Heck 2005.
11 Baudelaire 1992, pp. 373–74.
12 Taine 1869, p. 67: 'Comme un dieu indien qui est de loisir, il soulage sa fécondité en créant des mondes et, depuis les incomparables pourpres froissées et reployées de ses simarres jusqu'aux blancheurs neigeuses de ses chairs ou la soie pale de ses chevelures blondes, il n'y a pas un ton dans une de ses toiles qui ne soit venu se poser de lui-même en lui faisant plaisir.'
13 Reynolds 1996, pp. 201–13.
14 Renger 1974–75; Van Hout 2004.
15 Herremans and Van Hout 2012; Porter and Béland 2004.
16 Bellori 2005, p. 205.
17 I refer to instances of 'Rubens hatred' such as that expressed by the American painter Thomas Eakins: 'Rubens is the nastiest, most vulgar, noisy painter that ever lived ... His pictures always put me in mind of chamber pots and I would not be sorry if they were all burnt.' See Kirkpatrick 2006, pp. 121–22. See also William Blake's tirades in Wark 1997, appendix I, p. 308: 'All Rubens's Pictures are Painted by Journeymen & so far from being all of a Piece, are The most wretched Bungles.' 'To My Eye Rubens's Colouring is most Comtemptible. His Shadows are of a Filthy Brown somewhat the Colour of Excrement; these are fill'd with tints & messes of yellow & red. His lights are all the colours of the Rainbow, laid on Indiscriminately & broken one into another. Altogether his Colouring is Contrary to The Colouring of Real Art & Science.'
18 Delacroix 1996, p. 365.
19 Vollard 1938, p. 222.
20 Riley 1997, pp. 41–42.
21 Horace, *Ars Poetica*, 128–31.
22 McKim-Smith 1995.
23 Vincent to Theo van Gogh in a letter (552) written between 12 and 16 January 1886 and sent from Antwerp.
24 Vollard 1838, p. 210: 'Aussi bien, pour ce qui est des influences en peinture, je vais vous citer un trait personnel. Dans les commencements, je mettais des épaisseurs de vert et de jaune, croyant avoir par là plus de "valeurs". Un autre jour, au Louvre, je m'aperçois que Rubens, avec un simple frottis, avait obtenu davantage que moi avec toutes mes épaisseurs. Une autre fois, je découvre qu'avec du noir Rubens donnait de l'argent. Il va de soi que, les deux fois, j'ai profité de la leçon, mais cela veut-il dire que j'ai subi l'influence de Rubens?'
25 Ruskin 1843, vol. 1, chapter 2, *Of Truth of Colour*, p. 165, §12.

VIOLENCE
NICO VAN HOUT

PAGES 24-30

1 See Düsseldorf 2008–09 and Munich 2009A.
2 Schopenhauer 1839, pp. 374–75, quoted from Düsseldorf 2008–09, p. 166, source 53: 'Ich konnte vor innerem Grauen den Anblick kaum ertragen und auch nicht mich davon abwenden.'
3 Forster 1791, vol. 1, VII, p. 136: 'Nein, es war keine der Musen, die den Künstler zu solchen Ausgeburten begeisterte. An der dythyrambischen Wuth, die durch das Ganze strömt, an diesen trauben-ähnlichen Gruppen von Menschen, die als ekelhaftes Gewürm in einander verschlungen, eine verworrene Masse von Gliedern, und – schaudernd schreib' ich was ich sehe – einen kanibalischen Fleischmarkt vorstellen, erkennt man die wilde, bacchantische Mänas, die alle Bescheidenheit der Natur verläugnet, und voll ihres Gottes, den Harmonieschöpfer Orpheus zerreisst.'
4 Hasslin 1953, p. 73: 'Hilf Himmel, welch ein ästhetisches Gefühl hat so mancher gepriesener Künstler gehabt! Sind das Gegenstände, die eine Abbildung verdienen? Gegenstände, die ich in der Natur nicht sehen möchte.' That the horrendous, the violent and the devastating, as well as expressions of bodily pain, have no place in art is also the opinion of the philosopher Friedrich Schlegel. See Bock von Wülfingen 1947, p. 63.
5 Baudelaire 1992, pp. 57–58: 'ce genre de dessin, qui a quelque analogie avec celui de tous les grands coloristes, de Rubens par exemple, rend bien rend parfaitement le mouvement, la physionomie, le caractère insaisissable et tremblant de la nature, que le dessin de Raphaël ne rend jamais.'
6 Rubens possibly knew Titian's *Battle of Spoleto* from the print by Giulio Fontana (1569). The original in the Doge's Palace in Venice was destroyed by fire in 1577. See Poeschel 2001, p. 92.
7 Heinse 2012, p. 71: 'ein Stück voll heroischer Stärke aus dem Zeitalter des Theseus ... Gewalt in Männerschultern und Armen und Fäusten mit dem Mordgewehr, und Brust und Knie: und in den Bäumen, dem immer anderen Satz und Strang und Wurf der Streitrosse.'
8 In his *Salon de 1761*, Diderot refers to the print by Cornelis Galle I (Vorhelm Schneevogt 1873, p. 10, no. 79, Hollstein, vol. 7, no. 31): 'J'aime bien les tableaux ... dont on détourne la vue, pourvue que ce soit d'horreur, et non de dégout. Qu'y a-t-il de plus horrible que l'action et le sang-froid de la Judith de Rubens? Elle tient le sabre, et elle l'enfonce tranquillement dans la gorge d'Holopherne.' (Seznec and Adhémar 1957, vol. 1, p. 114). We observe the same reaction from the sculptor Falconet: see Weinshenker 1966, p. 16.
9 Providence 1975, p. 15.
10 The topographical backgrounds in this series were actually outsourced to Pieter Snayers, a painter of battle scenes. See Van Hout 2001A
11 For example, he copied figures from a print after Rubens's *Fall of the Rebel Angels*. See New York 1988, no. 55. Stanford University Museum of Art, inv. no. 67.50.
12 Lederballe 2000.
13 Burckhardt 1949, p. 142.
14 These hunting scenes were intended for the Archdukes Albert and Isabella, the Duke of Aarschot, the Duke of Hamilton, Maximilian of Bavaria and Philip IV of Spain, all of whom were passionate hunters. See Balis 1986.
15 Balis 1986, pp. 71–72.
16 On the influence of Rubens on Delacroix's hunting scenes, see Rudrauf 1956 and Kliman 1983. Delacroix drew inspiration for his animal scenes not only from Rubens but also from the bronzes by the animal artist Antoine-Louis Barye (1795–1875). See Paris 1998, pp. 77–78. I find it less likely that the static engravings by Tempesta and Stradanus and the three small, rare hunting etchings by Rembrandt had an impact on Delacroix.
17 In a letter from Tangiers of 8 February 1832, Delacroix states that 'everything that Gros and Rubens have invented is small beer in comparison' ('tout ce que Gros et Rubens ont inventé de furies n'est que peu de chose auprès'). See Joubin 1935, p. 311.
18 Balis 1986, p. 49.

19 This possibility was suggested in Paris 1998, p. 80. The 1615–16 canvas by Rubens was completely destroyed by fire in 1870.
20 Baudelaire 1868, p. 241: 'Jamais couleurs plus belles, plus intenses, ne pénétrèrent jusqu'à l'âme par le canal des yeux.'

PAGES 32–35

1 Another, more elaborate chalk study of this subject, executed in the 1630s, is to be found in the Stedelijk Prentenkabinet in Antwerp (Held 1986, no. 97).
2 Jaffé 1989, no. 1376.

PAGES 38–39

1 Renger 1974, pp. 150–51.
2 Renger 1974, p. 151; Robels 1996, p. 79; Balis 1986, pp. 46–49.
3 Rembrandt also etched a *Small Lion Hunt with One Lion* (*c.* 1629) and a *Small Lion Hunt with Two Lions* (*c.* 1632). See White and Boon 1969, nos 115 and 116.
4 Suggested by Luijten in London and Amsterdam 2000, under no. 42.
5 Held 1980, vol. 1, nos 298–300.
6 See Rooses 1897, p. 56. After the artist's death in 1640, we do encounter copies of *modelli* in the possession of former assistants, tapestry dealers and members of the painter's family.
7 Delacroix 1996, p. 121.
8 Delacroix 1996, p. 140, 6 March 1847.
9 Delacroix, 1996, p. 121: 'Sur la description, ce tableau semblera de tout point inférieur au precedent; cependant par la manière dont les groups sont disposes, ou plutôt du seul et unique groupe qui forme le tableau tout entier, l'imagination reçoit un choc, qui se renouvelle toutes les fois qu'on y jette les yeux, de même que, dans la *Chasse aux lions*, elle est toujours jetée dans la meme incertitude des lignes. Dans la *Chasse à l'hippopotame*, le monstre amphibie occupe le centre; cavaliers, chevaux, chiens, tous se precipitant sur lui avec fureur. La composition offre à peu près la disposition d'une croix de Saint-André, avec l'hippopotame au milieu. … Et ce qui est d'un effet incomparable, c'est cette grande partie du ciel qui encadre le tout de deux côtés, surtout dans la partie gauche qui est entièrement nue, et donne à l'ensemble, par la simplicité de ce constraste, un mouvement, une variété, et en meme temps une unité incomparables.'

PAGE 44

1 Drawing in brown ink over black chalk, Albertina, inv. no. 15097. Julius S. Held describes this pen-and-ink drawing – incorrectly, in my opinion – as 'crude' and 'without much imagination'. The many differences between the drawing and the painting indicate, after all, that this sheet represents a creative stage and was not intended as a copy (Held 1986, p. 114).
2 See Royalton-Kisch 1999, p. 13 and no. 2, pp. 66–67.
3 For example, the *Coup de Lance* in the Royal Museum of Fine Arts Antwerp, and *The Descent from the Cross* in the Palais des Beaux-Arts de Lille. See Van Hout 2011B and 2013.
4 Ehrlich White 1967 (pp. 39 and 50) wrongly assumes that Delacroix painted his copy after a reproductive print by François Deroy.
5 Ehrlich White 1967, no. 4; formerly Mme Noémi Renan Collection, Paris.
6 Ehrlich White 1967, pp. 37–39.
7 Delacroix 1996, p. 616; 13 January 1857: 'âgé de plus de cinquante ans, dans la mission dont il fut chargé auprès du roi d'Espagne, employait le temps qu'il ne donnait pas aux affaires, à copier à Madrid les superbes originaux italiens qu'on y voit encore. Il avait dans sa jeunesse copié énormément. Cet exercice des copies, entièrement negligé par les écoles modernes, était la source d'un immense savoir.'

PAGES 48–51

1 Du Camp 1885, p. 94.
2 Painted copies by Odilon Redon of 1855 (Musée des Beaux-Arts de Bordeaux) and by Pierre Andrieu (Palais Bourbon, Paris) and a drawn copy by Charles-François Daubigny of 1864 (Mildred Lane Kemper Art Museum, St Louis, Missouri).
3 Delacroix 1996, 26 April 1858, p. 717.

PAGE 52

1 James Ward's *View in Tabley Park* (1813–18; Tate Britain, London) and *The Morning Grey* (1853; Royal Academy of Arts, London) refer to *The Watering Place* by Rubens. Ward's *Three Views of the Head of a Native* (1815; British Museum, London) was possibly inspired by a version of Rubens's *Four Studies of a Male Head* now in the Getty Museum, Los Angeles (Held 1980, vol. 1, no. 441, copy 1) – an oil sketch documented from 1818 in the collection of the 13th Earl of Derby at Knowsley, Prescot – or by Rubens's *Two Studies of a Levantine Man* (Held 1980, vol. 1, no. 448). A design for *The Battle of Marston Moor, 1644* (1829; Cromwell Museum in Huntingdon) is painted in the style of Rubens's battle scenes.
2 The Metropolitan Museum of Art, New York, inv. no. 190.73; Baetjer 2009, no. 129.

PAGES 56–58

1 The institution was at that point known as the Musée Central des Arts, and occupied only the Grande Galerie and the Salon Carré.
2 Stanford University Museum of Art. See Los Angeles 1971, no. 76; Providence 1975, no. 75.
3 *The Mutiny on the Medusa*, a preparatory drawing for *The Raft of the Medusa*, was directly inspired by Rubens's *Small Last Judgement*; Eitner 1971, p. 51.
4 This is the current but disputed title, discussed at length in Van Hout 2001A, pp. 28–29.
5 Namur 2007, p. 24: 'le pas du sublime au ridicule a été complètement franchi'.
6 Andree 1977, no. 386.
7 Andree 1977, no. 417.
8 Ranke 1977, p. 68, compares Böcklin's subject-matter to the contemporary railway drawings by Turner and Menzel.

PAGES 62–65

1 See Van Hout 2011A. Similar compositions exist elsewhere: an oil sketch on canvas is to be found in the Palazzo Pitti and bears the inscription 'Langhiano'; a drawing in Chantilly has however been tentatively attributed to Jan Boeckhorst (Florence 1977, pp. 62–63); there is a painting in London (Von Simson 1986, p. 241 and no. 2); a drawing is preserved in the Nationalmuseum in Stockholm; another painting belongs to the Roselius collection in Bremen.

PAGES 66–75

1 Letter from Roger de Piles to Philip Rubens. See Ruelens 1883, p. 170: 'qui estonne tout Paris'.
2 De Piles 1681, pp. 88–89: '… personne ne le regarde attentivement qu'il ne soit frapé d'horreur, & qu'il ne descende, pour ainsi dire, tout vivant dans les enfers. Les ignorans, sans y penser, en font l'éloge aussi-bien que les plus savans Connoisseurs; les premiers détournant leurs yeux, âprès l'avoir regardé quelques tems, parce qu'ils n'en peuvent souffrir l'effet terrible, & qu'l leur semble effectivement voir de véritables damnés, & les savans, en changeant aussi-tost cette terreur en admiration …'.
3 De Piles 1681, p. 91.
4 Freedberg 1984, p. 226, note 31. This great monument was later moved to Mannheim, where it is still preserved.
5 A copy of the drawing is to be found in the Teylers Museum, Haarlem (inv. U+ 002).
6 British Museum inv. nos 1994,0514.33–36. Freedberg 1984, no. 52, (copies 2–5). Another, similar copy is preserved in the Louvre, Paris, Département des Arts graphiques (inv. RF50875). There is also a group of ten drawings in the Rubens Cantoor collection, Copenhagen. See Freedberg 1984, under no. 52, (copies 22–32).
7 The complete image of Le Brun's composition can be seen in a canvas by François Verdier (1652–1730) in the Palace of Versailles (inv. MV6266). See Thuillier 1967, p. 265, ill. 11.
8 Uhr 1990, pp. 26, 69, 142 and 159.
9 Corinth 1909, p. 55.
10 See Wyss 2008.

POWER

ALEXIS MERLE DU BOURG

PAGES 78–87

1 Intriguingly, in the engraving (fig. 12, after a portrait by Van Dyck), Rubens is seen assuming an attitude that is surprisingly deferential, given that his self-portraits show a much more supercilious character. These self-portraits are consistent with his reaction when his dignity or reputation came under threat, a reaction that can be clearly read in his letters. In selecting the pose, Van Dyck apparently intended to evoke the charm of a *cortegiano* familiar with court practices (of which Rubens was a supreme embodiment).
2 On Rubens as court painter, see in particular the synthesis by Alejandro Vergara, 'El universo cortesano de Rubens', in Madrid 1999, pp. 67–89.
3 The acquisition of privileges preventing the counterfeiting of his work, and the dedications penned by Rubens at the lower edge of his prints, indicate the employment of a strategy of self-promotion on an international scale. See Hottle 2004, pp. 55–85.
4 Throughout this section on 'Power', reference is made to the 'apologetic'

painterly language of Rubens. I use the term in relation to its more original sense of 'apologia', i.e. a work imbued with the quality of a vindication or a justification, rather than an act of deference or concession.

5 Sabatier 1984, in particular pp. 305ff.

6 With the exception of Van Dyck (Barnes et al. 2004, no. II 32, III 68 and IV 47) or Crayer (Vlieghe 1972, vol. 1, nos A253 and A255), the frontal equestrian portrait was a rarity in succeeding generations.

7 Van der Meulen 1994, vol. 1, no. 168 (a, b) and White 1999, pp. 117–23.

8 See De Vries 2004, pp. 147–58. The concept of *Pittura mista* ('mixed painting') refers to the combination of narrative, historical elements and allegorical, poetic elements within the same painted work.

9 This was the opinion of Eugène Delacroix, to whom the 'real protagonists' of Rubens's heterogeneous compositions were the supernatural beings (Delacroix 1848, p. 502).

10 Merle du Bourg 2004B, pp. 71ff., 227ff. and 283ff.

11 Ibid., pp. 191–92. The 'quarrel of the marvellous' debated the suitability and pre-eminence of Christian and mythological/pagan characters in epic poetry.

12 Seznec 1980; 1993 edition, pp. 374ff.

13 Dubos 1993, pp. 62ff.

14 Diderot 2007, especially p. 58.

15 Winckelmann 1825, pp. 46 and 58.

16 Sulzer 1771–74; French edition 1798–99, in particular pp. 272–73.

17 There still existed a few 'contrary' defenders of Rubens's allegorical language, including the painter and theorist Michel-François Dandré-Bardon, author of a vigorous, anti-Dubos *Apologie des Allégories de Rubens et de Le Brun*, Paris, 1777.

18 See the survey of 'quotations' from Rubens's compositions in the work of Watteau, Merle du Bourg 2004B, pp. 293–98.

19 See the enlightening article by Jérémie Benoît (Benoît 1993), pp. 76–92.

20 Wildenstein 1973, p. 180 (no. 1547), Paris 2004–05, pp. 64–65 and 68, and Los Angeles 2005, pp. 40 and 50–51.

21 Rubens's *The Triumph of the Eucharist* was originally executed as a series of oil *modelli* (1625–26; the remaining sketches are scattered in many museums). Converted into large cartoons, the works were used as designs for a series of tapestries (1626–28) for the Monasterio de las Descalzas Reales, Madrid, where they still hang today.

22 Ward's passionate admiration for Rubens is confirmed by the large body of paintings, drawings and engravings he executed after the works of the Flemish artist. See in particular Cambridge 1991, p. 5, nos 10 and 58, as well as cat. 16 of the present volume.

23 The rout of Ward's *Triumph* is discussed at greater length in Nygren 1976, pp. 129–59 and 272–74; Lalumia 1984, pp. 28–32; and Beckett 1995, pp. 76–90, 124, 156–160, and 220 no. 1.

24 On the *Eucharist* cycle, see De Poorter, 1978; Held 1980, vol. 1, pp. 139–43, no. 90–119; Antwerp 1997; pp. 78–88 and Brussels, 2007, pp. 224–29.

25 Peter C. Sutton (Sutton 1993), in particular pp. 19ff.

26 Thuillier and Foucart 1967, pp. 78–79. For the persuasive case of William Etty, see most recently R. Green in York 2011, pp. 67–68.

27 Paris 2004, pp. 85–92, in particular p. 88.

28 Chappuis 1973, nos 369, 455, 456, 457, 1128.

29 'No stories are told by Rubens, it's like journalism, historical film …': this was Picasso on the subject of the exhibition *Rubens et son temps* at the Musée de l'Orangerie, Paris, in 1936; quoted in Kahnweiler 1988.

30 See in particular Sebastián López 1984, p. 94.

31 Baumstark 1974; Florence 1977, no. 97; Heinen 2004, pp. 196–225.

32 There was a perceptible Francoist attempt in Spain to associate Rubens with the imperial (and racial) outlook of the regime. In 1940, to celebrate the third centenary of the artist's death, E. Lafuente Ferrari published in the review *Vértice* an article entitled 'Raza y universalidad de Rubens'. He asserts powerfully that this 'active and eminent member of our Empire … because he is Baroque, because he is a humanist, because he is Catholic, and in spite of all the differences that separate us from his race, the citizen of Antwerp and ambassador of King Philip is a glory that we claim as our own …'; quoted in Barrachina 1998, p. 200.

33 Karel Vereycken, 'Rembrandt et Comenius contre Rubens: la lumière d'Agapè', <solidariteetprogres.org/documents-de-fond-7/culture/article/rembrandt-et-comenius-contre-rubens-la-lumiere-d.html solidaritéetprogres.org> [accessed 19 February 2014]

PAGE 88

1 State Hermitage Museum, St Petersburg, inv. 508, signed and dated 1621; Musées royaux des Beaux-Arts de Belgique, inv. 4342.

2 The theory sometimes put forward of a commission by the son of the late soldier, Charles Albert de Longueval (1607–1663), is obviously unsustainable.

3 The portrait of Longueval was probably printed shortly after 11 July 1622, the date at which Vorsterman obtained his own 'privilege' as publisher in the Spanish Netherlands.

PAGES 90–91

1 Merle du Bourg 2004A, pp. 17ff.

2 Rooses and Ruelens 1887–1909, vol. 3, no. CCLXXXVI (letter from Peiresc to Rubens, 26 August 1622) and no. CCCLXXIV (letter from Rubens to Peiresc, 13 May 1625).

3 Muller 1993, p. 308.

4 The articulation of these warring aspects has divided opinion. Worth consulting, from among a sizeable bibliography, are Thuillier and Foucart 1967 (French edition, 1969); Millen and Wolf 1989; Weber and Müller Hofstede 1990; Warnke 1993; and Cohen 2003.

5 On the subject of the sketches see in particular Held 1980, vol. 1, pp. 89–122; Jaffé 1989, pp. 271–79; Renger and Denk 2002, pp. 392–443; Chrościcki 2005, pp. 221–49 (not unreservedly); and Gritsay and Babina 2008, pp. 255–63.

6 To give a famous example, the true meaning of *The Regent Militant: The Victory at Jülich* (which illustrates the 1609–10 intervention of France in the War of the Jülich Succession on behalf of Protestant allies in Germany) was long obscured by a 1709 engraving of Charles Simonneau (1645–1728), entitled *The Voyage of the Queen to Pont-de-Cé* (cat. 34.16), which identified the painting as an episode of August 1620, during the feud between Louis XIII and his mother.

7 The hand colouring with watercolour and gouache in the Royal Academy's collection of engravings from *La Galerie du Palais du Luxembourg* was an anonymous eighteenth-century addition. My thanks go to Katya Pisvin for the clarification she provided in this matter.

8 Paris 1982, no. 67 (Louvre).

PAGES 100–07

1 Pierpont Morgan Library, New York (published by Thuillier and Foucart 1967; edition used 1969, pp. 97–98).

2 Merle du Bourg 2004A, pp. 74ff. None of the attempts to find an Italian replacement for Rubens (from whom the project was never withdrawn) was successful.

3 'The French consider keeping the war alive in Flanders to be a State requirement, and maintaining the King of Spain in constant expenditure and disquiet, as they have proved by giving so much financial aid and so many troops to the Dutch since the beginning of the reign of Henri IV until today.' Rooses and Ruelens 1887–1909, vol. 3, no. CCCLXXI, letter from Rubens to the Infanta Isabella, 15 March 1625, in Italian.

4 Rooses and Ruelens 1887–1909, vol. 3, no. CCCLXXIV, letter from Rubens to Peiresc, 13 May 1625.

5 On the second gallery in the Palais du Luxembourg see in particular Jost 1964, pp. 175–219; Held 1980, vol. 1, pp. 123–36 (on the subject of preparatory sketches); Descheemaeker 1989, pp. 343–59; Jaffé 1989, pp. 310–13; the series of articles in *Rubens agli Uffizi* (edited by Marco Ciatti), Florence, 2001; and Galletti 2008, pp. 43–51.

6 National Gallery of Australia, Canberra (held at the Art Gallery of New South Wales, Sydney); Wallace Collection, London; Musée Bonnat, Bayonne; and The Metropolitan Museum, New York.

7 The term 'joyous entry' refers to the ceremonies and festivities by which cities welcomed the visit of a reigning monarch, prince or governor during the Middle Ages. The custom remained popular deep-rooted in the sixteenth and seventeenth centuries, especially in Flanders.

8 Martin 1972, no. 41.

9 We should not forget that Henri IV and Marie de Médicis were ancestors of William. The memory of the compositions surrounding the joyous entry of the Cardinal-Infante into Antwerp is also very evident, particularly in the figure of Minerva in *The Choice of Hercules* (ibid., no. 53), which can be spotted in our sketch.

10 On the relationship between Le Brun and the art of Rubens (and the failed acquisition by Louis XIV of the large unfinished painting from the Galerie Henri IV, now in the Uffizi), see Merle du Bourg 2004B, no. 26.

11 Merle du Bourg 2004B, pp. 232ff., and for an example relating to La Fosse missed by

me see Milovanovic 2005, no. 26.

12 Delacroix 1996, 8 June and 10 August 1850. *Apollo* in particular is imbued with reminiscence of Rubens's religious work (in particular his many versions of the *Fall of the Damned* and his profane work (worth mentioning here is the *Perfect Reconciliation of the Queen and Her Son* in the Galerie Médicis).

PAGES 108–17

1 For the interior design of the Banqueting House, its iconography and significance see most recently Donovan 2004, Martin 2005 and Martin 2011.

2 Martin 2005, vol. 1, in particular pp. 30–41, and vol. 2, appendix I, pp. 307–10.

3 Held 1980, vol. 1, no. 291.

4 Delacroix also made a copy of the London sketch when it was in the possession of the painter Sir David Wilkie (Wieseman 2004, pp. 58–59).

5 Rubens had got the measure of the Duke, an ostentatious character, as capricious as he was arrogant (Rooses and Ruelens 1887–1909, vol. 3, no. CCCXC, letter from Rubens to Valavez [Peiresc's brother], 26 December 1625).

6 Ibid., vol. 2, no. CCXXV, letter from Rubens to William Trumbull, 13 September 1621.

7 Martin 2005, vol. 1, pp. 73–74. Martin has his doubts.

8 Ibid., pp. 137–38, for a number of suggestions not mentioned here.

9 Lucas Vorsterman the Younger (1624–1666 or later), from Antwerp, had previously engraved various of Rubens's compositions for Whitehall including *The Apotheosis of James I* (Rome 1977, nos 334 and 335; Martin 2005, vol. 1, no. 4b, pp. 285–86 and 11b, copy 2).

10 Ibid., p. 138.

11 Here the resonances are made manifest by several borrowed figures. It should be noted, however, that these 'recollections' of Rubens are not always limited to quotations, more or less overt, from the London ceiling. Thus Thornhill in his sketch, when he depicted the luckless figures being cast into the abyss, could have been thinking of the damned in Rubens's tumultuous *Small Last Judgment*, in particular the one engraved by Jonas Suyderhoef from the painting in the Alte Pinakothek in Munich (Freedberg 1984, no. 51).

12 On the system of perspective employed by Rubens see in particular Held 1980, vol. 1, pp. 188, 200 and 218, and Martin 2005, vol. 1, pp. 61–62.

13 As often happens with Rubens's work, a large group of potential references for the London ceiling has flourished, including (hypothetically) Annibale Carracci, from whom Rubens is alleged to have borrowed the admirable figure of the hip-swaying guard – known through an Italian drawing owned and reworked by Rubens himself (between 1620 and 1630; Musée du Louvre, Paris) – in the Birmingham sketch (cat. 45) on display in the present exhibition (Wood 2010B, no. 162).

14 In 1754 the painter Joseph Highmore (1692–1780) published his *Critical Examination of Rubens's Paintings at the Banqueting House*; in it he reprimanded Rubens for his faulty perspective at Whitehall.

15 On the subject of the fierce debates that raged over the perspective used in ceiling decorations in Paris during the 1650s and 1660s, see Duro 1997, in particular pp. 167–68, and Le Blanc 2004, pp. 183–86 and p. 238.

PAGES 118–19

1 Genard 1867–96 and Martin 1972.

2 Martin 1972, nos 3 and 3a, and Wood 2010A, no. 49.

LUST

GERLINDE GRUBER

I am very grateful to Wencke Deiters, Sabine Pénot, Ron Spronk, Joost Vander Auwera, Nico Van Hout, Sabine van Sprang and Gerdien Verschoor for stimulating debate and for their kind support in this undertaking.

PAGES 122–29

1 Liessmann 2007, pp. 10.

2 Erdmann 1929.

3 Her pose is reminiscent of the classical crouching *Venus* and an unidentified statuette known to us from two sixteenth-century paintings by Bronzino. McCorquodale 1981, nos 83 and 30.

4 Bergman 1970, pp. 114ff., as quoted in Egil Törnquist, 'Bergman och bildkonst', *<http://ingmarbergman.se/universe/bergman-och-bildkonst-21118#_ftn6>* [accessed 19 February 2014] I am grateful to Nico Van Hout for alerting me to this.

5 Białostocki 1985, p. 192.

6 Carroll 1989; McGrath 1997, pp. 117–31; Heinen 2006, pp. 90–95; Heinen 2009.

7 Mittig 1985, pp. 48–88.

8 Healy 2004, pp. 39–48.

9 Hammer-Tugendhat 1994, pp 381–88.

10 Heinen 2006; McGrath 1997.

11 Paul Huvenne et al., *Rubens Cantoor. Een verzamelig tekeningen onstaan in Rubens' atelier*, exh. cat., Ghent, 1993, p. 17.

12 Recently again in Brunswick 2004, no. 7.

13 DeGrazia 1984, pp 168–76.

14 Healy 2004, pp. 39–40.

15 Wisława Szymborska, 'Rubens' Women', trans. from the Polish by Stanislaw Baranczak and Clare Cavanagh. The poem was published in the 1962 collection *Sól*. I am grateful to Nico Van Hout for alerting me to this.

16 Herman Parret, 'Beauté et Eros. Vénus à Venise', in Brussels 2003–04, pp. 142–53, 143.

17 De Clippel 2007–08, pp. 112–13.

18 'La Venus que esta de enmedio es retrato muy parecido de su misma muger que sin duda es lo mejor de lo que ahora hay aqui': Rooses and Ruelens 1909, vol. 6, 228, no. DCCCVXVI.

19 Ulrich Heinen, 'Peter Paul Rubens – Barocke Leidenschaften', in Brunswick 2004, p. 28.

20 'Je conclus que Rubens est la gloire de l'art, de son école, de son siècle et de tous les siècles à venir; qu'on doit admirer la fécondité de son imagination; qu'il est correct dans son dessein; qu'il est magnifique dans ses drapperies, et qu'il doit être le grand model au clair obscure quoiqu'il y est ideal; mais il me semble qu'il n'avoit pas rendu des sacrifices aux déesses de la beauté (Horae) et aux Grâces': Bock von Wülfingen, 30: letter from Winckelmann to Count von Cobenzl in 1768 (see Alexandre Pinchart, 'Correspondance artistique du comte de Cobenzl', in *Compte-rendu des séances de la Commission royale d'histoire*, 4, XI, Brussels, 1883, p. 205).

21 'Ou le beau sexe est communement bien nourri': (ibid., p. 205).

22 'Quelques femmes peintes par Rubens, qui, malgré le charactère [sic] flamand & incorrect, séduiront toujours par le charme du coloris': Etienne-Maurice Falconet, *Réflexions sur la sculpture*, Paris, 1761, p. 21.

23 Renger 1993, pp. 469–75.

24 Georg Forster, *Ansichten vom Niederrhein, von Brabant, Flandern, Holland, England und Frankreich... 1790*, Gerhard Stein (ed.), Berlin, 1958, p. 50, as quoted in Renger 1993, p. 471.

25 Renger 1993, p. 473.

26 Quintillian, *Institutio Oratoria*, XII.x.5. Renger already pointed to this possibility in Renger 1993, p. 470; Dittmann 2001.

27 Mechthild Fend, 'Inkarnat oder Haut? Die Körperoberfläche als Schauplatz der Malerei bei Rubens und Ingres', in Munich 2001, pp. 71–79.

28 Karel van Mander, *Het schilder-boeck* (facsimile of the first edition, Haarlem 1604), Utrecht 1969, fol. 49r, 30–33.

29 Van Hout and Balis 2012, pp. 72–73.

30 De Clippel 2008, especially p. 69.

31 Bayl 1964, p. 46.

32 Merle du Bourg 2004A, p. 150.

33 For an informative overview, see Merle du Bourg 2004B, pp. 134–222.

34 'Vie d'Antoine Coypel', in Lepicié 1752, II, 10: 'en attendant ils lui reprochèrent que son admiration pour le coloris de Rubens se faisoit trop connoitre dans le sein, et l'éloignoit de la nature', as quoted in Paris 1991, p. 146.

35 Storffer 1730, vol. 2, no. 101.

36 Mechel 1783, 118, no. 6.

37 Rosa 1796, vol. 2, p. 86, no. 5.

38 Held 1967.

39 Thøfner 2004; Belkin 2006; Ecker and Pataki 2007; De Clippel 2008; De Clippel 2009; De Clippel 2010, to name but a few.

40 De Piles 1990, pp. 85–88.

41 'Die verbeulten Körperpartien seiner jungen Frau so schonungslos darstellte', Thielemann 2012, p. 117, with a persuasive link to Italian art theory.

42 Gruber 2013, pp. 117–18.

43 Interview with Michael Auping on 9 December 2009.

44 Ecker and Pataki 2007, p. 130.

45 Heinen 2001.

PAGE 130

1 'Sine Cerere et Baccho friget Venus', in Erasmus, *Adagia*, no. 1297, as quoted in Heinen 2011, p. 189.

2 Phyllis Pray Bober and Ruth Rubinstein, *Renaissance Artists and Antique Sculpture: A Handbook of Sources*, 1986, second edition, London, 2010, no. 18, pp. 67–68.

PAGE 132

1 The first edition in Latin and German of 1567 included the emblem 'Ars Naturam adiuuans' / 'Kunst hilfft der Natur', but was not illustrated.

2 Carpi 2010, no. 15.

PAGES 135–37

1 Justus Lange takes the view that Syrinx is in fact only on the point of fleeing;

Kassel 2004, no. 18.
2 Vander Auwera 2004, p. 93.
3 Vander Auwera 2004, p. 81; Jakumeit-Pietschamm 2010, pp. 136–49
4 Vander Auwera 2004, pp. 96–97.
5 Otto van Veen's *Amorum Emblemata*, 1608, available online <http://emblems.let.uu.nl/v1608096.html> [accessed 4 March 2014]
6 Vander Auwera 2004, p. 96; Kassel 2004, no. 12.

PAGES 138–49

1 Alpers 1995, p. 109.
2 Rubens's drawings are to be found in the British Museum, London, and the Musée des Beaux-Arts d'Orléans.
3 Lücke and Lücke 2002, p. 510.
4 Hermance Marjon van der Meulen-Schregardus, 1975, p. 156, no. 79, no. XVI B.
5 Held 1986, pp. 151ff., no. 212.
6 Brunswick 2004, no. 9, p. 134.
7 Alpers 1995, p. 133.
8 Peter Paul Rubens, *Théorie de la figure humaine*, Nadeije Laneyrie-Dagen (ed.), Paris, 2003, p. 91; Alpers 1995, p. 173.
9 Alpers 1995, p. 136.
10 Rosenberg and Prat 1996, vol. 3, p. 838, do not agree with this attribution, whereas Grasselli remains convinced that this drawing is by Watteau (Grasselli 2001, p. 131).
11 Most recently in Barrett 2012, no. Pr-41.
12 Renger and Denk 2002, pp. 368–74.
13 Klessmann 1999, p. 193.
14 Held 1980, ill. 243, no. 256. I am grateful to Nico Van Hout for this information.
15 Musée du Louvre, Paris; on the back of the painting there is a note, in black paint: 'peint par P. P. Rubens en 1630, cabinet de M. de Villers'. See Garnier 1989, no. 46.
16 Gustin Gomez 2011, p. 180.
17 Laughton 1996, p. 31
18 Lücke and Lücke 2002, p. 511.
19 Edmond and Jules de Goncourt, 2012, p. 33.
20 Raux 2007, p. 22.
21 The reason for the doubtful attribution, see Roland Michel 2005, p. 219.
22 Raux 2005, p. 139.

PAGES 150–53

1 Hammer-Tugendhat 2009, p. 45.
2 Sabbe 1925, p. 57.
3 Rooses and Ruelens 1887–1909, vol. 2, p. 165; Magurn 1955, pp. 61–63.
4 Rooses and Ruelens 1887–1909, vol. 2, p. 150.
5 For more on this, see also Brunswick 2004, no. 88.
6 State Hermitage Museum, St Petersburg, inv. 496; Galleria Sabauda, Turin, inv. 1899, 265.
7 Locke 2001, p. 83.
8 Sterling 1932, p. 290.
9 Farwell 1975, pp. 225–29; Wilson-Bareau 1986, p. 36.
10 Françoise Cachin, in Paris 1983, no. 19, p. 86.

PAGES 154–63

1 For more on this, see Heinen 2006, with additional bibliography.
2 Werner Hofmann, foreword in Springer 2008, p. 11.
3 Strabo, *Geography*, IX.ii.13.
4 Homer, *The Odyssey*, XI.5.
5 For instance Antwerp 2004, p. 165.
6 Barnes et al. 2004, p. 82.
7 The story of Cimon and Iphigenia is the first told on the fifth day.
8 Inventory, no. 228. See Antwerp 2004, pp. 165, 332.
9 Hammer-Tugenhat 2009, p. 154.
10 Antwerp 2004, pp. 165–66.
11 Boston 2003, p. 169.
12 Hammer-Tugenhat 2004, p. 150 (quoting White 1999, pp. 207–08).
13 Paris 1991, p. 188.
14 De la Roque 1721, p. 81.
15 Muller 1982; Heinen 2001, pp. 70–109, particularly p. 99.
16 See, for instance, Sébastien Allard (ed.), *Dante et Virgile aux Enfers d'Eugène Delacroix*, exh. cat., Musée du Louvre, Paris, 2004, pp. 84–87.

PAGES 164–71

1 Bonnet, 2006.
2 'Carpeaux était le Rubens du marbre et de la pierre. La chair, en effet, est vivante' (Claretie 1882–84, vol. 1, p. 178).
3 Poletti and Richarme 2003, pp. 86–89.
4 Patrick Ramade, 'Etudes et copies', in Valenciennes 1999, p. 147.
5 Miquel and Miquel 2006, vol. 2, p. 350.
6 Munich 1996, p. 228.
7 Ballu 1877, p. 294.
8 Cincinnati 2004, no. 37.
9 Van Gogh Letters, Vincent to his brother Theo van Gogh, Nuenen, on or about Tuesday, 13 October 1885, (letter 535).
10 Vollard 1961, p. 68.
11 Chicago 1997, p. 67.
12 See Garb 1985.
13 Mary Louise Krumrine, 'Die Baseler Baigneuses', in Basel 1989, pp. 137–65.
14 Dittmann 2005, p. 186.
15 Berthold 1958, p. 14.
16 Andersen 2004, p. 116.

PAGE 172

1 Rey 1966, p. 82, as quoted in Laughton 1996, p. 31
2 One destroyed, one extant at the Chateau d'Arare, near Geneva.
3 Henri Loyrette, in Ottawa 1999, p. 259.
4 Louvre, inv. 20369. Renger 1994, p. 181.

COMPASSION

ARTURO GALANSINO

PAGE 178–87

1 Paul Claudel, *Le Soulier de satin*, 1987, p. 147.
2 Delacroix 1948, p. 242.
3 See Freedberg 1976, pp. 128–38.
4 Durante 2003, pp. 74–85
5 Pérez Sánchez 1977, pp. 66–109; Pérez Sánchez 1985, pp. 54–59; see also Vergara 1999.
6 The engraving was made by Lucas Vorsterman the Elder (1595–1675) after a 1633 work by Rubens now conserved at the Schloss Schleissheim, Munich.
7 On the Rubenist Francesco Rizi, see Lamas Delgado 2011, pp. 179–96; for Hidalgo's text see Calvo Serraller 1991, p. 605.
8 Lamas Delgado 2011, pp. 181–86.
9 *Galerie du Musée Napoléon publée par Filhol, et redigée par Joseph Lavallée*, 11 vols, Paris, 1804–28.
10 Merle du Bourg 2004B, pp. 79–80.
11 Merle du Bourg 2004B, pp. 83–84.
12 Merle du Bourg 2004B, pp. 84–91.
13 Merle du Bourg 2004B, pp. 227–42.
14 Merle du Bourg 2004B, pp. 240–41, 286–88.
15 Merle du Bourg 2004B, p. 287.
16 Rosenberg and Pratt, 1996, p. 1,351, no. R771
17 Weinshenker 1966, p. 5, letter V,27
18 Bliss 1975, pp. 197–221.
19 See *Diderot on Art*, vol. 2, New Haven and London 1995, p. 153.
20 Zurawski 1975, pp. 147–78.
21 Landers Althouse 1975, pp. 223–40.
22 On Delacroix, Rubens and sacred painting, see Elrich White 1967, pp. 37–51; Daguerre de Hureaux 1995, pp. 216–45; Judson 1997, pp. 106–21.
23 Delacroix 1948, p. 242
24 Reynolds 1996, pp. 31–35, 41–44, 55–61, 63–67. See also Danly Walther 1975, pp. 179–95. On Rubens's influence on English art, see White 1981, pp. 27–44.
25 Forster 1990, vol. 13, pp. 103–04.
26 Merke 1779, pp. 113–28.
27 Picon 2008, p. 445
28 Van Gogh Letters, Vincent to his brother Theo van Gogh, Antwerp, between 12 and 16 January 1886 (letter 552).
29 Ibid.
30 Van Gogh Letters, Vincent to his sister Willemien van Gogh, Saint-Rémy-de-Provence, Thursday, 19 September 1889 (letter 804).
31 On Van Gogh's *Pietá*, see Milan 2006, pp. 13–15, 17–24.
32 Milan 2006, p. 9.

PAGES 188–92 (KP)

1 Antonius Sanderus, *Chorographia Sacra Brabantiae*, The Hague, 1727, vol. 3, p. 200; Van Hout 2001, p. 13.
2 Reynolds 1996, pp. 63–67; Van Hout 2001, p. 4.
3 Descamps 1792, p. 175; Van Hout 2001, p. 14.
4 Judson 2000, p. 146.
5 Judson 1997, p. 110.
6 Delacroix 1948, pp. 240–41.
7 'Son Christ en croix ... rappelle les plus beaux crucifix de Rubens: resemblance de poésie et de couleur, comme de Giorgione à Titien'. Théophile Thoré-Bürger, March and April 1847, quoted in Johnson 1986, p. 220, no. 433.

PAGES 194–99 (KP)

1 Judson 2000, p. 168.
2 Van Hout et al. 2004, p. 47.
3 Hinterding 2000, p. 134.
4 Reynolds 1996, p. 33.
5 Bensey 2002, no. 9, p. 36.

PAGES 200–03 (KP)

1 Eisler 1967, p. 76.
2 Reynolds 1996, p. 38–39.
3 Ehrlich White 1967, p. 39.
4 Van Gogh Letters, Vincent to his sister Willemien van Gogh, Saint-Rémy-de-Provence, Thursday, 19 September 1889 (letter 804).

PAGES 204–06 (KP)

1 Wood 2005, p. 40.
2 Klemm 1986, p. 32.
3 Although the painting was most probably also available to him as an engraving, a large number of which he acquired. See Pietralata 2011, p. 70.

PAGE 208 (KP)

1 Freedberg 1984, p. 125.

PAGES 212–15 (KP)

1 Martin 1968, p. 38.
2 Martin 1968, p. 38.
3 Vienna 2012, p. 36.

PAGE 216 (KP)

1 The Abbé de Saint-Non's intended guide was not published during his lifetime. The draft form – a journal of notes – was later rediscovered, edited by Rosenberg and Brejon de Lavergnée, and published as *Saint-Non, Fragonard, Panopticon Italiano: Un diario di viaggio ritrovato, 1759–1761*, Rome, 1986. The quotation appears on p. 170.
2 Providence 1975, p. 153.
3 Reynolds 1996, introduction, p. xvl, and footnote 138 (cited by Edmond Malone in the introduction to Reynolds's complete works: Reynolds 1797, vol. 1, p. xli).
4 Cunningham 1843, vol. 1, pp. 400–01.
5 Ibid., vol. 1, pp. 443–44.

PAGE 220 (KP)

1 Van Gogh Letters, Vincent to his brother Theo van Gogh, Antwerp, Monday 14 December 1885 (letter 547).

ELEGANCE

DAVID HOWARTH

I would like to thank the Director and Trustees of the National Gallery, London, for allowing me to publish transcripts of material in the gallery files. Thanks are also due to Professor Sam Smiles, Dr Donato Esposito and Dr Tico Seifert. In addition I am grateful to Alan Crookham and Humphrey Wine of the National Gallery, and to Alexandra Lyons Greer of the Department of the History of Art, Edinburgh University.

PAGES 224–32

1 As recorded in the diary of Joseph Farington (1747–1821), Garlick and Macintyre 1976, vol. 3, no. 756, 22 January 1797, pp. 101–05.
2 Sampaio 2009, no. 16.
3 Sir Joshua Reynolds, quoted in Wark 1997, p. 86.
4 Wendorf 1990, pp. 240–45. See the National Gallery, London, dossier no. 853.
5 Mannings and Postle 2000, vol. 2, no. 1947, ill. 989.
6 Reynolds seems to have ladled out clotted cream supplied by Rembrandt for the dresses in *The Ladies Waldegrave* (1780; Scottish National Gallery, Edinburgh).
7 Historical Manuscripts Commission, Ninth Report, part 2, (1884), p. 482, Reynolds to a 'Mr Cunyngham', dated 25 November 1785, confiding plans to acquire the 'Rubens's portraits' of *St Peter* and *St Paul*, (both *c.* 1614), in the church of the Capuchins, Antwerp. Reynolds states he will send an artist who has been trained in his studio to understand the technique of Rubens: 'and will give him proper directions how to give the copy an old appearance, so that few among the connoisseurs shall distinguish the difference.' As has been suggested, Reynolds had a profound understanding of Flemish technique. An *Allegory of Charity* (between *c.* 1622 and *c.* 1627; Ashmolean Museum, Oxford) was presented in 1855 by the notable connoisseur Chambers Hall as a Van Dyck. Even as late as the 1931 catalogue it was assumed to be a Van Dyck upon which Reynolds had 'worked freely ... with his own hand'. Only today is it recognised as wholly the work of Reynolds. Mannings and Postle 2000, vol. 2, no. 2243.
8 Despite a lifelong admiration for Rubens, Reynolds's grandest ensemble, *The 4th Duke of Marlborough and His Family* (1778–79; Blenheim Palace, Oxfordshire), contests the laurels for the most ambitious of all portraits in England, not with a Rubens but with the Van Dyck *Pembroke Family* (*c.* 1633–35; Wilton House, Wiltshire).
9 The portrait of Sir Watkin is to be found in what is known as the 'vase' portrait, which comprises one of the pair of the Dilettanti commission. It would come as no surprise to discover that both Reynolds and Sir Watkin had discussed Rubens's 'four philosophers' as the *fons et origo* of the Dilettante pictures. Both knew the Rubens at first hand: Sir Watkin a great deal better than Reynolds.
10 Hilles 1929, p. 189, 22 April 1789, Reynolds to Cosway: 'Dear Sir, If you will trust me with your sketch of Rubens of Jupiter and Venus, for a few days, I shall take it as a great favour.'
11 Graves 1912.
12 Mannings and Postle 2000, vol. 2, no. 1529, ill. 1390.
13 Millar 1969, vol. 1, nos 879 and 880.
14 The most independent and creative response to the *Chapeau de Paille* in Britain was entitled *Summer*, painted by the Scotsman Andrew Geddes in about 1826. See Smailes 2001, pp. 62–64.
15 'et lundi nous avons eu la visite du chevalier Reynholes Peintre du Roy d'Angleterre, que vous connoissez mieux que nous, il nous en demandoit le prix, nous lui avons demandé 150 guinées, enfin il a voulu savoir le dernier prix et nous lui avons laissé a 125, dont il nous a offert inutilement 100 guinées'. Pilner and Beeckmans, Antwerp, to Thomas Harvey, Norwich, 5 August 1785. I am grateful to the National Gallery, London, for permission to quote this transcription, and that from Mrs Howe: both from dossier no. 852.
16 The National Gallery, London, dossier no. 852.
17 New York 1988, no. 40.
18 Parker and Mathey 1957, no. 290. The *trois crayons* technique was a bequest by Rubens to French eighteenth-century artists; probably developed from his knowledge of the artist Hendrick Goltzius (1558–1617).
19 New York 1988, no. 40.
20 Blumenfeld 2013, pp. 18, 20, 22, 34, 59–60, 67 and 71, n. 35 and 36.
21 Paris 1987, no. 139, pp. 288–89.
22 Percival 2012.
23 Aileen Ribeiro, 'Portraying the Fashion, Romancing the Past: Dress and the Cosways', in Lloyd 1995, pp. 101–05. Ribiero notes how Jefferys was first to reattribute it to Rubens.
24 Millar 1969, vol. 1, no. 716.
25 Lloyd 1995, p. 105.
26 Hilles 1936, p. 80: 'What was said of an ancient painter may be applied to these two artists, – that their figures look as if they fed upon roses.'
The other artist was Federigo Barocci.
27 Lawrence discounted Rubens in a letter to the budding art historian Mrs Jameson, written from Russell Square on 3 December 1829, only five weeks before he died: 'Dear Madam ... Rubens has been infinitely more the object of my admiration [than 'Vandyke'], but as you know, very little as example for portrait-painting.' Gower 1900, pp. 87–89.
28 Michiel C. Plomp, 'Collecting Rubens's Drawings', in New York 2005, pp. 37–62.

PAGE 234

1 Huemer 1977, no. 19 as 'Catarina Grimaldi' on the grounds that she was married in 1606, which fits the putative date of the Rubens; Jaffé 1977, ill. 264, also as 'Caterina Grimaldi'; Jaffé 1989, no. 58, as 'Maria Grimaldi'; Lille 2004, no. 15: 'Portrait of a lady with her dwarf [because] it is not possible to supply the woman portrayed here with a definite identity.'
2 Jaffé 1977, p. 77, states the sitter was 'newly married' in 1607; although it did not occur to him that the marriage might be central to the iconography of the painting.
3 McIntyre 2003, p. 397.
4 Especially in portraits of women, see Leca 2010, pp. 135–38.
5 Barnes 1997, p. 258, n. 32.
6 Antwerp 1999, no. 37.

PAGES 238–43

1 White 2007, no. 62, p. 211; Waagen 1838, vol. 1, pp. 173–74, 'as of Helena Fourment'; Jameson 1842, part 1, p. 263, no. 138, 'as of Isabella Brandt'; Oldenbourg 1921, p. 444, 'copy after Rubens of unidentified sitter'; Collins Baker 1937, p. 277, 'Rubens studio of unknown woman'.
2 White 2007, p. 209.
3 G. H. Steuart to William Stirling Maxwell, Baltimore, 22 February 1853; T-SK/29/6/212, Stirling of Keir Muniments, Glasgow City Archives. Steuart's identification of Van Havre's *Judgement of Paris* with the later of the two versions of this subject in the National Gallery, London, is not supported by the provenance of the National Gallery painting. See Martin 1986, no. 194. I must thank Archibald Stirling Esq. for this quotation, and Nerys Tunnicliffe, Glasgow City Archives, for checking its transcription.
4 Paris 1987, no. 139, pp. 288–89 where Rosenberg described it as a 'homage to Rubens' while acknowledging its humour.
5 The date for this portrait is disputed. Volk, in Providence 1975, no. 9, and p. 156, opts for *c.* 1769–72; Rosenberg, in Paris 1987, favours a date 'prior to 1779'; and Percival 2012, pp. 167–75, prefers *c.* 1767, when Fragonard visited the Luxembourg to copy the Marie de Médicis cycle. In the same publication, Percival examines Fragonard's dependence on works by Rubens (see pp. 19, 20, 22, 26, 32, 34, 36, 167, 169–70, 224 and 225) seeking to compare it with that of Alexander Roslin.
6 Paris 1987, no. 84. But Watteau was not alone among French artists of the eighteenth century in his admiration for Rubens's drawings. The Gros sale of 1778 contained a number of drawings by Fragonard that were copies after Flemish artists including Rubens.
7 New York 1988, no. 40.

PAGES 244–49

1 *The World*, 20 October 1789.
2 *Grove* 1996, p. 891.
3 London 1980, no. 3.
4 In 1806 appeared a catalogue of paintings at Corsham Court, which made a claim for Rubens that may have put Lawrence in mind of his visit: '[Rubens] was perhaps the most popular painter that ever pursued the profession … To a mind comprehensive and an imagination truly poetical, he added correct taste and consummate judgement.' Many of Lawrence's patrons, and they were counted in their hundreds, might themselves have seen this great President of the Royal Academy as 'the most popular painter' who had ever pursued the profession in England. Britton 1806, p. 89.
5 London 1980, no. 1. The picture cost 40 guineas.
6 Clifford 1976, p. 291, no. 20.
7 Garlick 1989, no. 36.
8 My thanks to Dr Donato Espositio for this information.
9 Jaffé 1989, no. 67. This portrait once belonged to the notable Hispanist Richard Ford, who knew both Lawrence and Wellington well.
10 Kauffmann 1982, no. 154.

PAGES 250–54

1 Jaffé 1989, no. 1,002.
2 Houghton Hall 2013, p.138, where it is remarked that Horace Walpole recorded how 'it was fitted for a panel in her own closet in Rubens's House'.
3 National Gallery Technical Bulletin, vol. 10, 1986, p.72.
4 Cardellini 2001, pp. 56–57.
5 However, as can be inferred from Martin 1986, no. 852, Rubens and Susanna were certainly close. The *staetmasse* of Rubens's estate shows that she sat for him, and that Rubens still owned at least four portraits of her at his death.
6 Stanley 1823, p. 5.

PAGE 256

1 Rome 1977, no. 57.
2 British Museum, London, inv. 1863,0110.86.
3 Luijten and Meij 1990, no. 47; Meij and De Haan 2001, no. 26.
4 For an overview of the quality of Rubens drawings owned by Lawrence, see Michiel C. Plomp, in New York 2005, pp. 37–62. For a more positive assessment, see Luijten and Meij 1990, no 47.

POETRY

TIM BARRINGER

My thanks to Stijn Alsteens, Daniella Berman, Gillian Forrester, Christiane Hille and Kate Roach for commenting upon earlier versions of this essay and to Alice Kelly for invaluable editorial assistance.

PAGES 260–73

1 See Rosenberg 1981, p. 17.
2 Empson 1935, p. 23; Alpers 1978, pp. 101–23.
3 On Het Steen, see Brown 1996, pp. 59–78.
4 Roger de Piles, *The Art of Painting with the Lives and Characters of above 300 of the Most Eminent Painters*, 2nd edition, London, 1744; quoted in Gordon 1981, p. 11.
5 A painting also known as *The Village Fête*.
6 Rubens to Nicolas-Claude Peiresc, 18 December 1634, in Rubens 1955, p. 393; quoted White 1987, pp. 234–35.
7 Sir Joseph Mead, 6 March 1630. See Rooses and Ruelens 1887–1909, vol. 5, pp. 287–88, quoted in Donovan 2004, p. 35.
8 Reynolds 1975, p. 86.
9 Reynolds 1975, p. 86.
10 Reynolds 1975, p. 69.
11 Reynolds 1975, p. 161.
12 Reynolds 1996, pp. 147–48.
13 Letter to Thomas Harvey, 22 May 1788; Sloman 2012, p. 27.
14 Rosenthal 1999, p. 193.
15 Hayes 1982, vol. 2, p. 467.
16 Whitley 1915, p. 61.
17 It is notable that J. M. W. Turner arrived at unusually lucid prose in his paean to the Rubensian aspects of Gainsborough's work: there, Turner found 'truth of forms arising from his close contact with nature, expression …'. Ziff 1963, p. 146.
18 Brown 2012.
19 Ziff 1963, pp. 124–47.
20 Dunlap 1834, vol. 2, p. 343.
21 See Forrester 1996 and Davies 1992 for further discussion of the disparities between Turner's lectures and his practice as a painter.
22 Leslie 1843, p. 329.
23 Leslie 1843, p. 97.
24 In *Salisbury Cathedral from the Meadows*, Constable may also have been alluding to another work he knew: Jacob van Ruisdael's *The Jewish Cemetery* (*c.* 1655), which was in London from 1815 and is now at the Detroit Institute of Arts.
25 Crow 1985, pp. 40–41.
26 The number 27 was added in the lower-right-hand corner of cat. 138.1 by Pierre-Jean Mariette (1694–1774), the most important collector of drawings in France at the time, as he prepared the catalogue of the collection of Pierre Crozat for auction in Paris in 1741. New York 2005, p. 264.
27 The fullest account is provided by Banks 1977, pp. 218–30, but see also later discussions by Plax 2000, pp. 108–53 and Ramade and Eidelberg 2004, p. 115.
28 Washington 1984, p. 396.
29 Crow 1985, p. 65.
30 Levey 1961.
31 See Tickner 2000, pp. 83–104.
32 Cork 1985, pp. 88–89.
33 The panel known as *The Watering Place* (fig. 44) was acquired by the National Gallery, London, in 1936. However, a composition Rubens derived from it, known as *A Shepherd with his Flock in a Woody Landscape* (oil on panel, 64.3 x 94.3 cm), was in the National Gallery's collection from 1913.

PAGES 274–76

1 On Titian/Giorgione and the pastoral, see Rosand 1988, pp. 2[illegible]–66.
2 Cafritz, Gowing and Rosand 1988, p. 115.
3 Blayney Brown 2005.
4 Leslie 1843, p. 346.
5 See Barringer 2012.
6 Leslie 1843, p. 346.

PAGES 278–87

1 See for example Joachim Patinir, *The Penitence of St Jerome* (1524; The Metropolitan Museum of Art, New York).
2 See, for example, Roelandt Savery's etching *Goatherd Between the Trees* (British Museum, London). See Brown 1996, p. 51.
3 Evers 1943; Natalya Gritsay, in Dukelskaya and Moore 2002, p. 116.
4 Vergara 1982, pp. 48–54.
5 See Houghton Hall 2013.
6 Walpole 1762, p. 85.
7 The vestibule of Boydell's Gallery contained chalk drawings by Josiah Boydell, Richard Earlom and Joseph and George Farington after works in Walpole's collection at Houghton. Boydell published a collection of engravings based on these drawings, *The Houghton Gallery*, in parts between 1774 and 1788. See Dias 2013, pp. 20–21.
8 Adler 1982, pp. 167–68.
9 Hayes 1982, vol. 1, p. 123, n. 54. The copy once at Nuneham that Gainsborough may have seen in 1758–59 is known to have been in the studio of Sir Joshua Reynolds in London, for restoration, at some time, providing another opportunity for Gainsborough to have seen it. See Birmingham 1995, pp. 50–51.
10 Hayes 1982, vol. 1, no. 107.
11 For a substantial account of the painting, with full bibliography, see Birmingham 1995. See also Rosenthal 1999, pp. 210–13.
12 See Parris and Fleming-Williams 1991, p. 214.
13 Huet 1911, p. 95; see Noon 2003, p. 197.
14 For a detailed discussion of the topography, see Brooks 1976, pp. 135–36.
15 Butlin and Joll 1984, pp. 58–61.
16 Butlin and Joll 1984, p. 61.

PAGES 288–91

1 Goodman 1982, p. 15.
2 Adler 1982, p. 142.
3 Adler 1982, p. 143; Goodman 1992, p. 66, no. 103.
4 Adler 1982, p. 142.
5 Delacroix's words were recalled by Antonin Proust in 'Edouard Manet: Souvenirs' (1897), quoted Cachin and Moffett 1983, p. 45.
6 Reff 1969, p. 46.

PAGES 292–95 (NVH)

1 Wood 2009.
2 See Nordenfalk 1938, pp. 43–47; Tietze-Conrat 1949–50, p. 435; Grossmann 1951, p. 25; and Lohse Belkin 1987, pp. 143–52. It was previously thought that Rubens used copies that he had drawn or purchased many years earlier in Rome. Others assumed that he worked from painted copies that were circulating in Antwerp. A few believed that Rubens based his two copies after Titian on several prints (in reverse) by Giovanni Battista Pocestà of 1636 (!).
3 '…qu'elle visita le peintre à son tour, dans les salles de la Maison hanséatique, ou il demeurait toujours et qu'il n'avait même pas fait décorer: les toiles originales et les copies du Titien en formaient le principal ornement' ('…that she in turn visited the painter in the rooms of the Hanseatic House where he had always lived but had never decorated: the original canvases and the copies after Titian were the main embellishment') (Michiels 1882, p. 304, quoted from Barnes, De Poorter, Millar and Vey 2004, p. 245).
4 British Museum, inv. 1957,1214.207.56.
5 'Bacchanal; sur le devant, une femme couchée, de son long, près d'une eau, la teste appuyée sur une urne; auprès d'elle un enfant qui pisse, avec quantité

de figures, de Vandeck. 20 liv' ('Bacchanal; in the foreground, a woman reclining, full-length, near a body of water, the head resting on an urn; next to her, a child pissing, with a number of figures, by Van Dyck, 20 pounds') (Grossmann 1951, p. 25).

6 See Barnes, De Poorter, Millar and Vey 2004, no. III.60.

7 Wood 2010, pp. 145 and 156–57.

8 Rubens possibly refers here to a passage in Pliny's *Natural History* (XXXI.xiii) that describes how every 5 January the water in Bacchus' shrine changes into wine and back into water when it is carried out of the temple.

9 'Nel Palazzo sonovi due copie, che fece Rubens di detti Quadri; ma si possono considerare come un libro tradotto in lingua Fiamminga, che conserva tutti i pensieri, avendo perduta tutta la grazia dell'originale' ('In the Palazzo there are two copies, which Rubens made of said paintings; but they can be considered as a book translated into the Flemish language, which preserves all the thoughts, having lost all the grace of the original) (D'Azara 1780, p. 69).

10 Van Hout 2001B, pp. 15–17.

PAGES 296–305

1 A version of *The Garden of Love* on panel now at Waddesdon Manor, Buckinghamshire, was attributed to Rubens for much of the twentieth century; see Waterhouse 1950, pp. 199–200. More recently, the painting's attribution has been questioned and it is widely agreed to be by another hand though close in date to Rubens. For a summary of recent research see Plock 2011. Further copies of the original composition are in the Staatliche Kunstsammlungen, Dresden; the Kunsthistorischesmuseum, Vienna; the Nationalmuseum, Stockholm; and in the Palazzo Reale, Naples. All are reproduced in Glang-Süberkrüb 1975, pp. 168–74 and discussed by her, pp. 102–09.

2 Rubens had probably seen *The Worship of Venus* in Rome, but he seems not to have made the copy until years later. A possible explanation is that he worked from copies brought to Antwerp by another artist (Anthony van Dyck has been suggested) who had, himself, copied Titian's pictures in Rome. Belkin 1998, pp. 269–72.

3 See Wood 2010, vol. 1, 187–88.

4 See Renger 2002, no. 313.

5 Goodman 1982, pp. 247–59, 249.

6 Goodman 1992, p. 44.

7 Goodman 1992, p. 29.

8 Goodman 1992, pp. 28–30.

9 White 1987, p. 271.

10 Antwerp 1993, p. 49.

PAGES 306–09

1 The fullest analysis is in New York 2004, pp. 260–65, which provides a full bibliography.

2 New York 2004, p. 263.

3 I am grateful to Stijn Alsteens, curator in the Department of Drawings and Prints at the Metropolitan Museum of Art, New York, for his help in preparing this entry and sharing his important insights into these works.

4 Goodman 1992, p. 43.

5 White 1987, p. 271.

6 See Wood 2010, vol. 1, part 1.

7 Conversation with the author, October 2013. Anne-Marie Logan and Michiel C. Plomp suggested (New York 2005, pp. 260–65) that the engraver, Jegher, might have been responsible for the pen drawing. It seems more likely that a member of Rubens's workshop added the work in pen and ink. Jegher would presumably have been responsible for transcribing the drawing onto the woodblock before cutting it but is unlikely to have been responsible for preparing the present drawings.

PAGES 310–13

1 The fullest account is in Washington 1984, pp. 367–72.

2 Plax 2000, p. 129.

3 Washington 1984, p. 298.

4 Watson 1953, pp. 240–42. See also Washington 1984, pp. 367–68, and Posner 1984, p. 167.

5 Leslie 1845, p. 210.

6 Hazlitt 1824, pp. 673–74, quoted in Salomon 2010, p. 52.

7 Edwards 2006, p. 43.

8 Posner 1984, p. 206. See also Parker and Mathey 1957, vol. 2, p. 739.

9 Quoted in Edwards 2006, p. 42.

10 The correspondences are explored in Rosenberg and Prat 1996, vol. 2, no. 484, p. 810.

11 Rosenberg and Prat 1996, vol. 2, no. 484.

12 See Washington 1984, pp. 149, 379.

13 Posner 1984, 208.

PAGES 316–18

1 See New York 2005, pp. 280–82, for this translation and discussion of its possible meanings.

2 Edwards 2006, p. 50.

BIBLIOGRAPHY

AACHEN 1883
Suermondt-Museum zu Aachen, Beschreibendes Verzeichnis der Gemälde, Aachen, 1883

AACHEN 1994
Ulrich Schneider et al., *Suermondt-Ludwig Museum Aachen*, Munich, 1994

ADHÉMAR 1954
Jean Adhémar, *Honoré Daumier*, Paris, 1954

ADLER 1980
Wolfgang Adler, *Jan Wildens, der Landschaftsmitarbeiter des Rubens*, Fridlingen, 1980

ADLER 1982
Wolfgang Adler, *Rubens: Landscapes and Hunting Scenes, Corpus Rubenianum Ludwig Burchard*, XVIII, vol. 1, Oxford and New York, 1982

ALPERS 1971
Svetlana L. Alpers, *The Decoration of the Torre de la Parada, Corpus Rubenianum Ludwig Burchard*, IX, Brussels, London and New York, 1971

ALPERS 1978
Paul Alpers, 'Empson on Pastoral', *New Literary History*, 10 (1978), pp. 101–23

ALPERS 1995
Svetlana L. Alpers, *The Making of Rubens*, New Haven and London 1995

AMSTERDAM 1964
Franse tekeningen von Claude tot Cèzanne uit Nederlandse verzamelingen, exh. cat., Rijksmuseum, Amsterdam, 1964

ANANOFF 1961–71
Alexandre Ananoff, *L'Oeuvre dessiné de Jean-Honoré Fragonard (1732–1806), Catalogue raisonné*, 4 vols, Paris, 1963

ANANOFF AND WILDENSTEIN 1980
Alexandre Ananoff and Daniel Wildenstein, *L'opera completa di Boucher*, Milan, 1980

ANDERSEN 2004
Wayne Anderson, *Cézanne and the Eternal Feminine*, Cambridge, 2004

ANDREE 1977
Rolf Andree, *Arnold Böcklin, Die Gemälde*, Basel and Munich, 1977

ANONYMOUS N.D.
Anonymous, *An Explanation of the Painting in the Royal Hospital at Greenwich, by Sir James Thornhill… Published By Order of the Directors of the Said Hospital, for the Benefit of the Charity-boys Maintained There. Sold by the Porter of the Hospital*, n.l., n.d. [*c.* 1730]

ANTWERP 1969
Schilderkunst in België ten tijde van Henri Leys (1815–1869), exh. cat., Royal Museum of Fine Arts Antwerp, 1969

ANTWERP 1978
Jordaens in Belgisch bezit, Marc Vandenven, exh. cat., Royal Museum of Fine Arts Antwerp, 1978

ANTWERP 1993
Jacob Jordaens (1593–1678), Roger-Adolf d'Hulst Nora de Poorter and Marc Vandenven, exh. cat., Royal Museum of Fine Arts Antwerp; Réunion des Musées Nationaux, Paris; Crédit Communal, Brussels, 1993

ANTWERP 1997
Rubenstextiel / Rubens's Textiles. Tentoonstelling georganiseerd naar aanleiding van 50 jaar Rubenshuis, Guy Delmarcel, Nora De Poorter et al., exh. cat., Hessenhuis, Antwerp, 1997

ANTWERP 1999
Anthony van Dyck as a Printmaker, Carl Depauw and Ger Luijten (eds), exh. cat. Museum Plantin-Moretus, Stedelik Prentenkabinet, Antwerp, and Rijksmuseum, Rijksprentenkabinet, Amsterdam, 1999–2000

ANTWERP 1999
Van Dyck 1599–1641, Christopher Brown and Hans Vlieghe, exh. cat., Royal Museum of Fine Arts Antwerp, and Royal Academy of Arts, London, 1999

ANTWERP 2004
A House of Art: Rubens as Collector, Kristin Lohse Belkin and Fiona Healy, exh. cat., Rubenshuis, Antwerp, 2004

ANTWERP 2013–14
Happy Birthday Dear Academie. 350 jaar Koninklijke Academie voor Schone Kunsten Antwerpen, MAS | Museum aan de Stroom, Antwerp 2013–14

ARMSTRONG 2002
Carol Armstrong, *Manet Manette*, New Haven, 2002

ASHTON 1988
Dora Ashton, *Fragonard in the Universe of Painting*, Washington DC, 1988

ATLANTA 2007
Inspiring Impressionism: The Impressionists and the Art of the Past, Ann Dumas (ed.), exh. cat., High Museum of Art, Atlanta, Denver Art Museum and Seattle Art Museum, 2007–08

BACOU 1974
Roseline Bacou, 'Donation Claude Roger-Marx', *Revue du Louvre et des Musées de France*, 24, 4–5 (1974), pp. 307–12

BAER 1986
Brigitte Baer, *Picasso Peintre-graveur: Catalogue raisonné de l'œuvre gravé et des monotypes*, 1946–1958, 3 vols, Bern, 1986

BAETJER 2009
Katharine Baetjer, *British Paintings in the Metropolitan Museum 1575–1875*, New York, 2009

BAILLO 1988
Joseph Baillio, 'Vigée Le Brun and the Classical Practice of Imitation', in *Paris: Center of Artistic Enlightenment, Papers in Art History from the Pennsylvania State University*, George Mauner (ed.), vol. 4, University Park, Pa., 1988

BAJOU 1998
Thierry Bajou, *La Peinture à Versailles. XVIIe siècle*, Paris, 1998

BALIS 1986
Arnout Balis, *Hunting Scenes, Corpus Rubenianum Ludwig Burchard*, XVIII, 2 vols, London and New York, 1986

BALLAS 2002
Giulia Ballas, *Cézanne, Baigneuse et baigneurs: thème et composition*, Paris, 2002

BALLU 1877
Roger Ballu, 'Les Artistes contemporaines – Diaz', *Gazette des Beaux-Arts*, 19, 2, 5 (1877), pp. 290–304

BANKS 1977
Oliver T. Banks, *Watteau and the North: Studies in Dutch and Flemish Baroque Influence on French Rococo Painting*, New York and London, 1977

BARCELONA 2006
Sophie Raux, 'Fragonard et les maîtres du Nord', in *Jean-Honoré Fragonard (1732–1806): orígenes e influencias: de Rembrandt al siglo XXI*, Jean-Pierre Cuzin, Katharina Schmidt and Sophie Raux, exh. cat., CaixaForum, Barcelona, 2006

BARKER 1999
'Women Artists and the French Academy: Vigée-Lebrun in the 1780s', in *Gender and Art*, Gillian Perry (ed.), New Haven and London, 1999

BARNES 1997
Susan Barnes, 'La società genovese nei ritratti di Van Dyck', in Boccardo and Di Fabio 1997

BARNES ET AL. 2004
Susan J. Barnes, Nora De Poorter, Oliver Millar and Horst Vey, *Van Dyck: A Complete Catalogue of the Paintings*, New Haven and London, 2004

BARRACHINA 1998
Marie-Aline Barrachina, *Propagande et culture dans l'Espagne franquiste, 1936–1945*, Grenoble, 1998

BARRELL 1980
John Barrell, *The Dark Side of the Landscape: The Rural Poor in English Painting, 1730–1840*, Cambridge, 1980

BARRETT 2012
Kerry Barrett, *Pieter Soutman: Life and œuvre*, Amsterdam and Philadelphia, 2012

BARRINGER 2012
Tim Barringer, *'The Wheat Field', in Landscape, Innovation and Nostalgia: The Manton Collection of British Art*, Jay Clarke (ed.), Williamstown, Mass., 2012, pp. 186–205

BARTSCH 1797
Adam Bartsch, *Catalogue raisonné de toutes les estampes qui forment l'œuvre de Rembrandt, et ceux de ses principaux imitateurs*, Vienna, 1797

BASAN 1767
François Basan, *Catalogue des estampes gravées d'après Pierre-Paul Rubens*, Paris, 1767

BASEL 1989
Paul Cézanne: Die Badenden, Mary Louise Krumrine, exh. cat., Kunstmuseum, Basel, 1989

BASEL 2001
Arnold Böcklin, Bernd Wolfgang Lindemann and Katharina Schmidt (eds), exh. cat., Kunstmuseum, Basel; Musée d'Orsay, Paris; and Neue Pinakothek, Munich, published in Heidelberg 2001–02

BAUDELAIRE 1868
Oeuvre complètes de Charles Baudelaire, Paris, 1868

BAUDELAIRE 1951
Charles Baudelaire, 'Exposition Universelle', in *Le Pays*, Paris, 26 May and 3 June 1855; reprinted in *Curiosités Esthétiques*, Paris, 1868 (1951 edition, p. 699)

BAUDELAIRE 1992
Charles Baudelaire, Ecrits sur l'art, Francis Moulinat (ed.), Paris, 1992

BAYL 1964
Friedrich Bayl, *Der nackte Mensch in der Kunst*, Cologne, 1964

BAZIN 1989
Germain Bazin, Théodore Géricault, *Etude critique, documents et catalogue raisonné*, vol 3, Paris, 1989

BEAN 1962
Jacob Bean, 'The Drawings Collection', *The Metropolitan Museum of Art Bulletin*, 20 (1962), pp. 157–75

BEAUVAIS 2000
Lydia Beauvais et al., *Inventaire général des dessins, école française: Charles Le Brun*, 2 vols, Paris, 2000.

BECKETT 1995
Oliver Beckett, *The Life and Work of James Ward, RA, 1769–1859. The Forgotten Genius*, Lewes, 1995

BELKIN 1998
Kristin Lohse Belkin, *Rubens*, London, 1998

BELKIN 2006
Kristin Lohse Belkin, 'La belle Hélène' and Her Beauty Aids: A New Look at *Het Pelsken*; in: *Munuscula Amicorum. Contributions on Rubens and His Colleagues in Honour of Hans Vlieghe*, Katlijne Van der Stighelen (ed.), Turnhout 2006, pp. 299–310

BELLORI 2005
Giovan Pietro Bellori, *The Lives of the Modern Painters, Sculptors and Architects*, Alice S. Wohl, Hellmut Wohl and Tommaso Montanari (eds), Cambridge, 2005

BELSEY 2002
Hugh Belsey, *Gainsborough at Gainsborough House*, London 2002

BENOÎT 1993
Jérémie Benoît, 'La Peinture allégorique sous le Consulat: structure et politique', *Gazette des Beaux-Arts*, 6, 121 (1993), pp. 76–92

BERTHOLD 1958
Getrude Berthold, *Cézanne und die alten Meister. Die Bedeutung der Zeichnungen Cézannes nach Werken anderer Künstler*, Stuttgart, 1958

BIALOSTOCKI 1985
Jan Bialostocki, 'Reflections on Erotism in some Rubens Pictures: Three Paintings in the Vienna Museum', in *Rubens and his World*, Antwerp, 1985, pp. 187–92

BINYON 1902
Laurence Binyon, *Catalogue of Drawings by British Artists ... in the Department of Prints and Drawings in the British Museum*, London, 1902

BIRMINGHAM 1995
Thomas Gainsborough: The Harvest Wagon, Paul Spencer-Longhurst and Janet M. Brooke, exh. cat., Birmingham Museum and Art Gallery, Birmingham, and Art Gallery of Ontario, Toronto, 1995

BJURSTROM 1981
P. Bjurstrom, Delacroix, *Lion Hunt in the Grace and Philip Sandblom Collection, Nationalmuseum Stockholm*, 1981

BLAYNEY BROWN 2005
David Blayney Brown, 'Commentary on Peter Paul Rubens's *Landscape with a Rainbow* (Inscription by Turner) 1802 by Joseph Mallord William Turner', catalogue entry, July 2005, in David Blayney Brown (ed.), *J. M. W. Turner: Sketchbooks, Drawings and Watercolours*, December 2012, <www.tate.org.uk/art/research-publications/jmw-turner/joseph-mallord-william-turner-commentary-on-peter-paul-rubenss-landscape-with-a-rainbow-r1129784> [Accessed 1 April 2014]

BLISS 1975
Diane Carole Bliss, 'Thomas Gainsborough', in Providence 1975, pp. 197–221

BLUMENFELD 2013
Carole Blumenfeld, *Une facétie de Fragonard: Les révélations d'un dessin retrouvé*, Montreuil, 2013

BOASE 1959
S. R. Boase, *English Art*, 1800–1870, Oxford, 1959

BOCCARDO 1997
Piero Boccardo, 'Ritratti di collezionisti e committenti', in Genoa 1997

BOCCARDO 1999
Piero Boccardo, 'Genoa and the Genoese at the time of Van Dyck', in Antwerp 1999

BOCCARDO AND DI FABIO 1997
Piero Boccardo and Clario Di Fabio (eds), *Pittura Fiamminga in Liguria*, secoli xiv–xvii, Aosta, 1997

BOCK VON WÜLFINGEN 1947
Ordenberg Bock von Wülfingen, *Rubens in der Deutschen Kunstbetrachtung*, Berlin, 1947

BONN 1999
Velázquez, Rubens und Lorrain. Malerei am Hof Philipps IV. Museo del Prado zu Gast in Bonn, exh. cat., Bundeskunsthalle, Bonn, 1999–2000

BONNET 2006
Jacques Bonnet, *Femmes au Bain*, Vanves, 2006

BÖRSCH-SUPAN 2007
Helmut Börsch-Supan, *Antoine Watteau 1684–1721*, Potsdam, 2007

BOSTON 1993
The Age of Rubens, Peter C. Sutton, exh. cat., Museum of Fine Arts, Boston, and Toledo Museum of Art (Ohio), 1993

BOSTON 2003
Rembrandt's Journey. Painter. Draftsman. Etcher, Clifford S. Ackley (ed.), exh. cat., Museum of Fine Arts, Boston, and The Art Institute of Chicago, 2003–04

BOTTINELLI 2004
Giorgia Bottinelli, *Faun Revealing a Sleeping Woman*, online entry (2004) <*www.tate.org.uk/art/artworks/picasso-faun-revealing-a-sleeping-woman-jupiter-and-antiope-after-rembrandt-p11360/text-summary*> [Accessed 6 March 2014]

BRETT 2010
Cécile Brett, 'Antonio Verrio à Londres: une carrière triomphale', in Toulouse 2010, pp. 85–97

BREWER 1801–18
James Norris Brewer, *The Beauties of England and Wales*, 18 vols, London, 1801–18

BRITTON 1806
John Britton, *An Historical Account of Corsham House in Wiltshire*, London, 1806

BROOKS 1976
Attfield Brooks, 'Further Topographical Notes', in Alastair Smart and Attfield Brooks, *Constable and His Country*, London, 1976

BRUNSWICK 2004
Nils Büttner and Ulrich Heinen, *Peter Paul Rubens, Barocke Leidenschaften*, exh. cat., Herzog Anton Ulrich Museum, Brunswick, published in Munich, 2004

BRUNTJEN 1985
S. Bruntjen, *John Boydell, 1719–1804: A Study of Art Patronage and Publishing in Georgian London*, New York, 1985

BRUSSELS 1880
Exposition historique de l'art belge, 1830–1880, exh. cat., Palais des Beaux-Arts et Musées Royaux, Brussels, 1880

BRUSSELS 2002
Rubens: exposition, Hôtel de ville de Bruxelles, Ville de Bruxelles, tentoonstelling, Stadbuis van Brussel, Stad Brussel, Renate Trnek, exh. cat., Brussels 2002

BRUSSELS 2003
Vénus dévoilée. La Vénus d'Urbino du Titien, Omar Calabrese (ed.), exh. cat, BOZAR, Brussels, 2003

BRUSSELS 2007
Rubens: A Genius at Work, Joost Vander Auwera, Sabine van Sprang et al., exh. cat. Musées royaux des Beaux-Arts de Belgique, Brussels, 2007

BRUSSELS 2012
Jordaens und die Antike, exh. cat., Musées royaux des Beaux-Arts de Belgique, Brussels, and Staatliche Museen Kassel, 2012

BRYSON 1981
Norman Bryson, *Word and Image: French Painting of the Ancien Régime*, Cambridge, 1981

BURCHARD 1963
Wolfgang Burchard, '"The Garden of Love" by Rubens', *Burlington Magazine*, 105 (1963), pp. 428–32

BURCHARD AND D'HULST 1963
Ludwig Burchard and Roger-Adolf d'Hulst, *Rubens Drawings*, 2 vols, Brussels, 1963

BURCKHARDT 1949
Jacob Burckhardt: Recollections of Rubens, H. Gerson (ed.), Mary Hottinger (trans.), London, 1949

BUTLIN AND JOLL 1984
Martin Butlin and Evelyn Joll, *The Paintings of J. M. W. Turner*, 2 vols, New Haven and London, 1984

CABANNE 1999
Pierre Cabanne, *Honoré Daumier. Painter of the Human Comedy*, Paris, 1999

CAFRITZ 1988
Robert C. Cafritz, 'Netherlandish Reflections on the Venetian Landscape Tradition', in Cafritz, Gowing and Rosand 1988, pp. 113–47

CAFRITZ, GOWING AND ROSAND 1988
Robert C. Cafritz, Lawrence Gowing and David Rosand, *Places of Delight: The Pastoral Landscape*, Washington DC, 1988

CALVO SERRALLER 1991
Francisco Calvo Serraller, *Teoría de la Pintura del Siglo de Oro*, Madrid, 1991

CAMBRIDGE 1985
The John Tillotson Bequest: Paintings and Drawings of the Barbizon School, exh. cat., Fitzwilliam Museum, Cambridge, 1985

CAMBRIDGE 1991
James Ward RA 1769–1859, Jane Munro, exh. cat., Fitzwilliam Museum, Cambridge, 1991–92

CARDELLINI 2001
Lucia Cardellini, 'Modelli Fiamminghi e Olandesi nella pittura di Elisabeth Vigée Le Brun', *Critica d'Arte*, 64, 9 (2001), pp. 56–67

CARROLL 1989
Margret D. Carroll, 'The Erotics of Absolutism: Rubens and the Mystification of Sexual Violence', *Representations*, 25 (1989), pp. 3–30

CARPI 2010
Dea Fortuna. Iconografia di un mito, Manuela Rossi (ed.), exh. cat., Museo Civico Giulio Ferrari, Carpi, 2010–11

CASSEL 2010
Sensualité et volupté. Le corps féminin dans la peinture flamande des XVIe et XVIIe siècles, exh. cat,. Musée de Flandre Cassel, 2010–11

CAVALLI-BJÖRKMAN, FRYKLUND AND SYDÉN 2010
Görel Cavalli-Björkman, Carina Fryklund and Káren Sidén, *Dutch and Flemish Paintings*, vol. 3, Flemish Paintings, *c.* 1600–c. 1800, Stockholm, 2010

CHAPPUIS 1973
Adrien Chappuis, *The Drawings of Paul Cézanne: A Catalogue Raisonné*, Greenwich, Conn., 1973

CHICAGO 1997
Renoir, Douglas Druick, exh. cat., The Art Institute of Chicago, 1997

CHROŚCICKI 2005
Juliusz A. Chrościcki, 'The Recovered Modello of P. P. Rubens's *Disembarkation at Marseilles*. The Problem of Control and Censorship in the Cycle *Life of Maria de' Medici*', *Artibus et Historiae*, 2005, pp. 221–49

CIATTI 2001
Marco Ciatti (ed.), *Rubens agli Uffizi. Il restauro delle Storie di Enrico IV*, Florence, 2001

CINCINNATI 2004
Drawn by the Brush: Oil Sketches by Peter Paul Rubens, Peter C. Sutton, Marjorie E. Wieseman and Nico Van Hout, exh. cat., Cincinnati Art Museum; Bruce Museum of Arts and Science, Greenwich, Conn.; Berkeley Art Museum and Pacific Film Archive, University of California, Berkeley, 2004

CLAYTON 2004
Martin Clayton, *Holbein to Hockney: Drawings from the Royal Collection*, London, 2004

CLIFFORD 1976
Timothy Clifford, 'Polidoro and English Design', *Connoisseur*, 192 (1976), pp. 282–91

COHEN 2003
Sarah R. Cohen, 'Rubens's France: Gender and Personification in the Marie de Médicis Cycle', *The Art Bulletin*, 85 (2003), pp. 490–522

COLLINS BAKER 1937
C. H. Collins Baker, *Catalogue of the Principal Pictures in the Royal Collection at Windsor Castle*, London, 1937

COLOGNE 2000
Faszination Venus. Bilder einer Göttin von Cranach bis Cabanel, Ekkehard Mai (ed.), exh. cat. Wallraff-Richartz Museum, Cologne, Alte Pinakothek, Munich, and Royal Museum of Fine Arts Antwerp, 2000–01

CONSTANS 1993
Claire Constans, *Versailles: Château de la France et orgueil des rois*, Paris, 1993

CONSTANS 1995
Claire Constans, *Musée national du château de Versailles. Les peintures*, 3 vols, Paris, 1995

CONSTANS AND BEAUVAIS 1999
Claire Constans and Lydia Beauvais 'Le roi gouverne par lui-même. 1661. Une esquisse de Charles Le Brun pour la voûte de la galerie des Glaces au Château de Versailles', *Revue du Louvre. La revue des musées de France*, 2 (1999), pp. 56–61.

COPENHAGEN 2000
Delacroix. Maleriets Musik, Thomas Lederballe (ed.), exh. cat., Ordrupgaard, Copenhagen, 2000

CORINTH 1909
Lovis Corinth, *Legenden aus dem Künstlerleben*, Berlin, 1909

CORK 1985
Richard Cork, *Art Beyond the Gallery in Early Twentieth-Century England*, New Haven and London, 1985

CROFT-MURRAY 1962
Edward Croft-Murray, *Decorative Painting in England 1537–1837*, vol. 1, London, 1970

CROW 1985
Thomas Crow, *Painters and Public Life in Eighteenth-Century Paris*, New Haven and London, 1985

CUNNINGHAM 1843
Allan Cunningham 1843, *The Life of Sir David Wilkie; with His Journals, Tours and Critical Remarks on Works of Art; and a Selection from His Correspondence*, Peter Cunningham (ed.), 3 vols, London, 1843

CUST 1900
Lionel Cust, *Anthony van Dyck: An Historical Study of His Life and Works*, London, 1900

D'AZARA 1780
Giuseppe Niccola d'Azara (ed.), *Opere di Antonio Raffaelle Mengs, Primo pittore della Maestà di Carlo III Re di Spagna*, vol. 2, Parma, 1780

D'HULST 1982
Roger-Adolf d'Hulst, *Jacob Jordaens*, Paris and Antwerp, 1982; English edition, Ithaca and London, 1982

D'HULSTE AND VANDENVEN 1989
Roger-Adolf d'Hulst and Marc Vandenven, *Rubens: The Old Testament, Corpus Rubenianum Ludwig Burchard*, III, Antwerp, 1989

DAGUERRE DE HUREAUX 1993
Alain Daguerre de Hureaux, *Delacroix*, Paris, 1993

DALLAS 1983
Picasso the Printmaker: Graphics from the Marina Picasso Collection, exh. cat., Museum of Art, Dallas, 1983

DANIELS 1974
Jeffery Daniels, 'English Baroque Sketches at Marble Hill', *Burlington Magazine*, 116, 856 (1974), pp. 421–22

DANLY WALTHER 1975
Susan Danly Walther, 'Sir Joshua Reynolds', in Providence 1975, pp. 179–95

DAUBERVILLE 2010–12
Guy-Patrice Dauberville, *Renoir: catalogue raisonné des tableaux, pastels, dessins et aquarelles*, vol. 3, 1895–1902 (Paris 2010), vol. 4, 1903–1910 (Paris 2012)

DAVIES 1957
Martin Davies, *National Gallery Catalogues: The French School*, 2nd edition, London, 1957

DAVIES 1992
Maurice Davies, *Turner as Professor: The Artist and Linear Perspective*, London, 1992

DAYOT 1908
Armand Dayot, *La Peinture anglaise, de ses origines à nos jours*, Paris, 1908

DE CLIPPEL 2007–08
Karolien De Clippel, 'Defining Beauty: Rubens's Female Nudes', in *Body and Embodiment in Netherlandish Art, Netherlandish Yearbook of History of Art*, 58 (2007–08), pp. 110–37

DE CLIPPEL 2008
Karolien De Clippel, 'Het barokke vrouwenlichaam', in *Jaarboek voor Vrouwengeschiedenis*, 28 (2008), pp. 61–83

DE CLIPPEL 2009
Karolien De Clippel, 'De Antwerpse Helena: Hélène Fourment en Peter Paul Rubens', *Kunstschrift*, 1 (2009), pp. 20–25

DE CLIPPEL 2010
Karolien De Clippel, 'Naked or not? Some thoughts on nudity and portraiture in seventeenth-century painting', in *Pokerfaced. Flemish and Dutch Baroque Faces Unveiled*, Katlijne Van der Stighelen, Hannelore Magnus, Bert Watteeuw (eds), Turnhout, 2010

DE GIORGI 2010
Raffaele de Giorgi, *'Couleur, couleur': Antonio Verrio un pittore in Europa tra Seicento e Settecento*, Florence, 2010

DE PILES 1681
Roger de Piles, *Dissertation sur les ouvrages des plus fameux peintres*, Paris, 1681

DE PILES 1699
Roger de Piles, *L'Abrégé de la vie des peintres*, Paris, 1699

DE PILES 1990
Roger de Piles, *Cours de peinture par principes* (1703), Nîmes, 1990

DE VRIES 2005
Lyckle de Vries, 'Rubens's Medici Cycle: Italian Art Theory and Flemish Painting', in Heck 2005, pp. 147–58

DEGRAZIA 1984
Diane de Grazia, *Le Stampe die Carracci con i disegni, le incisione, le copie e i dipinti connessi*, Bolgona, 1984

DELACROIX 1848
Eugène Delacroix, 'Peintres et sculpteurs modernes. Gros', *Revue des deux mondes*, 3 (1848), pp. 502–19

DELACROIX 1935
Correspondance Générale d'Eugène Delacroix, André Joubin (ed.), Paris, 1935

DELACROIX 1948
The Journal of Eugène Delacroix, Walter Pach (trans.), New York, 1948

DELACROIX 1996
Eugène Delacroix, *Journal 1822–1863*, preface by Hubert Damisch, introduction and notes by André Joubin, Régis Labourdette (ed.), revised edition, Paris, 1996

DELLA PERGOLA 1967
Paola Della Pergola, 'P. P. Rubens e il tema della Susanna al bagno', in *Bulletin Musées Royaux des Beaux-Arts de Belgique*, 16 (1967), pp. 7–20

DESCAMPS 1792
Jean-Baptiste Descamps, *Voyage pittoresque de la Flandre et du Brabant*, Nouvelle Edition, Paris, 1792

DESCHEEMAEKER 1989
Bernard Descheemaeker, 'Over enkele allegorische composities van Rubens en hun samenhang met de Hendrik IV-cyclus', in *Jaarboek van het Koninklijk Museum voor Schone Kunsten, Antwerpen*, 1989, pp. 343–59

DIAS 2013
Rosie Dias, *Exhibiting Englishness: John Boydell's Shakespeare Gallery and the Formation of a National Aesthetic*, New Haven, 2013

DÍAZ PADRÓN 1995
Matías Díaz Padrón, *El Siglo de Rubens en el Museo del Prado*, 2 vols, Madrid, 1995

DIDEROT 2007
Denis Diderot, *Essais sur la peinture. Salons de 1759, 1761, 1763*; new extended and corrected edition, edited and presented by G. May and J. Chouillet, Paris, 2007

DITTMANN 2001
Lorenz Dittmann, *Die Wiederkehr der antiken Götter im Bilde. Versuch einer neuen Deutung*, Paderborn, 2001, pp. 166–219

DITTMANN 2005
Lorenz Dittmann, *Die Kunst Cézannes*, Vienna, 2005

DONOVAN 2004
Fiona Donovan, *Rubens and England*, New Haven and London, 2004

DOUWES DEKKER 1983
H. T. Douwes Dekker, 'Gli Autoritratti di Elisabeth Vigée-Lebrun (1755–1842)', *Antichità viva*, 22, 4 (1983), pp. 31–35

DREIER 1977
F. Dreier, 'Anmerkungen zur Frierenden Venus von Peter Paul Rubens', *Niederdeutsche Beiträge zur Kunstgeschichte*, 16 (1977), pp. 45–51

DU CAMP 1855
Maxime du Camp, in *Les Beaux-Arts à l'Exposition universelle de 1855: Peinture. Sculpture*, Paris, 1855

DUBOS 1993
Jean-Baptiste Dubos, *Réflexions critiques sur la poésie et sur la peinture*, introduced by Dominique Désirat, Paris, 1993

DUBOURG 1911
Victoria Dubourg, *Catalogue de l'œuvre complet (1849–1904) de Fantin-Latour / établi et rédigé par Mme Fantin-Latour*, Paris, 1911

DUKELSKAYA AND MOORE 2002
Larissa Dukelskya and Andrew Moore (eds), *A Capital Collection: Houghton Hall and the Hermitage*, New Haven and London, 2002

DUNLAP 1834
William Dunlap, *History of the Rise and Progress of the Arts of Design in the United States*, 2 vols, New York, 1834

DUPONT 1958
Jacques Dupont, 'Le Pavillon de l'Aurore à Sceaux', *Bulletin de la société de l'histoire de l'art français*, 1958, pp. 67–72

DURANTE 2003
Stephanie-Suzanne Durante, 'The Ceilings of the Jesuits' Church, Antwerp', in London 2003, pp. 74–85

DURET 1902
Théodore Duret, *Histoire d'Edouard Manet et de son œuvre*, Paris, 1902

DURO 1997
Paul Duro, *The Academy and the Limits of Painting in Seventeenth-Century France*, Cambridge, 1997

DÜSSELDORF 2008–09
Himmlisch – Herrlich – Höfisch: Peter Paul Rubens, Johann Wilhelm von der Pfalz, Anna Maria Luisa de' Medici, Bettina Baumgärtel (ed.), exh. cat., Museum Kunst Palast, Düsseldorf, 2008–09

DUTUIT 1881
Eugène Dutuit, *Manuel de l'amateur d'estampes*, 6 vols, Paris and London, 1881–88

ECKER AND PATAKI 2007
Diana Ecker and Zita Ágota Pataki, 'Phantasie in Pelz: Bemerkungen zu Rubens' *Het Pelsken*', in *Rubens im Blick. Ausgewählte Werke unter Re-vision*, Eveliina Juntunen (ed.), Stuttgart, 2007, pp. 109–36

EDINBURGH 2007
Bruegel to Rubens: Masters of Flemish Painting, Desmond Shawe-Taylor and Jennifer Scott, exh. cat., The Queen's Gallery, Palace of Holyroodhouse, Edinburgh, Museum voor Oude Kunst, Brussels, and The Queen's Gallery, Buckingham Palace, London, 2007

EDWARDS 2006
JoLynn Edwards, 'Watteau Drawings: Artful and Natural', in Sheriff 2006, pp. 41–62

EHRLICH WHITE 1967
Barbara Ehrlich White, 'Delacroix's Painted Copies after Rubens', *The Art Bulletin*, 49, 1 (1967), pp. 37–51

EISELEIN 1825
Joseph Eiselein (ed.), *Johann Joachim Winckelmann, Sämtliche Werke: Einzige vollständige Ausgabe; dabei Porträt, Facsimile und ausführliche Biographie des Autors*, Donaueschingen, 1825–29

EISLER 1967
Colin Eisler, 'Rubens's Uses of the Northern Past: The Michiels Triptych and Its Sources', *Musées Royaux des Beaux-Arts de Belgique Bulletin*, 16 (1967)

EITNER 1960
Lorenz E. A. Eitner, *Géricault: An Album of Drawings in The Art Institute of Chicago*, Chicago, 1960

EITNER 1971
Lorenz E. A. Eitner, 'Dessins de Géricault d'après Rubens: la genèse du "Radeau de la Méduse"', *Revue de l'Art*, 14 (1971), pp. 51–56

ELLIS AND ROE 2007
Andrew Ellis and Sonia Roe (eds), *Oil Paintings in Public Ownership in Hampshire: Southampton and the Isle of Wight, The Public Catalogue Foundation*, London, 2007

ELLIS AND ROE 2008
Andrew Ellis and Sonia Roe (eds), *Oil Paintings in Public Ownership in the Victoria and Albert Museum*, London, 2008

EMPSON 1935
William Empson, *Some Versions of Pastoral*, London, 1935

ERDMANN 1929
Kurt Erdmann, 'Peter Paul Rubens "Nessus und Dejanira"', in *Zeitschrift für Bildende Kunst*, 1929, pp. 65–71

ERTZ 1979
Klaus Ertz, *Jan Brueghel der Ältere 1568–1625: Die Gemälde mit kritischem Œuvrekatalog*, Cologne, 1979

ERTZ AND ERTZ 2008–10
Klaus Ertz and Christa Nitze-Ertz, *Jan Brueghel der Ältere (1568–1625). Kritischer Katalog der Gemälde*, 4 vols, Lingen, 2008–10

EVERS 1942
H. G. Evers, *Peter Paul Rubens*, Munich, 1942

EVERS 1943
H. G. Evers, *Rubens und sein Werk, neue Forschungen*, Brussels, 1943

FARR 1958
Dennis Farr, *William Etty*, London, 1958

FINBERG 1961
Alexander Joseph Finberg, *The Life of J. M. W. Turner, RA*, Oxford, 1961

FLORENCE 1977
Rubens e la pittura fiamminga del Seicento nelle collezioni pubbliche fiorentine, Didier Bodart et al., exh. cat., Palazzo Pitti, Florence, 1977

FORSTER 1990
Georg Forster, *Werke. Sämtliche Schriften, Tagebücher, Briefe*, 16 vols, Berlin, 1990

FORRESTER 1996
Gillian Forrester, *Turner's Drawing Book: The Liber Studiorum*, London, 1996

FORSTER 1791
Georg Forster, *Ansichten vom Niederrhein, von Brabant, Flandern, Holland, England und Frankreich*, Berlin, 1791

FORT WORTH 1982
Elisabeth Louise Vigée Le Brun 1755–1842, Joseph Baillio, exh. cat., Kimbell Museum, Fort Worth, 1982

FRANKFURT 1982
Jean-Antoine Watteau: Einschiffung nach Cythera, exh. cat., Städtische Galerie im Städelschen Kunstinstitut, Frankfurt, 1982

FRANKFURT 1992
Daumier Drawings, Colta Ives, Margret Stuffmann and Martin Sonnabend, exh. cat., Städel Museum, Frankfurt, and The Metropolitan Museum of Art, New York, 1992

FREEDBERG 1976
David Freedberg, 'The Representation of Martyrdoms during the Early Counter-Reformation in Antwerp', *Burlington Magazine*, 118 (1976), pp. 128–38

FREEDBERG 1984
David Freedberg, *Rubens: The Life of Christ after the Passion, Corpus Rubenianum Ludwig Burchard*, VII, New York, 1984

GALLETTI 2008
Sara Galletti, 'Rubens et la galerie de Henri IV au palais du Luxembourg (1628–1630)', *Bulletin Monumental*, 166 (2008), pp. 43–51

GARLICK 1989
Kenneth Garlick, *Sir Thomas Lawrence*, Oxford, 1989

GARLICK AND MACINTYRE 1979
Kenneth Garlick and Angus Macintyre, *The Diary of Joseph Farington*, 16 vols, vol. 3 (September 1796 – December 1798), New Haven and London, 1979

GARNIER 1989
Nicole Garnier, *Antoine Coypel (1661–1722)*, Paris, 1989

GAYA NUÑO 1978
Juan Antonio Gaya Nuño, *La obra pictórica completa de Murillo, Clásicos del arte*, 59, Barcelona, 1978

GENARD 1869–76
Pierre Genard, 'Intrede van den Prins-Kardinaal Ferdinand van Spanje te Antwerpen, op 17 avril 1635', *Antwerpsch Archievenblad*, 6 (1869), pp. 400–72; 7 (1870), pp. 1–113; 13 (1876), pp. 215–345

GENOA 1997
Van Dyck a Genova, Grande pittura e collezionismo, Susan Barnes, exh. cat., Palazzo Ducale, Genoa, 1997

GERBERT 1978–79
Gerbert Frodl, 'Bewegung im Theater: Hans Makart und Gustav Klimt,' in *Mitteilungen der Österreichischen Galerie*, Vienna, 22–23, 66–67 (1978–79)

GHENT 1988
Musée des Beaux-Arts Gand, Robert Hooze, Brussels, 1988

GLANG-SÜBERKRÜB 1975
Annegret Glang-Süberkrüb, *P. P. Rubens: Der Liebesgarten: Eine Untersuchung über die Bedeutung der Konfiguration für das Bildthema im Spätwerk des Peter Paul Rubens*, Bern and Frankfurt, 1975

GLORIEUX 2004
Guillaume Glorieux, 'Watteau et la Nord', in Ramade and Eidelberg 2004, pp. 45–56

GLORIEUX 2011
Guillaume Glorieux, *Watteau*, Paris, 2011

GLÜCK 1920–21
Gustav Glück, 'Rubens Liebesgarten', *Jahrbuch der Kunsthistorischen Sammlungen in Wien*, 35 (1920–21), pp. 49–98

GONCOURT AND GONCOURT 2012
Edmond and Jules de Goncourt, 'L'ivresse de Silène, par Daumier', *Le Temps, Illustrateur Universel*, 3, 1860

GOODMAN 1982
Elise Goodman, 'Rubens's "Conversatie à la Mode": Garden of Leisure, Fashion, and Gallantry', *The Art Bulletin*, 64 (1982), pp. 247–59

GOODMAN 1992
Elise Goodman, *Rubens's 'The Garden of Love' as 'Conversatie à la Mode'*, Amsterdam and Philadelphia, 1992

GORDON 1981
Dillon Gordon, *Rubens, Gainsborough: Second Sight*, London, 1981

GORMANS 1998
A. Gormans, 'Jan Boeckhorsts Stürz der Verdammten,' *Aachener Kunstblätter*, 62 (1998–2002), pp. 283–317

GOWER 1900
R. S. Gower, *Sir Thomas Lawrence PRA*, London and New York, 1900

GRASELLI 1987
Margaret Morgan Grasselli, 'Watteau's Use of the Trois-Crayons Technique', in *Drawings Defined*, New York, 1987, pp. 189–91

GRASSELLI 2001
Margaret Morgan Grasselli, Review of Rosenberg and Prat 1996, *Master Drawings*, 39, 3 (2001), p. 331

GRAVES 1912
Algernon Graves, *Summary of and Index to Waagen*, London, 1912

GREEN 2011
Richard Green, 'Etty and the Masters', in York 2011, pp. 61–74

GRITSAY AND BABINA 2008
Natalya Gritsay and Natalya Babina, *Flemish Painting, Seventeenth and Eighteenth Centuries, State Hermitage Museum Catalogue*, St Petersburg, 2008

GROSSMANN 1951
Fritz Grossmann, 'Holbein, Flemish Paintings and Everhard Jabach,' *Burlington Magazine*, 93 (1951), pp. 16–25

GROVE 1996
Leonée Ormond, 'Lawrence, Thomas: Life and Work', *Grove Dictionary of Art*, London, 1996, p. 891

GRUBER 2013
Gerlinde Gruber, '"I want the paint to feel like flesh." Lucian Freud and Netherlandish Masters', in *Lucian Freud*, Sabine Haag and Jasper Sharp (eds), exh. cat., Kunsthistorisches Museum, Vienna, 2013, pp. 114–21

GRUNDY 1909
Cecil Reginald Grundy, *James Ward RA: His Life and Works*, London, 1909

GUIFFREY AND MARCEL 1907–1928
Jean Guiffrey and Pierre Marcel, *Inventaire général des dessins du Musée du Louvre et du Musée de Versailles*, 10 vols, Paris, 1907–28

GUSTIN GOMEZ 2011
Clémentine Gustin Gomez, *L'Avènement du plaisir dans la peinture française de Le Brun à Watteau*, Dijon, 2011

THE HAGUE 1997
Princely Patrons: The Collection of Frederick Henry of Orange and Amalia of Solms in The Hague, Peter van der Ploeg, Carola Vermeeren et al., exh. cat., Mauritshuis, The Hague, 1997

HAIRS 1965
Marie-Louise Hairs, 'Théodore van Thulden 1606–1669. Oeuvres signées ou attestées sur document', *Revue belge d'Archéologie et d'Histoire de l'Art*, 34 (1965), pp. 11–73

HAMBURG 2010
Rubens, van Dyck, Jordaens. Barock aus Antwerpen, Michael Philip (ed.), exh. cat., Bucerius Kunst Forum, Hamburg, 2010, and the National Museum of Art, Architecture and Design, Oslo, 2011

HAMMER-TUGENDHAT 1994
Daniela Hammer-Tugendhat, 'Erotik und Geschlechterdifferenz. Aspekte zur Aktmalerei Tizians', in *Privatisierung der Triebe? Sexualität in der frühen Neuzeit*, Daniela Erlach, Markus Reisenleitner and Karl Vocelka (eds), Frankfurt, 1994, pp. 367–446

HAMMER-TUGENDHAT 2009
Daniela Hammer-Tugendhat, *Das Sichtbare und das Unsichtbare. Zur holländischen Malerei des 17. Jahrhunderts*, Cologne, Weimar and Vienna, 2009

HASSLIN 1953
Johann Jacob Hasslin, *Köln – Stern im Westen*, Munich, 1953

HAYES 1963
John Hayes, 'Gainsborough and Rubens', *Apollo*, 78 (1963), pp. 89–97

HAYES 1975
John Hayes, *Gainsborough: Paintings and Drawings*, London, 1975

HAYES 1982
John Hayes, *The Landscape Paintings of Thomas Gainsborough*, 2 vols, Ithaca, New York, 1982

HAZLITT 1824
William Hazlitt, *Sketches of the Principal Picture-Galleries in England*, London, 1824

HEALY 2004
Fiona Healy, 'Das Unerwartete wahrnehmen, das zu Erwartende interpretieren: Die Liebe sehen, wie Rubens sie malte', in Munich 2004, pp. 39–40

HECK 2005
Michèle-Caroline Heck (ed.), *Le Rubénisme en Europe aux XVIIe et XVIIIe siècles*, Turnhout, 2005

HEINEN 2001
Ulrich Heinen, 'Haut und Knochen – Fleisch und Blut. Rubens' Affektmalerei', in *Rubens Passioni. Kultur der Leidenschaften im Barock*, Ulrich Heinen and Andreas Thielemann (eds), Göttingen, 2001, pp. 70–109

HEINEN 2004
Ulrich Heinen, 'Rubens's Pictorial Diplomacy at War (1637/1638)', in *Rubens and the Netherlands, Nederlands Kunsthistorisch Jaarboek*, Jan de Jong et al. (eds), 55, 2004 (2006), pp. 196–225

HEINEN 2006
Ulrich Heinen, '"Con ogni fervore": Love and Lust in Rubens's Library, Life and Work', in *Minuscula amicorum: Contributions on Rubens and His Colleagues in Honour of Hans Vlieghe*, Katelijne Van der Stighelen (ed.), vol. 1, Turnhout, 2006, pp. 79–101

HEINEN 2009
Ulrich Heinen, '"Auctores generis Venerem Martemque fatemur" – Peter Paul Rubens' Konzepte von Erotik und Gewalt', *Simpliciana. Schriften der Grimmelshausen-Gesellschaft*, 31 (2009), pp. 27–74

HEINEN 2011
Ulrich Heinen, 'Allegory as Pictorial Language in the Late Renaissance and Baroque Eras', in *Image-Thinking. Five Centuries of Images in Antwerp*, exh. cat., Museum Aan de Stroom, Antwerp, 2011, pp. 184–89

HEINSE 2012
Wilhelm Heinse, *Düsseldorfer Gemäldebriefe*, Hamburg, 2012

HELD 1959
Julius S. Held, *Rubens: Selected Drawings*, 2 vols, London, 1959

HELD 1967
Julius S. Held, 'Rubens's *Het Pelsken*', in *Essays in the history of art presented to Rudolf Wittkower*, Douglas Fraser, Howard Hibbard and Milton J. Lewine (eds), London, 1967, pp. 188–92

HELD 1980
Julius S. Held, *The Oil Sketches of Peter Paul Rubens: A Critical Catalogue*, 2 vols, Princeton, 1980

HELD 1982
Julius S. Held, 'Rubens's Glynde Sketch and the Installation of the Whitehall Ceiling', *Burlington Magazine*, 112, 806 (1970), pp. 274–81 (republished in A. W. Rosenthal, D. Rosand and J. Walsh Jr (eds), *Rubens and His Circle: Studies by Julius S. Held*, Princeton, 1982, pp. 126–37)

HELD 1986
Julius S. Held, *Rubens: Selected Drawings, with an Introduction and a Critical Catalogue*, second revised edition, Oxford, 1986

HERRMANN 1975
Luke Herrmann, *Turner: Paintings, Watercolours, Prints and Drawings*, Boston, 1975

HIGHMORE 1754
Joseph Highmore, *A Critical Examination of Rubens's Paintings at the Banqueting House*, London, 1754

HILLES 1929
F. W. Hilles, *Letters of Sir Joshua Reynolds*, Cambridge, 1929

HILLES 1936
F. W. Hilles, *The Literary Career of Sir Joshua Reynolds*, Cambridge, 1936

HIND 1915
Arthur Mayger Hind, *Catalogue of Dutch and Flemish Drawings preserved in the Department of Prints and Drawings in the British Museum*, 4 vols, London, 1915

HIND 1923
Arthur Mayger Hind, *A Catalogue of Rembrandt's Etchings; chronologically arranged and completely illustrated*, 2 vols, London, 1923

HINTERDING ET AL. 2000
Erik Hinterding, Ger Luijten and Martin Royalton-Kisch, *Rembrandt the Printmaker*, London, 2000

HOLLSTEIN 1949–2010
F. W. H. Hollstein, *F. W. H. Hollstein's Dutch and Flemish Etchings, Engravings and Woodcuts c. 1450–1700*, 73 vols, Amsterdam, 1949–87; Roosendaal, 1988–94; Rotterdam, 1995–2010

HOOG AND GUICHARNAUD 1984
Michel Hoog and Hélène Guicharnaud (eds), *Musée de l'Orangerie, Catalogue de la collection Jean Walter et Paul Guillaume*, Paris, 1984

HOTTLE 2004
Andrew D. Hottle, 'Commerce and Connections: Peter Paul Rubens and the Dedicated Print', in *Rubens and the Netherlands, Nederlands Kunsthistorisch Jaarboek*, Jan de Jong et al. (eds), 55, 2004 (2006), pp. 55–85

HOUGHTON HALL 2013
Houghton Revisited: The Walpole Masterpieces from Catherine the Great's Hermitage, Thierry Morel, Andrew Moore, John Harris and Larissa Dukelskaya, exh. cat., Houghton Hall, Norfolk, 2013

HUEMER 1977
Frances Huemer, *Portraits, Corpus Rubenianum Ludwig Burchard*, XIX (1), London, 1977

HUET 1911
René Paul Huet, *Paul Huet (1803–1869), d'après ses notes, sa correspondance, ses contemporains*, Paris, 1911

HYMANS 1893
Henri Hymans, *Lucas Vorsterman, 1595–1675, et son œuvre gravé: catalogue raisonné de l'œuvre de Lucas Emile Vorsterman, senior, graveur flamand*, Brussels, 1893

IÑIGUEZ 1981
Diego Angulo Iñiguez, *Murillo: Su vida su arte, su obra*, 3 vols, Madrid 1981

JACOBS 2009
Lynn F. Jacobs, 'Rubens and the Northern Past: The Michielsen Triptych and the Thresholds of Modernity', *The Art Bulletin*, 91, 3 (2009), pp. 302–24

JAFFÉ 1972
Michael Jaffé, 'Rubens's *Le Christ à la Paille* Reconsidered', *Apollo*, 95 (1972), pp. 107–114

JAFFÉ 1977
Michael Jaffé, *Rubens and Italy*, London, 1977

JAFFÉ 1989
Michael Jaffé, *Rubens. Catalogo Completo*, Milan, 1989

JAKUMEIT-PIETSCHMANN 2010
Caprice Jakumeit-Pietschmann, *Künstlerkonkurrenz in Antwerpen zu Beginn des 17. Jahrhunderts: Janssen, Jordaens and Rubens*, Weimar, 2010

JAMESON 1842
Mrs Jameson, *A Handbook to the Public Galleries of Art in or near London*, 2 parts, 1842

JEFFERYS 1757 AND 1772
Thomas Jefferys, *A Collection of the Dresses of Different Nations, Ancient and Modern; particularly Old English Dresses. After the designs of Holbein, Vandyke, Hollar, and others*, 4 vols, 2 parts, London, 1757 and 1772

JOACHIM AND HALLER OLSEN 1978
Harold Joachim and Sandra Haller Olsen, *French Drawings and Sketchbooks of the Nineteenth Century*, vol. 1, Chicago, 1978

JOBERT 1997
Barthélémy Jobert, *Delacroix*, Paris, 1997

JOHNSON 1981–89
Lee Johnson, *The Paintings of Eugène Delacroix: A Critical Catalogue*, 6 vols, Oxford, 1981–89

JOLL 1977
Evelyn Joll, *Turner: A Special Loan Exhibition of Twenty Rarely Seen Paintings*, London, 1977

JOST 1964
Ingrid Jost, 'Bemerkungen zur Heinrichsgalerie des P. P. Rubens', *Nederlands Kunsthistorisch Jaarboeck*, 15 (1964), pp. 175–219

JOUIN 1889
Henry Jouin, *Charles Le Brun et les arts sous Louis XIV. Le premier peintre sa vie son œuvre, ses écrits, ses contemporains, son influence. D'après le manuscrit de Nivelon et de nombreuses pièces inédites*, Paris, 1889

JUDSON 1997
J. Richard Judson, 'Comments on Rubens's Coup de Lance: Its Iconography, Style, and Importance for Eugène Delacroix', in *Rembrandt, Rubens, and the Art of Their Time: Recent Perspectives*, Roland E. Fleischer and Susan Clare Scott (eds), University Park, Pa., 1997

JUDSON 2000
J. Richard Judson, *Rubens: The Passion of Christ, Corpus Rubenianum Ludwig Burchard*, VI, Turnhout, 2000

JUYNBOLL 1961
Willem Rudolf Juynboll, 'Een olieverfschets van Eugène Delacroix', *Bulletin Museum Boymans-van Beuningen*, Rotterdam, 12, 1 (1961), pp. 1–11

KAHNWEILER 1988
Daniel-Henry Kahnweiler, *Huit entretiens avec Picasso*, Caen, 1988

KARLSRUHE 2003–04
Eugène Delacroix: Sonderausstellung des Landes Baden-Württemberg, exh. cat., Staatliche Kunsthalle Karlsruhe, 2003–04

KASSEL 2004
Pan und Syrinx, Eine erotische Jagd. Peter Paul Rubens, Jan Brueghel und ihre Zeitgenossen, exh. cat., Staatliche Museen Kassel, 2004

KAUFFMANN 1982
C. M. Kauffman, *Catalogue of Paintings in the Wellington Museum*, London, 1982

KAULBACH 2004
Hans-Martin Kaulbach, 'Europa in den Friedensallegorien des 16.–18. Jahrhunderts', in *Europa im 17. Jahrhundert. Ein politischer Mythos und seine Bilder*, K. Bussmann and E. A. Werner (eds), Stuttgart, 2004

KEITH 1999
Larry Keith, 'The Rubens Studio and the "Drunken Silenus supported by Satyrs"', *National Gallery Technical Bulletin*, 20 (1999), pp. 96–104

KELLER 1965
Horst Keller, 'Delacroix vor Rubens (ein Farbvergleich)', *Wallraf-Richartz Jahrbuch*, 17 (1965), pp. 423–25

KIRKPATRICK 2006
Sidney D. Kirkpatrick, *The Revenge of Thomas Eakins*, New Haven and London, 2006

KLEMM 1986
Christian Klemm, *Joachim von Sandrart: Kunst-Werke Und Lebens-Lauf*, Berlin, 1986

KLESSMANN 1999
Rüdiger Klessmann, Johann Liss. *Eine Monographie mit kritischem Oeuvrekatalog*, Ghent, 1999

KLIMAN 1983
Eve Kliman, 'Delacroix's Lions and Tigers: A Link between Man and Nature', *Art Bulletin*, 64 (1983), pp. 446–66

KOCKS 1981
Dirk Kocks, *Jean-Baptiste Carpeaux. Rezeption und Originalitat*, Sankt Augustin, 1981

KRÄFTNER ET AL. 2005
Johann Kräftner, Wilfried Seipel and Renate Trnek (eds), *Rubens in Wien. Die Meisterwerke. Die Gemälde in den Sammlungen des Fürsten von und zu Liechtenstein, des Kunsthistorischen Museums und der Gemäldegalerie der Akademie der bildenden Künste in Wien*, Vienna, 2005

KRAMM 1857–64
Christiaan Kramm, *De Levens en werken der hollandsche en vlaamsche Kunstschilders, Beeldhouwers, Graveurs en Bouwmeesters, van den vroegsten tot op onzen tijd*, 3 vols, Amsterdam, 1857–1864

KRAUSS 1967
Rosalind E. Krauss, 'Manet's Nymph Surprised', *Burlington Magazine*, 109 (1967), pp. 622–27

KRUMRINE 1992
Mary Louise Krumrine, 'Cézanne's "Restricted Power": Further Reflections on the Bathers', *Burlington Magazine*, 137 (1992), pp. 586–95

LAMAS DELGADO 2011
Eduardo Lamas Delgado, '"Un autre Rubens": l'influence du rubénisme dans la peinture courtisane espagnole à travers l'exemple de l'œuvre de Francisco Rizi (1614–1685)', *Revue Belge d'Archéologie et d'Histoire de l'Art*, 80, 1 (2011), pp. 179–96

LANDERS ALTHOUSE 1975
Roxane Landers Althouse, 'Théodore Géricault', in Providence 1975, pp. 223–40

LANGE 2004
Justus Lange, 'Ein Pan für jede Tonart? Pans Jagd auf die Nymphe Syrinx zwischen Mythos, Moral und Kunst', in Kassel 2004

LARKIN 1966
Oliver W. Larkin, *Daumier: Man of His Time*, New York, 1966

LAUGHTON 1991
Bruce Laughton, *The Drawings of Daumier and Millet*, New Haven, 1991

LAUGHTON 1996
Bruce Laughton, *Honoré Daumier*, New Haven and London, 1996

LE BLANC 2004
Marianne Le Blanc, *D'Acide et d'encre. Abraham Bosse (1604?–1676) et son siècle en perspectives*, Paris, 2004

LECA 2010
Benedict Leca, *Thomas Gainsborough and the Modern Woman*, London, 2010

LEDERBALLE 2000
Thomas Lederballe, 'Delacroix's Enthusiasm: Abduction as Genre in His Painting', in *Delacroix: The Music of Painting*, exh. cat., Ordrupgaard, Copenhagen, 2000, pp. 103–21

LEEDS 1989
Images of Women, Corinne Miller, Lynda Nead and Griselda Pollock, exh. cat., Leeds City Art Galleries, Leeds, 1989

LEHMANN 2007
Doris Helga Lehmann, '"Der eigentlich künstlerische Zug": Schönheit, Innovation und Paraphrase im Werk von Hans Makart', in *Hans Makart 1840–1884*, Erich Marx and Peter Maub (eds), Salzburg, 2007

LENNIE 1976
C. Lennie, *Landseer: The Victorian Paragon*, London, 1976

LEPPERT 1996
Richard Leppert, *Art and the Committed Eye: The Cultural Functions of Imagery*, Oxford, 1996

LESLIE 1843
Charles Robert Leslie, *Memoirs of the Life of John Constable Esq., Chiefly Composed of His Letters*, London, 1843

LEVEY 1961
Michael Levey, 'The Real Theme of Watteau's "Embarkation for Cythera"', *Burlington Magazine*, 106 (1961), pp. 180–85

LEVEY 2005
Michael Levey, *Sir Thomas Lawrence*, *New Haven and London*, 2005

LIEDTKE 1984
Walter A. Liedtke, *Flemish Paintings in The Metropolitan Museum of Art*, 2 vols, New York, 1984

LIESSMANN 2007
Konrad Paul Liessmann, 'Blutsverwandtschaft. Über Kunst und Erotik. Ein Annäherungsversuch', in *Eros in der Kunst der Moderne*, Evelyn Benesch (ed.), Vienna, 2007

LILLE 1968
Au temps du Roi Soleil. Les peintres de Louis XIV (1660–1715), Antoine Schnapper et al., exh. cat., Palais des Beaux-Arts de Lille, 1968

LILLE 2004
Rubens, Hans Vlieghe, exh. cat., Palais des Beaux-Arts de Lille, 2004

LITTI 2006
Sanna Litti, *The Feminine in German Song*, New York, 2006

LIVERPOOL 1994
Face to Face: Three Centuries of Artists' Self-portraiture, Xanthe Brooke, exh. cat., Walker Art Gallery, Liverpool, 1994

LLOYD 1995
Stephen Lloyd, *Richard and Maria Cosway: Regency Artists of Taste and Fashion*, Edinburgh, 1995

LOCKE 2001
Nancy Locke, *Manet and the Family Romance*, Princeton and Oxford, 2001

LOGAN 1977
Anne-Marie Logan, 'Rubens Exhibitions 1977', *Master Drawings*, 15 (1977), pp. 403–17

LOHSE BELKIN 1987
Kristin Lohse Belkin, 'Titian, Rubens and Van Dyck. A New Look at Old Evidence', in *Bacchanals by Titian and Rubens: Papers Given at a Symposium in the Nationalmuseum, Stockholm, 18–19 March 1987*, G. Cavalli-Björkman (ed.), (Nationalmusei Skriftserie, N.S. 10), Stockholm, 1987, pp. 143–52

LONDON 1972
The Age of Charles I: Painting in England 1620–1649, Oliver Millar, exh. cat., Tate Gallery, London, 1972

LONDON 1976
Constable. Paintings, Watercolours and Drawings, Leslie Parris, Ian Fleming-Williams and Conal Shields (eds), exh. cat., Tate Gallery, London, 1976

LONDON 1977
Rubens: Drawings and Sketches, John Rowlands (ed.), exh. cat., British Museum, London, 1977

LONDON 1980A
Sir Thomas Lawrence, Michael Levey, exh. cat., National Portrait Gallery, London, 1980

LONDON 1980B
John Hayes, *Thomas Gainsborough*, exh. cat., Tate, London, 1980

LONDON 1985
Renoir, exh. cat. Hayward Gallery, London, Galeries nationales du Grand Palais, Paris, and Museum of Fine Arts, Boston, 1985–86

LONDON 1986
Calvocoressi et al., *Oskar Kokoschka*, 1886–1980, Richard Calvocoressi et al., exh. cat., Tate Gallery, London, Kunsthaus Zürich, and Solomon R. Guggenheim Museum, New York, 1986–87

LONDON 1991
Constable, Leslie Parris and Ian Fleming-Williams (eds), exh. cat., Tate Gallery, London, 1991

LONDON 1996
Rubens's Landscapes: Making and Meaning, Christopher Brown, exh. cat., The National Gallery, London, 1996

LONDON 1999
The Light of Nature: Landscape Drawings and Watercolours by Van Dyck and His Contemporaries, Martin Royalton-Kisch, exh. cat., British Museum, London, and Rubenshuis, Antwerp, 1999

LONDON 2003
Peter Paul Rubens: A Touch of Brilliance, exh. cat., Courtauld Institute of Art, London, 2003

LONDON 2004
Cubism and Its Legacy: The Gift of Gustav and Elly Kahnweiler, Jennifer Mundy (ed.), exh. cat, Tate Modern, London, 2004

LONDON 2005
Rubens: A Master in the Making, David Jaffé and Elizabeth McGrath, exh. cat., The National Gallery, London, 2005

LONDON 2009
Van Dyck and Britain, Karen Hearn et al., exh. cat., Tate Britain, London, 2009

LONDON 2010
Thomas Lawrence, Regency Power and Brilliance, Cassandra Albinson, Peter Funnell and Lucy Peltz, exh. cat., National Portrait Gallery, London, 2010

LONDON 2011
Watteau: The Drawings, Pierre Rosenberg and Louis-Antoine Prat, exh. cat., Royal Academy of Arts, London, 2011

LONDON 2013
Daumier: Visions of Paris, exh. cat., Royal Academy of Arts, London, 2013–14

LONDON AND AMSTERDAM 2000
Rembrandt the Printmaker, Erik Hinterding, Ger Luijten, Peter Schatborn and Martin Royalton-Kisch, exh. cat., British Museum, London, and Rijksmuseum, Amsterdam, 2000

LOS ANGELES 1971
Géricault, Lorenz E. A. Eitner, exh. cat., Los Angeles County Museum, Los Angeles, 1971

LOS ANGELES 1997
Exiles and émigrés. The Flight of European Artists from Hitler, Stephanie Barron, Sabine Eckmann et al., exh. cat., Los Angeles County Museum of Art, Museum of Fine Arts, Montreal, and Neue Nationalgalerie, Berlin, 1997–98

LOS ANGELES 2005
Jacques-Louis David: Empire to Exile, Philippe Bordes, exh. cat., J. Paul Getty Museum, Los Angeles, and the Sterling and Francine Clark Art Institute, Williamstown, Mass., 2005

LOS ANGELES 2006
Rubens and Brueghel: A Working Friendship, Ann T. Woollett and Ariane van Suchtelen, exh. cat., The J. Paul Getty Museum, Los Angeles, and Royal Picture Gallery, Mauritshuis, The Hague, 2006

LÜCKE AND LÜCKE 2002
Hans-K. and Susanne Lücke, *Helden und Gottheiten der Antike. Ein Handbuch. Der Mythos und seine Überlieferung in Literatur und bildender Kunst*, Hamburg, 2002

LUIJTEN AND MEIJ 1990
Ger Luijten and A. W. F. M. Meij, *From Pisanello to Cézanne: Master Drawings from the Museum Boymans-van Beuningen, Rotterdam*, Rotterdam, 1990

MCCORQUODALE 1981
Charles McCorquodale, *Bronzino*, New York, 1981

MCGRATH 1984
Elizabeth McGrath, 'Rubens's "Susanna and the Elders" and Moralising Inscriptions on Prints', in Herman Vekeman and Justus Müller Hofstede (eds), *Wort und Bild in der Niederländischen Kunst und Literatur des 16. und 17. Jahrhunderts*, Erfstadt, 1984, pp. 73–90

MCGRATH 1997
Elisabeth McGrath, *Subjects from History, Corpus Rubenianum Ludwig Burchard*, XII, 2 vols, London, 1997

MCINTRYE 2003
Ian McIntyre, *Joshua Reynolds: The Life and Times of the First President of the Royal Academy*, London, 2003

MCKIM-SMITH 1995
Gridley McKim-Smith, 'Velázquez and Rubens: The Meaning of a Pigment, or a Date', *Shop Talk: Studies in Honour of Seymour Slive, Presented on His Seventy-fifth Birthday*, Cambridge, Mass., 1995, pp. 175–78

MADRID 1999
Velázquez, Rubens y Van Dyck: pintores cortesanos del siglo XVII, Jonathan Brown (ed.), exh. cat., Museo Nacional del Prado, Madrid, 1999–2000

MADRID 2011
Pintura barroca española, exh. cat., Museo Nacional del Prado, Madrid, 2011

MADRID 2012
The Young Van Dyck, Alejandro Vergara and Friso Lammertse (eds), exh. cat., Museo Nacional del Prado, Madrid, 2012

MADRID AND LONDON 1982–83
Bartolomé Esteban Murillo, 1617–1682, exh. cat., Museo Nacional del Prado, Madrid; Royal Academy of Arts, London, 1982–83

MAISON 1967
K. E. Maison, *Honoré Daumier: Catalogue Raisonné of the Paintings, Watercolours and Drawings*, 2 vols, London, 1967–68

MANNINGS AND POSTLE 2000
David Mannings and Martin Postle, *Sir Joshua Reynolds: A Complete Catalogue of His Paintings*, 2 vols, New Haven and London, 2000

MARTIN 1968
John Rupert Martin, *The ceiling paintings for the Jesuit Church in Antwerp, Corpus Rubenianum Ludwig Burchard*, I, London and New York, 1968

MARTIN 1972
John Rupert Martin, *The Decorations for the Poimpa Introitus Ferdinandi, Corpus Rubenianum Ludwig Burchard*, XVI, London and New York, 1972

MARTIN 1986
Gregory Martin, *National Gallery Catalogues: The Flemish School, c. 1600–1900*, London, 1970; new edition 1986

MARTIN 2005
Gregory Martin, *The Ceiling Decoration of the Banqueting Hall, Corpus Rubenianum Ludwig Burchard*, XV, Arnout Balis (ed.), 2 vols, London, 2005

MARTIN 2011
Gregory Martin, *Rubens in London. Art and Diplomacy*, London, 2011

MASSEAU 2009
Didier Masseau, *Elisabeth Vigée Le Brun: Souvenirs 1755–1842*, Paris, 2009

MAY 2005
Gita May, *Elisabeth Vigée LeBrun: The Odyssey of an Artist in an Age of Revolution*, New Haven and London, 2005

MAYER 1925
August L. Mayer, 'Leibl als Kopist in der Alten Pinakothek', *Kunst und Künstler*, 23 (1925), pp. 279–80

MAYHEW 1967
Edgar de Noailles Mayhew, *Sketches by Thornhill in the Victoria and Albert Museum*, London, 1967

MECHEL 1783
Christian von Mechel, *Verzeichniss der Gemälde der Kaiserlich Kgl. Bilder Gallerie in Wien verfasst von Christian von Mechel der Kaiserl. Kgl.u. anderer Akademien Mitglied nach der von ihm auf Allerhöchsten Befehl im Jahre 1781*, Vienna, 1783

MEIJ AND DE HAAN 2001
A. W. F. M. Meij and Maartje de Haan, *Rubens, Jordaens, Van Dyck and Their Circle: Flemish Master Drawings from the Museum Boijmans Van Beuningen, Rotterdam*, Rotterdam, 2001

MERCK 1779
Johann Heinrich Merck, 'Notizen von einer malerischen Reise nach Köln, Bensberg und Düsseldorf', *Teutscher Merkur*, 3 (1778), pp. 113–28

MERLE DU BOURG 2004A
Alexis Merle du Bourg, *Peter Paul Rubens et la France, 1600–1640*, Villeneuve d'Ascq, 2004

MERLE DU BOURG 2004B
Alexis Merle du Bourg, *Rubens au Grand Siècle, sa réception en France, 1640–1715*, Rennes, 2004

MÉROT 1994
Alain Mérot, *La Peinture française au XVIIe siècle*, Paris, 1994

MEXICO CITY 2012
Seventeenth-Century Flemish Art: Collection of the Royal Museum of Fine Arts Antwerp, exh. cat. Museo Nacional de Arte, Mexico City, 2012

MICHIELS 1882
Alfred Michiels, *Van Dyck et ses élèves*, Paris, 1882

MILAN 2006
La pietà dimenticata di Van Gogh: due Pietà a confronto, exh. cat., Museo Diocesano, Milan, 2006

MILES AND HANNAH 1961
H. Miles and A. Hannah, *Dutch and Flemish, Netherlandish and German Paintings, Glasgow Art Gallery and Museum*, 2 vols, Glasgow, 1961

MILLAR 1969
Oliver Millar, *Pictures in the Royal Collection: Later Georgian Pictures*, 2 vols, London, 1969

MILLAR 1995
Delia Millar, *The Victorian Watercolours and Drawings in the Collection of Her Majesty the Queen*, 2 vols, London, 1995

MILLEN AND WOLF 1989
Ronald Forsyth Millen and Robert Erich Wolf, *Heroic deeds and Mystic figures: A new reading of Rubens's Life of Maria de' Medici*, Princeton and Oxford, 1989

MILOVANOVIC 2005
Nicolas Milovanovic, *Les Grands Appartements de Versailles sous Louis XIV. Catalogue des décors peints*, Paris, 2005

MIQUEL AND MIQUEL 2006
Pierre Miquel and Rolande Miquel, *Narcisse Diaz de la Peña (1807–1876)*, 2 vols, Paris, 2006

MIRZOEFF 2006
Nicholas Mirzoeff, 'Flickers of Seduction: The Ambivalent and Surprising Painting of Watteau', in *Sheriff* 2006, pp. 123–32

MITTIG 1985
Hans-Ernst Mittig, 'Erotik bei Rubens', in *Der Garten der Lüste*, Renate Berger and Daniela Hammer-Tugendhat (eds), Cologne, 1985, pp. 48–88

MONBALLIEU 1976–78
Adolf Monballieu, 'Het probleem van het "Portret" bij Rubens' altaarstukken', *Gentse Bijdragen*, 24 (1976–78) pp. 159–68

MONGAN 1962
Agnes Mongan, *Great Drawings of All Time*, Ira Moskowitz (ed.) New York, 1962

MONTREAL 1960
The Montreal Museum of Fine Arts. Painting, Sculpture, Decorative Arts, Montreal, 1960

MOUREAU AND MORGAN GRASSELLI 1987
François Moureau and Margaret Morgan Grasselli (eds), *Watteau 1684–1721, Le peintre, son temps et sa legende*, Paris and Geneva, 1987

MULLER 1982
Jeffrey M. Muller, 'Rubens's Theory and Practice of the Imitation of Art', *The Art Bulletin*, 64, 2 (1982), pp. 228–47

MULLER 1993
Jeffrey M. Muller, 'Review of Heroic Deeds and Mystic Figures by R. F. Millen and R. E. Wolf', *Oud Holland*, 107, 3 (1993), pp. 305–10

MUNICH 1981
Neue Pinakothek München, Erläuterungen zu den ausgestellten Werken, Bayerische Staatsgemäldesammlungen, Munich, 1981

MUNICH 1994
Wilhelm Leibl: zum 150. Geburtstag Bayerischen Staatsgemäldesammlungen, Götz Czymmek and Christian Lenz, exh. cat., Neue Pinakothek, Munich, and Wallraf-Richartz Museum, Cologne, 1994

MUNICH 1996
Corot, Courbet und die Maler von Barbizon 'les amis de la nature', Christoph Heilmann, Michael Clarke and John Sillevis, exh. cat., Haus der Kunst, Munich, 1996

MUNICH 2001
Pygmalions Werkstatt: Die Erschaffung des Menschen im Atelier von der Renaissance bis zum Surrealismus, Barbara Eschenburg (ed.), exh. cat., Lehnbachhaus, Munich, 2001

MUNICH 2009A
Kurfürst Johann Wilhelms Bilder, Reinhold Baumstark (ed.), exh. cat., 2 vols, Alte Pinakothek, Munich, 2009

MUNICH 2009B
Vorbild und Neuerfindung. Rubens im Wettstreit mit Alten Meistern, Reinhold Baumstark et al. (eds), exh. cat., Bayerische Staatsgemäldesammlungen, Munich, 2009

MUNICH, BERLIN, LONDON AND NEW YORK 2007
Gustav Klimt, Alfred Weidinger (ed.), exh. cat., Munich, Berlin, London and New York, 2007

NAGLER 1835–52
G. K. Nagler, *Neues Allgemeines Künstlerlexikon*, 22 vols, Munich, 1835–52

NAMUR 2007
Les Relations de Monsieur Wiertz. Antoine Wiertz au coeur de son siècle, Paris and Namur, 2007

NAMUR 2007
Les Relations de Monsieur Wiertz. Antoine Wiertz au cœur de son siècle, exh. cat., Maison de la Culture de la province de Namur, Namur, 2007

NATTER 2012
Tobias G. Natter (ed.), *Gustav Klimt: The Complete Paintings*, Cologne, 2012

NÉRET 2009
Gilles Néret, *Renoir. Maler des Glücks*, Hong Kong, 2009

NEW YORK 1958
Renoir, Degas: A Loan Exhibition of Drawings, Pastels, Sculptures, exh. cat., Charles E. Slatkin Galleries, New York, 1958

NEW YORK 1983
Manet, 1832–1883, Françoise Cachin and Charles S. Moffett (eds), exh. cat., Metropolitan Museum of Art, New York, 1983

NEW YORK 1988
Creative Copies, Egbert Haverkamp-Begemann and Carolyn Logan, exh. cat., The Drawing Center, New York, 1988

NEW YORK 1992
Daumier Drawings, Colta Ives, Margret Stuffmann and Martin Sonnabend, exh. cat., The Metropolitan Museum of Art, New York, 1992

NEW YORK 2005
Peter Paul Rubens: The Drawings, Anne-Marie Logan and Michiel C. Plomp (eds), exh. cat., The Metropolitan Museum of Art, New York, 2005

NEW YORK 2009
Watteau, Music, and Theater, Katharine Baetjer (ed.), exh. cat., The Metropolitan Museum of Art, New York, 2009

NEW YORK 2012
Dürer and Beyond: Central European drawings before 1700 in the Metropolitan Museum of Art, Stijn Alsteens and Freyda Spira, exh. cat., The Metropolitan Museum of Art, New York, 2012

NIVELON 1700
Claude Nivelon, *Vie de Charles Le Brun et description detaillée de ses ouvrages*, Paris, *c.* 1700

NOON 2003
Patrick Noon, *Constable to Delacroix: British Art and the French Romantics*, London, 2003

NORDENFALK 1938
Carl Nordenfalk, 'Ein wiedergefundenes Gemälde des Van Dyck', in *Jahrbuch der Preussischen Kunstsammlungen*, 59 (1938), pp. 36–48

NYGREN 1980
E. Nygren, *The Art of James Ward RA (1769–1859)*, Ann Arbor, 1980

O'CONNELL 1985
Sheila O'Connell, 'Simon Gribelin (1661–1733), Printmaker and Metal-engraver', *Print Quarterly*, 2 (1985), pp. 27–38

OLDENBOURG 1921
Rudolf Oldenbourg, *P. P. Rubens, Des Meisters Gemälde*, Klassiker der Kunst series, 4th edition, Stuttgart, 1921

OP DE BEECK 1973
E. Op de Beeck, 'Suzanna en de twee ouderlingen, Rubens gravures voor Anna Roemer Visscher', in *Jaarboek van het koninklijk Museum voor Schone Kunsten*, 1973, pp. 207–21

OSLO 1973
Katalog over utenlandsk malerkunst, The National Museum of Art, Architecture and Design, Oslo, 1973

OTTAWA 1968
Jacques Jordaens 1593–1678, Michael Jaffé, exh. cat., National Gallery of Canada, Ottawa, 1968–69

OTTAWA 1999
Daumier 1808–1879, Henri Loyrette et al., exh. cat., Musée des Beaux-Arts du Canada, Ottawa, Galeries nationales du Grand Palais, Paris, and the Phillips Collection, Washington DC, 1999–2000

PANOFSKY 1966
Erwin Panofsky, '"Good Government" or Fortune?', *Gazette des Beaux-Arts*, 68 (1966), p. 309

PARIS 1932
L'Art de Versailles et les nouvelles acquisitions du musée, exh. cat., preface by Pierre de Nolha, Musée de l'Orangerie, Paris, April–May 1932

PARIS 1955
J. B. Carpeaux, 1827–1875, exh. cat., Petit Palais, Paris, 1955–56

PARIS 1975
Sur les traces de Jean-Baptiste Carpeaux, exh. cat., Grand Palais, Paris, 1975

PARIS 1982
Fantin-Latour, Douglas Druick, exh. cat., Galeries nationales du Grand Palais, Paris; National Gallery of Canada, Ottawa; California Palace of the Legion of Honor, San Francisco, 1982–83

PARIS 1983
Manet. 1832–1883, Françoise Cachin, exh. cat., Galeries nationales du Grand Palais, Paris, and The Metropolitan Museum of Art, New York, 1983

PARIS 1987
Fragonard, Pierre Rosenberg, exh. cat., Galeries nationales du Grand Palais, Paris, and The Metropolitan Museum of Art, New York, 1987–88

PARIS 1989
Le Beau Idéal, ou l'art du concept, Régis Michel (ed.), exh. cat., Musée du Louvre, Paris, 1989

PARIS 1991
The Loves of the Gods: Mythological Painting from Watteau to David, Colin B. Bailey, Philippe Le Leyzour and Pierre Rosenberg, exh. cat., Galeries nationales du Grand Palais, Paris, Philadelphia Museum of Art and Kimbell Art Museum, Fort Worth, 1991–92

PARIS 1998
Delacroix, les dernières années, exh. cat., Galeries nationales du Grand Palais, Paris, and Philadelphia Museum of Art, 1998–99

PARIS 2004
Dante et Virgile aux Enfers d'Eugène Delacroix, Sébastien Allard, exh. cat., Musée du Louvre, Paris, 2004

PARIS 2004–05
Le sacre de Napoléon peint par David, Sylvain Laveissière et al., exh. cat, Musée du Louvre, Paris, 2004–05

PARIS 2008A
Marie-Antoinette, Xavier Salomon, exh. cat., Grand Palais, Paris, 2008

PARIS 2008B
'L'Autoportrait comme récit historique. Le Rembrandt moderne', in *Lovis Corinth (1858–1925). Entre impressionisme et expressionism*, exh. cat., Musée d'Orsay, Paris, 2008

PARIS 2009
Renoir au XXe siècle, exh. cat., Galeries nationales du Grand Palais, Paris, Los Angeles County Museum of Art, and Philadelphia Museum of Art, 2009–10

PARIS 2011
Manet: The Man Who Invented Modernity, Stéphane Guégan (ed.), exh. cat., Musée d'Orsay, Paris, 2011

PARIS 2013
Jordaens 1593–1678, Alexis Merle du Bourg et al., exh. cat., Petit Palais, Musée des Beaux-Arts de la ville de Paris, 2013–14

PARKER 1933
Karl Theodore Parker, 'A Drawing by Fragonard after Rubens', *British Museum Quarterly*, 7 (1933), p. 105

PARKER AND MATHEY 1957
Karl Theodore Parker and Jacques Mathey, *Antoine Watteau: Catalogue complet de son œuvre dessiné*, 2 vols, Paris, 1957

PERCIVAL 2012
Melissa Percival, *Fragonard and the Fantasy Figure: Painting the Imagination*, Farnham, 2012

PÉREZ SÁNCHEZ 1977
A. Perez Sánchez, 'Rubens y la pintura barroca espanola', *Goya*, 140–41 (1977), pp. 86–109

PÉREZ SÁNCHEZ 1985
Alfonso Pérez Sánchez, 'Une vision nouvelle de la peinture espagnole du Siècle d'Or', *Revue de l'art*, (70) 1985, pp. 54–59

PERINI 1988
Giovanna Perini, 'Sir Joshua Reynolds and Italian Art and Art Literature. A Study of the Sketchbooks in the British Museum and in Sir John Soane's Museum', *Journal of the Warburg and Courtauld Institutes*, 51 (1988), pp. 141–68

PERRY 2005
Gill Perry, *Gender And Art*, New Haven, 2005

PETER-RAUPP 1980
Hanna Peter-Raupp, *Die Ikonographie des Oranjezaal (Studien zur Kunstgeschichte II)*, Hildesheim and New York, 1980

PIETRALATA 2011
Cecilia Mazzetti di Pietralata, *Joachim von Sandrart (1606–1688): i disegni*, Milan, 2011

PICON 2008
Jérôme Picon (Joris-Karl Huysmans), *Trois Primitifs*, Paris, 2008

PLAX 2000
Julie-Anne Plax, *Watteau and the Cultural Politics of Eighteenth-Century France*, Cambridge, 2000

PLOCK 2011
Philippa Plock, entry in the online catalogue of the Waddesdon Manor collection, Aylesbury, <http://www.waddesdon.org.uk/collection> [accessed 11 March 2014]

PLYMOUTH 2009–10
Sir Joshua Reynolds: The Acquisition of Genius, Donato Esposito, exh. cat., Plymouth City Museum and Art Gallery, 2009–10

POESCHEL 2001
Sabine Poeschel, 'Rubens's Battle of the Amazons as a War-Picture. The Modernisation of a Myth', *Artibus et Historiae*, 43 (2001), pp. 91–108

POHLEN 1985
Ingeborg Pohlen, *Untersuchungen zur Reproduktionsgraphik der Rubenswerkstatt*, München, 1985

POINTON 1979
Marcia Pointon, 'Gainsborough's Landscape of Retirement', *Art History*, 2 (1979), pp. 441–55

POLETTI AND RICHARME 2003
Michel Poletti and Alain Richarme, *Jean-Baptiste Carpeaux, sculpteur: Catalogue raisonné de l'oeuvre édité*, Paris, 2003

POSNER 1984
Donald Posner, *Antoine Watteau*, Ithaca, New York, 1984

PROVIDENCE 1975
Rubenism: An Exhibition by the Department of Art, Brown University, and the Museum of Art, Rhode Island School of Design, exh. cat., Providence, 1975

PROVOST AND CHILDS 1989
Louis Provost and Elizabeth Childs, *Daumier, A Thematic Guide to His Oeuvre*, Princeton, 1989

QUEBEC 2004A
Rubens et l'art de la gravure, Nico Van Hout (ed.), exh. cat., Royal Museum of Fine Arts Antwerp, and Musées national des Beaux-Arts du Québec, Quebec, 2004–05

QUEBEC 2004B
John R. Porter and Mario Béland, 'Echos de l'œuvre du maître. L'influence de Rubens sur l'art au Québec', exh. cat., Royal Museum of Fine Arts Antwerp, and Musée national des Beaux-arts du Québec, Quebec, 2004, pp. 156–71

RAMADE AND EIDELBERG 2004
Patrick Ramade and Martin Eidelberg, *Watteau et la fête galante*, Paris, 2004

RANKE 1977
Winfried Ranke, 'Böcklinmythen', in Andree 1977, pp. 64–91

RAUX 2005
Sophie Raux, 'Les Dessins de Fragonard d'après Rubens: transposition, interprétation, création', in Michèle-Caroline Heck, *Le Rubénisme en Europe aux XVIIe et XVIIIe siècles*, Turnhout, 2005, pp. 129–44

RAUX 2007
Sophie Raux, 'Le Voyage de Fragonard et Bergeret en Flandre et Hollande durant l'été 1773', *Revue de l'art*, 156, 2 (2007), pp. 11–28

RAYMOND 2013
Florence Raymond (ed.), *Antoine Watteau (1684–1721): La Leçon de la Musique*, Brussels, 2013

REFF 1969
Theodore Reff. '"Manet's Sources": A Critical Evaluation', *Artforum*, 8 (1969), pp. 40–48

RENGER 1974
Konrad Renger, 'Rubens Dedit Dedicavitque. Rubens' Beschäftigung mit der Reproduktionsgrafik. I. Teil: Der Kupferstich', *Jahrbuch der Berliner Museen*, 16 (1974), pp. 122–75

RENGER 1975
Konrad Renger, 'Rubens Dedit Dedicavitque. Rubens' Beschäftigung mit der Reproduktionsgrafik. II. Teil: Radierungen und Holzschnitte – die Widmungen', *Jahrbuch der Berliner Museen*, 17 (1975), pp. 166–213

RENGER 1981
Konrad Renger, 'Sine Cerere et Baccho friget Venus. Zu Bacchischen Themen bei Rubens', in *Peter Paul Rubens, Werk und Nachruhm*, issued by the Zentralinstitut für Kunstgeschichte and the Bayerische Staatsgemäldesammlungen, Munich, 1981, pp. 105–35

RENGER 1993
Konrad Renger, 'Rubens'sche Frauen. Lesesplitter zu einem Vorurteil', in *Hülle und Fülle, Festschrift für Tilmann Buddensieg*, Andreas Beyer (ed.), Alfter, 1993

RENGER AND DENK 2002
Konrad Renger and Claudia Denk, *Flämische Malerei des Barock in der Alten Pinakothek*, Cologne and Munich, 2002

REWALD 1996
John Rewald, *The Paintings of Paul Cézanne: A Catalogue Raisonné*, 2 vols, New York, 1996

REY 1968
Robert Rey, *Daumier: les grands peintres*, Paris, 1968

REYNOLDS 1975
Sir Joshua Reynolds, *Discourses on Art, Robert Wark* (ed.), New Haven and London, 1975

REYNOLDS 1984
Graham Reynolds, *The Later Paintings and Drawings of John Constable*, New Haven and London, 1984

REYNOLDS 1996
Sir Joshua Reynolds, *A Journey to Flanders and Holland*, Harry Mount (ed.), Cambridge 1996

REYNOLDS 1997
Sir Joshua Reynolds, *Discourses on Art*, Robert Wark (ed.), revised edition, New Haven and London, 1997

RIBERO 1995
Aileen Ribeiro, *The Art of Dress: Fashion in England and France 1750–1820*, New Haven and London, 1995

RILEY 1997
Bridget Riley, 'Colour for the Painter', in Colour: Art and Science, Trevor Lamb and Janine Bourriau (eds), Cambridge, 1997

ROBAUT 1885
Alfred Robaut, *L'Oeuvre complet de Eugène Delacroix: Peintures, Dessins, Gravures, Lithographies. Catalogué et reproduit par Alfred Robaut*, Paris, 1885

ROBELS 1996
Hella Robels, *P. P. Rubens Graphik*, Antwerp and Siegen, 1996

ROGELIO BUENDÍA 1994
José Rogelio Buendía, *Paintings of the Prado*, Boston, 1994

ROLAND MICHEL 1984
Marianne Roland Michel, *Watteau: An Artist of the Eighteenth Century*, New York, 1984

ROLAND MICHEL 1998
Marianne Roland Michel, 'The Rosenberg–Prat Catalogue of Watteau's Drawings', *Burlington Magazine*, 140 (1998), pp. 749–54

ROLAND MICHEL 2005
Marianne Roland Michel, 'Fragonard, exhibition catalogue by Jean-Pierre Cuzin', *Master Drawings*, 43, 2 (2005), pp. 217–21

ROME 1977
Rubens e l'incisione nelle collezione del Gabinetto nazionale delle Stampe, Didier Bodart, exh. cat., Villa della Farnesina alla Lungara, 8 February – 30 April 1977, Rome, 1977

ROOSES 1886–92
Max Rooses, *L'Oeuvre de P. P. Rubens*, 5 vols, Antwerp, 1886–92

ROOSES 1897
Max Rooses, 'Staet ende inventaris van den sterffhuyse van Mynheer Albertus Rubens ende Vrouwe Clara del Monte,' *Rubens-Bulletijn*, 5 (1897), pp. 29–30

ROOSES 1906
Max Rooses, *Jordaens' Leben und Werke*, Stuttgart, 1906

ROOSES AND RUELENS 1887–1909
Max Rooses and Charles Ruelens (eds), *Codex diplomaticus Rubenianus, Correspondance de Rubens et documents épistolaires concernant sa vie et ses œuvres*, 6 vols, Antwerp, 1887–1909

ROSA 1796
Joseph Rosa, *Gemälde der k.k. Gallerie. Zweyte Abtheilung. Niderländische Schulen*, 2 vols, Vienna, 1796

ROSAND 1988
David Rosand, 'Giorgione, Titian and the Pastoral Vision', in Cafritz, Gowing and Rosand 1988, pp. 20–81

ROSENBERG 1981
Donald Rosenberg, *Oaten Reeds and Trumpets: Pastoral and Epic in Virgil, Spenser and Milton*, East Brunswick, New Jersey, 1981

ROSENBERG 1999
Pierre Rosenberg, 'Watteau's Copies after Old Masters', in *Watteau and His World: French Drawing from 1700 to 1750*, Alan Wintermute (ed.), London and New York, 1999

ROSENBERG AND BREJON DE LAVERGNÉE 1986
Pierre Rosenberg and Barbara Brejon De Lavergnée, *Panopticon italiano: un diario di viaggio ritrovato, 1759–1761*, Rome, 1986

ROSENBERG AND PRAT 1996
Pierre Rosenberg and Louis-Antoine Prat, *Antoine Watteau 1684–1721. Catalogue raisonné des dessins*, 3 vols, Milan, 1996

ROSENBERG AND STEWART 1987
Pierre Rosenberg and Marion C. Stewart, *French Paintings 1500–1825*, San Francisco, 1987

ROSENTHAL 1983
Michael Rosenthal, *Constable: The Painter and His Landscape*, New Haven and London, 1983

ROSENTHAL 1999
Michael Rosenthal, *The Art of Thomas Gainsborough: 'A Little Business for the Eye'*, New Haven and London, 1999

ROSENTHAL AND MYRONE 2002
Michael Rosenthal and Martin Myrone, *Gainsborough*, London, 2002

ROTTERDAM 1963
Museum Boymans-van Beuningen: Catalogus schilderijen na 1800, Rotterdam, 1963

ROTTERDAM 1983
Malerei aus erster Hand-Ölskizzen von Tintoretto bis Goya, Jeroen Giltay et al., exh. cat., Museum Boijmans Van Beuningen, Rotterdam, and Herzog Anton Ulrich Museum, Brunswick, 1983–84

ROWLANDS 1977
John Kendall Rowlands, *Rubens: Drawings and Sketches*, London, 1977

RUBENS 1955
The Letters of Peter Paul Rubens, Ruth Saunders Magurn, (trans. and ed.), Cambridge, Mass., 1955

RUDRAUF 1956
Lucien Rudrauf, 'Imitation et invention dans l'art d'Eugène Delacroix. Delacroix et Rubens', in *Mélanges Georges Jamati*, Paris, 1956, pp. 277–84

RUELENS 1883
Charles Ruelens, 'La Vie de Rubens par Roger de Piles', *Rubens-Bulletijn*, 2 (1883), pp. 157–75

RUHMER 1984
Eberhard Rumer, *Der Leibl-Kreis und die Reine Malerei*, Rosenheim, 1984

RUSKIN 1843
John Ruskin, *Modern Painters*, 9 vols, 1843–60

SABATIER 1984
Gérard Sabatier, 'Versailles, un imaginaire politique', in *Culture et idéologie dans la genèse de l'Etat moderne*, (transactions of the conference held in Rome, 15–17 October 1984), Rome, 1985, pp. 295–324

SABBE 1925
Maurits Sabbe, 'De Antwerpsche vriendenkring van Anna Roemers Visscher', in *De Moretussen en hun kring*, Antwerp, 1925

ST ANDREWS 1985
Sir David Wilkie: Sketches and Studies. A Bicentenary Exhibition, exh. cat., Crawford Arts Centre, St Andrews, 1985

SALINGER 1949
Margaretta Salinger, 'Representations of Saint Teresa', *The Metropolitan Museum of Art Bulletin*, New Series, 8, 3 (1949), pp. 97–108

SALOMON 2010
Xavier F. Salomon, *Masterpieces of European Painting from the Dulwich Picture Gallery*, New York, 2010

SAMPAIO 2009
Luisa Sampaio, *Painting in the Calouste Gulbenkian Museum*, Lisbon, 2009

SCEAUX 2000
Le Pavillon de l'Aurore. Les dessins de Le Brun et la coupole restaurée, Serge Pitiot et al., exh. cat., Orangerie du domaine de Sceaux, 2000

SCHAFFER 2007
Nikolaus Schaffer, 'Biografie von Hans Makart', in *Hans Makart 1840–1884*, Erich Marx and Peter Laub (eds), Salzburg, 2007, pp. 9–50

SCHAMA 1999
Simon Schama, *Rembrandt's Eyes*, New York, 1999

SCHLOSS HALBTURN 1986
Hans Makart und der Historismus in Budapest, Prag und Wien, exh. cat., Schloss Halbturn, Vienna, 1986

SCHMID 1918
H. A. Schmid, 'Böcklin und die Alten Meister', *Die Kunst*, 1918

SCHNEEVOGT 1873
C. G. Voorhelm Schneevogt, *Catalogue des estampes gravées d'après P. P. Rubens*, Haarlem, 1873

SCHOPENHAUER 1839
Johanna Schopenhauer, *Jugendleben und Wanderbilder, Besuch der Düsseldorfer Gemäldegalerie*, 1839

SEBASTIÁN LÓPEZ 1984
Santiago Sebastian Lopez, *El Guernica y otras obras de Picasso: contextos iconográphicos*, University of Murcia, 1984

SENIOR 1936
Elisabeth Senior, 'Drawings Made in Italy by Fragonard', *The British Museum Quarterly*, 11, 1 (1936), pp. 5–9

SÉRULLAZ 1963
Maurice Sérullaz, *Mémorial de l'exposition Eugène Delacroix organisée au Musée du Louvre à l'occasion du centenaire de la mort de l'artiste*, Paris, 1963

SÉRULLAZ 1971
Maurice Sérullaz, *Eugène Delacroix*, New York, 1971

SÉRULLAZ 2004
Arlette Sérullaz, *Delacroix, Cabinet des dessins 5*, Musée du Louvre, Département des arts graphiques, Paris, 2004

SETA 2013
Cesare de Seta, 'Manet e i "Voyages d'Italie"', in Manet. *Ritorno a Venezia*, exh. cat., Musée d'Orsay, Paris, and Palazzo Ducale, Venice, 2013, pp. 52–67

SEZNEC 1993
Jean Seznec, *La Survivance des dieux antiques. Essai sur le rôle de la tradition mythologique dans l'humanisme et dans l'art de la Renaissance*, second edition, Paris, 1993

SEZNEC AND ADHÉMAR 1957
Jean-Joseph Seznec and Jean Adhémar (eds), *Diderot Salons*, 4 vols, Paris and Oxford, 1957–67

SHERIFF 1995
Mary D. Sheriff, 'The im/modesty of her sex: Elisabeth Vigée-Lebrun and the Salon of 1783', in *Consumption of Culture, 1600–1800: Image, Object, Text*, John Brewer and Ann Bermingham (eds), Oxford and New York, 1995

SHERIFF 2006
Mary D. Sheriff (ed.), *Antoine Watteau: Perspectives on the Artist and Culture of His Time*, Newark, Delaware, 2006

'S HERTOGENBOSCH 1991
Alain Roy, Theodoor Van Thulden. *Un peintre baroque du cercle de Rubens*, exh. cat., Noordbrabants Museum, 's Hertogenbosch, and Musée des Beaux-Arts de Strasbourg, 1991–92

'S HERTOGENBOSCH 2000
Dans la lumière de Rubens – Peintres baroques des Pays-Bas du Sud, exh. cat., Noordbrabants Museum, 's Hertogenbosch, and Musée des Beaux-Arts de Valenciennes, 2000–01

SLOMAN 2012
Susan Sloman, *Gainsborough's Landscapes: Themes and Variations*, London, 2012

SMILES 2009
Sam Smiles (ed.), *Sir Joshua Reynolds: The Acquisition of Genius*, Plymouth, 2009

SMITH 1829–42
John Smith, *A Catalogue Raisonné of the Works of the Most Eminent Dutch, Flemish, and French Painters*. 9 vols, London, 1829–42

SMITH 1840
S. Smith, *The Royal Gallery of Pictures*, 1840

SPRINGER 2008
Peter Springer, *Voyeurismus in der Kunst*, Berlin, 2008

STANLEY 1823
George Stanley, *Memorandum of the Picture called the Chapeau de Paille by P. P. Rubens exhibiting at Mr Stanley's Rooms, No. 21 Old Bond Street*, 5th edition, London, 1823

STEINBART 1959
Kurt Steinbart, 'Das Werk des Johann Liss in alter und neuer Sicht', *Saggi e memorie di storia dell'arte*, 2 (1959), pp. 203–06

STEWART 1983
J. Douglas Stewart, *Sir Godfrey Kneller and the English Baroque Portrait*, Oxford, 1983

STORFFER 1730
Ferdinand à Storffer. *Neu eingerichtetes Inventarium der Kayl. Bilder Gallerie in der Stallburg welches nach denen Numeris und Maasstab ordiniret und von Ferdinand à Storffer gemahlen worden*, 3 volumes on parchment, vol. 2, archive of the Gemäldegalerie, Kunsthistorisches Museum, Vienna, 1730

STUKENBROCK 1994
Christiane Stukenbrock, 'Wilhelm Leibl und die Niederländische Malerei des 17. Jahrhunderts', in Munich and Cologne 1994, pp. 114–23

SULLIVAN 1986
Edward J. Sullivan, *Baroque Painting in Madrid: The Contribution of Claudio Coello, With a Catalogue Raisonné of His Works*, Columbia, 1986

SULTANO AND WERKNER 2003
Gloria Sultano and Patrick Werkner, *Oskar Kokoschka. Kunst und Politik 1937–1950*, Vienna, 2003

SULZER 1771–74
Johann Georg Sulzer, *Discours sur l'allégorie, in De l'allégorie, ou Traités sur cette matière; par Winckelmann, Addison, Sulzer, etc. Recueil utile aux gens de lettres, et nécessaire aux artistes*, Paris, vol. 2, 1798 or 1799 (translation of the article on allegory appearing in *Allgemeine Theorie der schönen Künste in einzeln, nach alphabetischer Ordnung*, 21 vols, Leipzig, 1771–74)

TAINE 1869
Hippolyte Taine, *La Peinture dans les Pays-bas*, Paris, 1869

TAYLOR 1955
Basil Taylor, *Animal Painting in England from Barlow to Landseer*, Harmondsworth and Baltimore, 1955

THIELEMANN 2012
Andreas Thielemann, 'Rubens' Traktat De imitatione statuarum', in *Imitatio als Transformation. Theorie und Praxis der Antikennachahmung in der Frühen Neuzeit*, U. Rombach and P. Seiler (eds), Petersberg, 2012, pp. 95–150

THOMPSON 1949
Francis Thompson, *A History of Chatsworth, Being a Supplement to the 6th Duke of Devonshire's Handbook*, London and New York, 1949

THØFNER 2004
Margit Thøfner, 'Helena Fourment's *Het Pelsken*', *Art History*, 27 (2004), pp. 1–33

THORÉ-BÜRGER, MARCH AND APRIL 1847
Théophile Thoré-Bürger, 'Salon de 1847', *Le Constitutionnel*, 17 March and 14 April

THUILLIER 1967
Jacques Thuillier, 'Le Brun et Rubens', *Bulletin Koninklijke Musea voor Schone Kunsten van België*, 16 (1967), pp. 247–68

THUILLIER AND FOUCART 1967
Jacques Thuillier and Jacques Foucart, *Le Storie di Maria de' Medici di Rubens al Lussemburgo*, Milan, 1967; French edition: Paris 1969

TICKNER 2000
Lisa Tickner, *Modern Life and Modern Subjects: British Art in the Early Twentieth Century*, New Haven and London, 2000

TIETZE-CONRAT 1949–50
E. Tietze-Conrat, 'Das "Skizzenbuch" des Van Dyck als Quelle für die Tizianforschung', in *Critica d'arte*, 8 (1949–50), pp. 435–36

TOKYO 1985
The Impressionist Tradition: Masterpieces from The Art Institute of Chicago, exh. cat., The Seibu Museum of Art, Tokyo, Fukoka Museum and Kyoto Municipal Museum of Art, 1985–86

TOULOUSE 2010
Antonio Verrio. Chroniques d'un peintre italien voyageur (1636–1707), Axel Hémery (ed.), exh. cat., Musée des Augustins, Toulouse, 2010

TURNER 1980
The Correspondence of J. M. W. Turner, John Gage (ed.), Oxford, 1980

UHR 1990
Horst Uhr, *Lovis Corinth*, Berkeley, 1990

VALDIVIESO 1990
Enrique Valdivieso, *Murillo: sombras de la tierra, luces del cielo*, Madrid, 1990

VALDIVIESO 2010
Enrique Valdivieso, *Murillo: catálogo razonado de pinturas*, Madrid, 2010

VALENCIENNES 1978
Peintures et Sculptures Jean-Baptiste Carpeaux, exh. cat. Musée des Beaux-Arts de Valenciennes, 1978

VALENCIENNES 1999
Carpeaux: peintre, Patrick Ramade et al., exh. cat., Musée des Beaux-Arts de Valenciennes, Musée du Luxembourg, Paris, and Van Gogh Museum, Amsterdam, 1999–2000

VALENCIENNES 2008
Carpeaux, Daumier; dessiner sur le vif, Emanuelle Delapierre, exh. cat., Musée des Beaux-Arts de Valenciennes, 2008–09

VAN DE VELDE 1977
Carl Van de Velde, 'Archivalia betreffende Rubens' Madonna met Heiligen voor de Kerk der Antwerpse Augustijnen' in *Jaarboek Koninklijk Museum voor Schone Kunsten Antwerpen*, Antwerp, 1977

VAN DE VELDE AND VAN HOUT 2013
Hildegard Van de Velde and Nico Van Hout, *The Golden Cabinet – Royal Museum at the Rockox House*, Visitors' Guide, Antwerp, 2013

VAN DEN WIJNGAERT 1940
Frank van den Wijngaert, *Inventaris der Rubeniaansche Prentkunst*, Antwerp, 1940

MARJON VAN DER MEULEN-SCHREGARDUS 1975
Hermance Marjon van der Meulen-Schregardus, *Petrvs Pavlvs Rvbens antiqvarivs. Collector and Copyist of Antique Gems*, Alphen aan de Rijn, 1975

MARJON VAN DER MEULEN-SCHREGARDUS 1994
Hermance Marjon van der Meulen-Schregardus, *Rubens Copies after the Antique, Corpus Rubenianum Ludwig Burchard*, XXIII, 3 vols, London, 1994

VAN GOGH LETTERS
www.vangoghletters.org

VAN HOUT 2001A
Nico Van Hout, 'Henri IV valait bien une Galerie! Rubens's Unfinished Luxembourg Project', in Ciatti 2001, pp. 23–40

VAN HOUT 2001B
Nico Van Hout, 'Reconsidering Rubens's Flesh Colour', *Bóletin del Museo del Prado*, 19, 37 (2001), pp. 7–20

VAN HOUT 2001C
Nico Van Hout, 'On the invention and execution of the Coup de Lance', *Rubensbulletin*, 3, 2011, pp. 1–39

VAN HOUT 2010
Nico Van Hout, *Rubens doorgelicht, Meekijken over de schouder van een virtuoos*, Antwerp, 2010; English edition: *Rubens Unveiled, Notes on the Master's Painting Technique*, Antwerp, 2012

VAN HOUT 2011A
Nico Van Hout, 'A Rubens Discovery in Oslo', *Rubensbulletin*, 2011, pp. 88–93 (online publication) <*www.kmska.be/en/Onderzoek/Rubens/Rubensbulletin.html*> [accessed 31 March 2014]

VAN HOUT 2011B
Nico Van Hout, 'On the Invention and Execution of the Coup de Lance', *Rubensbulletin*, 2011, pp. 2–39 (online publication) <*www.kmska.be/en/Onderzoek/Rubens/Rubensbulletin.html*> [accessed 31 March 2014]

VAN HOUT 2012
Nico Van Hout, 'Jordaens and the Rubens Descent of the Cross in Lille', *Rubensbulletin*, 2012, pp. 34–49 (online publication) <*www.kmska.be/en/Onderzoek/Rubens/Rubensbulletin_4.html*> [accessed 31 March 2014]

VAN HOUT AND BALIS 2012
Nico Van Hout and Arnout Balis, *Rubens Unveiled: Notes on the Master's Painting Technique*, Antwerp, 2012

VAN MULDERS 2004
Christine van Mulders, 'Die Zusammenarbeit zwischen Peter Paul Rubens und Jan Brueghel d.Ä.', in Kassel 2004, pp. 59–79

VAN THIEL 1976
Peter J. J. van Thiel, *All the Paintings of the Rijksmusum in Amsterdam: A Completely Illustrated Catalogue by the Department of Paintings of the Rijksmuseum*, Amsterdam, 1976

VANDER AUWERA 2004
Joost Vander Auwera, 'Pan und Syrinx bei Rubens, Jordaens und Janssen. Erotik und Antikenstudium in Konkurrenz', in Kassel 2004, pp. 81–98

VARSHAVSKAYA AND YEGOROVA 1995
Maria Varshavskaya and Xenia Yegorova, *Peter Paul Rubens: The Pride of Life*, Bournemouth and St Petersburg, 1995

VENTURI 1936
Lionello Venturi, *Cézanne, son art, son œuvre*, 2 vols, Paris, 1936

VERGARA 1982
Lisa Vergara, *Rubens and the Poetics of Landscape*, New Haven and London, 1982

VERGARA 1999
Alexander Vergara, *Rubens and His Spanish Patrons*, Cambridge and New York, 1999

VERSAILLES 1963
Charles Le Brun, 1619–1690, peintre et dessinateur, Jennifer Montagu and Jacques Thuillier, exh. cat., Château de Versailles, 1963

VERSAILLES 1999
Jean-Marc Nattier, Xavier F. Salomon, exh. cat., Musée national des châteaux de Versailles et de Trianon, 1999–2000

VERSAILLES 2002
Les Grands Décors peints de Louis XIV. Esquisses et dessins, Nicolas Milovanovic, exh. cat., Musée national des Château de Versailles et de Trianon, 2002–03

VIDAL 2006
Mary Vidal, 'Style as Subject in Watteau's Images of Conversation', in *Sheriff* 2006, pp. 76–93

VIENNA 1961
Katalog der Gemäldegalerie der Akademie der bildenden Künste, Vienna, 1961

VIENNA 1977
Peter Paul Rubens 1577–1640. Ausstellung zur 400. Wiederkehr seines Geburtstages, exh. cat., Kunsthistorisches Museum, Vienna, 1977

VIENNA 2008
Oskar Kokoschka. Exil und neue Heimat 1934–1980, Antonia Hoerschelmann et al., exh. cat., Albertina, Vienna, 2008

VIENNA 2012
Gustav Klimt: 150 years, Agnes Husslein-Arco and Alfred Weidinger (eds), exh. cat., Belvedere Gallery, Vienna, 2012

VLIEGHE 1972
Hans Vlieghe, *Gaspar de Crayer, sa vie et ses œuvres*, 2 vols, Brussels, 1972

VLIEGHE 1973
Hans Vlieghe, *Saints, Corpus Rubenianum Ludwig Burchard*, VIII, Brussels, 1973

VLIEGHE 1987
Hans Vlieghe, *Rubens Portraits of Identified Sitters Painted in Antwerp, Corpus Rubenianum Ludwig Burchard*, XIX, (2), London and New York, 1987

VOLLARD 1938
Ambroise Vollard, *En écoutant Cézanne, Degas, Renoir*, Paris, 1938

VOLLARD 1961
Ambroise Vollard, *Auguste Renoir, Gespräche u. Erinnerungen*, Zurich, 1961

VON SANDRART 1675
Joachim von Sandrart, 'The Life of Rubens, Painter' in *Teutsche Academie*, 1675

VON SIMSON 1986
Otto von Simson, 'Der Raub der Leukippiden. Rubens begegnet der Antike', in *Von Geschichte umgeben. Joachim Fest zum 60. Geburtstag*, Berlin, 1986, pp. 233–44

VOORHELM SCHNEEVOOGT 1873
Carl Godried Voorhelm Schneevoogt, *Catalogue des estampes gravées d'après P. P. Rubens avec l'indication des collections où se trouvent les tableaux et les gravures*, Haarlem, 1873

WAAGEN 1838
Gustav Waagen, *Works of Art and Artists in England*, 3 vols, 1838

WAAGEN 1854
Gustav Waagen, *Treasures of Art in Great Britain*, 3 vols, 1854

WALPOLE 1762
Horace Walpole, *Anecdotes of Painting in England*, Twickenham, 1762

WALTER AND GUILLAUME 1966
Musée de l'Orangerie, Catalogue de la collection Jean Walter et Paul Guillaume, Paris, 1966

WARNKE 1993
Martin Warnke, *Laudando praecipere. Der Medicizyklus des Peter Paul Rubens*, Groningen, 1993

WASHINGTON 1984
Watteau 1684–1721, Margaret Morgan Grasselli and Pierre Rosenberg (eds) exh. cat., National Gallery of Art, Washington DC, Galeries nationales du Grand Palais, Paris, and Schloss Charlottenburg, Berlin, 1984

WATERHOUSE 1950
Ellis K. Waterhouse, *The James A. de Rothschild Collection at Waddesdon Manor: Paintings*, Fribourg, 1950

WATERHOUSE 1966
Ellis Waterhouse, *Gainsborough*, London, 1966

WATSON 1953
F. J. B. Watson, 'New Light on Watteau's "Les Plaisirs du Bal"', *Burlington Magazine*, 95 (1953), pp. 240–42

WEBER AND MÜLLER HOFSTEDE 1990
Kristine Weber and Justus Müller Hofstede, '"Non si fa niente contra la verita". Historischer Schauplatz und ikonographische Inszenierung im Vermählungsbild von Rubens' Medici Zyklus', in *Wallraf-Richartz-Jahrbuch. Westdeutsches Jahrbuch für Kunstgeschichte*, 51, 1990

WEINSHENKER 1966
A. B. Weinshenker, *Falconet: His Writings and His Friend Diderot*, Geneva, 1966

WENDORF 1990
Richard Wendorf, *The Elements of Life*, Oxford, 1990

WESTHEIDER 2010
Ortrud Westheider, 'Die frierende Venus. Rubens' Kunst, zu enthüllen und zu verschleiern', in Hamburg 2010, pp. 36–43

WHITE 1967
Barbara Ehrlich White, 'Delacroix's Painted Copies after Rubens', *The Art Bulletin*, 49 (1967), pp. 37–51

WHITE 1981
Christopher White, 'Rubens and British Art', in *'Sind Briten hier?' Relations Between British and Continental Art 1680–1880*, Munich, 1981, pp. 27–43

WHITE 1987
Christopher White, *Peter Paul Rubens: Man and Artist*, New Haven and London, 1987

WHITE 1999
Christopher White, *Rembrandt as an Etcher: A Study of the Artist at Work*, New Haven, 1999

WHITE 1999B
Christopher White, *Dutch, Flemish and German Paintings before 1900. Catalogue of the Collection of Paintings in the Ashmolean Museum, Oxford*, Oxford, 1999

WHITE 2007
Christopher White, *The Later Flemish Pictures in the Collection of Her Majesty The Queen*, London, 2007

WHITE AND BOON 1969
Sir Christopher White and Karel G. Boon, *Rembrandt's Etchings: An Illustrated Critical Catalogue*, 2 vols, Amsterdam, 1969

WHITLEY 1915
William Thomas Whitley, *Thomas Gainsborough*, New York, 1915

WICHMANN 1977
Siegfried Wichmann, *Arnold Böcklin, 1827–1901, Schlachten, Amazonen- und Brückenkampf*, Sindelfingen, 1977

WIESEMAN 2004
Marjorie E. Wieseman, 'Pursuing and Possessing Passion: Two Hundred Years of Collecting Rubens's Oil Sketches', in Cincinnati 2004, pp. 43–71

WILDENSTEIN AND WILDENSTEIN 1973
Daniel and Guy Wildenstein, *Documents complémentaires au catalogue de l'œuvre de Louis David*. Paris, 1973

WILSON 1985
Michael Wilson, *National Gallery Catalogues: French Paintings Before 1800*, London, 1985

WILSON-BAREAU 1986
Juliet Wilson-Bareau, 'The Hidden Face of Manet: An investigation of the artist's working process', *Burlington Magazine*, 128, 997 (1986), pp. 26–47

WINCKELMANN 1825
Johann Joachim Winckelmann, *Versuch einer Allegorie, besonders für die Kunst*, Dresden, 1766, in *Johann Winckelmanns sämtliche Werke. Einzige vollständige Ausgabe*, Josef Eiselein (ed.), vol. 9, Donaueschingen, 1825

WINTERFELD 1999
Anita-Maria von Winterfeld, *Arnold Böcklin. Bildidee und Kunstverständnis im Wandel seiner künstlerischen Entwicklung*, Basel and Munich, 1999

WOOD 2005
Giovanni Baglione, Joachim von Sandrart, Roger de Piles, *Lives of Rubens*, with an introduction by Jeremy Wood, London, 2005

WOOD 2009
Jeremy Wood, 'Rubens' Italienische Kopien. Ein chronologischer Abriss', in Munich 2009B, pp. 57–81

WOOD 2010A
Jeremy Wood, *Copies and Adaptations from Renaissance and Later Artists. Italian Artists I. Raphael and His School, Corpus Rubenianum Ludwig Burchard*, XXVI.I, 2 vols, London and Turnhout, 2010

WOOD 2010B
Jeremy Wood, *Copies and Adaptations from Renaissance and Later Masters. Italian Artists II. Titian and North Italian Art, Corpus Rubenianum Ludwig Burchard*, XXVI.II, 2 vols, London and Turnhout, 2010

WURZBACH 1906–11
Alfred von Wurzbach, *Niederländisches Künstler-Lexikon auf Grund archivalischer Forschungen bearbeitet*, 3 vols, Vienna, 1906–11

WUYTS 1991
Leo Wuyts, *Bij de iconografie van twee Rubensschilderijen: De Bewening van Christus en Christus op het stro*, Antwerp, 1991

YORK 2011
William Etty: Art and Controversy, Sarah Burnage et al., exh. cat., York Art Gallery, 2011–12

ZIFF 1963
Jerrold Ziff, '"Backgrounds, Introduction of Architecture and Landscape": A Lecture by J. M. W. Turner', *Journal of the Warburg and Courtauld Institutes*, 26 (1963), pp. 124–47

ZIRPOLO 2010
Lilian H. Zirpolo, *Historical Dictionary of Baroque Art and Architecture*, Toronto and Plymouth, 2010

ZURAWSKI 1975
Simone Alaida Zurawski, 'François Boucher and Jean-Honoré Fragonard', in Providence 1975, pp. 147–78

ZURICH 1958
Sammlung Emil G. Bührle. Festschrift zu Ehren von Emil G. Bührle zur Eröffnung des Kunsthaus-Neubaus und Katalog der Sammlung Emil G. Bührle, exh. cat., Kunsthaus, Zurich, 1958

ZURICH 1987
Eugène Delacroix, Günter Metken, exh. cat., Kunsthaus Zürich, and Städtische Galerie im Städelsches Kunstinstitut, Frankfurt, 1987–88

LENDERS TO THE EXHIBITION

AACHEN
Suermondt-Ludwig Museum

AMSTERDAM
Amsterdam Museum
Rijksakademie van Beeldende Kunsten
Rijksmuseum

ANTWERP
Royal Museum of Fine Arts

BERLIN
Gemäldegalerie, Staatliche Museen zu Berlin
Kupferstichkabinett, Staatliche Museen zu Berlin

BIRMINGHAM
The Barber Institute of Fine Arts, University of Birmingham
Birmingham Museums and Art Gallery

BOSTON
Museum of Fine Arts

BRUSSELS
Musées royaux des Beaux-Arts de Belgique

CALAIS
Musée des Beaux-Arts

CAMBRIDGE
Fitzwilliam Museum

CARDIFF
Amgueddfa Cymru – National Museum Wales

CHICAGO
The Art Institute of Chicago

COLOGNE
Wallraf-Richartz Museum and Fondation Corboud

DIJON
Musée des Beaux-Arts de Dijon

EDINBURGH
Scottish National Gallery of Modern Art

FIRLE
Trustees of the Firle Estate Settlement

GHENT
Museum voor Schone Kunsten

KASSEL
Museumslandschaft Hessen Kassel

KINGSTON LACY
Kingston Lacy, the National Trust

LIVERPOOL
Lady Lever Art Gallery

LONDON
British Museum
Michael Tollemache Fine Art
Tate
Royal Academy of Arts
The National Gallery
The Royal Collection
Dulwich Picture Gallery
Victoria and Albert Museum

MADRID
Museo Nacional Centro de Arte Reina Sofía
Museo Nacional del Prado

MONTREAL
The Montreal Museum of Fine Arts

MUNICH
Alte Pinakothek
Neue Pinakothek

NEW YORK
The Metropolitan Museum of Art

OSLO
The National Museum of Art, Architecture and Design

PARIS
Musée de l'Orangerie
Musée des Arts Décoratifs
Musée du Louvre
Musée du Petit Palais
Musée National des Châteaux de Versailles et de Trianon

PHILADELPHIA
Philadelphia Museum of Art

RENNES
Musée des Beaux-Arts de Rennes

ROTTERDAM
Museum Boijmans Van Beuningen

'S-HERTOGENBOSCH
Het Noordbrabants Museum

ST PETERSBURG
State Hermitage Museum

SOUTHAMPTON
Southampton City Art Gallery

STOCKHOLM
Nationalmuseum

SUDBURY
Gainsborough's House

VALENCIENNES
Musée des Beaux-Arts de Valenciennes

VIENNA
Akademie der bildenden Künste
Kunsthistorisches Museum
Österreichische Galerie Belvedere

WASHINGTON DC
National Gallery of Art

YORK
York Museums Trust

ZURICH
Fondation E. G. Bührle Collection
Kunsthaus Zürich

and others who wish to remain anonymous

PHOTOGRAPHIC ACKNOWLEDGEMENTS

All works copyright the artists, their heirs and assigns.

All works of art are reproduced by kind permission of the owners. Every attempt has been made to trace the photographers of works reproduced. Specific acknowledgements are as follows:

Aachen, Suermondt-Ludwig Museum: cat 23 (Anne Gold)
Amsterdam, Amsterdam Museum: cats 131–34
Amsterdam, Collection Rijksmuseum: cats 11, 38, 71, 72, 88, 141
Amsterdam, Van Gogh Museum (Vincent van Gogh Foundation): fig. 31

Basel, Kunstmuseum Basel/Martin P. Bühler: figs 16, 17
Berlin, bpk: figs 5, 7, 33, 56 (Bayerische Staatsgemäldesammlungen); cats 2, 12, 81 (Bayerische Staatsgemäldesammlungen); cat. 135 (Kupferstichkabinett, Staatliche Museen zu Berlin, Jörg P. Anders)
Berlin, © Gemäldegalerie Photo Jörg P. Anders: cat. 93
Birmingham, The Barber Institute of Fine Art, University of Birmingham: cat. 122
Birmingham, © Birmingham Museums Trust: cats 15, 45
Boston, © 2014 Museum of Fine Arts: cat. 14
Brussels, © IRPA-KIK, Brussels (Saint James's Church, Antwerp): fig. 30
Brussels, © Musées royaux des Beaux-Arts de Belgique/J. Geleyns/Ro scan: cat. 56

Calais, © F. Kleinefenn: cat. 63
Cambridge, © Fitzwilliam Museum, Cambridge: cats: 61, 77
Cardiff, Amgueddfa Cymru – National Museum Wales: cat. 111
Chicago, Art Institute of Chicago: cat. 18 (© The Art Institute of Chicago); cat. 79 (© unknown Photographer/Art Institute of Chicago)
Cologne, © Kunst-Station Sankt Peter Köln, 2014: fig. 29
Cologne, Photo © Rheinisches Bildarchiv Köln: cat. 36 (rba_c024300), cat. 69 (rba_c004648)

Dijon, © Musée des Beaux-Arts de Dijon. Photo François Jay: cat. 27
Dorset, © National Trust Images/Derrick E. Witty: cat. 104

Edinburgh, Scottish National Gallery of Modern Art, on long-term loan: cat. 30

Florence, © 2013 Scala: cats 37, 94, 108, 128, 138.1–2 (The Metropolitan Museum of Art/Art Resource/Scala, Florence); cat. 33 (The State Hermitage Museum, St Petersburg)

Ghent, © Lukas-Art in Flanders vzw: figs 25, 27 (photo Hugo Maertens, Cathedral Church of Our Lady, Antwerp); cat. 70 (photo Hugo Maertens, Museum voor Schone Kunsten, Ghent); fig. 26 (photo Hugo Maertens, Royal Museum of Fine Arts Antwerp); cats 4, 5, 6, 7, 8, 9, 10, 19, 25, 26, 31, 32, 39, 44, 51, 53, 57, 60, 65, 66, 83, 84, 91, 96, 103, 114, 117, 139 (photo Hugo Maertens and Dominique Provost, Royal Museum of Fine Arts Antwerp)

Isle of Arran, National Trust for Scotland: fig. 57

Kassel, Museumslandschaft Hessen Kassel, Gemäldegalerie Alte Meister/Ute Brunzel: cat. 55

Lisbon, © Calouste Gulbenkian Foundation, Museu Calouste Gulbenkian, photo Catarina Gomes Ferreira: fig. 39
Liverpool, © National Museums Liverpool, Lady Lever Art Gallery: cat. 119
Lodi, Fondazione Cosway, courtesy of Dr Tino Gipponi: fig. 37
London, © akg-images/Schloss Weissenstein, Pommersfelden: fig. 55
London, The Bridgeman Art Library: cat. 35 (Southampton City Art Gallery)
London, © The Trustees of the British Museum: fig. 12; cats 3, 24, 64, 87, 100, 101, 102, 137, 143
London, By Permission of the Trustees of the Dulwich Picture Gallery: cats 136, 140
London, © The National Gallery 2014: figs 35, 38, 40, 44–46; cats 58, 75, 115
London, Private Collection: cat. 145
London, Royal Academy of Arts, Photo: Roy Fox: cat. 126 (Private Collection, c/o Michael Tollemache Fine Art, London); cat. 211 (Trustees of the Firle Estate Settlement); cats 34.1–24, 47
London, The Royal Chelsea Hospital: fig. 15
London, Royal Collection Trust, © Her Majesty Queen Elizabeth II 2014: fig. 42; cats 86, 106, 109, 113
London, Samuel Courtauld Trust, Courtauld Institute of Art Gallery: fig. 43
London, © Tate, London 2013: fig. 47; cats 46, 49, 110, 126; cat. 52 (© Fondation Oskar Kokoschka/DACS 2013)
London, © Victoria and Albert Museum: fig. 52; cats 16, 48, 50, 123, 124, 125

Madrid, Collection Museo Nacional Centro de Arte Reina Sofía: cat. 73 (© Succession Picasso/DACS, London 2014)
Madrid, © Museo Nacional del Prado: figs 1, 6, 11, 54: cats 54, 95, 97, 130
Mexico City. © José Ignacio González Manterola: fig. 4
Montreal, The Montreal Museum of Fine Arts/Brian Merrett: cat. 82

New Haven, Yale Center for British Art © The Wyndham Lewis Memorial Trust/Bridgeman Images: fig. 49
New York, Ali Elai, Camerarts (private collection): cat. 80
New York, © The Frick Collection: fig. 36

Oslo, The National Museum of Art, Architecture and Design, Børre Høstland: cats 21, 57. 92
Ottawa, © National Gallery of Canada/© Jonathan Clark Fine Art, Representatives of the Artist's Estate: fig. 50

Paris, © Petit Palais: cats 22, 142 (Roger-Viollet)
Paris, Private collection/Pascal Lemaître Photographer: cat. 41
Paris, © RMN-Grand Palais/Musée des Arts Décoratifs: cat. 144 (Jean Tholance)
Paris, RMN-Grand Palais. Photo © Musée des Beaux-Arts de Rennes, dist. RMN-Grand Palais: cat. 1 (Jean-Manuel Salingue)
Paris, © RMN-Grand Palais/Musée des Beaux-Arts de Valenciennes: fig. 3 (René-Gabriel Ojéda/Thierry Le Mage); cat. 76 (René-Gabriel Ojéda)
Paris, © RMN-Grand Palais/Musée du Louvre: fig. 22 (Daniel Arnaudet/Jean Schormans); figs 23, 41 (Gérard Blot); figs 8, 14 (Angèle Dequier); fig. 2 (Adrien Didierjean); fig. 13 (Christian Jean/Hervé Lewandowski); fig. 58 (Hervé Lewandowski); fig. 48, cat. 74 (Stéphane Maréchalle); cat. 146 (Michel Urtado)
Paris, © RMN-Grand Palais/Musée National du Château Versailles: cats 40, 116 (Gérard Blot)
Paris, © RMN-Grand Palais/Musée de l'Orangerie: cat. 78 (Franck Raux)
Philadelphia, Philadelphia Museum of Art: fig. 34 (John G. Johnson Collection, 1917); cat. 62 (Purchased with funds (by exchange) from the bequest of Edna M. Welsh and the gift of Mrs. R. Barclay Scull, 1990)

Rotterdam, loan museum Museum Boijmans Van Beuningen (Collection Koenigs): cats 89, 107 (Photographs Studio Tromp, Rotterdam); Museum Boijmans Van Beuningen: cats 85, 121 (Photographs Studio Tromp, Rotterdam)

St Petersburg, © The State Hermitage Museum, Pavel Demidov: cat. 120
Stockholm, © 1963 AB Svensk Filmindustri, Still Photographer: Harry Kampf: fig. 18
Stockholm, © Hans Thorwid, Nationalmuseum, Stockholm: cat. 13; © Erik Cornelius, Nationalmuseum, Stockholm: cat. 129
Sudbury, Gainsborough's House, Sudbury, Suffolk: cat. 90

Toronto, © 2014 Art Gallery of Ontario: fig. 53
Toulouse, Musée des Augustins/Daniel Martin: fig. 28

Vatican City, Vatican Museums and Galleries © Stefano Baldini/The Bridgeman Art Library: fig. 32
Vienna, Gemäldegalerie der Akademie der bildenden Künste: cat. 98
Vienna, Kunsthistorisches Museum: figs 21, 24; cats 68, 127
Vienna, Österreichische Galerie Belvedere: cats 28, 29, 99

Washington DC, Courtesy National Gallery of Art: cats 17, 59, 105

York, York Museums Trust (York Art Gallery): cat. 43

Zurich, Foundation E. G. Bührle Collection (J.-P. Kuhn, SIAR): cat. 42
Zurich, © 2014 Kunsthaus Zürich. All rights reserved: cat. 20

INDEX

All references are to page numbers; those in **bold** type indicate catalogue plates, and those in *italic* type indicate essay illustrations

SUPPORTERS OF THE ROYAL ACADEMY

MAJOR SUPPORTERS

The President and the Trustees of the Royal Academy Trust are grateful to all its donors for their continued loyalty and generosity. They would like to extend their thanks to all those who have made a significant commitment, past and present, to the galleries, the exhibitions, the conservation of the Permanent Collection, the Library collections, the Royal Academy Schools, the Learning programme and other specific appeals.

HM The Queen
Her Majesty's Government
The 29th May 1961 Charitable Trust
The Aldama Foundation
The American Associates of the Royal Academy Trust
The Annenberg Foundation
Barclays Bank
BAT Industries plc
Sir David and Lady Bell
The late Tom Bendhem
The late Brenda M Benwell-Lejeune
John Frye Bourne
British Telecom
The Brown Foundation
John and Susan Burns
Mr Raymond M Burton CBE
Sir Trevor Chinn CVO and Lady Chinn
The Trustees of the Clore Foundation
The John S Cohen Foundation
Sir Harry and Lady Djangoly
The Dulverton Trust
Alfred Dunhill Limited
The John Ellerman Foundation
The Eranda Foundation
Ernst & Young
Esso UK plc
Esmée Fairbairn Charitable Trust
The Fidelity UK Foundation
The Foundation for Sports and the Arts
Friends of the Royal Academy
Jacqueline and Michael Gee
The Getty Grant Programme
Mr Thomas Gibson
Glaxo Holdings plc
Diane and Guilford Glazer
Mr and Mrs Jack Goldhill
Maurice and Laurence Goldman
The Horace W Goldsmith Foundation
HRH Princess Marie-Chantal of Greece
Mr and Mrs Jocelin Harris
The Philip and Pauline Harris Charitable Trust
The Charles Hayward Foundation
Heritage Lottery Fund
IBM United Kingdom Limited
The Idlewild Trust
Lord and Lady Jacobs
The JP Jacobs Charitable Trust
The Japan Foundation
Gabrielle Jungels-Winkler Foundation
Mr and Mrs Donald Kahn
The Lillian Jean Kaplan Foundation
The Kresge Foundation
The Samuel H Kress Foundation
The Kirby Laing Foundation
The Lankelly Foundation
The late Mr John S Latsis
The David Lean Foundation
The Leverhulme Trust
Lex Service plc
The Linbury Trust
Sir Sydney Lipworth QC and Lady Lipworth CBE
John Lyons Charity
Ronald and Rita McAulay
McKinsey and Company Inc
John Madejski OBE DL
The Manifold Trust
Marks and Spencer
The Paul Mellon Estate
The Mercers' Company
The Monument Trust
The Henry Moore Foundation
The Moorgate Trust Fund
The late Mr Minoru Mori HON KBE and Mrs Mori
Museums and Galleries Improvement Fund
National Westminster Bank
Stavros S Niarchos
Simon and Midge Palley
The Peacock Charitable Trust
The Pennycress Trust
PF Charitable Trust
The Pidem Fund
The Pilgrim Trust
The Edith and Ferdinand Porjes Trust
The Porter Foundation
John Porter Charitable Trust
Rio Tinto
John A Roberts FRIBA
Sir Simon and Lady Robertson
The Ronson Foundation
Rothmans International plc
RTZ Corporation plc
Dame Jillian Sackler DBE
Jillian and Arthur M Sackler
Mr Wafic Rida Saïd
Mrs Jean Sainsbury
The Saison Foundation
The Sammermar Trust
The Basil Samuel Charitable Trust
Mrs Coral Samuel CBE
Sea Containers Ltd
Shell UK Limited
Miss Dasha Shenkman
William and Maureen Shenkman
The Archie Sherman Charitable Trust
The late Pauline Sitwell
The Starr Foundation
Sir Hugh Sykes DL
Alfred Taubman
Sir Anthony and Lady Tennant
Ware and Edythe Travelstead
The Trusthouse Charitable Foundation
The Douglas Turner Trust
Unilever plc
The Weldon UK Charitable Trust
The Welton Foundation
The Weston Family
The Malcolm Hewitt Wiener Foundation
The Maurice Wohl Charitable Foundation
The Wolfson Foundation

and others who wish to remain anonymous

PATRONS

The Royal Academy is extremely grateful to all its Patrons, who generously support every aspect of its work.

CHAIR
Robert Suss

PLATINUM
Celia and Edward Atkin CBE
Mr and Mrs Christopher Bake
Mr and Mrs Patrick Doherty
Ms Ghizlan El Glaoui
Mr Stephen Gosztony
Mr Hideyuki Osawa
Mr Maurice Pinto
Mr and Mrs Jake Shafran
David and Sophie Shalit

GOLD
Mr and Mrs Thomas Berger
Christopher and Alex Courage
Mrs Elizabeth Hosking
Mr Michael Jacobson
Miss Joanna Kaye
Lady Rayne Lacey
Jacqueline and Marc Leland
The Licensing Company, London
Sir Sydney Lipworth QC and Lady Lipworth CBE
Mr and Mrs Ronald Lubner
Sir Keith and Lady Mills
Jean and Geoffrey Redman-Brown
Richard Sharp
Jane Spack
David Stileman
Mr Robert John Yerbury

SILVER
Lady Agnew
Miss H J C Anstruther
Ms Dina Aslanyan
Mrs Emma Avignon
Mrs Jane Barker
Catherine Baxendale
The Duke of Beaufort
Mrs J K M Bentley, Summers Art Gallery
Mr Nigel Boardman
Eleanor E Brass
Mr and Mrs Richard Briggs OBE
Mrs Elie Brihi
Mrs Marcia Brocklebank
Sir Francis Brooke BT
Jeremy Brown
Mr and Mrs Zak Brown
Lord Browne of Madingley
Mr F A A Carnwath CBE
Sir Roger Carr
Jean and Eric Cass
Suzy Castleman
Sir Charles and Lady Chadwyck-Healey
Mrs Ann Chapman-Daniel
Sir Trevor and Lady Chinn
Mr and Mrs George Coelho
Denise Cohen Charitable Trust
Sir Ronald Cohen
Ms Linda Cooper
Mark and Cathy Corbett
Mr and Mrs Ken Costa
Keith Craig
Andrew Crawley
Julian Darley and Helga Sands
Gwendoline, Countess of Dartmouth
Mr Daniel Davies
Peter and Andrea De Haan
The de Laszlo Foundation
Dr Anne Dornhorst
Lord and Lady Douro
Mr and Mrs Jim Downing
Ms Noreen Doyle
Mrs Janet Dwek
Mrs Sheila Earles
Lord and Lady Egremont
Bryan Ferry
Benita and Gerald Fogel
Mr Sam Fogg
Mrs Rosamund Fokschaner
Mrs Jocelyn Fox
Arnold Fulton
The Lord Gavron CBE
Mrs Mina Gerowin Herrmann
Jacqueline and Jonathan Gestetner
Lady Getty
Mr Mark Glatman
Lady Gosling
Piers Gough CBE RA
Mr Gavin Graham
Mrs Mary Graves
HRH Princess Marie-Chantal of Greece
Mr Jim Grover
Mrs Margaret Guitar
Mrs Jennifer Hall
Mr James Hambro
Richard and Janeen Haythornthwaite
Sir John Hegarty and Miss Philippa Crane
Sir Michael and Lady Heller
Lady Heseltine
Alan and Mary Hobart
Mr Philip Hodgkinson
Anne Holmes-Drewry
Mr Philip Hudson
Mr and Mrs Jon Hunt
Judy and Robert Huret
S Isern-Feliu
Mrs Caroline Jackson
Sir Martin and Lady Jacomb
Mrs Raymonde Jay
Ignacio Jayanti
Alistair Johnston and Christina Nijman
Fiona Johnstone
Mrs Ghislaine Kane
Dr Elisabeth Kehoe
Skip Keesal
Princess Jeet Khemka
Mr D H Killick
Mr and Mrs James Kirkman
Mrs Aboudi Kosta
Mr and Mrs Herbert Kretzmer
Norman A Kurland and Deborah A David
Joan H Lavender
Mr George Lengvari and Mrs Inez Lengvari
Lady Lever of Manchester
Miss R Lomax-Simpson
The Hon Mrs Virginia Lovell
Mr and Mrs Henry Lumley
Mrs Josephine Lumley
Gillian McIntosh
Andrew and Judith McKinna
Mr Nicholas Maclean
Sir John Mactaggart
Madeline and Donald Main
Scott and Laura Malkin
Mr Charles Martin
Mr and Mrs Richard C Martin
Zvi and Ofra Meitar Family Fund
Professor Anthony Mellows OBE TD and Mrs Anthony Mellows
Dr Ann Naylor
Ann Norman-Butler
Mr Michael Palin
John Pattisson
Nicholas B Paumgarten
Mr and Mrs D J Peacock
Mr and Mrs A Perloff
Mr Philip Perry
David Pike
Mr and Mrs Anthony Pitt-Rivers
Mr Basil Postan
John and Anne Raisman
Lady Renwick
Mrs Bianca Roden
Rothschild Foundation
Miss Elaine Rowley
Mr and Mrs K M Rubie
Mr Adrian Sassoon
Mr and Mrs Kevin Senior
Christina, Countess of Shaftesbury
Mr Robert N Shapiro
Victoria Sharp
Major General and Mrs Jonathan Shaw
Mr Richard Simmons CBE
Alan and Marianna Simpson
The Lady Henrietta St George
Lady Tennant
Dr Gillian Tett
Anthony Thornton
The Tavolozza Foundation
Mr Anthony J Todd
Miss M L Ulfane
John and Carol Wates
Mrs Angela Webb
Edna and Willard Weiss
Anthony and Rachel Williams
Mrs Isobel Williams
Mrs Adriana Winters

PATRON DONORS
Stephen Barry Charitable Settlement
Mr Eugene Ludwig
The Michael H Sacher Charitable Trust
H M Sassoon Charitable Trust

and others who wish to remain anonymous

BENJAMIN WEST GROUP PATRONS

CHAIR
Lady Judge

PLATINUM
Mr Tony Davis
David Giampaolo
Charles and Kaaren Hale
Mr and Mrs John R Olsen

GOLD
Mr Steve Cardell
Lady Judge
Mr Christian Levett
Ms Alessandra Morra
Mr Peter Williams

SILVER
Lady J Lloyd Adamson
Mr Dimitry Afanasiev
Mrs Spindrift Al Swaidi
Poppy Allonby
Ms Ruth Anderson
Ms Sol Anitua
Mr Andy Ash
Marco and Francesca Assetto
Mrs Leslie Bacon
Naomi and Ted Berk
Mrs Michal Berkner Jenrick
Micaela and Christopher Boas
Jean and John Botts
Mr Simon Brocklebank-Fowler
Ms Pauline Cacucciolo
Mrs Sophie Cahu
Brian and Melinda Carroll
Mrs Caroline Cartellieri Karlsen
Mr and Mrs Paul Collins
Vanessa Colomar de Enserro
Ms Karla Dorsch
Mr and Mrs Jeff Eldredge
Mrs Stroma Finston
Cyril and Christine Freedman
Ms Alexandra Hess
Katie Jackson
Suzanne and Michael Johnson
Syrie Johnson
Lord and Lady Leitch
Mrs Stephanie Léouzon
Ms Ida Levine
Mrs Valerie Nataliya Levine
Mrs Rose-Marie Lieberman
Mr Guido Lombardo
Charles G Lubar
Ted and Patricia Madara
Cornelius Medvei
Dean Menegas
Mrs Victoria Mills
Neil Osborn and Holly Smith
Lady Purves
Mrs Diana Quasha
Broocks Robertson
Mr Aaron Rosenstein
Mrs Candice Schneider
Mr James B Sherwood
Mrs Sahim Sliwinski-Hong
Mr Stuart Southall
Sir Hugh and Lady Sykes
Mr Ian Taylor
Miss Lori Tedesco
Mr and Mrs Julian Treger
Frederick and Kathryn Uhde
Mr Craig D Weaver
Prof Peter Whiteman QC
Mr and Mrs John Winter
Ms Regina Wyles

and others who wish to remain anonymous

SCHOOLS PATRONS

CHAIR
Mr Keir McGuinness

PLATINUM
Mr Mark Hix

GOLD
Sam and Rosie Berwick
Mrs Sarah Chenevix-Trench
Ms Cynthia Corbett
Rosalyn and Hugo Henderson
Christopher Kneale
Mr William Loschert
Mr Keir McGuinness
Carol Sellars

SILVER
Lord and Lady Aldington
Mrs Elizabeth Alston
Mr and Mrs Jonathan and Sarah Bayliss
Ms Sara Berman
Rosalind Clayton
Mr Richard Clothier
Ms Davina Dickson
Mrs Dominic Dowley
Miss Roxanna Farboud
Mrs Catherine Farquharson
Mrs Catherine Ferguson
Mr Mark Garthwaite
Mrs Michael Green
Mr and Mrs G Halamish
Mr Lindsay Hamilton
Mrs Lesley Haynes
Professor and Mrs Ken Howard OBE RA
Mark and Fiona Hutchinson
Mr Charles Irving
Mrs Marcelle Joseph
Mr and Mrs S Kahan
Mr Paul Kempe
Nicolette Kwok
Mrs Anna Lee
Mr and Mrs Mark Loveday
The Hon Mrs Lowther
Philip and Val Marsden
The Lord and Lady Myners
Mr William Ramsay
Peter Rice Esq
Anthony and Sally Salz
Ms Adrienne Showering
Brian D Smith
Mr Simon Thorley QC
Mr Ray Treen
Mrs Diana Wilkinson

PATRON DONOR
Mrs Dounia Nadar

and others who wish to remain anonymous

CONTEMPORARY CIRCLE PATRONS

CHAIR
Susie Allen-Huxley

PLATINUM
Robert and Simone Suss

GOLD
Joan and Robin Alvarez
Mr Jeremy Coller
Lady Alison Deighton
Mr and Mrs O Masek
Mr and Mrs Scott Mead
Mr and Mrs Simon Oliver
Mr Kevin Sneader and Ms Amy Muntner
Ms Miel de Botton
Manuela and Iwan Wirth

SILVER
Mrs Charlotte Artus
Jeremy Asher
Mr David Baty
Viscountess Bridgeman
Alla Broeksmit
Dr Elaine C Buck
Ms Debra Burt
Mr Tremayne Carew Pole
Jenny Christensson
Nadia Crandall
Mr Stefan Cross QC
Mrs Georgina David
Helen and Colin David
Patrick and Benedicte de Nonneville
Mollie Dent-Brocklehurst
Mrs Sophie Diedrichs-Cox
Chris and Angie Drake
Mrs Jennifer Duke
Mr and Mrs Eric Dusansky
Mr Timothy Ellis
Mr David Fawkes
Mr Stephen Garrett
Simon Gillespie
Mrs Susan Hayden
Zane Jackson, Director of Three Point Enterprises
Mr Gerald Kidd
Mrs Fiona King
Mr and Mrs John Koch
Mrs Julie Lee
Mr Jeff Lowe
Mrs Sarah Macken
Mrs Sophie Mirman
Victoria Miro
Mr Stuart C Nelson
Mr and Mrs Jeremy Nicholson
Mrs Tessa Nicholson
Dr Carolina Minio Paluello
Mrs Tineke Pugh
Mrs Catherine Rees
Frances Reynolds
Mrs Yosmarvi Rivas Rangel
Mrs Karen Santi
Edwina Sassoon
Richard and Susan Shoylekov
Mrs Veronica Simmons
Jeffery C Sugarman and Alan D H Newham
Mrs Arabella Tullo
Anna Watkins
Cathy Wills
Mrs Debora Wingate
Mr and Mrs Maurice Wolridge

PATRON DONOR
Ms Cynthia Wu

and others who wish to remain anonymous

LIBRARY AND COLLECTIONS CIRCLE

Patron Donors
Mr Mark W Friend
Mr Loyd Grossman
Miss Jo Hannah Hoehn
Mr and Mrs Robert Hoehn
Pam and Scott Schafler
Mr John Schaeffer
Mr and Mrs Bart Tiernan
Jonny Yarker

and others who wish to remain anonymous

INTERNATIONAL PATRONS

PLATINUM
Mr Thaddaeus Ropac
Mrs Sabine Sarikhani

and others who wish to remain anonymous

YOUNG PATRONS

CHAIR
May Calil

Kalita al Swaidi
Mrs Sharis Alexandrian
Miss Maria Allen
Ms Katharine Arnold
Miss Joy Asfar
Ms Vanessa Aubry
Ms Elif Bayoglu
Mr Alexander Bradford
Ms Katharine Butler
Rosanna Bossom
May Calil
Mr Alessandro Conti
Mr Stefano Donati
Mr Rollo Gabb
Miss Fernanda Gilligan
Laura Graham
Mr and Mrs Raoul Fraser
Marc Koch
Amanda Kearn Lambert
Julie Lawson
Lily Le Brun
Mr James Lindon
Mr John Madden
Ignacio Marinho
Isabella Marinho
Mr Turi Munthe
Mr Edoardo Roberti
Mr Mandeep Singh
Ms Eleonora Soares
Ms Chloe Stead
Mr Ralph Taylor
Ms Zeynep Uzuner
Miss Burcu Yuksel

and others who wish to remain anonymous

TRUSTS, FOUNDATIONS AND CHARITABLE GIVING

Artists Collecting Society
The Atlas Fund
The Albert Van den Bergh Charitable Trust
The Bomonty Charitable Trust
The Charlotte Bonham-Carter Charitable Trust
William Brake Charitable Trust
R M Burton 1998 Charitable Trust
C H K Charities Limited
P H G Cadbury Charitable Trust
The Carew Pole Charitable Trust
The Clore Duffield Foundation
John S Cohen Foundation
The Evan Cornish Foundation
The Sidney and Elizabeth Corob Charitable Trust
The Dovehouse Trust
The Gilbert and Eileen Edgar Foundation
The John Ellerman Foundation
Lucy Mary Ewing Charitable Trust
JM Finn and Co.
The Margery Fish Charity
The Flow Foundation
The Garfield Weston Foundation
Gatsby Charitable Foundation
The Golden Bottle Trust
Sue Hammerson Charitable Trust
The Charles Hayward Foundation
Heritage Lottery Fund
Hiscox plc
Holbeck Charitable Trust
The Harold Hyam Wingate Foundation
The Ironmongers' Company
The Emmanuel Kaye Foundation
The Kindersley Foundation
The de Laszlo Foundation
The Leche Trust
The Maccabaeans
The McCorquodale Charitable Trust
The Machin Foundation
The Paul Mellon Centre
The Paul Mellon Estate
The Mercers' Company
Margaret and Richard Merrell Foundation
The Millichope Foundation
The Mondriaan Foundation
The Monument Trust
The Henry Moore Foundation
The Mulberry Trust
The J Y Nelson Charitable Trust
The Old Broad Street Charity Trust
The Peacock Charitable Trust
The Pennycress Trust
PF Charitable Trust
The Stanley Picker Charitable Trust
The Pidem Fund
The Edith and Ferdinand Porjes Charitable Trust
Mr and Mrs J A Pye's Charitable Settlement
Rayne Foundation
The Reed Foundation
T Rippon & Sons (Holdings) Ltd
Rootstein Hopkins Foundation
The Rose Foundation
Schroder Charity Trust
The Sellars Charitable Trust
The Archie Sherman Charitable Trust
Paul Smith and Pauline Denyer-Smith
The South Square Trust
Spencer Charitable Trust
Oliver Stanley Charitable Trust
Peter Storrs Trust
Strand Parishes Trust
The Joseph Strong Frazer Trust
The Swan Trust
Thaw Charitable Trust
Sir Jules Thorn Charitable Trust
The Bruce Wake Charity
Celia Walker Art Foundation
Warburg Pincus International LLC
Weinstock Fund
Wilkinson Eyre Architects
The Spencer Wills Trust
The Maurice Wohl Charitable Foundation
The Wolfson Foundation

AMERICAN ASSOCIATES OF THE ROYAL ACADEMY TRUST

BURLINGTON HOUSE TRUST
Mrs James C Slaughter

BENJAMIN WEST SOCIETY
Mrs Deborah Loeb Brice

BENEFACTORS
Mr Michael Moritz and Ms Harriet Heyman
Mrs Elizabeth R Moran

SPONSORS
David Hockney OM CH RA

PATRONS
Mr and Mrs Steven Ausnit
Mr Donald A Best
Mr Richard C Colyear
Mr Lawrence S Friedland
Mr Oliver R Grace Jr
The Hon Samuel K Lessey Jr
Mr Henry S Lynn Jr
Mrs John P McGrath
Mrs Diane A Nixon
Mr and Mrs Wilson Nolen
Stanley D Scott
Mrs Mary Sharp Cronson
Mr Morton I Sosland
Ms Louisa Stude Sarofim
Martin J Sullivan OBE
Mr Frederick B Whittemore

DONORS
Mr and Mrs Charles N Atkins
Ms Alyce Faye Cleese
Mr Richard E Ford
Mrs Kay Foster
Mr and Mrs Gordon P Getty
Mr and Mrs Ellis Goodman
Mrs Judith Heath
The Hon. and Mrs Earle Mack
Ms Christine Mainwaring-Samwell
Mrs Charles W Olson III
Cynthia Hazen Polsky and Leon B Polsky
Mrs Eileen Powers
Mr Paul K Rooney
Mr and Mrs Elihu Rose
Mrs Sylvia Schever
Mrs Georgia Shreve
Mrs Martin Slifka
Mrs Frederick M Stafford
Mr and Mrs Robert K Steel

CORPORATE AND FOUNDATION SUPPORT
Henry C Beck Jr Charitable Trust

British Airways plc
Crankstart Foundation
Sunny and Frederick Dupree Children's Trust
The Charles and Carmen de Mora Hale Foundation
Leon Levy Foundation
Andrew W Mellon Foundation
Morris and McVeigh LLP
Siezen Foundation
Smart Family Foundation
Starr Foundation

CORPORATE MEMBERS OF THE ROYAL ACADEMY

Launched in 1988, the Royal Academy's Corporate Membership Scheme has proved highly successful. Corporate membership offers benefits for staff, clients and community partners and access to the Academy's facilities and resources. The outstanding support we receive from companies via the scheme is vital to the continuing success of the Academy and we thank all members for their valuable support and continued enthusiasm.

PREMIER LEVEL MEMBERS

American Express®
Barclays plc
Bird & Bird LLP
BNY Mellon
Catlin Group Limited
Christie's
Deutsche Bank AG
FTI Consulting
GlaxoSmithKline plc
Insight Investment
JTI
JM Finn & Co.
Jones Lang LaSalle
KPMG
Linklaters
Neptune Investment Management
Schroders Private Banking
Smith & Williamson
Sotheby's

CORPORATE MEMBERS

The Boston Consulting Group UK LLP
Brunswick
Capital Group
Chestertons
Close Brothers
Credit Agricole CIB
F & C Asset Management plc
GAM
Lazard
Lindsell Train
Marie Curie
Moelis & Company
Ridgeway Partners
The Royal Society of Chemistry
Trowers & Hamlins
UBS
Vision Capital LLP
Weil, Gotshal & Manges

ASSOCIATE

Bank of America Merrill Lynch
BNP Paribas
Bloomberg LP
Bonhams 1793 Ltd
British American Tobacco
Clifford Chance LLP
DONG Energy
Ernst & Young
Generation Investment Management LLP
Heidrick & Struggles
John Lewis Partnership
Lubbock Fine Chartered Accountants
Morgan Stanley
Pentland Group plc
Rio Tinto
Simon-Kucher & Partners
Sykes & Son Limited
Timothy Sammons Fine Art Agents

SUPPORTERS OF PAST EXHIBITIONS

The President and Council of the Royal Academy would like to thank the following supporters and supporters for their generous contributions towards major exhibitions in the last ten years:

2014

Giovanni Battista Moroni
2009–2016 Season supported by JTI
Anselm Kiefer
BNP Paribas
Radical Geometry: Modern Art of South America from the Patricia Phelps de Cisneros Collection
2009–2016 Season supported by JTI
Christie's
Dennis Hopper: The Lost Album
Lead Series Supporter JTI
Nikon UK
Premiums, RA Schools Annual Dinner and Auction and RA Schools Show 2014
Newton Investment Management
246th Summer Exhibition
Insight Investment
Dream, Draw, Work: Architectural Drawings by Norman Shaw RA
Lowell Libson Ltd
Collections and Library Supporters Circle
Renaissance Impressions: Chiaroscuro Woodcuts from the Collections of Georg Baselitz and the Albertina, Vienna
JTI
Edwards Wildman
Sensing Spaces: Architecture Reimagined
Scott and Laura Malkin
AKT II
Arauco

2013

Bill Woodrow RA
Lead Series Supporter JTI
The Henry Moore Foundation
Daumier
2009–2013 Season supported by JTI
Australia
National Gallery of Australia
Qantas Airways
The Woolmark Company
Richard Rogers RA: Inside Out
Ferrovial Agroman
Heathrow Airport
Laing O'Rourke
Mexico: A Revolution in Art, 1910–1940
2009–2013 Season supported by JTI
Art Mentor Foundation Lucerne
Conaculta
James and Clare Kirkman
Mexican Agency for International Development Cooperation
Catherine and Franck Petitgas
Sectur
Visit Mexico
Mercedes Zobel
245th Summer Exhibition
Insight Investment
George Bellows
2009–2013 Season supported by JTI
Edwards Wildman
Premiums 2013, RA Schools Annual Dinner and Auction and RA Schools Show 2013
Newton Investment Management
Manet: Portraying Life
BNY Mellon, Partner of the Royal Academy of Arts

2012

Mariko Mori
JTI
RA Now
JTI
Bronze
Christian Levett and Mougins Museum of Classical Art
Daniel Katz Gallery
Baron Lorne Thyssen-Bornemisza
John and Fausta Eskenazi
The Ruddock Foundation for the Arts
Tomasso Brothers Fine Art
Jon and Barbara Landau
Janine and J. Tomilson Hill
Embassy of the Kingdom of the Netherlands
Eskenazi Limited
Lisson Gallery
Alexis Gregory
Alan and Mary Hobart
Richard de Unger and Adeela Qureshi
Rossi & Rossi Ltd
Embassy of Israel
244th Summer Exhibition
Insight Investment
From Paris: A Taste for Impressionism – Paintings from the Clark
2009–2013 Season supported by JTI
Edwards Wildman
The Annenberg Foundation
Premiums, RA Schools Annual Dinner and Auction and RA Schools Show 2012
Newton Investment Management
Johan Zoffany RA: Society Observed
2009–2013 Season supported by JTI
Cox & Kings
Building the Revolution: Soviet Art and Architecture 1915–1935
2009–2013 Season supported by JTI
The Ove Arup Foundation
The Norman Foster Foundation
Richard and Ruth Rogers
David Hockney RA: A Bigger Picture
BNP Paribas
Welcome to Yorkshire: Tourism Partner
Visit Hull & East Yorkshire: Supporting Tourism Partner
NEC

2011

Degas and the Ballet: Picturing Movement
BNY Mellon
Region Holdings
Blavatnik Family Foundation
Eyewitness: Hungarian Photography in the Twentieth Century. Brassaï, Capa, Kertész, Moholy-Nagy, Munkácsi
2009–2013 Season supported by JTI
Hungarofest
OTP Bank
243rd Summer Exhibition
Insight Investment
Premiums, RA Schools Annual Dinner and Auction and RA Schools Show 2011
Newton Investment Management
Watteau: The Drawings
2009–2013 Season supported by JTI
Region Holdings
Modern British Sculpture
American Express Foundation
The Henry Moore Foundation
Hauser & Wirth
Art Mentor Foundation Lucerne
Sotheby's
Blain Southern
Welcome to Yorkshire: Tourism Partner

2010

GSK Contemporary – Aware: Art Fashion Identity
GlaxoSmithKline
Pioneering Painters: The Glasgow Boys 1880–1900
2009–2013 Season supported by JTI
Glasgow Museums
Treasures from Budapest: European Masterpieces from Leonardo to Schiele
OTP Bank
Villa Budapest
Daniel Katz Gallery, London
Cox & Kings: Travel Partner
Sargent and the Sea
2009–2013 Season supported by JTI
242nd Summer Exhibition
Insight Investment
Paul Sandby RA: Picturing Britain, A Bicentenary Exhibition
2009–2013 Season supported by JTI
The Real Van Gogh: The Artist and His Letters
BNY Mellon
Hiscox plc
Heath Lambert
Cox & Kings: Travel Partner
RA Outreach Programme
Deutsche Bank AG

2009

GSK Contemporary
GlaxoSmithKline
Wild Thing: Epstein, Gaudier-Brzeska, Gill
2009–2013 Season supported by JTI
BNP Paribas
The Henry Moore Foundation
Anish Kapoor
JTI
Richard Chang
Richard and Victoria Sharp
Louis Vuitton
The Henry Moore Foundation
J W Waterhouse: The Modern Pre-Raphaelite
2009–2013 Season supported by JTI
Champagne Perrier-Jouët
GasTerra
Gasunie
241st Summer Exhibition
Insight Investment
Kuniyoshi. From the Arthur R. Miller Collection
2009–2013 Season supported by JTI
Canon
Cox & Kings: Travel Partner
Premiums and RA Schools Show
Mizuho International plc
RA Outreach Programme
Deutsche Bank AG

2008

GSK Contemporary
GlaxoSmithKline
Byzantium 330–1453
J F Costopoulos Foundation
A G Leventis Foundation
Stavros Niarchos Foundation
Cox & Kings: Travel Partner
Miró, Calder, Giacometti, Braque: Aimé Maeght and His Artists
BNP Paribas
Vilhelm Hammershøi: The Poetry of Silence
OAK Foundation Denmark
Novo Nordisk
240th Summer Exhibition
Insight Investment
Premiums and RA Schools Show
Mizuho International plc
RA Outreach Programme
Deutsche Bank AG
From Russia: French and Russian Master Paintings 1870–1925 from Moscow and St Petersburg
E.ON
2008 Season supported by Sotheby's

2007

Paul Mellon's Legacy: A Passion for British Art
The Bank of New York Mellon
Georg Baselitz
Eurohypo AG
239th Summer Exhibition
Insight Investment
Impressionists by the Sea
Farrow & Ball
Premiums and RA Schools Show
Mizuho International plc
RA Outreach Programme
Deutsche Bank AG
The Unknown Monet
Bank of America

2006

238th Summer Exhibition
Insight Investment
Chola: Sacred Bronzes of Southern India
Cox & Kings: Travel Partner
Premiums and RA Schools Show
Mizuho International plc
RA Outreach Programme
Deutsche Bank AG
Rodin
Ernst & Young

2005

China: The Three Emperors, 1662–1795
Goldman Sachs International
Impressionism Abroad: Boston and French Painting
Fidelity Foundation
Matisse, His Art and His Textiles: The Fabric of Dreams
Farrow & Ball
Premiums and RA Schools Show
The Guardian
Mizuho International plc
Turks: A Journey of a Thousand Years, 600–1600
Akkök Group of Companies
Aygaz
Corus
Garanti Bank
Lassa Tyres